Fatimid Cosmopolitanism

Fatimid Cosmopolitanism

*History, Material Culture,
Politics and Religion*

Edited by
Gregory Bilotto, Farhad Daftary and Shainool Jiwa

I.B.TAURIS
LONDON · NEW YORK · OXFORD · NEW DELHI · SYDNEY
in association with
THE INSTITUTE OF ISMAILI STUDIES
LONDON, 2025

I.B. TAURIS
Bloomsbury Publishing Plc
50 Bedford Square, London, WC1B 3DP, UK
1359 Broadway, 12th Floor, New York, NY 10018, USA
29 Earlsfort Terrace, Dublin 2, Ireland

In association with
The Institute of Ismaili Studies
Aga Khan Centre, 10 Handyside Street, London N1C 4DN
www.iis.ac.uk

BLOOMSBURY, I.B. TAURIS and the I.B. Tauris logo are trademarks
of Bloomsbury Publishing Plc

First published in Great Britain 2025

Copyright © Islamic Publications Ltd., 2025

Gregory Bilotto, Farhad Daftary, Shainool Jiwa and Contributors have asserted
their rights under the Copyright, Designs and Patents Act, 1988, to be identified
as Editors and Authors of this work.

Cover design: Paul Smith
Cover image © Courtesy of the Bodleian Libraries, University of Oxford,
MS. Arab. c. 90, fols. 30b–31a.

This work is published open access subject to a Creative Commons
Attribution-NonCommercial-NoDerivatives 4.0 licence (CC BY-NC-ND 4.0,
https://creativecommons.org/licenses/by-nc-nd/4.0/). You may re-use, distribute,
and reproduce this work in any medium for non-commercial purposes, provided you
give attribution to the copyright holder and the publisher and provide a link to the
Creative Commons licence.

Bloomsbury Publishing Plc does not have any control over, or responsibility for, any
third-party websites referred to or in this book. All internet addresses given in
this book were correct at the time of going to press. The author and publisher regret
any inconvenience caused if addresses have changed or sites have ceased to exist,
but can accept no responsibility for any such changes.

A catalogue record for this book is available from the British Library.

A catalog record for this book is available from the Library of Congress.

ISBN: HB: 978-0-7556-5779-7
PB: 978-0-7556-5778-0
ePDF: 978-0-7556-5781-0
eBook: 978-0-7556-5780-3

Typeset by RefineCatch Limited, Bungay, Suffolk
Printed and bound in Great Britain

To find out more about our authors and books visit www.bloomsbury.com
and sign up for our newsletters.

The Institute of Ismaili Studies

The Institute of Ismaili Studies, established in 1977, has an extensive programme of multilingual and interdisciplinary research and publications, dating back to 1983. Informed by rigorous scholarly research, we endeavour to make available texts relating to Islam and Muslim communities in their historical and contemporary contexts. Our focus is on Ismaili and related Shi'i studies, Qur'anic studies, as well as Islam's diverse devotional, literary, intellectual, artistic, and esoteric traditions. Many of these publications highlight the relationship of faith and practice to broader dimensions of society, culture, and modern life.

IIS publications take the form of monographs; critical editions and translations of significant primary or secondary texts; edited volumes and conference proceedings; reference works such as bibliographies, manuscript catalogues, and encyclopaedias; occasional papers and essays; and trade non-fiction works aimed at lay audiences.

Authors of the Institute's publications hail from various parts of the world and express a range of views and ideas, which are not necessarily those of the Institute itself.

A full list of the publications of the Institute of Ismaili Studies can be found on our website at www.iis.ac.uk.

Contents

List of Contributors   xi
Preface by Gregory Bilotto   xiii
List of Abbreviations   xxi

SECTION I: FATIMID RELIGION AND STATECRAFT

1. Ismaili Neoplatonism: The Cosmopolitan Legacy of the Fatimid Ismaili *Daʿwa*   3
   Khalil Andani
2. Who was Nasir-i Khusraw's Patron in Yumgan? Notes on the Political Vectors of the Late Fatimid *Daʿwa*   27
   Daniel Beben
3. The Reign of the Fatimid Imam-caliph al-Hakim bi-Amr Allah: Historiographical Considerations   45
   Shainool Jiwa
4. The Fatimid *Kitab al-Majalis waʾl-musayarat* as *Responsa* to Internal Controversy and External Propaganda   67
   Hasan al-Khoee
5. (Re)-making Time, (Re)-making Place: Some Considerations on Early Fatimid *Taʾwil* and Sacred Space   91
   Jamel A. Velji
6. Fatimid Public Pronouncements: Messages from a Shiʿi Dynasty to a Cosmopolitan Empire   103
   Paul E. Walker

SECTION II: THE FATIMID LEGACY RECONSIDERED

1. The Modern Rediscovery of the Fatimid Artistic and Architectural Legacy in Egypt   125
   Dina Ishak Bakhoum
2. A Dynasty for All Seasons: The Fatimids in Modern and Contemporary Cosmopolitanism Discourses   147
   Delia Cortese

3. Wladimir Ivanow and Fatimid Studies 161
   Farhad Daftary
4. The Untold Problem of Ibn al-Haytham's Scientific
   Legacy in Islamic Art History 171
   Valérie Gonzalez
5. The Fatimids and the Indian Ocean: Evidence from the
   Book of Curiosities 191
   Yossef Rapoport

SECTION III: FATIMID CEREMONY AND SYMBOLISM

1. The Fatimid Crescent: Understanding a Complex Religio-
   Political Cosmos through Lunar Symbolism 209
   Ali Asgar Hussamuddin Alibhai
2. The Power of Six: Astral, Solomonic and Imami Imagery
   in Fatimid Art 235
   Bernard O'Kane
3. The Cosmopolitan Ecosystem of the Festival Costumes of
   515/1122 255
   Paula Sanders
4. Back to Black Background: The Rediscovery of Black
   Background and the Aesthetic of Darkness – A Global
   Visual Spectacle during the Fatimid Age 273
   Avinoam Shalem
5. Displaying the Hidden: Fatimid Public Texts in Floriated
   Kufic 293
   Yasser Tabbaa

SECTION IV: ART AND ARCHAEOLOGY

1. A Fatimid Mermaid 315
   Doris Behrens-Abouseif and Juan de Lara
2. 'The Work is Blessed, Unique': The Fatimid Silver Casket
   of Sadaqa b. Yusuf 335
   Anna Contadini
3. Fatimid Jewellery Hoards from Palestine in the Light of
   the Cairo Geniza Documents 373
   Ayala Lester
4. The Fatimid Rock Crystal Ewers: Innovation or Variation?
   A Historical and Iconographical Investigation 387
   Marcus Pilz

5. Fatimid Archaeology and Excavations in Cairo: What We Really Know about the Ismaili Capital City and Fustat 409
Stéphane Pradines
6. Reassessing Fatimid Figuralism: Ettinghausen, Grabar and a Medieval Lustre Workshop 431
Jennifer A. Pruitt

Image Credits 457
Select Bibliography 461
Index 467

List of Contributors

Ali Asgar Hussamuddin Alibhai University of Texas at Dallas
Khalil Andani Augustana College, USA
Dina Ishak Bakhoum Independent Scholar
Daniel Beben Nazarbayev University, Kazakstan
Doris Behrens-Abouseif SOAS, University of London
Gregory Bilotto Metropolitan Museum of Art, New York
Anna Contadini SOAS, University of London
Delia Cortese Middlesex University, London
Farhad Daftary The Institute of Ismaili Studies, London
Juan de Lara University of Oxford
Valérie Gonzalez SOAS, University of London
Shainool Jiwa The Institute of Ismaili Studies, London
Hasan al-Khoee The Institute of Ismaili Studies, London
Ayala Lester Independent Scholar
Bernard O'Kane American University in Cairo
Marcus Pilz Vesta Coburg Art Collections
Stéphane Pradines Aga Khan University-ISMC
Jennifer A. Pruitt University of Wisconsin-Madison
Yossef Rapoport Queen Mary University London
Paula Sanders Rice University, Houston, Texas
Avinoam Shalem Columbia University, New York
Yasser Tabbaa Independent Scholar
Jamel A. Velji Claremont McKenna College, USA
Paul E. Walker University of Chicago

Preface
Gregory Bilotto

> There is no specific word for 'Mediterranean' in the Geniza records. The ancient Arab term 'The Sea of the Romans' (as opposed to the 'Sea of the Indians', the Indian Ocean) never occurs in them, and one has the impression that in the writings of the Muslim geographers of this period[,] it appears as a traditional scientific term rather than a name in living use. The Mediterranean was 'The Sea' par excellence, and as such, of course, it is mentioned in our records countless times.[1]

Shelomo Goitein offered this observational analysis in his voluminous work on the myriad Arabic and Hebrew texts preserved in the '*janaza*' (Arabic) or 'Geniza' (Hebrew), a store in the Ben Ezra Synagogue in Old Cairo, meant to literally 'bury' but in actuality 'safeguard' documents that might mention the word of God (figure 1). The cache of documents, written during the 5th to 7th/11th to 13th centuries – contemporary with the Fatimids in Egypt (368–567/969–1171) and their successors, the Ayyubids (567–658/1171–1260) – recorded numerous aspects of contact with foreign cultures (beyond Egypt), daily life, economics, familial affairs, trading and travelling, among other topics, across the Fatimid state and further afield. These once-discarded texts, e.g., court and legal records (the most valuable owing to their detail), letters, marriage dowries, receipts, etc., have offered an invaluable glimpse into the international and cosmopolitan world cultivated by the Fatimids. Perhaps the quote by Goitein on the familiarity of 'The Sea' for the Fatimids can elucidate further on this cosmopolitanism because it was in their role as an omnipotent maritime power, even while initially ruling from Ifriqiya (figure 2), that the Fatimids developed highly successful trading and missionary (*da'wa*) networks – stretching the breadth of the Mediterranean and even reaching parts of Eastern Zanj, and of Malabar in Hind – with all goods and raw materials passing through the imperial marketplace, Fustat (Cairo), allowing the state to collect lucrative customs and duties,

Figure 1 A view of the southern facade of the Ben Ezra Synagogue in Fustat (Kom Ghorab), Egypt. Although initially erected in the 4th/9th century, it was rebuilt/restored several times, notably under Fatimid rule during the 5th to 6th/11th to 12th centuries.

Figure 2 A view of the former Fatimid inland port and harbour at Mahdiyya. The harbour quays and parts of the defences are original, surviving from the Fatimid era. The Ismaili influence of the Fatimids was connected to their trading links, including the maritime trade that began from this port.

and ensuring its place as a model multicultural manufacturing centre and import-export terminal.

Aside from the Geniza contracts or receipts, evidence of this strategic economic system was detailed in several texts of the Fatimid period, particularly the *Safar-nama* (Travelogue), written by the Ismaili *da'i*, Nasir-i Khusraw, when he meticulously described the exotic luxuries and wealth of the markets of Cairo during his stay in Egypt between 439 and 441/1047 and 1049.

> ... and no one ever saw such a market anywhere else. Every sort of rare goods from all over the world can be had there.[2]

> The city and markets were so arrayed that, were they to be described, some would not believe that drapers' and moneychangers' shops could be so decorated with gold, jewels, coins, goldspun fabrics, and linen that there was no room to sit down.[3]

> I saw such personal wealth there that were I to describe it, the people of Persia (Khurasan and Ma wara' al-Nahr) would never believe it. I could discover no end or limit to their wealth, and I never saw such ease and security anywhere.[4]

It was this intimate knowledge of and interconnectedness with the Mediterranean that invigorated the empire's enormous wealth, the intercultural dialogue with other states, both Muslim and Christian, and the seemingly 'free movement' of people, including artisans, merchants, skilled labourers and traders who travelled and settled in major Fatimid metropolises following the pluralistic Cairo blueprint, such as Aden, Aswan, Caesarea, Mahdiyya, Tiberias and Tunis. Despite periods of division and conflict, a considerable part of this urban success can be attributed to the inclusive environment of varying ethnicities and religions. As the Fatimid maritime specialist David Bramoullé remarked in his recent work:

> L'Égypte devint peu à peu une véritable plate-forme du commerce médiéval vers laquelle convergeaient marchandises et marchands de toutes origins. Les califes du Caire surent sans doute mieux que leurs prédécesseurs exploiter la position de ce territoire à l'interface de la Méditerranée et la mer Rouge, deux mers rendues de plus en plus complémentaires, Il ne s'agissait en aucun cas d'un simple fait de géographie ou du fruit du hasard, mais du résultat d'un processus qui

permettait à la dynastie de devenir un acteur tout à la fois omniprésent du commerce maritime, mais aussi très dépendant de ce dernier.[5]

He notes the connection between the 'omnipresent' dynasty with 'merchandise and merchants of all origins', and it was this arrangement that would undoubtedly facilitate a natural inclination for tolerance and prosperity. In other words, the overwhelming success of the Fatimid economic model, and therefore the state's power, was inextricably linked to ensuring a cosmopolitan global environment, with diverse merchants and traders passing throughout the land plying their produce and wares with limited barriers. Through this international maritime trading network, the Fatimid state emerged during an age with other rival caliphal empires – notably the Abbasids and the Umayyads of al-Andalus – perhaps not as the lone maritime 'superpower', but indeed overall, probably the most tolerant and multicultural.

The conference 'Fatimid Cosmopolitanism: History, Material Culture, Politics, and Religion', held at The Institute of Ismaili Studies (IIS) on 6–9 December 2021, addressed this cosmopolitan Fatimid milieu, with thirty-eight scholars from diverse backgrounds, both early career and well-established, covering numerous areas of current research in Fatimid studies beyond the traditionally Western-centric approach prevalent with its study set in the past. The event was successful in providing a common platform for these scholars of diverse disciplines – ranging from archaeology to history, numismatics to theology, and material culture to the living legacy – initiating collaboration for future academic endeavours and a broader appeal to a non-specialist audience, which resulted in over 2,000 registered participants. The specific topics, ranging from archaeological investigation to primary source texts – including those of the Geniza – to the exploration of the ceremonial and symbolic, to rethinking the legacy of the sixth Fatimid Imam-caliph, al-Hakim bi-Amr Allah, presented new material and analysis in what is a rapidly evolving field. The conference also benefitted from the recent publication of an exceptional Fatimid treatise, *Kitab Ghara'ib al-funun wa-mulah al-'uyun* (ca. 411–442/1020–1050),[6] detailing how the Fatimids perceived their maritime state while navigating 'The Sea' and the world beyond, as well as from seventeen years of archaeological investigation in Cairo led by Stéphane Pradines and funded by IFAO and AKTC, which has resulted in new perceptions about Fatimid architecture and urban life.[7]

The London event also sought to build on the foundation of a previous conference, 'L'Égypte fatimide: son art et son histoire', convened by Marianne Barrucand and held at l'Université de Paris-Sorbonne on 28–30 May 1998. The Paris conference proceedings, published in 1999 under the same title,[8] were the first significant international acknowledgement of Fatimid studies, and while primarily arts-centric, the assembled scholars successfully developed its importance and consequently elevated the field on the world stage. Additionally, an accompanying exhibition of Fatimid art, 'Trésors fatimides du Caire'[9] was curated at l'Institut du monde arabe in 1998 and then shown in Vienna as 'Schätze der Kalifen: Islamische Kunst zur Fatimidenzeit',[10] at the Künstlerhaus from 1998–1999. These exhibitions complemented and enhanced the work of the conference, but more importantly, were the sole international events of their kind exclusively dedicated to Fatimid art – a distinction only surpassed by 'The World of the Fatimids' held at the Aga Khan Museum, Toronto, in 2018.[11]

The present volume, now published more than twenty-five years after the Paris conference, contains twenty-two texts demonstrating the interdependence and international exchange characterising the Fatimid state, both internally and externally. In essence, these texts explore the cosmopolitan Fatimid environment through artistic, cultural, doctrinal, economic, intellectual, political and social interactions. This publication reflects current research in Fatimid studies, which has advanced substantially since 1998 through ongoing archaeological investigation, historical documentation, scientific and technological innovation, and a greater understanding of and broader interest in the field. While the volume has sought to further enhance research by building on the previous conference, it also aims to encourage future academic work in Fatimid studies. Hence, the contributions have been arranged in four thematic sections, 'Religion and Statecraft', 'Ceremony and Symbolism', 'Art and Archaeology', and 'The Fatimids Reconsidered', as these reflect the structure and focus of the conference.

I wish to express gratitude to my co-editors, Farhad Daftary and Shainool Jiwa, who have supported me through each phase of organising the conference and publishing its proceedings. I thank all the conference presenters, moderators, and those who have submitted texts for publication in this peer-reviewed volume. My colleagues on the conference organising committee, Shainool Jiwa, Sarah Campbell, Russell Harris, Naushin Shariff and Susheel Gokarakonda, and the volume editors, Isabel Miller, Patricia Salazar who organised the images, as well as Tara

Woolnough, have supported me in realising this publication and I offer my special appreciation to Zayn Kassam, the IIS director, for her ongoing commitment to Fatimid studies.

I also want to recognise the incredible achievement of the late Ghada al-Hijjawi al-Qaddumi, who sadly died in 2021. She completed her PhD at Harvard University under the supervision of Oleg Grabar, and her published thesis, a translation, annotation and analysis of the 6th/12th-century *Kitab al-Hadaya wa'l-tuhaf*, has had a profound influence in the field of Fatimid studies,[12] drawing us closer to understanding the international exchange and global reach of Fatimid court life: '. . . [these exchanges and events] characterised the hospitality and sophistication of the periods of high culture of Islamic civilisation'.[13] I had the pleasure of visiting her at home in Kuwait City, Kuwait, in April 2019, where she expressed an enthusiastic desire to participate in the then-forthcoming conference by offering insights on further unpublished texts related to this essential Fatimid treatise. I thank her for many kindnesses. Unsurprisingly, her essential publication was frequently referenced during the 1998 and 2021 conferences and certainly will remain an indispensable primary source for future scholarship.

Gregory Bilotto, July 2024

NOTES

1. S. D. Goitein, *A Mediterranean Society: The Jewish Communities of the Arab World as Portrayed in the Documents of the Cairo* Geniza, vol. 1, *Economic Foundations* (Berkeley, 1999), p. 42.
2. Nasir-i Khusraw, *Safar-nama*, tr. Wheeler M. Thackston as *Nasir-i Khusraw's Book of Travels* (Costa Mesa, CA, 2001), p. 69; for the full account, see pp. 66–72.
3. Ibid., p. 71; the description relates to celebrating a royal birth.
4. Ibid.
5. David Bramoullé, *Les fatimides et la mer (909–1171)* (Leiden, 2020), p. 471; for an excellent overview of Fatimid naval power and commercial seafaring, see his complete work.
6. Yossef Rapoport, and Emilie Savage-Smith, *Lost Maps of the Caliphs: Drawing the World in Eleventh-Century Cairo* (Oxford, 2018); Emilie Savage-Smith, amazingly, only identified its importance by chance just before a sale at Christie's, London in 2000.
7. See the chapter in this volume by Stéphane Pradines, who directed the nearly two-decades-long Cairo excavations through l'Institut français d'archéologie orientale and the Aga Khan Trust for Culture.
8. Marianne Barrucand, ed. *L'Égypte fatimide: son art et son histoire* (Paris, 1999).
9. *Trésors fatimides du Caire* (Paris, 1998).
10. W. Seipel, ed. *Schätze der Kalifen: Islamische Kunst zur Fatimidenzeit* (Milan, 1998).
11. Assadullah Souren Melikian-Chirvani, ed., *The World of the Fatimids* (Toronto, London, Munich, 2018).

12 Ghada al-Ḥijjawi al-Qaddumi, *Book of Gifts and Rarities: Kitab al-Hadaya wa al-Tuhaf* (Cambridge, 1996).
13 Ibid., p. 3; the Fatimid courtier al-Qadi b. al-Zubayr, who witnessed and recorded many exchanges and events at the royal court and other localities, almost surely wrote the text. However, his work spans the Dar al-Islam from the age of the Prophet Muhammad until the decline of Fatimid rule, covering the 1st to 6th/7th to 12th centuries. Therefore, following his reliance on earlier Muslim chroniclers from the previous centuries, the volume probably was written as a comprehensive text to compare courtly life during the preceding periods of Islam with the 'more powerful' Fatimid court.

Abbreviations

AI   *Annales Islamologiques*

BSOAS   *Bulletin of the School of Oriental and African Studies*

EIr   *Encyclopaedia Iranica*, ed. E. Yarshater et al.

EIs   *Encyclopaedia Islamica*, ed. F. Daftary, the late Wilferd Madelung

EI2   *The Encyclopaedia of Islam*, ed. H.A.R. Gibb et al. New edition.

JRAS   *Journal of the Royal Asiatic Society*

SECTION I
FATIMID RELIGION AND STATECRAFT

1

Ismaili Neoplatonism: The Cosmopolitan Legacy of the Fatimid Ismaili *Daʿwa*

Khalil Andani

The Shiʿi Ismaili Muslim tradition of Islam manifests a significant number of distinctive features that differentiate the Ismaili interpretations of Islam from other competing Muslim schools of law and theology. One of these distinctive elements was a specific Ismaili theological worldview known as 'Ismaili Neoplatonism'. Ismaili Neoplatonism was the result of Ismaili philosophers adapting and refining the metaphysical teachings of Plotinus and Proclus as translated into Arabic and edited during the 3rd/9th century through the translation movement.[1]

Modern scholars have presented theories on the origins, functions and legacies of Ismaili Neoplatonism in the Ismaili *daʿwa* (summons). According to the current scholarly narrative argued by Stern, Madelung and Daftary, Ismaili Neoplatonism was first adopted by the Eastern Ismaili *daʿwa* for the purpose of missionary activity directed at the ruling educated elite in Persia.[2] It is believed that the Fatimid Ismaili Imam-caliphs in North Africa were initially against the use of Neoplatonic philosophy and condemned it wholesale.[3] However, because the Fatimid Imam-caliphs sought the spiritual allegiance of the Eastern Ismaili communities, they changed course and allowed Fatimid *daʿi*s to employ Neoplatonic ideas to win over these constituencies.[4] Finally, it is further claimed that within the Nizari tradition of post-Fatimid Ismailism, Ismaili Neoplatonism became obsolete, was formally repudiated, and died out.[5]

The above narrative on the origins and function of Ismaili Neoplatonism deserves closer scrutiny. The general claim that Ismaili Neoplatonism basically reflected a clever 'marketing strategy' to win over converts is not based on any textual evidence; it is an inference of modern scholars based on interpreting the available material. In this chapter, I argue that Ismaili Neoplatonism as a sophisticated form of Islamic thought did not simply serve a missionary purpose for the Ismaili *daʿwa* and was not adopted by Ismaili thinkers simply because it was fashionable. Rather, the Neoplatonic worldview provided the strongest metaphysical basis for Ismaili theological, cosmological and soteriological truth-claims within a rational and universalist framework. The cosmopolitan and philosophical merits of Islamic Neoplatonism allowed this worldview to endure long past the demise of the Fatimid caliphate and well into the modern period of Ismaili history.

First, the prevalent hypothesis that the Fatimid Imam-caliphs were initially against Neoplatonism and later allowed it for the sake of converting the Eastern Ismaili communities is re-evaluated. This narrative is based on scant evidence, a conflation between *falsafa* and philosophy in general, and is contradicted by the presence of Neoplatonic teachings in Fatimid *daʿwa* writings composed under the Fatimid Imam-caliph, al-Muʿizz (r. 341–365/953–975). The Ismaili *daʿi*s, however, naturalised Neoplatonism into *daʿwa* teaching because of their own universalist approach to the revelatory and rational sciences. Ismaili philosophers upheld Neoplatonism due to the rational and metaphysical coherence of its worldview, not as a matter of dogma or popularity; they further expounded uniquely Ismaili conceptions of *tawhid* and divine guidance (Prophetology and Imamology) in fully Neoplatonic terms. Finally, Ismaili Neoplatonism outlived the demise of the Fatimid caliphate and, contrary to certain claims, did not fade away but continued as a viable worldview simply taken for granted. Neoplatonism became pervasive amongst many notable post-classical Muslim philosophers and mystics beyond Ismailism. The Ismaili form of Neoplatonism continued in the Nizari Ismaili tradition through the teachings of ʿAbd al-Karim al-Shahrastani (d. 548/1153) and Nasir al-Din al-Tusi (d. 672/1274) in the Alamut period and endured among post-Alamut Nizari thinkers, for whom it provided the metaphysical basis for Ismaili Imamology and soteriology. Finally, Ismaili Neoplatonism is currently undergoing a resurgence as contemporary Ismaili scholars and philosophers draw upon it to address theological and philosophical questions. Today, Ismaili Neoplatonism thus stands as one of the most enduring cosmopolitan legacies of the Fatimids and the Ismaili *daʿwa*.

Neoplatonic Philosophy, *Falasafa* and the Ismaili *daʿwa*: Revising the Narrative

The earliest Ismaili *daʿi*s to affirm a Neoplatonic worldview in the first half of the 4th/10th century were the Brethren of Purity (fl. late 3rd/9th century to mid-4th/10th century) as well as the *daʿi*s Muhammad b. Ahmad al-Nasafi (d. 332/943) in Transoxania, Abu Hatim al-Razi (d. 322/934) in Rayy, and Abu Yaʿqub al-Sijistani (d. after 361/971) in Sistan and Khurasan. Their Neoplatonic worldview envisages a hierarchical conception of reality. God, or *Allah*, is the absolutely simple and absolutely transcendent, uncaused Originator of all existents – what Plotinus calls the One. From God, the Originator, there proceeds an eternal divine act of creation or origination (*al-ibdaʿ*); the immediate product of God's originating act is the 'first creation' (*al-khalq al-awwal*) or 'first originated being' (*al-mubdaʿ al-awwal*) known as the Universal Intellect (*al-ʿaql al-kulli*) or First Intellect (*al-ʿaql al-awwal*). The Intellect is a perfect substance that encompasses all intelligible forms and essences. From the First Intellect, there emanates the 'second creation' known as the Universal Soul (*al-nafs al-kulliyya*). The Universal Soul is a perpetually moving or active spiritual substance continuously receiving intelligible forms emanating from the Intellect. The Soul's spiritual motion emanates Prime Matter and Form through which individual souls and the physical world come into existence.

The above scheme is the most basic account of the Neoplatonic worldview found among Muslim thinkers. However more complex schemas, like al-Farabi's (d. 339/950) model of ten intellects were also popular. The Ismaili version of Neoplatonism displayed important refinements including: rejecting common philosophical labels for God like 'First Cause', 'Perfect' and 'Good'; developing a discourse of dual negation to talk about God by negating every positive attribute ('God is not perfect') and its privative negation ('God is not imperfect') on the grounds that both statements apply only to creatures and are category errors for God; emphasising the concept that God's creative act of origination is an act of will (*mashiʾa*) and command (*amr*) as opposed to an involuntary production; framing God's Command or Word as a logical, supra-hypostatic or perspectival intermediary between God and the originated Intellect where God's Command/Word has no positive ontological status and is unified with the Intellect's substance.[6] The outcome of these Ismaili philosophical deliberations was immensely fruitful and inaugurated Ismaili Neoplatonism, which Henry Corbin once called 'the most daring metaphysical thought in Islam.'[7] Many Muslim groups among the mystics and philosophers came to hold some version of Islamic Neoplatonism – including al-Kindi (d. 260/873) and his followers, the Ismailis, the Sunni mystics of al-Andalus, the post-classical Sunni followers of Ibn al-ʿArabi (d. 638/1240), Persian Sunni Sufis, the Muslim Peripatetic *falasifa* in the tradition of Ibn Sina (d. 428/1077), the Illuminationist thinkers of the school of al-Suhrawardi (d. 587/1191), and various Twelver Shiʿi mystical philosophers in the Safavid period.

In a 1955 article, Samuel M. Stern argued that the Fatimid Imam-caliph al-Muʿizz disapproved of Ismaili Neoplatonism. His claim is based on an account in al-Qadi al-Nuʿman's *Majalis wa'l-musayrarat* where Imam al-Muʿizz was visited by one of his followers from a region (*jazira*) in which many of the Ismailis 'follow the doctrine of the philosophers (*aktharuhum yadhhabuna madhhab al-falasifa*)'. The Imam asked his visitor to present to him the teachings of the Ismaili *daʿi* who taught the doctrines of these 'philosophers' (*falasifa*). However, the visitor 'did not convey the views of philosophy according to its people (*kalam al-falsafa kama dhakarahu ahlahu*) nor did he explain God's religion as he had claimed (*wa la huwa abana ʿan din Allah kama zaʿama*).' 'He produced from the confused mixing that which removes (one) from the religious community and invites to unbelief (*wa jaʾa min al-takhlit bi-ma yukhriju ʿan al-milla wa yadʿu ila al-kufr*).' The report goes on to say that many of the followers of the Fatimid *daʿwa* in that region were attached to this philosophical doctrine and al-Muʿizz realised that he could not repudiate it without risking the loss of their allegiance. The visitor then asked the Imam-caliph to name his ancestors, which he did. The visitor, however, referred to different names. When confronted with this divergence, the visitor remarked that 'it is said among us that the Imam has seven names: a corporeal name, psychic name, spiritual name, natural name, real name, exoteric name and esoteric name.'[8]

Stern concluded that these Ismailis who subscribed to the 'doctrine of the philosophers' (*madhhab al-falasifa*) that the Imam-caliph condemned as unbelief (*kufr*) were the Ismaili Neoplatonist *daʿi*s like al-Nasafi and al-Sijistani: 'The paragraph would fit Abu Yaʿqub al-Sijzi to perfection; I do not know, however if the specific doctrine about the seven names is attested for Abu Yaʿqub.'[9] Thus, Stern believed that Imam al-Muʿizz judged the Ismaili Neoplatonist *daʿi*s to be promoters of *kufr* that exceeded the bounds of God's religion; but the Imam hesitated to officially condemn these beliefs due to political expediency and allowed them to continue. Stern's interpretation continues to dominate modern scholarship. Hollenberg refers to this anecdote as 'the clearest evidence ... that the Fatimids *consciously* rejected a Neoplatonised form of earlier doctrine.'[10] Furthermore, several scholars including Walker, Brett, Daftary and

Hollenberg suggest that at some later point, the Imam-caliph authorised his *daʿi*s to start teaching Neoplatonism in their *daʿwa* works to win over these philosophically inclined Ismaili communities. As summarised by Hollenberg, 'al-Muʿizz employed Neoplatonica in order to convince the Iranian dissident Ismailis to join ranks with the Fatimid *daʿwa* . . . as a concession to the eastern Ismaili dioceses, al-Muʿizz instructed his spokesmen to sate the Easterners' appetite for philosophy by incorporating *falsafa* into Fatimid doctrine."[11]

The first issue is that Stern's inference – that those Ismailis who reportedly followed the doctrine (*madhhab*) of the 'philosophers' (*falasifa*) are the Ismaili Neoplatonists – is based on almost no evidence. Stern concluded that the account matches al-Sijistani and similar *daʿi*s 'to perfection', but this claim was not substantiated anywhere. The only teaching of the heretical Ismaili group concerns the Imam having seven names (corporeal psychic, spiritual, natural, real, exoteric and esoteric) – but this doctrine cannot be found in the extant writings of al-Sijistani or al-Razi. Otherwise, the major distinctive traits of Ismaili Neoplatonic belief are absent from the account. Furthermore, the account specifically speaks of those who follow the *madhhab al-falasifa* and the *kalam al-falsafa*, which they 'mixed' with God's religion. Many scholars simply assumed that *falsafa* here means all forms of philosophy, and especially 'Neoplatonic philosophy', and that *falasifa* refers to Neoplatonists. But this determination does not account for the multivalent meanings of the words *falsafa/falasifa* in classical Islam and paints all forms of Islamic philosophical activity with an overly broad brush. As explained by Frank Griffel and Ulrich Rudolph, the term *falsafa* has multiple meanings in Muslim discourse. The first meaning of *falsafa* is 'a collective term that refers to the sum total of all scientific disciplines, where "science", is understood to mean those branches of knowledge that are universal to humans.'[12] The second meaning of *falsafa* is one that prevailed among the *mutakallimun* (rational theologians) in the classical period: 'a clearly identifiable set of teachings . . . a heretical doctrine concerning improper ideas about God and the world which he created.' This sense of *falsafa* was mostly negative as scholars like al-Ghazali, al-Shahrastani and Fakhr al-Din al-Razi wrote about *falsafa* in this respect as a series of metaphysical and theological theses that constitute an 'independent religious tradition' alongside Islam and Christianity.[13] A third meaning of *falsafa* refers to intellectual practices and textual traditions as understood by al-Kindi and his successors. This sense of *falsafa* is more neutral as it is one means of acquiring knowledge that is not necessarily antithetical to revelatory wisdom.[14]

It is therefore inappropriate to simply translate *falsafa* as simply 'philosophy' or 'Neoplatonic philosophy'. The account of Imam al-Muʿizz condemning *falsafa* uses the terms *madhhab al-falasifa* and *kalam al-falsafa*; the word usage here points to a distinct set of theological doctrines and claims in accordance with the second definition of *falsafa* surveyed above – which many Muslims saw as problematic. Therefore, what the Fatimid Imam-caliphs condemned as *kufr* cannot be taken as Ismaili Neoplatonism. In fact, the Ismaili Neoplatonist *daʿi*s did not call themselves *falasifa* and never referred to their project as *falsafa*. Thus, there remains no direct evidence that the Imam-caliph was ever against Ismaili Neoplatonism.

Furthermore, the Ismaili Neoplatonist *daʿi*s attacked views of the '*falasifa*'. We find clear condemnations of the *falasifa* with respect to specific theological doctrines in the works of al-Sijistani. For example, in his *Kitab al-Iftikhar*, al-Sijistani condemns the Abbasid caliph al-Maʾmun for translating the books of 'the Greek, naturalist, divesting philosophers' (*al-falasifa al-yunaniyyin al-dahriyyin al-muʿattilin*) who deny the Prophethood of Muhammad and deny the resurrection.[15] He criticises other theistic philosophers, whom he calls the 'pseudo-philosophers' (*al-mutafalasifun*), for believing that God is a mere cause (*ʿilla*) and a substance (*jawhar*) – which he attacks as an implicit form of agnosticism (*taʿtil*).[16] Al-Sijistani also refutes the 'partisans of philosophy' (*ashab al-falsafa*) for not believing in the resurrection (*qiyama*) and even questions the point of learning their *falsafa* when it brings no benefit to their souls.[17] Al-Sijistani makes similar critiques in his *Kitab al-Maqalid*, referring to 'the divesters among the philosophers' (*muʿattila min al-falasifa*) who say that God is a cause,[18] 'the ignorant among the philosophers' (*al-juhal min al-falasifa*) who say that God is a substance,[19] and 'the ignorant among the pseudo-philosophers' (*al-juhal min al-mutafalasifin*) who deny the reality of God's Command.[20] Al-Sijistani's attacks on *falsafa* and the *falasifa* should *not* be interpreted as a hostility towards all philosophy or philosophical activity in general. But it proves that Ismaili Neoplatonism was not known as *falsafa* and that we are dealing with two distinct philosophical traditions. A more value-neutral meaning of *falsafa* in classical Islam is the dedicated study of various branches of the philosophical sciences – metaphysics, ethics, mathematics, physics, etc. The Ismailis were not hostile to this idea of philosophy. In fact, al-Sijistani specifically refers to these philosophical sciences as *hikma* and argues at length that the revealed prophetic message (*al-risala*) and philosophical wisdom (*hikma*) are fully harmonious as both share the same knowledge structure and facilitate the same spiritual goals for humanity: 'Thus, when the prophetic message (*al-risala*) necessitates what philosophical wisdom (*al-hikma*) [also] necessitates in terms of their divisions and the divisions of each category, then the prophetic message is within the essence of philosophical wisdom (*nafs al-hikma*) since they do not contradict each other in anything.'[21] Given that both the Fatimid Imam-caliphs and Ismaili Neoplatonist *daʿi*s attacked the belief-system (*madhhab*) of certain *falasifa*, there remains no evidence that Imam al-Muʿizz even condemned the Ismaili Neoplatonists in the first place. The current historical narrative seems to be plagued by a case of mistaken identity between two different groups of Islamic thinkers – the *falasifa* with their heretical views and the Ismaili Neoplatonist *daʿi*s with their espousal of a refined Neoplatonism.

The second issue in the standard narrative is the existence of multiple extant Fatimid *daʿwa* works dating to the Imamate of al-Muʿizz. In these works, the Imam's highest-ranking *daʿi*s and the Imam himself endorse the core theses of Ismaili Neoplatonism. These include the *Kitab al-Fatarat* and *Saraʾir wa asrar al-nutuqaʾ* attributed to Jaʿfar b. Mansur al-Yaman (d. ca. 346/957), the *bab al-abwab* (highest deputy of the Imam), the *Risala al-mudhhiba* attributed to al-Qadi al-Nuʿman, and the *Kitab Taʾwil al-shariʿa* composed by the Imam-caliph al-Muʿizz himself.[22] Consider the following remarks in the opening page of the *Kitab al-Fatarat* ascribed to the Imam's own *bab*, Jaʿfar b. Mansur al-Yaman:

> Verily the Creator, originated 'he first' not from anything and in simple 'nowhereness'. It does not have form, nor is it intelligible . . . The wise ones named it [the first origination] 'intellect' and the Messenger (peace be upon him) named it '*Pen*'. . . . And [the word] became an intermediary between the Creator and intellect, being *the Pen* (Qurʾan 68:1, 96:4), except that from [the vantage point of] the Creator, it was the act of drawing, and from the [vantage point of the] origination, it was that which was drawn. The Creator is purely one, exalted above attributes and qualities. . . . From the intellect, there is an effect, that which is acted upon [by the intellect]. It is the Universal Soul. He named her '*Tablet*'.[23]

This statement summarises the worldview of Ismaili Neoplatonism quite accurately including the distinctive Ismaili doctrine of God's command as a perspectival (but not ontological) intermediary between God and the originated Intellect. In the *Kitab Ta'wil al-shari'a*, the Imam-caliph al-Mu'izz explicitly teaches a Qur'anic exegesis (*ta'wil*) that evokes Neoplatonic concepts. For example, the Imam was asked about the Prophet's Night Journey from the Sacred Mosque (*al-masjid al-haram*) to the Farthest Mosque (*al-masjid al-aqsa*) as given in Qur'an 17:1. The Imam replied: 'The Sacred Mosque is the [Universal] Soul and the Farthest Mosque for the Prophets is the [Universal] Intellect.'[24]

If Imam al-Mu'izz truly deemed Ismaili Neoplatonism to be *kufr* (unbelief), there is no conceivable explanation as to why he himself and his highest *da'is* would adopt Neoplatonism wholesale and make it an essential part of *da'wa* teaching for all Ismailis, both inside and outside the Fatimid domains. Highly committed religious groups, such as the Ismaili *da'wa*, would not simply forfeit their core theology and adopt what they deem as heresy for popularity. Finally, there is no evidence that the preaching of Ismaili Neoplatonism – with its highly intricate and esoteric theses about God, creation and the cosmos of hierarchical Neoplatonic hypostases – was how the Fatimid *da'is* even won converts in the first place. The Fatimid *da'wa* manual of al-Nisaburi (d. after 386/996) tells us that *da'wa* instruction about the celestial ranks (*hudud*) is part of the esoteric knowledge and Ismaili initiates are only to be taught this esoteric knowledge after giving their oath of allegiance to the Imam and mastering the exoteric branches of knowledge.[25]

Having challenged the dominant narrative, we may reconsider why the Fatimid *da'wa* rapidly adopted the Neoplatonic ideas of the Eastern Ismaili *da'is*. Hollenberg proposes that the Fatimid *da'is* were engaged in a sort of 'riposte' to demonstrate the intellectual superiority of the Fatimid Imam-caliph and his *da'wa* over the Eastern Ismailis who did not recognise the Fatimids.[26] While this is surely a possibility, I would suggest a more benign and intellectually holistic reason. The earliest Ismailis conceived the dimensions of knowledge and reality in terms of a tripartite framework: the exoteric (*zahir*), the esoteric (*batin*) and the esoteric of the esoteric (*batin al-batin*). The exoteric comprises the verbal teachings of the prophets and the physical dimension of the Cosmos. The esoteric comprises the inner meanings of the various symbols and structures in the religious laws and physical world – inner meanings which are articulated, expounded, described and rationally formulated by the Imams and their deputies throughout history and the Ismaili *da'wa* in the present time. The third level, the esoteric of the esoteric, refers to universal immutable truths that Ismailis call 'God's Religion' (*din Allah*) and identify with the inner reality of the angels, prophets and God's vicegerents on earth.²⁷ This supreme esoteric level lies beyond the conventional *zahir-batin* polarity. It should be observed that the theological, metaphysical and cosmological doctrines taught by the Ismaili *daʿwa* at any given time occupied the intermediary level, the *batin,* and not the highest level of the *batin al-batin*. This means that private Ismaili teachings as articulated in theological discourse such as metaphysics, cosmology and *taʾwil*, only hold a secondary status before the unspeakable essential truths of the *batin al-batin*. This *batin al-batin* cannot be exhausted by any specific articulation of esotericism, which only partially and symbolically indicates the former without being identical to it. On this basis – the differentiation between the intermediary *batin* and the higher *batin al-batin* – the Ismaili *daʿwa* taught several concurrent theo-cosmological worldviews as intermediary *batin*. These include the 'Ismaili Gnosticism' model of the pre-Fatimid and early Fatimid *daʿi*s, the Ismaili Neoplatonism of the Eastern *daʿi*s and the Fatimid *daʿi*s under Imam al-Muʿizz, and even the later Satpanth Ismaili Indic theo-cosmologies presented in the *ginan* literature of South Asia.

This tripartite framework (*zahir, batin, batin al-batin*) enabled the Ismaili *daʿwa* to envision all human knowledge as stemming from prior forms of religious and philosophical heritage within a universalist cosmopolitan paradigm. In their view, every exoteric and esoteric truth among the religions and sciences is symbolically oriented towards God's Religion or the *batin al-batin* and originated from divine inspiration. Abu Hatim al-Razi teaches that 'every branch of wisdom in this world, great or small, takes its origin from Prophets who bequeathed it to the wise and scholarly after them, until it became a matter of instruction among mankind.'²⁸ Thus, when the Ismaili *daʿi*s adapted knowledge systems originating from 'foreign' traditions, such as Greek philosophy, Neoplatonism, Late Antique gnosticism, or Indic spiritual traditions (Vaishnavism, Sant, Bhakti, Vedanta), the Ismaili *daʿwa* was self-consciously integrating and recovering that knowledge in their own Ismaili epistemic framework. Instead of conceiving of the Fatimid adaption of Ismaili Neoplatonism as a bid to *convert* or *compete* against other Ismaili schools of thought, I would propose that the Fatimid *daʿi*s envisioned themselves as simply *restoring* a body of ancient truths they took to have originated with the prophets and Imams of Antiquity.

Neoplatonism as Metaphysical Infrastructure for Ismaili Theology

The emergence of Ismaili Neoplatonism in the philosophical teachings of the Ismaili *daʿwa* was a gradual and multifaceted process that took place over centuries. I would offer the following heuristic of three phases through which Ismaili Neoplatonism manifested among its proponents: 1) adoption, 2) consolidation, 3) application. Considering the development of Ismaili Neoplatonism through these three phases helps one attend to how Ismaili Neoplatonism functions in the works of various Ismaili *daʿis* throughout different periods of Ismaili history. The first phase, adoption, is found in the extant works of Abu Hatim al-Razi, Abu Yaʿqub al-Sijistani and the attributed works of Jaʿfar b. Mansur al-Yaman. In these works, while the Neoplatonic framework is clearly present, some of the terminology is still being worked out and one sees the presence of the older pre-Neoplatonic gnostic motifs like *al-sabiq/al-tali, kuni-qadar*, etc. The adoption phase is when various interpretations of Ismaili Neoplatonism are being ironed out and debated – as was the case in the intra-Ismaili debates of al-Razi, al-Nasafi and al-Sijistani. Most of the energy in these discussions is about defining terms and rationally defending the objective reality of Neoplatonic metaphysics. The second phase, consolidation, starts to take place in the late 4th/10th century and occurs during the 5th/11th century. It is manifested in the writings of Hamid al-Din al-Kirmani (d. after 411/1020) and Nasir-i Khusraw (d. after 462/1070). These thinkers, having read and interpreted the *daʿwa* writings of earlier generations, make a series of theological and philosophical judgements to standardise a Neoplatonic metaphysical model for themselves. Al-Kirmani maintained the apophatic theology of his predecessors with some of his own refinements but argued for a Neoplatonic model of ten intellects that clearly drew on Abu Nasr al-Farabi.[29] Meanwhile, Nasir-i Khusraw, his teacher al-Muʾayyad fiʾl-Din al-Shirazi (d. 470/1078), and other Fatimid *daʿis* maintained the classical Neoplatonic cosmology of al-Sijistani and Jaʿfar b. Mansur al-Yaman. Regardless of this difference, the works of al-Kirmani and Nasir show an effort to standardise their metaphysics and systematically offer syllogistic cosmological arguments for the existence of God, the Universal Intellect and the Universal Soul/Secondary Intellects.[30] The third phase, application, is found among all of the Ismaili Neoplatonists. This is when the Ismaili *daʿis* evoke their Neoplatonic worldview and apply its truth-claims to theological matters such as Prophethood, Imamology, *qiyama* and the *ta'wil* of Islamic ritual. Eminent examples of this application phase are to be found in al-Sijistani's *Kitab al-Iftikhar,* Ja'far b. Mansur al-Yaman's *Sara'ir wa asrar al-nutuqa',* the *Majalis* of al-Mu'ayyad, and Nasir-i Khusraw's *Wajh-i din.* In these texts, the *daʿi*s present revelatory exegesis (*ta'wil*) of various Islamic articles of faith (*usul al-din*), laws (*shariʿa*), rituals (*ʿibadat*) and Qur'anic narratives (*qisas*) of the prophetic missions by way of symbolically linking these exoteric structures to the Ismaili *daʿwa* ranks and the Neoplatonic hierarchy.

The outcome of the Ismaili *daʿwa*'s incorporation of Neoplatonic thought is that the philosophical explanations of core Ismaili theological commitments were suffused with and presupposed a Neoplatonic structure of reality. Far from being a case of cosmetic marketing, Ismaili Neoplatonism provided a cosmopolitan theological framework allowing Ismaili philosophers to articulate esoteric truths in universalist cosmic terms. It suffices to present two concrete examples of how Ismaili religious commitments are suffused with Neoplatonic structures: *tawhid* (monotheism) and divine guidance (Prophethology and Imamology).

Tawhid

All schools of Islamic thought were concerned with upholding *tawhid*, the absolute oneness of God. The Qur'an proclaims that God is absolutely one (*ahad, wahid*), that nothing resembles God (Q. 42:11), and that God is the absolute creator or originator of all things. At the same time, the Qur'an refers to God by many names – such as the knowing, the living, the powerful, the merciful, the wise, the seeing, the hearing, etc. Muslim theological schools conceived *tawhid* in various mutually contradictory ways due to differing interpretations of the Qur'anic material. The Sunni *kalam* schools (Ashʿari and Maturidi) and the Hanbali traditionalists interpret many of the divine names as predications referring to entitative attributes (*sifat maʿnawiyya*) that subsist in God's Essence. This means that God possesses an eternal uncreated life, eternal uncreated power, eternal uncreated knowledge, eternal uncreated speech, etc., as ontological attributes. For Sunnis, God's existence comprises an ontological multiplicity of uncreated attributes and a divine essence. Meanwhile, the Muʿtazilis deny that God has real-distinct attributes and hold that God's Essence is identical to His knowledge, power, life, hearing, seeing, etc.[31] All Sunni *kalam* theologians further believe that God directly and temporally interacts with the created world, which is wholly physical consisting of bodies made up of atoms and accidents; the Ash'aris and Hanbalis affirm occasionalism – that God is the direct creator and agent of every event in the Cosmos. Against the ideas of Sunni *kalam* theology and cosmology, the Ismailis argued for an alternative paradigm.

The Ismaili *da'is* asserted the absolute oneness and radical transcendence of God beyond all creaturely qualities, descriptions, names and attributes. This means that God is absolutely singular (*fard, ahad*) without entitative attributes or internal multiplicity, timelessly eternal (*azal*) beyond all change, unrestricted beyond all limits, self-sufficient and transcendent without any similarity to His creation. Everything other than God is a physical or spiritual creation whose existence always depends upon God. God transcends the various ontological categories and binaries that apply to His creation, such as cause/effect, substance/accident, spirit/matter, existence/non-existence, thingness/nothingness, etc. This Ismaili apophatic theology raises several theological and hermeneutical challenges. First: how does an absolutely transcendent, metaphysically simple, timeless and immutable God relate to His creatures? Second: on what basis can Muslims continue to refer to God using the Qur'anic divine names – such as the one, the powerful, the living, the king, or the knowing? The Ismaili *da'is* drew on the worldview of Neoplatonism to answer these questions and rationally uphold the Ismaili doctrine of *tawhid*. In Ismaili Neoplatonism, God's absolute unity entails that God's pure oneness cannot be the direct source of creaturely multiplicity; rather, God's pure oneness directly originates a single creation or a single effect only. The single and direct creation of God is the Universal Intellect. This was later called the 'Rule of One'.[32] Similarly, God's timelessness means that God does not create in time at a specific moment; rather, God is eternally originating His direct creation. God's eternal creative action is what Ismailis call the Divine Command (*amr*) or Word (*kalima*). Accordingly, the eternal first creation of God is the Universal Intellect, whose existence is both eternal and dependent upon God and whose essence is united to God's eternal action. As to the second question, since God utterly transcends having real-distinct attributes, including life, knowledge, power, wisdom, etc., there must be an entity among God's creatures that *does* possess these great-making attributes to the most perfect degree.[33] Ismailis identify this perfect creation who encompasses these perfect attributes with the Universal Intellect.[34] This Neoplatonic concept of the Universal Intellect allows the Ismailis to affirm the reality of the divine names used throughout the Qur'an and Islamic prayers in two complementary ways. Firstly, the divine names as *real predicates* or *literal descriptions* properly refer to the Universal Intellect whose multiple perfections correspond to the divine names; this means that the Universal Intellect is *literally described* by many of the 'Ninety-Name Names' of God. In the words of al-Kirmani, the First Intellect is 'entirely living (*hayy*), entirely powerful (*qadir*), entirely knowing (*'alim*), entirely eternal (*azali*), entirely all-encompassing (*muhit*), entirely perfect (*kamil*), complete (*tamm*) and singular (*wahid*).'[35] Since God is absolutely transcendent and limitless, the Universal Intellect functions theologically and cosmologically as the 'Face of God' that rational creatures can understand and conceptualise. Secondly, the Ismaili philosophers also apply these divine names to God Himself by construing each divine name as a metonymic predication describing God's creative action as opposed to God's Essence. To refer to God as the living, the powerful, the knowing, or the merciful truly means that God is the source and giver of life, power, knowledge, and mercy, which exist in the Universal Intellect and the Neoplatonic hierarchy. In the words of al-Shahrastani: 'He [God] is 'existent' in the sense that He existentialises every existence, is 'Necessary of Existence' in the sense that He necessitates every existent, is 'knowing' in the sense that He causes whatever is knowing to know, and is 'powerful' in the sense that He empowers whatever is powerful.'[36]

Without positing certain Neoplatonic intermediaries – such as the Universal Intellect/Soul or the First/Secondary Intellects, Ismaili philosophers would be unable to rationally defend their doctrine of *tawhid* both metaphysically and linguistically.

Divine Guidance

All Muslims affirm that God has revealed His guidance through His Messengers in the form of a revelatory message (*al-risala*). The popular Muslim belief is that God verbally dictates literal words, such as the Arabic Qur'an, to an angelic messenger, who descends to earth and conveys God's message to the Prophet as auditory speech. In this popular view, the Prophet repeats verbatim the precise linguistic words that God has dictated. However, the Ismaili view that God is absolutely transcendent, timeless and immutable negates this literalistic view of divine guidance where God conveys physical speech to His creatures at specific temporal moments. Ja'far b. Mansur al-Yaman belittled the popular Muslim views as the beliefs of the masses who are ignorant of the hierarchical ranks (*hudud*) in God's creation.[37] The Ismaili *da'i*s formulated a metaphysical model of divine guidance based on the Neoplatonic worldview. In Ismaili Neoplatonic cosmology, the Universal Soul is receiving intelligible emanations from the Universal Intellect, whose essence is eternally united to God's creative action – His Word or Command; the Universal Soul produces human souls and the natural world while continuously showering the Intellect's emanation of the Divine Word upon them. Most human souls, due to being imperfect and attached to materiality, are unable to fully accept the spiritual emanations from the Universal Intellect/Soul as they lack spiritual receptivity. However, in every period of humanity, there is at least one human soul whose spiritual perfections render it receptive to the emanations of the Universal Intellect and Universal Soul; this soul is a prophet. Nasir-i Khusraw writes: '[This soul] becomes the Messenger of the Universal Soul amongst other souls to those souls who remain incapable of accepting the influences of the Universal Soul. The name of this reception which the soul of the Prophet receives from the influences of the Universal Soul is the prophetic message (*risalat*).'[38]

Thus, all the prophets of God received non-verbal divine inspiration (*wahy*) from God only through the mediation of the Universal Intellect and Universal Soul. This divine inspiration flows to them as spiritual ideas and meanings, which each prophet creatively translates into human discourse appropriate to his audience. Thus, Nasir-i Khusraw states: 'All the Messengers who came brought the message of the Universal Soul through the divine support of the Universal Intellect from the Creator's Word (*paygham-i nafs-i kull bi-ta'yid-i 'aql az kalimat-i bari*).'[39] The Ismaili *da'i*s rationally explained divine guidance as a spiritual process involving the Neoplatonic intermediaries – Universal Intellect and Universal Soul – where a prophet is a perfect human soul directly receptive to their spiritual emanations. After the prophets, the Imams continued to receive spiritual emanation and divine support (*ta'yid*) (known as the Holy Spirit) from the Universal Intellect and Universal Soul. The Neoplatonic worldview allowed Ismaili thinkers to rationally explain the necessity and process of divine guidance through prophets and Imams while maintaining the radical transcendence of God.

The Continuity of Ismaili Neoplatonism in the Post-Fatimid Nizari Ismailism

It has been claimed that Ismaili Neoplatonism in the post-Fatimid Nizari Ismaili tradition was sidelined and completely fell out of fashion.[40] But this claim is somewhat exaggerated and fails to register how Ismaili Neoplatonism continued to exist but functioned in novel ways to serve the theological and spiritual concerns of post-Fatimid Ismaili communities. Several prominent non-Ismaili thinkers and traditions adopted Neoplatonic ideas directly or indirectly from the Ismailis. These include al-Ghazali in his post-crisis Sufi works, the Sunni mystics of al-Andalus, Ibn al-'Arabi (d. 638/1240) and his commentators, and certain Twelver Shi'i mystical philosophers like Haydar Amuli (d. after 787/1385) and Mulla Sadra (d. 1050/1640). Overall, the Neoplatonic worldview became quite popular in the post-Fatimid era among numerous Muslim philosophers and mystics including Afdal al-Din Kashani (d. 610/1213-14), Jalal al-Din Rumi (d. 672/1273), 'Aziz al-Din Nasafi (d. ca. 661/1262), Mahmud Shabistari (d. after 740/1339), Muhammad Lahiji (d. 912/1506-07), Mir Damad (d. 1040/1630), Mulla Muhsin Fayd Kashani (d. 1091/1680), Shah Wali Allah Dihlawi (d. 1174/1762), and Ibrahim al-Kurani (d. 1101/1690).

In the early Nizari period, Ismaili Neoplatonism featured quite prominently in the writings of 'Abd al-Karim al-Shahrastani (d. 548/1153), who was most likely a Nizari Ismaili practising *taqiyya* for most of his life. Al-Shahrastani's important treatises – including his *Kitab al-Musara'a* refuting Ibn Sina's metaphysics and his unfinished *tafsir* – display his indebtedness to and deployment of Ismaili Neoplatonism to achieve his ends. For example, al-Shahrastani counters Ibn Sina's cosmology with his rendering of classical Ismaili Neoplatonic thought where God transcends attributes, names, existence and non-existence, and the cosmic hierarchy unfolds starting with God's Command, the Universal Intellect and the Universal Soul: 'It is also necessary for the universal soul to have a universal intellect, and the intellect has a universal intellection from which emanates the absolute good upon everything by the medium of the soul, and existence ends up in it, just as existence originated *from* it, as an ordered series connected to the Command of the Creator, Who is exalted and sanctified above His glory falling within the hierarchy of existents or contrariety in beings.'[41] In his *tafsir*, al-Shahrastani presents an esoteric exegesis (*ta'wil*) of the twenty-eight letters of the Arabic alphabet in which every letter refers to a rank in the Neoplatonic and religious hierarchies: the *alif* symbolises God's Command; the *ba'* symbolises the First Intellect; the *ta'* represents the Universal Soul. This entire hermeneutic presupposes Neoplatonic emanation, as al-Shahrastani states: 'As for the unity of the Intellect, it is from the emanation (*fayd*) of the Command . . . and the light of the Intellect is from it . . . As for the secondary rank of the [Universal] Soul, it is from the emanation of the Intellect and the Command. Thus, there obtains a marriage between the Intellect and the Soul through the guardianship (*wilaya*) of the Command.'[42] Far from fading into the shadows, there is a fully functional Ismaili Neoplatonism in the writings of al-Shahrastani and he employs this worldview to construct novel metaphysical and exegetical arguments.

It is al-Shahrastani's version of Ismaili Neoplatonism – with its emphasis on the cosmic triad of God's Command, the Universal Intellect and the Universal Soul – that appears in the Nizari writings of Nasir al-Din al-Tusi (d. 672/1274). The *Rawda-yi taslim*, a joint work of al-Tusi and several Nizari *da'i*s, teaches metaphysics, cosmology, ethics, Imamology and soteriology infused with the Neoplatonic model specific to the Fatimid Ismailis and al-Shahrastani.[43] For example, the second *tasawwur* explains the emergence of God's Command, the origination of the First Intellect and the emanation of the Universal Soul. The third *tasawwur* relies on the Command-Intellect-Soul model to answer questions about God's creative action. Various subsequent *tasawwurat* dealing with nature, matter, human souls, etc. are reliant on this Neoplatonic model. This is especially true of Prophethology and Imamology: 'The sublime Word, the First Intellect, and the Universal Soul each have a locus of manifestation (*mazhar*) in this world. The locus of manifestation of the Sublime Word is the Imam . . . The locus of manifestation of the First Intellect is the supreme *hujjat* (proof) of the Imam . . . The locus of manifestation of the Universal Soul is the Prophet.'[44] In this Neoplatonic schema, the Imam's metaphysical reality or 'Light' is God's Command – the eternal creative action and primordial manifestation of God.

In the post-Alamut period when most Nizaris had to practise *taqiyya* and the Ismaili community was not at the liberty to publicise its literature, one continues to find the classical Ismaili Neoplatonic worldview being evoked in extant Nizari treatises. However, the primary function of the Neoplatonic worldview in this era was to provide the metaphysical infrastructure for Ismaili Imamology and soteriology. Instead of the highly intricate metaphysical arguments of al-Sijistani, al-Kirmani and Nasir-i Khusraw, one instead finds that Ismaili Neoplatonism is assumed or taken for granted as a background truth. Thus, the post-Alamut Nizari *da'i*s did not repudiate Neoplatonism at all; but they were no longer focussed on proving its veracity as a worldview. Their primary concern was the recognition of God through the person of the Imam with the aid of the *da'wa* hierarchy, for which the Ismaili Neoplatonic worldview was a necessary premise. The 8th–9th/14th–15th century Nizari treatise, *The Epistle of the Right Path*, summarises the Ismaili Neoplatonic schema by quoting the following words of the Nizari Imam 'Abd al-Salam:

> The first thing that the Exalted God brought forth was the Command. As a result of the Command, the Universal Intellect was produced. The Universal Soul was produced as a result of the Universal Intellect and the hyle, or prime matter, the heavens, the four natures, minerals, plants and animals were produced as a result of the Universal Soul. In reality, the purpose of creating these substances is humankind's existence. Then, the issuance of the existents from the Exalted God, who is the first origin, is through the mediation of something which, in the parlance of this community, is called his Command or his Word, may He be exalted. Thus, the first cause is the Command and the first effect is the Universal Intellect, for the Exalted God is pure from being a cause or an effect.[45]

This passage shows how the Nizari Imams, even a century after Alamut's destruction, continued to teach Ismaili Neoplatonism. The treatise goes on to explain the true nature of the Imam as the *mazhar* (locus of manifestation) of God's Command and the speaker-prophet (*natiq*) as the locus of manifestation of the First Intellect. The cosmological necessity of the Imam's existence in the physical world is premised on the Ismaili Neoplatonic worldview. Based on the Neoplatonic principle that the trace of the cause must exist within its effect, God's Command as the ultimate cause of the Cosmos necessarily entails that the Command is reflected within the physical world through a locus of manifestation – this being the Imam.

Later in the treatise, the author explains that the Imam is never concealed from his highest ranking *da'i*s – the *bab* (gate) and *hujja* (proof), who are the earthly reflections of Neoplatonic principles: 'It is impossible for the world to be bereft of the Universal Intellect and the Universal Soul and for them to be unaware of the Imam of the time, for they are the possessors of divine support (*ta'yid*). Their epiphanies are the *bab* (gate) and the *hujjat* (proof).'[46] A glance at other post-Alamut Nizari works also reveals the continued presence of Ismaili Neoplatonism, positioned to metaphysically substantiate Ismaili notions of prophethood and imamate. Notable examples appear in the *Haft Bab* of Abu Ishaq

Quhistani,[47] several post-Fatimid Syrian Ismaili treatises,[48] and the 12th/18th century Pamiri Ismaili work known as *Kalam-i Pir*.[49]

Ismaili Neoplatonism in the Contemporary Period

There are important instances of Neoplatonic ideas in contemporary Ismaili teachings from the recent Nizari Ismaili Imams, *pir*s and several Ismaili thinkers. Pir Shihab al-Din Shah, the eldest son and spiritual deputy of Imam 'Ali Shah Aga Khan II (d. 1302/1885), composed an authoritative treatise elucidating Ismaili theology for the Imam's Persian and Indian *murid*s. In this work, Shihab al-Din emphasises the Ismaili Neoplatonic and apophatic concept of God transcending all attributes and modalities: 'It is not permissible for you anymore to speculate whether He [God] is this kind or that. That is because God's Essence has not and will not be recognised. That is why whatever you say about God is your creation and has no relationship to God's Essence … Establishing an attribute for God is not possible as God's Essence cannot be known.'[50] The only types of 'attribute' that the author permits for God are metonymic predications that describe God's creations as opposed to His Essence – the same position upheld by premodern Ismaili philosophers.[51] Shihab al-Din further teaches that God's first and greatest creation is the 'Light of *Hadrat-i Mawla*', which is the 'Light' or metaphysical essence of the Imams and the Prophet: 'A light from the Light of God was extracted several thousand years before the creation of this world and [its] people; the Light of *Hadrat-i Mawla* is that light which had recognised and worshipped God in the way that God had desired. In this aspect, God willed that the Light of *Hadrat-i Mawla* be the possessor of all of His powers.'[52] In these passages, Shihab al-Din affirms a distinctively Ismaili Neoplatonic cosmology in which God is absolutely transcendent and God's first creation – the spiritual Light of 'Ali and Muhammad – is the locus of divine attributes and the intermediary through which God creates the Cosmos. This first-created Light is reflected or epiphanised in the person of the historical Imam, who is but a *mirror* (not incarnation) of God's attributes, while God's Essence remains wholly transcendent and inaccessible: 'In this manner, within our guidance, you recognised the station of *Hadrat-i Mawla*, who is the locus of manifestation (*mazhar*) of all of the divine attributes and God has made him the bearer of all of His powers and dominion. However, God is the one God about whom not a word must be uttered.'[53] All of this appears to be a modern restatement of

Ismaili Neoplatonism 21

the classical Ismaili Neoplatonic doctrine of God transcending attributes and the First Intellect being the locus of the divine names and predications.

The forty-eighth Imam, Sir Sultan Muhammad Shah Aga Khan III (d. 1376/1957), explained some of his theological ideas in his memoirs using Ismaili Neoplatonic terms: 'The creation according to Islam is not a unique act in a given time but a perpetual and constant event; and God supports and sustains all existence at every moment by His will and His thought.'[54] Michel Boivin observed that this is a modern restatement of the Ismaili metaphysics of God's Command/Will as the eternal cause of all created beings.[55] Aga Khan III also spoke of the 'Holy Spirit' as the source of spiritual illumination and enlightenment, an idea invoking the premodern Ismaili concept of the Holy Spirit as a luminous divine support (*ta'yid*) emanating from the Universal Intellect and Soul. Aga Khan III further described the physical Universe as a 'manifestation of the Universal Soul.' He also depicted this Universal Soul as 'the all-powerful Soul of God' connected to every created soul, the 'Soul that sustains, embraces, and is the Universe' who conveys divine inspiration to God's Messengers. Such descriptions evoke the Ismaili Neoplatonic views of Prophethood examined earlier.

The late 49th Imam, Shah Karim al-Husayni Aga Khan IV, also evoked Neoplatonic ideas on many occasions. At the 1975 Paris Conference, Aga Khan IV reinforced the concept of the Imam as the *mazhar* (locus of manifestation) in the context of various levels of inspiration between God and man. He also emphasised the absolute transcendence of God as the Ismaili position on *tawhid*.[56] In his own religious discourse, Aga Khan IV often referred to God using terms that emphasise transcendence, such as 'He who is above all else', which appeared at least ninety-five times in his *firman*s over the past sixty-five years.[57] Likewise, Aga Khan IV mentioned the technical terms 'Light (*nur*) of imamate' or the 'Light (*nur*) of 'Ali' over seventy-eight times and mentioned 'the Light' (*nur*) some 650 times in his *firman*s; 'light' was one of the most common symbols used by Ismaili philosophers to describe God's Command and the First Intellect. An oft-repeated spiritual idea taught by the late Imam in his *firman*s is that the Ismaili aspirant (*murid*) may attain a closeness to 'He who is above all else' (God) *through* the 'Light (*nur*) of imamate' or 'Light of 'Ali.' Thus, the late Ismaili Imam's teaching presents the Light of the imamate as the highest Neoplatonic intermediary between the absolutely transcendent God and created existents. Aga Khan IV explicitly mentioned the term 'Universal Intellect' ('*aql-i kull*) with its full Neoplatonic resonances in his 1985 address in Pakistan: 'The Divine Intellect, '*aql-i kull*, both transcends and informs the human intellect ... It is the light of the intellect which distinguishes the complete human being from the human animal.'[58] The late Aga Khan explicitly affirmed the Neoplatonic doctrine of 'eternal creation' in several *firman*s delivered during his Silver Jubilee: 'Remember that in Islam, Allah is eternal, His creation knows no limits in time, nor in dimension, nor in location ... therefore, Allah's creation, like Himself, is eternal.'[59] A great deal of Aga Khan IV's public discourse on Islam and his imamate revolved around the idea that God created humanity 'from a Single Soul', which evokes the Ismaili concept of the Universal Soul.

Apart from the recent Ismaili Imams, there are several Nizari Ismaili scholars, *wa'izin* and academic philosophers of religion, who have followed suit and employed Ismaili Neoplatonism in their theological and philosophical discourse. 'Allama Nasir al-Din Hunza'i has written numerous books on mystical and philosophical topics in which Ismaili Neoplatonism features prominently alongside Sufi ideas. Rai Jehangir Merchant has produced a synthesis of certain motifs in the Qur'an and the Ginan literature using Ismaili Neoplatonism as an interpretative lens.[60] M. Ali Lakhani's various writings on tradition, modernity and the late Aga Khan's public discourse draw upon a traditional Islamic Neoplatonic worldview.[61] The present author (Khalil Andani) has brought Ismaili Neoplatonism into contemporary philosophical debates by presenting new Ismaili responses to key issues in analytic theology and philosophy of religion, such as the problem of evil, the metaphysical viability of classical theism, the efficacy of petitionary prayer and the reconciliation of creation and evolution.[62]

In conclusion, far from being a mere missionary strategy for the Fatimid Ismaili *da'wa*, Neoplatonism came to colour the entire Ismaili theological paradigm from the 4th/10th century onwards. Ismaili Neoplatonism continued long past the demise of the Fatimid caliphate due to its universalist and cosmopolitan orientation, which both Ismailis and non-Ismailis found to be a valuable worldview paradigm. In the words of Dermot Moran, 'Neoplatonism is the longest and most enduring intellectual tradition in the history of philosophy and yet perhaps the most neglected.'[63] This chapter demonstrates a similar situation for the Ismaili version of Neoplatonic thought in Ismaili history. Apart from the imamate itself, Ismaili Neoplatonism is one of the most enduring legacies of the Fatimid caliphate and classical Islam. As Henry Corbin once instructed: 'Its voice, at once original and traditional, should be heard again today—a task of which it seems that the young Ismailis are aware.'[64]

NOTES

1. On al-Sijistani's access to an Arabic Neoplatonic source, see Alexander Treiger, 'The Intellect is a Point and a Circle: A Case Study in the Textual Relationship of Abu Ya'qub al-Sijistani's *Kitab al-Maqalid* and the *Longer Theology of Aristotle*', *Intellectual History of the Islamicate World*, 10 (2022), pp. 326–354.
2. Farhad Daftary, *The Isma'ilis: Their History and Doctrines* (Cambridge, 2007), pp. 225, 232.
3. Samuel M. Stern, 'Heterodox Isma'ilism at the time of al-Mu'izz', *BSOAS*, 17 (1955), pp. 15–16.
4. See David Hollenberg, 'The Empire Writes Back: Fatimid Ismaili *Ta'wil*', in Farhad Daftary and Gurdofarid Miskinzoda, ed., *The Study of Shi'i Islam* (London, 2014), p. 137.
5. Daryoush Mohammad Poor, 'Extra-Ismaili Sources and a Shift of Paradigm in Nizari Ismailism', in Orkhan Mir-Kasimov, ed., *Intellectual Interactions in the Islamic World: The Ismaili Thread* (London, 2020), pp. 222–230.
6. See details in Ismail K. Poonawala, 'An Early Doctrinal Controversy in the Iranian School of Isma'ili Thought and its Implications', *Journal of Persianate Studies*, 5 (2012), pp. 17–34.
7. Henry Corbin, *History of Islamic Philosophy* (London, 1992), p. 327.
8. Stern, 'Heterodox Isma'ilism', pp. 22–23.
9. Ibid., p. 15.
10. David Hollenberg, 'Neoplatonism in Pre-Kirmanian Fatimid Doctrine', *Le Museon*, 122 (2009), p. 161.
11. Hollenberg, 'The Empire Writes Back', p. 137.
12. Frank Griffel, *The Formation of Post-Classical Philosophy in Islam* (New York, 2021), p. 95.
13. Ibid., pp. 85–94.
14. Ibid., p. 95.
15. Abu Ya'qub al-Sijistani, *Kitab al-Iftikhar*, ed. Ismail K. Poonawala (Beirut, 2000), p. 175.
16. Ibid., pp. 94–95, 98.
17. Ibid., pp. 180–181, 186.
18. al-Sijistani, *Kitab al-Maqalid al-malakutiyya*, ed. Ismail K. Poonawala (Beirut, 2011), p. 70.
19. Ibid., p. 72.
20. Ibid., p. 111.
21. Abu Ya'qub al-Sijistani, *Ithbat al-nubuwwat*, ed. Wilferd Madelung and Paul E. Walker (Tehran, 2016), p. 184.
22. Hollenberg, 'Neoplatonism in Pre-Kirmanian Fatimid Doctrine', p. 163. Nadia E. Jamal is currently editing the *Kitab Ta'wil al-shari'a* and shared selected excerpts with me.
23. *Kitab al-Fatarat*, ed. and tr. in Hollenberg, 'Neoplatonism in Pre-Kirmanian Fatimid Doctrine', p. 188.
24. Abu Hanifa al-Qadi al-Nu'man, *Kitab Ta'wil al-shari'a*, ed. Nadia E. Jamal (typescript), Chapter 5, Section 37. Jamal kindly shared the excerpted text with me.
25. Ahmad b. Ibrahim al-Nisaburi, *al-Risala al-mujaza al-kafiya fi adab al-du'at*, ed. and tr. Verena Klemm, Paul E. Walker as *A Code of Conduct* (London, 2011), pp. 42–44, 61–62.

26 Hollenberg, 'The Empire Writes Back', p. 147.
27 Ja'far ibn Mansur al-Yaman, *Kitab al-'Alim wa'l-ghulam*, ed. and tr. James W. Morris as *The Master and the Disciple* (London, 2002), pp. 92–95.
28 Abu Hatim al-Razi, *A'lam al-nubuwwa*, ed. and tr. Tarif Khalidi as *The Proofs of Prophecy* (Provo, UT, 2011), p. 221.
29 On al-Kirmani's role and ideas, see Paul E. Walker, *Hamid al-Din al-Kirmani: Ismaili Thought in the Age of al-Hakim* (London, 1999).
30 For al-Kirmani's arguments for God, the First Intellect, and secondary Intellects, see Hamid al-Din al-Kirmani, *Rahat al-'aql*, ed. Mustafa Ghalib (Beirut, 1983), the first four large chapters (*al-sur*). For Nasir-i Khusraw's cosmological arguments for the Universal Soul, Universal Intellect and God, see his *Zad al-musafirin*, ed. Sayyid Isma'il 'Imadi Hairi and Sayyid Mohammad 'Imadi Hairi (2nd ed., Tehran, 2014), chapters (*qawl*) 13–16.
31 On these kinds of theology, see Richard M. Frank, *Early Islamic Theology: The Mu'tazilites and al-Ash'ari: Texts and Studies on the Development and History of Kalam*, vol. 2 (Aldershot, 2007). See also Khalil Andani, 'Divine Unicity (tawhid)', in B. N. Wolfe et al., ed., *St Andrews Encyclopaedia of Theology*, 2024. https://www.saet.ac.uk/Islam/DivineUnicity. For an exhaustive philosophical defence of Ismaili *tawhid*, see Khalil Andani, 'Apophatic Tawhid: A Philosophical Account of Shi'i Isma'ili Theology', in Wahid M. Amin, Aaron W. Hughes, Sajjad H. Rizvji, ed., *Islamic Perspectives on God and (Other) Monotheism(s)* (Birmingham, 2025), pp. 154–190.
32 Hamid al-Din al-Kirmani, *Rahat al-'aql*, p. 201. See also al-Kirmani, *Kitab al-Riyad*, quoted in Poonawala, 'An Early Doctrinal Controversy', p. 29. For more on the Rule of One, see Khalil Andani, 'Necessitated Evil: An Islamic Neoplatonic Theodicy from the Ismaili Tradition', in Mohammed Rustom and Muhammad U. Faruque, ed., *From the Divine to the Human* (New York, 2023), pp. 50–51.
33 al-Kirmani, *Rahat al-'aql*, pp. 181–191.
34 al-Sijistani, *Ithbat al-nubuwwat*, p. 25.
35 al-Kirmani, *Rahat al-'aql*, p. 189.
36 'Abd al-Karim al-Shahrastani, *Kitab al-musara'a*, ed. and tr. Wilferd Madelung and Toby Mayer as *Struggling with the Philosopher* (London, 2001).
37 Ja'far b. Mansur al-Yaman, *Sara'ir wa asrar al-nutuqa*', ed. Mustafa Ghalib (Beirut, 1984), p. 25.
38 Nasir-i Khusraw, *Khwan al-ikhwan*, ed. Yahya al-Kashshab (Cairo, 1940), p. 231.
39 Nasir-i Khusraw, *Gusha'ish va raha'ish*, ed and tr. F. M. Hunzai as *Knowledge and Liberation: A Treatise on Philosophical Theology* (London, 1998), p. 107. Translation slightly modified.
40 Poor, 'Extra-Ismaili Sources', pp. 226–233.
41 al-Shahrastani, *Struggling*, p. 32.
42 'Abd al-Karim al-Shahrastani, *Mafatih al-asrar wa masabih al-abrar*, ed. Muhammad 'Ali Azarshab (Tehran, 2008), vol. 1, p. 121.
43 Nasir al-Din al-Tusi, *Rawda-yi taslim*, ed. and tr. S. J. Badakhchani as *Paradise of Submission* (London, 2005).
44 Ibid., p. 113. Translation slightly modified and abbreviated.
45 Shafique Virani, 'The Right Path: A Post-Mongol Persian Ismaili Treatise', *Iranian Studies*, 43 (2010), p. 203.
46 Ibid., pp. 211–212.
47 Abu Ishaq Quhistani, *Haft Bab*, ed. and tr. Wladimir Ivanow (Bombay, 1959).
48 Simonetta Calderini, 'Studies in Isma'ili Cosmology: The Role of Intermediary Worlds', (PhD, University of London, 1991).
49 Wladimir Ivanow (ed. and tr.), *Kalam-i pir* (Bombay, 1935).
50 Sayyid Shihab al-Din Shah al-Husayni, *The Supreme Admonitions: Khitabat-e-'Aliya*, tr. Mast-e-'Ali Badakhshi (2023), pp. 17–18; For the Persian text, see Shihab al-Din ibn 'Ali

51. Shah (Khalil Allah), *Kitab-i Khitabat-i 'Aliyya: dar masa'il akhlaq va qa'id-i Isma'iliyya* (Bombay, 1963), accessed 6/13/2024: https://www.agakhanlibrary.digital/da-volume?docid=AKL_04900000150539. All citations of this work refer to the English translation.
51. Ibid., p. 19.
52. Ibid., pp. 20–21. Translation slightly modified
53. Ibid., p. 33. Translation slightly modified.
54. Sir Sultan Muhammad Shah Aga Khan III, 'Islam, The Religion of My Ancestors', in *The Memoirs of the Aga Khan: World Enough and Time* (New York, 1954), pp. 174–175. Reproduced by *The NanoWisdom Archives*. Last modified January 6, 2012: http://www.nanowisdoms.org/nwblog/1225/.
55. Michel Boivin, *La Renovation du Shi'isme Ismaélien en Inde et au Pakistan* (New York, 2003), pp. 116–117.
56. Eqbal Rupani, *Paris Conference* (Paris Ismailia Association, 1975), p. 6.
57. All referenced *firman*s of Aga Khan III and Aga Khan IV are from Ismaili private collections to which the author had direct access to perform analysis and gather data. The author used digital humanities methods to obtain precise word counts.
58. Aga Khan IV, 'Inauguration of the Faculty of Health Sciences and Aga Khan University Hospital, Pakistan', Karachi, Pakistan, 11 November 1985. Accessed 11 July 2022: https://www.aku.edu/about/chancellor/Pages/inauguration-fhs-and-akuh-khi.aspx
59. Aga Khan IV, June 13, 1983, quoted in Khalil Andani, 'Evolving Creation: An Ismaili Muslim Interpretation of Evolution', *Zygon*, 57 (2022), pp. 443–466, 448.
60. Jehangir Merchant, 'Light upon Light – *Nurun ala Nur*', *Ilm*, 2 (1976), pp. 43–49.
61. M. Ali Lakhani, *Faith and Ethics: The Vision of the Ismaili Imamat* (London, 2018).
62. See Khalil Andani, 'Evolving Creation: An Ismaili Muslim Interpretation of Evolution', *Zygon*, 57 (2022), pp. 443–466; 'Divine Simplicity and the Myth of Modal Collapse: An Islamic Neoplatonic Response', *European Journal of Analytic Philosophy*, 18 (Interactions between analytic and Islamic philosophy/theology), pp. 5–34; 'Neoplatonic Prayer: The Isma'ili Hermeneutics of salat According to al-Sijistani and Nasir-i Khusraw', in Mohammed Rustom, ed., *Islamic Thought and the Art of Translation* (Leiden, 2023), pp. 277–297.
63. Alexander J. B. Hampton and John Peter Kenney, ed., *Christian Platonism: A History* (Cambridge, 2021).
64. Corbin, *History of Islamic Philosophy*, p. 327.

2

Who was Nasir-i Khusraw's Patron in Yumgan? Notes on the Political Vectors of the Late Fatimid *Daʿwa*

Daniel Beben

The Persian poet and Fatimid *daʿi*, Nasir-i Khusraw (d. after 464/1072), is widely celebrated for having introduced Ismailism to the Upper Oxus districts of present-day eastern Tajikistan and northeastern Afghanistan. Yet very little is known of the final years of Nasir-i Khusraw's life and career, during which he continued his work on behalf of the Fatimid *daʿwa*. While the outlines of Nasir's earlier years are relatively well known on account of his renowned travelogue, the *Safar-nama*, the text concludes with his return from Egypt and says nothing of his subsequent career as a *daʿi*. Of the final years of his life, spent in exile in the present-day Badakhshan province of Afghanistan, only a handful of details are well established. Among them is that, at some point, he was patronised by a local ruler, the amir of Badakhshan, to whom Nasir dedicated his last dated work, the *Jamiʿ al-hikmatayn* (462/1070). A second fact is that Nasir resided for much of his period of exile in Yumgan, a locality to which he refers often in his poetry and where his burial place is found.

Previous scholarship has almost unanimously chosen to merge these two details, assuming that Yumgan was an internal district of Badakhshan and, thus, that the amir to whom Nasir refers in his *Jamiʿ al-hikmatayn* was the sovereign of Yumgan who served as his patron during his residence there.[1] This assumption is not unreasonable, given that Yumgan today does indeed constitute a subordinate district within the province of Afghan Badakhshan. However, it overlooks the accounts presented in the local Badakhshani tradition, which tell us a rather different story regarding Nasir-i Khusraw's patrons, and which suggest that our present understanding of the political relationship between Badakhshan and

Yumgan may be anachronistic when applied to the context of the 5th/11th century. While the Badakhshani tradition presents a great diversity of stories concerning Nasir-i Khusraw, there are nonetheless several details that appear with remarkable consistency throughout these narratives: namely, that Yumgan was politically autonomous from Badakhshan at the time of Nasir's arrival there, that the rulers of both Badakhshan and Yumgan at differing times served as patron to Nasir, that Nasir experienced some manner of a break or disruption in his relationship with the ruler of Badakhshan and, finally, that it was the ruler of Yumgan, and not Badakhshan, with whom Nasir developed the closest and most consequential relationship.

To be sure, the local hagiographical traditions concerning the life of Nasir-i Khusraw found in Badakhshan, at least in their attested form, were composed many centuries after the fact and clearly present many facets that are best not accepted uncritically at face value. Nonetheless, there is a substantial body of circumstantial evidence to suggest that the claims presented in the Badakhshani tradition on this point, in their broadest outlines, are historically feasible and, in fact, should be preferred to the assumptions presented in most modern scholarship regarding Nasir-i Khusraw's patronage. While this matter is of obvious interest for scholarship on the figure of Nasir-i Khusraw himself, beyond this, I would like to suggest that the vicissitudes of Nasir's patronage may offer some broader insight into the political dimensions of the *da'wa* outside the borders of the Fatimid state.

Nasir-i Khusraw and his Patrons

Nasir-i Khusraw dedicated his last dated work, the *Jami' al-hikmatayn*, to a local ruler whom he refers to ornately as 'the Amir of Badakhshan 'Ayn al-Dawla Zayn al-Milla, Fakhr al-Umma, Shams al-A'ali, Abu'l-Ma'ali 'Ali b. al-Asad b. al-Harith, the client (*mawla*) of the Commander of the Faithful (*amir al-mu'minin*)'.[2] The work was occasioned when Nasir received from the amir a copy of a poem by the Ismaili author al-Jurjani, of whom very little is otherwise known today, with a request to explain its meaning. The fact of 'Ali b. al-Asad's familiarity with the work of al-Jurjani, coupled with Nasir's copious praise of him, has generally been taken as sufficient evidence that 'Ali b. al-Asad was the primary supporter of Nasir's *da'wa* work in the region. However, Nasir's references to 'Ali b. al-Asad in the *Jami' al-hikmatayn* constitute the only known mention of this ruler in contemporary sources, and scarcely anything is otherwise known of him. There are, however, a number of overlooked accounts to be found about this figure in the later Badakhshani tradition, which are unanimous in stating that 'Ali b. al-Asad, in fact, served at best only temporarily as Nasir's patron, and that Nasir found a second and more committed patron in the person of the ruler of Yumgan.

The earliest version of the narrative of Nasir-i Khusraw's two patrons is found in a text, first appearing in the late 10th/16th century, which purports to be an autobiography of Nasir-i Khusraw, titled *Risalat al-nidamat fi zad al-qiyamat*. The text first appeared as an appendix to the notice on Nasir in the *Khulasat al-ashʿar va zubdat al-afkar* of Taqi al-Din Kashi, a biographical dictionary of poets completed in 985/1577-78.[3] Subsequently, variants of this text appeared in a wide range of literary sources and biographical dictionaries. The work was almost universally accepted as the authoritative account of Nasir's biography down to the late 19th century, when his authorship of it was conclusively rejected. The text has subsequently received little scholarly attention, its credibility as a source for the biography of Nasir-i Khusraw having been broadly discredited.

I have discussed the *Risalat al-nidamat* at some length elsewhere, where I have argued that, while the text may not necessarily reveal a great deal about the historical life of Nasir-i Khusraw, it does serve as an informative source for the confessional politics surrounding his legacy in the early modern era.[4] In particular, I demonstrated how it is likely that the text was probably crafted in connection with Nasir's shrine in Yumgan, at a time when the site is known to have come under the control of non-Ismaili caretakers, with the intention of dissociating Nasir from Ismaili beliefs for the purpose of attracting patronage for the shrine. The text begins with an account of Nasir's early life and education, followed by a narrative of how he found employment as the chief minister of the Abbasid caliph al-Qadir bi'llah (historically known for his anti-Ismaili policies), who sent him on a diplomatic mission to the Daylam region in Persia to meet with the leader of the Ismailis, referenced here under the derogatory term *malahida*, or heretics. The account relates that Nasir and his brother were captured and imprisoned by the chief of the *malahida*, who compelled Nasir under threat of death to compose a treatise defending the doctrines of the Ismailis, the contents of which the pseudo-Nasir entirely disavows in this account.

The text continues with relating how Nasir and his brother escaped from the *malahida* and fled from place to place, eventually arriving in

Badakhshan. There they were received by the king of Badakhshan, whose name is given as ʿAli b. al-Asad Husayni ʿAlavi, who is described as the 'Pride of the Family of the Prophet' (*fakhr-i Al-i Rasul*), and thus a sayyid. The name is clearly a reference to the ruler to whom Nasir-i Khusraw dedicated his *Jamiʿ al-hikmatayn*, although the reference to him being a sayyid appears to be an innovation, as Nasir himself made no mention of this fact (and almost certainly would have mentioned it were it the case, considering the high praise he otherwise lavishes upon him). According to the narrative, ʿAli b. al-Asad honoured Nasir and elevated him to a high position as his minister, so that his station equaled that which he held previously in Baghdad.

Before long, however, the treatise that Nasir was compelled to compose during his captivity among the *malahida* reached Badakhshan and came to the attention of the chief *qadi* of the realm, named Nasr Allah, who issued a *fatwa* calling for the execution of Nasir, forcing him to flee once again, this time to the province of Yumgan. There the ruler of Yumgan, named Jahanshah b. Giv Yumgani, gave refuge to Nasir and offered him a high position in his own administration; this time, however, Nasir concedes that he has grown too old for such matters and expresses his desire to retire from the world. The text then relates how Nasir chose a cave for his residence and spent twenty-five years there engaged in constant fasting and ascetic practices. The text concludes with a lengthy and detailed description of the arrangements for Nasir's burial, revealing itself at the end to have been dictated by Nasir on his deathbed to his brother, who is charged with preparing Nasir's grave.

Yet while many aspects of the *Risalat al-nidamat* are clearly ahistorical, such as the account of Nasir's employment under al-Qadir bi'llah and the narrative of his imprisonment at the hands of the *malahida*, it is not evident that we must dismiss the work in its entirety as an early modern fabrication; in particular, there is reason to believe that there may be a kernel of veracity in the account of Nasir's relationships with various rulers in the Badakhshan region. Having, most likely, originated in Yumgan, the text would be well situated to reflect some historical memory of events that transpired in the region in Nasir's time. Of the fact that Nasir arrived in the region in flight from persecutors, and that accusations of heresy or irreligiosity continued to beleaguer him even while in exile, there is little doubt, as he bemoans these developments often in his poetry and other writings, and thus is it not unlikely that these accusations may have caused any strain in his relations with his patrons there.[5] Furthermore, the text demonstrates no evident bias or agenda against the figure of 'Ali b. al-Asad that might have obliged the author to downplay his role as Nasir's patron; on the contrary, this figure is elevated in the text to the status of a sayyid, and is shown to have been absolved by Nasir of any blame for having been misled by the slander spread by his persecutors.

But perhaps the strongest evidence in support of the *Risalat al-nidamat*'s narrative of Nasir-i Khusraw's patronage is the fact that an account of Nasir's relationship with a ruler of Yumgan by the name of Jahanshah is attested already in another source dating to a century and a half earlier than the *Risalat*. The source in question is a scroll presently held in a private collection in the Rushan region of Badakhshan, containing a genealogy (*nasab-nama*) and biography of Jahanshah (referred to here as Malik Jahanshah), dated to 830/1426-27.[6] The account relates how Malik Jahanshah gave up his power and wealth in order to serve Nasir-i Khusraw, subsequently spending thirty years in his service, taking the new name of 'Umar Yumgi. The *nasab-nama* mentions nothing of 'Ali b. al-Asad, and it is not until the later appearance of the *Risalat al-nidamat* that we find the earliest attestation of the narrative of Nasir's exile from Badakhshan to Yumgan. It does, however, indicate the antiquity of the tradition concerning Nasir's relationship with a local ruler in Yumgan other than the one to whom he dedicated his *Jami' al-hikmatayn*.

While the *Risalat al-nidamat* presents a clear anti-Ismaili agenda, nonetheless the account of Nasir-i Khusraw maintaining relationships with separate rulers in Badakhshan and Yumgan also features in later Ismaili hagiographical traditions, in which Malik Jahanshah/'Umar Yumgi is depicted as one of Nasir-i Khusraw's chief disciples and successors.[7] By contrast, the figure of 'Ali b. al-Asad is relegated to a relatively minor place in later Ismaili sources, and is not credited with any role in the subsequent spread of the *da'wa* after Nasir. Stories of Jahanshah are preserved in non-Ismaili sources from Badakhshan as well: a particularly embellished account is offered by the early 20th-century anthologist Shah 'Abd Allah Badakhshi, who describes Jahanshah as a powerful king whose realm extended from Balkh in the west to Chinese Turkestan in the east, and from Hisar-i Shadman (the present-day town of Hisor in southwestern Tajikistan) in the north to Kashmir in the south.[8] Despite their evident exaggeration, such accounts nonetheless illustrate the much greater significance attached to the figure of Jahanshah in popular memory in the region in comparison with 'Ali b. al-Asad.

Badakhshan and Yumgan

Is there any historical basis to the notion that Badakhshan and Yumgan were separate kingdoms with separate rulers in the time of Nasir-i Khusraw? To be sure, references to Yumgan (alternatively Yumghan or Yamgan) are extremely sparse for the pre-modern period. However, the little information available indicates that it was clearly autonomous from Badakhshan at least in the centuries prior to Nasir-i Khusraw's life there. The earliest known reference to Yumgan is found in the 7th century AD travel account of the Chinese Buddhist pilgrim Xuanzang, who unambiguously describes Badakhshan and Yumgan as separate kingdoms with their own rulers.[9] Following this, the 3rd/9th century geographer Ibn Khurdadhbih refers to Yumgan as among the districts that paid tax revenue directly to the Abbasid governor of Khurasan, implying that it held equal autonomy alongside the other districts of the region.[10]

Regretfully, there are no known references to Yumgan in the sources from the two centuries preceding Nasir-i Khusraw's arrival in the region. While numismatic evidence reveals that the Samanids appointed governors of Badakhshan in the 4th/10th century, we have no indication of whether Yumgan was included in their remit.[11] However, there is evidence from Nasir-i Khusraw's own works to indicate that Yumgan was autonomous from Badakhshan in his time.[12] Nasir refers to Yumgan often in his poetry, invariably mentioning it as his place of residence.[13] By contrast, Badakhshan is mentioned far less frequently and appears in the majority of cases only in the context of the poetic motif of the 'ruby of Badakhshan' (*la'l-i Badakhshan*).[14] Badakhshan is never mentioned in Nasir's poetry in a manner that would imply it was the place where he actually lived; in one passage, in which Nasir gives a number of sites throughout the region in which his *da'wa* has been heard, Badakhshan is listed as a place alongside Yumgan and a number of other districts.[15] This would seem to suggest that Nasir considered Yumgan and Badakhshan as two items in the same category, rather than one being subordinate to the other.

Furthermore, biographical accounts of Nasir-i Khusraw for several centuries after his death unanimously mention his place of exile and burial as Yumgan, and not Badakhshan. The 7th/13th century geographer Zakariyya al-Qazwini in his account of Yumgan, which is primarily dedicated to a discussion of Nasir-i Khusraw's connection with the region, refers to it as an 'inaccessible territory among the mountains *bordering on*

Badakhshan', while a separate entry in his work on Badakhshan itself mentions nothing of Nasir.[16] Likewise, the historian Rashid al-Din, writing in the early 8th/14th century, relates how Nasir fled from Balkh 'to the mountain of Yumgan'.[17] Altogether, not a single known reference to Nasir-i Khusraw composed within the first three centuries after his death refers to him as having resided in Badakhshan, nor do they refer to Yumgan as a dependency of the former.[18] If Yumgan had been merely an internal district of Badakhshan, then this raises the question of why accounts of Nasir throughout this period were so consistent in mentioning only Yumgan and not Badakhshan as his place of residence and burial, considering that the latter name would have likely been much more familiar to readers outside the region.

It is not until the late 9th/15th century that we find the earliest reference to Yumgan as an internal district of Badakhshan. This is found in the work of the anthologist Dawlatshah Samarqandi, who writes in his account of Nasir-i Khusraw in his *Tadhkirat al-shuʿara* that his grave is located 'in the valley of Yumgan, which is among the dependencies of Badakhshan'.[19] Similarly, writing in the early 10th/16th century the historian Ghiyath al-Din Khwandamir says in his *Habib al-siyar* that Nasir fled from Balkh and took refuge in 'one of the mountains among the mountains of Badakhshan'.[20] Thereafter, sources produced outside Badakhshan regularly describe Nasir-i Khusraw's burial place, and Yumgan itself, as being located in Badakhshan; however, as noted previously, sources produced in the vicinity of Badakhshan continued to place an emphasis on a distinction between Yumgan and Badakhshan when discussing the biography of Nasir-i Khusraw. This shift in the status of Yumgan in the sources can be explained by the fact that the scope of territory designated by the term Badakhshan expanded significantly after the Mongol conquests. In the pre-Mongol era, the name Badakhshan referred to but one of a series of small kingdoms situated in the eastern reaches of what was then termed the region of Tukharistan.[21] However, following the Mongol conquests, Badakhshan in the late 7th/13th century came under the rule of an autonomous dynasty, under which Badakhshan expanded significantly to encompass a number of previously independent neighbouring territories, and many authors subsequently applied this expanded geographical definition anachronistically to the time of Nasir-i Khusraw.

In summary, while we have no contemporary evidence to directly corroborate the narrative of Nasir-i Khusraw's dual patrons found in later Badakhshani sources, our knowledge of the geographical situation at the time suggests that this possibility is feasible. If Nasir indeed was not under the protection of the ruler of Badakhshan throughout his period of residence in Yumgan, then this would help to explain Nasir's seemingly inexplicable decision to not only choose the peripheral region of eastern Tukharistan for his place of exile, but furthermore, one of the most isolated and peripheral sites *within* this region. Nasir complains frequently of his surroundings in Yumgan in his poetry and laments his lack of access to the cultural resources of his native Khurasan.[22] Yet, if the ruler of Badakhshan was in fact his chief patron throughout this time, then Nasir presumably would have enjoyed the option of living in the relatively greater comfort of the capital of his kingdom (situated near the present-day capital of Faydabad), which undoubtedly would have also served as a more effective hub for his conduct of the *daʿwa*. This raises the question: given ʿAli b. al-Asad's evident personal interest in Ismaili thought, what truth might there be, then, to the claim that in fact it was not him, but rather the ruler of Yumgan who served as Nasir's primary patron? In order to address this question, we must begin by examining more closely the available evidence concerning these two men and their historical connections with the region.

ʿAli b. al-Asad and Malik Jahanshah: Their Ancestry and Relationship

Aside from Nasir-i Khusraw's reference to him, there is no other information available from contemporary sources regarding the figure of ʿAli b. al-Asad himself. However, there is some evidence available to suggest that this figure represented a dynasty that had been involved in ruling over the Badakhshan region intermittently for nearly two centuries prior to Nasir's arrival there. The geographer al-Yaʿqubi in his *Kitab al-Buldan* from 278/891 mentions a local ruler of the district of Rustabik (modern-day Rustaq) in present-day Badakhshan by the name of al-Harith b. Asad b. Bik, after whom the Bikiyya horses are named.[23] This same al-Harith b. Asad is mentioned slightly earlier by Ibn Khurdadhbih as the ruler of the neighbouring Khuttalan and is described as a nephew of Daʾud b. Abu Daʾud b. ʿAbbas, thus connecting him with the Banijirid clan who ruled Balkh in the later part the 3rd/9th century.[24]

Our knowledge of the rulers of Badakhshan from this time onwards is limited almost entirely to numismatic evidence. The Banijirids periodically minted coinage from the district of Andarab, in present-day southwestern

Badakhshan, first as independent rulers and then, from 287/900 to 294/907, as vassals of the Samanids.[25] Thereafter, the Banijirids disappear from the record, and coinage from the region for most of the remainder of the 4th/10th century carries only the names of the Samanid amirs.[26] However, during the reign of the Samanid *amir* Nuh II (r. 366–387/976–997), we find coins produced in the name of al-Harith b. Harb, the only Samanid governor of Badakhshan to have his own coinage.[27] Some of his coins also carry the name of Abu'l-Hasan Muhammad Simjuri, the Samanid governor of Khurasan who was known for his ruthless persecution of the Ismailis.[28]

Following the downfall of the Samanids at the end of the 4th/10th century, Badakhshan came under the control of the Ghaznavids, a change which appears to have been accompanied by a shift in the line of governors ruling the region. A report from the year 422/1031 gives the name of the Ghaznavid governor of Badakhshan as Ahmad b. ʿAli b. Nushtigin, 'Master of the Royal Stables', whose name does not suggest any connection with the previous Samanid governors of the region.[29] This individual may have been the father of Malik Jahanshah, as the 9th/15th-century *nasab-nama* reports his father's name as Mir Ahmad, son of ʿAli. Meanwhile, numismatic evidence shows that the neighbouring region of Khuttalan down to the year 431/1040 was ruled by another Ghaznavid governor by the name of Abu'l-Asad al-Harith.[30] This figure's name indicates that it is likely he was a descendant of the former line of governors of Badakhshan and, moreover, may have been the grandfather of Nasir-i Khusraw's patron, the amir of Badakhshan, ʿAli b. al-Asad al-Harith. Altogether, the repeated appearance of the names Harith and Asad among the governors of Badakhshan and neighbouring Khuttalan might be taken to suggest that these individuals belonged to a single lineage, descended from the Banijirid clan.

The *Tarikh-i Bayhaqi* reports that in the year 431/1040, Khuttalan was attacked by the Qarakhanids and its governor, presumably the aforementioned Abu'l-Asad, was forced to take refuge in Balkh.[31] However, an ensuing Qarakhanid assault on Balkh itself was repelled, and later that same year Abu'l-Asad was installed once again in Khuttalan, where for the next several years he minted coins as an independent ruler.[32] In the meantime, the Ghaznavids, not long after having repelled the Qarakhanid invasion, suffered a series of defeats at the hands of the Saljuqs in Khurasan, culminating in the Saljuq conquest of Balkh later that same year.[33] By 435/1043, the Saljuq prince Alp Arslan ruled over almost the entirety of the Tukharistan region, to the borders of Badakhshan.³⁴ Khuttalan remained outside the Saljuq orbit for some time and several coins dated to 437/1045-46 depict Abu'l-Asad as a vassal of the Qarakhanid ruler Ibrahim b. Nasr; however, shortly thereafter, Abu'l-Asad transferred his vassalage to the Saljuq khan, Chaghri Beg Da'ud (r. 429–451/1038–1059).³⁵

The fate of Abu'l-Asad from this point forward is unclear, and it is not known how long he remained in control of Khuttalan. Ibn al-Athir reports that, in the year 456/1064, the ruler of Khuttalan rebelled against the Saljuqs and was killed in an ensuing siege.³⁶ After this, Khuttalan was annexed directly to the Saljuq domains and there are no further references to a local dynasty in the region. It is uncertain if Ibn al-Athir's account refers to a member of Abu'l-Asad's lineage; however, some references in the *Jami' al-hikmatayn* allude to the report that 'Ali b. al-Asad's family had experienced some calamity in the past, as Nasir refers to the amir having 'forcefully subdued the enemies of his most illustrious ancestors'.³⁷

In summary, at the time of Nasir-i Khusraw's arrival in the region, the Saljuqs were well established as the preeminent power in the lands to the west of Badakhshan, while the Qarakhanids retained their strongholds in the Ferghana valley and the Tarim basin to the north and east of Badakhshan, respectively. However, the political situation in Badakhshan and among its immediate neighbours during this time is almost entirely obscure, and we have no clear indication of what may have taken place in the four decades between Bayhaqi's report from 422/1031 of a local Ghaznavid governor in the region by the name of Ahmad b. 'Ali, and Nasir-i Khusraw's reference to 'Ali b. al-Asad in 462/1070. It is probable that, following their annexation of Khuttalan in 456/1064, the Saljuqs thereafter came to exercise some degree of influence over Badakhshan as well. They had clearly annexed the region no later than the reign of Sultan Ahmad Sanjar (r. 511–552/1118–1157), as coins bearing his name were minted in Badakhshan (unaccompanied by the name of any local governor).³⁸ While there is evidence that the Qarakhanids oversaw mining operations in the eastern Pamirs down to the early 6th/12th century, it would appear that the Pamir range served as the boundary between their realm and that of the Saljuqs.³⁹

Altogether, the most likely scenario is that 'Ali b. al-Asad served in Badakhshan in the capacity of a Saljuq vassal or frontier warden, perhaps having accepted this modest post as a means of reconciling with the Saljuqs following his forebear's revolt. This appointment evidently came at the expense of the family of Ahmad b. 'Ali, who previously served as governor of Badakhshan under the Saljuqs' former opponents, the Ghaznavids, and who may have subsequently found themselves reduced to the more marginal kingdom of Yumgan. However, it would also appear that ʿAli b. al-Asad's position in Badakhshan was still not altogether secure, as Nasir-i Khusraw refers cryptically in the *Jamiʿ al-hikmatayn* to 'a time when he had been driven by a misfortune from his rule (*mulk*),' before once again being restored to it.[40]

Amongst these developments, Nasir-i Khusraw returned from Egypt and arrived in Balkh in 444/1052, at the height of Saljuq ascendency in Khurasan. To say the least, this was an inopportune time to begin a career as an Ismaili *daʿi* in the region, as his subsequent persecution and exile vividly demonstrates. Nasir was forced into exile in Yumgan no later than 454/1062, at a time when the region may have still been safely beyond the Saljuq orbit.[41] However, following their annexation of neighbouring Khuttalan in 456/1064, it is likely that Saljuq interest in the Badakhshan region would have intensified, especially considering that the region would have now become a frontier with their long-standing opponents, the Qarakhanids. Both powers maintained a stringent hostility towards the Ismaili *daʿwa* and were known for their violent persecutions of Ismailis within their realms. On at least one occasion, in 488/1095, it would appear that the Saljuq sultan, Malik Shah, engineered the downfall of his rival, the Qarakhanid ruler of Samarqand, Ahmad Khan, by deploying accusations of Ismaili sympathies.[42] Nasir-i Khusraw, who had previously served as a clerk under the Saljuqs in the city of Marw before his adoption of Ismailism, was unsparing in his criticisms of their dominion in his poetry.[43] Considering the foregoing context, it is thus not at all difficult to imagine that ʿAli b. al-Asad, as a representative of a local dynasty who had long served as governors under Sunni powers with the reputation for marked hostility towards the Ismailis, and who probably now found himself under an increasing level of scrutiny from the Saljuqs, may have harboured doubts regarding the choice to extend his patronage to Nasir-i Khusraw.

That being said, we can probably discount the precise sequence of events presented in the *Risalat al-nidamat*, which claims that Nasir went to Yumgan only after suffering a break in his relationship with the ruler of Badakhshan. As noted above, Nasir appears to have been already settled in Yumgan no later than 454/1062, eight years before composing his *Jamiʿ al-hikmatayn*.[44] Furthermore, Nasir's references to ʿAli b. al-Asad give no overt indication that he served in any position at the latter's court, as the

Risalat al-nidamat suggests, or even that he had been in the physical presence of the amir at all; rather, Nasir refers only to exchanging letters with ʿAli b. al-Asad, and it is possible that their relationship may have been conducted entirely through correspondence. Despite this, I would suggest that what is most significant and 'reliable' in regard to the account in the *Risalat al-nidamat* is not its depiction of any particular events in the career of Nasir-i Khusraw, but rather, what these depictions suggest concerning local understanding and memory of the fundamental *character* of Nasir's relationships with various rulers in the region. Altogether, both the Ismaili and non-Ismaili traditions preserved in Badakhshan about Nasir-i Khusraw concur: that it was the independent ruler of Yumgan with whom Nasir had the closest, most enduring, and most consequential relationship.

Conclusion: The *Daʿwa* and the Politics of Imperial Exclusion

In light of the above, I would like to offer here an alternative hypothesis regarding the chronology of Nasir-i Khusraw's patronage: that from early on in his exile, Nasir was under the protection of a local ruler in Yumgan, and that it was only sometime later that he extended overtures towards the ruler of neighbouring Badakhshan (who appears to have entertained a genuine interest in Ismaili beliefs), but that these overtures ultimately proved to be abortive, thus compelling Nasir to remain in Yumgan. This leaves one final question to address: if the scenario posited above is correct, then what reasons might have motivated the ruler of Yumgan to be more receptive to Nasir-i Khusraw than the ruler of Badakhshan? Of course, one can only speculate as to the exact motives of any individual in such circumstances, not to speak of one whose very existence remains a matter of conjecture. Instead, I will offer here simply a heuristic framework to explain what factors might have informed such a scenario.

From its height in the middle of the 4th/10th century, the Ismaili *daʿwa* achieved significant if temporary success in its efforts to establish relations with the political elites of the Buyid and the Samanid states, and later those of the Qarakhanids and the Ghurids as well.[45] However, despite a string of transitory successes, these efforts failed to result in any enduring shifts in support of Ismailism in the political centres of Persia and Central Asia. Instead, in nearly all cases, the same pattern can be seen, in which a ruler or other high-ranking member of the elite is persuaded of the *daʿwa*, only to shortly after find himself sidelined, with the former recipients of his patronage then subjected to persecution or massacre.

Where the *da'wa* achieved much more lasting success was not among central elites, but rather, among local elites on the imperial periphery. This pattern is most vividly in evidence in the early Nizari movement in Persia, which acquired its most enduring support in the mountainous territories of the southern Caspian region and the Quhistan region of eastern Persia, areas long known for their centrifugal political tendencies and histories of resistance to outside rule. This pattern can be clearly seen later in Badakhshan as well, where Ismaili activity also frequently correlated with movements towards local autonomy. One prominent example comes from an account of an Ismaili-led uprising in Badakhshan that lasted for several years until it was suppressed by the Timurid governor, Sultan Ways Mirza, in 915/1509.[46] Notably, the revolt is mentioned as having been centred in the district of Ragh, a region that had previously hosted another major anti-Timurid insurrection just several years earlier (in which Ismaili participation is not recorded).[47] The Ragh region is also subsequently recorded as being in a state of frequent rebellion against the rulers of Badakhshan in the 12th/18th century.[48] I have further discussed elsewhere how the patronage extended by the rulers of Shughnan to representatives of the *da'wa* starting in the late 12th/18th century was connected to the efforts by these local rulers to assert autonomy from Badakhshan.[49]

The system of caliphal authorisation that emerged from the 3rd/9th century onwards, which underpinned the political foundations of the Sunni tradition, was equally awesome in its ability to legitimise and empower rulers, as it was in its ability to marginalise and exclude those who fell out of its favour. Moreover, the impact of this effect would be felt not only by the ruler alone, but by all elites and relevant constituencies in the realm. As the foregoing examples demonstrate, the success of the Ismaili *da'wa* in a given region was not solely dependent upon the personal inclinations of a ruler, but rather, on the degree to which those inclinations could align with the interests of other constituencies. For those who benefitted from a relationship with the imperial centre and the Sunni establishment, a ruler's dalliance with the *da'wa* could be readily perceived as an existential threat. By contrast, those who may have found themselves conclusively marginalised from imperial politics, or whose primary interest was to retain autonomy against imperial encroachment, the *da'wa*, with the alternative religious and political cosmology that it offered, could present a powerful source of symbolic capital when articulating claims to political autonomy.

If Nasir-i Khusraw's patron in Yumgan can, in fact, be connected to the Ahmad b. ʿAli who previously served as the Ghaznavid governor of Badakhshan (a connection which admittedly remains far from certain), then this would suggest that his family had suffered a remarkable decline in fortune in the intervening period, and thus may have found common cause with local actors in Yumgan with an interest in maintaining autonomy from Badakhshan. By contrast, the evidence available for ʿAli b. al-Asad suggests that his family may have experienced something of an opposite trajectory, their political fortunes having recently rebounded after they had experienced a period of exclusion and marginalisation, and thus they would have had reason to be far more reticent in engaging with the *daʿwa*. Thus, despite the amir's evident personal interest in Ismaili beliefs, ultimately it was not in the political centre of Badakhshan but rather in the more marginal kingdom of Yumgan, and later in yet even more peripheral districts, where Nasir-i Khusraw's *daʿwa* efforts took the strongest root.

NOTES

1. Among other studies, see Farhad Daftary, *The Ismaʿilis: Their History and Doctrines* (2nd ed., Cambridge, 2007), p. 206; Alice Hunsberger, *Nasir Khusraw, the Ruby of Badakhshan: A Portrait of the Persian Poet, Traveller and Philosopher* (London, 2000), p. 8 et passim; Marcus Schadl, 'The Shrine of Nasir Khusraw: Imprisoned Deep in the Valley of Yumgan', *Muqarnas*, 26 (2009), p. 70; Azim Nanji, 'Nasir-i Khusraw', *EI2*. The sceptical Wladimir Ivanow is the only modern biographer of Nasir-i Khusraw to have expressed doubt as to whether Yumgan was politically subject to Badakhshan in Nasir's time, although he does not consider the issue at length; see his *Problems in Nasir-i Khusraw's Biography* (Bombay, 1956), p. 14.
2. Nasir-i Khusraw, *Jamiʿ al-hikmatayn*, tr. Eric Ormsby as *Between Reason and Revelation: Twin Wisdoms Reconciled* (London, 2012), p. 277; see also pp. 31–33.
3. Mir Taqi al-Din Kashi, *Khulasat al-ashʿar va zubdat al-afkar*, British Library, MS no. Or. 3506, ff. 73a–103b.
4. See further my discussion in 'The *Kalam-i pir* and Its Place in the Central Asian Ismaʿili Tradition', *Journal of Islamic Studies*, 31 (2020), pp. 83–92.
5. For an overview, see Hunsberger, *Nasir Khusraw*, pp. 220–240. It should be noted here that the narrative in the *Risalat al-nidamat* entails a shift in the depiction of this persecution: whereas Nasir-i Khusraw in his own writings sought to defend his Ismaili creed against accusations of blasphemy, the pseudo-Nasir in the *Risalat al-nidamat* seeks to defend himself against accusations of having been an Ismaili altogether.
6. A description and facsimile of the document has been published in Yayoi Kawakhara and Umed Mamadsherzodshoev, ed., *Documents from Private Archives in Right-Bank Badakhshan* (Tokyo, 2015), pp. 115–119 (Barrushan 10). I have discussed this document at greater length elsewhere; see Daniel Beben, 'Beyond Sayyid-hood: Genealogy and

Narrative in the *Nasab-nama* of Malik Jahanshah and the Ismaʿili Tradition of Badakhshan', in Daniel Beben and Jo-Ann Gross, ed., *Genealogical History in the Persianate World* (London, 2025), pp. 33–62.

7   I have surveyed these traditions further in 'Beyond Sayyid-hood'. Treatments of these narrative traditions have also appeared in two unpublished theses: Shaftolu Gulamadov, 'The Hagiography of Nasir-i Khusraw and the Ismaʿilis of Badakhshan' (PhD, University of Toronto, 2018), pp. 254–258; Nourmamadcho Nourmamadchoev, 'The Ismaʿilis of Badakhshan: History, Politics and Religion from 1500 to 1750' (PhD, School of Oriental and African Studies, University of London, 2014), pp. 47–48.

8   Shah ʿAbd Allah Badakhshi, *Armaghan-i Badakhshan*, ed. Farid Bizhan (Tehran, 1385 Sh./2006), pp. 95–98. The fact that the author here refers to 'Chinese Turkestan' (*Turkistan-i Chin*) indicates that this tradition probably originated only after the Qing conquest of the Tarim Basin in the mid-18th century. Badakhshi says that Jahanshah died in 456/1064; however, there is no evident basis for this date and it is incompatible with the claim offered in the Ismaili tradition that Jahanshah spent several decades in Nasir-i Khusraw's service.

9   Xuanzang (Hiuen Tsiang), *Si-yu-ki. Buddhist Records of the Western World*, tr. Samuel Beal (London, 1884), pp. 291–292.

10 Ibn Khurdadhbih, *Kitab al-Masalik al-mamalik*, ed. M. J. de Goeje (Leiden, 1889), p. 37.

11 I discuss the Samanid-era governors further below. The numismatist Michael Mitchiner tentatively proposed the existence of a Samanid mint in Yumgan; see his *Oriental Coins and Their Values*, vol. 1: *The World of Islam* (London, 1977), p. 141. However, this claim has now been established to have been based on a misreading and in fact there is no evidence for such a mint; see Stephen Album, *A Checklist of Islamic Coins* (3rd ed., Santa Rosa, CA, 2011), p. 152.

12 Aside from his *Jamiʿ al-hikmatayn*, Nasir-i Khusraw's surviving prose works do not make any direct reference to either Badakhshan or Yumgan.

13 For a discussion of some of these references, see Hunsberger, *Nasir Khusraw*, pp. 245–251.

14 Nasir-i Khusraw, *Diwan*, ed. Mujtaba Minuvi and Mahdi Muhaqqiq (8th ed., Tehran, 1388 Sh./2010), p. 84 (#39/22); p. 295 (#138/6); p. 437 (#208/44).

15 *Sukhanam rikht-i ab-i div-i laʿin; bi Badakhshan u Jurm u Yumg u Baraz*; Nasir-i Khusraw, *Diwan*, p. 153 (#69/36).

16 Zakariyya al-Qazwini, *Athar al-bilad wa akhbar al-ʿibad* (Beirut, 1380/1960), p. 489. Italics added for emphasis.

17 Rashid al-Din, *Jamiʿ al-tawarikh: Tarikh-i Ismaʿiliyan*, ed. Muhammad Rawshan (Tehran, 1387 Sh./2008), pp. 75–76.

18 For a survey of other references, see Daniel Beben, 'The Legendary Biographies of Nasir-i Khusraw: Memory and Textualization in Early Modern Persian Ismaʿilism' (PhD, Indiana University, 2015).

19 Dawlatshah Samarqandi, *Tadhkirat al-shuʿara*, ed. Fatima ʿAlaqa (Tehran, 1385 Sh./2007), pp. 112–113.

20 Ghiyath al-Din Khwandamir, *Habib al-siyar fi akhbar afrad bashar*, ed. Muhammad Dabir Siyaqi (Tehran, 1333 Sh./1955), vol. 2, pp. 456–457.

21 For further references for this discussion, see Daniel Beben, 'The History of Badakhshan from the 7th to the 19th Century', in David Ludden, ed., *The Oxford Research Encyclopedia of Asian History* (New York, 2023), available online at https://doi.org/10.1093/acrefore/9780190277727.013.406.

22 Hunsberger, *Nasir Khusraw*, p. 228.

23 al-Yaʿqubi, *Kitab al-Buldan*, ed. M. J. de Goeje (Leiden, 1892), pp. 288–292.

24 Ibn Khurdadhbih, *Kitab al-Masalik waʾl-mamalik*, p. 180. On the Banijirids, see C. E. Bosworth, 'Banidjurids', *EI2*.

25 J. L. Bacharach, 'Andarab and the Banijurids', *Afghanistan Journal*, 3 (1976), pp. 147–150.

26 Florian Schwarz, *Sylloge Numorum Arabicorum Tübingen: Balh und die Landschaften am oberen Oxus* (Berlin, 2002), pp. 36–56.
27 Mitchiner, *Oriental Coins and Their Values*, pp. 140–143.
28 On Simjuri's role in the massacres of Ismailis in this period, see Nizam al-Mulk, *Siyar al-muluk*, tr. Hubert Darke as *The Book of Government or Rules for Kings* (London, 1978), p. 226.
29 Abu'l-Fadl Muhammad Bayhaqi, *Tarikh-i Bayhaqi*, ed. 'Ali Akbar Fayyad (Mashhad, 1350 Sh./1971), p. 254.
30 Michael Fedorov, 'New Data on the Appanage Rulers of Khuttalan and Wakhsh', *Iran: Journal of the British Institute of Persian Studies*, 44 (2006), pp. 197–206.
31 Bayhaqi, *Tarikh-i Bayhaqi*, p. 612.
32 Fedorov, 'New Data on the Appanage Rulers of Khuttalan and Wakhsh', pp. 198–199.
33 Sadr al-Din 'Ali al-Husayni, *Akhbar al-dawla al-Saljuqiyya*, tr. C. E. Bosworth as *The History of the Seljuq State* (London, 2011), p. 16.
34 al-Husayni, *Akhbar al-dawla al-Saljuqiyya*, p. 25.
35 Fedorov, 'New Data on the Appanage Rulers of Khuttalan and Wakhsh', pp. 199–200.
36 Ibn al-Athir, *al-Kamil fi'l-ta'rikh*, ed. C. J. Tornberg (Leiden, 1851–76), vol. 10, p. 22.
37 Nasir-i Khusraw, *Jami' al-hikmatayn*, p. 33.
38 Schwarz, *Balh und die Landschaften am oberen Oxus*, p. 58.
39 Mira A. Bubnova, *Drevnie rudoznattsy Pamira* (Dushanbe, 1993), pp. 60–67; Mira A. Bubnova, 'L'extraction des minerals et le mode de vie des mineurs au XIe siècle: L'exemple du Pamir Oriental', *Cahiers d'Asie Centrale*, 9 (2001), pp. 177–187.
40 Nasir-i Khusraw, *Jami' al-hikmatayn*, p. 97.
41 While the exact date of Nasir-i Khusraw's move to Yumgan is unknown, there are some references in his writings that can provide a *terminus ante quem* for his residence there. In one of his *qasida*s, in which he also refers to his residence in Yumgan, Nasir eulogises the Fatimid capture of Mecca; see Nasir-i Khusraw, *Diwan-i ash'ar*, p. 208 (#96/20). This evidently refers to the conquest of Mecca by the Fatimid client 'Ali al-Sulayhi, which occurred in 454/1062; see Michael Brett, *The Fatimid Empire* (Edinburgh, 2017), pp. 197–198. In addition, in his *Zad al-musafir*, composed the previous year (453/1061), although he makes no direct reference to Yumgan, in an aside Nasir lambasts opponents who have accused him of irreligion and expelled him from his homeland; see Nasir-i Khusraw, *Zad al-musafir*, ed. Sayyid Muhammad 'Imadi Ha'iri (Tehran, 1384 Sh./2005), p. 371 (the date of composition is given on p. 254).
42 Ibn al-Athir, *al-Kamil fi'l-ta'rikh*, vol. 10, pp. 164–165.
43 For example, see Nasir-i Khusraw, *Diwan*, p. 79 (#37).
44 It should also be noted in this regard that, in the colophon in the printed edition of the *Jami' al-hikmatayn*, the *nisba* of Nasir-i Khusraw is given as al-Yumghani; see Nasir-i Khusraw, *Jami' al-hikmatayn*, ed. Henry Corbin and Muhammad Mu'in (Tehran and Paris, 1953), p. 316. However, as the editors note, this colophon is not found in the only known manuscript of the work, but rather was reproduced from a later manuscript containing abstracts of the text compiled by another author. Nasir-i Khusraw does not elsewhere employ the *nisba* Yumghani in his own writings, but rather Qubadiyani, referring to his town of birth in present-day southwestern Tajikistan.
45 For an overview of this history, see Daniel Beben, 'The Ismailis in Central Asia', in *The Oxford Research Encyclopedia of Asian History* (New York, 2018), available online at https://doi.org/10.1093/acrefore/9780190277727.013.316.
46 Mirza Muhammad Haydar Dughlat, *Tarikh-i Rashidi*, ed. 'Abbasquli Ghaffari Fard (Tehran, 1383 Sh./2004), pp. 346–347, 357–358.
47 Ibid., pp. 329, 347–348.
48 Sang Muhammad Badakhshi and Fadl 'Ali Bek Surkh-Afsar, *Tarikh-i Badakhshan*, ed. and tr. A. N. Boldyrev (Moscow, 1997), ff. 40a–41b.

49 Daniel Beben, 'Religious Identity in the Pamirs: The Institutionalization of the Ismaʿili *Daʿwa* in Shughnan', in Dagikhudo Dagiev and Carole Faucher, ed., *Identity, History and Trans-Nationality in Central Asia: The Mountain Communities of Pamir* (London, 2018), pp. 123–142.

3

The Reign of the Fatimid Imam-caliph al-Hakim bi-Amr Allah: Historiographical Considerations

Shainool Jiwa

Introduction

The complex reign of the enigmatic figure of al-Hakim bi-Amr Allah (r. 384–411/996–1021), the sixth Fatimid Imam-caliph, has attracted considerable attention. Projections of al-Hakim in 20th-century Western scholarship present a paradoxical figure, from one who encouraged fantastical claims about his status and indulged in acts of wanton cruelty, to one who resolutely upheld justice and elicited popular support, as is evident in the article on al-Hakim in the first edition of the *Encyclopaedia of Islam*.[1] While significant strides have been made since the early 20th century, assessments of al-Hakim in current scholarship, as summarised by Michael Brett's recent survey of the field, nonetheless remain 'widely' differing.[2] Portrayals of al-Hakim include those that present him as a messianic 'God-King',[3] as a ruler seeking to end the imamate and turn the Fatimid state into an 'ordinary' dynasty,[4] as regent seeking to end the problem of a patrimonial state,[5] as a figure increasingly withdrawn from affairs of both state and *daʿwa*,[6] or as a Muslim ruler working to the 'best of his ability' to fend off the crises impending Egypt by adopting agricultural and economic reforms.[7]

Despite continued interest in the study of al-Hakim, the historiographical problems facing researchers remain and they are twofold in nature. The idiosyncrasies associated with al-Hakim's reign and personality – including his approach towards asceticism and variations in policy and statecraft – have seen repeated attempts at deciphering his motivations by both medieval and modern historians, including those within the Ismaili *daʿwa*, which fostered legends around the figure of the Imam-caliph. Secondly, al-Hakim's reign coincided with a resurgent Abbasid caliphate (forming an early era of the 'Sunni revival') fixated on rolling back the Fatimid advance in the early 5th/11th century through polemic, with the Imam-caliph al-Hakim therefore often bearing the brunt of anti-Fatimid propaganda in pro-Abbasid historiography which continued to proliferate in writings of the Ayyubid and Mamluk periods. Consequently, the emergence of a complex and highly tendentious historiographical tradition concerning al-Hakim, in which verifiable historical material is enmeshed with patently fabricated accounts, remains a significant obstacle in the study of his reign. As Paul Walker has recently observed:

> Sorting out all of this information, separating myth from fact, bias from reality, for a figure of such complexity, replete with ambiguity built into his very character, who was the subject of obvious and subtle hostility from both mediaeval and modern writers, friends and foe, is not simple, and perhaps is not even possible.[8]

In responding to this challenge this paper takes a two-pronged approach to address the historiographical intricacies of studying the life and times of al-Hakim.[9] Firstly, it proposes the adoption of close source textual analysis of specific events of al-Hakim's reign on a case-by-case basis. Secondly, it situates the necessity of examining prevailing regional trends to contextualise those specific developments within a broader framework. In this paper, these approaches are brought together to revisit the question of al-Hakim's reputed injunction to inscribe the public cursing of the Companions of the Prophet in public venues throughout Cairo. The initial findings of this exploratory study reveal that when subjected to historiographical critique, some widely reproduced reports concerning aspects of al-Hakim's rule are in fact, not exceptional to his personality, as has been portrayed, but deeply interrelated with the political and religious developments in Fatimid Egypt, with the Abbasid East, as well as the Umayyad West.

The Curse Inscriptions of 395/1005

One of the events during the reign of al-Hakim that is most widely commented on, ostensibly occurred in 395/1005. As widely noted in the secondary literature, in this year, al-Hakim is reported to have ordered a programme of public inscriptions that pronounced curses or insults (*la'n* or *sabb*) on the Companions of the Prophet.[10] These are variously reported as being either directed at the Caliphs, Abu Bakr (r. 11–13/632–634) and

'Umar (r. 13–28/634–644) in particular, or the Companions in general as well as others, including the Umayyad and Abbasid caliphs. Inscriptions were accordingly written on mosques, markets, bathhouses, on main roads and alleyways, and elsewhere. The 'inscriptions' were however akin to public writing such as wall-art or graffiti, including writings on placards (*lawh*) that were publicly displayed. They do not necessarily correlate to the kind of formal stone inscriptions famous in Fatimid architecture.[11] As per the established narrative, two years later al-Hakim is said to have revoked the order, commanding Fatimid officials to ensure the erasure of the inscriptions and decreed that anyone who partook in the public cursing of the Companions was to be reprimanded and punished. This is considered to be the precursor for his subsequent injunction upholding the Qur'anic principle that there is 'no compulsion in religion' (2:256).

The Significance of the Inscriptions

Studies on al-Hakim discuss the appearance of these inscriptions, and they account for their significance in varied ways. Firstly, the inscriptions are taken to symbolise a period of al-Hakim's sectarian anti-Sunni policies,[12] instituted as part of his efforts to emphasise his own vision of the *imama* and to strengthen the role of the Ismaili *da'wa* both within and beyond the Fatimid state.[13] By extension, the curse inscriptions are taken as representing efforts by al-Hakim to territorially and visually convey Fatimid power as predicated on Shi'i ideas of legitimacy,[14] to 'Ismailise' the urban space.[15] Secondly, if the appearance of the inscriptions is taken as reflecting al-Hakim's religious policies, their erasure is deemed to demonstrate al-Hakim's pragmatism when threatened.[16] This is intractably linked to the revolt of Abu Rakwa (d. 397/1007).[17] Claiming Umayyad descent and proclaiming his own status as Imam, Abu Rakwa launched a rebellion against the Fatimids with the support of the Banu Qurra in 395/1004. Having initially achieved significant victories against Fatimid forces such that he threatened Cairo itself, Abu Rakwa suffered irreversible defeats in 396/1006, culminating in his final capture and execution in 397/1007.[18] As some sources indicate that part of Abu Rakwa's cause for rebellion was the defence of the Companions, al-Hakim's erasure of the inscriptions was therefore considered to have been motivated by his fear of antagonising the Sunni population at the height of the rebellion,[19] or as a gesture aimed at indicating greater reconciliation with the Sunni population once the revolt had been ended.[20] Thirdly, the appearance and erasure of inscriptions are regarded as further evidence of al-Hakim's instability, serving as one example of several injunctions that were promulgated and rescinded.²¹

The Sources on the 'Curse Inscription'

The sole known contemporary source on the appearance and erasure of these inscriptions is that by Yahya b. Sa'id al-Antaki (d. 458/1066). Yahya was a Melkite Christian historian who felt persecuted during al-Hakim's reign, and therefore left for Byzantine Antioch where he subsequently wrote his history.²² In his entry for the year 395/1005, he states:

> And it was ordered [by al-Hakim] that curses should be written on the congregational and other mosques, walls and roads, against Abu Bakr, 'Umar, 'Uthman, Mu'awiya b. Abi Sufyan and other Companions, as well as caliphs from the Banu 'Abbas. This became oppressive for the Muslims from the Sunni *madhhab*, and they were filled with dread and shame.²³

On the erasure of the inscriptions, al-Antaki records that in 397/1007:

> Al-Hakim decreed [*rasama*] the scraping [*kasht*] of the writing upon the paths [*durub*], and others, that cursed Abu Bakr and those others whose names had been written.²⁴

Among other widely referenced Sunni sources of the 6th–7th/12th–13th centuries including those of Ibn Zafir (d. 613/1216), Ibn Hammad (d. 628/1231), Ibn Khallikan (d. 681/1282) and Ibn al-Athir (d. 630/1233), claims that al-Hakim ordered the curse inscriptions are also documented. A close analysis of the latter three of these texts reveals that they are in fact replications of *one* principal report, which, it is likely, originated in Sunni circles in 6th/12th-century Alexandria.

In his *Akhbar Muluk Banu 'Ubayd* ('History of the 'Ubaydid Kings'), the 7th/13th-century Maghribi author Ibn Hammad (Ibn Hamadu) provides a legend-filled account of al-Hakim's reign. His rendition of these materials testifies to the nature of the myths circulating particularly about al-Hakim, and about the Fatimids at large in the 7th/13th century. This includes an Arabian Nights-like account of an out-of-control camel race that led one of its participants, who was lost in an unknown land, to a source of immense amounts of jewels. After undertaking an arduous journey through the desert, living off scrubland, he brought the treasures to al-Hakim's court, where the Imam-caliph accepted the gifts gratefully. Such hoards are, for Ibn Hammad, a principal source of the wealth of the Fatimid caliphate.[25] In his introduction to al-Hakim's biography, Ibn Hammad refers to the curse inscriptions:

> Al-Hakim was generous with money, and a shedder of blood (*jawadan bi'l-mal, saffakan li'l-dima'*). He killed many eminent people of his *dawla* and others in cold blood. His biography [*sira*] is the strangest of biographies (*min a'jab al-siyar*)[26] ... In his days there unfolded many strange affairs ... among these was that during the height of his caliphate, he ordered the writing of curses against the Companions on the walls of mosques, palaces, roads, and alleys, and he wrote *sijill*s to all his governors (*al-a'mal*) ordering for such cursing, and that was in 395. Then he ordered their removal, decried it, and forbade its inscriptions in 397. This continued for a while, and he ordered the public beating of anyone who cursed the Companions.[27]

In his entry on al-Hakim in the *Wafayat al-a'yan*, the Iraqi-born biographer Ibn Khallikan begins with an introduction to al-Hakim that notably contains near verbatim parallels of the summative biography found in Ibn Hammad with only slight variants:

> Al-Hakim was generous with money, and a shedder of blood (*jawadan bi'l-mal, saffakan li'l-dima'*). He killed many from the eminent people of his *dawla* and others in cold blood. His biography (*sira*) was of the strangest/wonderous of biographies (*min a'jab al-siyar*), promulgating each time orders that people were obliged to follow ...
>
> Of them, he ordered in the year 395 the writing of curses against the Companions (*sabb al-sahaba*) – God's contentment upon them – on the walls of the mosques, palaces and roads; and he wrote to all his governors in the lands of Egypt ordering them for such curses; then he ordered for the removal of these, censured it and forbade it in the year 397; and proceeded after that to beat any who cursed the Companions, [ordering] their punishment and public parading.[28]

The Iraqi historian Ibn al-Athir similarly provides extended coverage of al-Hakim's reign in his *al-Kamil*, though his principal foci for these years are Iraq, Iran and the campaigns of Mahmud of Ghazna (d. 421/1030). Across the yearly entries that variously relate events in al-Hakim's reign, including his entry for the year 395/1004-05, he makes no mention of the curse inscriptions. However, it is in his summative biography of al-Hakim for the year 411/1021 when accounting for al-Hakim's demise that Ibn al-Athir recounts the event, reproducing once more almost verbatim the account found in Ibn Hammad and Ibn Khallikan:

> Al-Hakim was generous with money, and a shedder of blood (*jawadan bi'l-mal, saffakan li'l-dima'*). He killed many of the eminent people of his *dawla* and others. So, the record of his biography [*sira*] is strange/wonderous (*siratihi 'ajiba*). One of these was that at the peak of his caliphate (*fi sadr khilafatih*), he ordered the writing of curses against the Companions – God's contentment upon them – on the walls of the mosques and markets, and he wrote to all his governors (*al-a'mal*) about such curses, and that was in 395. Then, after a while, he ordered for the halting of the cursing, and the disciplining (*ta'dib*) of any who cursed them or mentioned them in a vile way.[29]

Though Ibn Hammad, Ibn Khallikan and Ibn al-Athir share direct textual parallels in their treatment of al-Hakim, none of them indicate the source of their report. That information however can be gleaned from al-Maqrizi – who *also* relates a segment of the common account – regarding al-Hakim's treatment of the Christians, but not the curse inscriptions. It is here that al-Maqrizi names his source as Abu'l-Hasan al-Rawhi, the author of the *Bulghat al-zurafa' fi ta'rikh al-khulafa'*.[30]

The *Bulghat al-zurafa'* provides an extended account of the history of the caliphates up until the 6th/12th century, beginning with the life of the Prophet Muhammad, continuing with entries on the Umayyads, the Abbasids, the Umayyads of Spain and the Fatimids, among others. Organised by reign and, as is common to his treatment of other caliphs, al-Rawhi's entries on the Fatimids are in the main brief and summative statements – reminiscent of early Arabic historiographical works that provide the dates of birth and death, a short account of notable events, and listing of key officials including judges, chamberlains and parasol-bearers.

Though his work has been in circulation since the 20th century, Abu'l-Hasan al-Rawhi's identity and death date remain unclear.[31] It is likely he was a Sunni scholar from Alexandria who came from a family of Sunni jurists (*faqih*s), an identity principally established because his father and grandfather are cited as among the circles of *hadith* narrators in Alexandria in the late 6th/12th century.³² As Brett has recently noted, Alexandria emerged as bastion of Sunni Islam in the final half-century of the Fatimid caliphate, in a period when Sunni ascendency was marked by the emergence of Sunni generals as well as the proliferation of Sunni *madrasa*s.³³ It is in the *Bulghat al-zurafa*'s treatment of al-Hakim that al-Rawhi provides the full quote which was in all probability the source narrative later adapted by Ibn Hammad, Ibn Khallikan and Ibn al-Athir. Here, al-Rawhi states about al-Hakim that:

> He was generous with money, and a shedder of blood (*jawadan bi'l-mal, saffakan li'l-dima'*). He killed many of the eminent people of his *dawla* and others. So, his biography (*sira*) is one of the strangest of biographies . . . In his days there unfolded many strange affairs. Of them was that at the peak of his caliphate (*fi sadri khilafatihi*), he ordered the writing of curses against the Companions on the walls of mosques, palaces, roads, and alleys, and he wrote *sijill*s to all his governors about such cursing, and that was in 395. Then he instructed their removal, censured the practice, and ordered its implementation in the year 397. For a while thereafter those who cursed the Companions were beaten and publicly paraded.³⁴

While al-Rawhi's affinity, and the provenance of his work, remain uncertain, it should be noted that it is likely it was the principal Egyptian source for later historians deriving from the circles of Alexandrian Sunni *faqih*s. While this does not negate its veracity, it reveals that many of the seemingly widely circulating formulations about critical aspects of al-Hakim's reign are in fact reproductions of a single source which had its own dynamic of textual transmission.

The presence of al-Rawhi's narrative in Ibn al-Athir's work has added significance. Thoughout his *Kamil*, Ibn al-Athir regularly relates significant information about Fatimid Egypt in the reign of al-Hakim. These include accounts of al-Hakim's accession and the struggle between Ibn 'Ammar and the Turks in 386/996,³⁵ Barjawan's accession and his subsequent demise in 390/1000,³⁶ as well as extensive coverage of the rebellion of Abu Rakwa,³⁷ concluding with a brief review of al-Hakim's biography in the year of his death.³⁸ However, throughout this coverage, including under the year 395/1005, there is no mention of the curse inscriptions until the concluding statement taken from al-Rawhi. This absence of the curse inscriptions is conspicuous, especially because Ibn al-Athir reports even incidental events such as inflation in Egypt at the time.³⁹ Notably, indicating his propensity for relating information pertaining to sectarian affairs, in his entry for the year 393/1003, Ibn al-Athir recounts the appointment of the Fatimid governor Abu Muhammad al-Aswad, known as Tamzula. He says that this governor once paraded and punished a Maghribi with the following proclamation, 'This is the punishment (*jaza'*) from the one who loves Abu Bakr and 'Umar'.[40]

Ibn al-Athir's silence regarding the curse inscriptions in his annalistic narrative – as contrasted to his summative biographical treatment of al-Hakim – can be similarly compared to that of Ibn al-Qalanisi. Living in Damascus just after the Fatimid period (ca. 465–555/1073–1160), Ibn al-Qalanisi provides detailed accounts of events in Fatimid Cairo during al-Hakim's reign. These include reports on al-Hakim's succession and reports on Sitt al-Mulk's efforts to have her cousin appointed;[41] the rise of Ibn 'Ammar and the Kutama;[42] Barjawan's relationship with al-Hakim and his eventual demise,[43] rivalries at the Fatimid court between various factions, as well as transcripts of letters sent by al-Hakim to Syria.[44] In his summative statement of al-Hakim's biography, written in his entry for 411/1021 – the year of al-Hakim's demise – Ibn al-Qalanisi characterises the Imam-caliph negatively, depicting him as a proud figure who loved to spill blood.[45] However, across his entire rendition on al-Hakim either under the year 395/1005, or in his summative statement, Ibn al-Qalanisi makes no reference to the ordering of the curse inscriptions, leading one to surmise that he had not come across this information.

The Question of Ascription: Al-Maqrizi, Idris 'Imad al-Din and Ibn Khaldun

The most cited account pertaining to the 'curse inscriptions' of al-Hakim, and the seemingly sole account which specifies that some of the inscriptions were written in gold, is that of al-Maqrizi,[46] who mentions the event both in his *Itti'az* and the *Khitat*. In his entry under the year 395/1005 in the *Itti'az* he states:

> There was written on the walls of the mosque, and on the Old Mosque on its exterior, interior, and all its niches, and the doors of the hostels, tomb-complexes, graves, and the desert, insults and curses toward the *salaf* (*sabb al-salaf wa la'nahum*). These were inscribed, coloured in with paints and gold. This was also done on the doors of markets and houses.[47]

Nonetheless, al-Maqrizi's account does not ascribe the curse inscriptions to an order from al-Hakim. Similarly, the only Shi'i Ismaili source that relates the events at length, that of the Yemeni Tayyibi Ismaili *da'i*, Idris 'Imad al-Din,[48] associates the appearance of the curse inscriptions to hubris among the Shi'a in Egypt during this period, rather than resulting from an order of the Imam-caliph. Idris thus notes:

> The Shi'a emerged victorious against those who opposed them during the time of al-Hakim, and they publicly cursed those who put themselves forward against 'Ali Commander of the Believers, and [they cursed] those who opposed him, who argued against him, who went to war with him. And they called them by their names, so much so that plentiful became the insults against Abu Bakr, Umar, 'Uthman, Talha, Zubayr and others, during that time. This [cursing] went from private to public (*zahara min al-sirr ila'l-i'lan*). The curses appeared and were inscribed on the pulpits, and on sheets, and on the doors of the bathhouses, and wherever people gathered. So, the Imam al-Hakim denounced this, and pronounced the following words, ordering it to be read to those in the cities and the countryside, telling everyone to remain with their own *madhdhab*.[49]

This groundswell of Shi'i zealousness noted by Idris is reiterated by the 9th/15th-century Maghribi Sunni historian, Ibn Khaldun (d. 808/1406). While he recounts al-Hakim's *rafidi* (rejectionist) beliefs as being well known,[50] he makes no reference to the curse inscriptions, either by al-Hakim, or otherwise. He does however report that Shi'i-led sectarian strife was active in al-Hakim's time, stating thereafter that al-Hakim was opposed to this, and therefore issued his edict of tolerance:

> It was raised to him [al-Hakim] that a group from the 'rejectionists' (*rawafid*) assaulted the Sunnis during the *tarawih*, as well as in the funerary prayers, by stoning them. Consequently, a *sijill* was read out from the *minbar* of *Misr* [Fustat] which included... 'The Commander of the Believers recites to you the verses of God's Clear Book, "There is no coercion in religion" (2:256)... None are to curse anyone from the *salaf*.'[51]

Ibn Khaldun and Idris were one generation apart and belonged to distinct North African and Yemeni historiographical traditions respectively. Yet, the striking parallels in their exposition of Shi'i-led strife as the cause of the issuance of al-Hakim's decree of tolerance, and their quoting the text of the decree, could suggest their sharing of a common-source of information. Idris' version – that largely correlates with that of al-Maqrizi and parallels aspects of Ibn Khaldun's – is reflected more widely than would have been otherwise assumed.

Challenging the prevailing view that held al-Hakim directly responsible for the inscriptions for various reasons, Heinz Halm (in 1986 and 2003) questioned whether it was al-Hakim himself who had ordered the curse inscriptions.[52] He notes that the specific phrasing of al-Maqrizi's text does not state that a formal decree (*sijill*) was issued by al-Hakim.[53] Al-Maqrizi thus relates that 'there was written on the doors of the mosques' (*wa kutiba 'ala abwab al-masajid*), in distinction to references to other policies that expressly stipulate al-Hakim's decree.[54] As regards al-Antaki's account above, Halm states that al-Antaki must have *presumed* that the appearances of such writing in public spaces could only have been possible on al-Hakim's orders, but that 'this assumption is not mandatory and is emphatically denied by the Ismaili tradition'.[55] Halm accordingly refers to the account of Idris 'Imad al-Din, which states that it was the zealous elements among the Shi'a of Egypt that triggered the appearance of the inscriptions, which al-Hakim then decreed to be removed over the following years. Halm adds that al-Hakim's agency is clearly apparent in the erasure of the inscriptions two years later.[56] Several decades earlier, the Egyptian historian 'Abd al-Mun'im Majid (1920–1990) similarly pointed out that the sources do not confirm the view that al-Hakim had ordered the curse inscriptions, attributing the appearance of the inscriptions to the activities of the Shi'a in Egypt instead.[57] While the majority view in contemporary scholarship continues to maintain that al-Hakim ordered the inscriptions, a close analysis of the sources questions the claim. This is further corroborated in relation to wider developments in the Islamic world during this period, especially as regards the hardening of sectarian boundaries between Sunni and Shi'i communities in civic contexts.

The Context of the Inscriptions: Sunni-Shi'i Rivalry in the 5th/11th century

The major markers of the evolving relationship between the Shi'i Ismaili Fatimid caliphate and the Sunni population of its realms over its two centuries of rule have been well documented.[58] While known for its largely tolerant attitude towards its Sunni subjects, as exemplified in the *aman* document of al-Muʿizz (r. 341–365/953–975) that upheld the permissibility of practices of the Sunni *madhhab*s, the Fatimid stipulation of the requirement of state law as applying to particular ritual practices such as the calculation of the new moon, the pronouncement of the Shiʿi *adhan* and prayers, nonetheless resulted in tension in the Sunni establishment. The reign of al-Hakim is consequently contrasted with those of preceding Imam-caliphs, especially that of his father al-ʿAziz bi'llah (r. 365–386/975–996), as instituting an overt phase of anti-Sunni policies, which were subsequently repealed in favour of an emphasis on tolerance. Walker cites several instances, including the arrest and execution of a Syrian man in 391/1001 who proclaimed that he did not acknowledge ʿAli and the apprehending of 13 people in 393/1003, for praying the *duha* prayer, considered in Shiʿi ritual law as an innovation.[59] Al-Hakim's edicts against the consumption of food items such as *mulukhiyya* are at times deemed to be a reaction against some revered figures in Sunni history. The curse inscriptions of 395/1005 are however, considered the pinnacle representation of al-Hakim's Sunni antipathy. Consequently, their removal in 397/1007 is said to mark a new phase of rapprochement with the Sunni population.

This distinctive aspect of al-Hakim's reign, however, is often read narrowly, and in isolation from broader trends then permeating the Islamic world. It is apparent that the curse inscriptions of 395/1005 – regardless of their ascription – and the sectarian strife to which they are closely linked, are a particular Egyptian manifestation of developments that were also being manifested in other regions, including Iraq and Ifriqiya. The late 4th/10th and early 5th/11th century saw the formation of a stronger sense of communal identity, crystallising especially around the symbolic values attached to the principal figures of the Sunni and Shiʿi traditions – Abu Bakr, ʿUmar and other Companions for the former, or ʿAli b. Abi Talib and the family of the Prophet Muhammad for the latter. In as much as reverence for such figures served as public symbols of these communities, it became the cornerstone of the contest between the rival traditions.

Pivotal to the tightening of confessional boundaries – especially for the emerging Sunni traditions – was the role of the Abbasid caliph al-Qadir bi'llah (r. 381–422/991–1031), in recasting the Abbasid caliphs as the spokesmen of Sunni Islam.[60] The decline of Buyid authority in Baghdad, and the transfer of their capital to Shiraz during the reign of the Buyid amir, Baha' al-Dawla, around 390/1000 had enabled al-Qadir to take a lead in formulating the boundaries of acceptable Sunni tradition, which entailed the refutation of the Muʿtazila and the Shiʿa, among others.

Notably, al-Qadir's reign coincided with that of al-Hakim, which witnessed the burgeoning success of the Fatimid *daʿwa* in Iraq. In seeking to halt its advance, al-Qadir facilitated the provision of anti-Ismaili polemical tracts including that of al-Baqillani (d. 403/1013). He also promulgated the 'Baghdad Manifesto' in 402/1011, which branded the Fatimids as impostors and heretics, and negated their lineage from the Prophet Muhammad.[61] Al-Qadir's anti-Shiʿi and anti-Ismaili polemic was bolstered by the emergence of rulers such as Mahmud of Ghazna (r. 388–421/998–1030) in the eastern Islamic lands, who pledged allegiance to al-Qadir, and whose campaigns in India unleashed assaults against the adherents of the Fatimid *daʿwa* in Sind. Al-Qadir and Mahmud thus forged a symbiotic relationship, each reinforcing the prestige of the other.[62]

A recurring feature of the history of the eastern Islamic world during this period is accounts of repeated urban clashes between the Sunni and Shiʿi communities in Iraq. Riots, repeatedly described in the sources as 'strife' (*fitna*) in the 4th–5th/10th–11th centuries in Baghdad were often sparked off around Shiʿi ceremonies of commemoration or conflicting doctrinal issues, such as the validity of the recension of the Qurʾan by Ibn Masʿud (*Mushaf Ibn Masʿud*), which the Shiʿi communities of Iraq held in esteem, but was considered problematic by the Sunni establishment.

Thus, for 391/1001, Ibn al-Athir records a *fitna* erupting between the Shiʿa of the Karkh district of Baghdad and the Turkish contingents, supported by the *ahl al-sunna* of Baghdad.[63] Two years later, he reports, the *fitna* in Baghdad had intensified. Hence, the Buyid amir, Bahaʾ al-Dawla, sent his leading general (*ʿamid al-juyush*) to quell the disturbance and forbade the public profession of any *madhhab*, Sunni or Shiʿi.[64] Three years later, in 398/1006 al-Qadir commissioned a group of scholars to condemn the Qurʾanic recension of Ibn Masʿud. Soon thereafter, a Shiʿi at Karbala was executed for publicly censuring those who had burned the *Mushaf* of Ibn Masʿud.[65] The following year, insults by the Hashimi family (that is, the Abbasids) against the leading Twelver Shiʿi of Iraq, Shaykh al-Mufid (d. 413/1022), led to open riots.[66] As per the reports of Ibn al-Jawzi (d. 597/1200), during the *fitna* of 398/1007–08 the Shiʿi population in Baghdad invoked the name of the Fatimid Imam-caliph al-Hakim, chanting, '*Ya Hakim Ya Mansur.*'[67] Meanwhile, the Fatimid *daʿwa* in Iraq secured the support of the ʿUqaylid ruler of Mosul, Qirwash b. al-Mukhallad (d. 444/1052), who publicly invoked al-Hakim in 401/1010, and extended this act to all the areas in his domain including Anbar, Ctesiphon and Kufa, prompting al-Qadir to issue the anti-Fatimid 'Baghdad Manifesto'.[68] While Qirwash's allegiance to the Fatimids was short-lived due to Abbasid and Buyid censuring, the Sunni-Shi'i rivalry raged on. Consequently, in 408/1018, al-Qadir pronounced impositions on the Shi'a and Mu'tazila:

> In this year there was further *fitna* in Baghdad between the people of Karkh from the Shi'a and the *ahl al-sunna*, and the situation worsened. Al-Qadir bi'llah rued the Mu'tazila, the Shi'a, and others, due to the opposing doctrines that they believed in their *madhhab*s and forbade discussion (*al-munazara*) about any of them. Whoever did so was ill-treated and punished.[69]

Sectarian strife also broke out in other Iraqi cities such Wasit, where in 408/1018, Shi'i Daylami soldiers clashed with their Sunni Turkish counterparts, the latter supported by the *ahl al-sunna* of the city due to the Daylami's Shi'i inclinations.[70] Events in Syria also reveal sectarian tensions. While these were evident in the reigns of the Fatimid Imam-caliphs al-Mu'izz and al-'Aziz, in al-Hakim's reign they escalated, mirroring the *fitna* in Baghdad and elsewhere. Thus, in the same entry that relates the Sunni-Shi'i *fitna* of Baghdad of 393/1003, Ibn al-Athir reports that in Fatimid-controlled Damascus, a Maghribi was arrested and publicly paraded due to his 'love' of Abu Bakr and 'Umar.[71]

However, the bloodiest sectarian strife during this period occurred in North Africa. Under the year 407/1016-17, Ibn al-Athir provides an extended narrative on the massacre of the Shi'a of Ifriqiya, which is linked to the issue of curses and the status of the early Companions of the Prophet:

> In this year in Muharram, the Shi'a were killed in all the lands of Ifriqiya. The reason was that al-Mu'izz b. Badis rode through Qayrawan, and the people were greeting him and invoking prayers for him. He passed a group and asked about them. He was told, 'These are the *rafida*, and they curse Abu Bakr and 'Umar.' He said, 'God's contentment be upon Abu Bakr and 'Umar.' Thereupon, the commonalty (*al-'amma*) went to the *darb al-maqli* from Qayrawan, where the Shi'a used to gather, and killed some of them. . . . Then the Shi'a were killed and torched, their houses demolished throughout Ifriqiya. A group of them gathered in the palace of [the Fatimid Imam-caliph] al-Mansur near Qayrawan, and fortified themselves

there but the *'amma* besieged them, and tightened [their siege]. Their hunger became fierce, and they agreed to leave, but the people killed them until the last of them had died. Those in al-Mahdiyya sought refuge in the mosque, but they were all killed. In the Maghrib, the Shiʻa were called the Mashariqa as named after Abi ʻAbd Allah al-Shiʻi, who was from the Mashriq. Most of the poets mentioned this event, some of them with replete joy, and others with tearful sorrow.[72]

Though not as destructive or bloody, the outbreaks of *fitna* between segments of the Shiʻi and Sunni population of North Africa and Iraq had precedents in Egypt. Following the Fatimid conquest in 358/969, al-Maqrizi relates outbreaks of civil strife in 361/972, noting the denigration of the status of ʻAli b. Abi Talib through the association of him with Muʻawiya by anti-Shiʻi segments of the population:

> In Ramadan [June–July 972], a blind, old woman who was singing in the street was arrested and imprisoned. Some people rejoiced and publicly praised the Companions [of the Prophet]. They shouted, 'Muʻawiya is the maternal uncle of the believers and of ʻAli.' So Jawhar had it proclaimed in the ʻAtiq Mosque, 'O people, watch your words and abandon loose talk. Indeed, we have imprisoned the old woman for her own protection. So let no one utter a word without knowing that grievous punishment will befall him.' Thereafter, the old woman was set free.[73]

Using Muʻawiya as a means to provoke Shiʻi segments of the Egyptian population was also recorded during the pre-Fatimid era under Ikshidid rule:

> Egypt was not devoid of strife at the tombs of Kulthum and Nafisa bint al-Hasan b. Zayd b. al-Hasan b. ʻAli b. Abi Talib on the day of ʻAshura' during Ikhshidid and Kafurid times. Kafur's *sudan* [i.e. the 'black' troops] were biased against the Shiʻa; they would harass people on the streets by asking them, 'Who is your maternal uncle?' If they answered, 'Muʻawiya', they would honour them. If, however, they remained silent, they would be hostile to them and would seize their clothes and possessions, to the extent that Kafur had to appoint someone to supervise the desert gates and prohibit people from leaving.[74]

On the other hand, following the arrival of the Fatimids in Egypt, its Shiʻi communities felt emboldened in their public appearances, as evident in al-Maqrizi's entry for the year 363/973-74:

> On the day of 'Ashura' a group of [Twelver] Shi'a, along with their followers, returned from the shrines at the tombs of Kulthum bint Muhammad b. Ja'far b. Muhammad al-Sadiq and Nafisa. Accompanying them was a group of Maghribi horsemen and foot soldiers, mourning and weeping for al-Husayn. They broke waterpots in the markets, ripped the waterskins of the water carriers and cursed those who shopped on that day. A group of people protested at this. Then Abu Muhammad al-Hasan b. 'Ammar went to them and separated the two groups. If he had not done so the trouble would have intensified, for the people had shut their shops and suspended the markets. The Shi'a felt strengthened by al-Mu'izz's presence in Egypt.[75]

The Curse Inscriptions in Context

The occurrence of Sunni-Shi'i animosities over the first decades of the 5th/10th century can be attributed to multiple factors, including the crystallisation of confessional identity, the role of varied authorities in sparking controversy as a means of legitimising their own authority – whether that of the Zirids in Ifriqiya, or of al-Qadir and the pro-Abbasid establishment in Iraq. They share several characteristics, most notably their urban and populist nature in which the principal actors and agents in the strife remain largely unknown, anonymised in the chroniclers as simply being the actions of the *awwam* (commoners). In this context, the renditions provided by al-Maqrizi and especially Idris 'Imad al-Din of the curse inscriptions of al-Hakim's reign – where they are initiated by elements of the population themselves, fit more characteristically than is apparent at first sight. That there was popular feeling behind the appearance of the inscription becomes evident in the account regarding al-Hakim's subsequent order for their erasure in 397/1007:

> On 9 Rabi' al-Akhar [2 January], al-Hakim ordered the erasure of all that had been written on the mosques, doors, and elsewhere, insulting the *salaf*. These were erased. The *mutawalli* of the police went around ensuring none remained.[76]

However, as noted by Walker, the command prohibiting the cursing of the Companions had to be repeatedly re-issued. Thus, four months later, as part of a wider series of reforms that are described by Walker as favouring, 'a wide latitude for the accommodation of both Shi'i and Sunni practice',[77] the same decree that allowed for participation in Sunni ritual practices and calculation according to sighting the moon, admonished thus, 'No one is to curse the Companions, or object to any person's attributing to them what he attributes or swears about them what he swears.'[78] Six years later, the prohibition was again emphatically pronounced when, as related by al-Maqrizi, 'The people were banned from cursing the *salaf*, and a man was beaten for this and paraded.'[79] Thereafter, 'a decree was read in the palace, containing the invocation of God's mercy on the *salaf* from among the Companions, and prohibition from taking any interest in such matters.'[80] Similarly, during one of his rides in 402/1011-12, al-Hakim saw a placard with the curse inscriptions upon it, and had it removed:

> Al-Hakim saw upon his route, while he was out riding, a signboard (*lawhan*) on which a curse on the Companions was inscribed. He disavowed it and halted until it was brought down. Other similar signboards followed in succession. All of them were brought down. Similar writings on the walls were erased until there they no longer had any trace. The rejection of any who opposed this was emphasised, with vows of punishment [decreed] against them.[81]

The populist nature of these inscriptions and their continued appearance despite repeated state censure validates the view that these were communally engendered public expressions.

Regardless of the attribution of origin, the appearance of the curse inscriptions themselves are often taken as a symbol of the idiosyncratic nature of al-Hakim's rule. A cross-reading of a range of sources demonstrates that their manifestation and context were not exclusive to al-Hakim's reign.

While the *fitna* between the Shi'i and Sunni communities of Baghdad seemingly escalated in the early 5th/11th century, its earlier manifestations are recorded in several Iraqi and Iranian cities in the mid-4th/10th century. Under the year 348/959, Ibn al-Athir records the eruption of riots between the communities in Baghdad leaving many dead,[82] civil strife that seemingly recurred in 349/960.[83] Punctuated by similar civil disturbances in Isfahan and Basra in 351/962,[84] riots in Baghdad are again recorded in 353/964 escalating to a major disturbance in 362/972 where, Ibn al-Athir reports, the subsequent conflagration in the Karkh quarter led to 7000 fatalities.[85] It is in the context of these repeated *fitna*s that curse inscriptions attributed to the Buyid ruler Muʿizz al-Dawla (d. 356/967) come to the fore. Following his entry into Baghdad in Jumada I 334/December 945 and until his demise, Muʿizz al-Dawla was at the apex of power in the city. According to Ibn al-Athir's account, it was in 351/962, during his reign, that a series of curse inscriptions appeared, this time directly attributed to the Buyid ruler's command. Under the heading, 'What was written upon the mosques of Baghdad' for this year, Ibn al-Athir states:

> In this year in Rabiʿ al-Akhar, the commonality from amongst the Shiʿa in Baghdad, on the orders of Muʿizz al-Dawla, wrote upon the mosques, what appeared (*kataba ʿamatu'l-Shiʿati bi Baghdad bi amri Muʿizz al-Dawla ʿalaʾl-masajid ma hadhihi suratahu*):
>
> May God curse (*laʿan Allah*) Muʿawiya b. Abi Sufyan, and may He curse he who usurped Fadak from Fatima – God's Contentment upon Her; and [upon] he who prevented al-Hasan [b. ʿAli b. Abi Talib], upon him be peace, from being buried in the grave of his grandfather [i.e. the Prophet]; and [upon] he who expelled Abu Dharr al-Ghiffari, and [upon] he who expelled al-ʿAbbas [b. ʿAbd al-Muttalib] from the *shura*.
>
> Because the caliph was under orders (*mahkuman ʿalayhi*), he could not prevent this. And as for Muʿizz al-Dawla, this was upon his command. When evening came, people erased some of them (*hakkahu baʿd al-nas*). But al-Muʿizz al-Dawla wanted them to be renewed. But his *wazir*, Abu Muhammad al-Muhallabi, indicated to him that in place of those that had been erased it should be written: 'May God curse the oppressors of the family of the Messenger of God (*laʿan Allah al-zalimina li ali-rasuli'llah*)', and no one should be mentioned in the curses except Muʿawiya. So, this was done.

The narrative on the appearance of the curse inscriptions of Baghdad in 351/962, predating those attributed to al-Hakim's reign by just over forty years, presents characteristics reflected in the narratives of those in Cairo. These include the writing on mosques, the cursing of those Companions of the Prophet held in Shiʿi history as responsible for the setting aside of ʿAli b. Abi Talib and the oppression of the family of the Prophet Muhammad and, critically, the involvement of the commonality. Moreover, they became a feature of heightened urban strife between the confessional communities. Furthermore, they establish that one of the supposedly distinct features of al-Hakim's reign had other recorded precedents.

Conclusion

The reign of al-Hakim bi-Amr Allah – and the Fatimids more broadly – remains a rich area for further scholarship. The sectarian conflict that was becoming an endemic feature of regional developments, from Ifriqiya to India, as illustrated in this paper, inevitably influenced the policies and decisions of al-Hakim. While al-Hakim's reign has been juxtaposed with the tolerance of his forebears, there were also examples of sectarian strife in the time of his predecessors in Ifriqiya and in Egypt. Placing the reign of al-Hakim in its broader regional and historical context allows for a more textured understanding of a reign that has often been exceptionalised. A close-textual analysis of a wide range of sources, and a broadening of the analytic frame are critical for unravelling the complexity and connectivity of the dynamics throughout the Islamic world in the 4th-6th/10th–12th centuries, of which the Fatimids were an integral part.

NOTES

1. E Graefe, 'al-Hakim bi-Amr Allah', *EI*. See e.g. 'If this is the striking feature of his whole attitude, it was complicated by a sense of unrestricted power, which grew more and more in this strange personality, and a boundless capriciousness, with which cruel traits were strongly mingled.' 'His liberality is nowhere denied, and scenes have been preserved from the years of the low Nile for example, in which he is depicted in the midst of his people, accessible to every request and anxiously endeavouring to check the ravages of famine.'
2. Michael Brett, *The Fatimid Empire* (Edinburgh, 2017), pp. 129–133.
3. P. J. Vatikiotis, 'Al-Hakim bi-Amrillah: The God-King Idea Realised', *Islamic Culture*, 29 (1955), pp. 1–18.
4. S. N. Makarem, 'Al-Hakim bi-Amrillah's Appointment of his Successors', *al-Abhath*, 23 (1970), pp. 319–324.
5. Th. Bianquis, 'Al-H'akim bi Amr Allah où la folie de l'unité chez un soverain Fat'imide', *Les Africains*, 11 (1978), pp. 107–133.
6. Paul E. Walker, *Caliph of Cairo: Al-Hakim bi-Amr Allah*, as cited in Brett, *Fatimid Empire*, p. 132.
7. M. A. Shaban, *Islamic History* (Cambridge, 1976), vol. 2, pp. 206–209.
8. Paul E. Walker, 'al-Hakim bi-Amr Allah', *EI3*.
9. More recent efforts involved in untangling distinct historiographical problems associated with the coverage of al-Hakim in medieval sources include Najam Haider, 'On Lunatics and Loving Sons: A Textual Study of the Mamluk Treatment of al-Hakim', *JRAS*, 18 (2008), pp. 109–139.
10. See e.g. M. Canard, 'al-Hakim Bi-Amr Allah', *EI2*; De Lacy E. O'Leary, *A Short History of the Fatimid Khalifate* (London, 1923), p. 142; Paul E. Walker, *Caliph of Cairo: Al-Hakim Bi-Amr Allah, 996–1021* (Cairo, 2009), pp. 191–193; idem, *Exploring an Islamic Empire: Fatimid History and its Sources* (London, 2002), p. 100.
11. For the latter see Irene A. Bierman, *Writing Signs: The Fatimid Public Text* (Berkeley, CA, 1998), pp. 76–77, covering her discussion on the curse inscriptions.
12. Brett, *Fatimid Empire*, p. 135.

13 S. A. Assaad, *The Reign of al-Hakim bi Amr Allah (386/996–411/1021): A Political Study* (Beirut, 1974), pp. 91–92.
14 Bierman, *Writings Signs*, pp. 76–77.
15 J. A. Pruitt, 'Method in Madness: Recontextualizing the Destruction of the Churches in the Fatimid Era', *Muqarnas*, 30 (2013), p. 124.
16 J. A. Pruitt, 'Method', pp. 124–125. On the sources' indication of the relationship between the inscriptions and Abu Rakwa's revolt see also Walker, *Caliph of Cairo*, p. 173.
17 H. Halm, 'al-Walid b. Hisham', *EI2*.
18 Ibid.
19 Brett, *Fatimid Empire*, p. 137.
20 Paula Sanders, *Ritual, Politics and the City in Fatimid Cairo* (Albany, NY, 1994), p. 57.
21 See e.g. M. Canard, 'al-Hakim bi-Amr Allah', *EI2*.
22 On al-Antaki see M. Canard, 'al-Antaki', *EI2*; Paul E. Walker, *Exploring an Islamic Empire, Fatimid History and its Sources* (London, 2002), p. 141.
23 Yahya b. Saʿid al-Antaki, *Taʾrikh al-Antaki*, ed. ʿUmar ʿAbd al-Salam Tadmuri (Tripoli, 1990), p. 256.
24 al-Antaki, *Taʿrikh*, p. 268.
25 Muhammad b. ʿAli b. Hammad (Hamadu), Ibn Hammad, *Akhbar muluk Banu ʿUbayd wa siratuhum*, ed. ʿAbd al-Halim ʿUways and al-Tihami Naqra (Cairo, 1401/1980), pp. 101–102.
26 The term *ʿajib* carried the meaning of both wonderous or strange depending on the context; the genre of works dedicated to *ʿajaʾib* (wonders) is a well-known theme in medieval Arabic literature.
27 Ibn Hammad, *Akhbar*, p. 97.
28 Ibn Khallikan, *Wafayat al-aʿyan wa anba abna al-zaman*, ed. Ihsan ʿAbbas (Beirut, 1397/1977), vol. 5, p. 293.
29 Ibn al-Athir, *al-Kamil fiʾl-taʾrikh*, ed. Muhammad Yusuf al-Daqqaq (Beirut, 1407/1987), vol. 8, p. 129.
30 Abuʾl-Hasan al-Rawhi, *Bulghat al-zurafaʾ fi taʾrikh al-khulafaʾ*, ed. ʿImad Ahmad Hilal, Muhammad ʿAbd al-Rahman and Suʿad ʿAbd al-Sattar (Cairo, 2004/1425).
31 The editors of the recent critical edition of al-Rawhi's work, named above, who worked under the supervision of Ayman F. Sayyid, sought to ascertain his identity and the year of his death from the internal evidence of the work. They tentatively concluded, through reference to occasional verbatim eyewitness accounts, that it is likely he was alive in the final years of the Fatimid era in 567/1172, though with the caveat that he may have lived on into the Ayyubid period with his demise dated to after 575/1180. See their discussion in al-Rawhi, *Bulghat*, pp. 19–26.
32 See the editors' introduction in al-Rawhi, *Bulghat*, pp. 23–26.
33 Brett, *Fatimid Empire*, p. 210.
34 al-Rawhi, *Bulghat*, pp. 308–309.
35 Ibn al-Athir, *al-Kamil*, vol. 7, pp. 479–480.
36 Ibid., p. 482.
37 Ibn al-Athir, *al-Kamil*, vol. 8, pp. 42–46.
38 Ibid., p. 129.
39 Ibid., p. 49.
40 Ibid., p. 26.
41 Ibn al-Qalanisi, *Taʾrikh Dimashq*, ed. Suhayl Zakkar (Damascus, 1403/1983), vol. 1, p. 74.
42 Ibid., pp. 75–76.
43 Ibid., p. 90.
44 See e.g., Ibn al-Qalanisi, *Taʾrikh Dimashq*, vol. 1, p. 98.

45 Ibn al-Qalanisi, *Ta'rikh Dimashq*, vol. 1, p. 127.
46 On al-Maqrizi, see F. Rosenthal, 'al-Makrizi', *EI2* and for his importance in Fatimid historiography see Walker, *Exploring*, pp. 152–154 and 164–169, Shainool Jiwa, *Towards a Shi'i Mediterranean Empire: Fatimid Egypt and the Founding of Cairo* (London, 2009), pp. 32–38, and Nasser Rabbat, *Writing Egypt: Al-Maqrizi and his Historical Project* (Edinburgh, 2023).
47 al-Maqrizi, *Itti'az al-hunafa bi-akhbar al-a'imma al-Fatimiyyin al-khulafa*, ed. Muhammad Hilmi Muhammad Ahmad (Cairo, 1416/1996), vol. 2, p. 53. An almost identical entry is found in al-Maqrizi, *al-Mawa'iz wa'l-i'tibar fi dhikr al-khitat wa'l-athar* (Beirut, 1418), vol. 4, p. 73.
48 On Idris 'Imad al-Din, see I. Poonawala, 'Idris b. al-Hasan', *EI2*; Walker, *Exploring*, pp. 12–13; Shainool Jiwa *The Founder of Cairo: The Fatimid Imam-Caliph al-Mu'izz and his Era* (London, 2013), pp. 27–34.
49 Idris 'Imad al-Din, *'Uyun al-akhbar wa funun al-athar*, ed. Mustafa Ghalib (Beirut, 1404/1984), vol. 6, p. 292.
50 Ibn Khaldun, *Ta'rikh Ibn Khaldun (Diwan al-mubtada' wa'l-khabar fi ta'rikh al-'Arab wa'l-Barbar)*, ed. Khalil Shahada (Beirut, 1421/2000), vol. 4, p. 76.
51 Ibid., pp. 76–77.
52 Heinz Halm, 'Der Treuhänder Gottes', *Der Islam*, 63 (1986), pp. 11–72; Heinz Halm, *Die Kalifen von Kairo: Die Fatimiden in Ägypten 973-1074* (Munich, 2003), p. 193.
53 Ibid., p. 193. This is implicitly compared to other instances of the institutions of al-Hakim's policies which are regularly expressed as resulting from his order or his decree.
54 al-Maqrizi, *Itti'az*, vol. 2, p. 53.
55 Halm, 'Der Treuhänder', p. 36.
56 Ibid., pp. 36–37.
57 'Abd al-Mun'im Majid, *al-Hakim bi-Amr Allah, al-khalifa al-muftara 'alayh* (2nd ed., Cairo, 1982), pp. 86–87.
58 Wilferd Madelung, 'The Religious Policy of the Fatimids Toward their Sunni Subjects in the Maghrib', in M. Barrucand, ed., *L'Égypte Fatimide, son art et son histoire* (Paris, 1990), pp. 97–104.
59 Walker, *Caliph of Cairo*, p. 192.
60 Shainool Jiwa, 'The Baghdad manifesto (402/1011): A Re-examination of Fatimid-Abbasid rivalry', in F. Daftary and S. Jiwa, ed., *The Fatimid Caliphate: Diversity of Traditions* (London, 2017), p. 36; Hugh Kennedy, *The Prophet and the Age of the Caliphates: The Islamic Near East from the Sixth to the Eleventh Century* (3rd ed., London, 2015), pp. 206–208; John Donohue, *The Buwayhid Dynasty in Iraq 334H./945 to 403H./1012: Shaping Institutions for the Future* (Leiden, 2003), pp. 279, 283–287.
61 Jiwa, 'Baghdad Manifesto', pp. 22–79; Farhad Daftary, *The Isma'ilis: Their History and Doctrines* (2nd ed., Cambridge, 2007), p. 101; idem, *Ismailis in Medieval Muslim Societies* (London, 2005), p. 77.
62 C. E. Bosworth, 'Mahmud b. Sebuktigin', *EI2*; Daftary, *Medieval Muslim Societies*, p. 68.
63 Ibn al-Athir, *al-Kamil*, vol. 8, p. 19.
64 Ibid., p. 26.
65 D. Sourdel, 'al-Kadir Bi'llah', *EI2*.
66 Ibn al-Athir, *al-Kamil*, vol. 8, p. 49.
67 Abu'l-Faraj 'Abd al-Rahman ibn al-Jawzi, *al-Muntazam fi ta'rikh al-muluk wa'l-umam*, ed. Muhammad A. 'Ata and Mustafa A. 'Ata (Beirut, 1412/1992), vol. 15, p. 59. For further on this event see Donohue, *The Buwayhid Dynasty*, p. 284.
68 Jiwa, 'The Baghdad Manifesto', p. 47.
69 Ibn al-Athir, *al-Kamil*, vol. 8, p. 121.
70 Ibid.

71 *al-Kamil*, p. 26.
72 Ibid., p. 114.
73 al-Maqrizi, *Itti'az al-hunafa' bi-akhbar al-a'imma al-Fatimiyyin al-khulafa'*, ed. Jamal al-Din al-Shayyal (Cairo, 1967), vol. 1, pp. 131–132; tr. Shainool Jiwa, *Mediterranean Empire*, p. 100.
74 al-Maqrizi, *Itti'az*, vol. 1, p. 146; tr. Jiwa, pp. 115–116.
75 al-Maqrizi, *Itti'az*, vol. 1, p. 146; tr. Jiwa, p. 115.
76 al-Maqrizi, *Itti'az*, vol. 2, p. 69.
77 Walker, *Caliph of Cairo*, p. 193.
78 Ibid., p. 193.
79 al-Maqrizi, *Itti'az*, vol. 2, p. 98.
80 Ibid., Cf. Walker, *Caliph of Cairo*, p. 85.
81 al-Maqrizi, *Itti'az*, vol. 2, p. 98.
82 Ibn al-Athir, *al-Kamil*, vol. 7, p. 263.
83 Ibid., p. 267.
84 Ibid.
85 *al-Kamil*, vol. 7, pp. 336–337.

4

The Fatimid *Kitab al-Majalis wa'l-musayarat* as *Responsa* to Internal Controversy and External Propaganda

Hasan al-Khoee

Introduction

The importance of the *Kitab al-Majalis wa'l-musayarat* of al-Qadi Abu Hanifa al-Nu'man (d. 363/973) for the history of the Fatimids in North Africa and the western Mediterranean in the 4th/10th century is now well established.[1] Most probably composed sometime in the decade before 358/969,[2] as an extensive text centred on the life and pronouncements of the Fatimid Imam-caliph al-Mu'izz li-Din Allah (r. 341–365/953–975), written by the Fatimid's most prominent scholar who was himself an intimate of al-Mu'izz and a regular at court, the *Kitab al-Majalis*' contemporaneity with the events it describes and its 'insider status' has provided historians with a critical core of information on Fatimid history since its availability to academic scholarship.[3]

Despite this importance however, and perhaps due to the *Majalis*' discursive form and distinct structure, questions regarding its function and objective remain open. Similarly open are questions of form and genre, since the *Kitab al-Majalis* largely eschews the categorisations afforded to Arabic literary works of the period.[4] In accounting for its objective,[5] it has thus been situated as a *sira* (biography) of al-Mu'izz,[6] or notably by Hamdani as a product of al-Nu'man's efforts in Fatimid state formation through his construction of a 'historical' personage of the reigning Imam-caliph.[7] The work has similarly been classified by Brett as constituting a *sunna* of al-Mu'izz,[8] while also falling within the rubric of a type of Fatimid legal literature.[9] Walker has importantly, however, adduced the text's principal function as being that of legitimisation, when suggesting a further purpose was the 'portrayal of Fatimid rule in its best light' and an 'appeal for the sympathy and political loyalty of their subjects'.[10] While important and critical contextualisation has been provided, albeit often in brief, consideration of the distinct objectives of *Majalis* as emerging from its singular thematic focuses remain largely unanswered.[11]

In this present chapter, I propose that one of the principal functions of the *Kitab al-Majalis* was the provision of official Fatimid *respona* to questions and controversies relating to the history and policies of the first four Fatimid Imam-caliphs and those pertaining to the Shi'i doctrinal underpinnings of the caliphate. By *responsa* I here refer to, as shorthand, the provision of 'officially' sanctioned discourses that carried a distinct theological weight within the polity, having been approved by the Imam-caliph himself, as predicated on Imami Shi'i doctrine concerning the divinely-sanctioned knowledge of the Imam.[12] The interlocutors to whom the *Majalis* responds are diverse, with the subjects ranging from those questions and controversies emanating from constituents of Fatimid state or adherents of the Ismaili *da'wa*, to those external accusations directed against the Fatimids by adversaries and neighbouring powers, including especially the Umayyads of al-Andalus. Consequently, with the output of al-Nu'man standing as having been 'approved' by al-Mu'izz, the *Majalis* can be classified as an 'official record' of the Fatimid state regarding the positions, policies and doctrines of its Imam-caliphs as manifest in their own recent history, rendering the text a literary artefact seemingly exceptional in early medieval Muslim statecraft.[13]

This assertion of the function of the *Majalis* is predicated upon identification of the text's singular thematic concerns. It is apparent there that al-Nu'man through his choices, when either reproducing the statements of al-Mu'izz or his predecessors, or when presenting his own expositions of these, is repeatedly focused on providing either direct or implicit answers to queries, anxieties, controversies or accusations relating to myriad themes pertaining to Fatimid history, doctrine or statecraft. These can concern, variously, questions or controversies about specific historical events in Fatimid history or about doctrine and theology. They can similarly relate to issues in the conduct of Fatimid government, whether concerning court protocol, the activity of state officials, military strategy or general statecraft. The answers appear in tandem with larger thematic discourses that undergird the text serving to elaborate the doctrines of the Shi'i Fatimid imamate but which in turn also regularly deal with especially contentious notions, including those specific to the *da'wa*.

The identification of this function of the *Kitab al-Majalis* bears considerably on conceptions of Fatimid statecraft. It is a common-place that both the Fatimid state and the Shiʿi Ismaili *daʿwa* through which it was created and which it in turn subsequently catalysed, were subject to distinct waves of polemic and propaganda from their adversaries, both contemporary and in later medieval historiography.[14] While this hostility as an endemic feature of later medieval historiography is well known, the thematic focuses of the *Kitab al-Majalis* demonstrate the extent to which the Fatimids, as early as the Ifriqiyan era, sought to *respond* in the struggle for public perception. The following seeks, therefore, to outline the nature of the *Kitab al-Majalis* with specific focus on the issuance of *responsa* in the text before turning to its detailed treatment of two, apparently especially, contentious issues: those concerning the ceremonial act of 'kissing the ground' (*taqbil al-ard*) and those pertaining to questions regarding variations in the policies and deeds of the Imam-caliphs themselves.

The *Kitab al-Majalis* and al-Qadi al-Nuʿman

The *Kitab al-Majalis* constitutes an extended series of episodic discourses as organised and presented by al-Nuʿman. While the thematic focus is varied, the work follows an approximate chronological order, beginning with al-Nuʿman's first conversation with al-Muʿizz after his arrival in al-Mansuriyya as *qadi* in 336/948, and ending approximately with an account of the circumcision ceremonies in 351/962. The multitude of 'episodes' presented in it appear in the form of shorter or lengthier textual blocks that typically provide the speeches, statements, testimonies or letters of the Imam-caliph al-Muʿizz or his father the Imam-caliph al-Mansur biʾllah (r. 334–341/946–953), and less commonly those of their predecessors al-Qaʾim bi-Amr Allah (r. 322–334/934–946) and al-Mahdi biʾllah (r. 297–322/909–934). These are often, though not always, embedded within a large narrative 'report' (*khabar*) provided by al-Nuʿman which delivers a specific historical context behind the statement. The issuance of such pronouncements is usually placed whilst the Imam-caliph al-Muʿizz is holding court (*majlis*), or during an excursion (*musayara*), but can include a range of other scenarios. The statements are in the main ostensibly witnessed directly by al-Nuʿman himself, or are otherwise – and especially in the case of accounts pertaining to al-Mansur or earlier Imam-caliphs – related by al-Nuʿman as having been transmitted to him via intermediaries, with statements attributed to al-Mansur often transmitted directly on the authority of al-Muʿizz.[15] Often in relation to each 'episode', after the narrative frame and the relating of a pronouncement of an Imam-caliph, al-Nuʿman then himself provides an exposition (thus a '*sharh*') in which he draws from the Qurʾan, *hadith*, the traditions of the earlier Shiʿi Imams and the Fatimid Imam-caliphs themselves, or a range of other historical or literary sources, to clarify the inner truths (*haqaʾiq*) of the given pronouncement of the Imam-caliph. As detailed further below, the topics covered are extensive and include for instance: Arabic grammar, the Qurʾan and *hadith*, history and literature, government and politics, ethics and morality, law and legal hermeneutics, questions of theology and doctrine as especially relating to the Shiʿi notion of *imama* and those specific to the Ismaili *daʿwa*, and include furthermore distinct discourses on varied aspects of Muslim history.

Within the text, treatment of specific episodes are either brief or extended as mentioned earlier. A number stand especially prominent however, serving as sites for extensive reporting of the statements of al-Muʿizz or expositions of the statements and deeds of earlier Imam-caliphs. Included here is coverage of the Byzantine embassies to al-Muʿizz's court in 346/958,[16] the campaign of the Fatimid general Jawhar al-Katib (d. 381/992) to the Maghrib in 347–348/958–959,[17] and Fatimid diplomacy pertaining to the Byzantine conquest of Crete in 349/960.[18] Especially prominent are accounts concerning Fatimid-Umayyad rivalry, catalysed by direct naval conflict in 344–345/955–956 and as followed by the first direct diplomatic overtures between the Fatimid court and that of Umayyad Andalus.[19] The latter provides especially a significant source for attestation of external accusations against the Fatimids, and serves as a loci for numerous responses by al-Muʿizz and al-Nuʿman.

The centrality of al-Nuʿman as the leading judge, *daʿi*, historian and jurist (*faqih*) of the Fatimid empire, whose works laid the foundations for the crystallisation of Fatimid legal theory and law, has been well established.[20] In contextualising the work, it is important nonetheless to note that the *Kitab al-Majalis* serves a secondary function of standing as a de-facto *curriculum vitae* of al-Nuʿman himself, with aspects of the *qadi*'s own biography and literary output looming large in the text.[21] Beyond his role as principal eyewitness of many of the statements, various narratives demonstrate both al-Nuʿman's credentials and critically his high status in the eyes of the Imam-caliphs.[22] Especially important for the present discussion are the extended bibliographic discussions of al-Nuʿman's works, and the rendering of their status as authoritative. The *Majalis* thus provides extensive coverage of the context of the composition of some of al-Nuʿman's most important works, including the historical and highly influential *Iftitah al-Daʿwa* amongst a range of other compositions,[23] and includes furthermore al-Muʿizz's distinct praise for his most influential legal text, the *Daʿaʾim al-Islam*.[24] Central in this bibliographic presentation, and undergirding the identification of the *Majalis* as the *responsa* of the state, is the authoritative role bestowed on al-Nuʿman's literary output by repeated explicit attestation of al-Muʿizz's approval of their contents. Thus beyond the composition of specific works produced by the order of the Imam-caliph, al-Nuʿman reiterates in the *Majalis* his process of recording the Imam-caliphs' statements – notably in 'meaning' (*maʿna*) and not verbatim (*lafz*)[25] – and composing his works and then submitting them to al-Muʿizz for approval,[26] receiving thereafter guidance and correction.[27]

The Responses of the *Kitab al-Majalis*

In determining the function of the *Kitab al-Majalis*, it becomes apparent that a significant range of themes and concerns permeating the work repeatedly and prominently relate primarily to contested subjects.

As expected, questions on the *Imama* are central. In that the work also serves a didactic function of demonstrating, in application, the central doctrines of the Ismaili *daʿwa*, treatments of the core tenets of Shiʿi Ismaili doctrine undergird the entirety of the text. These thus include discourses on: the necessity of the imamate and the religio-political role of the Imam-caliphs as guides and 'shepherds' of the *umma*,[28] on their cosmographic and soteriological functions;[29] and include discourses on infallibility and the function of the Imams as mediums of authoritative knowledge, one of the prime themes of the text.[30] Embedded in them, however, are distinct series of discourses that demonstrate concern with delineating the parameters of contested doctrine. These include treatments of particular questions including the succession of Imams whilst of minor age, those pertaining to the *baraka* of the Imam's physical presence, or those – as reflected in Zaydi doctrine – concerning multiple contemporaneous imamates.[31] Especially conspicuous however are rejections of 'extremism' (*ghuluww*) in the doctrines of the imamate, often attributed in the text to 'dissident' or 'erroneous' *daʿi*s within the broader *daʿwa*, censure of whom emerges repeatedly.[32] Included here specifically are discourses delimiting the nature of the knowledge (*ʿilm*) of the Imams and those defining their hierarchical status in relation to the offices of Prophethood and Messengership.[33]

The treatment of questions of *imama* extended to those pertaining to the historical figures of the Imam-caliphs themselves, and seemingly treat especially notions of succession. While the Fatimid line of succession was largely uncontested in terms of open conflict or violence, Haji has shown through reference to the contemporary text of the *Sirat Jawdhar* that claims of potential succession from alternative lines of al-Mahdi's descendants remained an operative factor in al-Muʿizz's reign.[34] Within the *Majalis*, the demonstration of al-Muʿizz's attributes of imamate are potent, yet indicate that there were questions of contestation. These become most apparent when demonstrating the legitimacy of al-Muʿizz's succession, most pertinently in relation to charting his close relationship with his grandfather al-Qa'im and his great-grandfather al-Mahdi, and further by establishing his intimacy with his father al-Mansur and cementing his status as al-Mansur's legatee (*wasi*).[35] Though less prominent, similar treatments are given for the succession of al-Mansur.[36]

Beyond broader treatments of *imama*, the doctrines of the *daʿwa* or the phenomenon of errant *daʿi*s, note can here be made of the presence of responses in the *Majalis* to those discourses seemingly exclusively emanating from the adherents of the *daʿwa* itself. These include questions on the religious dues paid to the Imam and the mechanisms for doing so.[37] They also encompass treatments of the expectations held by adherents of the *daʿwa* about conquest and the continuing expansion of the Fatimid realms. One recurring theme – anticipating the conquest of Egypt – are responses to questions regarding the conquest of the 'East' (*al-sharq*), and especially the reasons for the delay. The *Majalis*' repeated positioning of al-Muʿizz's responses thereafter, including his affirmation of the prediction of the conquest, stand perhaps indicative of its contemporary prominence.[38]

The *Kitab al-Majalis*' function in the provision of response becomes further apparent in its treatment of broader legal and theological questions and controversies, as then pertinent throughout the 4th/10th-century milieu. Coverage of al-Muʿizz's extended pronouncements thus encompass distinct treatments of the meaning of monotheism (*tawhid*),[39] God's decree (*al-qada*'),[40] God's justice ('*adala*),[41] on the notion of 'proofs' (*burhan*), and include expositions on the especially contentious subject of the relationship between 'faith' (*iman*), 'action' ('*amal*) and Islam.[42] Excursuses on legal questions pertaining to the role of '*aql* as a source of knowledge, and thus law, are similarly treated.[43] Aspects of the history of Islam, and those specifically related to Shi'i salvation history, are similarly considered. These include discourses on the dating and significance of the event of Ghadir Khumm,[44] and include a sustained discourse on the causes for the division of the Shi'a and the question of the crises of succession that afflicted the community after Imam Ja'far al-Sadiq (d. 148/765).[45]

Perhaps one of the most distinctive features of the *Majalis* coverage however is its turn inwards to deal with specific questions and controversies pertaining to social life and the conduct of government. The *Majalis* thus regularly turns its attention to treating religio-social controversies as emerging from 'popular' customs. A perhaps unexpected extended series of episodes in the text – likely to be indicative of phenomena in the 4th/10th century – are criticisms and polemics, in relation to popular practises of divination, appearing especially in the censuring of astrologers (*al-munajjimun*), and reliance on their predictions, which are collectively and repeatedly described as manifestations of falsehood (*kidhb*).[46] Also apparent is censuring regarding the practice of women wailing at burials – one appearing perhaps more conspicuous in the text in that al-Nu'man's role as *qadi* seemingly involved regulation of it.[47] Also notable here are indications of popular celebrations of the Spring Equinox in Ifriqiya, where the 'excuse' for licentious behaviour is censured, as contrasted with al-Mu'izz's affirmation of the glories of the Spring itself as a sign of God's Power (*qudra*).[48]

Particularly significant for the present discussion, questions regarding government and especially the conduct of Fatimid state officials also emerge as significant themes. Here, the object of the principal thrust is dealing with issues of how to conceptualise oppressive or corrupt agents (*'ummal*) or governors (*wula'*) operating under the aegis and authority of the Fatimid Imam-caliph, with the bulk of the crimes seemingly concerning extortion in the extraction of taxes. Al-Mu'izz's disassociation and condemnation of the oppression (*zulm*) of such figures is clear.[49] Elsewhere, he explicitly pronounces on the damage to legitimacy rendered by such figures, in that their 'evil deeds are attributed to us (*fasayyi'atihim mansubata ilayna*)'.[50] In contrast, methods for the amelioration of the activities of such officials are also found in the text. These include statements by al-Mu'izz concerned with clarifying the mechanisms for raising complaints to him, injunctions on the necessity of informing the Imam-caliph in regard to the deeds of the malevolent, and broader attestations on the accessibility and open door of the Imam-caliph.[51]

Responses to accusations and propaganda emanating from sources outside the Fatimid domains – and beyond those indicated above – appear especially in those extended narratives pertaining to Fatimid relations with neighbouring powers. Central here are the extended series of discourses between al-Muʿizz and his Umayyad interlocutor, operating on behalf of the Andalucian Umayyad Caliph, ʿAbd al-Rahman al-Nasir (r. 300–350/912–961). The dispatch of an intermediary by al-Nasir, to negotiate a truce with the Fatimids following the conflict between the Fatimids and the Umayyads in 344/955, thus provides the occasion for the relaying of an extended series of direct accusations covering a distinct range of themes. These include those relating to the execution of the Fatimid *daʿi* Abu ʿAbd Allah al-Shiʿi,[52] on the distinction of Fatimid liturgical prayer in the Friday prayer that sees the pronouncement of 'blessings' (*salawat*) on the Imam-caliph,[53] on the central role of Berbers in the Fatimid army,[54] on accusations that the Fatimids prevented Umayyad pilgrims from performing the *hajj*,[55] and they encompass a series of almost jingoistic claims regarding the superiority of Umayyad Andalus as compared to Fatimid Ifriqiya in terms of economy, craftsmen and quality of inhabitants.[56] As presented in the *Majalis*, each instance in the narrative provides an occasion for al-Muʿizz to provide a response. ʿAbd Allah's execution is thus situated as the extension of God's Ordinance, the *salawat* on the Imam as an extension of the practise of offering up prayers for the family of the Prophet; the Berbers are praised and al-Nasir (often in the text referred to by the antonym of his regal name, and thus *al-khasir* 'the loser') is castigated for his ingratitude, while the question of preventing the performance of the *hajj* is wholly repudiated. Indicative of the nature of accusation and response is thus al-Nasir's claim as to the flight of people from Ifriqiya to al-Andalus. Al-Muʿizz's reply castigates those who did migrate as doing so out of a desire to live licentious lives in Umayyad domains and critically, that almost all Ifriqiyan or Maghribi towns (thus under the Fatimids) had in turn their own communities of Andalucian emigrants, who had 'departed in fright (*kharaja hariban*)', out of fear of God's punishment for living in lands of immorality.[57]

The *Majalis* and the Question of *Taqbil al-Ard*

Of the *responsa* issued by al-Nuʿman in the *Kitab al-Majalis*, particularly indicative of the larger function of the work is his treatment of the question of *taqbil al-ard* (kissing the ground). Constituting a gesture of *proskynesis*, this refers to the prescribed ceremonial practice where a figure attending an audience (*majlis*) of the Fatimid Imam-caliph at court, or in a variety of other contexts as expounded below, proceeded to 'kiss the ground' in front of the him.

The performance of proskynesis in the presence of the Imam-caliph, as demonstrated by Canard and Sanders, was an established feature of the Fatimid ceremonial idiom during both their Ifriqiyan and Egyptian eras.[58] In the broader early medieval Muslim context, the performance of *taqbil al-ard* in front of the Abbasid caliph as a feature of 4th/10th-century ceremonial in Baghdad and thereafter has been established by Al-Azmeh and El-Cheikh.[59] Conclusions posited regarding the general marginality of performance as stemming from reluctance to adopt the practice in the Abbasid milieu remain unstable however, especially in consideration of its widespread adoption in the Saljuq and Ayyubid eras. More recently, Cardoso has situated the nature of the practice in the Umayyad Andalucian context, noting specifically its general absence in court ceremonial apart from those instances when *taqbil al-ard* was expected of delegates from subordinate Christian courts arriving at the court of the Umayyad caliph.[60]

Al-Nuʿman's treatment of the subject in the *Majalis* makes apparent however that the practice was subject of significant opprobrium from opponents of the Fatimid dynasty. Notably, the treatment appears in an extended narrative where al-Nuʿman narrates how he himself was ordered by the Imam-caliph al-Mansur to *halt* his custom of kissing the ground before him. When the then *amir* al-Muʿizz nonetheless encourages al-Nuʿman to uphold the custom, and with al-Muʿizz himself noted by al-Nuʿman as being those amongst the princes and other *awliya'* who uphold the custom, al-Nuʿman subsequently embarks on a *sharh*. This demonstrates that his continuing *taqbil al-ard* – despite al-Mansur's prohibition – was permitted as predicated on the principle that the 'forbidding of a good act (*maʿruf*) is not an absolute necessity [to follow]'.[61] The prohibition is thus presented as a test for al-Nuʿman, affirmed furthermore when al-Mansur no longer censures the practice.[62] Here, the idea is established that the gesture stands commendable as a symbol of thankfulness for and glorification of the position of the Imam.[63]

The narrative introduction and *sharh* thus provides al-Nuʿman with what appears to be the principal focus of the episode – the provision of his *respona* to the opprobrium expressed by opponents of the practice. While their identity is anonymised, they are here described as the 'ignorant (*al-juhhal*)', the 'oppressive ignorant (*al-zalimun al-jahilun*)' and 'a people with no intellect (*qawmin la ya'qilun*)'.[64] Supposition can be made that such criticism emanated from circles of the most committed opponents of the Fatimids in Ifriqiya and especially Qayrawan, namely the establishment of the Maliki *'ulama*. As per al-Nu'man's own recapitulation, the criticism of the opponents held that *taqbil al-ard* was analogous to the act of prostration in prayer (*sujud*), that it consequently demonstrated the performance of worship of a figure other than God (*min dun illahi*), and that it therefore thrust both practitioners and recipients into the realm of disbelief (*kufr*).[65] Critically, for al-Nu'man, in regard to all the propaganda and polemic directed at the dynasty, it was in particular this accusation that became:

> of the heaviest of criticisms that the ignorant have placed upon us (*min a'zam ma tazri 'alayna'l-juhhal*). But they are more worthy of criticism and in ignorance are superior, and we have made clear their ignorance so that they may be guided.[66]

In his treatment, al-Nu'man proceeds to unpack his response by providing a focused reply to the criticism. This cumulatively affirms the permissibility of the act by distinguishing it from *sujud* through appeal to Qur'anic precedence and core principles of jurisprudence.

In the first instance, al-Nu'man declares that prostration (*sujud*) itself is not analogous to worship and specific appeal is made to Qur'anic precedence. Al-Nu'man thus adduces Q. 12:100 where, and anticipating the dream pronounced in Q. 12:4, the Prophet Yusuf sees his brothers and his father – the Prophet Ya'qub – prostrate before him following their arrival in Egypt.[67] In reference, al-Nu'man here asks, 'Did these prophets render disbelief (*kufr*) with this *sujud*?'[68]

Despite this distancing of *sujud* from necessarily indicating worship, al-Nu'man is also emphatic in denying the correlation of *taqbil al-ard* with the act of *sujud* itself. He thus pronounces, 'Nonetheless, we do not say that we perform *sujud* for anyone aside from God, God Almighty is Above this'.[69] Similarly and further on, al-Nu'man expounds on the nature of Q. 12:100 where the *sujud* to Joseph is situated not as worship, but rather one of 'obedience', 'glorification' and 'submission to his command'.[70] By extension, and in his conclusion of the treatment, al-Nu'man attests that none of the Imam-caliphs ever ordained that *sujud* be directed towards them: 'God is Above this, and His *Awliya'* are too exalted for them to allow this, or prescribe it for anyone from their companions.'[71]

In providing the response, al-Nuʿman also proceeds to reject the analogy of *taqbil al-ard* with *sujud* due to the attested similarity in gesture. This is rendered when he provides a potential analogy between the act of 'kissing the hands' and the ritual bow (*rukuʿ*), which constitutes a feature of the ritual prayer (*salat*). Al-Nuʿman thus posits that given those same opponents themselves 'kiss the hands of the Imams', then by analogy they too have a performed a *rakʿa*.⁷²

The central thrust of al-Nuʿman's response however – and testifying to his jurisprudential background – is his emphasis first on the distinction between physical acts pertaining to *taqbil al-ard* and *sujud*, and secondarily and more importantly, his appeal to the notion of 'intention' (*niyya*).⁷³ In distinguishing the gesture, al-Nuʿman thus argues that the dissimilarities between the two acts are far enough so as to render them wholly inequivalent. This is most emphatically argued when he locates *taqbil al-ard* as an inadmissible substitution for the *sujud* in prayer:

> If these ignoramuses were asked about a man who kissed the earth during his prayer (*salat*) in the cycle of prostration, but does not place his forehead upon it as the prostraters (*sajidun*) do, is that a *sujud*? They will never say that it is a *sujud*.⁷⁴

Most important for al-Nuʿman however is the question of intention. Here, in that the *niyya* for *taqbil al-ard* is not one of worship nor the act of performing *sujud*, al-Nuʿman appeals to the pivotal importance of *niyya* in the performance of acts, as consensually accepted across the developing schools of *fiqh*:

> So how for someone who does so [i.e. kiss the ground], and who has no intention (*la yanwi*) to perform a *sujud, can* they claim he has performed one? With them, if a man in reality performed a *sujud* and had no intention of doing so, then he would not be considered a *sajid*; just as if someone avoided eating throughout the day and into the night, but had no intention of fasting, then he would not be considered amongst those who have fasted.⁷⁵

It is in this regard that al-Nuʿman turns to address the *hadith* literature pertaining to the forbidding of the performance of *sujud* to a figure or being other than God. Referencing a distinct variant of a noted *hadith* where the Prophet expressly forbids performing *sujud* to humans, this version elsewhere being found in the *Musnad* of Ahmad b. Hanbal (d. 241/855),⁷⁶ al-Nuʿman provides an exposition of the meaning of *sujud* here, as attested to have been performed by the Abyssinians to the Negus and witnessed by the first Muslim emigrants (*muhajirun*). Here, al-Nu'man, referencing the *hadith* but not necessarily accepting its veracity (thus noting 'if it is affirmed'), locates the impermissibility of the gesture as stemming from the religious background (and thus intention) of its performers, identified as 'Magians' who had not yet received the *da'wa* of the Prophet.[77]

The *Majalis* and the Question of Variance in the Policies of the Imam-Caliphs

Further indicative of the function of the *Majalis* to provide responses is its repeated treatment of what seemingly appears a contentious question to those living within the Fatimid realms: the variation in the policies and even personalities of the Imam-caliphs. In its repeated treatment of the subject, the *Majalis* thus makes it apparent that disparities and distinctions in the policies of individual Imam-caliphs, if not apparent reversals of policy, had emerged as a distinct subject for questioning for those in the Fatimid empire. To provide the *responsa*, two distinct but interrelated themes are established across the text. The first is that which establishes a principle that can be termed 'convergence and not divergence', one that the *Majalis* explains by saying that the decisions of the Imam-caliphs despite their external differences, nonetheless remain in *i'tilaf* (convergence) and not *ikhtilaf* (divergence, or more literally 'disagreement'). Relatedly, the second posits that all decisions of the Imam-caliphs must be read as representations of a collective continuum of decisions, which are necessarily adapting to specific times, circumstances and space.

The ostensible proximate cause – and that necessitating the provision of a response – was most probably the significant variance in the stance of al-Mu'izz himself in relation to the treatment of recalcitrant tribes and rebels in Ifriqiya. Al-Mu'izz's policy of issuing amnesties (*aman*) has been noted, and in this the policies of the Imam-caliph seemingly marked a significant departure from those of his father and predecessor, al-Mansur bi'llah. As constituting part of his broader effort in the defeat of the widespread rebellion of Abu Yazid returned to below, al-Mansur's hostility towards rebel and enemy tribes emerges as a notable feature of his approach in pacifying hostile regions. In that the climax of Abu Yazid's rebellion was less than eight years before al-Mu'izz's own accession, supposition can be made – and as also variously indicated in the *Majalis*

– that questions about al-Muʿizz's departure of policy emanated especially from those veterans who had served alongside his father, whether amongst the Saqlabi or Arab generals of the Fatimid army, or from the Kutami Shaykhs.

The treatment in the *Majalis* of the question of variation in policy is recurrent. In the first instance, al-Muʿizz's 'leniency' (*hilm*) and compassion (*raʾfa*) are located as integral and laudable attributes of the Imam-caliph.[78] To situate however this difference in personality between al-Mansur and al-Muʿizz – one that was reflected in state policy – al-Nuʿman again provides a distinctive eyewitness narrative to allow for exposition. He describes his practice while serving as *qadi*, of hearing legal cases in the portico (*saqifa*) of the palace of al-Mansuriyya, as ordered by al-Mansur. In the narrative, al-Nuʿman proceeds to relate how he subsequently raised questions to the *amir* al-Muʿizz as to the suitably of the public setting, especially for the 'women or the weak'. The young al-Muʿizz then successfully petitioned al-Mansur for amelioration, with the Imam-caliph subsequently providing the funds for the construction of a dedicated court.[79]

In reaching his exposition, the objective of the episode, al-Nuʿman seeks to demonstrate that while al-Muʿizz demonstrated kindness and mercy in taking this position (*raʿiyy*), there was nevertheless 'neither change nor disagreement (*ikhtilaf*)' between al-Muʿizz and al-Mansur.[80] Rather, according to al-Nuʿman, 'It is all *ʿilm*, *hikma* and accord (*iʾtilaf*).'[81] The justification for this is that both approaches are represented as upholding central doctrinal principles, al-Mansur's representing the necessity for the public manifestation (*izhar*) of justice, while al-Muʿizz's representing the seeking of 'ease' for the people.[82]

The principle of *iʿtilaf* and not *ikhtilaf* is elsewhere reiterated when the pronouncements (*qawl*) of al-Mansur and al-Muʿizz are cast as one 'without difference (*ikhtilafan fih*)'.[83] Thus in relation to their differences in personality and approach to government, al-Nuʿman stipulates that with regard to al-Mansur and al-Muʿizz, 'severity has a place wherein it is apposite; and leniency has a place wherein it is apposite'.[84] Consequently, al-Nuʿman is careful to point out that making comparison of these attributes of the Imam-caliphs is erroneous, in that each requires consideration of its suitability.[85] The notion of the unanimity of decision is furthermore developed in episodes which seek to demonstrate congruence of the decisions of al-Mansur and al-Muʿizz.[86]

The idea of 'convergence and not divergence' as it appears in the *Majalis* is critically predicated on a central notion, that of relating the changes, transformations and distinctions in the policies of the Imam-caliphs as being relevant to specific contexts. Returning again to the question of the variations in the stances of al-Mansur and al-Muʿizz, elsewhere in the *Majalis* al-Nuʿman pronounces on discussions regarding the activities of brigands, rebels and those sowing 'corruption on the earth' (*al-fasadi fi'l-ard*) during an audience with al-Muʿizz. Al-Muʿizz, it is related, declares that he had asked an individual what should be done with such figures. In turn, the respondent is said to have replied simply, 'Just as al-Mansur did – meaning killing them and burning them with fire.'[87] The need to situate evolutions in policy as relevant to specific contexts becomes the central focus of al-Muʿizz's response:

> The time in which al-Mansur acted like so, was a time when this was appropriate (*yahsunu dhalik*), for the Earth was trampled with evil, and great had become for people their trials. There was no choice for this repugnancy to be deflected except with what he [al-Mansur] deflected it with. However, if God Almighty and Glorious has removed that trial, and extinguished the fires of that discord (*fitna*), what is incumbent upon us is to welcome this blessing by reconciling those whom we can reconcile (*nasfaha ʿamma kana lana an nasfaha*).[88]

That the policies and commands of the Imams are conditional on time and context is consequently integrated into the second critical feature of the *responsa*, that all decisions and commands need to be situated in a shared continuum of time. A specific exposition of this notion appears in the *Majalis* in relation to what appears as another controversy, this time relating to the relative policies of al-Qaʾim and al-Mansur. This seemingly concerns an apparent repudiation by al-Mansur of al-Qaʾim's decision regarding the fate of unnamed rebels. The *Majalis* thus narrates al-Muʿizz discussing the subject with an audience (*jamaʿa*) seated before him, asking them their opinion, and furthermore 'what the people say about it', before asking whether the audience themselves thought that al-Mansur in his act had expressed 'a rejection of the action of al-Qaʾim and a changing of his decree?'[89]

In the development of the subsequent discourse, the *Majalis* thus has al-Muʿizz himself pronounce that the variance of al-Mansur's command from that of al-Qaʾim was a result of time, and the manifestation (*tabyin*) of distinct conditions that brought about a variation in circumstance. Consequently, in that time and context necessarily impact the commands of the Imams, al-Muʿizz pronounces that the acts of the Imam-caliphs cannot be considered in isolation but rather as one continuous whole, for 'al-Qaʾim and al-Mansur in this matter are like one soul, and their orders therein are conjoined without a break (*mutassil ghayr munqatiʿ*)'.⁹⁰

While predicated on the assertion of 'convergence and not divergence' and the continuum of all actions, the *Majalis* nonetheless upholds that variations are natural as a reflection of the personalities of the Imam-caliphs. In perhaps one of the more distinct iterations of the imamology of the *Majalis* al-Muʿizz, as narrated by al-Nuʿman, proceeds to pronounce a discourse predicated wholly on:

> the variance in the conditions of the Imams, in terms of what people see in regard to determination (*zabt*), capacity (*al-kifaya*), and in upholding the affairs of the imamate (*waʾl-qiyam bi-umur al-aʾimma*).⁹¹

While brief, the discourse is nonetheless emphatic since al-Muʿizz situates variation in personality as typical of the figures of all divinely-appointed guides. Reference to Q. 46:35 is thus made to note the varied states of the prophets themselves, as demonstrated by the distinction in the Qurʾan to those messengers who were afforded the title as being 'the messengers of firm resolve (*uluʾl-ʿazmi minaʾl-rusul*)'.⁹² Consequently, in that prophets and messengers themselves could be of varied nature, al-Muʿizz pronounces:

> So are the Imams. From them are those possessing determination and firmness, and from them are those of compassion and mercy, and of them are possessors of firmness and fortitude, and of them are those unable to carry the severity of their affair. Each one of them is suited for their time, and is beneficial for his place, for God Almighty and Glorious is the one who chose them.⁹³

Al-Qaʾim and the Rebellion of Abu Yazid

The most emphatic treatment in the *Majalis* of the question of distinction in stance and variation in policy, concerns however what seemingly stood as a principal subject of controversy, namely the events surrounding the rebellion of the ʿIbadi preacher, Abu Yazid al-Nukkari (d. 336/947). Integral to the broader conception of Fatimid salvation history, in which the leading figure receives the soteriological appellative of *al-Dajjal* (The

Liar), the rebellion of Abu Yazid al-Nukkari began in 322/944 and lasted until 336/947, seizing significant heartlands of the Fatimid domains and laying siege to the capital al-Mahdiyya, dominating the last years of al-Qa'im bi-Amr Allah's reign. The widespread devastation it inflicted both on Ifriqiya and on Fatimid forces in particular, is widely covered both in the medieval chronicles and in histories specifically of Fatimid Ifriqiya.[94] As noted by Halm, it seems the Berber Kutama as the foremost followers of the Fatimid Ismaili da'wa and the backbone of the Fatimid infantry, suffered most acutely. Provisions of security (aman) if issued to towns and cities, seem not to have been applied to Kutami garrisons, the massacres of which are reflected in the sources. Integral to treatments of the rebellion are those concerning the role of the Imam-caliph al-Qa'im. In contrast to his time as wali 'ahd to his father al-Mahdi bi'llah, when al-Qa'im was in the forefront of most major Fatimid campaigns, al-Qa'im's own defensiveness in the face of the rebellion has therefore been the subject of commentary.[95]

Despite the final and emphatic victory of al-Mansur over Abu Yazid in 336/947, the treatment of his rebellion in the Kitab al-Majalis makes it apparent that questions regarding the conduct of the Fatimid military and the decisions of al-Qa'im during the initial phase of the rebellion were still circulating and being debated in al-Mu'izz's reign. As expected, much of these seem to stem from the circles of the Kutama who, if not veterans themselves, would have been the sons and descendants of those lost in battle. The role of the Kutama, as awliya' and the beloved among followers of the Imam, is prominent in the Majalis.[96] Enmeshed in this, however, are attestations of the trials and tribulations suffered by Kutami tribesmen during the rebellion, including the imprisonment and enslavement of their women and children at the hands of Abu Yazid's forces.[97] Questions on the role of al-Qa'im are thus found throughout the text. Thus, in an audience of al-Mu'izz that included Kutami shaykhs, when the topic of Abu Yazid was once more raised, 'they [the shaykhs] mentioned the delays (takhalluf) of al-Qa'im in advancing against this.'[98]

To provide the response to questions still being asked about the rebellion, the Majalis deploys a distinctive range of discourses. The causes of the rebellion, beyond the heretical assumption of authority by the 'accursed Dajjal' himself, are thus variously situated as the result of the corruption of officials.[99] That the rebellion itself was a test (imtihan) and trial (mihna) for the awliya' and a source of purification of their sins is further stressed. Similarly, that al-Qa'im was 'inactive' is implicitly rejected, especially in consideration of his personal expenditure during the course of the rebellion.[100] Most consistent, however, are assertions that the success of the rebellion in the reign of al-Qa'im and its eventual defeat at the hand of al-Mansur were emphatically linked to God's decree (*qadar*) and consequently each Imam acted as apposite to each circumstance, their collective actions thus again representing a continuum. As such, questions as to action or inaction become redundant.

That the rebellion of Abu Yazid was decreed is rendered apparent in attestations of its prediction long before its eruption. Such predictions, featuring centrally in narratives on the construction of the Fatimid capital al-Mahdiyya, in which its successful resistance to Abu Yazid's siege marks a distinct turning point in the course of the rebellion.[101] The theme of inevitability is joined to assertions of the predestined decree that it would be only at al-Mansur's hands that victory was attained.[102] Responses conceptualising al-Qa'im's actions during the course of the rebellion are thus located within the context of salvation history, where amelioration of the *fitna* stood as a marker in the history of the Fatimid age, one to be realised only by al-Mansur. This is succinctly situated in the *Majalis* in the provision of another episode, here relating a conversation between al-Mu'izz and his father al-Mansur, and providing afterwards al-Mu'izz's own elucidation and al-Nu'man's exposition. Al-Nu'man, in transmitting a tradition on the authority of the Imam-caliph, thus relates a question al-Mu'izz asked his father, al-Mansur: 'What if al-Qa'im bi-Amr Allah had endeavoured to do what you did, and acted as you were able to act, so he realised it [i.e. success], so that authority was again unified and affairs were set in order?'[103]

In his reply to the question, al-Mansur seemingly rebukes the questioner, pronouncing the necessity to 'seek refuge in God' and 'indeed seek God's forgiveness (*bal fastaghfiri'llah minh*)' for asking it.[104] It is in al-Mansur's subsequent statement that a conception of the determining role of salvation history becomes apparent,[105] which in turn provided the medium for al-Mu'izz's own elaboration:

> It was not for al-Qa'im to bring about an affair that God had permitted (*adhina*) to [continue] until its end ... God tested (*imtahana*) His Servants with the *fitna*, and determined a time for the expiration of the trial (*mihna*) ... So he [al-Qa'im] was unable to bring closer what God had made distant, and he was unable to act except with patience, and with submission, and contentment, until

he met God in a state of patience ... so when God decreed for the lifting of the *mihna* and the expulsion of the *fitna*, it was not for al-Mansur to delay (*yatakhallaf*) in arising for the affair due to a shortage in numbers and a weakness of power, and whomsoever God decrees to be victorious can have no victor against him.[106]

With al-Nuʿman's own subsequent eyewitness elaboration demonstrating furthermore al-Qaʾim's knowledge that all options available to him presented 'nothing save pain' (*ina*'), the *Majalis* then provides a further statement by al-Muʿizz relating al-Qaʾim's knowledge that the *fitna* could not 'end through his hands (*la yanqatiʿ ʿala yadayhi abada*)'.[107] Collectively, the demonstration cements the broader response that there can be no censure of God's decree.

Conclusion

The identification of the function of the *Kitab al-Majalis* as a medium for the provision of official *responsa* leads to further conclusions on the nature of the Fatimids' Ifriqiyan polity. These include those pertaining to the strategies deployed in ameliorating the tensions inherent between the proclamation of a divinely-sanctioned salvific polity on the one hand, and the genesis of a pragmatic political order on the other. Above all, however, the thematic focuses of the *Majalis* reflect a polity that had an 'ear to the ground', conscious of 'public' perception and the nature of the opposition and propaganda directed against it. The identification of this objective of al-Nuʿman's work can in turn lead to some reconsideration of the nature of the early Fatimid state in Ifriqiya. In his study of the practices of the Fatimid *khutba*, a wholly public performance which the Fatimid Imam-caliphs took 'seriously', Walker has demonstrated how participation in public rituals, predicated on assertions of the legitimacy of their authority, was central to the outlook of the Ifriqiyan Fatimid Imam-caliphs.[108] A consideration of the distinctive role of the *Kitab al-Majalis* adds to this knowledge the evidence of the impetus towards public discourse and legitimisation. This allows for some reconsideration on the nature of the polity itself, which rather than standing as an exclusivist state resting wholly on Berber (i.e. Kutama and Sanhaja) military power and economic hegemony, and possessing otherwise little local 'appeal', emerged as one highly conscious of 'public' perception and whose statecraft was critically predicated on acts of public legitimisation and persuasion.

NOTES

1. Abu Hanifa al-Nuʿman, *Kitab al-Majalis waʾl-musayarat*, ed. al-Habib al-Faqi, Ibrahim Shabbuh and Muhammad al-Yaʿlawi (Tunis, 1978).
2. The absence in the *Majalis* of any reference to the events surrounding the Fatimid conquest of Egypt in 356/969 provides a generally acceptable *terminus ante quem* for al-Nuʿman's sealing of the work. The editors of the critical edition, al-Faqi, Shabbuh and Yaʿlawi, suggest the date range of 358–360/968–971 based on the internal evidence including the lack of a reference to Jawhar's conquest of Egypt, but also considering that the *Majalis* indicates al-Nuʿman's sons Muhammad and ʿAli – both soon to be prominent *qadi*s in Fatimid Egypt – were still unmarried at the time of writing (al-Nuʿman, *Kitab al-Majalis*, editors introduction, pp. 17–18). For Poonawala's affirmation of the end date see Ismail K. Poonawala, 'The Chronology of al-Nuʿman's Works', in Kumail Rajani, ed., *The Sound Traditions: Studies in Ismaili Texts and Thought* (Leiden, 2022), p. 427.
3. For studies predicated principally on the information found within the *Kitab al-Majalis*: On Fatimid foreign and diplomatic relations with the Byzantines and the Umayyads of Spain, see Samuel M. Stern, 'An Embassy of the Byzantine Emperor to the Fatimid Caliph al-Muʿizz', *Byzantion*, 20 (1950), pp. 239–258; Mohammed Yalaoui, 'Controverse entre le Fatimide al-Muʿizz et l'Omeyyade al-Nasir, d'après le Kitab al-Majalis w-al Musayarat du Cadi Nuʿman', *Cahiers de Tunisie*, 26 (1978), pp. 7–33. For the contours and complexities of the Fatimid *daʿwa* beyond its borders, see Samuel M. Stern, 'Ismaʿili Propaganda and Fatimid Rule in Sind', *Islamic Culture*, 23 (1949), pp. 298–307; Idem, 'Heterodox Ismailism at the time of al-Muizz', *Bulletin of the School of Oriental and African Studies*, 17 (1955), pp. 10–33; for distinct political developments in al-Muʿizz's reign see Farhat Dachraoui (Farhat al-Dashrawi), 'La captivité d'Ibn Wasul, le rebelle de Sidjilmassa, d'après le Cadi an-Nuʿman', *Cahiers de Tunisie*, 4 (1956), pp. 295–299; and more recently for the Shiʿi Ismaili legal hermeneutics elaborated in the *Kitab al-Majalis* see Agostino Cilardo, 'Ismaili and Sunni Elaborations of the Sources of Law: The *Kitab al-Majalis waʾl-musayarat* by al-Qadi Abu Hanifa al-Nuʿman and the *Risala* of al-Shafiʿi: A Comparative Study', in Orkhan Mir-Kasimov, ed., *Intellectual Interactions in the Islamic World: The Ismaili Thread* (London, 2019), pp. 109–145. For a listing of catalogue entries of the mss. of the *Kitab al-Majalis* see Ibid., p. 109, fn1. These are besides use of the *Majalis* in broader chronographic treatments of Fatimid Ifriqiyan history, or on the evolution of Fatimid doctrine under the aegis of al-Muʿizz, as in Wilferd Madelung, 'The imamate in Early Ismaili Doctrine', *Shii Studies Review*, 2 (2018), pp. 74–75.
4. Thus al-Faqi *et al.* locate the text as a 'work of history, *sira*, *ʿaqida* and *adab*' (al-Nuʿman, *Kitab al-Majalis*, editors introduction, p. 19).
5. al-Nuʿman himself in his introduction to the *Majalis* situates his desire, in composing the work, to reap the rewards reserved for the 'load-carrying preacher' (*al-mubbaligh al-hamil*) and the 'truthful narrator' (*al-sadiq al-naqil*) of the knowledge of the Imams to others and for future generations (al-Nuʿman, *Kitab al-Majalis*, pp. 45–46). He adds however that he composed this work in particular – as distinct from his *sira* of al-Muʿizz – in order to retain those aspects of knowledge and wisdom of the Imam-caliph that would not naturally fall into a *sira*-type work (Ibid., p. 47).
6. al-Nuʿman, *Kitab al-Majalis*, editors introduction, p. 6.
7. Hamdani thus situates the *Majalis* as representing part of al-Nuʿman's effort to present a realistic historical image of a ruling Imam in his overall construction of a 'exoteric' (*zahiri*) paradigm, in contrast to the idealised soteriological presentations of the Imams in other Shiʿi literature. See Sumaiya A. Hamdani, *Between Revolution and State: The Path to Fatimid Statehood* (London, 2006), p. 111 and also pp. 97–110 for Hamdani's preceding treatment of the *Majalis*.

8   Michael Brett, *The Fatimid Empire* (Edinburgh, 2017), pp. 69, 74.
9   Brett summarised the work as belonging to the 'question and answer' genre then emerging in legal literature. While sharing aspects of the hypothesis presented here, this brief evaluation seems not to account for the distinctive thematic focus of the text.
10 Paul E. Walker, *Exploring an Islamic Empire: Fatimid History and its Sources* (London, 2002), p. 138.
11 This is not withstanding the detailed coverage of the text by the editors, nor the highly commendable extensive index that renders the critical edition significantly navigable.
12 For the more recent translation of Madelung's still authoritative article on the doctrines of the Ismaili Fatimid imamate see now Wilferd Madelung, 'The imamate in Early Ismaili Doctrine', pp. 62–155. On early Ismaili doctrines of the imamate more broadly see Heinz Halm, *The Empire of the Mahdi: The Rise of the Fatimids*, tr. Michael Bonner (Leiden, 1996), pp. 16–22; Farhad Daftary, *The Ismaʿilis: Their History and Doctrines* (2nd ed., Cambridge, 2007), pp. 128–137. For a summation of the centrality of authoritative knowledge in the Ithna ʿAshari and Ismaili conceptions of the imamate see Najam Haider, *Shiʿi Islam: An Introduction* (Cambridge, 2014), pp. 38–49.
13 In that caliphal, or dynastic, patronage of the *akhbariyyun* was a standard feature of Muslim historiography especially following the 2nd/8th century with figures from Ibn Ishaq (d. 150/767) to al-Baladhuri (d. ca. 279/892) either patronised or members of the 'pro'-Abbasid establishment, and that works were often produced with dynastic legitimisation in mind (e.g. the anonymous *Akhbar al-ʿAbbas*); such works rarely contained direct or formal imprint of caliphal sanction, which furthermore post-*mihna* would have different legal status in contrast to a statement of a Fatimid Imam-caliph. For such earlier patronage see e.g. Chase Robinson, *Islamic Historiography* (Cambridge, 2003), p. 26.
14 Daftary, *Ismaʿilis*, pp. 4–10. See also Walker, *Exploring*, pp. 8–9; cf. Shainool Jiwa, 'The Baghdad Manifesto (402/1011): A Re-Examination of Fatimid-Abbasid Rivalry', in F. Daftary and S. Jiwa, ed., *The Fatimid Caliphate: Diversity of Traditions* (London, 2018), pp. 22–79.
15 For al-Nuʿman's reliance on intermediaries for reports on al-Mansur see e.g. al-Nuʿman, *Kitab al-Majalis*, p. 71.
16 Ibid., pp. 367–370.
17 e.g. Ibid., pp. 255–257, 388–395, 483–485.
18 Ibid., pp. 442–446.
19 Ibid., pp. 164–196.
20 For a recent summative biographical overview of al-Nuʿman see al-Qadi al-Nuʿman, *Disagreements of the Jurists: A Manual of Islamic Legal Theory*, ed. and tr. Devin J. Stewart (New York, 2015), pp. ix–x, and, also p. xxxv for earlier references on al-Nuʿman. Poonawala's collection of studies on al-Nuʿman remain the most comprehensive treatments of his life and output, see now Poonawala, 'The Chronology of al-Nuʿman's Works', pp. 337–583.
21 As also noted by Hamdani, *Revolution and State*, p. 104.
22 See for instance al-Nuʿman, *Kitab al-Majalis*, pp. 82, 353–359 and especially p. 311 where in mention of al-Muʿizz's dream of the sword al-Nuʿman seeks to demonstrate the importance and perpetuity of his service to the Imam-caliphs. The *qadi* is nonetheless not averse to recording censures and reprimands received at the hands of the Imam-caliphs and especially al-Mansur, the episodes nonetheless retaining didactic function (Ibid., pp. 75, 77–79, 535). Included furthermore are narratives that implicitly relate the distinctions of al-Nuʿman's family through reference to al-Muʿizz's concern for and benefactions to them, see Ibid., pp. 543–555 for al-Muʿizz's interest in al-Nuʿman's sons' marriages, cf. p. 546. ʿAli b. al-Nuʿman furthermore appears in conjunction with al-Nuʿman's account of his composition of an *urjuza* for al-Muʿizz. Ibid., p. 462. Their occurrence is seemingly in part motivated by the presence of the rivalry and even

23 hostility of others at court towards al-Nuʿman, see Ibid., pp. 307, 348–351 and especially pp. 353–359).
23 For the *Iftitah* and the *Manaqib wa'l-mathalib* see Ibid., pp. 117–118; see pp. 360–361 for al-Nuʿmans *Kitab al-Dinar*.
24 *Kitab al-Majalis*, pp. 305–306.
25 This point is reiterated across the text e.g. at Ibid., pp. 224, 301.
26 For example, on the *Kitab al-Dinar*, see Ibid., pp. 360–361. On his general practise of presenting his works to al-Muʿizz cf. Ibid., pp. 297, 396.
27 See for instance Ibid., pp. 430, and 545 for al-Muʿizz's signed comment on a copy of a text submitted by al-Nuʿman.
28 Ibid., pp. 118, 120, 137, 347, 485. On the *walaya* of the Imams cf. Ibid., p. 108.
29 Ibid., pp. 208, 420. For the Imams as intercessors (*shufaʿa'*) for their followers see Ibid., pp. 86, 274 and 401.
30 Ibid., pp. 274, 404, 433, 487. The necessity of seeking the knowledge and wisdom (*hikma*) of the Imam-caliphs, as an impetus for the believers, recurs repeatedly as in Ibid., pp. 153–154, 224, 274, 388, cf. p. 312.
31 The legitimacy of succession of a minor to the office of the imamate is thus treated in al-Muʿizz's discourse on the age of Imam ʿAli b. al-Husayn, Zayn al-ʿAbidin, at p. 521, cf. p. 482. For the question of multiple imamates see Ibid., p. 514. On the *baraka* of the Imams, pp. 292–294.
32 Thus on the activities, deviance and express censure of 'errant' *daʿi*s see Ibid., pp. 105, 157, 198, 237, 407–411, 420, 452, 497–498, 524. See Ibid., p. 419 for their designation as *ghulat*, and pp. 548–550 for al-Muʿizz's express condemnation.
33 On the *ghuluww* as rendered by belief in the Imam's knowledge of the unseen see Ibid., pp. 84, and 419 but cf. pp. 271–272. On the status of the Imams vis-à-vis Prophethood, Ibid., pp. 522–524, 548–550.
34 Hamid Haji, *Inside the Immaculate Portal: A History From Early Fatimid Archives: a new edition and English translation of Mansur al-ʿAzizi al-Jawdhari's biography of al-Ustadh Jawdhar* (London, 2012), pp. 7–8.
35 Thus on the provision of the 'testimonies' (*wasiyya*) of al-Mansur to al-Muʿizz see *Kitab al-Majalis*, pp. 96, 241, cf. pp. 501–502. For the love of al-Mahdi for al-Muʿizz, p. 541, and of al-Qa'im for al-Muʿizz, pp. 125, 468–469.
36 Ibid., p. 296.
37 Ibid., p. 519.
38 Thus on the expected conquest of the East, see Ibid., p. 138 and for the cause for the delay Ibid., p. 371 and 475–477. The promise of al-Muʿizz appears at Ibid., p. 508.
39 Ibid., p. 159.
40 Ibid., pp. 268–269.
41 Ibid., pp. 142–145.
42 Ibid., pp. 382–383, 521–522.
43 Ibid., pp. 423, 521–522.
44 Ibid., pp. 328–329.
45 Ibid., pp. 123–125. For further historical discussions including pertaining to the significance of the appointment of Imam ʿAli b. Musa al-Rida, as successor (*wali ʿahd*) by the Abbasid Caliph al-Ma'mun, see Ibid., p. 403.
46 Ibid., pp. 132, 327, 431–432, 439, 508, 532.
47 Ibid., pp. 102–103, 535, cf. p. 131.
48 Ibid.
49 Ibid., pp. 250–251.
50 Ibid., pp. 361–362. Notable here are condemnations of the excesses – when seeking to arrogate authority – of the Fatimid Saqlabi generals Muzaffar and Qaysar (Ibid., pp. 434–435), who were accordingly executed in 349/960, as per *Sirat Ustadh Jawdhar*.
51 Ibid., pp. 250, 487–488 thus in a speech to the Kutama shaykhs.

52 Ibid., p. 183.
53 Ibid., p. 192.
54 Ibid., p. 190, cf. p. 344.
55 Ibid., p. 193.
56 Ibid., pp. 180, 190.
57 Ibid., p. 191. Al-Muʿizz here adds moreover that 'emigration can simply arise out of desire and choice.'
58 Marius Canard, 'Le cérémonial fatimite et le cérémonial byzantin: essai de comparaison', *Byzantion*, 21 (1951), pp. 355–420, 370–382, 417; Paula Sanders, *Ritual, Politics and the City in Fatimid Cairo* (Albany, NY, 1994), pp. 13–17. That al-Nuʿman sought to defend the practice was also noted by Sanders, as reflected exclusively on al-Nuʿman's more limited treatment in his *Kitab al-Himma*, see Ibid., p. 17.
59 See Aziz Al-Azmeh, *Muslim Kingship: Power and the Sacred in Muslim, Christian and Pagan Polities* (London, 1996), p. 140; Nadia Maria El-Cheikh, 'The Institutionalisation of ʿAbbasid Ceremonial', in John Hudson and Ana Rodríguez, ed, *Diverging Paths? The Shapes of Power and Institutions in Medieval Christendom and Islam* (Leiden, 2014), pp. 351–370, 353, 364–365.
60 Elsa Cardoso, *The Door of the Caliph: Concepts of the Court in the Umayyad Caliphate of al-Andalus* (Abingdon, UK, 2023), pp. 195–199. I would like to thank the author for sharing with me an advanced copy of the relevant segments in anticipation of the publication.
61 al-Nuʿman, *Kitab al-Majalis*, p. 58.
62 Ibid., p. 59.
63 Ibid., p. 59. Cf. Sanders, *Rituals*, p. 17.
64 *Kitab al-Majalis*, p. 59.
65 Ibid.
66 Ibid., p. 60.
67 Q. 12:100: 'And he placed his parents on the dais and they fell down before him prostrate (*wa kharru lahu sujjada*), and he said: O my father! This is the interpretation of my dream of old (tr. Pickthall).' Notably, alongside debates as to the meaning of God's command to Iblis to prostrate to Adam as repeated throughout the Qurʾan as in Q. 2:34, Q. 17:61, Q. 18:50, Q. 20:116, Q. 15:29–33 and Q. 38:72–77, this verse of Q. 12:100 serves as a distinct site of debate for contemporary exegetes as to the meaning of the *sujud* of Yusuf's brothers, as demonstrated by Totolli. See Roberto Tottoli, 'Muslim Attitudes Towards Prostration (sujud): I. Arabs and Prostration at the Beginning of Islam and in the Qurʾan', *Studia Islamica* (1998), pp. 5–34, 26–27.
68 *Kitab al-Majalis*, p. 59.
69 Ibid.
70 Ibid., p. 60.
71 Ibid.
72 Ibid., p. 59.
73 On the centrality of *niyya* see Paul R. Powers, *Intent in Islamic Law: Motive and Meaning in Medieval Sunni Fiqh* (Leiden, 2006), especially pp. 19–43.
74 al-Nuʿman, *Kitab al-Majalis*, p. 59.
75 Ibid.
76 Totolli, 'Muslim Attitudes', p. 12.
77 *Kitab al-Majalis*, p. 59.
78 Thus Ibid., pp. 69, 76, 210–213, 232–234, 259, 391.
79 Ibid., pp. 69–70.
80 Ibid.
81 Ibid.
82 Ibid., pp. 69–70.
83 Ibid., p. 77.

84　Ibid.
85　Ibid.
86　Thus when *amir* and upon being asked by al-Mansur as to his choice for an *amir* for one of the frontiers (*al-thughur*), al-Muʿizz's choice converges with that of al-Mansur, Ibid., pp. 71–72.
87　Ibid., p. 232. The additional statement seems here to be by al-Nuʿman.
88　Ibid.
89　Ibid., p. 277.
90　Ibid., p. 278. The analogy is then provided of how an Imam-caliph, in the same reign, could appoint an official and then, 'it is made apparent to him thereafter that which obligates his removal (*thumma yubbayinu lahu baʿda dhalika ma yujab ʿazlahu*).' This is furthermore situated in reliance on the notion of *tabyin* as based on Q. 49:6.
91　Ibid., p. 283.
92　Ibid.
93　Ibid., p. 284.
94　The most sustained coverage and narrative remains that of Halm, *Empire*, pp. 298–325. See now also Mounira Chapoutot-Remadi, 'Abu Yazid al-Nukkari', *EI3*.
95　See e.g. Brett, *Empire*, p. 163.
96　Distinct praise for the Kutama is thus found on pp. 96, 203, 249, cf. p. 255 on al-Muʿizz's love (*mahabba*) for them and especially p. 321.
97　Ibid., p. 322.
98　Ibid., p. 215.
99　Thus on al-Qaʾim's own statements as to the excesses of officials as factors in the rebellion see Ibid., pp. 119, 429.
100　Ibid., p. 551.
101　Thus also in the *Majalis*, where al-Mahdiyya's fortifications were established by al-Mahdi for that 'one hour of one day (*li-maqam saʿatan min al-nahar*)', Ibid., p. 542.
102　Ibid., p. 325. For al-Mansur's dream, in which a map indicating the extent of Fatimid possessions is gradually blackened until erased clear by al-Mansur himself, see Ibid., p. 113.
103　Ibid., p. 248.
104　Ibid.
105　Ibid. Thus the Imam-caliph al-Mansur pronounces, 'It was not for al-Qaʾim to act except in the way that he did (*ma kana li'l-Qaʾim an yafʿala illa ma qad faʿalah*), and it was for not me to act [in any other way] except for the way I did.'
106　Ibid, p. 249.
107　Ibid.
108　Paul E. Walker, *Orations of the Fatimid Caliphs: Festival Sermons of the Ismaili Imams* (London, 2009), p. xii.

5

(Re)-making Time, (Re)-making Place: Some Considerations on Early Fatimid *Ta'wil* and Sacred Space*

Jamel A. Velji

Suffusing Qur'anic discussions of the natural world is its repeated insistence that earthy, material and heavenly topographies – the sky, the heavens, the alternation of night and day, and even the ships on the sea[1] – are only ephemeral signs pointing to the permanence and transcendence of the divine reality. The conceptual framework of this system of signification rests in large part on the Qur'anic grammar of the apocalypse: that, at the end of time, these seemingly fixed realities that govern our quotidian existences will unravel, giving way to the true reality of God's unicity. These conceptions of signs, significations and their relationship with what constitutes divine truth provides a useful heuristic framework for exploring some of the literary dimensions inherent to Fatimid *ta'wil*, a method of signification that operates to create new meaning by re-inscribing the *zahir*, the apparent, with aspects of the hidden, the *batin*. Before going further, I should note that I am not interested in showing any kind of systemisation of this hermeneutic, though of course there are patterns inherent to the production of this literature by certain individuals. My interest is, rather, in highlighting how this hermeneutic of the hidden can address at once a multiplicity of concerns, ranging from the political to the spiritual, the manifest to the ephemeral.[2] This paper adds to recently published studies outlining some of the features of *ta'wil*.[3] I hope to do so by focusing on the rather blank canvas of the concept of religious 'space' to explore some of the features of this hermeneutic among two early Fatimid authors, focusing in particular on how an examination of space can touch on the theme of cosmopolitanism.

Religion and Space

Religion is, *pace* Durkheim, an eminently social phenomenon.[4] And yet it is in the spatial world where these social interactions occur. As Knott points out, social relations – relations with people, objects and with the natural world – take place in space, and so religion, too, 'must also exist and express itself in and through space, and must play its part in the constitution of spaces'.[5] Knott continues, 'The spatial underpinning of religion is witnessed at all levels, from the expression of hierarchical relations ... to the local, national and global extension of religious structures and institutions by their repeated reproduction in new settings through mission or migration.'[6] It should be mentioned here that space is not only a blank canvas through which religions operate. 'Religious spaces are constitutive components of religion and religious experience, not simply the settings in which they occur.'[7] Thus an analysis of religious space or, more precisely, the dynamic processes by which space can be constructed as religious, can tell us a great deal about the nature of religion itself.

The discussion here begins with a few basic observations about Qur'anic space. The Qur'an commonly re-ascribes what we know in our quotidian spatial field as that which, in reality, indicates something else. Trees, mountains, the sky, the heavens, rain, various foods we eat, the crops we grow, the insects we encounter, our social relations and the roads we travel are just some of these objects that point to the reality of the divine who has created these terrestrial and celestial phenomena – arguing, in turn, for the necessity of obedience to the divine message.[8] Those who obey this message are promised a reward in special, eternal spaces characterised by luxury, lack of want, tranquility and constant satiation, whereas those who do not are foisted into eternal spaces of endless cycles of deprivation, torment and pain. This transition from this world to the next is punctuated by the earthly apocalypse, during which the organisational principles of earthly and heavenly space give way to the disclosure of true reality for all to see at the end of time. The beginning of Sura 82, for instance, states:

> When the sky is torn
> When the stars are scattered
> When the seas are poured forth
> When the tombs are burst open
> Then a soul will know what it has given

and what it has held back
Oh, O human being
what has deceived you about your generous
lord
who created you and shaped you and made
you right⁹

And it continues to discuss admission into heaven and hell. It states that those who deny religion (which at this time also meant acceptance of the reckoning)¹⁰ will be admitted to hell, while those who embraced it will be admitted to heaven.

A cursory spatial reading of the beginning of this sura would reveal that the space of the apocalypse encompasses the totality of the earth and even beyond: from the highest point of what we can see, the sky and the stars, to what is beneath the earth, the tombs – and presumably everything in between. The normally silent earth becomes the locus of the apocalypse's ontological reversal, and that which is normally hidden in one's soul is shown to them.¹¹ In Sura 99, the *zalzal*, or the quaking, the quaking earth discloses all the secrets hidden within it, and it will actually be the place where the resurrected are brought forth, the text says 'straggle forth',¹² and shown the true reality of the final judgment. At the end of time the organising principles of earthly existence disintegrate, giving way to the permanent spaces of the afterworld. It is important to note that one of the most powerful proofs for this Qur'anic argument is death itself: that our lives have an appointed time that is not known to us but is known to the divine – an 'appointed time', in the Qur'an frequently tethered to the fixed time for all things, including the Hour.¹³ Our ephemerality, and Qur'anic assertions of the ephemerality of earthly time, serve then as proofs and foils for the promise of the permanence of otherworldly space – a space of no time.

The 'Where' of *Ta'wil*

A key point often overlooked in the study of Fatimid *ta'wil* is this: that for the Fatimid hierarchy, the *da'wa*, the organisation of the world was a reflection of the Fatimids' utopian aspirations. As Daftary writes: 'the hierarchy traceable in the Fatimid texts seems to have had reference to a paradigmatic or utopian situation, when the Ismaili Imam would rule the entire world, and not to any actual *hudud* existing at any given time.'

Further, he writes, 'All Ismaili authors agree that the world, presumably the non-Fatimid part of it, was divided into twelve *jaza'ir* (s. *jazira*; lit., island) for *da'wa* purposes, with each *jazira* representing a separate and somewhat independent region for the penetration of the *da'wa*.'[14] This means that the *da'wa* hierarchy and the organisation of the *da'wa* saw the totality of the known world as the arena that religion moves through and reconstructs.

It is thus no coincidence that early *ta'wil* texts often ascribe celestial, cosmological and historical events with new referents – referents that only the initiated can see. One early text of *ta'wil*, Ja'far b. Mansur al-Yaman's *Kitab al-'Alim wa'l-ghulam* (Book of the Master and Disciple), states, for instance:

> [91] Now, all of the pairs I have described to you have *an inner and outer aspect* (57:3), a symbol (*mathal*) and what is symbolised. Thus the outer aspect (the visible planets, sun and moon) of *the seven heavens* (55:12, etc.) are symbols, while their inner aspect is *the seven natiqs* (among the prophets), *the possessors of determination among the (divine) messengers* (46:35). The outer aspect of *the seven earths* (55:12) is likewise a symbol, while its inner aspect is *the Imams of right guidance* (21:73; 32:24)[15]

The initiated acquire spiritual knowledge to perceive the hidden symbolic realities of things through the hermeneutics of unveiling – not just of the sacred text but through the universe itself. If the Qur'an repeatedly signals that our quotidian existence is framed through temporary cosmic realities that ultimately point to the reality of divine unicity (ships on the sea; alternation of night and day; spring and its connections to resurrection), *ta'wil* makes a similar argument, investing the known world with spiritual referents for those who could see beyond the *zahir* into the horizon of the *batin* and those authorised to dispense it.

Just as the rupturing of quotidian space is a primary feature of the Qur'anic apocalypse, early promises of utopian transformation undergirded Fatimid claims to religio-political power. Pulsating with promises of an imminent earthly transformation often expressed in apocalyptic terms, the *Kitab al-Kashf*,[16] or 'Book of Unveiling', envisions a world in which the eschatological figure is often elided with the Qur'an's descriptions of the end of time. The *Kashf*'s *ta'wil* of many of these passages transforms the earth's unravelling topography to argue that these apocalyptic descriptions point, in fact, to the potentially imminent arrival of the eschatological figure. While I have discussed many of the following passages at length in other places,[17] what I wish to point out here is just how wide-ranging the *Kashf*'s use of space is in constructing its argument – a rhetorical move accomplished by harnessing and re-signifying the Qur'an's vast spatial expanses. In one place in the text, for instance, the heaven that is 'split open and becomes rose-coloured like oil'[18] (Qur'an 55:37) is interpreted to refer to the manifestation of the *qa'im* and his world. The text states that the horizon will bloom for him, and while those who oppose him will try to flee from him, the *qa'im* is equated to the approaching punishment 'that cannot be prevented' (Qur'an 52:8).[19] Yet it is not just the advent of the *qa'im* that is reinscribed as apocalyptic unveiling. Celestial and terrestrial phenomena are elided with the hierarchy of the *da'wa* as well. In reproducing Qur'an 52:1–8, for instance, which declares:

> By the mountain
> By a Scripture inscribed
> In unrolled parchment
> By the much-visited House
> By the ceiling raised high
> By the ocean ever-filled
> Your Lord's punishment is approaching
> It cannot be prevented[20]

The text says that the mountain is the *natiq*, or the speaking prophet. The scripture inscribed is the knowledge (*'ilm*). The unrolled parchment is the *hujja*, or the 'proof'[21] – and the much-visited House is the progeny (of the Prophet). The ceiling raised high is the totality, and the ever-filled ocean is the gate (*bab*). The approaching punishment is the *qa'im* who we are told, once again, 'cannot be prevented'.[22] In another place in the text, the mountains that vanish and become like a mirage (Qur'an 78:20) point, in fact, to the disappearing *hujja*s, proofs of the Imam in his absence.[23] Their authority will vanish as the eschatological figure, elided with the end of time, manifests. The *Kashf* also tells us that the earth that is 'pounded to dust, pounded and pounded',[24] (Qur'an 89:21) is also equated to the *hujja*, the proof of the *qa'im*, who will appear and then yield his authority to the eschatological figure at the end of time.[25]

Even when the *Kashf* is not engaged in an active resignification of apocalyptic imagery, its spatial field often concerns the entire earth and its contents. Since we are in a time of increased awareness of how our different kinds of behaviour have variously affected shifts in global climate patterns, I thought it would be particularly appropriate to cull an example from the *Kashf* that speaks about water and then bees.

In interpreting the Qur'an 67:30, for instance, which states: 'Say, "Just think: if all your water were to sink deep into the earth who could give you flowing water in its place?"'[26] the text states that 'Ali b. Abi Talib is a likeness of water. Just as the living is made alive through water, it states, the world is made alive through knowledge (*'ilm*) from the Knower. In other words, just as water surrounds us and we rely upon it, often taking it for granted, likewise the universe is suffused with signs that point to 'Ali and his salvific knowledge. The text then states that the flowing water means the *qa'im* from the family of Muhammad.[27]

The *Kashf* then cites 16:68, a verse about bees: *'And your Lord inspired the bee, saying, "Build yourselves houses in the mountains and trees and what people construct."'* It then states:

> The bees are the Imams, the places [var: sweeteners] of God's knowledge because they are the repositories of God's guidance and His light. *[T]he mountains* are the *da'i*s (callers) who are [at] the station of the proofs (*hujja*s). *And in the trees* are the *da'i*s who are under the *hujja*s. *In what people construct*, means the places the *da'i*s use to multiply.
>
> God says to the Imams, *'Then feed from all kinds of fruits and follow the ways made easy for you by Lord'* (16:69).[28] The fruits are the knowledge and the ways of God are the work. *'From their bellies comes a drink of different colours in which there is healing for people'* (16:69). He says that there is no contradiction in the judgment that will separate people from one another. *Indeed, in that is a sign* (16:69). By the *hujja* He means the proof (*al-burhan*).[29]

Bees, trellises, trees, hives and fruits all become the open spatial field of the Fatimid mission. The bees are likened to the Imams, the storehouses of God's wisdom. The bees set up hives which are proofs, the *hujja*s – once again we see how they are equated to mountains. Note that there is a hierarchy of *da'i*s here: hives in the trees are a rank lower in the *da'wa* than the *da'i*s who are at the station of the *hujja*s. And the hives constructed out of human-made materials – perhaps we can say in the midst of the social world – are the places where the *da'i*s multiply. The nourishment for the bees is knowledge, and the paths that the bees fly through, the paths that God makes easy for the bees, become the spatial field for work, the work of religion. The honey that emerges from their bellies serves as proof for this system in two ways. First, it is a tangible proof for the veracity of this system which operates across spaces in plain sight to disseminate healing knowledge and guide the work of true religion. Second, the various colours of honey serve as a likeness for how people will be separated into categories as they are judged by the *qa'im*.

As we know, the transition from movement to state necessitated a sharing of space with different religious communities. The utopian hierarchy iterated in early Fatimid texts like the *Kashf* – a utopia that spanned all known space, and often equated terrestrial and celestial phenomena with the imminent disclosure of the *da'wa* – needed to be revised to accommodate shifting realities on the ground. A central question, then, is what happened to these spatial and theoretical constructions as the hidden became manifest – or only partially manifest – as the Fatimids transitioned from movement to state?[30]

To get at this question, I want to take a brief look at some of the work of al-Qadi al-Nu'man, the intellectual idealogue of the Fatimid state, who wrote a number of esoteric and exoteric works during his long service to the Imam-caliphs. Al-Nu'man's corpus is quite substantial, so it would not be appropriate to generalise, but I would like to point to a few examples of how a spatial analysis might aid in thinking about the relationship between space and cosmopolitanism.

First, in the *Kitab Asas al-ta'wil*, or 'Foundations of Spiritual Hermeneutics', there is a focus on events that happened during the time of the prophets, such as Adam, Noah, Abraham and Moses. Indeed, past prophetic history is re-read to construct the present. Through *ta'wil*, these past events acquire meaning that gestures to the establishment of the contemporary structure of the *da'wa*. In other words, al-Nu'man spends a significant amount of time discussing how events in prophetic history point to the structure and function of the Fatimid hierarchy. One fine example is al-Nu'man's discussion of Noah's ark:

> Noah built the ark as an example for a foundation (*asas*, a rank of the *da'wa* just after the speaker-prophet, custodian of the hidden knowledge) of his *da'wa*, and set up its borders (*hudud*) to establish the *batin* by the command of God so as to save believers through the life of spiritually enlightened knowledge from drowning in ignorance and error, just as the ark in the *zahir* is a refuge from literal drowning. And so, with the *asas*, he built a foundation for his *da'wa* and his *hudud* and set up the *da'wa* for the believers using the storehouses of

hidden knowledge. God made this knowledge clear to them and informed them of what will happen to them regarding their matters and the matters of the deceivers. He set up the ark and He will begin to work through it, and He has said,

(So he began to build the Ark,) *and whenever leaders of his people passed by, they laughed at him. He said, 'You may scorn us now, but we will come to scorn you: you will find out who will receive a humiliating punishment, and on whom a lasting suffering will descend.'* (11:38–39).[31]

And He made the manifest ark a proof by which believers are shown the way, and as a likeness for His *batin* (*Asas*, 2011: 57).[32]

The story of the ark is generally known as one in which true believers, the minority of people who adhere to God's word, are saved and the majority of people who refuse to believe in the truth are not. But al-Nu'man re-signifies this story so that the salvific substrate of the ark becomes transformed into spiritually enlightened knowledge. The ark's borders are likened to the *batin*, to hidden knowledge, and function both as barriers to the outside, to the unsaved masses, and as a hierarchical system of a particular structure ordering that knowledge. Those within the ark are surrounded by and saved through the spiritually enlightened knowledge dispensed by the *asas* and the *da'wa*. This *ta'wil* is suggestive in many ways of how space becomes bounded and transformed – from a narrative of imminent terrestrial transformation to one in which a minority community with claims to the truth had to navigate complex inter-religious dynamics when they found themselves ruling over a population that did not adhere to their own religious worldview.

It is striking, too, that the bulk of this text is concerned with the ascribing and delineating of an esoteric hierarchy to Qur'anic and extra-Qur'anic sources. Unlike the *Kashf*, where there is a sense of eschatological urgency and the totality of the final judgment, here *ta'wil* gently hangs over many of these stories; it infuses them, or almost stands parallel to them. While this might be due to a multiplicity of reasons, two will be highlighted here. The first is the issue of eschatology: that the Fatimids came to power following an apocalyptic revolution. This reinterpretation of prophetic history might have been a necessary step in articulating the tenets of various authoritative structures. In other words, reinterpreting the past and endowing events with *ta'wil* that corresponded to a specific esoteric hierarchy, in which particular functions were delineated as the Fatimids transitioned from movement to state, helped to institutionalise a movement that initially was grounded in a *Mahdist* impulse. The *da'wa* hierarchy infusing the hidden was preserved, but perhaps needed to be systematised, and here prophetic history was a substrate by which this could be readily achieved.

Ritual and legal spaces, too, were spaces that reflected the Fatimids' cosmopolitan realities. One unique set of texts for the study of *ta'wil* and its relationship to legal discourse was also penned by al-Qadi al-Nu'man, who wrote both the *Da'a'im al-Islam*, the Fatimid legal compendium, as well the *ta'wil* of his own legal work, the *Ta'wil al-da'a'im*. This movement from the *zahir* to *batin* written by the same author is remarkable for scholars and students of *ta'wil* and the study of religion more broadly, as it illuminates how the *qadi* produced different discourses for distinct audiences – the initiated and the uninitiated –the *Ta'wil al-da'a'im* being disclosed only to Ismaili insiders.[33]

The *Da'a'im al-Islam*, which has an entire chapter on the details of the Pilgrimage, states, for instance: 'Abu Ja'far Muhammad b. 'Ali: He said, "Every faithful one who goes around the House {this is the Ka'ba} seven times ... prays two *raka'at*, performs the circumambulation properly, and offers the prayers correctly, shall be forgiven [his sins] by God".'[34]

Here is how al-Nu'man talks about this in the *Ta'wil al-da'a'im*:

> The likeness of the House is the Master of Age, whoever is a Prophet or an Imam. The likeness of circumambulating it is the likeness of the people of the *da'wa* of truth holding fast to the Imam of their time, their seeking refuge in him, their drawing near to him, and their striving for the grace of God and the knowledge and wisdom that he has. The likeness of the pilgrims who circumambulate the Ka'ba, who in the *zahir* have completed seven circumambulations, is the likeness of the people of the *da'wa* of truth acknowledging the seven Speaker-Prophets and seven Imams, those Imams between each of the seven speaker-prophets who succeed one another.[35]

Correct religion is mediated by proper spatial interaction with the sacred in both cases. In the first, performing the obligation of the Pilgrimage, including the circumambulation of the Ka'ba with its attendant prayers correctly, results in the expiation of sins. In the movement from the *zahir* to the *batin*, the sacred centre acquires additional meaning. The likeness of the Ka'ba as the Master of the Age means that the sacred centre of Islam is now imbued with motion. Its circumambulation is likened to the people of the *daʿwa* expressing their *walaya* to him. The performance of the seven circumambulations in the *zahir* results in the proper completion of the rite; in the *batin*, this is analogous to the proper acknowledgment of not just the Master of the Age, but of Fatimid authority and sacred history. Shared religious spaces, legal narratives and prophetic histories like that of Noah's ark, then, acquired a multiplicity of interpretations for multiple audiences, validating Fatimid claims to authority on multiple registers.

What can this, admittedly all too brief, discussion of space tell us about Fatimid religion? First, looking at these and other texts through the prism of space can illuminate in very interesting ways the dynamic construction of religion by certain authors. The *Kashf*'s spatial field is replete with eschatological images, for instance, anticipating the imminent emergence of the *qaʾim* and ranks of the *daʿwa* for those who possessed true knowledge. Those who could truly see would be prepared for the transition from earthly time to a time of no time; everything in the world such as mountains, trees and bees were indications of the coming of this new age. As regards al-Nuʿman's writings, discussions of space also indicate that when apocalyptic ideas had to be revised, shared prophetic narratives as well as ritual and legal structures served as substrates for *taʾwil*. Vast utopian expanses gave way to the realities of the cosmopolitanism of shared religious spaces. *Taʾwil*, then, infused stories of the past to establish the present; it infused ritual structures and shared religious spaces to reify the hierarchy of the Fatimid state; and continued to provide believers with a sense of a process of constant unveiling, even in a majority Sunni context. As al-Nuʿman wrote reams on the law for general audiences, this notion of *taʾwil* continued, pointing to the importance of maintaining for the believers a special mode of interpretation that powerfully displaced normative understandings of shared spaces, attesting to the continued appeal of this hermeneutic and of the forces from which it was issued.

NOTES

* My thanks to Shainool Jiwa and Gregory Bilotto for kindly inviting me to deliver a paper at the IIS's Fatimid Cosmopolitanism conference. I am grateful to Bassam Frangieh and Shawki El-Zatmah for reviewing selections of the translations that appear here.

1 A particularly vivid example is Qurʾan 2:164.

2 'In some Ismaili examples that have come down to us, no such connection, or at least no obvious link, can be seen; the *batin* in such cases is truly and really esoteric, a realm of knowledge in which no outsider can participate. *Taʾwil* in this sense implies moving

from a shared understanding based on common language, religious teaching, and culture into a secret world where interpretation can lead almost anywhere and in any direction.' Paul Walker, 'The Doctrine of *Ta'wil* in Fatimid Ismaili Texts', in Rodrigo Adem and Edmund Hayes, ed., *Reason, Esotericism, and Authority in Shi'i Islam* (Leiden, 2021), p. 138. See also the discussion in David Hollenberg, *Beyond the Qur'an: Early Isma'ili Ta'wil and the Secrets of the Prophets* (Columbia, SC, 2016), p. ix ff.

3   In addition to Hollenberg, see Tahera Qutbuddin, 'Principles of Fatimid Symbolic Interpretation (*Ta'wil*): An Analysis Based on the *Majalis Mu'ayyadiyya* of al-Mu'ayyad al-Shirazi (d. 470/1078)', in Adem and Hayes, ed., *Reason, Esotericism, and Authority in Shi'i Islam*, pp. 151–189. See also Bulbul Shah, 'Al-Qadi al-Nu'man and the Concept of *Batin*', in Todd Lawson, ed., *Reason and Inspiration in Islam: Theology, Philosophy and Mysticism in Muslim Thought, Essays in Honour of Hermann Landolt* (London, 2005), pp. 117–126.
4   Emile Durkheim, *The Elementary Forms of Religious Life*, tr. K. E. Fields (New York, 1995), p. 9.
5   Kim Knott, *The Location of Religion: A Spatial Analysis* (New York, 2005), p. 21.
6   Ibid.
7   Jeanne Halgren Kilde, 'Introduction: Thinking About Religious Space: An Introduction to Approaches', in Jeanne Halgren Kilde, ed., *The Oxford Handbook of Religious Space* (New York, 2022), p. 3.
8   Among the many studies on Qur'anic conceptions of space, see, for instance, Angelika Neuwirth, 'Cosmology', *Encyclopaedia of the Qur'an*; Anna Gade, 'Space, Time, and the Boundaries of Knowledge', in her *The Qur'an, An Introduction* (Oxford, 2010), pp. 217–267; Irvin Cemil Schick, 'Text', in Jamal J. Elias, ed., *Key Themes for the Study of Islam* (Oxford, 2010), pp. 321–335; Christian Lange, *Paradise and Hell in Islamic Traditions* (Cambridge, 2016), pp. 37–70.
9   Michael A. Sells, *Approaching the Qur'an* (Ashland, OR, 1999), p. 52.
10 Ibid., p. 95.
11 Ibid., p. 53.
12 Ibid., p. 108.
13 The term *ajal* is used throughout the Qur'an to refer to God's creation of a fixed time for things, including nations (7:34); people who disbelieve (16:61); when the meeting time with God will be (29:5); and the term of one's life (39:42), for instance.
14 Farhad Daftary, *The Ismailis: Their History and Doctrines* (2nd ed., Cambridge, 2007), p. 217.
15 Ja'far b. Mansur al-Yaman, *Kitab al-'Alim wa'l-ghulam*, ed. and tr. James Morris as *The Master and the Disciple: An Early Islamic Spiritual Dialogue* (London, 2001), p. 82.
16 *Kitab al-Kashf*, ed. Mustafa Ghalib (Beirut, 1984).
17 See, for instance, Velji, *An Apocalyptic History of the Early Fatimid Empire* (Edinburg, 2016), pp. 27–60 and idem, 'Making Authority from Apocalypse', in Mark Juergensmeyer and Margo Kitts, ed., *Buddhist Violence and Religious Authority: A Tribute to the Work of Michael Jerryson* (Sheffield, UK and Bristol, CT, 2022), pp. 150–152.
18 Saheeh International translation.
19 *Kashf*, pp. 29–30. Abdel Haleem's translation with minor amendments. See a parallel discussion of this in Velji, 'Making Authority', p. 151.
20 Abdel Haleem's translation with minor amendments.
21 I have chosen to translate the term here as 'proof' of the authority of the Imam in his absence, though Brett illustrates how this term could refer to a range of persons in the *da'wa*, including the awaited *mahdi* figure. See Michael Brett, *The Rise of the Fatimids: the world of the Mediterranean and the Middle East in the fourth century of the hijra, tenth century CE* (Leiden, 2001), p. 125 ff.
22 *Kashf*, pp. 29–30.

23 Ibid., pp. 147–148; Velji *Apocalyptic History*, p. 48.
24 Abdel Haleem's translation.
25 *Kashf*, p. 70; see also Velji *Apocalyptic History*, p. 54.
26 Abdel Haleem's translation.
27 *Kashf*, p. 42.
28 Abdel Haleem's translation with minor amendments.
29 *Kashf*, p. 42.
30 The concept of the 'hidden transcript' is iterated most famously by James C. Scott in his *Domination and the Arts of Resistance* (New Haven, 1990). More recently, Anver Emon has discussed this concept as well as what happens when the hidden transcript becomes manifest in his 'Is ISIS Islamic? Why it Matters for the Study of Islam', *The Immanent Frame*, March 27, 2015. https://tif.ssrc.org/2015/03/27/is-isis-islamic-why-it-matters-for-the-study-of-islam/ Accessed April 21, 2023.
31 Abdel Haleem's translation.
32 Velji, 'Making Authority from Apocalypse', p. 152.
33 Daftary, *The Ismaʿilis*, p. 215.
34 I have used Poonawala's edition and translation here. Al-Qadi al-Nuʿman, *The Pillars of Islam, Daʾaʾim al-Islam*, vol. 1, "*Ibadat*: Acts of Devotion and Religious Observances', tr. Asaf A.A. Fyzee. Completely revised and annotated by Ismail K. Poonawala (New Delhi, 2002), p. 390.
35 *Taʾwil al-daʿaʾim*, ed. ʿArif Tamir (Beirut, 1995), vol. 2, pp. 232–233. See also Velji, *An Apocalyptic History*, pp. 97–104.

6

Fatimid Public Pronouncements: Messages from a Shiʿi Dynasty to a Cosmopolitan Empire*

Paul E. Walker

Among other measures set in motion at the commencement of his caliphate, al-Mahdi, the very first of the Fatimids to rule, gave an order that the names of those who had built the various mosques, cisterns, palaces and bridges in his realm be removed and his name inscribed on them instead.[1] He had announced himself and his dynasty in a quite traditional fashion, replacing any mention of those who preceded and substituting his own. Unfortunately, we do not know more about what might have been inscribed besides the name alone. No example survives. But we are perhaps entitled to expect that it may have contained some clue to the Shiʿi beliefs of the new state. Abu ʿAbd Allah al-Shiʿi, the great *daʿi* who brought victory to the Fatimids, even prior to the advent of al-Mahdi, had given a general order to include in all *khutba*s in the territory a blessing on Muhammad and his family.

> He had the *khatib*s of the mosques of Raqqada and al-Qayrawan lead the way. He also wrote to other regions to the same effect. Abu ʿAbd Allah ordered that the *khutba* include blessings on Muhammad, on his family, on the Commander of the Believers ʿAli, on al-Hasan and al-Husayn, and on Fatima the radiant, may the blessings of God be on them all.[2]

Therefore, the essential elements of a Shiʿi *khutba* were already present in this way before the first one for al-Mahdi as the new Imam-caliph, which occurred on the Friday immediately following his arrival in Raqqada in Rabiʿ II 297/January of 910.

> When the morning dawned on Friday the day following his arrival, he sent out a note ordering that he be prayed for from the *minbar*s,

and he dispatched it to the *khatib*s of Raqqada and al-Qayrawan telling them to invoke, after the blessing on Muhammad, a blessing on ʿAli, and Fatima and al-Hasan and al-Husayn, and the Imams among their progeny, as Abu ʿAbd Allah had ordered.³

That note, according to al-Qadi al-Nuʿman, now stipulated the following prayer as part of the Friday *khutba*:⁴

> O God, bless Your servant and Your deputy, the one responsible for the affairs of Your servants in Your land, the servant of God (*ʿabd Allah*), Abu Muhammad, the Imam al-Mahdi biʾllah, Commander of the Believers, just as You blessed his forefathers Your deputies, the rightly guided, the *mahdi*s,⁵ who have discharged the duty of truth and in regard to it acted justly. O God, and just as You chose him for Your guardianship and for Your deputyship (*li-khalifatika* [i.e. Your caliphate]) and You made him the defence of Your religion and its foundation, and for Your creation a refuge and sanctuary, so grant him victory over Your apostate enemies, and heal through him the breasts of the believers. Conquer through him the easts of the land and its wests as You promised him; support him against the iniquitous rebels, O God of creation, Lord of the worlds.⁶

Although this passage by itself states the key portion of Fatimid claim to rule, the Shiʿi dimension is less obvious without further blessings on ʿAli, Fatima, Hasan and Husayn as was done routinely in public pronouncements (such as the ritual Friday and Feast sermons [*khutba*s]) from then on until the end of the Fatimids two and a half centuries later.⁷

Festival sermons of the Imam-caliph

The following examples taken from these annual festival sermons⁸ clearly illustrate the new dynasty's claim. What is uniquely Fatimid in them is the reference to the Prophet as the 'grandfather', e.g. of the current Imam-caliph, or, as it most often appears, as 'our grandfather', as in the invocation of God's blessings on 'our grandfather' (*jaddina*). The meaning, of course, is ancestor or forefather, but it carries a special connotation in conjunction with references to ʿAli b. Abi Talib, who is always called 'our father' (*abuna, abina*).⁹ References and characterisations of ʿAli are particularly important as a sign of the ancestral lineage of the Fatimids and of the Shiʿi assertion of legitimacy for its imamate. ʿAli bears the title 'Commander of the Believers', which, for the Shi'a, applies to him alone among the Companions of the Prophet since they do not recognise any of the others as valid successors to the imamate. In his position as heir to the Prophet, both physically and spiritually, he also carries the title of legatee (Ar., *wasi*). In Qirwash's *khutba*, cited below, he is called the 'Lord of the Legatees' (*sayyid al-wasiyyin*). Another appellation denoting his close family relationship to Muhammad, which for the Shi'a means in reference to 'Ali, is as a brother. For them, the Prophet had adopted him as his own brother. He was, moreover, in the same position as Aaron had been with respect to his brother Moses. The Prophet had stated, according to a *hadith* of special importance to the Shi'a, that, "'Ali is to me as Aaron was to Moses.'

Here follow some examples from public proclamations:

> ... and bless [O God] the first to respond to him (i.e. the Prophet), 'Ali, the Commander of the Believers and Lord of the Legatees, the establisher of excellence and mercy, the pillar of knowledge and wisdom, the root of the noble and righteous tree generated from the sacred and pure trunk. And [blessings be] on his successors, the lofty branches of that same tree, and on what comes from it: the fruit that grows there.[10]

> God bless our grandfather, Muhammad, the guide to the shining path, and our father, the Commander of the Believers, 'Ali b. Abi Talib, his brother and son of his paternal uncle, whom he sanctioned for the position of executor, and the chaste Imams among the descendants of both, the clear evident proofs of God to His creatures.[11]

> And bless, O God, our father, the Commander of the Believers, 'Ali b. Abi Talib, who held the place with respect to him that had Aaron with Moses, the one who spoke to God.[12]

And here is another that includes not only the Prophet and 'Ali but also Fatima and her two sons Hasan and Husayn:

> O God, bless Your servant and Your messenger with a perpetually perfect blessing, increase him with an honour to his honour and a nobility to his nobility. Bless also all of the Companions of the Cloak (*ashab al-kisa'*), the pure ones, the immaculates: 'Ali, the Commander of the Believers, Fatima the radiant, mistress of the women of the two worlds, and al-Hasan and al-Husayn, the two most noble and

most righteous, and [bless] the rightly guided Imams among the progeny of al-Husayn, the luminaries of guidance, the full moons of the darkness, the masters of mankind, friends of the Most Merciful, the proofs of times, and pillars of the faith.[13]

It should thus be amply clear that the Fatimids were never reluctant to insist on their Shi'i roots, nor to hide or disguise their lineal connection to the Prophet and to 'Ali. See, as a good example, the first Fatimid *khutba* in Egypt following their conquest in 385/969 which states clearly:

> O God, bless Your servant and Your deputy, the fruit of prophecy, scion of the rightly guided guiding family, the servant of God, the Imam Ma'add Abu Tamim al-Mu'izz li-Din Allah, Commander of the Believers, just as You blessed his pure forefathers and his predecessors, the rightly guided Imams.
>
> O God, raise high his rank and advance his word, make his proofs clear, bring the community together in obedience to him and their hearts loving friends of his, make guidance follow his sanction, have him inherit the eastern parts of the land and its west, have him be master of the beginning of things and their outcomes, for truly You speak and Your word is the truth.
>
> Your religion has been subject to vexation. When that which is sacred to You was defiled, *jihad* on Your behalf extinguished, pilgrimage to Your house and visitation of the tomb of Your messenger . . . disrupted, he made his preparations for the *jihad*, got ready everything necessary and sent the armies to support You. . . . So, O God, support the armies that he has sent and the detachments that he charged with fighting the polytheists, contending with the heretics, defending the Muslims, building up of the border territories and the holy places, eradicating injustice, suspicions and greed, and spreading justice throughout the nations.[14]

Nevertheless, there are historically several problems that arise from this situation. One curiosity involves the name of the dynasty and of the specific religious tradition behind it. In modern usage we nearly always refer to the dynasty as the 'Fatimids' and to the religious group as the 'Ismailis'. And yet there is little evidence of either term in the many public pronouncements issued by them until much later during the last phases of their rule. They simply did not call themselves 'Fatimids' or 'Ismailis', preferring, it would appear, a neutral language that associated them with broader claims. They were in their own words 'the rightly guiding guides', stressing the term *mahdi*, here used in the plural. Although there exist a few instances of *fatimi* (Fatimid) in the first century or so, it is not until the final decades that either this term[15] or 'Ismaili'[16] begins to appear more frequently in public documents.

Another issue is the lack of reference in public to the names of the Imams who preceded al-Mahdi. It was standard practice for the speaker to invoke in the *khutba* God's blessing on the Prophet and the Imams, name by name. But the list never included the names of those between Muhammad b. Ismaʿil b. Jaʿfar al-Sadiq and al-Mahdi. Clearly the Imams after al-Husayn b. ʿAli are his offspring, not those of al-Hasan. However, they are seldom mentioned by name in the surviving *khutba*s, even those in the period prior to the concealment of those immediately before al-Mahdi, a concealment that commenced with Ismaʿil, the son of Jaʿfar al-Sadiq, or with his son Muhammad b. Ismaʿil, who was the first never to have appeared in public. In Qirwash's sermon from North Mesopotamia in 401/1010, they are in all simply 'the righteous Imams, the best and most excellent, those of them that stood forth and appeared and those of them that were concealed and hidden.' In the first *khutba* by the Imam-caliph al-Mansur, he calls his own grandfather, al-Mahdi, the 'son of the Rightly Guided Ones (*al-Mahdiyyin*), the noble son of the most noble' without going further into the matter. That seems to have been, to judge from these *khutba*s, the preferred policy for public pronouncements. Only in a *khutba* of al-Amir (r. 495–524/1101–1130) are any of them cited by name. There he refers to the Imams prior to al-Mahdi as, "ʿAli b. al-Husayn Zayn al-ʿAbidin, and Muhammad b. ʿAli Baqir ʿUlum al-Din, and Jaʿfar b. Muhammad al-Sadiq al-Amin, and the true Imam Ismaʿil, and Muhammad his son, possessor of the nobility of the authentic caliphate, and those who had all excellences and superiority, *and [bless] the Imams who were concealed from the enemy*, ... the piercing stars of truth, the suns rising from the places of setting.' These latter he names one by one starting with al-Mahdi.

Failure to supply these names caused serious problems and offered an opportunity for anti-Fatimid propaganda, a weakness eventually fully exploited by the Abbasids, who insisted that the Fatimids were not in fact descendants of the Prophet and ʿAli. A great deal of modern scholarship has also been dedicated to explaining the origins of the dynasty in part because the Fatimids themselves never adequately explained their exact genealogical origins. However, it may have been originally a doctrinal matter in that the period in question was what the Ismailis refer to as a *dawr al-satr*, an era of concealment (as opposed to the *dawr al-zuhur*, era of open proclamation of the imamate). Since the Imams of that period did not declare their imamate publicly, they are not to be named, even in the subsequent open period.

Still the success or failure of the Fatimids to endure as long as they did was, it is likely, not contingent on such factors. More serious was the potential for clashes with their opponents and detractors caused by their Shi'ism. The Fatimids simply never governed a population that was majority Shi'i. At some points they had a substantial loyal following, although often not of Ismailis who remained a distinct minority. Most of their subjects were Sunni (or non-Muslim Christians). Not a few of these Sunnis were in fact quite hostile to Shi'ism.

A critical issue for the Fatimids was how much of Shi'i doctrine and practice could they insist on. In contrast to other examples of a *da'wa* (a missionary appeal) in Islamic history, which ceased to proselytise once in power, the Fatimids retained an active *da'wa*, even incorporating it into a state-run bureaucracy. Converting non-Ismailis to Ismailism remained an important goal, although there is little enough evidence of success, especially in later periods. But overly aggressive promotion of Shi'ism often resulted in a dangerous counter-reaction from the Sunnis. One highly significant case was the Imam-caliph al-Hakim's order to publicly curse the Companions of the Prophet who had denied 'Ali his right to succeed to leadership immediately after the Prophet. The issues associated with such cursing were, and are, often a flash point for conflict between Sunni and Shi'i. For the Sunnis this kind of condemnation of Abu Bakr, 'Umar and the others is totally unacceptable and cannot be tolerated. However, it is, for most of the Shi'a, standard fare.

Al-Hakim's venture in this particular case proved a near disaster and he soon rescinded his order, replacing it with a new command whereby his subjects were to speak only about the good things the Companions had done while the Prophet was alive and to ignore their transgression during the period after his death.

Several other points of potential conflict received a similar generally tolerant treatment. A serious issue for example was the commencement of the new month, so crucial for ritual purposes, such as the start and close of Ramadan. Ismailis determine the beginning of the month, not by the actual sighting of the new moon, but by astronomical calculation. Sunnis insist on physically witnessing the new moon. Thus it could happen that, in a mixed population, the Ismailis might begin the feast ending Ramadan a day before their Sunni neighbours who would still be under the rule of fasting. Here again al-Hakim eventually decreed that both practices were to be allowed, hoping thereby to prevent conflict.

These are but two of several additional problems the Fatimids faced in ruling over a Sunni population in respect to their Shi'ism. The issues involved were always matters requiring a delicate and sensitive balance between the very claims of the dynasty to absolute legitimacy, which were based on Shi'i principles, and the necessity for compromise and accommodation to maintain some degree of loyalty from their non-Ismaili citizenry.

Coins and coinage

So far most of the material and the examples cited here have come from *khutba*s or decrees, which were public in nature but, even so, restricted as far as general access is concerned. The audience for either one was limited. A much better case of public distribution of a message is the coinage. Legends stamped on a coin would have been hard to miss and it is quite likely that anyone with basic literacy knew what the coins had to say. The earliest Fatimid coins carry a Qur'anic verse and the name of the current Imam-caliph, plus sometimes the motto *al-hamdu li-llah rabbu'l-'alamin* ('Praise be to God Lord of the Universe'), which was, or was to become, the motto (and signature) of all the Fatimids. Coin inscription of this type did not convey a distinctly Shi'i message. However, under the fourth Imam-caliph, al-Mu'izz, for a two-year period, his coins declared, 'There is no god but God, alone without associate; Muhammad is the apostle of God and 'Ali b. Abi Talib is the heir (*wasi*) of the Apostle and the most excellent deputy and husband of the Radiant Pure One.' The reverse contained the name of al-Mu'izz with his titles among which was 'the inheritor of the glory of the Rightly Guiding Imams'.

Apparently that message was too aggressive because it was replaced by "Ali is the most excellent of the heirs and is the deputy (*wazir*) of the best of those sent [by God].' And that was also later shortened by the next Imam-caliph to "Ali is the best of God's elite' (*khayr safwat Allah*), still quite Shi'i but perhaps not so blatantly. Under al-Hakim beginning in 386/996 and continuing to the end of the dynasty, the Shi'ism on Fatimid coins was confined to the declaration that "Ali is the *wali* of God' (*'Ali wali Allah*). Here then is a quintessential example of how to encode Shi'ism in a message that can also be taken by those not Shi'i in a different sense. For Sunnis to say that "Ali is a friend (*wali*) of God' is not particularly offensive (if it is at all). To the Shi'a the meaning of *wali* in this context is entirely different, not 'friend' but rather 'guardian'. "Ali is God's guardian', as in, the guardian of God's earthly community, its supreme leader. Use of words and phrases that admit of a double meaning, such as is evident in this case, could and did avoid some elements of the conflict.

Messages internal to the members of the *da'wa*

One issue that has not yet been discussed here and which often served as a matter of contention in the hands of the opponents of the Fatimids is the secrecy imposed on its followers by the Ismaili *da'wa*. The Ismaili Shi'a are famous for a doctrine that insists, for the outward literal aspects of scripture, and the law based on it, there are esoteric hidden meanings that are not available to the ordinary Muslim. It is accessible solely through the *da'wa* and then only contingent on a carefully controlled and regulated process that required both an initial oath of allegiance and payment of whatever dues might be stipulated by the agent (*da'i*) in charge. The oath alone contained a firm clause commanding that nothing revealed should ever be passed on to anyone not authorised to receive it. One version has the novice state, in part:

> that he will uphold the external and the internal and that he will support the Imam of his time and will not forsake him, that he will not reveal any secret of the faith to a person not worthy of it or to anyone who has not sworn the oath of covenant, that he will not betray any of the brethren of believers who have joined him in swearing the oath, that he will treat as a friend those who have accepted the Imams and as an enemy those who are enemies of theirs, that he will stay away from their enemies, that he will offer good counsel on behalf of God and His representative, upon whom be peace, and that, if he should go back on his oath, there will apply to him what applies to those who rescind or violate an oath, that he will appeal for the Imam of their time, ascribe knowledge to him and not a letter of that to himself.

In a newly recovered treatise from the earliest period of the Fatimids, we now have an explanation of the connection between the willing payment of various dues, as in the *zakat* and *sadaqa* tithes, and access to these esoteric meanings. It states:

... the person who produces that [the offering] out of the goodness of his own self, God will cleanse thereby his spirit and purify his money, and thus it will be lawful for his *da'i* and mentor to reveal to him the interpretive (*ta'wili*) sciences and make known to him the truths hidden from the enemies of God's religion.[17]

The enemies of the Fatimids tried to understand this doctrine of theirs but lacking much real evidence of what it stipulated, or, being unwilling to accord it any credence, they preferred to exploit it to prove that Ismailism was, in its secret doctrine, highly heretical and un-Islamic. Thus, the problem of secrecy rose to the forefront. Detractors attempted to pin on the Fatimids a label of Batinism, of believing that once one knows the esoteric meanings, the exoteric, literal outward wording of, say, a ritual prescription, no longer applied, and that Ismailis need not observe the works required by Islamic law.

But, while the issue itself never went away and therefore was always a factor in Fatimid dealings with either their own non-Ismaili subjects or their opponents at large, there is little or no evidence to support this charge. All written testimony from the Fatimid period, from both the restricted literature produced by the *da'wa*, which was kept away from public scrutiny and remains until now jealously guarded from outsiders, and any works or commentary by contemporary non-Ismailis from that era, suggest no such doctrine. Instead, the secret doctrine about which we now have considerable detailed knowledge indicates the opposite. The Ismailis remained bound by the law in its outward form. A standard pronouncement from a leading authority, as an example, insists that both outward and inner be observed and that one without the other is unacceptable; both are required. In fact, Sunni Muslims are in error because they recognise only the outward and do not acknowledge (or do not know) the inner meanings. It is they who are heretical.

How much of any of this debate ever entered the public domain is questionable. The Ismailis naturally did not talk about it because to do so would have required that they reveal what they had pledged to conceal. Sunnis, by contrast, made the most of this issue but primarily solely from a safe distance, that is, from outside the Fatimid domain. Anti-Fatimid polemic and its rhetoric used all potential weaknesses in Fatimid pronouncements and claims, even though often without foundation in fact. And the Abbasids over time increased the vehemence of their anti-Ismaili propaganda. A particular blatant example is the manifesto issued in 402/1011 in Baghdad to denounce the Fatimid genealogical claim to descent from 'Ali and the Prophet. Part of what caused them to act in that fashion at that moment was the declaration by Qirwash, the ruler of Mosul, in favour of al-Hakim in the previous year. Both actions were deliberately spread as widely as possible by the delivery of copies of either decree. We now know exactly what Qirwash's *khutba* said obviously because copies of it circulated throughout Iraq and elsewhere.[18] The same would have been true of the Abbasid Manifesto.

Enemies and opponents

Many public pronouncements feature condemnations of various enemies of the Fatimids. An early text is a *khutba* that requests God to 'grant him [the Imam] victory over Your apostate enemies (*a'da'ika al-mariqin*), and heal through him the breasts of the believers, conquer through him the easts of the land and its wests as You promised him, support him against the iniquitous rebels.' Those who oppose the Fatimid cause are in fact enemies of God. That much is made clear again and again. In the earliest sermon given by al-Mansur he says, 'Bring down upon his [meaning his father, al-Qa'im's] enemies, in the east and the west, on land and on the sea, the most severe assaults and retributions that You have done or caused to occur with any of those who were enemies of Yours, with destructive misfortune, dishonoring exemplary punishments; destroy them by annihilation and burn them in the fire of hell.'

The Fatimids similarly employed a special kind of rhetoric to denounce their opponents and much of this was quite public. One important early example is the sermon by the future Imam-caliph al-Qa'im in Alexandria during the first Fatimid attempt to conquer Egypt. In front of an Egyptian non-Ismaili audience, he said, in part, referring to the Abbasids:

> The lying apostate community, reneging on its intentions, deviating from the command of their Lord, suppose that it has been correct in what it claims about its caliphs whom they insist are the caliphs of the Lord of the worlds, such as a youth not yet mature, like the boy lacking knowledge, or like the child who, according to their claim, governs Islam. And yet among them women bring them wine from every valley and region on the backs of horses and in the bottoms of ships. As God the Exalted said: 'They take their priests and monks as lords besides God' [Q 9:31]. They spend the funds of orphans and the poor, wrongly on their part and unjustly, for singing lute players,

skilled tamburists, and ma'zatanists,[19] and talented drummers. You have seen their governors of cities, how one of them mounts the wooden pulpit of the Prophet's *minbar* to preach to the people but he does not preach to himself. Rather he descends from that position and inquires of those in that land for male and female singers, tamburists, 'ud players, thieves, short-change artists and shavers of weights so that those can be brought to serve him. God curses the unjust and prepares for them a blazing fire. That man is someone who neither commands the good nor prohibits the bad.

Another example comes from the time of al-Hakim and the *da'i* al-Kirmani, who provides a list of disqualifying attributes of all those in his era who falsely claim, according to him, to be the Imam of the Muslim community. In contrast to most of his writings, which were highly restricted, this work was addressed openly to the Buyid vizier of Baghdad. At one point al-Kirmani denounces specifically the 'Imam' of the Abbasids, the Zaydis, the Ibadis, the Umayyads and the Qarmatians (of al-Ahsa'), one by one. Perhaps the most interesting case is that of the Abbasids whose 'Imam' he identifies simply as: 'Ahmad b. Ishaq, who resides in Baghdad'. According to our Fatimid author he is unqualified for the imamate because:

> He is not a lineal descendant of al-Husayn; he is not pure in soul due to his consumption of forbidden things (*suht*) and his setting the price of wine that is sold for him on his estates in Baghdad and its hinterland and for the ignorance deeply rooted in him due to the lack of knowledge; the existence in him by his own admission of things connected to the imamate that he does not know and his utilisation of resources in ways not religiously commendable; being devoid of the knowledge associated with religious declaration of God's absolute oneness and his reliance on the leaders of the Postponers (al-Murji'a), such as Abu Bakr al-Baqillani, and others; contempt for the regulations of God; not commanding the good and forbidding the bad in his own household and entourage, let alone for any other Muslims; being devoid of the designation of the person who occupies the place of the Apostle and instead having been put in office by the august Amir Baha' al-Dawla, may God's mercy be upon him.

One curiosity on the Fatimid side was this use of the term Murji'a. Its meaning in this context is radically different from the name of the early

Islamic sect. The Murji'a, in Ismaili parlance, are all those who denied 'Ali his exclusive right to succeed the Prophet immediately by 'postponing' (the meaning of *murji'a* is 'those who postpone') his claim and accepting his caliphate only after those of Abu Bakr, 'Umar and 'Uthman. Thus, most Muslims would be Murji'a by that standard, that is, all but the Shi'a. However, such rhetoric, as with certain additional elements, was not always suitable for public use and tended to appear more in private *da'wa*-based writings, either that or where the exact meaning and its implication might have been missed or misunderstood. Al-Kirmani's addressee in this treatise was known to be himself a Shi'i and thus it is likely such a reference carried for him the meaning intended (though others may have missed it).

Decrees and documents from the chancery

Turning now from the kinds of representation cited above to the chancery which had, in the long run and aggregate, the principal public responsibility as the leading voice of Fatimid aspirations, at least those announced openly, we encounter in the first instance a formal bureau of government. The great Mamluk era expert on chancery practice, the author of the monumental *Subh al-a'sha*, al-Qalqashandi, comments favourably on the Fatimid chancery, noting that:

> When the Fatimids gained control over the territory of Egypt, they devoted an extreme amount of attention to the chancery (*diwan al-insha'*) and its clerks (*kuttab*). Its value greatly increased because of them, and its repute spread far and wide. The chancery was staffed by them with a collection of the most talented and eloquent of clerks, including among them both Muslims and Dhimmis.[20]

A history of the Fatimid chancery has not yet been written although the material for it is abundant. Its work is often mentioned explicitly in the historic chronicles, perhaps even more often than any other single bureau of government. Two treatises by members of the *diwan al-insha'* – Ibn Khalaf's *Mawadd al-bayan*[21] and al-Sayrafi's *al-Qanun diwan al-rasa'il*[22] – survive. The former was a substantial collection of guides and examples assembled for the use of clerks. The latter lays out the rules for the running of a successful chancery. Names of heads of the bureau are often given in the sources, frequently in association with various decrees which the person in question composed. Examples of a full range of chancery products exist, many copied by al-Qalqashandi himself as illustrations of how to write a particular type of document (for examples: letters to foreign powers or decrees of appointment to office). In all we have perhaps as many as 300 examples. His report about the extreme importance of the Fatimid chancery and the skill of its clerks, which gained the dynasty eminence both at home and abroad, is worth emphasising. The government fully realised and appreciated their value. Although we now possess copies of some 300, thousands more once existed.[23] To provide some evidence of how much, here are, first, a list of the kinds and range of products emanating from the chancery, and second, a list of those only in one of the categories: decrees of appointment to a government office.

Types of communications produced by the chanceries[24]

Permissions and licenses, safe conduct passes, oaths, messages, commissions, investitures, congratulations, royal letters, sermons, dispatches, decrees, contracts, edicts, peace treaties, treaty commitments, letters and correspondences, business contracts, royal mandates, edicts and regulations, pardons, official announcements, assemblies, benevolences, proclamations, truces, admonitions, and advice.

Fifty-six types of Governmental office that each require a decree of appointment[25]

Daʿi al-duʿat, mazalim, wazir, naʾib wazir, qadi, daʿwa, governors (of Cairo, Fustat, District of Qus, Gharbiyya, Alexandria, ʿAsqalan), *Zamm al-aqarib, naqib, amir al-hajj, amir al-jihad, hisba,* judge of Qus and superintendant of the Saʿid, deputy of the judge in Dimyat, judge of the Gharbiyya, judge and superintendent of ʿAsqalan, professorship (Alexandria), superintendency over the poll tax of the Lower Saʿid, comptroller for the Upper Egyptian Districts, commissary of sheep (small cattle) and the kitchens, Open Decree of superintendency of taxable inheritance and statutory portions.

Prominent experts working in the Fatimid chancery were often not Ismaili, and more than a few not even Muslim. And that may be especially significant. The messages promoted via a chancery document of whatever type were intended in most instances for an audience of mixed religious loyalties: Sunnis, Shiʿis (of different persuasions), Jews, Christians, foreign powers and others. Even so, the text in question needed to uphold the basic Fatimid claim to rule. And yet seemingly any of these clerks could, at will, draft a text that conformed to the religious doctrines supporting the Ismaili imamate, that expressed the wishes and policies of the Fatimid state, and yet that sounded fairly normal and uncontroversial, thus avoiding arousing enmity needlessly. In short, the skill of the clerks was impressively adaptive to the needs of both politics and religion. That al-Qalqashandi, long after this dynasty and its Shi'ism had governed in Egypt, would carefully preserve so many examples of its chancery products, as if to show a future Shi'i government how to write for a Fatimid ruler the documents he might require, offers a strikingly case of intertextuality in practice.

At this point in modern scholarship about the Fatimid chancery, Marina Rustow's masterful exploration of all the actual physical evidence of its work and products – what survives – provides a detailed account of it based on many examples now found mostly in fragments in the Cairo Geniza with, in addition, a few whole documents from other locations, offering a richly annotated study of what she calls *The Lost Archive* subtitled 'traces of a Caliphate in a Cairo synagogue'.[26] But although highly informative and entertaining to read, her principal perspective focuses on the actual document, less on Fatimid imperial policy and messaging. Nevertheless, her analysis and reconstruction of the chancery, in part via al-Sayrafi's treatise *al-Qanun*, and how it is to be run, is as complete as anyone could ask for.

Here it might be useful to examine the role of the 'clerk', in Arabic *katib*, but basing ourselves on a couple of specific examples: a) the former slave and later commander-in-chief, Jawhar, and b) Ibn Surin, a Christian in the chancery, who it is said wrote the famous/infamous order to destroy the Church of the Holy Sepulchre. Both also happen to provide an interesting context for the present theme of cosmopolitanism.

Curiously, although Jawhar would eventually command the formidable army that conquered Egypt on behalf of the Fatimids which he thereafter actually ruled for four years, nevertheless he is often in our sources simply titled not 'commander' (Arabic *qa'id*) but rather 'clerk' (*katib*), clearly based on his earlier profession. He entered service to the Imam-caliphs as someone who composed documents and messages on their behalf.[27] And yet in origin he was of Slavic extraction as a slave brought over from Sicily. Only much later had he risen so high in their esteem that they deemed him fully skilled as a manager and as a consequence appointed him to lead the army (of course, by then, being also manumitted).

Clearly then a *katib* was, as in his case, not merely a 'scribe'. A document he wrote quite often was drafted by him employing his own words and depending for its force on his personal verbal skill and rhetorical eloquence. That is often shown in our historical accounts by fairly explicit direct references stating that the author of this or that decree was not the Imam-caliph but rather his *katib*, the latter's name remaining attached to the text as its author. For Jawhar's verbal skill we also have the testimony of no less than Abu Hayan al-Tawhidi who quotes from him a short piece of rhymed *saj*.[28] Apparently his fame as a wordsmith passed well beyond and outside the domain of the Fatimids.

However, perhaps the best example of Jawhar's authority is his famous *aman* (guarantee of safety) for the people of Egypt the text of which he composed personally in response to a plea from them to avoid a military assault by the approaching Fatimid army.[29]

Here are some key passages from that document:

> This letter is from Jawhar, *al-Katib*, servant of the Commander of the Believers al-Muʿizz li-Din Allah, to all the people of Egypt.... On your behalf they have said that you request a document that includes your assurance of safety for yourselves, your property and lands, and all matters pertaining thereto.... So let us thank God for what he has arranged for you and thank him for protecting you. Be untiring in what is required of you. Make haste toward obeying him who is your guardian, the one who restores your happiness and wellbeing. He ... has produced the victorious armies and triumphant military for no other purpose than to strengthen and protect you.... He wants thereby to restore the Pilgrimage which has fallen into abeyance.... Next, he will make the coinage good again and restore its fineness ... Our master and our lord the Commander of the Believers, has instructed his servant to spread justice and expand fairness, root out injustice and stop enmity, deny injury and extol cooperation, uphold what is right and aid the oppressed with compassion and kindness, administer fairly, be generous in associations and gracious in relationships....
>
> I am to administer matters of inheritance in accord with the Book of God and the Sunna of His prophet.
>
> I am also to undertake the repair of your mosques and embellished them with carpets and lighting and to pay their *muʾadhdhin*s, keepers and those who lead people in prayer in them the stipends

due them, given to them generously and without cessation or interruption. All is to be paid solely from the state treasury.

I here respond to these . . . of your concerns. . . . Islam is one legal system and one law followed by all and it keeps you in accord with your legal school. It leaves you free to fulfil obligations as you have done based on information, to gather in your congregational and other places of prayer, firmly holding to the practice of the earliest generations of the community among the Companions. . . . The call to prayer, prayers, fasting in the month of Ramadan, breaking the fast, and maintaining night vigils, alms taxes, the Pilgrimage and holy war will run according to the command of God, His Book and what His prophet, . . . has set forth in his law. And the treatment of the protected peoples will continue as it has in the past.

I am hereby responsible for God's complete universal eternal and everlasting assurance of safety, perfect and all inclusive, renewed and confirmed through the days, the passing of the years for yourselves, your property, your families, your livestock, your estates, your residences, the least and the most of what is yours. . . . You will be guarded, kept safe and protected. . . . You will find joy in it through obedience to our master and our lord the Commander of the Believers. . . .

Ibn Zulaq continues:

He [Jawhar] wrote down in his hand on this very document: 'Jawhar the clerk and servant of the Commander of the Believers, . . . said: I have written this *aman* as instructed by command of our master and our lord the Commander of the Believers, with the obligation to fulfil all of it for those of the land and others who accept the conditions stipulated therein. . . .

The case of Ibn Surin is radically different, although obviously this man possessed similar clerical skills. But critically he was a Nestorian Christian who had nevertheless risen high in the ranks of the chancery (second only to the director in charge who happened to be also the son of Jawhar). What of his work we might recover is not known.[30] However, he is famous for having composed the order to destroy Christendom's most important church. The Imam-caliph al-Hakim had begun a general policy of church and synagogue destruction, eventually of vast proportions.[31] Still the Church of the Holy Sepulchre in Jerusalem and its destruction is the one that profoundly shocked the Christian world and was to be remembered for centuries. However, in Muslim sources it merited a simple line or two: an order was given to Ibn Surin in the chancery to draft an order to send to an agent in Jerusalem for him to instigate a mob to undertake the raising of the building.[32] It is hard not to wonder how a practising Christian could actually write such a decree and, perhaps appropriately, in a near contemporary Christian account, the clerk's subsequent pained regret shines forth prominently. Here is how the matter is reported in that source:

> ... al-Hakim ordered that a decree be written to the governor of Jerusalem that the Church of the Resurrection should be demolished. The scribe wrote to the governor a letter, and this is a copy of it: 'An order of the Imam has been issued to you to demolish the [church of] the Rubbish Mound (the Qumama),[33] and to make its roof the earth and its length a breadth.' The writer of the decree was a Nestorian Christian known as Ibn Surin. When the aforementioned [scribe] had dispatched the decree which he had written, he became as one drunk who awakes from his drunkenness, and he thought within himself about what he had done and he said: 'I wrote with my hand that the Church of the Resurrection should be demolished. Why did I not endure death before doing this, and why did I not endure having my right hand cut off and [then] I would not have written this? If I had refrained from writing it, what would have been done to me beyond beheading me, and I could not have wished for a martyrdom greater than this.' He used to say this and similar things to it and to repeat this by heart night and day. Through the intensity of his sorrow, he became ill and was confined to a sick-bed, and he used to say: 'O my right hand, how did you dare to do this terrible thing? I, also, shall do to you what you deserve, and I shall not cease from afflicting you.' He began to lift his hand and to strike the ground with it, and he did not cease from this throughout the days of his illness until his fingers were cut to pieces and he died.[34]

Jawhar and Ibn Surin are but two examples of the great number of clerks who served the Fatimid dynasty over the two and a half centuries of its existence.[35] Many others achieved some degree of fame. Two of them, as mentioned earlier, wrote works on the chancery in addition to the edicts and other documents they composed. Ultimately, perhaps the most famous was the last, al-Qadi al-Fadil, who eventually left behind a substantial collection of what he had written, which was preserved, and admired, by later generations.[36]

One final but curious note about the role of the chancery might be added here. We have seen that policy always elevated the words of the Imam-caliph above those of the chancery clerks (although it is not clear in every case which is which). After all the clerks did speak on behalf of their masters. But, near the end of the dynasty, we hear of a general policy requiring that in an appointment decree — a document known to have come out of the chancery, it was necessary that the ruler add a short personal note on the over leaf (*al-turra*), normally in his own hand. But the one example that survives has the five-year-old al-Fa'iz (r. 549–555/1154–1160) contribute such a note expressing his personal approval of the appointment.[37] We are surely entitled to suspect that even this was the work of a chancery clerk.

NOTES

* The material and examples assembled and discussed in what follows come from *khutba* sermons, from Fatimid coin legends, from various kinds of Ismaili literature produced by its *daʿwa*, and, most notably, from the products of the state chancery.
1 Ibn ʿIdhari al-Marrakushi, *Kitab al-Bayan al-mughrib fi akhbar al-Andalus wa'l-Maghrib*, ed. George S. Colin and Evariste Lévi-Provençal as *Histoire de l'Afrique du Nord et de l'Espagne Musulmane intitulée Kitab al-Bayan al-Mughrib* (Leiden, 1948–1951), p. 159.
2 al-Qadi al-Nuʿman, *Iftitah al-daʿwa wa ibtida' al-dawla*, ed. Farhat Dachraoui (Tunis, 1975), pp. 249–250, and confirmed by Ibn ʿIdhari, *al-Bayan*, p. 151.
3 As had already been cited in the *Iftitah al-daʿwa*, pp. 249–250.
4 *Iftitah al-daʿwa*, pp. 293–294.
5 The words here are: *ʿala khulafaʾika al-rashidin al-mahdiyyin*. The last term, the *mahdi*s, meaning 'those who were rightly guided', which is also the plural of *mahdi*, is particularly significant as becomes apparent when it reappears regularly in the texts of later *khutba*s, all the way to the end of the dynasty.
6 Another translation of the same passage can be found in Heinz Halm, *Das Reich des Mahdi. Der Aufstieg der Fatimiden (875–973)* (Munich, 1991), tr. M. Bonner as *The Empire of the Mahdi. The Rise of the Fatimids* (Leiden, 1996), p. 138, tr., p. 147.
7 For additional examples, see below some official references to the Prophet, ʿAli, Fatima, Hasan and Husayn.
8 For general details of Fatimid *khutba*s and the specific texts of those that survive, see my *Orations of the Fatimid Caliphs: Festival Sermons of the Ismaili Imams* (London, 2009).
9 See, for example, the *khutba*s of al-Amir where this type of reference appears prominently in both parts of the sermon. Additional examples occur in those of al-Mansur from 335/946-47 and 336/947-48.
10 Qirwash's *khutba* (no. 11).
11 Ibid.
12 *Khutba* of al-Amir (no. 12).
13 From the *khutba* by al-Mansur on the ʿId al-fitr of 335/947 (no. 5).
14 al-Maqrizi, *Ittiʿaz al-hunafaʾ bi-akhbar al-aʾimma al-fatimiyyin al-khulafaʾ*, ed. Ayman F. Sayyid (Damascus, 2010), vol. 1, pp. 114–115, with variations given by Idris ʿImad al-Din, *ʿUyun al-akhbar wa funun al-athar*, ed. in 7 volumes by Ahmad Chleilat,

Mahmoud Fakhoury, Yousef S. Fattoum and Ayman F. Sayyid (Damascus, 2007–2014), pp. 684–685; Shihab al-Din Ahmad al-Nuwayri, *Nihayat al-arab fi funun al-adab: al-Juz' al-thamin wa'l-'ishrun*, ed. Muhammad Muhammad Amin and Muhammad Hilmi Muhammad Ahmad (Cairo, 1992), vol. 28, pp. 131–132 (the editor has recorded there variations from the version in the *Itti'az*).

15 For example, a decree ordered by the vizier al-Ma'mun (early 6th/12th century) in favour of the noted scholar Ibn Hasdai, who was being accorded official status by the state, uses the phrase *al-dawla al-fatimiyya*.

16 A sample decree for the appointment of the caretaker of the royals (*zamm al-aqarib*) now found in al-Qalqashandi refers specifically to *al-Ashraf al-Isma'iliyya*. (*Subh al-a'sha fi sina'at al-insha'*, Cairo, 1912–1938, vol. 10, p. 396).

17 Passage from a tract by Abu'l-'Abbas (brother of Abu 'Abd Allah al-Shi'i) entitled *Mafatih al-ni'ma* on the relationship of paying alms taxes (*zakat* and *sadaqa*) and other dues with access to the esoteric knowledge controlled by the *da'wa* and its agents, now found in *Affirming the imamate: Early Fatimid Teachings in the Islamic West; An Arabic critical edition and English translation of works attributed to Abu 'Abd Allah al-Shi'i and his brother Abu'l-'Abbas*, ed and tr. Wilferd Madelung and Paul E. Walker (London, 2021).

18 The full text and translation are available in my *Orations of the Fatimid Caliphs*.

19 Players of the short-necked lute.

20 al-Qalqashandi, *Subh al-a'sha*, vol. 1, p. 96.

21 'Ali b. Khalaf, *Mawadd al-bayan*, published in fascimile (Frankfurt, 1986); edited by Hatim Salih al-Damin in *al-Mawrid*, vols 17 (1988) & 19 (1990); edited by Husayn 'Abd al-Latif (Tripoli, Libya, 1984).

22 Ibn al-Sayrafi, *al-Qanun fi diwan al-rasa'il*, ed. Ayman F. Sayyid (Cairo, 1990).

23 Rustow, see below, estimates that she has found clear evidence of perhaps 1500, for the most part of course now represented by a mere surviving fragment of the original.

24 This list translates al-Qalqashandi's own Arabic list.

25 The list given here is not merely theoretical but is based on a survey of surviving exemplars. In short, we have, in each instance, a copy of at least one decree drafted and issued from the Fatimid chancery for the position in question.

26 Marina Rustow, *The Lost Archive: Traces of a Caliphate in a Cairo Synagogue* (Princeton, 2020).

27 A good example of his role much earlier is the following report: . . . . ولما انهزم اللعين الدجال أمر المنصور بالله صلوات الله عليه عبده جوهرًا الكاتب بإنفاذ السجلّات على البريد إلى جميع الآفاق بالفتح، وكتب إلى الأستاذ [جوذر] سجلًّا عظيمًا وفي داخله رقعة بخطّ المنصور بالله صلوات الله عليه فيها: '. . . يا جوذر'.

المصدر: سيرة جوذر، ص ٢٧

'After the cursed Deceiver was routed . . . . Then al-Mansur bi'llah ordered his slave Jawhar the secretary (al-Katib) to send by post official letters to all the regions announcing the victory. He also wrote to the Ustadh [Jawdhar] a significant document in which was enclosed a letter in the hand of al-Mansur bi'llah expressing the following. . . .' Note here that there is a clear difference between the words of the clerk and those of the Imam.

28 I owe this reference to Hasan al-Khoee who kindly supplied it via email along with the Arabic text as it appears both in al-Maqrizi's *Itti'az* and in Wadad Qadi's edition of al-Tawhidi's *Basa'ir*, vol. 1, p. 184.

29 Report from Ibn Zulaq, an Egyptian author contemporary to the event, who says, 'He [Jawhar] responded favourably to what they sought and wrote down for them the following.' Hereafter we have the text verbatim.

30 One example of his work is the following item reported by al-Maqrizi in his *Itti'az*, vol. 2, pp. 32–34:

وأمر بكتابة سجلّ أنشأه أبو منصور بن سورين كاتب الإنشاء، قُرئ بسائر الجوامع في مصر والقاهرة والجيزة والجزيرة، نصّه بعد البسملة:

... مِن عبد الله ووليه المنصور أبي علي الإمام الحاكم بأمر الله

وكُتب سجلّات على نسخة واحدة وأنفذت إلى سائر النواحي والأعمال.

المصدر: اتّعاظ، ٢: ٣٢ – ٣٤

31 One estimate has thirty thousand destroyed during this period. In general, on this matter see my *Caliph of Cairo: Al-Hakim bi-Amr Allah, 996–1021* (Cairo and New York, 2009), pp. 209–212.

32 *Itti'az*, vol. 2, p. 95.

33 Apparently, within the local context and non-Christian views, the area of the church preserved an original indication that it had been a garbage heap at the time of Jesus's crucifixion, hence the name Qumama instead of Qiyama.

34 From *History of the Patriarchs of Alexandria*, in the part relating to al-Hakim by Michael, bishop of Tinnis, vol. 2, pt. 2: 'Khaël III-Senouti II (A.D. 880-1066)', tr. and annotated by Aziz Suryal Atiya, Yassa 'Abd al-Masih & O.H.E. (Burmester, UT, 1948), p. 193. Thanks here to Hasan al-Khoee for reminding me of this passage.

35 I have collected from various sources the names of thirty-five individuals who were, at one time or another, clerks in the chancery.

36 He also, it must be added, served not only the Fatimids but their Ayyubid successors. On him see the entry in *EI2* by C. Brockelmann and C. Cahen.

37 al-Maqrizi, *Itti'az*, ed. Sayyid, vol. 3, pp. 265–266.

SECTION II
THE FATIMID LEGACY RECONSIDERED

1

The Modern Rediscovery of the Fatimid Artistic and Architectural Legacy in Egypt

Dina Ishak Bakhoum

Fatimid artistic and architectural legacy in Egypt: continuity

The artistic and architectural legacy of the Fatimids in Egypt (358–566/969–1171)[1] is manifested through the establishment of al-Qahira (Cairo), the capital they founded on the eastern side of the Nile, northeast of the earlier capitals of al-Fustat, al-ʿAskar and al-Qataʾiʿ built between the mid-1st/7th and late-3rd/9th century by the Muslim rulers who preceded them. It is in al-Qahira that the most famous Fatimid military, secular and religious architecture was built with some of it still standing in situ. It includes: part of the recently discovered first Fatimid mudbrick city walls built during the late 4th/10th century by Jawhar al-Siqilli, and the later Fatimid walls and gates (480–485/1087–1092) constructed during the mandate of the Armenian vizier Badr al-Jamali under the reign of the Imam-caliph al-Mustansir (r. 427–487/1036–1094) expanding the city of Cairo;[2] al-Azhar mosque (359/970), enlarged during the Fatimid period as well as by subsequent Muslim rulers and active till today; the Mosque of the Imam-caliph al-Hakim bi-amr Allah (380–393/990–1003) initially built outside the northern city walls and then incorporated within the city after its expansion during the late 5th/11th century;[3] the Mashhad al-Juyushi (478/1085) constructed on the hill of al-Muqattam by the vizier Badr al-Jamali, whose title was Amir al-Juyush (hence the name of the *mashhad*); the Mosque of al-Aqmar (519/1125) founded by the vizier Maʾmun al-Bataʾihi during the reign of al-Amir (r. 495–524/1101–1130), constructed next to the eastern Fatimid palace (the eastern and northern palaces do not exist anymore and only traces of them could be found; some items that belonged to these structures are displayed in the Museum of Islamic Art in Cairo as well as other international museums); the mosque constructed by the vizier al-Salih Tala'iʿ (555/1160) outside Bab Zuwayla, the southern gate of the city; the *mashhad ru'ya* of Sayyida Ruqayya (527/1133), a grand-daughter of the first Shiʿi caliph ʿAli and the mausoleums of Sayyida Atiqa and Muhammad al-Jaʿfari (516/1222) are in what today is known as al-Khalifa area, and the mausoleum of Yahya al-Shabih (545/1150), a descendant of the Prophet is in the area known today as the Southern Cemetery; at the bottom of the Muqattam hills there are several Fatimid structures including the Mosque of al-Lu'lu'a (406/1016) and the shrine of Ikhwat Yusuf (519/1125).[4]

The Upper Egyptian city of Aswan also houses the famous Fatimid necropolis as well as archaeological remains of other types of Fatimid architecture. This necropolis and its Fatimid mausolea were subject to a project carried out by the German Archaeological Institute (Deutsches Archäologisches Institut Kairo), whose results were recently published in a co-edited volume by Philipp Speiser and Giorgio Nogara titled *Die Nekropole der Fatimiden in Assuan: Bauforschung, Restaurierung und Site Management* (2021). Moreover, salvage excavation work by the Swiss Institute (Schweizerisches Institut für Ägyptische Bauforschung und Altertumskunde in Kairo) carried out in Aswan through a joint mission with the Egyptian Ministry of Antiquities (now Ministry of Tourism and Antiquities) is revealing more information regarding the Fatimid city in Aswan.[5]

Other cities in Lower and Upper Egypt house mosques that date to the Fatimid period such as for example the mosque of Qus near Luxor with its Fatimid *minbar*. Many of these structures have been heavily modified revealing little of the original Fatimid features.

Although few buildings from the Fatimid period survived in Egypt, especially when compared to the number of surviving Mamluk structures in Cairo for example, the Fatimid mosques, shrines, mausolea, city walls and gates as well as the works of art now housed at the Museum of Islamic Art in Cairo and in international museums worldwide attest to their great architectural, artistic and spiritual significance.

Fatimid architecture in Egypt shows a continuous use of earlier artistic and architectural motifs from the Byzantine, Coptic and early Islamic periods. Nonetheless, the interchange between both Christian and Islamic art and architecture has received only some scholarly attention and deserves more interdisciplinary research,[6] especially because a great deal has been written regarding the Christians during the Fatimid period in Egypt.[7] The Fatimids developed the design motifs they used from earlier periods, producing innovative forms that have become characteristic of the Fatimid period. For example, the keel arch with radiating flutes, a motif specifically associated with Fatimid architecture, is 'a variation on a late classic theme used widely in Coptic art';[8] it takes the shell motif that was also widely used during the Coptic period and stylises it creating a new motif.[9]

The earliest known appearance of certain elements such as *muqarnas* decoration (also referred to as stalactite or honeycomb decoration) in Egypt was found on Fatimid buildings of the 5th/11th and 6th/12th centuries but its exact origins and the way it developed on different architectural elements is debatable.[10]

What can be clearly noticed is how certain architectural and decorative motifs specific to the Fatimid period continued to aspire and to be used, adapted and modified during the Ayyubid, Mamluk, Ottoman as well as the modern periods in Egypt. As Fatimid forms became thoroughly integrated in Islamic architecture, neo-Islamic architecture in Egypt, even if it contained motifs originally stemming from Fatimid architecture, is referred to as neo-Mamluk because the overall shape, form and source of inspiration come from buildings dating to the Mamluk period.

Examples of neo-Islamic architecture in Egypt that are strictly, and strikingly neo-Fatimid are very scarce. The two main examples that will be discussed here are the facade of the Coptic Museum in Cairo (1929) influenced by the discovery of the facade of the Fatimid mosque of al-Aqmar (al-Muʿizz street, Cairo, Egypt, 519/1125)[11] and the mausoleum of Aga Khan III (1877–1957) in Aswan (constructed ca. 1960) inspired by the Fatimid *mashhad* of al-Juyushi (Cairo, 478/1085). These neo-Fatimid buildings will be discussed, shedding light on the modern history of rediscovering their Fatimid sources of inspiration, the context and setting of their construction and the motives behind the selection of their Fatimid design motifs.

The facade of the Mosque of al-Aqmar and the facade of the Coptic Museum

'Eine freudige Ueberraschung für die Kunsthistoriker' ('A joyful surprise for the art historians'). These were the words of the German architect Julius Franz (1831–1915), published in his book *Kairo* (1903),

Figure II.1.1 The Fatimid mosque of al-Aqmar (519/1125): the 'rediscovered' facade shortly after its restoration by the *Comité de conservation des monuments de l'art arabe*.

describing the discovery of the central and left-hand side of the facade of al-Aqmar mosque (figure II.1.1), which was hidden behind buildings constructed at an unknown period in front of the mosque.[12] In 1901 demolishing these buildings and revealing part of the facade was possible as a result of negotiations and efforts carried out by the *Comité de conservation des monuments de l'art arabe* (in Arabic *Lagnat Hifz al-Athar al-'Arabiyya*, known also at the time as The Commission for the Preservation of Monuments of Arab Art).[13]

The *Comité de conservation des monuments de l'art arabe* (hereafter the *Comité*) was established in December 1881 under the Ministry of *Awqaf* through a khedival decree/superior order (*amr 'ali*) issued by Khedive Muhammad Tawfiq (Méhmét Thewfik) and co-signed by him and by the Minister of *Awqaf*, Muhammad Zaki (Mohamed Zéki).[14] In 1881 Franz, who was a court architect and at the foundation of the *Comité*, the director of the *Awqaf*'s technical office, established by Khedive Isma'il around the 1860s, became a member of the *Comité* and its main leading architect until his retirement in late 1880s, remaining however active with the *Comité* after his retirement.[15]

Although the *Comité*'s overarching mandate was the conservation and restoration of Egypt's Islamic monuments,[16] I have argued that the activities and publications of the *Comité* and its Egyptian and European members as well as those it collaborated with qualifies them to be considered as significant patrons and forefathers of the field of studying Egypt's Islamic art and architecture.[17] Their actions including scholarly research as well as in-situ discoveries have greatly contributed to our knowledge as will be demonstrated through the story of the facade of al-Aqmar mosque.

Decades before the interventions of the *Comité* on the Mosque of al-Aqmar, Émile Prisse d'Avennes (1807–1879), wrote the following about the mosque in the text accompanying his masterwork *L'Art arabe*: 'Cette mosquée, située dans le quartier de Sébatyeh, ne mérite pas une description particulière ; elle fut construite par ordre du soultan Ebn-Aly-el-Mansour, qui mourut assassin à l'île de Roudah.'[18]

Nonetheless, the *Comité* paid attention to this small mosque as it had done to many other less monumental Islamic buildings. In the sixth Bulletin of the *Comité* covering the works carried out in 1889 (and published in 1890), and which included its minutes of meetings and technical reports, it published a report on the mosque referencing also al-Maqrizi's account of its foundation and history. It is noted in the report that the house, which belongs to the *Awqaf* and which abuts the facade, is causing damage to the monument, suggesting therefore to ask for the permission of the *Awqaf* administration to destroy the house and expose the facade, arguing that the 'door and the ornaments are monumental and must be conserved'.[19] The report was written and signed by Pierre Grand Bey (d. 1918; member of the *Comité* and at the time Directeur général des Villes et Bâtiments / Director General of Cities and Buildings at the Ministry of Public Works) and Max Herz (1856–1919; member of the *Comité* and at the time its chief architect).[20] Herz's plan of the mosque was attached to the report, and is most likely the first architectural plan of it; it shows the mosque's hypostyle design and how its main facade does not run parallel to the *qibla* wall but respects the street alignment, a feature whose first known appearance is in this mosque and which was followed in later mosques.[21] Moreover, the houses abutting the facade are shown in hatched lines. After discussions between the *Comité*, the *Awqaf* Administration and the Ministry of Public Works, the decision was taken to expropriate the houses and the shops (in front of the central and left-hand side, not the right-hand side), and pay the necessary compensation.[22]

The discovery of the facade, indeed 'a joyful surprise for art historians', impacted our understanding of Fatimid architecture and design motifs. K. A. C. Creswell (1879–1974), the famous art historian of Islamic art and architecture, commenting on this discovery explains that the mosque's 'supreme interest [. .] lies in its facade, which is the first in Egypt to exhibit an ambitious architectural scheme'.[23] The facade's lavish decorative scheme with its keel arches and radiating flutes, a lamp, a star and a door/window as well as Qur'anic inscriptions and roundels inscribed with the names Muhammad and 'Ali have attracted the attention of numerous scholars raising debate on the possible interpretations and meanings of these different elements. Caroline Williams has written an article titled 'The Cult of 'Alid Saints in the Fatimid Monuments of Cairo. Part I: The Mosque of al-Aqmar' in which she analysed the facade's inscriptions and 'the esoteric significance of the mosque's plan of decoration', explaining 'how handicapped we are in the study of the Fatimid monuments by the wholesale loss and destruction of Isma'ili texts.'[24] Her interpretation links the use of specific Qur'anic and foundational inscriptions on the facade, the use of the name of 'Ali and the name of the mosque, al-Aqmar (the moonlit or moon), as well as a decorative repertoire that recalls Shi'i symbolism to the aim of reviving the cult of the 'Alid saints, especially at a time of political turmoil. She notes that this strategy was used earlier by the Fatimid vizier Badr al-Jamali in the city of Ascalon, where he 'discovered' the head of al-Husayn (in 484/1091) and aimed at turning the city into a 'popular religious center' at a time of weakness of the Fatimid empire.[25]

Doris Behrens-Abouseif in her article 'The facade of the Aqmar Mosque in the context of Fatimid Ceremonial' stresses the location of the mosque in the very close vicinity of the Fatimid palace and differs from Caroline Williams in her interpretation of the symbolism of the facade's carved decorative elements focusing on the political and memorial context of its construction. She argues that the message of the mosque: 'celebrated a specific monument in Fatimid history: the return of splendor to the city and its palace under Caliph al-Amir' and concludes that '[a]fter decades of obscurity the caliph, like a light, revealed himself in a splendid ceremonial to a rejoicing population in a revived capital. The ceremonial had been choreographed by Vizier al-Ma'mum. Both caliph and vizier have therefore been recorded on the facade not only in the text of the inscription but also through the themes of its carving.'[26]

A brief interpretation by Lucy-Anne Hunt in her article 'Churches of Old Cairo and Mosques of al-Qahira: A case of Christian-Muslim Interchange' takes a different direction. She notes: 'Here [in the facade of al-Aqmar] a new awareness of the potency of the iconic image as a supplement to inscriptions suggests a knowledge of the symbolism inherent in the Christian use of the sanctuary screen door to mark the entry into a sacred space.'[27]

It is worth mentioning here that al-Maqrizi noted that originally there was a Christian monastery on the site of the mosque,[28] but no archaeological works have taken place in this area to confirm or negate this matter. If material evidence is found to verify al Maqrizi's account, then it can be assumed that architectural elements found on site could have also inspired al-Aqmar's facade. Is it possible that some pieces of stone found on site were incorporated in the facade? This cannot be ascertained but what seems to be clear is that decades before the debates on al-Aqmar's facade took place, its decorative scheme intrigued the curiosity and interest of scholars and designers such as Marcus Simaika Pasha (1864–1944) an Egyptian Copt who played a major role in the creation of the Coptic Museum and is widely considered as its founder, although this is debatable.[29]

Simaika's name is however carved as the founder of the Coptic Museum on a facade built in 1929 (figure II.1.2) as the hall of the icons at what was known at the time as the Coptic Patriarchal Museum; this facade is now the entrance of the museum. Its overall architectural scheme used the Aqmar mosque's facade as a model (but this time in a symmetrical form). To date, we do not have any written or iconographic archival evidence regarding the designer or architect of this facade but I have argued that Marcus Simaika was the mastermind behind its design. And while nothing can be found in Simaika's memoirs regarding the choice of design for the facade two scholars contemporary with him, namely Louis Hautecœur (1884–1973) and Gaston Wiet (1887–1971) have given us some clues regarding this matter. In their co-authored book *Les Mosquées du Caire* (1932) when discussing the Mosque of al-Aqmar they write in a footnote: 'S. E. Morcos Simaika pacha, directeur du musée copte, en a conclu que la façade d'el-Akmar devait reproduire les façades d'églises copte et s'en est inspiré pour construire la salle des icones de son musée.'[30]

The design of the facade at the Coptic Museum has recreated the symmetric form of al-Aqmar's facade, which was lost at that time and

Figure II.1.2 The facade of the Coptic Museum constructed in 1929 inspired by the facade of the Mosque of al-Aqmar.

which was later reconstructed by the Bohras in the 1990s (figure II.1.3).[31] And although the facade of the Coptic Museum is in its overall shape similar to the facade of al-Aqmar mosque, the designer has used as models several archaeological objects discovered at Coptic sites, in addition to those from the facade of al-Aqmar mosque, but that bear similarities to Coptic ones such as the shell motif and the keel arch with radiating flutes. Elements that are clearly Fatimid or Islamic such as the *muqarnas* niches and the Qur'anic inscriptions were not incorporated in the facade of the Coptic Museum.

I will not dwell into the different scholarly interpretations regarding Simaika's choice for the facade of the Coptic Museum as I have discussed this in other publications.[32] What I would like to highlight here are two points. The first is that the modern discovery of al-Aqmar's facade, the discovery of objects dating to the Coptic period, and the similarities that could be recognised between both, are factors that allowed for the creation of the hybrid and innovative facade of the Coptic Museum. The second is that the construction of the facade of the Coptic Museum, with its overall Fatimid design frame along with Coptic artistic and architectural motifs, triggered scholars contemporary with Simaika to study the influence of Coptic art on Islamic art and architecture and to publish their ideas on

Figure II.1.3 The Fatimid mosque of al-Aqmar: the facade after reconstructing its right-hand side in the 1990s.

this subject. This is attested to in an article by Zaky Mohamed Hassan (1908–1957), an art historian expert in Islamic art and architecture, and at the time curator at the Museum of Arab Art (later renamed as the Museum of Islamic Art). The article was published in 1937 in the *Bulletin de l'Association des Amis de l'Art Copte* and is titled 'Ba'd al-ta'thirat al-qibtiyya fi'l-funun al-islamiyya'. Another is an article written by Creswell two years later and titled 'Coptic Influences on Early Muslim Architecture' and published in the *Bulletin de la Société d'Archéologie Copte*.

Both articles were published in bulletins dedicated to Coptic studies and were not further pursued in publications dedicated to Islamic art.

The *mashhad* of al-Juyushi in Cairo and the mausoleum of Aga Khan III in Aswan

Another site that calls for further research especially regarding the interchange between the Christians and the Fatimids is the Muqattam hills and the area directly beneath it. For the Copts the site is associated with numerous miracles, most notably the moving of the hill during the Fatimid period; the area also housed the monastery known as Dayr

Figure II.1.4 *Mashhad* al-Juyushi (478/1085) on the Muqattam hills.

al-Qusayr as well as other hermitages and cemeteries.[33] For the Fatimids, the area houses several shrines, mosques and cemeteries. On the top of the hill/mountain lies the *mashhad* of al-Juyushi (figure II.1.4),[34] the one used by the architect Farid Shafeʻi (1907–1985) as a model for the design of the mausoleum of Aga Khan III, constructed in Aswan between 1956 and 1960 (figure II.1.8).[35] The mausoleum lies on the west bank of the Nile close to the historic Coptic Monastery, Dayr Anba Hadra, also known as St. Simeon Monastery.

While some similarities between the mausoleum in Aswan and other Fatimid mausolea could be traced it is the *mashhad* of al-Juyushi that shows the most striking similarities (figures II.1.5a and 5b, II.1.6a and 6b).

The scholarly attention on the *mashhad* of al-Juyushi and its modern rediscovery was initiated during the 19th century by epigraphists, art historians and architects.

Although the building was mentioned by Mehren in his *Câhirah og Keràfat* (1869), it was Max van Berchem (1863–1921), the famous epigraphist and historian of Arabic inscription, 'who was the first to have brought attention to it' as noted by Oleg Grabar.[36] In a photograph taken by the Italian photographer Beniamino Facchinelli (1839–1895) we see Max van Berchem inside the building during one of his visits to study the

Fatimid Artistic and Architectural Legacy in Egypt 135

Figures II.1.5a and II.1.5b The interior of the *mashhad* al-Juyushi and the interior of the mausoleum of Aga Khan III.

Figures II.1.6a and II.1.6b The six-pointed star in the apex of the dome of *mashhad* al-Juyushi and of the mausoleum of Aga Khan III.

Figure II.1.7 *Mashhad* al-Juyushi, interior view of the *mihrab*, during exploration of the site. Max van Berchem standing left.

mashhad (figure II.1.7).[37] Facchinelli took other photographs of the building,[38] and some of these photographs were used by Max van Berchem in the article he published on the structure in 1889.[39] It is in this article – and possibly specifically for it – that the first drawings of the *mashhad* al-Juyushi were made and published. It is thanks to Julius Franz that the

138 Fatimid Cosmopolitanism

plan and the section of the building were surveyed and drawn. The same drawings are found in the *Comité*'s archives.[40] Creswell, who resurveyed and redrew the plan and section of the building, compared some aspects of his plan to that of the plan published by van Berchem referring to it as 'the Comité's plan published by van Berchem.'[41] This could indicate that

Figure II.1.8 The Mausoleum of Aga Khan III on the west bank of the Nile in Aswan (ca. 1960).

van Berchem's interest in this building is what triggered the *Comité* and its technical section to undertake this task. Van Berchem in fact ends his article with the following recommendation: 'Ce monument, par sa haute antiquité et par ses formes originales, mérite d'être recommandé aux bons soins du Comité de conservation des monuments de l'art arabe.'[42]

Possibly in response to this suggestion, the *Comité* did indeed take action to consolidate the building during the following years.[43] These were not major restoration works and were considered as 'petits travaux' that would ensure the safeguarding of the building.[44]

Although van Berchem's article is titled 'Une Mosquée du temps des Fatimites au Cairo. Notice sur le Gami' El Goyushi', in the text he clearly identifies the building as a *mashhad* based on the foundation inscription. Scholars have however differed regarding the purpose and function of this building.

In Oleg Grabar's article 'The Earliest Islamic Commemorative Structures, Notes and Documents' he argues that the *mashhad* of al-Juyushi 'created for prayer is used with a commemorative function emphasised by the foundation inscription.'[45] Analysing the Qur'anic inscriptions in the building vis à vis the political context and taking into consideration the location of the *mashhad* on the Muqattam hills with a view over the whole city of Cairo, he notes: '[I]t may be suggested that its purpose was to symbolize the victory achieved only a few years earlier by Badr al-Jamali in the name of the caliph al-Mustansir over the rebellions and disorders which for a long time plagued the Fatimid empire.'[46]

Farid Shafe'i in his article titled 'The Mashhad of al-Juyushi. (Archaeological Notes and Studies)' (1965),[47] which he published after designing the mausoleum of Aga Khan III, argues that the mosque with its minarets and roof domes in such a remote place away from the city could have been used as a watchtower 'disguised in a shape of a mosque'[48] but Behrens-Abouseif questions 'why a watchtower needs to be disguised'.[49]

Yusuf Raghib, who studied Fatimid mausolea, also dedicated an article to the *mashhad* al-Juyushi titled 'Un oratoire fatimide au sommet du Muqattam'.[50] In this work, Raghib analyses all earlier scholarly works regarding the building, agreeing with Grabar's interpretation of the building being a commemorative structure for Badr al-Jamali's victories.

This modern rediscovery of the *mashhad* al-Juyushi has, like the rediscovery of the facade of al-Aqmar, affected not only our knowledge of Fatimid art and architecture in Egypt but also the development of the neo-Fatimid style in Egypt and elsewhere during the 20th century. Academic studies as well as the photographs and drawings of the *mashhad* produced since the late 19th century allowed architects to use its newly explored artistic and architectural forms as sources of inspiration. This can be clearly seen in the design of the mausoleum of Aga Khan III in Aswan by the architect Farid Shafeʿi. Selecting a Fatimid building, rather than one from any other Islamic period in Egypt, for the mausoleum of an Ismaili Imam whose ancestors were the Fatimids needs no further elaboration. To my knowledge Farid Shafeʿi did not however publish his rationale for specifically taking this building as a model for the mausoleum of Aga Khan III in Aswan. In the introduction to his book on 'Arab architecture', he only explains how his interest in Islamic art and architecture, which he considered a hobby, combined with his profession as an architect, is what allowed him to design this mausoleum.[51]

Comparing the plan of the *mashhad* al-Juyushi with that of the mausoleum of Aga Khan III in Aswan it can be noticed what kind of modifications Shafeʿi carried out to the original design, with the biggest change being not incorporating the minaret and the adjacent room (considered by Creswell as a later added mausoleum though this was later refuted by Shafeʿi). Otherwise, the layout of the building, with the central dome flanked by two rooms and having in the centre an open courtyard is similar in both plans. The plan of this *mashhad* as well as other Fatimid structures recalls those of some Coptic churches, a matter that is not discussed in articles dedicated to the study of the building.

It is in Barbara Finster's article titled 'On masjid al-Juyushi on the Muqattam' where we find an examination of the possible 'architectural origins of the plan' and a comparison with 'contemporary Coptic churches', arguing that it 'may have been designed by a Coptic architect' which also touches upon the importance of the Muqattam for both Muslims and Christians.[52] My initial research suggests that there are a number of other Coptic structures that could be included in this study. Building on this article and as noted above the matter deserves more interdisciplinary research looking at a variety of other Coptic structures, and discussing in more detail the relationship between the Fatimids and the Copts and the artistic and architectural works they produced, particularly during the time of the patron of the building, Badr al-Jamali, as well as the sanctity of the Muqattam hills for both the Christians and the Muslims.[53]

Moving to the architectural and decorative features of the interior, we also see striking similarities between the *mashhad* and the mausoleum such as the type of keel arch used in the *mihrab* and the triple arch area (figures II.1.5a, 5b, II.1.6a, 6b) as well as the six-pointed star at the apex of the dome.[54]

The construction of the mausoleum in Aswan, on the west bank of the Nile, near the historic Coptic Monastery of Anba Hadra recalls the building of *mashhad* al-Juyushi on the Muqattam hills, a site of significance to the Copts. The choice of Aswan in particular is most likely due to the existence of the famous necropolis on the eastern bank of the Nile, housing many domed mausolea from the Fatimid period. The cemetery is still used by the local community as a burial site.

Conclusion

While the interest in Egypt's Islamic and Coptic art and architecture can be traced to centuries ago, it is during the 19th century that we can observe a turning point in how systematically these artistic and architectural legacies were studied, surveyed and explored. The work of the *Comité de conservation des monuments de l'art arabe* and the production of photographs, drawings and studies either by its members and/or the professionals it collaborated with greatly contributed to our knowledge of Islamic art and architecture in Egypt. The two studies presented here are cases in point.

The discovery of the facade of the Mosque of al-Aqmar, which had a design and decoration not known to art historians or art connoisseurs prior to 1901, fills a gap in the art historical timeline of Fatimid and Islamic art and architecture in Egypt, triggering questions on the meaning of its decorative scheme as well as the interchange between Fatimid and Coptic art and architecture. Scholarly rediscovery in the late 19th century of the *mashhad* al-Juyushi which is situated in a remote spot on the Muqattam hills above Cairo, has also raised questions and generated debates on the function of the building, its context and founder.

It was these modern discoveries / rediscoveries that have provided architects and designers with new sources of inspiration for their 'neo-Fatimid' designs. Nevertheless, comparing these seemingly strikingly and strictly neo-Fatimid buildings with their sources of inspiration shows that the designers created hybrid structures that build on the Fatimid legacy of continuity, innovation and interchange.

Finally, one would like the examples presented here to trigger more research regarding the entanglement between Coptic and Fatimid art as well as the construction of Christian and Islamic structures in areas that have common sanctity for both.

NOTES

1. For a good overview of Fatimid art and architecture in North Africa and Egypt, see, for example, Jonathan Bloom, *Arts of the City Victorious* (New Haven, CN, 2007).
   For a focus on Fatimid art, see Anna Contadini, *Fatimid art at the Victoria and Albert Museum* (London, 1998).
   For an overview on the Fatimids in Egypt, see Ayman F. Sayyid, *al-Dawla al-Fatimiyya fi Misr, tafsir jadid* (Cairo, 1992) and Paul Walker, *Exploring an Islamic Empire: Fatimid History and its Sources* (London, 2002).
   For a variety of topics on Fatimid art and history in Egypt, see Marianne Barrucand, ed., *L'Égypte Fatimide: son art et son histoire* (Paris, 1999).
2. For more on the walls, see Stéphane Pradines's chapter in this volume as well as his earlier publications such as Pradines, ed., *Earthen Architecture in Muslim Cultures: historical and anthropological perspectives* (Leiden, 2018). For a historical overview on early Fatimid walls see Abu'l-ʿAmyam, 'Aswar madinat al-Qahira wa hitatuha. Sur Gawhar sanat 358h/969m', *Annales Islamologiques*, 36 (2002), pp. 23–94.
3. The Mosque of al-Hakim was restored and parts of it reconstructed by the Dawoodi Bohras during the 1970s. For more on the Bohra's restorations see Paula Sanders, 'Bohra Architecture and the Restoration of Fatimid Culture', in Marianne Barrucand, ed., *L'Égypte Fatimide: son art et son histoire* (Paris, 1999), pp. 159–165, and Sanders, *Creating Medieval Cairo* (Cairo, 2008), pp. 115–142; see also Aliasger Najam Madraswala, 'The Ihya' of al-Jamiʿ al-Anwar: Religious Values in the Restoration of Sacred Islamic Monuments', (PhD, Oxford Brookes University, 2020). Other Fatimid buildings that were also restored and reconstructed by the Bohras include the *mashhad* al-Juyushi, the Mosque of al-Aqmar and the Mosque of al-Lu'lu'a. For al-Hakim's architectural patronage, see Jennifer Pruitt's PhD thesis, 'Fatimid architectural patronage and changing sectarian identifies (969-1021)', (Harvard University, 2009). To what extent could the restorations and reconstructions by the Bohras (which they consider as revival) be considered as neo-Fatimid architecture is a question that will not be discussed in this chapter.
4. For some of these mausolea as well as additional ones see Caroline Williams, 'The Cult of 'Alid Saints in the Fatimid Monuments of Cairo. Part II: the Mausolea', *Muqarnas*, 3 (1985), pp. 39–60.
5. For more, see Gregory William's paper presented at the Fatimid Cosmopolitanism conference, in which he discussed the salvage archaeology carried out in Aswan and the archaeological finds there from the Islamic era.
6. This will be briefly discussed in this chapter. See Doris Behrens-Abouseif and Juan de Lara's chapter in this volume titled 'A Fatimid Mermaid'. See also Anthony Cutler, 'The Parallel Universes of Arab and Byzantine Art', in Marianne Barrucand, ed., *L'Égypte Fatimide: son art et son histoire* (Paris, 1999), pp. 635–648. See Johannes den Heijer et al., 'Christian Art and Culture', in Asadullah Souren Melikian-Chirvani, ed., *The World of the Fatimids* (Toronto, London and Munich, 2018), pp. 190–217 and also the work of Lucy-Anne Hunt on the interchange between Christian and Islamic art such as for example Hunt, 'Churches of Old Cairo and Mosques of al-Qahira: A case study of Christian-Muslim Interchange', *Medieval Encounters: Jewish, Christian and Muslim Culture in Confluence and Dialogue*, 2 (1996), pp. 43–66 (thanks are due to Gertrud J.M.

van Loon for drawing my attention to this article). Some scholars have also touched upon this theme focusing for example on a specific element; for example, Bloom in his book *Arts of the City Victorious*, also touches upon the Fatimid and Coptic connection in woodwork. Nevertheless, to my knowledge nothing more holistic and interdisciplinary was carried out regarding this theme.

7 See the work of den Heijer and for example the special issue of *Medieval Encounters* (21, 2015) titled 'Non-Muslim Communities in Fatimid Egypt (10-12th centuries CE)', edited by den Heijer et al.
8 Doris Behrens-Abouseif, *Islamic Architecture in Cairo, An Introduction* (Leiden, 1998), p. 10.
9 For more see Ramez Wadie Boutros, 'La Symbolique de la conque dans l'Égypte chrétienne et musulmane', *Le Monde Copte*, 20 (1992), pp. 81–87.
10 See for example Jonathon Bloom, 'The Introduction of the Muqarnas into Egypt', *Muqarnas*, 5 (1988), pp. 21–28.
11 I have discussed the facade of the Coptic Museum vis-à-vis the facade of al-Aqmar mosque as well as themes linked to the foundation of the Coptic Museum in two other articles. See note 29. For the chapter here I will only highlight relevant parts for the theme here and will present additional information not discussed in these earlier articles.
12 Julius Franz, *Kairo* (Leipzig, 1903), pp. 29–31.
13 The demolition of these houses can be followed through the Bulletins of the *Comité de conservation des monuments de l'art arabe*. These Bulletins will be shortened to BC. For the demolitions of these houses, see BC, 18 (1901), pp. 92 and 104.
   Numerous scholars have written about the *Comité* and some of its members; these include but are not limited to: Donald Malcom Reid, Philipp Speiser, Alaa El-Habashi, Mercedes Volait, István Ormos, among others. The author of this chapter also wrote her PhD on the *Comité*, see Bakhoum, 'Les restaurations du Comité de conservation des monuments de l'art arabe en Égypte : « conservation » ou « reinvention » des monuments ?', (PhD, Université Paris 1 Panthéon Sorbonne & Universiteit Leiden, 2021).
14 BC, 1 (1882-1883^2), pp. 8–9.
15 For more on Franz, see Elke Pflugrad-Abdel Aziz, *Islamisierte Architektur in Kairo. Carl von Diebitsch und der Hofarchitekt Julius Franz – Preußisches Unternehmertum in Ägypten des 19. Jahrhundert* (Bonn, 2003) [based on PhD 1992].
16 Fifteen years after the foundation of the *Comité*, Coptic monuments with a functioning nature (hence not purely archaeological sites) were added to its mandate but with funding from the Coptic Patriarchate (not from the Ministry of *Awqaf*) as well as other secular sources.
17 I have discussed this topic in my PhD and presented it at the Third Conference of the School of Mamluk Studies which took place in Chicago in June 2016 in a paper titled 'The Comité de Conservation des Monuments de l'Art Arabe and its Members: Patrons of the Study of Mamluk Architecture in Egypt'. http://mamluk.uchicago.edu/past-conferences.html (last accessed June 2020).
18 Émile Prisse d'Avennes, *L'art arabe [d'après les monuments du Kaire depuis le VIIe siècle jusqu'à la fin du XVIIe]* (Paris, 1877), [text], p. 99. Translation: 'This mosque, situated in the area of Sabtiyya does not deserve a particular description; it was constructed by the order of the Sultan Ibn Ali al-Mansur, who was assassinated on the island of Roda'. Translations from French or Arabic into English are by the author of this chapter unless otherwise indicated.
19 BC, 6 (1889), pp. 112–113.
20 For more on Max Herz see István Ormos, *Max Herz Pasha 1859-1919: His Life and Career* (Cairo, 2009).
21 BC, 6 (1889), plate no. II. Behrens-Abouseif, *Islamic Architecture in Cairo*, p. 72.

22 BC, 14 (1898), pp. 22 and 170–171; BC, 16 (1899), p. 31; BC, 17 (1900), pp. 46 and 79–80.
23 K. A. C. Creswell, *The Muslim Architecture of Egypt*, vol. 1 (Oxford, 1952), p. 243.
24 Caroline Williams, 'The Cult of 'Alid Saints in the Fatimid Monuments of Cairo. Part I: The Mosque of al-Aqmar', *Muqarnas*, 1 (1983), p. 46.
25 Ibid., p. 42.
26 Doris Behrens-Abouseif, 'The facade of the Aqmar Mosque in the Context of Fatimid Ceremonial', *Muqarnas*, 9 (1992), p. 37.
27 Lucy-Anne Hunt, 'Churches of Old Cairo and Mosques of al-Qahira: A case study of Christian-Muslim Interchange', *Medieval Encounters: Jewish, Christian and Muslim Culture in Confluence and Dialogue*, 2 (1996), p. 55.
28 al-Maqrizi, *al-Mawaʿiz waʾl-iʿtibar fi dhikr al-khitat waʾl-athar*, ed. Ayman F. Sayyid (London, 2013), vol. 4, p. 79.
29 Dina Ishak Bakhoum, 'Recreating the Facade of a Fatimid Mosque at the Coptic Patriarchal Museum: A Step Towards its Nationalization?', in Kim Bowes and William Tronzo, ed., *The Memoirs of the American Academy in Rome (Special Edition)*, 62 (2017), pp. 99–118 and 'Egypt's Coptic Museum: From Patriarchal to National', in Virginie Rey, ed., *The Art of Minorities. Cultural Representation in Museums of the Middle East and North Africa* (Edinburgh, 2020), pp. 181–204. The debate regarding Simaika being the founder of the Coptic Museum took place contemporary to his time (see Bakhoum, 'Recreating the Facade of a Fatimid Mosque'). For more on the Coptic Museum, its foundation and its founder, and the discussion between Donald M. Reid and István Ormos regarding who founded the Coptic Museum, see Donald M. Reid, *Whose Pharaohs? Archaeology, Museums, and Egyptian National Identity from Napoleon to World War I* (Cairo, 2002), pp. 275–278; Ormos, *Max Herz Pasha*, vol. 2, pp. 334–346 and Reid, *Contesting Antiquity in Egypt: Archaeologies, Museums, and the Struggle for Identities from World War I to Nasser* (Cairo, 2015), pp. 202–206. See also Julien Auber de Lapierre, 'Le Musée copte du Caire, une utopie architecturale', *Annales Islamologiques*, 50 (2016), pp. 235–266.
30 Louis Hautecœur and Gaston Wiet, *Les mosquées du Caire* (Paris, 1932), p. 248, fn. 2; Translation: 'S. E. Morcos Simaika pacha, director of the Coptic Museum, was convinced that the façade of al-Aqmar mosque reproduced elements from Coptic churches and that this inspired him to construct the façade of the hall of the icons'.
31 For more on the mosque see Jaʿfar us Sadiq M. Saifuddin, *Al Aqmar: A Living Testament to the Fatemiyeen* (Croydon, 2000). For the restorations by the Bohras, see Paula Sanders, 'Bohra Architecture and the Restoration of Fatimid Culture', in Marianne Barrucand, ed., *L'Égypte Fatimide: son art et son histoire* (Paris, 1999), pp. 159–165, and her *Creating Medieval Cairo* (Cairo, 2008), pp. 115–142.
32 Bakhoum, 'Recreating the Facade of a Fatimid Mosque' and 'Egypt's Coptic Museum'.
33 For more on this miracle see Maryann M. Shenouda 'Displacing Dhimmi, Maintaining Hope: Unthinkable Coptic Representations of Fatimid Egypt', *International Journal of Middle East Studies*, 39 (2007), pp. 587–606, and Gaétan du Roy et al., 'Le miracle du Muqattam à travers les siècles. Origines et reinvention d'une légende copte', *Annales Islamologiques*, 52 (2018), pp. 193–217.
34 For more on the building see also Jaʿfar us Sadiq M. Saifuddin, *Al Juyushi: A Vision of the Fatemiyeen* (Croydon, 2002).
35 https://www.walycenter.org/images/stories/archives/TWC-Archives-farid-shafei.pdf (last accessed 31 Oct. 2022). In 2011, the author of this chapter in her capacity at the time as the Conservation Programme Manager at the Aga Khan Cultural Services-Egypt / the Aga Khan Trust for Culture directed the conservation project of the mausoleum.
36 Oleg Grabar, 'The Earliest Islamic Commemorative Structures', *Ars Orientalis*, 6 (1966), pp. 27–28.

37 http://facchinelli.huma-num.fr/items/show/210
38 http://facchinelli.huma-num.fr (search: al-Guyushi)
39 Max van Berchem, 'Une mosquée du temps des Fatimites au Caire. Notice sur le gami' el Goyushi', *Mémoires de l'institut Égyptien*, 2 (1889), pp. 605–619.
40 Markaz Tasjil al-Athar al-Islamiyya wa'l-Qibtiyya, Archives of the Supreme Council of Antiquities, folder no. 304.
41 Creswell, *Muslim Architecture of Egypt*, vol. 1.
42 van Berchem, 'Une Mosquée', p. 619.
43 See for example BC, 7 (1890), pp. 25, 109 and 112; BC, 8 (1891), pp. 25 and 36.
44 BC, 10 (1903), pp. 68–69.
45 Grabar, 'The Earliest Islamic Commemorative Structures', p. 28.
46 Ibid.
47 Farid Shafe'i, 'The Mashhad of al-Juyushi (Archaeological Notes and Studies)', in *Studies in Islamic Art and Architecture in Honour of Professor K.A.C. Creswell* (Cairo, 1965), pp. 237-252.
48 As per Bloom's discussion of al-Shafe'i's interpretation, *Arts of the City Victorious*, p. 134.
49 Behrens-Abouseif, *Islamic Architecture in Cairo*, p. 67.
50 Yusuf Ragib, 'Un oratoire fatimide au sommet du Muqattam', *Studia Islamica*, 65 (1987), pp. 51–67.
51 Farid Shafe'i, *al-'Imara al-'arabiyya* (Cairo, 1994), p. 21.
52 Barbara Finster, 'On Masjid al-Juyushi on the Muqattam', *Archéologie islamique*, 10 (2000), pp. 65–78. Bloom in his *Arts of the City Victorious*, p. 133 notes that the plan of the *mashhad* 'is an elaborated version of the shrine type, exemplified by the earlier Hadra Sharifa or later Mausoleum of Sayyida Ruqqaya, rather than a mosque type, although some scholars have seen parallels between its plan and that of contemporary Coptic churches'. Bloom gives reference to Janine Sourdel-Thomine and Bertold Spuler, *Die Kunst des Islam* (Berlin, 1973), p. 249 (this section on the *mashhad* as well as other sections were written by Michael Rogers) and to Barbara Finster, 'On Masjid al-Juyushi'.
53 For the state of the Christians during the time of Badr al-Jamali, see den Heijer, 'Considération sur les communautés chrétiennes en Égypte fatimide: l'État et l'Église sous le vizirate de Badr al-Jamali (1074-1094)', in Marianne Barrucand, ed., *L'Égypte Fatimide: son art et son histoire* (Paris, 1999), pp. 569–578.
54 For more on the use of the six-pointed star in Fatimid architecture, see Bernard O'Kane's chapter in this volume.

2

A Dynasty for All Seasons: The Fatimids in Modern and Contemporary Cosmopolitanism Discourses*

Delia Cortese

Cosmopolitanism is a slippery word. Over time it has acquired different meanings and constructs depending on the context and the agenda that have called for its use that betray a deliberate orientation towards the attainment of a particular goal. The word, applied to describe *post facto* conditions of living in multicultural settings, is typically used to imply or assume inclusivity, pluralism, universalistic ideals, mobility and tolerance. What can, at first, read as a positive appraisal of what it means to live a cosmopolitan life can also betray an essentially Euro/Western-centred vision of this phenomenon. It is not by chance that the word cosmopolitanism is often linked to the lifestyles of elites (the intellectual elites) that in many regions emerged as, or were perceived to have been, a by-product of the colonial experience. By contrast, when considered from the perspective of those who find themselves to be categorised as cosmopolitan we see that the term is far from having always a positive value. Cosmopolitanism has in most cases been the result of a default outcome due to forced diasporas caused by conflict, persecution, disease and economic pressures. Cosmopolitanism for many has been – and still is – the embellishment at the end of a tragedy, something endured first and, perhaps, willingly or unwillingly, positively matured later.[1]

Debates about Muslim cosmopolitanism display a similar polarisation in the way meanings are constructed around its understanding when seen from an Islamic perspective. Among its advocates, it is projected onto the concept of *umma*, recast as ultimate example of a universal community shaped by an inbuilt cosmopolitan nature. They hark back to an idealised vision of the Islamic past where mobility meant intellectual interactions and fruitful cultural encounters and exchanges. In recent times the idea of an inherent 'cosmopolitan' nature in Islam has been reclaimed by those

Muslims keen to correct the obscurantism, sectarianism and violence that is often ascribed to Muslim societies by non-Muslims observers. However, at the opposite end of the spectrum, there is the Islamic understanding of cosmopolitanism as something 'foreign', imposed by external forces onto the Muslim commonwealth – the Crusades, colonial administration, recent West-led wars – hence provoking systems of resistance warding Muslims against inclusivity, pluralism, universalistic ideals, mobility, tolerance.[2]

Defenders of Islamic cosmopolitanism have been drawing resources from the past to present evidence gathered through the lens of the Muslim urbanite cosmopolis from pre-modern Islamic history. Until recently, as the ultimate example of Islamic rule in the West, al-Andalus was hailed as the home of the exemplar cosmopolitan society to follow in order to bridge the gap between two seemingly contrasting realms: that of 'the East' and 'the West'. For many al-Andalus has become a byword for vibrant economic and cultural exchanges brought about by an international movement of people as well as peaceful religious coexistence. But could this be in fact misplaced nostalgia for an idealised past? In post-9/11 Muslim discourse, what amounts to a predominantly Western-centred construct of al-Andalus has been replaced with a counter-nostalgia where Islamic Spain stands for loss and longing. Al-Andalus is invoked as model for the foundation of new political subjectivities of anti-colonial resistance. Extreme expressions call for the restoration of this lost caliphate, holy war and the expulsion of non-Muslims. In the case of al-Andalus, either way, to showcase cosmopolitanism as a filter through which one could reclaim, as model, a phase in history has proved at best idealistic and at worst dangerous.[3]

Where then could one find an example from Islamic history that could satisfy today varied Islamic cosmopolitanism orientations without triggering the 'wrong' type of nostalgia? An example from the Islamic past where the positives and negatives of cosmopolitanism coexist yet without forcing a polarised stance? Enter the Fatimids. In this paper I will share some examples of how the Fatimids have in recent times become part of some of today's Muslim universalist discourses. I will look at how, and to what extent, the Fatimids feature as part of today's Muslim assimilation of divergent voices. Those who have an investment in projecting their cosmopolitan orientations, how do they go about using the Fatimids so as to display them in a particular way? What agendas do they betray if any? To what extent and in what way is the analysis of this use of 'The Fatimids' useful for the understanding of new or alternative expressions of cosmopolitanism? In attempting to address these questions I will look first at few examples of modern political and cultural discourses in which we can detect the erasure of the Fatimids' Ismaili identity – and in some instances the dynasty altogether – from cosmopolitan orientations. I will then look at the re-inscription of the Fatimids in cosmopolitanism discourses by considering a variety of examples, including those drawn from material currently available in the digital cosmopolis.

Obfuscating, Camouflaging, Erasing the Fatimids: The Case of Egypt

By the 19th century, Egypt had affirmed itself, among the Arab regions, as the country universally acknowledged as the cultural, intellectual and academic beacon of Sunni Islam. This prestigious position however made historical revisionism imperative: Egypt's distinctive Shi'i past, particularly the Ismaili brand that the Fatimids embodied, had to go. In Cairo, therefore, a number of strategies to 'erase' the Fatimids from collective memory were adopted, which we see reflected in the way in which the foreign-protected Ottoman regime of Egypt came to represent the country to its subjects and the world.[4] In Egypt the respective agendas of European colonial and Ottoman imperial spheres converged, among other expressions, in 1881 with the formation of a *Comité de conservation des monuments de l'art arabe* (Committee for the Preservation of the Monuments of Arab Art) established to list all the 'Arab' monuments in Egypt that this body considered worthy of preservation. The establishment of the *Comité* led to the foundation of the National Museum of Arab Art. The initial fund of its collection was made of mainly salvaged architectural artefacts in the broad Cairo area that, before being eventually housed in a dedicated venue, had been stored in the then dilapidated and disused al-Hakim Mosque, named after the Fatimid Imam-caliph who completed it in 403/1013. In time, more artefacts were added to the museum's collection via a reworking of the *waqf* (pious endowments) system and finally via purchase.[5] The first catalogue of the museum's collection was published in 1885. In its introduction a brief chronological outline of Islamic Egypt is provided where the Fatimids are featured as one of the ruling dynasties of the past. Referred to as caliphs, rather than rulers or sultans as per the other dynasties, the nature of their caliphate is not explained and no mention is made of the Ismaili form of Islam that the Fatimids endorsed. The only reference to Shi'ism associated with the Fatimids occurs in the context of introducing the Ayyubids, with Salah al-Din presented as the champion of Sunnism against the Shi'ism of the Fatimids.⁶ Both the list of artefacts and the selected images in the catalogue betray the privileging of objects belonging to the Mamluk period and subsequent eras as best representative of 'Arab' art. In fairness, in the catalogue, religious connotations in general are hardly ever mentioned in relation to objects beyond specific ritual use or settings. In fact, the emphasis on 'Arab-ness' rather than on Islam served to promote a secular model of art that was in keeping with the Western curatorial standards of the time. In historical introductory notes featured in later promotional pamphlets for the museum, Fatimid rule is described with the emphasis on the might of their artistic patronage 'despite' its Shi'i affiliation.⁷

In forming its collection, the museum's curators had relied on whatever artefacts had survived the ravages of the past. Likewise, the pre-modern landscape of 19th-century Cairo was informed by what were the only extant landmarks of earlier ages as opposed to the many more which had previously disappeared. Most of what was left belonged to the Mamluk period. In time architectural interventions on the capital's urban assets and cityscape added an extra neo-Mamluk flavour to its skyline. As a result, deliberately or by default, 19th-century Egyptians collectively came to accept the Mamluk period as representative of their national past. As this perception of the past gained ground the uncomfortable Shi'i origins and history of the city became more and more obfuscated. On the international scene a tangible example of this understanding of pre-modern Cairo as essentially Mamluk, at the expense of the Fatimid foundation of the city, can be found in shows that became the ultimate way for Western regimes to advertise ideologically-charged cosmopolitan orientations. These were the universal exhibitions that took place in Europe between the early 1860s and 1900. These were mega-shows that formed a new way to celebrate colonial national might and industrial innovation while show-casing to broad audiences at home what the rest of the world looked like, with a before-and-after subtext. For the Paris Exposition of 1867 Charles Edmond, who wrote the general catalogue accompanying the show, sought to present the official version of Egypt's history and architecture. The event and the literature that accompanied it gave birth to the idea of what constituted Islamic architecture that became the standard one in the West whereby the visual representation of Egypt's Islamic historic past was confined to the Mamluk era. ⁸

At the 1889 Exposition Universelle of Paris a pavilion called '*Rue du Caire*' was staged consisting of the reconstruction of an imaginary street lined by twenty-five replicas of historic Islamic buildings located in old Cairo. None were Fatimid except a copy of a gate of the Mosque of al-Azhar – originally built by the Fatimids in 361/972 – that was included in the show to reflect a time when this institution had already been transformed into the most famous Sunni theological university in the world. In his catalogue for the exhibition Alphonse Delort de Gléon (d. 1899), the architect promoter and curator of the display and connoisseur of Egypt, did not mention the Fatimids at all. In keeping with the by-now established practice of presenting the urban histories of Fustat and Cairo as those of one city, Delort de Gléon dated the foundation of Cairo back to the early Arab conquests, with its heart around the mosques of 'Amr and Ibn Tulun. He attributed to Salah al-Din the construction of the city's famous Fatimid gates. With reference to the mosque, he called al-Hakim a sultan of the 8th/14th century, that is, confusing the Fatimid Imam-caliph with one namesake ruler of the Mamluk period.[9] In paying tribute to the bastion of Sunni Islam there was no room for celebrating Cairo's indebtedness to its Ismaili Shi'i Fatimid founders, not even in a fantasy. Similar displays had been held in other locations, famous among them the World's Columbian Exposition of Chicago in 1893.[10] The expositions staged also 'tableaux' illustrating other Arab countries that had come under Fatimid direct or indirect rule, but again the Fatimids were neither showcased or acknowledged.

Fast forward to the 1950s. In 1952 Jamal 'Abd al-Nasir – Nasser (d. 1970) as he became known around the world – led the Free Officers' revolution that overthrew the Egyptian monarchy and ended colonial rule. The revolution he spearheaded – political, constitutional and cultural – culminated with Nasser becoming President of Egypt in 1954. During this period of transformation cultural winds of change were already blowing as shown, among other things, by the National Museum of Arab Art being renamed the Museum of Islamic Art. As the concept of 'national' identity in the name of which the idea of the museum had been conceived in first place was shifting relevance, the 'ownership' of its collection changed from being race-based to being religiously identifiable. The shift would suit Nasser's manoeuvre to assert himself as the ruler at the centre of the *umma*. From being a signifier of 'only' a local Egyptian Arab culture the renaming of the museum repositioned Egypt as the heart of Islamic civilisation. To out-manoeuvre the religious fundamentalists in their claim to exclusivity over Islam, Nasser – in keeping with his secularist vision – symbolically distanced himself from their '*ism*' by inclining towards the '*ic*' thus privileging an understanding of Islam as a cultural force rather than an ideological one.

In 1969 Nasser staged a lavish set of celebrations to mark 1000 years since the foundation of Cairo. The president turned the occasion into an opportunity to promote himself as a world leader through the projection of Cairo as an historically international cosmopolitan capital at a time of crisis throughout the Arab world. Once again nationalist and secularist agendas underscored the reasons behind the commemoration. One of the events organised to mark the occasion was the staging in Cairo of an academic symposium titled *Colloque International sur l'Histoire du Caire*. The proceedings of the conference feature Nasser's inaugural speech in which the president's words betrayed the internal political tensions around the decision to take 358/969 as the first reference for the reckoning of the city's millennium. Marking as it did the year of the Fatimid general Jawhar's arrival in Egypt and his foundation of the city, the dating was no doubt problematic because of its implications. Commemorating it would inevitably draw attention to the achievements of the city's founders, a Shi'i Ismaili dynasty. The wisdom of celebrating *this* millennium was debated in the parliament with Nasser finally agreeing to it by endorsing the rationale presented by the Ministry of Culture. In their respective opening addresses delivered on 29 March 1969 neither Nasser nor the Minister of Culture mentioned the Fatimids, something that turned the dynasty into the proverbial elephant in the room. In the rest of the volume the space given to the dynasty is relatively peripheral and mostly incidental in sharp contrast to their foundational role in Cairo's history.[11] A separate celebratory coffee-table-like volume was published in several languages as a memento of the occasion. It features an introduction where the Fatimids' contribution to Cairo's history and the artistic splendour they brought is acknowledged as a prelude to the Mamluks' achievements and as a way to sharpen contempt for the Ottomans and the colonial powers. The collectively authored narrative goes as far as crediting the Fatimids for bringing the caliphate to Egypt thus turning the country from that time onwards into the beating heart of Arab-Islamic culture and political life. What is not mentioned however is the Shi'i Ismaili character of that caliphate.[12]

Re-inscribing the Fatimids

The late 1970s and the early 1980s saw the Fatimids being re-inscribed in broad Islamic political and cultural discourses. In those years the Egyptian government granted the leadership of the Shi'i Ismaili Da'udi Bohras, with their headquarters in India, permission to set in motion a massive Bohra-financed restoration programme of various Fatimid landmarks in the capital. Since then the Bohras have reclaimed their Fatimid past, through taking symbolic ownership of Cairo's Fatimid architecture with their distinctive, if controversial, restoration programme.[13] While re-inscribing Islamic pluralism upon the Cairo landscape, the Bohras have also endowed their adoption of a neo-Fatimid style in new mosques and other applications with an authoritativeness, as a unifying visible vocabulary to share across their scattered cosmopolitan community.[14] The programme spearheaded by the Bohras was matched by the launch of a series of Ismaili-led conservation initiatives carried out by the Aga Khan Development Network, mainly in Cairo. Here the rationale behind the AKDN's intervention was to sponsor projects designed to bring about a holistic regeneration of socially and economically deprived areas in order to flag out the pluralistic orientation of a community that is comfortable with its global dimension.[15] Either way, the programmes have served to showcase and re-establish in the eyes of audiences – domestic and international – a direct nexus between Egypt and its Shi'i Ismaili past.

In the first part of 2007 we find the Fatimids hitting the news in the context of discourses reflecting the political polarisation surrounding the Sunni – Shi'i rivalries that have been dominating the geopolitics of the Middle East. At that time an unlikely apologist for the Fatimid dynasty and its age came forward in the person of the late Libyan leader Mu'ammar Qadhdhafi (d. 2011). Although himself a Sunni, Qadhdhafi emerged as a champion of the Fatimids in a series of speeches where he glorified them as beacons of tolerance and cultural advancement. Tapping into the cosmopolitan understanding underpinning the concept of *umma*, Qadhdhafi dismissed the divide between Muslims as Persian Shi'is and Sunni Arabs. For him, all Muslims could be said to be Shi'is, in the original meaning of the word as 'follower, partisan'. He reiterated that reverence for the *ahl al-bayt* (the Prophet's family) was not exclusive to Shi'is but something that all Muslims had. In the same way, adhering to the *sunna* of the Prophet was not exclusive to Sunnis. To Qadhdhafi, it appeared that the only triumph the descendants of the Prophet achieved was the realisation of the Fatimid empire in North Africa and that, therefore, Fatimid Shi'ism was part of North African identity and culture. Qadhdhafi saw Egypt as the heart of the Fatimid caliphate that spearheaded a cultural dominance which that country had been enjoying ever since.[16] What was

Qadhdhafi's real agenda behind his seemingly pro-Fatimid rhetoric? His newly found Islamic ecumenism and the calling for a Fatimid revival, at least in spirit and in the name of Muslim unity, was intended in fact as an oblique derogatory comment against other Arab governments of his day, the Saudi one *in primis*.

By endorsing the Fatimids Qadhdhafi deliberately implied that the direct descendants of the Prophet had more right to rule than the Saudi royal family. In response to this provocation the Saudis resorted to condemning Qadhdhafi's praise of the Fatimids in local media with articles that ridiculed their era. The Permanent Committee for Scholarly Research and Deliverance of Formal Opinions, a Saudi official body of state-appointed religious scholars, attacked the Fatimids in a *fatwa* of 8 April 2007 which stated that '(Fatimid rulers) *were infidel, godless, depraved atheists who renounced Islam and believed in Zoroastrianism*'.[17] The *fatwa* alarmed the community of the Sulaymani Ismailis based in Najran, on the Saudi border with Yemen, who trace their historical religious roots to the Fatimids. To these Ismailis the *fatwa*, which rang as a deliberate insult, became a cause of alarm since it took aim at a period of Islamic history relevant to their identity. In turn it might have served the Saudi regime as an expedient pretext for their repression. In 2008 Human Rights Watch reported cases of Saudi abuses against members of the Ismaili community of Najran.[18] Religious scholars in Egypt, though Sunnis, reacted negatively to the *fatwa* which – as they saw it – debased an important chapter of their country's history.

In tandem with these disputes, varied examples of discourses emerging around the Fatimids may be found disseminating through and in the digital sphere. Digital cosmopolitanism can be described as a social world with an open horizon in which new cultural models take shape in encounters between the local and the global. Virtual expressions of cosmopolitan relations happen in technologically mediated networks of symbolic exchanges, communications and interactions across the internet. The internet opens up spaces for specific types of soft cultural cosmopolitan relationships found in expressions of curiosity and openness arising in the online consumption of other cultures as well as in greater self-reflection emerging out of discursive intercultural encounters. Like cosmopolitanism which has its roots in the communicative structures embedded in social interactions, virtual cosmopolitanism is contingent upon the socio-technological capabilities of the internet to mediate, reciprocate and bridge cross-cultural connections within and across national boundaries.

For this reason, the idea of virtual cosmopolitanism as being facilitated by mediated social spaces is framed by a debate on the explicit effects of the internet on shared social capital.[19]

These effects can be seen in the way the Fatimids have become a fixture of this social capital. For example, in one episode of the YouTube channel *Home Team History*, which on its Facebook page defines itself as a '*multimedia platform ... that incorporates African history into popular culture*', the Fatimids are capitalised upon as positive example from the past to inform Black history via the coverage of the 'Black' contingents of the Fatimid army. The topic is obviously treated in a selective, revisionist and apologetic manner to fit one core agenda: the recognition of the contribution of Black people to world history. To this end strategies include: the use of the term 'conscript' to avoid the slave/non-slave question relating to the specific status of the Black soldiers from specific ethnic backgrounds in the Fatimid army. In keeping with this approach, Arab sources are denounced for calling Black people in the service of the Fatimids both *Sudani* and *'abid* interchangeably thus perpetuating an understanding that a Black person was automatically understood to be a slave and 'different'. The division between the *Maghariba* (that is, the North African elements in the Fatimid army), the *Mashariqa* (the Eastern contingents) and the *Sudani* is challenged with the claim that all contained Black elements of sorts. Apologetically, the Black people acting for the Fatimid regime are described as loyal, as major players in Fatimid history and brilliant fighters against the Crusaders. Ultimately, it is concluded, that the Fatimids owed their success to Black soldiers, claimed here to have been the most numerous element in the Fatimid army. The Fatimids are here re-imagined, becoming a source of empowerment for the real public that is behind a virtually connected cosmopolitan Black community.[20]

Adding to this presence in the virtual world, is this rich repertoire of digital resources represented by online games, a domain that the Fatimids entered in the early 2000s.[21]

Sega-published Creative Assembly's 2006 *Medieval: Total War* (MTW) released *Medieval II* where the Fatimids made their major debut in the game world as a faction. Subsequently, in wishing to challenge the orientalist portrayal of Muslim Arabs as the ultimate enemies, Sid Meier injected inclusiveness and a more balanced portrayal of the Islamic past into his products in his *Civilization* game series (Firaxis Games).[22] Here the Fatimids can be played via modding (mod), the process through which players can alter aspects of the game to meet their own specifications and strategies. For example a mod focuses on the North African phase of the dynasty during the reigns of the Imam-caliphs al-Mahdi and al-Muʿizz. Another mod that features the Fatimids is *Abbasid, Fatimid & Almohad Caliphates* (2019) released by a third party as an add-on in Europa Universalis IV (EU4) published by Paradox Interactive. Beyond MIITW, *Civilization* and EU4, other game sets featuring the Fatimids are *Field of Glory II: Wolves at the Gates* (2019), *Field of Glory II: Medieval – Swords and Scimitars* (2021) and *VR Historical journey to the age of the Crusaders: Medieval Jerusalem, Saracen Cities, Arabic Culture, East Land* (2020). For all of these the historical context is that of the conflicts, rivalries and alliances between Byzantines, Crusaders and Muslims between 5th/11th and 7th/13th centuries. Differently contextualised in Paradox Development Studio's *Crusader Kings II: Monarch's Journey* the Fatimids are also represented via the Sulayhids, that is, a dynasty that acted as their vassals in Yemen in the 5th–6th/11th–12th centuries, with Queen Arwa (d. 532 /1138) modded into an avatar.

Conclusion

Within digital Islamic cosmopolitanism, discourses embedding the Fatimids have again been serving a variety of agendas. At one end of the spectrum, there is for example a Twelver Shiʿi preacher who, as part of an anti-Abbasid tirade in a YouTube video for the Muslim Youth Foundation, encourages young Shiʿis to look at the individuals serving the Fatimids as champions of a meritocratic regime and exhorts them to follow their example in scholarly endeavour and specialism.[23] At the opposite end, YouTube channels like *Come to Islam,* in exalting the Saljuqs and Salah al-Din as the champions of Sunni Islam, claim that the success of the Crusaders in 493/1099 in Jerusalem was due to a weakness caused by the betrayal of Islam on the part of the Fatimids, deemed worse than the Crusaders themselves.[24] By contrast, reflecting on the importance of transmitting the Fatimids' legacy to new generations through storytelling, the digital channel *The Ismaili TV* directs audiences to the Fatimids as beacons of tolerance, inclusivity, protecting their subjects, as well as being precursors of values and attitudes appropriate for the 20th and 21st centuries. Among these: the emphasis on the intellect as enabling a better understanding among people; the paramount importance they gave to knowledge, opening learning and debating.[25]

To what extent and in what way is the analysis of the use of 'The Fatimids' useful for the understanding of new/alternative expressions of cosmopolitanism? Digital media offer boundary-flexible immersive pedagogical opportunities that can be deployed to illuminate today's perspectives, uses and 'reconstruction' of the past, as well as attract new, diverse, pluralistic audiences to historical debates. To the digital cosmopolitans, digital media offer the opportunity to shift across diverse kinds of history and diverse societies for solace as much as for ideological reasons. Within an Islamic framework, we see that, as in the case of the Fatimids, digital media can offer the opportunity to undo a perception of Islamic history and doctrines as monolithic. These 'experiences' of the past can in turn have an impact on the present in a real way. On the one hand we witness an engagement with an Islamic dynasty and an age noted for tolerance, inclusivity, intellectualism, promotion of the arts and indeed cosmopolitanism. On the other this very engagement can lead to the perpetuation of stereotypes: the 'sect' factor; the 'mystery' around esoteric doctrines and secrecy; the trope of the 'mad caliph'; a perceived hedonistic lifestyle and resultant decadence. In digital games, warfare is the typical format used to re-enact medieval scenarios and in this the use of the Fatimids is no exception.[26] With that, through re-enactment, the memory of old rivalries and religion-inspired conflicts risk being perpetuated in order to be used as precedents to settle perceived old scores and unfinished business. The opportunities and challenges that digital media can offer as a tool at the service of historical research are now at the heart of what constitutes an established field of study. So far attention has been paid primarily to themes relating to medieval Europe. In challenging a cultural homogenisation that tends to subsume diverse cultures under a single dominant Western model, exploring the digital Fatimids offers an opportunity to represent Islamic history as integral part of a growing range of cosmopolitan possibilities that extend beyond the digital realm.

NOTES

* I am grateful to Dr Simonetta Calderini, University of Roehampton-London, and James Baillie, University of Wien, for their comments and suggestions.
1 In between these polarised positions, cosmopolitanism is used, for example, to indicate a utopian, universal community of world citizens. To navigate across the varied shades of cosmopolitanism and its applications in the political, economic and moral spheres see Maria Rovisco, and Magdalena Nowicka, ed., *The Ashgate Research Companion to Cosmopolitanism* (Farnham, 2011). In recent years the debates between those who

advocate and reject cosmopolitanism have resulted in the production of a vast body of literature. To name but few contributors see Kwame A. Appiah, *Cosmopolitanism: Ethics in a World of Strangers* (New York, 2006); Richard J. Arneson, 'Extreme Cosmopolitanisms Defended', *Critical Review of International Social and Political Philosophy*, 19 (2016), pp. 555–573; Tom Bailey, ed., *Contestatory Cosmopolitanism* (New York, 2017); Gillian Brock, 'Cosmopolitanism Versus Non-cosmopolitanism: The State of Play', *The Monist*, 94 (2011), pp. 455–465; Martha C. Nussbaum, *The Cosmopolitan Tradition: A Noble but Flawed Ideal* (Cambridge, 2019).

2 In recent years the relationship between Muslims, Islam and cosmopolitanism/s has been the subject of growing scrutiny. The academic literature is now abundant, with contributions from different perspectives and reflecting varied geographical realities. What follows is a small selection of these contributions, based on their closer relevance to this paper. For a brief critique of the Eurocentric understanding of cosmopolitanism and Muslim neo-liberal attitudes to it see Derryl N. MacLean, 'Introduction: Cosmopolitanisms in Muslim Contexts', in Derryl N. MacLean and Sikeena Karmali Ahmed, ed., *Cosmopolitanisms in Muslim Contexts, Perspectives from the Past* (Edinburgh, 2012), pp. 1–6. For a concise yet insightful discussion that engaged with recent scholarly debate reflecting the fluid meanings attached to the word 'cosmopolitanism' and its varied applications to an Islamic context see Mara A. Leichtman and Dorothea Schulz, 'Introduction to Special Issue: Muslim Cosmopolitanism: Movement, Identity, and Contemporary Reconfigurations', *City & Society*, 24 (2012), pp. 1–6. The polarisation of Islam vis-à-vis a positive or negative appraisal of cosmopolitanism with a focus on Muslim South East Asia is reflected in Khairudin Aljunied, ed., *Muslim Cosmopolitanism. South East Asian Islam in Comparative Perspective* (Edinburgh, 2017) and its counterpart Joshua Gedacht and R. Michael Feener, ed., *Challenging Cosmopolitanism. Coercion, Mobility and Displacement in Islamic Asia* (Edinburgh, 2020).

3 For a critical review of cosmopolitanism in Middle Eastern studies see Will Hanley, 'Grieving Cosmopolitanism in Middle East Studies', *History Compass*, 6 (2008), pp. 1346–1367. The myth of al-Andalus as positive role model of cosmopolitanism has been challenged in works by, among others, Kenneth Wolf, Maya Soifer Irish, Bruna Soravia and, above all, Eduardo Manzano Moreno.

4 For a critical overview of British-Ottoman trans-imperial cosmopolitanism, articulated as a cultural and civilisational view of a universalist Muslim public conduct based on consensus in matters of belief, ritual and form of devotion see Seema Alavi, *Muslim Cosmopolitanism in the Age of Empire* (Boston, 2015), pp. 1–31. On the nuanced nature of 'Ottoman cosmopolitanism' see Ulrike Freitag, '"Cosmopolitanism" and "Conviviality"? Some conceptual considerations concerning the late Ottoman Empire', *European Journal of Cultural Studies*, 17 (2013), pp. 375–391.

5 On the history of the museum, its implications for orientalist critique and 'cosmopolitisation' of its art collection with its conceptual transitioning from 'Arab' to 'Islamic' see Jean-Gabriel Leturcq, 'The Museum of Arab Art in Cairo (1869–2014): A Disoriented Heritage', in François Pouillion and Jean-Claude Vatin, ed., *After Orientalism, Critical Perspectives on Western Agency and Eastern Re-appropriations* (Leiden, 2015), vol. 2, pp. 145–161.

6 Max Herz, *Catalogue Sommaire des monuments exposés dans le musée national de l'Art arabe* (Cairo, 1895), English tr. *Catalogue of the National Museum of Arab Art* (London, 1896), pp. XXII–XXIV.

7 '*But the fatimids (sic) who overtook Egypt . . . introduced in the country . . . chiism. Yet the reign of this dynasty was rather a period of welfare, stability and religious forbearance*', Mohamed Mostapha, *The National Museum of Arab Art in Cairo* (Cairo, 1949), [p. 7].

8 The imperial European-Colonial and Ottoman convergences and the idea that they shaped Cairo as a constructed Mamluk medieval city are discussed in Paula Sanders,

Creating Medieval Cairo. Empire, Religion, and Architectural Preservation in Nineteenth-century Egypt (Cairo, 2008). Sanders' core arguments and methodological approach in this book have been reviewed by István Ormos in an article entitled 'The Comité de conservation des monuments de l'art arabe: Towards a Balanced Appraisal', *The Arabist: Budapest Studies in Arabic*, 40 (2019), pp. 47–140. I am grateful to Prof. Ormos for sharing his article with me and for his comments as well as suggestions.

9   See Alphonse Delort de Gléon, *L'Architecture arabe des khalifes d'Egypte à l'Exposition universelle de Paris en 1889: la rue du Caire* (Paris, 1889). Even when listing the sequence of Egypt's early Islamic ruling dynasties he says, *'Après Amrou, c'est Touloun, puis Saladin, Hakim, Beybars, Hassan, Barkouk, Kaïtbay, El-Achraf, etc., qui, les uns après les autres, rivaliseront de magnificence pour doter le Caire de monuments merveilleux'*, p. 5.

10 On all aspects relating to this show see the excellent István Ormos, *Cairo in Chicago. Cairo Street at the World's Columbian Exposition of 1893* (Cairo, 2021).

11 [Ministry of Culture of the of the Arab Republic of Egypt] *Colloque International sur l'Histoire du Caire, 27 mars-5 avril 1969*, ed. André Raymond, Magdi Wahba and Michael Rogers (Cairo, 1972). The only article in the collection specifically dedicated to the Fatimids is by Keppel A. Creswell (pp. 125–130) where the religious denomination that the Fatimids endorsed is not mentioned. In his contribution Bernard Lewis (1916–2018) speaks of the Fatimids in terms of their failures which merited them to be forgotten. The Ismaili character of the dynasty is discussed only at page 437 (of a total pp. 473) in an article by S. M. Stern (1920–1969) on Cairo as the centre of the Ismaili movement. For the speeches of Nasser and the Minister of Culture, (Tharwat Okasha), cf. pp. 15–18.

12 [Ministry of Culture of the of the Arab Republic of Egypt], *Cairo: The Life-Story of 1000 years* (Leipzig, 1969), pp. 17–20.

13 On the Fatimids' re-inscription into Cairo's landscape via the Bohra-led restoration programme and the controversies regarding the project's approach to conservation see Paula Sanders, 'Bohra Architecture and the Restoration of Fatimid Culture', in Marianne Barrucand, ed., *L'Egypte Fatimide: son art et son histoire* (Paris, 1999), pp. 159–165 and Sanders, *Creating Medieval Cairo*, pp. 115–142.

14 On the strategies adopted by the Bohras to affirm a uniform neo-Fatimid identity across communities see Olly Akkerman, 'The Bohras as Neo-Fatimids: Documentary Remains of a Fatimid Past in Gujarat', *Journal of Material Cultures in the Muslim World*, 1 (2020), pp. 291–313 and her *A Neo-Fatimid Treasury of Books. Arabic Manuscripts among the Alawi Bohras of South Asia* (Edinburgh, 2022).

15 On the scope and activities of AKDN see Daryoush Mohammad Poor, *Authority without Territory. The Aga Khan Development Network and the Ismaili imamate* (London, 2014). See also, F. Daftary, E. Fernea and A. Nanji, ed., *Living in Historic Cairo: Past and Present in an Islamic City* (London, 2010). On the Ismailis' cosmopolitan identity see Sara Shroff, *Muslim Movements Nurturing a Cosmopolitan Muslim Identity: The Ismaili and Gulen Movement* (sic, this refers to the wording used here. The author writes 'Movement' instead of 'Movements' as it should be) (MA, Georgetown University, 2009), pp. 20–62.

16 Muʿammar al-Qadhdhafi's pro-Fatimid statements received extensive press coverage worldwide. Media reports include Andrew Hammond, 'Arab history spat highlights Sunni-Shiʿite rift', *Reuters*, 14 May 2007; 'Gaddafi sees Muslims as Shiites "by default" Says Egypt Heart of Fatimid Culture', *al-Arabiyya News*, 11 October 2007, last accessed 13 June 2024 https://english.alarabiya.net/articles/2007%2F10%2F11%2F40254; Mshari Al-Zaydi, 'The Return of the Fatimids', *Asharq al-awsat*, 26 March 2009, https://eng-archive.aawsat.com/mshari-al-zaydi/opinion/the-return-of-the-fatimids, last accessed 13 June 2024. An extract from one of al-Qadhdhafi's speeches extolling the Fatimids is featured in 'Qaddafi's views on Fatimid state' posted in April 2019, available on YouTube at https://www.youtube.com/watch?v=tTPiNkpnZpE&t=53s (last visited 10 June 2022).

17 Cited in Andrew Hammond, 'Arab History'.
18 The Sulaymanis belong to the Tayyibi Musta'lian branch of Ismailism and, within it, to a group that emerged in the late 10th/16th century as an offshoot of the Bohras. They live predominantly in Yemen with a community based in Najran, a border district inside Saudi Arabia. Press coverage of their plight includes Robert F. Worth, 'Muslim Sect Sees Struggle Through Christian Lens', *The New York Times* (20 October 2010). https://www.nytimes.com/2010/10/21/world/middleeast/21saudi.html, last accessed 13 June 2024. The text of the 2008 HRW report is accessible at https://www.hrw.org/reports/2008/saudiarabia0908/saudiarabia0908web.pdf
19 Debates over the internet as space where cosmopolitanism can find both shape and expression occupy a growing field of academic research. Contributors include Edward Spence, 'Cosmopolitanism and the Internet', https://www.researchgate.net/publication/ 2535783_Cosmopolitanism_and_the_Internet, 2002 (last visited 10 June 2022); 'The Internet and Cosmopolitanism'. http://sro.sussex.ac.uk/id/eprint/81574/1/The%20Internet%20and%20Cosmopolitanism.pdf, pp. 1–13 The latter article provides a comprehensive survey on the state of study in the field up until around 2015. See also Marc Verboord, 'Internet Usage and Cosmopolitanism in Europe: a Multilevel Analysis', *Information, Communication & Society*, 20 (2017), pp. 460–481.
20 'Black Soldiers in the Fatimid Caliphate Military', *Home Team History*, https://www.youtube.com/watch?v=h_CM7ehKyiI, November 2020, (last visited 10 June 2022).
21 Within the growing field of 'Game studies' papers see Vít Šisler, 'Digital Arabs: Representation in Video Games', *European Journal of Cultural Studies*, 11 (2008), pp. 203–220. On the effects of negative representation of Muslims and Arabs in video games focused on contemporary themes, see Adhitya M. Maheswara, 'Representation of Middle Eastern Islamic Locality in Video Games', *IBDA Jurnal Kajian Islam dan Budaya*, 19 (2021), pp. 141–151.
22 See the *TopHat's Fatimid pack* (2018) produced by TopHatPaladin. For an appraisal of pros and cons of Sid Meier's *Civilization* see Šisler, 'Digital Arabs', p. 210.
23 Cf. for example the speech by Sayed Jawad Qazwini posted in February 2018 on https://www.youtube.com/watch?v=nHxoUx9AuKE (last visited 20 June 2022)
24 See for example https://www.youtube.com/watch?v=sSzb74iOZT8 posted in July 2018 (last visited 20 June 2022).
25 Launched in the spring of 2020 The Ismaili TV (https://tv.ismaili) is an online streaming platform delivering content 24/7 destined for the worldwide Ismaili community.
26 Cf. Šisler, 'Digital Arabs', p. 205.

3

Wladimir Ivanow and Fatimid Studies

Farhad Daftary

It is no exaggeration to say that Wladimir Ivanow ushered in modern scholarship in Ismaili and Fatimid studies almost single-handedly. In order to properly situate and evaluate Ivanow's contributions to these fields it is necessary to set Ismaili studies within their proper historical context.

The Ismailis, as well as the Ismaili Imams who ruled over a vast empire as Fatimid caliphs, were studied and judged almost exclusively on the basis of evidence collected, or often fabricated, by their adversaries. This is mainly because the vast literature produced by the Ismailis themselves, especially during the Fatimid period of their history (297–567/909–1171), was not accessible to outsiders, even if they so desired it to be. As a result, a variety of myths and misrepresentations were disseminated regarding Ismaili motives, teachings and practices. In fact, it was in the immediate aftermath of the foundation of the Fatimid caliphate in 297/909 that the Sunni establishment launched what amounted to an official anti-Ismaili and anti-Fatimid campaign. The overall aim of this prolonged literary campaign, fully supported by the Abbasid caliphs, was to discredit the entire Ismaili movement from its origins so that the Ismailis could be condemned readily as *malahida*, or heretics, who had deviated from the true religious path. Muslim theologians, jurists and heresiographers, as well as historians, participated variously in this campaign. In particular, Sunni polemicists fabricated the necessary evidence that would lend support to the condemnation of the Ismailis on specific doctrinal grounds, while also refuting the 'Alid genealogy of the Fatimid Imam-caliphs.

By spreading defamations as well as forged accounts of Ismaili teachings, the anti-Ismaili authors in fact produced in the course of the 4th/10th century a 'black legend'. Ismailism was now depicted as the arch-heresy (*ilhad*) of Islam, carefully designed by a certain 'Abd Allah b.

Maymun al-Qaddah,[1] or some other non-ʿAlid impostor, or possibly even a Jewish magician disguised as a Muslim, aiming to destroy Islam from within. By the 5th/11th century, this hostile fiction, with its elaborate details and stages of initiation, had been accepted as an accurate and reliable description of Ismaili-Fatimid motives, doctrines and practices, leading to further anti-Ismaili polemics and heresiographical accusations as well as intensifying the animosity of other Muslims towards the Ismailis and their Fatimid Imam-caliphs.

Many of the essential components of this anti-Ismaili 'black legend' may be traced to a certain Sunni polemicist known as Ibn Rizam who lived in Baghdad during the first half of the 4th/10th century. Ibn Rizam's polemical treatise has not survived, but it was extensively used by another anti-Ismaili polemicist, the Sharif Abu'l-Husayn Muhammad b. ʿAli, better known as Akhu Muhsin, who produced his own anti-Ismaili works. The tracts of Ibn Rizam and Akhu Muhsin have survived only fragmentarily in the writings of later historians.[2] The same 'black legend' served as the basis of the famous Baghdad manifesto issued in the time of the sixth Fatimid Imam-caliph, al-Hakim bi-Amr Allah (r. 386–411/996–1021), in 402/1011.[3] This declaration, sponsored by the reigning Abbasid caliph al-Qadir (r. 381–422/991–1031), was essentially a public refutation of the ʿAlid ancestry of the Fatimids. Be it as it may, this anti-Ismaili campaign, especially its depiction of ʿAbd Allah b. Maymun al-Qaddah as the founder of Ismailism and the progenitor of the Fatimid Imam-caliphs, became astonishingly successful throughout the Islamic world until the breakthrough in modern Ismaili studies.

The orientalists of the 19th century, led by Silvestre de Sacy (1758–1838), began their more scholarly study of Islam in general, and to some extent the Ismailis and the Fatimids, on the basis of the textual sources of the Muslims themselves, including especially the Arabic manuscripts acquired by various major European libraries. As these manuscripts had been written mostly by Sunni authors, the orientalists, too, studied Islam and its subdivisions according to Sunni perspectives and treated Shiʿi Islam in general as the 'heterodox' interpretation of Islam. With his lifelong interest in the Druze religion, de Sacy also concerned himself with the early history of the Ismailis and the Fatimids, without access to any Ismaili texts. In his major work on the Druzes,[4] he devoted a long introduction to the origins and early history of the Ismailis and the rise of the Fatimids. There, de Sacy based himself exclusively on the anti-Ismaili polemical accounts of Ibn Rizam and Akhu Muhsin, as preserved especially by the historian al-Nuwayri (d. 732/1332). Therefore, he unwittingly endorsed their malicious views and presented the controversial ʿAbd Allah b. Maymun al-Qaddah as the real founder of Ismailism and the non-ʿAlid ancestor of the Fatimids.

De Sacy's distorted evaluation of the Ismailis and the Fatimids established the frame within which other orientalists studied the medieval history of the Ismailis. It was within such a context that Étienne M. Quatremère (1782–1857), one of the most learned orientalists of the period, produced a number of historical studies on the Fatimids.[5] There also appeared for the first time a history of the Fatimids by Ferdinand Wüstenfeld (1808–1899), which was a compilation from a range of Arabic chronicles without any extracts from Ismaili sources.[6] The unsatisfactory state of the field of Fatimid studies is clearly attested to by the fact that the next Western monograph on the Fatimids, written some four decades later by De Lacy Evans O'Leary (1872–1957) of Bristol University, still did not cite any Ismaili sources.[7] It was under such circumstances that Wladimir Ivanov emerged on the scene and made major contributions to the field.

The modern progress in Ismaili studies was made possible by the recovery and study of a large number of Ismaili manuscript sources. The Ismailis produced a diversified and rich literature, especially during the Fatimid period of their history. These texts were guarded secretly in numerous collections in Yemen, Syria, Persia, Central Asia and India. Already in the 19th century, a few of these textual sources had surfaced in Syria and were sent to Paris, the capital of Orientalism, and more such resources were recovered in the opening decades of the 20th century from Yemen and Central Asia. However, all these early finds were few and far in between. This situation changed drastically in the 1930s, however, mainly through the efforts of Ivanow and a few Ismaili Bohra scholars.

Ivanow was born in 1886 in St Petersburg.[8] He studied Arabic and Persian as well as Islamic and Central Asian history with eminent Russian scholars, such as V. V. Barthold (1869–1930), graduating in 1911 from the Faculty of Oriental Languages of St Petersburg University. In 1915, he joined the Asiatic Museum of the Russian Academy of Sciences as an assistant keeper of oriental manuscripts. Described as 'a fanatical lover of manuscripts',[9] he collected over a thousand Arabic and Persian manuscripts from Central Asia for the Asiatic Museum. It was, indeed, Ivanow's lifelong interest in Islamic manuscripts that equipped him for his subsequent pioneering work in Ismaili studies.

It was also at the Asiatic Museum that Ivanow had his first contact with Ismaili literature. There, he catalogued a small collection of Ismaili manuscripts acquired for the Asiatic Museum by I. I. Zarubin (1887–1964),[10] the renowned Russian scholar of Iranian languages and ethnology. In 1918, Ivanow was once again sent to Central Asia to collect more manuscripts for the Asiatic Museum's so-called Bukharan Collection. He would never return to St Petersburg in the aftermath of the unsettled conditions of the Russian Revolution. Subsequently, after a brief stay in Persia, Ivanow found himself in India. Initially, he spent several years in Calcutta, where he catalogued (in four volumes) the extensive collections of the Persian manuscripts held in the Asiatic Society of Bengal's Library. In 1930, Ivanow relocated to Bombay, signalling a new phase in his life and academic career, now devoted exclusively to Ismaili and Fatimid studies.

Meanwhile, Ivanow had established friendly relations with some members of the Nizari Khoja Ismaili community of Bombay, who would introduce him to their Imam, Sultan Muhammad Shah Aga Khan III (1877–1957). In 1931, the Ismaili Imam formally commissioned Ivanow to study the literature, history and intellectual contributions of the Ismailis. Henceforth, Ivanow readily found access to the private collections of Ismaili manuscripts held in various localities. He indefatigably recovered these rare sources, made them available to other scholars, while engaged in his own research and publications on various aspects of Ismailism, including its Fatimid phase. At the same time, Ivanow established scholarly contacts with three Tayyibi Ismaili Bohra scholars, Asaf A. A. Fyzee, Husayn al-Hamdani and Zahid 'Ali, who were in possession of significant collections of Ismaili manuscripts and who made these resources available to Ivanow and other scholars.

Asaf A. A. Fyzee (1899–1981), in fact, made modern scholars aware of the foundation of an independent school of Ismaili jurisprudence, which had been established during the Fatimid period mainly through the efforts of al-Qadi al-Nu'man (d. 363/974). Zahid 'Ali (1888–1958) would produce, on the basis of a variety of Ismaili sources, the first scholarly book on Fatimid history, written in Urdu;[11] while Husayn al-Hamdani (1901–1962) shared his family's collection of manuscripts with numerous libraries, and scholars such as Paul Kraus (1908–1961). It was, indeed, through the pioneering efforts of Ivanow and the above-mentioned small group of Bohra scholars, all educated in England, that modern scholarship in Ismaili studies had commenced in the 1930s in India.

Henceforth, through a vast network of Ismaili friends and connections, Ivanow began to identify a large number of Ismaili texts, which he described in the first catalogue of its kind published in 1933.[12] This catalogue, citing some 700 separate titles, attested to the hitherto unknown rich and diversified nature of Ismaili literature and intellectual traditions. This catalogue also enumerated the works of the renowned da'is of the Fatimid period who were at the same time the scholars and authors of their community, notably Abu Hatim al-Razi (d. 322/937), Ja'far b. Mansur al-Yaman (d. ca. 346/957), Abu Ya'qub al-Sijistani (d. after 361/971), al-Qadi al-Nu'man (d. 363/974), Hamid al-Din al-Kirmani (d. after 411/1020), al-Mu'ayyad fi'l-Din al-Shirazi (d. 470/1078) and Nasir-i Khusraw (d. after 462/1070).[13] The initiation of modern scholarship in Ismaili studies, including Fatimid studies, may in fact be traced to the appearance of this very catalogue, which provided for the first time a scientific framework for research in this new field of Islamic studies. By 1963, when he published an expanded edition of his Ismaili catalogue,[14] Ivanow had identified a few hundred more titles, while the field of Ismaili studies as a whole had witnessed nothing less than a revolution, thanks largely to his own efforts. Numerous Ismaili texts of the Fatimid and other periods in Ismaili history had now begun to be critically edited, preparing the ground for further scholarship.

The bulk of Ivanow's own research and publications were related to the Nizari branch of Ismailism. As is known, the literary heritage of the Nizaris, outside Syria and as preserved by the Persian-speaking Nizaris of Persia, Afghanistan and Central Asia, was written entirely in the Persian language. However, from early on, Ivanow also concerned himself with the Fatimids and the Ismaili texts of the Fatimid period. As the earliest fruits of such efforts, we may cite two highly important Arabic texts related to the Fatimids, viz., the *Istitar al-Imam* and the *Sira* of al-Hajib Ja'far b. 'Ali.[15]

An important early historical source authorised by the Fatimids themselves, the *Istitar al-Imam*, written by the da'i Ahmad b. Ibrahim al-Nisaburi (d. after 386/996), deals with the settlement of the early Ismaili Imam 'Abd Allah in Salamiyya, and the eventful journey of 'Abd Allah al-Mahdi, the future founder of the Fatimid caliphate, from Syria to North Africa. The *Sira*, containing the autobiography of Ja'far b. 'Ali, chamberlain to the Fatimid Imam-caliph 'Abd Allah al-Mahdi (d. 322/934), was compiled later by a certain Muhammad b. Muhammad al-Yamani. Born in 260/874, Ja'far b. 'Ali had accompanied al-Mahdi on his fateful journey from Salamiyya to Qayrawan (289–297/902–909), where he was installed to the Fatimid caliphate.

Subsequently, Ivanow published an important article on the organisation of the Ismaili *da'wa* under the Fatimids,[16] followed by his major work on the Fatimids, comprised of a historical study as well as editions and translations of numerous extracts of the Ismaili texts related to the Fatimids.[17] Here, Ivanow also attempted a preliminary deconstruction of what he called the myth of 'Abd Allah b. Maymun al-Qaddah,[18] to which he subsequently devoted a full monograph. This book represented the first effort by a Western scholar to study the Fatimids on the basis of Ismaili sources.

While continuing with his systematic efforts to recover Ismaili manuscripts and study them, Ivanow correctly identified the need for institutional resources and support. In this context, he was instrumental in founding in 1946 the Ismaili Society of Bombay, under the patronage of Aga Khan III and with Ivanow himself as the editor of the Society's various series of publications. It was also through his efforts that the Ismaili Society came to possess an important library of manuscripts. The Ismaili Society's series of publications were launched by a monograph by Ivanow, which contained substantial evidence for deconstructing and dissipating the myth of 'Abd Allah b. Maymun al-Qaddah as the founder of Ismailism and ancestor of the Fatimid Imam-caliphs.[19] This book also showed, once and for all, the reasons as to why the Sunni polemicists had chosen this non-'Alid figure for the fictitious role assigned to him.

As noted, Ivanow generously shared his knowledge as well as the manuscript resources of the Ismaili Society with other scholars. In particular, he established a very close working relationship with the French Islamicist Henry Corbin (1903–1978). As revealed in the correspondence between these two scholars,[20] Ivanow readily prepared (hand-written) copies of the manuscripts at his disposal and sent them to Corbin, who launched his own 'Bibliothèque Iranienne' series of publications in which several Ismaili texts appeared simultaneously in Tehran and Paris.[21] Corbin then represented a new generation of scholars interested in Ismaili-Fatimid studies. Another early member of this generation was the Egyptian scholar Muhammad Kamil Husayn (1901–1961), who edited several Ismaili texts of the Fatimid period in his own 'Silsilat Makhtutat al-Fatimiyyin' series, published in Cairo. Through Ivanow's efforts, Professor M. Kamil Husayn edited for the first time the *da'i* al-Kirmani's major theological-philosophical work, *Rahat al-'aql*, which appeared in both the Ismaili Society's series and Husayn's own series.[22] This was one of the most significant Ismaili texts of the Fatimid period, belonging to the so-called Persian school of philosophical theology in Ismailism, or philosophical Ismailism.

Ivanow was, in fact, the earliest scholar of Ismaili studies to have identified the distinctive Persian school of Ismailism, influenced extensively by various philosophical traditions, that came into being during the Fatimid times.[23] He also presented aspects of a long drawn-out theological debate among some of the earliest members of this Persian school, notably Muhammad b. Ahmad al-Nasafi (d. 332/943), who introduced philosophical thought into Ismailism, Abu Hatim al-Razi and Abu Yaʿqub al-Sijistani, with al-Kirmani acting as an arbiter of their views more than a century later from the standpoint of the Fatimid daʿwa. These daʿis of the Iranian lands elaborated complex metaphysical systems of thought with a distinct Neoplatonised emanational cosmology, representing the earliest tradition of philosophical theology in Shiʿi Islam.[24]

In fact, Ivanow devoted some of his early research to Nasir-i Khusraw (d. after 462/1070), the last great member of this Persian school propounding philosophical Ismailism. He published the first monograph in English on this Fatimid daʿi, traveller and philosopher.[25] Nasir-i Khusraw is also one of the greatest poets of the Persian language. He was in fact the only daʿi of the Fatimids who wrote all of his works in Persian. Subsequently, Ivanow edited, with an English translation, Nasir's *Shish fasl* (Six Chapters), published for the first time in the Ismaili Society's series.[26] He also facilitated the publication of Nasir-i Khusraw's *Gusha'ish va raha'ish*, on the basis of a single manuscript located in a private collection in Tehran.[27]

Ivanow's early studies culminated in what was effectively the first modern survey of Ismaili history in terms of its main phases – a categorisation instituted by Ivanow himself and henceforth adopted by other scholars.[28] In this monograph, the Fatimid period was treated as one of the main phases of Ismaili history. Here, Ivanow also covered briefly but rather comprehensively, aspects of Ismaili teachings under the Fatimids, when Ismailism found its greatest and most lasting success outside the domains of the Fatimid Ismaili state, notably in Yemen, Syria, Persia and Central Asia.

By the 1960s, Ivanow had produced an incredible body of work, comprised of studies, editions of Ismaili texts, their English translations, and pioneering research in several aspects of Ismaili studies.[29] It is no exaggeration to state that in no other field of Islamic studies has the work of a single individual been as pathbreaking as that of Ivanow in modern Ismaili studies. As Asaf Fyzee, his associate of four decades, observed, Ivanow's work will endure and constitute the basis in almost every aspect of Ismaili studies.[30] Wladimir Ivanow died in 1970 in Tehran, where he had spent the last decade of his life. Doubtless, Ivanow stands as one of the key founders of modern scholarship in Ismaili-Fatimid studies.

NOTES

1 F. Daftary, "Abd Allah b. Maymun al-Qaddah', *EIs*, vol. 1, pp. 369–370.
2 See especially, Shihab al-Din Ahmad b. ʿAbd al-Wahhab al-Nuwayri, *Nihayat al-arab fi funun al-adab*, vol. 25, ed. M. J. al-ʿAl al-Hini (Cairo, 1984), pp. 187–317; Abu Bakr ʿAbd Allah b. al-Dawadari, *Kanz al-durar wa-jamiʿ al-ghurar*, vol. 6, ed. S. al-Munajjid (Cairo, 1961), pp. 6–21, 44–156; Taqi al-Din Ahmad b. ʿAli al-Maqrizi, *Ittiʿaz al-hunafaʾ bi-akhbar al-aʾimma al-Fatimiyyin al-khulafaʾ*, ed. J. al-Shayyal (Cairo, 1967), vol. 1, pp. 22–29, 151–202; ed. Ayman F. Sayyid (Damascus, 2010), pp. 20–29, 173–230; partial English tr., *Towards a Shiʿi Mediterranean Empire: Fatimid Egypt and the Founding of Cairo*, tr. Shainool Jiwa (London, 2009), pp. 122–180.
3 The text and list of the signatories of this manifesto may be found in Ibn al-Jawzi, *al-Muntazam*, ed. F. Krenkow (Hyderabad, 1357–1362/1938–1943), vol. 7, p. 255; Ibn Khaldun, *The Muqaddimah*, tr. F. Rosenthal (2nd ed., Princeton, 1967), vol. 1, pp. 45–46; Ibn Taghribirdi, *al-Nujum al-zahira fi muluk Misr waʾl-Qahira* (Cairo, 1348–1392/ 1929–1972), vol. 4, pp. 229–231.
4 See A. I. Silvestre de Sacy, *Exposé de la religion des Druzes* (Paris, 1838), vol. 1, introduction, pp. 20–246.
5 See F. Daftary, *Ismaili Literature: A Bibliography of Sources and Studies* (London, 2004), pp. 369–370.
6 F. Wüstenfeld, *Geschichte der Fatimiden Chalifen nach den Arabischen Quellen*, in *Abhandlungen der königlichen Gesellschaft der Wissenschaften zu Göttingen, Historisch-philologische Classe*, 26, Band 3 (1880), pp. 1–97; 27, Band 1 (1881), pp. 1–130; 27, Band 3 (1881), pp. 1–126; published separately (Göttingen, 1881; reprinted, Hildesheim and New York, 1976).
7 De Lacy E. O'Leary, *A Short History of the Fatimid Khalifate* (London, 1923; repr., Delhi, 1987). See also Paul E. Walker, *Exploring an Islamic Empire: Fatimid History and its Sources* (London, 2002), pp. 189 ff.
8 For Ivanow's biographies, see W. Ivanow, *Fifty Years in the East: The Memoirs of Wladimir Ivanow*, ed. F. Daftary (London, 2015), pp. 39–96; F. Daftary, 'Ivanow, Vladimir Alekseevich', *EIr*, vol. 14, pp. 298–300.
9 I. Iu. Krachkovskii, *Among Arabic Manuscripts: Memoirs of Libraries and Men*, tr. T. Minorksky (Leiden, 1953), p. 68.
10 V. A. Ivanov, 'Ismailitskie rukopisi Aziatskogo Muzeya. Sobranie I. Zarubina, 1916 g.', *Bulletin de l'Académie Impériale des Sciences de Russie*, série 6, 11 (1917), pp. 359–386.
11 Zahid ʿAli, *Tarikh-i Fatimiyyin-i Misr* (Hyderabad, 1367/1948; reprinted, Karachi, 1963).
12 W. Ivanow, *A Guide to Ismaili Literature* (London, 1933).
13 Ibid., pp. 33–50, 89–93.
14 W. Ivanow, *Ismaili Literature: A Bibliographical Survey* (Tehran, 1963), pp. 23–50, 159–162, citing the literature of the Fatimid period.
15 Ahmad b. Ibrahim al-Nisaburi, *Istitar al-Imam*, and Muhammad b. Muhammad al-Yamani, *Sirat Jaʿfar b. ʿAli al-hajib* under the title of *Mudhakkirat fi harakat al-Mahdi*

al-Fatimi, edited by W. Ivanow, in *Majallat Kulliyyat al-Adab, al-Jami'a al-Misriyya/ Bulletin of the Faculty of Arts*, University of Egypt, 4, part 2 (1936), pp. 89–133.

16 W. Ivanow, 'The Organization of the Fatimid Propaganda', *Journal of the Bombay Branch of the Royal Asiatic Society*, New Series, 15 (1939), pp. 1–35; reprinted in Bryan S. Turner, ed., *Orientalism: Early Sources*, Volume I, *Readings in Orientalism* (London, 2000), pp. 531–571.

17 W. Ivanow, *Ismaili Tradition Concerning the Rise of the Fatimids* (Bombay, 1942). This book, as well as several other early works of Ivanow, all appeared in the series of publications of the Islamic Research Association founded in Bombay in 1933, through the efforts of Ivanow himself.

18 Ibid., pp. 127–156.

19 W. Ivanow, *The Alleged Founder of Ismailism* (Bombay, 1946). He later published a revised edition of this work under the title of *Ibn al-Qaddah (The Alleged Founder of Ismailism)* (Bombay, 1957).

20 See S. Schmidtke, ed., *Correspondance Corbin – Ivanow. Lettres échangées entre Henry Corbin et Vladimir Ivanow de 1947 à 1966* (Paris and Louvain, 1999).

21 See Daniel de Smet, 'Henry Corbin et études Ismaéliennes', in M. A. Amir-Moezzi et al., ed., *Henry Corbin, philosophies et sagesses des religions du livre* (Turnhout, 2005), pp. 105–118; D. Shayegan, 'Corbin, Henry', *EIr*, vol. 6, pp. 268–272.

22 Hamid al-Din al-Kirmani, *Rahat al-'aql*, ed. M. Kamil Husayn and M. M. Hilmi (Leiden and Cairo, 1953). See also F. Daftary, 'Hamid-al-Din Kermani', *EIr*, vol. 11, pp. 639–641.

23 W. Ivanow, *Studies in Early Persian Ismailism* (Leiden, 1948), especially pp. 115–180.

24 See Paul E. Walker, *Early Philosophical Shiism: The Ismaili Neoplatonism of Abu Ya'qub al-Sijistani* (Cambridge, 1993).

25 W. Ivanow, *Nasir-i Khusraw and Ismailism* (Bombay, 1948). The Russian scholar Andrey E. Bertel's produced the next monograph in Russian on the same subject, and using the same title; see his *Nasir-i Khosrov i ismailizm* (Moscow, 1959). See also S. Niyozov, 'A Comparative Analysis of W. Ivanow's and A. Bertel's works on Nasir-i Khusraw and Ismailism: Toward Rethinking Central-Asian Ismaili Studies', in S. Prozorov and H. Elnazarov, ed., *Russkie uchënye ob ismailizme/Russian Scholars on Ismailism* (St Petersburg, 2014), pp. 160–208.

26 Nasir-i Khusraw, *Shish fasl, ya Rawshana'i-nama-yi nathr*, ed. and English tr. W. Ivanow (Leiden, 1949).

27 Nasir-i Khusraw, *Gusha'ish va raha'ish*, ed. Sa'id Nafisi (Leiden 1950; 2nd ed., Tehran, 1961). The same text was edited and translated into English by F. M. Hunzai, with an introduction and commentary by Parviz Morewedge, as *Knowledge and Liberation: A Treatise on Philosophical Theology* (London, 1998).

28 W. Ivanow, *A Brief Survey of the Evolution of Ismailism* (Leiden, 1952), especially pp. 28–30.

29 For details, see F. Daftary, 'Bibliography of the Works of Wladimir Ivanow', in Ivanow, *Fifty Years in the East*, pp. 185–207. See also D. Dagiev, *Central Asian Ismailis: An Annotated Bibliography of Russian, Tajik and Other Sources* (London, 2022), pp. 175–181.

30 A. A. A. Fyzee, 'Wladimir Ivanow (1886–1970', *Journal of the Asiatic Society of Bombay*, New Series, 45–46 (1970–1971), p. 93.

4

The Untold Problem of Ibn al-Haytham's Scientific Legacy in Islamic Art History

Valérie Gonzalez

Ibn al-Haytham's Scientific Legacy

Al-Hasan b. al-Haytham (354–430/965–1040) was a scientific luminary of Fatimid culture whose work irradiated throughout Islam and beyond. His treatise *Kitab al-Manazir* (Book of Optics), which famously advanced both the physiology and phenomenology of vision, resonated beyond these domains in the sphere of art.[1] As is well known, Renaissance Italy engaged in a re-positioning of the ontotheological role of man in Christian metaphysics, in which Ibn al-Haytham's optics were instrumentalised in order to create figurative representations imitating the the various forms of the appearance of nature as the eye perceives them. Thus was born the so-called 'scientific linear perspective', becoming the conceptual and stylistic canon of Western art until its de-mythification in the 19th century. Due to this momentous transcultural collusion between art and science which it occasioned in global cultural history, Ibn al-Haytham's legacy has received a great deal of attention from both scientific and art historical experts. However, the reference to this legacy in art history has not been without pitfalls. The present essay endeavours to discuss these pitfalls.

Decolonising the Art Historical View of Ibn al-Haytham's Optics

Addressing the question of Ibn al-Haytham's scientific impact on visual culture in the medieval and early Modern period presents the risk of reinvigorating a bygone, albeit lingering, Eurocentric epistemology. The reason for this lies in the historical connection of Arab science to Renaissance art and aesthetics, which constitutes the very foundations of this epistemology. To recall the latter, until postcolonialism linear perspective and mimesis or the lack of thereof formed unchallenged criteria for interpreting and appraising both Western and non-Western art, without properly heeding the fact of cultural difference. If, in theory, postcolonialism led to the discarding of the imperialist values of this normativity, in practice its conceptual parameters continue to guide area studies. Non-Western art historical narratives, such as those on painting and portraiture in Islam, all too often revolve around the measurement of the perspectival or mimetic level an artwork may present.[2] Equally affected by symptoms of Eurocentricity, the approach to the said question of Ibn al-Haytham's legacy in these narratives calls for decolonisation.

Eurocentric symptoms manifest themselves through two main epistemic attitudes. The first consists in seeking to explain why Florentine artists built upon Ibn al-Haytham's scientific oeuvre to construct their own aesthetic system while their Muslim counterparts, although the owners of this oeuvre, did not do so, neither in the Middle Ages nor the early Modern period. In thus problematising comparatively the issue of the impact of Ibn Haytham's discoveries in the creative domain scholars have perpetuated, as we shall see, an imbalanced epistemology that is detrimental to Islam.

The second attitude is the uncritical presupposing that the Kitab al-Manazir reflects or is evidence of the Islamic modes of art-making and seeing as culturally determined features of Islamic aesthetics. In practice, scholars exhibiting this attitude have at all costs sought to establish links between Ibn al-Haytham's discoveries and Islamic visuality.[3] In particular, they make use of his aesthetic proto-phenomenology without reflecting on the nature and workings of the phenomenological method themselves, and by extension, without envisaging the very possibility of the invalidity of their presupposition. Such a possibility is in fact unthinkable for this scholarship because its tenets adhere to a reductive conception of the concept of aesthetics itself. According to this conception, in any culture texts with an aesthetic content necessarily converge with that culture's approach to plastic expression. But although in Renaissance Italy theoretical and applied aesthetics collided, in other global contexts historic or contemporary, like pre-modern Islam, aesthetic theories may mostly remain at the abstract level of philosophical ideas about the senses and the material world, with seldom repercussions in artistic practice.[4] This second attitude consequently betrays an overreliance on the Renaissance aesthetic model, which translates itself into a compensatory desire to seek some form of influence of Ibn al-Haytham's findings on Islamic visual-artistic culture equivalent to that which they acquired in medieval Florence. A deconstruction of these two attitudes aims to expose the deficiencies of this Eurocentric understanding of the effect of Ibn al-Haytham scientific phenomenon within the framework of the art world.

Eurocentrism Manifest: Epistemic Creation of an Islamic Non-Event

Contrasting the Renaissance's creative appropriation of Ibn al-Haytham's optics with the non-existence of an analogous event in Islam somehow implies a thought along these lines: 'Western culture accomplished something that Muslim culture did not', and 'unlike the Christians who seized upon the opportunity of exploiting Ibn al-Haytham's great discoveries, Muslims somehow missed it'. Was something amiss in the Muslim world? Scholars have been struggling with this unsettling question, whereas the true issue resides in the contrasting manner of problematising the artistic impact of these discoveries which raises the question in the first place. This problematisation indeed engenders what I call 'an Islamic non-event', which interestingly resonates with the Freudian theory of the penis envy similarly premised upon a fabricated absence as a result of a biased correlativity.[5] A look at an article that Gülru Necipoğlu wrote in 2015 in response to Hans Belting's comparative study of Islamic and Renaissance aesthetics in his widely read book, *Florence and Baghdad*, supports the approach of this problematic view.[6]

In her essay, Necipoğlu writes: 'I, too, have interpreted the nonperspectival mode of geometric construction codified in the Topkapi Scroll ...'[7] Here the non-event emerges from the use of this term 'nonperspectival' to describe the *ghiri* design, a geometric form of patterned art unrelated to figural representation about which, consequently, it makes no sense to evoke perspective. This terminological misuse is actually caused by an uncritical submission to the untenable correlation between Islamic and Christian European art that imposes the presence or absence of perspective and representation as the supreme condition of making art. Considering the basic semantics of the notion of absence, which signifies the lack of some element that should be present, describing the *ghiri* as a non-perspectival design codified on a given material posits perspective and representation as criteria against which this design would have been constructed. These criteria having no relevance and being non-existent in the making of geometric art in Islam, which constitutes a totally autonomous plastic expression functioning according to mathematical rules, the idea of the lack or absence of perspective created by their discreditation in the artistic conceptualisation of the *ghiri* repertoire is therefore baseless. In other words, because this absence of perspective cannot be a missing presence of perspective, it is a false absence, namely a non-event. The same reasoning would apply to a description of the Renaissance naturalistic figuration as a 'non-abstract' or 'non-geometric' art form. Significantly, such a description has never been produced, has it?

Clearly, the contrasting correlation responsible for the creation of non-evental Islamic aesthetics in the discussion of Ibn al-Haytham's impact on the art world appears not only illogical, but also Eurocentric in more ways than one.[8] First, it inequitably foregrounds the Western order of artistic evolution marked by the momentous invention of perspective, overshadowing in the process the conception of this order by Muslims which is marked by their own creative breakthroughs.[9] Second, this foregrounding entails another less obvious, albeit no less Eurocentric, superimposition on Islam of another pattern typical of the Renaissance cultural-artistic order, namely that of the agency of the artist of genius. This requires some explanation.

Due to the pivotal role of the *Kitab al-Manazir* in its art, Renaissance Europe gave Ibn al-Haytham a special epistemic status close to that of intracultural intellectual figures like Leon Battista Alberti or Pico della Mirandola, despite the fact that the former and the latter lived centuries apart in different historical-religious contexts. This status is precisely the product of the system of individual agency revolving around the artist of genius at the origins of the Renaissance cultural-artistic construct. Artists past and present thus characterised make, to a certain extent, their own aesthetic decisions and personally choose their own source material, be it of philosophical, religious, poetic, scientific or other order.[10] Therefore, in global cultures shaped by this model of agency, inventions and breakthroughs are attributed to persons or identified groups of people such as, say, the pictorial technique of sfumato attributed to Leonardo da Vinci, the inner self-expression to the Chinese literati painters or the ready-made to Marcel Duchamp. However, this individual-based organisational system clashes with the artistic-cultural ordering of Ibn al-Haytham's medieval milieu built upon the opposite model of collective agency. Following the latter, the artist of genius is the collective body. Equally present in historic and contemporary cultures such as the traditional Oceanian and pre-Columbian civilisations, collective agency produces creative forces, movements and currents that overpower individual agency and own the cultural-artistic construct. Although in any society practitioners of art who are geniuses exist and work in the fullness of their individual abilities, this logic of creativity nevertheless signifies that they mainly operate according to rules of practice and aesthetic values that have been established by the collective body. For this reason, one cannot identify an individual or group of individuals behind the invention of, say, the medieval Islamic art of carved stucco or *muqarnas* designs, just as one cannot detect any historical initiative that would have made the *Book Optics* the chosen source of ideas for an identifiable artist or circle of artists in a particular Muslim polity.

This promulgation of the Renaissance order of things at the expense of its Muslim counterpart de-legitimises the problematisation of Ibn al-Haytham's legacy under scrutiny. This means that, to become legitimate, this problematisation must be re-formulated in new decolonised terms. Yet, this requirement comes up against a seemingly unbreakable epistemic circularity that paradoxically provides the problematisation with some legitimacy, given that Ibn al-Haytham's scientific presence in the intellectual background of both Islam and Renaissance Europe invites one to look at the presence of his cultural role in both contexts. What, without this presence, would otherwise be the point of drawing parallels between the birth of Renaissance perspective and the rise of Islamic pattern art which is older by several centuries? In aesthetic terms, these two phenomena separated by time and space have nothing in common. How then to break this circularity at the source of the problematisation's Eurocentricity?

The solution is plainly the elimination of the contrasting evental/non-evental view as the problematisation's premise, and the re-centring of the inquiry on the unsolved question of the agency of Ibn al-Haytham's legacy in the formation of Islamic artistic visuality. By thus getting the Muslim part of the story out this blank zone in which this view plunges it, the Renaissance invention of linear perspective itself recovers its proper place in the trans-spatiotemporal history of Ibn al-Haytham's scientific findings, precisely as a later historical event with absolutely no relation to the latter's fate in Islamic culture. Thus, not only the fallacious Islamic non-event disappears, but also the unsolved question finally comes into sharp focus. The state of affairs in the studies concerning this question is now to be examined, beginning with Hans Belting's application of the concept of the symbolic form to Islamic visual aesthetics in *Florence and Baghdad*.

Application to Islam of the Symbolic Form as a Structuring / Structuralist Cultural Model

A reputed expert in Western art, Belting offers an unprecedented reflection on the sciences and the arts in Islam, but it does so in the comparativist framework just discussed. One of his directions of thought attempts to discover Islamic symbolic forms that would equate in significance to Renaissance perspectival mimesis. Purposely echoing Panosky's famous aphorism of the 'perspective as symbolic form' in Western art, Belting thus discerns in the *mashrabiyya* and *muqarnas* two such forms of central significance in Islam.[11] (figures II.4.1 & II.4.2) However, one may challenge this quest for symbolic equivalents between early Modern European and traditional Islamic art in the first place. Does not the very idea that a particular aesthetic-metaphysical symbol may characterise Islamic visuality subliminally reinforce another typical Eurocentric mode of culture structuring? If we think of the history of symbolisation, we are brought back to the foundations of European aesthetic classicism since the Renaissance, when perspective became the visual mark of the way the Western world identifies itself, that is the symbolic expression born out of

Figure II.4.1 Detail of a *pishtaq*'s *muqarnas* decoration in the complex of Shaykh Tayfur Abu Yazid al-Bistami. Bastam, Iran, 6th–8th/ 12th–14th century. Carved stucco.

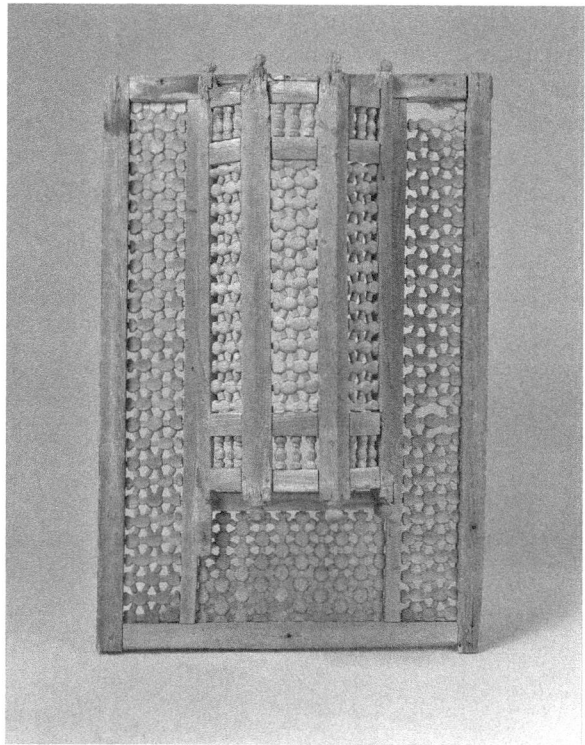

Figure II.4.2 *Mashrabiyya* screen. Egypt, 18th–19th century. Metropolitan Museum of Art, New York.

conscious acts of autoreferentiality and self-representation.[12] It is this Western history of the concept of perspective as a symbolic form that flags up the potential Eurocentricity of its use as a critical model in a non-Western context.[13]

In his enterprise of seeking to symbolise Islamic visual culture, Belting does not determine his choice of Islamic symbolic forms on the basis of the identification of Islamic autoreferential acts. His choice of the *mashrabiyya* and *muqarnas* is the product of his own assessment, meaning *he sees* in these motifs Islamic symbolic forms par excellence. Even though this assessment allows him to highlight some of the chief aspects of Islamic visuality, the fact is that he projects onto the latter an external reorganising Europeanising *regard* with, unavoidably, certain distortions in the process.

Above all, it is not truly possible to itemise historic Islamic art in order to extract the most symbolic parts of the whole because of its specific aggregative structure which consists of writing, patterning, geometrising and representation. Each of these distinct art forms conveys in equal measure the Islamic conception of visuality so that calligraphic friezes, patterned tiled walls or Persian paintings are no less revelatory of this conception than *mashrabiyya* and *muqarnas*. (figure II.4.3) Furthermore, in admitting that one may loosely borrow Cassirer-Panofsky's concept of the symbolic form just to locate the visual expression most representative of Islamic metaphysics, calligraphy would still be the better choice. Not only for Muslims calligraphy renders the sacred in material form, however, from a phenomenological viewpoint, the unprecedently ubiquitous transmedial nature of the Arabic script generates a unique type of perception engaging the double act of seeing and reading which forms the core of the Islamic aesthetic experience. Problematically, Belting's selection of symbols leaves aside this fundamental structuring element of Islamic visuality which is writing.

Yet, the idea of the *mashrabiyya* as a symbolic form actually fits contemporary Islamic visuality. In our hyper-globalised world, visual cultures of all kinds distinguish themselves on the international scene by means of idiosyncratic patterns consciously selected from complex

Figure II.4.3 Star-shaped tile. Kashan, Iran, 663/1265. Metropolitan Museum of Art, New York.

traditional repertoires and plastically manipulated in order to enhance their semiotic power. Like the Shang and Zhou bronze designs in Chinese contemporary architecture or the brightly coloured geometric motifs in South African art, a few hyper-recurrent motifs such as the *mashrabiyya*, stand for Islamic culture in the current global standardised language of aesthetic appearances. But again, if one sought to single out the most autoreferential of all, it would rather be the geometric interlace at large, present everywhere Islam visually signals itself, in the plastic arts, public architecture of all genres, offices, metros, etc. We may talk about 'the geometric interlace as symbolic form of contemporary Islamic visuality'. But is there a connection between this artistic phenomenon and Ibn al-Haytham's science of optics and aesthetics?

Ibn al-Haytham in the Discourse on Islamic Art: A Fundamental Misunderstanding

The routine reference to the *Kitab al-Manazir* in the history of Islamic art is symptomatic of the second attitude mentioned above, namely the presupposition that this oeuvre had an influence on Islamic art-making and seeing, or that it can be used to explain them. By contrast, the historians of Islamic science and philosophy like Abdelhamid Sabra, Roshdi Rached, Nader El-Bizri and many others, do not relate this scientific heritage in any way to Islamic art or to a specifically Islamic conception of aesthetic experience. El-Bizri even remarked that, although Ibn Haytham had elaborated his theory of vision and light in the intellectual environment of Fatimid Egypt, where light had considerable theological significance, the Ismaili approach to light had no place in his enterprise, and neither did any other Islamic conception of light for that matter.[14] For as El-Bizri clearly says, the *Kitab al-Manazir* belongs to fundamental science:

> Even though Ibn al-Haytham's mathematical and optical research was foundational in the domains of the exact sciences and their scientific applications, it was not in itself metamorphosed into artistic theoretical or practical spheres. Ibn al-Haytham's preoccupations were centred on experimental methods of inquiry and controlled testing, which combined geometry with physics (natural philosophy; *philosophia naturalis*), and rested on studies in optics that aimed at investigating the optimal veridical conditions of visual perception, which would ground the reliable empirical recording and analysis of accurate observational data.[15]

These different understandings of Ibn al-Haytham's findings in these two fields indicate a problem and raise two questions: did the historians of science only partially comprehend Ibn al-Haytham's contribution to knowledge? And does the *Kitab al-Manazir* after all contain material that informs the Islamic gaze, its conception of art and its aesthetic experience, especially considering the remarkable intersectionality between art and science in Islam? Although with some nuances, as we shall see, the answer to these two questions is straightaway a negative therefore those art historical discourses replete with citations of Ibn al-Haytham's writings fall short of any critical efficacy. Worse, they mislead because they conflate the dual science of optics and the phenomenology of perception, premised upon the observation of human nature, with 'cultural optics' and the aesthetic experience premised upon the civilisational determinants of visuality as a cultural construct.[16]

An Unheeded Double Differentiation: Scientific Optics and Phenomenology of Perception versus Cultural Optics and Aesthetics

In her 2015 article previously cited, Necipoğlu says:

> Regardless of the debate on whether or not theories of vision and aesthetics had an impact on artistic production, such texts offer precious glimpses into widespread sensibilities that framed visual hermeneutics. Despite their often underestimated value, Islamic narrative sources and poetry provide valuable insights into aesthetic values that informed the modalities of the gaze and attitudes toward the visual arts.

This statement discloses thinking that results in a fundamental misunderstanding about Ibn al-Haytham's aesthetics in the scholarship on Islamic art. Prioritising exhaustiveness at the expense of critical discernment in the manipulation of primary texts, it brings together in a single corpus eclectic material ranging from theology, science, poetry and philosophy, to ethics and theoretical aesthetics. Ibn al-Haytham's oeuvre occupies a leading position in this corpus vaguely called 'Islamic narrative sources' that, it is contended, expresses, thematises or theorises concepts and processes immanent in Islam such as sensibilities, values, visual hermeneutics, the aesthetic gaze and artistic philosophy. However, this reasoning fails to heed the epistemic-ontological differentiation between the two radically distinct realms of humanistic expression and scientific practice. A note on the *Kitab al-Manazir*'s content is necessary to address this issue.

Among Ibn al-Haytham's breakthroughs what stands out for its novel epistemology is the study of embodied modes of the acquisition of knowledge that sustain the phenomenon, not the philosophy, of being in the physical world. Centuries later, Edmund Husserl designated this endeavour 'transcendental phenomenology' which he defined in terms of 'Philosophy as Rigorous Science'.[17] The phenomenological method, the contemporary phenomenologist Dermot Moran further explains, can be used in a wide range of scientific fields.[18] After the ancient Greeks, Ibn al-Haytham is consequently not only the medieval father of modern optics and phenomenology, but also the frontrunner of the newer branches of cognitive science generically called 'neuroscience', which focus on the entwinement of the sensory experience and the functioning of the brain. In particular, Ibn Haytham opened up the pathway to neuroaesthetics when he undertook to dissect the process of the arousal of a sense of beauty, not as a psychological subjective process but as an intersubjective phenomenon.[19] He even pushed this investigation further by examining the condition of the beautiful that, in the constitution of any object itself, induces what he believed was the intersubjective experience of beauty, regardless of taste and culture. We could say that, had he been born today and had access to the new forms of technology, Ibn al-Haytham would be a neuroscientist specialising in neuroaesthetics.

In sum, Ibn al-Haytham's analyses of vision and perception fall under the heading of what I would call 'scientific aesthetics', as opposed to Islamic or other cultural 'applied aesthetics' in the creation and experience of art. As such, Ibn al-Haytham's aesthetic theory may constitute a neutral critical apparatus for the study of Islamic visuality, exactly as its more advanced modern phenomenological and neuroaesthetic versions may do, but it is not evidence of this visuality as has been wrongly assumed. And yet, his phenomenology of beauty has a tricky, edgy, side to it in the sense that, in some of its aspects, it amounts to cultural aesthetics.

Ibn al-Haytham's Phenomenology of Beauty Versus Cultural Aesthetics

In her book *What is Islamic Art?* Wendy M.K. Shaw produces an account of Islamic perception and naturally consults the *Kitab al-Manazir*.[20] Yet, she avoids engaging in phenomenological knowledge, which leads her to misconstrue Ibn al-Haytham's theorisation of the beautiful as a theoretical proposition of beauty anchored in Islamic perceptual culture. Thus she argues that this culture emphatically favours a free and open subjectivity, declaring that: 'emphasizing subjectivity, Ibn al-Haytham offers a paradigm of beauty rooted in manifold possibilities that can only be differentiated through subjective experience'.[21] Clearly, Shaw confuses his phenomenological notion of intersubjectivity, which corresponds to Husserl's 'transcendental ego' and shared human experience of the lifeworld in intersubjectivity, with the psychological subjectivity at stake in the representationalist attitude.[22] Ibn al-Haytham had no interest in these subjective products of 'the faculty of judgement', to employ his own terminology, as he intended instead to uncover what he thought of as the universal truth regarding the objective constitution of beauty in objects and subjects. However, paradoxically, Shaw strikes a just note when she uses the term 'paradigm' that, in the context of her misinterpretation, signifies a cultural paragon and not a scientific model. This is why.

Although in respect of Ibn al-Haytham's scientific commitment the concept of 'paradigm' thus conceptualised appears out of place, his conclusions on beauty specifically promote the mathematical concepts of geometric harmony and proportions inherited from the Greeks. As such, these conclusions reflect a system of aesthetic values which are intrinsically non-objective and non-scientific, even though they involve the mathematical notion of proportionality. Furthermore, to repeat a cliché, universal beauty does not exist. Disproportion and disharmony in forms may definitely be considered as beautiful or visually appealing. Suffice it to cite certain human representations in African statuary or in Jean-August Dominique Ingres' paintings in which purposely elongated or exaggerated body parts breaking with the natural harmony of human anatomy for the purpose of expressiveness were certainly not thought of as ugly. Interestingly, the latter illustrates the Western practice of deconstructing the same proportion-based ideal of pleasant appearances, which was of Greek origin, that paradoxically constitutes the pillar of Ibn al-Haytham's 'scientific beauty'.

Viewed in this light, yet in contradiction with Ibn Haytham's goal of scientific objectivity, the theory of beauty in the *Kitab al-Manazir* constitutes a cultural paradigm. In this respect, it reverberates through medieval Islamic culture forged by a multidisciplinary approach to geometry anchored in the Greek aesthetic and scientific heritage. Still, there is no way around the fact that Ibn al-Haytham's aesthetic phenomenology as a whole excludes the following from its scope: location, culture, Islam, the Fatimid space and, a fortiori, most of the immanent cultural concepts and processes Necipoğlu mentions in her article. Crucially, Ibn al-Haytham himself did not relate geometry and proportionality to the geometric aesthetics found in Islamic art. Consequently, leaving aside the overarching consensual argument of geometry as common denominator to all aspects of medieval Islamic intellectual and creative life, it can be asserted that Ibn al-Haytham's scientific aesthetics have little bearing on artistic conceptualisation and visuality in Islam.

Ibn al-Haytham's Oeuvre Misused

The art historical discourses citing Ibn al-Haytham present essentially three shortcomings. The first one is the *lapalissade* and other *perogrulladas*, namely truisms passed off as critical insights.[23] This problem occurs when art historians, legitimately albeit inefficiently, appropriate Ibn al-Haytham's scientific findings as analytical instruments by definition applicable to anything in any context. The misappropriation consists precisely in re-expounding these known findings in propositions in which this 'anything' takes on the identity of an Islamic artwork as in, say, 'the façade of the Blue Mosque in Istanbul can be seen when light reaches the eye following Ibn al-Haytham's theory of vision ...'. The result is an unproductive self-evident truth whereby the cultural particularities of the architecture vanish from the discussion under the erasing effect of scientific generality. In *Reframing the Alhambra*, Olga Bush employs this technique to argue that 'the principles of the "widespread sensibilities" that informed the creation of the Alhambra may be articulated coherently by reference to Ibn al-Haytham's optics', thus proffering numerous *perogrulladas* such as:

> Since the judgements involved in discerning geometric design are secondary to the perception of colour, according to Ibn al-Haytham, one may also study such visible properties such as shape, size, position, order, and such pairs as separation and continuity or motion and rest, as dependent upon the use of colour.... The alternation of colours in the vault also contributes to what Ibn al-Haytham discussed as the separation and contiguity of the constitutive parts of the object, that is 'the boundaries of the objects and of the intervals between the boundaries;.... As Ibn al-Haytham

observed, one differentiates between an object's colour and that of its surroundings.[24]

The second shortcoming concerns the geopolitical placement of the un-placeable scientific content of Ibn al-Haytham's oeuvre in Islamic material culture. Olga Bush's placing of this content in al-Andalus through her investigation of the Alhambra typifies this issue. She presents, for instance, geometry and proportionality observable in the palace as evidence of the local impact of Ibn al-Haytham's aesthetics. However, in the broad perspective of the history of Islamic geometric designs this view loses all substance. Geometric art emerged before Ibn al-Haytham was born, in the Umayyad period, and has been spreading since then continuously throughout the Muslim world up to today. Similarly, other Muslim polymaths and philosophers before and after Ibn al-Haytham had engaged in the theorisation of geometry and mathematical proportions, such as al-Kindi (ca. 185–252/801–866) and the Brethren of Purity (3rd or 4th/9th or 10th century).

Furthermore, contradictions in regionalising discourses of this type only confirm the impossibility of limiting the Ibn al-Haytham phenomenon to specific places when viewed through the prism of the Islamic artworld. While, to make her case regarding the Alhambra, Bush reports historical evidence for the *Kitab al-Manazir*'s intellectual-scientific impact on the Iberian world, Necipoğlu deems that 'Ibn al-Haytham's treatises remained confined largely to the realm of the scientific gaze in the post-Mongol Islamic East, where the pictorial arts were more closely allied with aesthetic discourses on poetics, music and calligraphy'.[25] Overlooking the biased view of an Islamic West less penetrated by Ibn al-Haytham's science than the Islamic East, this statement by Necipoğlu and the narratives she builds based on it exemplify a vain effort to link Ibn al-Haytham's optics to specific currents of Islamic art and visuality. Weaving together the *Kitab al-Manazir*'s medieval theories with the early Modern Islamic philosophies of the visual produces a regionalist visual history conflating scientific and cultural optics that are then seen as embedded in the Islamic East's abstractive styles of painting, as Necipoğlu expounds: 'the predilection of abstraction in the pictorial arts may have responded in part to religious constraints. However, this predilection was generally theorised as a matter of aesthetic preference in the early Modern literature on the visual arts where the power of the abstractive inner gaze ... reigns supreme in Islamic aesthetic culture'.[26] This approach argues that Ibn al-Haytham's scientific gaze 'with its humanistic emphasis on the mental dimensions of visual perception' served as the conceptual foundations of these cultural developments.[27]

Among the many issues destabilising this regionalist narrative are misconceptions about both Ibn Haytham's intentions and results. First, he did not place any 'humanistic emphasis' on the noetic process in perception, which would imply an intentional act of valorising the intellective faculty in a hierarchised, i.e. non-scientific and cultural conception of bodily and mental perceptive functions. Valorisation is a philosophical-ethical endeavour incompatible with the descriptive nature of Ibn al-Haytham's scientific enterprise. Therefore, overlooking the truistic observation about the awareness of the role of mental faculties in perception in both Islamic art and Ibn al-Haytham's optics, the latter cannot be related in any way to the philosophical-ethical inner gaze in the theories of Muslim theologians and poets. It can be even less related to the Islamic East's pictorial abstraction.

Second, the abstract conception of representation underpinning the painting of the Islamic East stems from a metaphysics of images that has nothing whatsoever to do with mental cognition as Ibn al-Haytham conceives of it in his neutral observational account of the perceptive phenomenon. According to his account, cognition emerges from a wide range of mental operations of both representational and abstract order, through which the pre-logic information obtained in the sensory experience is processed. In particular, he explains, the eidetic operation maintains mentally visible and living things which at some point vanish from the optical field, so that cognition is by no means intrinsically abstract. In addition, because of its scientific nature, Ibn al-Haytham's demonstration does not deal with the cultural-artistic Islamic preference for one or the other among the mind's representational and abstract powers.

There is Imagination and Imagination(s)

A final misuse of the *Kitab al-Manazir* in Islamic art history to be discussed concerns the concept of imagination. According to Ibn al-Haytham: 'to imagine the forms of objects previously seen at the time of remembering them, and in the absence of these objects, is clear proof that the forms perceived by sight exist in the soul and are imprinted in the imagination.'[28] This definition concerns what may be described as 'the reconstituting eidetic imagination' involving the aforementioned eidetic faculty in the experience of the visible. Nurtured by memory and habits, this type of imagination has the pragmatic function of allowing for the mental reconstitution of things that have disappeared from sight or are only partially seen because of optical obstacles. Dermot Moran explains the same imagining function in Husserlian phenomenology:

> Perception is the primal or 'originary' form of intuiting, whereas memory and imagination are reproductive modifications of perception. Memory is a form of 'calling to mind' or presenting (*Vergegenwärtigung*) that no longer has the distinctive bodily presence that characterises perception. Imagining is yet another form of presenting which posits an object somewhat detached from perceptual surroundings.[29]

Eidetic imagination is consequently to be distinguished from the other types of imagination operating in the more expansive region of the imagined such as the poetic, meditative, spiritual, psychedelic and other meandering imaginations and unbridled reveries which aim to create alternative realities, re-invent reality or depart from reality seeking to attain the metaphysical realm. Failing to differentiate between these different types of imagination, Islamic art scholarship misuses Ibn al-Haytham's approach to this concept. For example, Wendy M.K. Shaw misinterprets an illustration of *Kalila wa Dimna* as she writes: 'the story also reflects Ibn al-Haytham's thought in distinguishing between the external, glancing function of vision and the internalised imprint of contemplation *retreating from exteriority* in the space of the mind' (my emphasis).[30] Clearly, this confuses Ibn al-Haytham's intersubjective phenomenology of imagination, based on the body-mind relationship as the conduit of information perceptually received, with the psychology of subjective imagination that she presents as evidence of an Islamic inclination for free imagining and contemplation. Ibn al-Haytham's epistemological pivot was precisely that exterior subjects intersubjectively deal with and are tethered to the sensory experience. Similarly, in his phenomenology contemplation signifies the entwinement of intense looking and thinking that is demanded by objects which are complexly constituted, not 'a retreat from the seen'. For as a phenomenologist, Ibn al-Haytham did not delve into the infinitely conjugated and culturally forged psychological derivations that direct perception in one particular direction or another.

There is no Analytical Use of the *Kitab al-Manazir* in Islamic Art History other than as a Generic Phenomenological Tool

If Ibn al-Haytham's scientific work has any usefulness for Islamic art history, it is as a generic phenomenological instrument of analysis. For example, one may refine the hermeneutics of the numerous elusive Islamic aniconic art forms, such as the *mihrab* or certain geometric configurations that seem to conjure up mental images, by invoking the theory of the eidetic faculty that he posited.[31] However, the appropriate use of this or any other of Ibn al-Haytham's findings on perception requires two things: a minimal knowledge of the phenomenological method itself, and a conscious approach to these findings as a proto-phenomenology enabling only a sketchy delineation of certain general processes of reception that the material of Islamic art may induce or engage, and not as way of accessing its meaning. For owing to the scientific applicability of Ibn al-Haytham's oeuvre, the sole observation of its workings in this or another cultural context can only lead to truisms, namely to the illustration of certain scientific phenomena already long proved and established through a demonstrated application to specific instances of objects or situations, and not to the understanding of those instances themselves which is instead the goal of analytical exercise.

NOTES

1 Among abundant publications see: Ibn al-Haytham (Alhazen), *The Optics of Ibn al-Haytham, Books I–III, On Direct Vision*, tr. Abdelhamid I. Sabra (London, 1989); Ibn al-Haytham, *Kitab al-Manazir*, Books I–III, ed. Abdelhamid I. Sabra (Kuwait, 1983), and Books IV–V (Kuwait, 2002); Abdelhamid I. Sabra, 'Sensation and Inference in Alhazen's Theory of Perceptual Vision', in *Studies in Perception: Interrelations in the History of Philosophy and Science* (Columbus, OH, 1978), pp. 160–185; Roshdi Rashed, *Geometry and Dioptrics in Classical Islam* (Wimbledon, 2005); Elaheh Kheirandish, *The Arabic Version of Euclid's Optics: Kitab Uqlidis fi ikhtilaf al-manazir* (New York, 1999). I first identified the connection between Ibn al-Haytham's theory on perception and phenomenology in Valérie Gonzalez, *Beauty and Islam, Aesthetics of Islamic Art and Architecture* (London, 2001), Chapter 1, 'Beauty and the Aesthetic Experience in Classical Arabic Thought', pp. 5–25, and in 'Universality and Modernity of Ibn al-Haytham's Thought and Science', with an introduction by Azim Nanji, © 2002 The Institute of Ismaili Studies. Nader El-Bizri further discusses this connection in 'A Philosophical Perspective on Alhazen's Optics', *Arabic Sciences and Philosophy*, 15 (2005), pp. 189–218.

2 See my critique of the Eurocentric studies on Persianate painting in 'The "Visible Voice" or "Vocal Visibility" of the Subalterns in Early Modern Safavid and Mughal Painting', in Andrew J. Newman, ed., *Iranian/Persianate Subalterns in the Safavid Period: Their Role and Depiction, Recovering 'Lost Voices'* (Berlin, 2022), pp. 149–192, and, including a

reflection on postcolonialism, in *Aesthetic Hybridity in Mughal Painting, 1526-1658* (London, 2015), pp. 39–48, and 72–87, pp. 96–102.

3 In brief, visuality designates the compound of conceptions related to the visual in art and philosophy, and to the mode of seeing in a given cultural context.

4 On Islamic theoretical aesthetics see José Miguel Puerta Vílchez, *Aesthetics in Arabic Thought*, tr. Consuelo Lopez-Morillas (Leiden, 2017).

5 Simon O'Meara is to be credited for this brilliant parallel between this non-event and Sigmund Freud's theory that he made during a conversation I had with him about Ibn al-Haytham and Islamic art history. See https://thepsychologist.bps.org.uk/volume-31/june-2018/freud-and-penis-envy-failure-courage.

6 Hans Belting, *Florence and Baghdad: Renaissance Art and Arab Science*, tr. Deborah Lucas Schneider (Cambridge, MA, 2011), and Gülru Necipoğlu, 'The Scrutinizing Gaze in the Aesthetics of Islamic Visual Cultures; Sight, Insight and Desire', *Muqarnas*, 32 (2015), pp. 23–62.

7 Ibid., p. 28.

8 This concept of 'non-eventual aesthetics' is the pendant, by negation, to 'eventual aesthetics' that, for example, lends its name to a journal of philosophy: https://independent.academia.edu/EventalAestheticsJournal.

9 About the first breakthrough in Islamic art history, see Valérie Gonzalez, 'Aporia in Umayyad Art or the Degree Zero of the Visual Forms' Meaning in Early Islam', *Journal of Material Cultures in the Muslim World*, 1 (2020), pp. 6–33. https://doi.org/10.1163/26666286-12340002.

10 This discussion pertains to the broad field of the study of social facts variably involving the single subject or plural subjects. See Margaret Gilbert's work, in particular, 'Shared Intention and Personal Intentions', *Philosophical Studies*, 144 (2009), pp. 167–187.

11 Panofsky was famously inspired by Ernst Cassirer, *The Philosophy of Symbolic Forms* (New Haven, CN, 1965), for his book, *Perspective as Symbolic Form*, tr. Christopher S. Wood (Princeton, NJ, 1997).

12 Cassirer's seminal philosophical work expounds this functioning of symbolisation. See also Samuel Y. Edgerton, *The Mirror, the Window and the Telescope: How Renaissance Perspective Changed Our Vision of the Universe* (Ithaca, NY, 2009), and Margaret Iversen, 'The Discourse of Perspective in the Twentieth Century: Panofsky, Damisch, Lacan', *Oxford Art Journal*, 28 (2005), pp. 193–202.

13 This vast question of the symbolic form would actually require a separate thorough inquiry, especially in the light of the studies on the opposite process to symbolisation: de-symbolisation. See Joëlle Mesnil's outstanding 1988 dissertation, *La désymbolisation dans la culture contemporaine*, Revista de Filosofia, septiembre 2015, https://www.revistadefilosofia.org/66-25.pdf. Like symbolisation, the critique of de-symbolisation is based on the observation of Western culture, but I strongly believe that it is also at stake in historic Islam. That is a rich topic for a future study.

14 El-Bizri, 'A Philosophical Perspective on Alhazen's Optics', p. 214, n. 53.

15 Nader El-Bizri, 'By Way of an Overture: Classical Optics and Renaissance Pictorial Arts', in Angela Bartram and Nader El-Bizri, ed., *Recto Verso: Redefining the Sketchbook* (Aldershot, 2014), p. 18.

16 The concept of 'cultural optics' has been explored by Martin Jay in *Downcast Eyes, The Denigration of Vision in Twentieth-Century French Thought* (Berkeley, CA, 1993).

17 Edmund Husserl, 'Philosophy as Rigorous Science', in *Edmund Husserl: Phenomenology and the Crisis of Philosophy*, tr. Quentin Lauer (New York, 1965), pp. 289–341. See also Donn Welton, ed., *The Essential Husserl: Basic Writings in Transcendental Phenomenology* (Bloomington, IN, 1999).

18 Dermot Moran, 'What is the Phenomenological approach?', *Phenomenology and Mind*, special issue, Francesca Boccuni and Stefano Bacin, ed., 'Methods of Philosophy', 15

(2018), pp. 72–91. Text online by SCRIBD. See also by this author, *Introduction to Phenomenology* (London, 2000).
19 About the notions of 'intersubjectivity' and 'the transcendental ego' in Husserlian phenomenology and that also underpin Ibn al-Haytham's epistemology, see Jan Almäng's published dissertation, 'Intentionality and Intersubjectivity', *Acta Philosophica Gothoburgensia*, 21 (2007), pp. 1–210. Re. neuroscience, see John Onians, *Neuroarthistory: from Aristotle and Pliny to Baxandall and Zeki* (New Haven, CN, 2008).
20 Wendy M. K. Shaw, *What is Islamic Art? Between Religion and Perception* (Cambridge, 2019). See my review of this book in *al-Masaq*, 32 (2020), pp. 1–4. DOI: 10.1080/09503110.2020.1712811.
21 Shaw, *What is Islamic Art?*, p. 181
22 Here 'attitude' is to be understood as a philosophical term, as in 'the natural attitude', to which the phenomenological stance opposes itself.
23 The terms '*lapalissades*' and '*perogrulladas*' derive from the name of literati specialised in telling comical tautologies: the French Jacques de La Palisse (1470–1525) and a certain Pedro Grullo in Spain's medieval popular literary lore. See https://en.wikipedia.org/wiki/Jacques_de_La_Palice, and https://definicion.de/perogrullo/.
24 Olga Bush, *Reframing the Alhambra, Architecture, Textiles and Court Ceremonial* (Edinburgh, 2018), pp. 42, 44–45 and 51.
25 See Bush, *Reframing the Alhambra*, pp. 41–42; Necipoğlu, 'The Scrutinizing Gaze', p. 28.
26 Ibid., p. 23.
27 Ibid., p. 24.
28 Sabra, tr., *The Optics of Ibn al-Haytham, Books I–III* (London, 1989), pp. 211–212.
29 Moran, 'What is the Phenomenological approach?', text online by SCRIBD, p. 8.
30 Shaw, *What is Islamic Art?*, p. 161.
31 See my analysis of this type of mental process in the case of the *mihrab* in Valérie Gonzalez, 'Semiotic Outside, Phenomenological Inside: A Double Viewing of Mosque Architecture and its *Mihrab*-Centred Interior', in Idries Trevathan, ed., *Mosque, Approaches to Art and Architecture* (London, 2024), pp. 81–94.

5

The Fatimids and the Indian Ocean: Evidence from the *Book of Curiosities**

Yossef Rapoport

About a millennium ago, at some time between 410 and 442/1020 and 1050, in Fatimid Cairo, a large, illustrated book on the heavens and the earth was completed by an anonymous author. Modern scholars were unaware of its existence until its recent discovery and subsequent acquisition in 2002 by the Bodleian Library at Oxford. The Arabic title of the treatise is *Kitab ghara'ib al-funun wa-mulah al-'uyun*, and is today referred to as the *Book of Curiosities*. It contains a remarkable series of early maps and astronomical diagrams, most of which are unparalleled in any Greek, Latin or Arabic material. The treatise is composed of two parts. The first is on the heavens, moving the reader from the outermost sphere of the stars through the spheres of the five planets visible to the naked eye down to the sub-lunar world of winds and comets. The second part is on the earth, beginning with calculation of the earth's circumference, then moving to maps of the inhabited world, islands of the Indian Ocean and the Mediterranean, and major lakes and rivers of the world, ending with strange plants and animals inhabiting the earth. Taken together, the discovery of this manuscript made significant contributions to the history of cartography, to the history of astronomy and astrology, and to our knowledge of Mediterranean and Indian Ocean medieval networks of communication.[1]

The *Book of Curiosities* is a rare example of a medieval Islamic treatise that has maritime spaces as its main focus of attention, chiming with the maritime orientations and strategies of the Fatimid empire. The treatise has a highly original and systematic account of the world's major bodies of water, providing maps for three great seas known at the time (the Mediterranean, the Caspian and the Indian Ocean), and cartographic and textual descriptions of major islands, peninsulas, lakes and rivers. Given the geographical location of the Fatimid empire, it is not surprising that most of the maps depict the eastern half of the Mediterranean, bounded in the west by an imaginary line drawn between Mahdiya and Sicily. This Eastern Mediterranean, as depicted in the *Book of Curiosities*, was as Byzantine as it was Muslim. The Byzantine southern coasts of Anatolia, the coasts of the Aegean and many of its islands, as well as Cyprus, are described with as much detail as the Egyptian or Syro-Palestinian coasts under Fatimid control, and with the use of Greek navigation terminology.

While the Eastern Mediterranean was Fatimid Egypt's backyard, the maps of the Indian Ocean, the Indus and the Oxus attest to the truly global ambitions and networks of communications of the early Fatimids. Far beyond the physical borders of their Mediterranean empire, these maps demonstrate the strategic importance of the Indian Ocean, where Ismaili missionaries had been active since the 3rd/9th century. Of particular importance is a map of the Indus river, which uniquely depicts an overland itinerary from Fatimid-controlled Sind to China, via northern India and Tibet. Other medieval routes to China – either the sea route through the Straits of Malacca or the Central Asian Silk Road – are not as prominent, suggesting that the maps represent a time when a Tibetan 'Musk Route' eclipsed its more famous alternatives.[2]

The map of the Indian Ocean shows the Gulf of Aden as a gateway to the ports and islands of the East African coasts. Fatimid commercial relations with East Africa are very rarely documented, and recently the Fatimid impact on the region during the formative period of its Islamisation has been cast into doubt. However, the detailed depiction of East Africa in the *Book of Curiosities* points to an unexpected level of familiarity, based on information gathered from navigation along the coasts of the Horn of Africa. We have here what may be the first recorded references in Arabic to the islands of Zanzibar (al-Unguja), Mafia, and several localities and capes along the coasts of modern Somalia. Prior to the late 9th/15th century, no other medieval text describes the East African coasts in such detail. Viewed from Fatimid Cairo, the Indian Ocean was as much about East Africa as it was about India and China.

The Route to China

The map of the Indian Ocean depicts it as an enclosed oval sea, a form that parallels the form of the Mediterranean in the preceding map in the treatise. The absence of any major gulfs and bays was a result of the cartographic method chosen by the author, which privileged clear display of labels over accuracy in the depiction of actual coastlines. It corresponded to the way coast-hugging mariners thought out their journeys as a sequence of landing points. Scale and orientation were removed not because they were unknown, but because they were of lesser importance as one travelled following the shoreline.

The map of the Indian Ocean is made up of two halves, an Asian one and an East African one (on which more later). The Asian half, occupying the right-hand side of the map, shows Indian and Chinese localities along the shores, with a sea route to China indicated by a volcano and several islands in the Bay of Bengal and the Sea of China. Most of the names here are familiar from the 3rd/9th-century work of the Abbasid geographer Ibn Khurradadhbih and from *The Account of China and India* by Sulayman the Merchant, composed in 236/851.[3] They include the Nicobar Islands, the island of Tiyuma (identified as Pulau Tioman off the coast of Malaya), and the island of Sandarfulat, one of the last stopping points on the route to Canton. There is also a large island, mostly lost in the gutter, which is almost certaimly Sri Lanka.

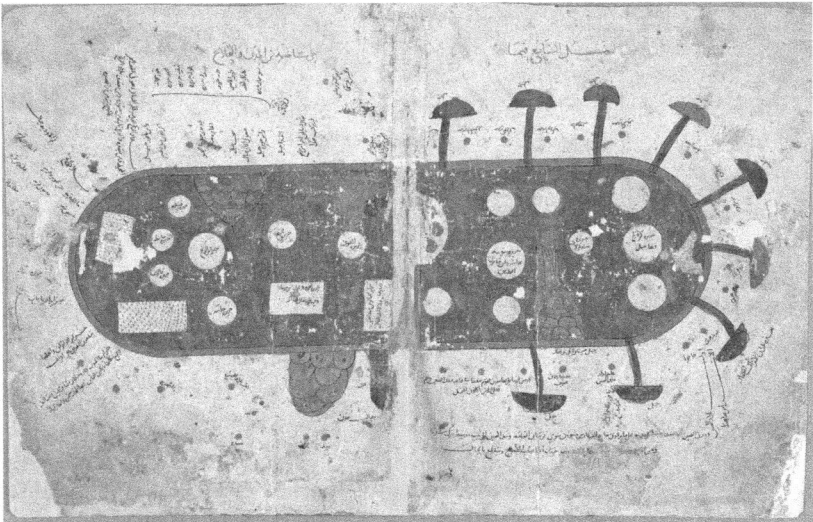

Figure II.5.1 Map of the Indian Ocean from the *Book of Curiosities*. Bodleian Library, Oxford.

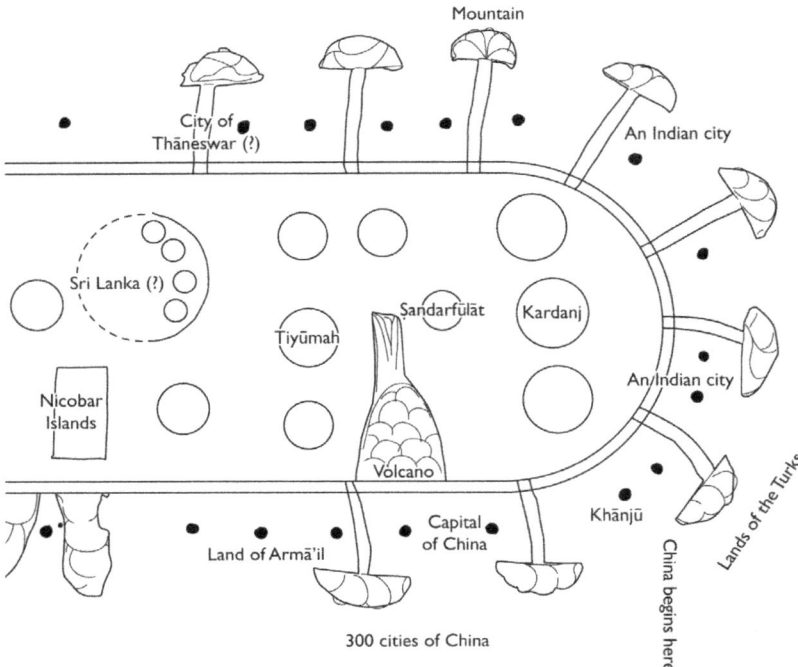

Figure II.5.2 Interpretative diagram for right-hand section of the map of the Indian Ocean from the *Book of Curiosities*.

China itself is located along the rim, at the bottom right. It is separated from India by the 'Lands of the infidel Turks'. A long label at the bottom of the map, partly illegible, states that there are 300 cities in China, a number familiar from the account of Ibn Khurradadhbih. Several Chinese place-names are indicated but are badly deformed. Coming from the direction of India, the first label is *Tahu*, which may be a corruption of *Khanju*, likely Ch'uan-chou (Quanzhou), later known to the Arabs as the port of Zaytun.[4]

The historical context of this material is that of the 3rd/9th century, when Arab and Persian vessels frequently made the entire journey from Basra to Canton.[5] This route, through the Straits of Malacca, was facilitated by advancement in navigational techniques and better understanding of the monsoon seasons, and was also driven by political instability on the overland trade routes in Central Asia. But this sea route came to a dramatic halt at the end of the 3rd/9th century, probably due to the Huang Chao uprising against the Tang, leading to the massacre of thousands of foreigners in Guanzhou (Canton) around 265/879, including Muslims, Christians, Jews and Zoroastrians. The merchant, Abu Zayd al-Sirafi, who wrote a supplement to the *Account of China and India* around 303/915-16, reported that this rebellion was a severe blow to Cantonese trade. By the 4th/10th century, the long voyages across the breadth of the Indian Ocean, like those reported by Sulayman, were replaced by shorter, segmented trips, from the Red Sea or Persian Gulf to Gujarat or Malabar. While Muslims continued to play a major role in every circuit of Indian Ocean commerce, these circuits were not part of direct trade between the Middle East and China.[6]

It is remarkable that the famous Central Asian Silk Road is not represented at all in the *Book of Curiosities*. Central Asia itself is depicted in the map of the Oxus river (Amu Darya). The map shows the river emerging from a brown mountain at the top, then forming an almost complete loop before emptying into the green Aral Sea in the centre of the page. Other rivers are also shown, including the Syr Darya, also flowing to the Aral Sea, and the Ab-i Qaysar that emerges in the red mountains. This map indicates some of the major cities on the Silk Road, such as Balkh and Faryab on the bottom left. But they are not part of an itinerary going towards China, which is not mentioned at all on this map.

From the perspective of Fatimid Cairo, the route to China and the potential wealth that came with it passed not through the Silk Road or the Straits of Malacca, but rather through the Ismaili amirates of Sind. In the 350s/960s, in tandem with the Fatimid conquest of Egypt, Ismaili *daʿis* sent from Yemen took over the city of Multan, on the banks of the Indus, and by the end of the 4th/10th century Multan and al-Mansura, the other major city of Sind, were Fatimid vassal states. It was during this period of expansion that the poet Ibn Hani' fantasised about Fatimid forces moving even beyond Baghdad, leading Indian kings to lose sleep and their elephants, symbols of their military might, 'lowing like a young camel'.[7] India figured prominently in the Fatimid imagination as a source of worthy enemies, but also a fertile land for conversion as well as a font of cosmological wisdom.

A map of the Indus and the Ganges rivers, which is unique to this treatise, depicts an itinerary that begins in Muslim Sind and the Indus valley, traverses northern India and then follows an overland route to China, almost certainly through Tibet. The map curiously represents the major rivers of northern India – the Indus, the Ganges and perhaps also the Brahmaputra – as one continuous river system that runs from east to west across the northern part of the Indian subcontinent. This single river originates in the mountains of Tibet,[8] shown as a red landmass at the top of the map, and then flows down what may possibly be taken to be the actual course of the Brahmaputra in eastern Bengal. The labels at the centre of the page refer to Hindu cities along the banks of the Ganges, such as Benares, Prayag (Allahabad) and Qannawj (Kannauj), the capital of the Gurjara-Pratihara dynasty (r. 836–1037 CE).[9] After receiving six tributaries, the river bends southwards, and then clearly represents the Indus. The bottom part of the page shows Multan and al-Mansura, the Muslim capitals of Sind, along the lower Indus. The river eventually empties into the Indian Ocean, marked by a green square.

The map is dominated by two itineraries, one from Multan to Kannauj in northern India, and a second from Kannauj to China. The itinerary from Multan to Kannauj begins with a label describing Multan itself and giving historical information about the city, including its association with the Prophet Yahya (John). There are eight place-names in this itinerary, but they cannot be identified with certainty. They all appear to be localities in northern India, ruled by non-Muslim, Indian kings. The last stop on the itinerary is the city of Kannauj itself, which is the most prominent locality on the map, described as the capital of India and the seat of its ruler, whose army consists of 2,500 elephants.

Given the uncertainty in the identification of the place-names, it is difficult to trace the precise route of this itinerary from Multan to Kannauj. But both the visual depiction and the geographical literature of the time suggest a desert route, away from the river valleys, in what is the shortest direct line. Buddhist sources refer to an important trade route that proceeded away from the Indus delta, via Arur (al-Rur) and across the desert to Mathura, where it joined the main Indian trade route down the Ganges.[10] Al-Biruni, who died in 440/1048, reports that Multan had become the western terminus point of this desert route.[11]

The depiction of a detailed itinerary from Multan to Kannauj is a striking visual attestation to the religious, political and economic links between Fatimid Egypt and Sind ca. 390/1000. Even before the rise of the Fatimids, Sind had become practically independent, with a local dynasty of Arab tribal rulers residing in a nearby garrison, and commanding a strong army supported by elephants.[12] Multan also attracted substantial numbers of Hindu pilgrims who came to revere the Sun-god statue, first

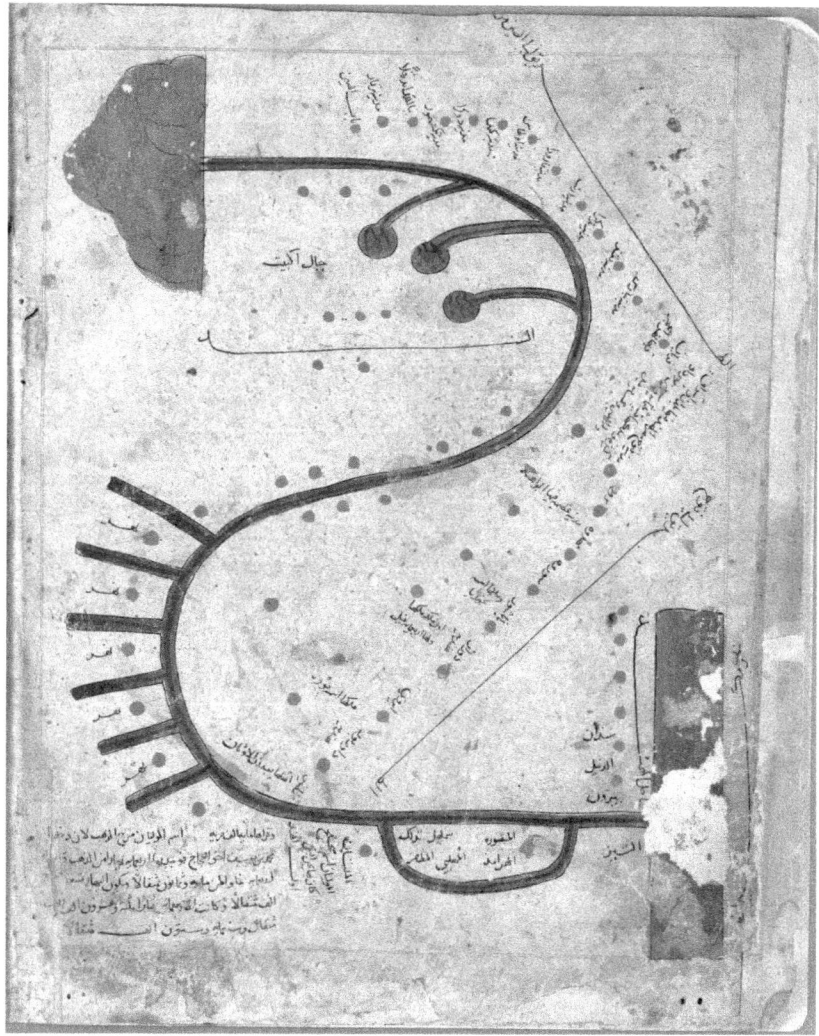

Figure II.5.3 Map of the Indus-Ganges river system from the *Book of Curiosities*. Bodleian Library, Oxford.

described by a Chinese traveller in the mid-7th century CE.[13] This was a major source of revenue for Multan's rulers. According to al-Mas'udi and Ibn Hawqal, the Sun-god provided protection against the local Hindu powers – the rulers of Multan threatened to smash the statue in case of Indian attack.[14] Relations between Hindus and Muslims involved trade and pilgrimage. In the wake of the Arab conquest of the Sind valley, India

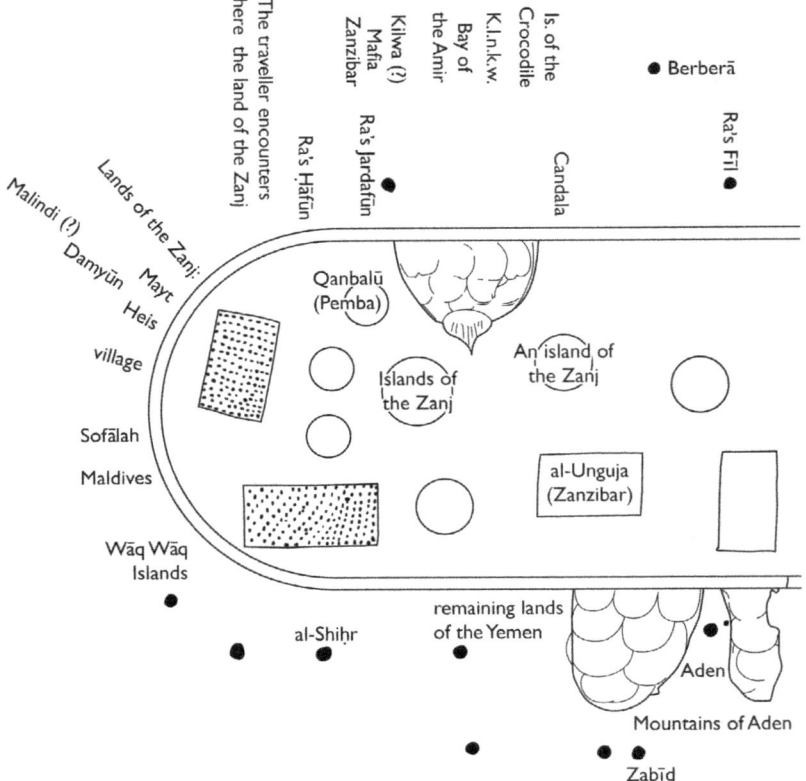

Figure II.5.4 Interpretative diagram for left-hand section of the map of the Indian Ocean from the *Book of Curiosities*.

was re-incorporated into the global economy, with Hindus now actively involved in trade alongside Muslims, pushing aside the networks of the Buddhist merchants.[15] Kannauj in particular became the nodal point for trade routes criss-crossing northern India. Its visual prominence in the *Book of Curiosities* map is in complete accord with al-Biruni's slightly later description of its central location.[16]

The Fatimid Imam-caliphs pursued a policy of active intervention in Sind, and gained control of its main cities. Ismaili *daʿi*s were sent to Sind from Yemen in the late 3rd/9th century, and one of them, known as al-Haytham, attracted disciples in Multan.[17] In the 350s/960s Multan was captured by an Ismaili *daʿi* called Jalam (or Halam) b. Shayban, who seized the city, and then proceeded to destroy the Sun-god's statue and kill its priests, building an Ismaili mosque on the site and closing the Sunni, Umayyad-era, mosque.[18] Jalam was acting under the direct orders of the Fatimid Imam-caliph, as attested by a letter from al-Muʿizz to an agent in Multan, criticising lax attitudes towards the practices of the converts who joined the local Ismaili community.[19] A second letter congratulates Jalam for his capture of the city and destruction of the Sun-idol.[20] Al-Muqaddasi, who visited Sind in the late 4th/10th century, reports that Multan was under the control of the Fatimid Imam-caliph, and that 'envoys and presents go regularly from Multan to Egypt'.[21] Fatimid control is also attested by a series of coins minted in the distinct Fatimid concentric pattern.[22] There is also a record of an exotic gift from India presented to al-ʿAziz in 385/995.[23] Multan and al-Mansura remained under Fatimid control until they were captured by Mahmud of Ghazna in 410/1010 (Multan) and 416/1025 (al-Mansura).[24]

The second section of the itinerary on the map, from Kannauj to China, shows that the horizons of the Fatimids extended beyond central India. This itinerary is entitled 'the road to China', and consists of an overland passage from northern India to China not found in any other Islamic source. The itinerary initially follows the river – in reality, the Ganges, although it is not named – eastwards from Kannauj. The first label is *Frayan*, undoubtedly Prayag (Allahabad), which lies at the confluence of the Ganges and the Jumna.[25] The next locality is written as *N-b-a-r-s*, certainly Benares. The third locality is written as *B-t-z*, which is likely to be *Putra*, a shortened form of Pataliputra (Patna). The route then turns away from the river, with a dozen further localities named, including 'the city of *Awlhas*' possibly Lhasa in Tibet. The terminus of the itinerary is a locality labelled 'The Gate of China'.

Although identification of place-names is speculative, the map almost certainly depicts a Tibetan route to Xi'an, the capital of central China. Muslim and non-Muslim sources report increased use of a Tibetan route in the 4th/10th and 5th/11th centuries.[26] When the Tibetans gained control of Dunhuang and the Gansu corridor in 786 CE, they ushered a period of intense traffic between Tibet, India and China. Tibetan influence continued even after the Tang re-took Dunhuang in 848 CE. According to Sen Tansen's study of Indian-Chinese Buddhist networks, travellers climbed the mountains of Nepal to Kathmandu, then passed through Lhasa and the Tibetan plateau, finally reaching the Chinese terminus at Xi'an.[27]

How well informed was this map? The misconception of Indian rivers demonstrates that the author of the *Book of Curiosities* did not travel through India himself. His lack of familiarity with the course of the Indus and the Ganges constrasts with earlier Islamic geographers who were aware of the distinction between them, even if confused about the course of the Indus.[28] The labels describe Kannauj as the capital of India and the seat of its ruler, and this seems to originate at a time when the Gurjara-Pratihara power was at its height, between 850 and 950 CE. By the end of the 4th/10th century, however, the empire had shrunk to the territory immediately surrounding Kannauj, and it was then sacked by Mahmud of Ghazna in 408/1018. By al-Biruni's day it was still commercially important, but no longer the capital of the kingdom.[29] The map also precedes the Ghaznavid conquests during the first decades of the 5th/11th century, and thus reflects the knowledge of India circulating in Egypt in the second half of the 4th/10th century, perhaps during the period of the most intense Fatimid involvement and interest in Muslim Sind, during the 350s/960s.

The Indus–Ganges river map visually shows how much Sind mattered to the Fatimids. Before the discovery of the *Book of Curiosities* we had only occasional glimpses of Fatimid involvement in Muslim Sind, mainly through the cryptic letters sent by the Imam-caliph al-Muʿizz to his *daʿi*s in India. But here we can visually see that from a Fatimid perspective, Multan was the gateway to central India, and from there to China. Multan coming under Ismaili-Fatimid control gave the Fatimids the opportunity to rival the other great empires of the medieval world economically, in the same way the Abbasids were made rich by their pole position in the global trade networks, and in particular through the direct maritime trade with China.

East Africa

As mentioned above, the map of the Indian Ocean in the *Book of Curiosities* is made up of two halves, which are quite independent of each other and joined up in an arbitrary fashion, with Yemen lying next to China. The left half of the oval depicts the Gulf of Aden and East Africa, in several distinct segments. Yemen is located at the bottom of the map, with Aden and its mountains prominently indicated. Capes and landmarks along the African coast of the Gulf of Aden, in what is today northern Somalia, lie at the top of the map, directly opposite Aden and its mountains. The easternmost cape is Raʾs Hafun, the prominent mountain protruding into the sea on the eastern Somali coast. The next cape is Raʾs

Jardafun, described as a very large mountain. This is the cape at the tip of the Horn of Africa, known today as Ra's 'Asir and in European literature as Guardafui.[30] The sequence of capes suggests that this map was based on first-hand knowledge of sailing along the East African coast of the Gulf of Aden. A third segment, on the left-hand side and outside the rim, is a list of villages along the East African coast. Inside the oval of the Indian Ocean we find the islands of Zanzibar (written Unjuwa for Unguja, the Swahili name for Zanzibar),[31] Pemba (Qanbalu)[32] and a generic 'Island of the East Africans (Zanj)'. A list of islands and bays of the Zanj is also given at the top of the page, above the map itself. This list includes Zanzibar again, and eight other place-names, including that of the nearby island of Mafia.

A final segment of the Indian Ocean map, located on the bottom left, between the villages of the East African coast and Yemen, has islands thought to lie at the extreme southern end of the Indian Ocean: Sofala, the Maldives and the Waq Waq. The region of Sofala in modern Mozambique was famed for its gold trade from at least the 4th/10th century.[33] Below Sofala, a label indicates the islands of al-Dibajat (the Maldives). A semi-legendary account of these islands, complete with coconut trees and a naked queen, is found elsewhere in the treatise in a chapter on the islands of the infidels.[34] Further down we find the Waq Waq islands, whose inhabitants are said to be pirates. The Waq Waq islands were the subject of much of the lore of the Indian Ocean, and the author of the *Book of Curiosities* too has an account of the Waq Waq human-shaped fruits in a chapter devoted to wondrous plants. There he describes the islands as 'bordering on Sofala, one of the isles of the Zanj'.[35]

The Indian Ocean map of the *Book of Curiosities* is a testimony to a resurgent trade between Egypt and East Africa along a maritime route that ran along the African coastline, from the Gulf of Aden and down to the Lamu archipelago. Like the Greek or Roman merchants who sailed to East Africa a millennium earlier, the Fatimids moved down the African coastline and established direct contacts with East African trading emporia.[36] Numismatic evidence of Fatimid trade with East Africa comes from the Mtambwe hoard found in the island of Pemba, which included eight Fatimid dinars and three imitation dinars of Fatimid type, dating from 358 to 458/969 to 1066.[37] The *Book of Curiosities* demonstrates that an Egyptian Fatimid author was able to provide a detailed account of the capes and villages along the coasts of Berbera in the Gulf of Aden, and to provide a southward itinerary towards the trading emporia of Zanzibar and Pemba.

The most tangible result of this Fatimid connection to East Africa is the sudden emergence of a market for African luxury materials in Cairo, resulting in some of the best known Fatimid artefacts. The extraordinary expansion of ivory carving in the Mediterranean world from the 350s/960s, including in Fatimid Egypt, may be linked to this increased level of commerce with East Africa.[38] The East African origin of Fatimid ivory is supported by Nasir-i Khusraw's *Safar-nama*, in which he reports seeing elephant tusks from Zanzibar in the markets of Fustat.[39] Similarly, exquisite Fatimid rock crystal vessels, the centrepiece of almost any catalogue of Fatimid art, also point to an East African connection. The surviving examples from Fatimid Egypt were carved from unusually large and pure pieces, suggesting that the Fatimid fascination with rock crystal artefacts was driven by the availability of a new source of raw material.[40] There seems little doubt that Fatimid rock crystal originated in East Africa, most probably in the river valleys of northern Madagascar.[41] Al-Biruni also wrote that the finest crystal was brought to Basra from the islands of East Africa and from the Maldives.[42] Nasir-i Khusraw reported that in the Lamp Market in Cairo he saw lamps made of Maghribi rock crystal, but 'it is said that near the Red Sea there is an even finer and more translucent crystal than the Maghribi'.[43]

The prominence of Yemen on the Indian Ocean map is in line with the crucial strategic importance it held for the Fatimid dynasty. By the 4th/10th century Aden had emerged as a major emporium, a concomitant result of a shift in trade routes from the Persian Gulf to the Red Sea. Al-Muqaddasi described Aden as 'the anteroom of China, entrepot of Yemen, treasury of the West'.[44] The Ismaili *daʿi* and poet Nasir-i Khusraw, who travelled in the Fatimid empire between 438/1046 and 444/1052 when he returned home to Khurasan, also tells us that the main trade routes of the Indian Ocean bifurcated at Aden, leading either to India in the east or to Zanzibar and Ethiopia in a south-westerly direction.[45] The depiction in the *Book of Curiosities* pre-dates the control of Yemen by the Ismaili Sulayhid dynasty, which rose to power in the late 430s/1040s and in 480/1087 established its capital in Dhu Jibla. Yet it highlights Yemen's earlier strategic importance for the spread of the Ismaili *daʿwa* and the promotion of Fatimid influence in the Indian Ocean.

Conclusion

The Indian Ocean map does not have a military orientation, and has no information on the capacity of ports, availability of water or references to fleets of galleys. The absence of a naval perspective is in line with what we know of the slow southward advance of the Fatimids. No Fatimid galleys travelled to Aden at the time the *Book of Curiosities* was composed. The first reference to the presence of Fatimid navy patrols in the Red Sea comes only in 512/1118, when five galleys (*harariq*) were sent to 'Aydhab to accompany merchants travelling to Suakin.[46] Convoys of ships travelling from Egypt, carrying the merchants known as Karimi, did not appear in the Red Sea until well into the 6th/12th century.[47] The Red Sea as a whole is surprisingly and inexplicably absent from any of the maps of the *Book of Curiosities*.

While the Mediterranean was the realm of naval warfare against a renascent Byzantium, the Indian Ocean was not a militarised space; the Fatimid ambitions in the Indian Ocean related not to military conquest, but to the propagation of the Ismaili *da'wa* and the extension of Fatimid suzerainty to the key commercial nodes of Yemen and Sind.[48] Knowledge of India and of East Africa was probably carried back and forth by *da'i*s travelling the routes to Aden, Sind and beyond. The Ismaili missionary network was a means for the exchange of wide-ranging knowledge about the world, with each *da'i* expected to have sufficient understanding not only of the exoteric and esoteric aspects of the faith, but, in addition, knowledge of the lands and peoples in their area of operation. A surviving manual for Ismaili missionaries recommends that the *da'i* should 'travel and observe the various "islands" so that he be acquainted with the nature of the inhabitants and the kind of knowledge they desire',[49] as well as with their religion.[50] In an example coming from the *Book of Curiosities* itself, a missionary *naqib* called Ahmad b. al-Marzuban is cited as the author's informant on the marvellous trees of Nubia.[51]

The representation of the Indian Ocean in the *Book of Curiosities* captures a very specific moment in Fatimid history and in the history of global communications. The overland Tibetan route to China that is central to this treatise declined after the fall of the Ismaili outposts of Multan and al-Mansura, during the early decades of the 5th/11th century, and there is also only meagre textual evidence of Egyptian contacts with East Africa in the following centuries.[52] The overland route to China through Sind and Tibet was soon replaced by a revived maritime route, extensively attested to in the letters of the Cairo Geniza. After 472/1080, coinciding with the consolidation of the Sulayhid Ismaili dynasty in Yemen, Jewish merchants made their way by boat from Egypt to Aden, India and then to the furthest islands of south-east Asia, carrying an astounding range of goods. The maps of the *Book of Curiosities* pre-date the lively Geniza letters, and attest to the importance of the amirates of Sind and of the East African emporia for the global ambitions of the Cairo caliphate up to the first decades of the 5th/11th century.

NOTES

* This essay is an updated abridgement of chapters 7 and 8 in Y. Rapoport and Emilie Savage-Smith, *Lost Maps of the Caliphs* (Chicago, 2018).
1 Ibid.; Y. Rapoport and E. Savage-Smith, *An Eleventh-century Egyptian Guide to the Universe* (London, 2014).
2 On the encounters between the Islamic world and Tibet, see A. Akasoy et al., ed., *Islam and Tibet. Interactions along the Musk Route* (Farnham and Burlington, VT, 2011).
3 For Sulayman's account of this route, see J. Sauvaget, ed., *Akhbar al-Sin wa'l-Hind. Relation de la Chine et de l'Inde, rédigée en 851* (Paris, 1948).
4 'al-Sin', *EI2*. Khanfu has alternatively been identified with Fuzhou rather than Quanzhou: D. D. Leslie, 'Chinese Cities in Arabic and Persian Sources', *Papers for Far Eastern History*, 25 (1982), p. 8.
5 V. Hansen, *The Silk Road* (Oxford, 2012), pp. 164–165; H. Park, *Mapping the Chinese and Islamic Worlds* (Cambridge, 2012), pp. 56–90.
6 'al-Sin', *EI2*; T. Sen, *Buddhism Diplomacy and Trade. The realignment of Sino-Indian relations, 600–1400* (Honolulu, 2003), pp. 167, 181; Abu'l-Hasan 'Ali al-Mas'udi, *Kitab Muruj al-dhahab*, ed. C. Barbier de Meynard and P. de Courteille, rev. C. Pellat (Beirut, 1965), vol. 1, p. 308, n. 336.
7 Tahera Qutbuddin, 'Fatimid Aspirations of Conquest and Doctrinal Underpinnings in the Poetry of al-Qa'im bi-Amr Allah, Ibn Hani' al-Andalusi, Amir Tamim b. al-Mu'izz and al-Mu'ayyad al-Shirazi', in Ramzi Baalbaki et al., ed., *Poetry and History: The Value of Poetry in Reconstructing Arab History* (Beirut, 2011), p. 218.
8 The label is wrongly written as:'.k.b.y.t. jibal, undoubtedly a mistake for *al-Tubbat jibal*. It is typical of the pervasive copying mistakes in the manuscript.
9 The label is wrongly written '*Futuh*' instead of '*Qannawj*'. The Sanskrit name of the city, Kanaakubdja or Kanyakubdja, was rendered by Arab geographers as Qannawj or Qinnawj. See, 'Kanawdj or Kannawdj', *EI2*.
10 Derryl N. MacLean, *Religion and Society in Arab Sind* (Leiden, 1989), pp. 59–63; 'Arur', *EI2*.
11 al-Biruni, *Kitab Ta'rikh al-Hind. Alberuni's India*, ed. E. Sachau (London, 1888), pp. 161, 164. For al-Biruni's itineraries, see also D. C. Sircar, *Studies in the Geography of Ancient and Medieval India* (Delhi, 1971), p. 241; J. E. Schwartzberg, with the collaboration of Shiva G. Bajpai et al., *A Historical Atlas of South Asia* (2nd. ed., New York, 1992), plate IV.3 (2).
12 A. Wink, *Al-Hind, the Making of the Indo-Islamic world*. vol. 1, 'Early Medieval India and the Expansion of Islam, 7th–11th Centuries' (Leiden, 1990), pp. 186–187, citing al-Istakhri, *Kitab al-Masalik wa'l-mamalik*, ed. de Goeje (Leiden, 1870, rpr. 1967), pp. 173–175.
13 *Hudud al-'alam*, tr. by V. Minorsky as *The Regions of the World : A Persian Geography 372AH-982 AD*, ed. C. E. Bosworth (London 1970), pp. 89–90, 123.

14 Y. Friedmann, 'Multan', *EI2*; A. Wink, *Al-Hind*, vol. 1, p. 187; R. C. Majumdar, ed., *The History and Culture of the Indian People*, vol. 4, 'The Age of Imperial Kanauj' (Bombay, 1955), pp. 125, 402.
15 Johan Elverskog, *Buddhism and Islam on the Silk Road* (Philadelphia, 2010), p. 40.
16 al-Biruni, *Kitab Ta'rikh Hind*, ed. E. Sachau (London, 1888), p. 157.
17 Wink, *Al-Hind*, vol. 1, p. 213.
18 'Multan', *EI2*; Wink, *Al-Hind*, vol. 1, pp. 214–215; Finbarr Barry Flood, *Objects of Translation: Material Culture and Medieval 'Hindu-Muslim' Encounter* (Princeton, NJ, 2009), p. 155; F. Daftary, *The Isma'ilis: Their History and Doctrines* (2nd ed., Cambridge, 2007), p. 166 (where the date is given as 347/958).
19 Flood, *Objects of Translation*, p. 42; S. M. Stern, 'Heterodox Isma'ilism at the time of al-Mu'izz', *BSOAS*, 17 (1955), pp. 23–25.
20 Flood, *Objects of Translation*, p. 30; Stern, 'Heterodox Isma'ilism at the time of al-Mu'izz', pp. 25–26.
21 Wink, *Al-Hind*, vol. 1, p. 216; al-Muqaddasi, *Ahsan al-taqasim fi ma'rifat al-aqalim*, ed. de Goeje (Leiden, 1877, rpr. 1906), p. 485.
22 Wink, *Al-Hind*, vol. 1, p. 216; Flood, *Objects of Translation*, p. 50 (circulation of Egyptian artefacts in Sind, including an Abbasid dinar minted in Egypt between 227–233/842–847).
23 Yaacov Lev, 'A Mediterranean Encounter: The Fatimids and Europe, Tenth to Twelfth Centuries', in Ruthy Gertwagen and Elizabeth Jeffreys, ed., *Shipping, Trade and Crusade in the Medieval Mediterranean: Studies in Honour of John Pryor* (Farnham, UK, 2012), p. 145.
24 Wink, *Al-Hind*, vol. 1, pp. 216, 218.
25 'Allahabad', *EI2*.
26 T. Sen, *Buddhism, Diplomacy and Trade*, pp. 171–174.
27 Ibid., p. 173, Map (Kathmandu – Zongga – Tingri – Shigatse – Gyantse – Lhasa – Nagqu – Zhutuokalun – Chang'an).
28 'Mihran', *EI2*.
29 Wink, *Al-Hind*, vol. 1, pp. 284–285.
30 'Guardafui', *EI2*.
31 al-Idrisi, *Nuzhat al-mushtaq fi ikhtiraq al-afaq*, ed. A. Bombaci et al. (Naples, 1970), p. 61; 'Zandjibar', *EI2*.
32 'Mtambwe Mkuu', *EI2*.
33 'Sofala', *EI2*.
34 Y. Rapoport and E. Savage-Smith, ed. and tr., *An Eleventh-Century Egyptian Guide to the Universe. The 'Book of Curiosities'* (Leiden, 2014), p. 482. Compare G. R. Tibbetts, *A Study of the Arabic Texts Containing Material on Southeast Asia* (Leiden, 1979), pp. 50, 80; J. Sauvaget, ed., *Akhbar al-Sin wa'l-Hind*, p. 3 (no. 4); Mas'udi, *Muruj al-dhahab*, vol. 1, pp. 179–180 (nos. 366-68); Idrisi, *Nuzhat al-mushtaq*, p. 69.
35 Y. Rapoport and E. Savage-Smith, *An Eleventh-Century Egyptian Guide to the Universe*, p. 519. G.R. Tibbetts and Shawkat Toorawa, 'Wakwak', *EI2*. The illustration of the Waq Waq trees in the Bodleian copy is a late medieval addition.
36 M. Horton and J. Middleton, *The Swahili: The Social Landscape of a Mercantile Society* (Oxford, 2000), pp. 33, 78–80. For the Roman era, see L. Casson, ed., *Periplus Maris Erythraei* (Princeton, NJ, 1989).
37 'Mtambwe Mkuu', *EI2*. The 2000 locally minted silver coins contained the names of local rulers with rhyming couplets on their reverse (M. Horton, 'Artisans, Communities, and Commodities: Medieval Exchanges between North-western India and East Africa', *Ars Orientalis*, 34 (2007), p. 75; Horton, 'The Swahili Corridor', *Scientific American*, 257 (1987), p. 81). There is also an intriguing numismatic correlation between the miniscule coinage found in Shanga, on the East African coasts, and a series of Fatimid silver coins from Sind, carrying the name of the Fatimid Imam-caliphs al-Mu'izz and al-'Aziz,

acquired by the British Museum in 1980. The two series of coins from Shanga and Sind share a unique and consistent die-alignment, where the obverse and reverse are precisely at 3, 6, 9 or 12 o'clock, a feature that is absent from the rest of the Islamic world at this time (Horton and Middleton, *The Swahili*, p. 50; Horton, 'Artisans, Communities, and Commodities', p. 75).

38. Horton and Middleton, *The Swahili*, p. 80.
39. Nasir-i Khusraw, *Safarnama*, tr. W. M. Thackston, Jr., as *Naser-e Khosraw's Book of Travels* (1986), p. 53.
40. A. Contadini, *Fatimid Art at the Victoria and Albert Museum* (London, 1998), pp. 16–18.
41. S. Pradines, 'The Rock Crystal of Dembeni, Mayotte Mission Report 2013', *Nyame Akuma*, 80 (2013), pp. 59–72.
42. A. Contadini, *Fatimid Art*, p. 18.
43. Nasir-i Khusraw, *Safarnama*, p. 53. Horton also suggests that the high-quality Fatimid dinars were made from gold brought from the regions between the Zambezi and Limpopo basins (M. Horton, 'The Swahili Corridor', p. 76.)
44. Roxani Margariti, *Aden and the Indian Ocean Trade: 150 Years in the Life of a Medieval Arabian Port* (Chapel Hill, NC, 2007), p. 27; al-Muqaddasi, *Ahsan al-taqasim fi ma'rifat al-aqalim*, p. 85.
45. Nasir-i Khusraw, *Safarnama*, p. 43.
46. David Bramoullé, 'The Fatimids and the Red Sea (969–1171)', in Dionisius A. Agius et al., ed., *Navigated Spaces, Connected Places: Proceedings of Red Sea Project V* (Oxford, 2012), p. 132; E. Vallet, *L'Arabie marchande: État et commerce sous les sultans Rasulides du Yémen, 626–858/1229–1454* (Paris, 2010), p. 485.
47. In the Fatimid period the term refers to convoys travelling to the Indian Ocean from Egyptian ports, not exclusively Muslim ones (Margariti, *Aden and the Indian Ocean Trade*, p. 152; Bramoullé, 'The Fatimids and the Red Sea', p. 135).
48. See the insightful remarks in C. Picard, 'Espaces maritimes et polycentrisme dans l'Islam abbasside', *Annales Islamologiques*, 45 (2011), p. 43. Picard argues that the Indian Ocean came to be identified with Islamic civilisation.
49. Ahmad b. Ibrahim al-Naysaburi, *A Code of Conduct: A Treatise on the Etiquette of the Fatimid Ismaili Mission*, ed. and tr. by Verena Klemm and Paul E. Walker (London, 2011), p. 55 (no. 59).
50. al-Naysaburi, *A Code of Conduct*, p. 56 (no. 62).
51. Rapoport and Savage-Smith, *An Eleventh-Century Egyptian Guide*, p. 518.
52. S. D. Goitein and M. A. Friedman, *Indian Traders of the Middle Ages: Documents from the Cairo Geniza: India Book* (Leiden, 2008), p. 21.

SECTION III

FATIMID CEREMONY AND SYMBOLISM

1

The Fatimid Crescent: Understanding a Complex Religio-Political Cosmos through Lunar Symbolism

Ali Asgar Alibhai

On the day of ʿArafa in 362/973 CE, the Fatimid Imam-caliph al-Muʿizz (r. 341–365/953–975) ordered that a *shamsa* be displayed in the *iwan* (great hall) of the royal palace in Cairo.[1] *Shamsa*s were ornamented textile-based decorative hangings that caliphs and rulers traditionally commissioned in the medieval Islamic world to be attached over the drapery (*kiswa*) of the Kaʿba during the *hajj* season as an additional embellishment. Correlating its dazzling likeness to the sun (*al-shams*), the medieval Islamic lexicon aptly named this ornament *shamsa* since it was shaped like a medallion and sparkled by means of its elaborately embroidered, gilded and jewelled composition. Since Abbasid times, when the Caliph al-Mutawakkil (d. 247/861) initiated the tradition, *shamsa*s functioned to legitimise the ruler and symbolise his authority, since he would have it sent long distances across the empire to Mecca, where Muslims coming from all parts of the medieval Islamic world gathered annually. Al-Muʿizz's *shamsa* was paradoxical in that, though it was a design inspired by the sun, it was ornamented with a series of waxing crescent moons (*ahilla*), a celestial visual motif that was tied to notions of time and authority in medieval Islamic and Fatimid intellectual discourse.

Through an interdisciplinary analysis of the Fatimid *shamsa* and the waxing crescent moon (*hilal*), this chapter looks closely at medieval Arabic primary sources and argues that ornamentation in medieval Fatimid art, particularly official and courtly objects and architecture, often conveyed multiple meanings rather than a single, fixed interpretation. That is to say, Fatimid rulers purposefully used ornamental motifs on the art they commissioned to convey a range of meanings that could be found in the interpretive frameworks of the broader medieval Islamic world as well as inner Ismaili discourses.² It can be suggested that al-Muʿizz intentionally commissioned his *shamsa* with the *hilal* motif because of its mimetic and didactic potential in conveying the message of his divine authority over temporal time and space. In this instance, the calligraphic and geometric ornamentation chosen for the *shamsa*'s visual beauty was not purely a device for pleasure but a carrier and conveyer of direct meaning.

This chapter, through a deconstruction of the visual descriptions of al-Muʿizz's *shamsa*, posits that viewing ornament in medieval Islamic art was an active, communicative process rather than a passive experience. While intended to evoke viewing pleasure, engaging with ornament also required the viewer to assume the task of intentional and mindful interpretation. Ornament functioned as more than a mere bridge between the observer and personal interpretations; instead, the *hilal* motif on the Fatimid *shamsa* demonstrates an intellectual, political and spiritual ambition to convey specific meanings. By employing the mimetic symbol of the *hilal*, al-Muʿizz aimed to communicate to a broad audience, diverse in geographic and ideological background, coming from various schools of Islamic thought. The common symbol of the *hilal* invited viewers to uncover layered meanings, each level influenced by their unique intellectual and religious contexts. Here, the viewer's pleasure in beholding the ornament becomes the vehicle through which the intended message is conveyed.

The waxing crescent motif in medieval Islamic visual culture evoked a diverse array of meanings for multiple audiences ranging from the elite (*al-khass*) to the common folk (*al-ʿam*) in both Fatimid and larger Islamic communities. Most Muslim onlookers who saw al-Muʿizz's *shamsa* displayed in Mecca, understood that the motif symbolised notions of time, since sighting the physical, waxing, crescent moon served medieval Islamic societies as the temporal marker of the beginning of the season of the *hajj* and other important events. Qurʾan 2:189³ makes this interpretation and the resulting practice abundantly clear: the sighting of the waxing crescent moon was (and still is) a common way for Muslims to determine important dates like the beginning and end of Ramadan and the start of Dhuʾl-Hijja, the twelfth month of the lunar calendar in which the Hajj is performed. However, as this study suggests, while the sighting of the waxing crescent moon (*ruʾyat al-hilal*) was a traditional method used for marking time in medieval Muslim societies, the *hilal* and its connection to telling time carried an added significance for the elite of Fatimid society.

The Fatimids were unique among medieval Muslims in their use of an astronomically calculated and fixed calendar to mark time, diverging from the broader contemporary practice of relying on moon sightings as the basis for measuring the calendar.[4] While most medieval Muslims determined the telling of time anecdotally and based on the recurring natural instant of actually seeing the new moon when it was in its waxing form in the sky, the Fatimids understood time through a rational approach, understanding time through fixed calculations, a notion that was grounded in Ismaili interpretations of jurisprudence as well as spiritual hermeneutics. For the Fatimids, the waxing crescent moon also signified the Imam-caliph's universal authority and his doctrinal role as the 'Master of Time' (*sahib al-zaman*).[5] This doctrine led them to rely on a calculated calendar rather than physical moon sightings.

The argument that medieval Islamic ornament frequently conveyed multivalent symbolism rather than singular forms of iconic symbolism remains a vital topic in Islamic art scholarship.[6] Since the 19th century, Orientalists and European scholars and theorists have shown a keen, albeit biased, interest in Islamic art, characterising its ornament – often referred to as 'the arabesque' – as the decorative elements found in calligraphic, vegetal, geometric or figural patterns.[7] Within this discourse, two major interpretations have dominated academic circles: Islamic ornament's purpose is either highly formalist or abundantly spiritual.[8] These conflicting views about the nature of Islamic ornament have generated a secondary debate regarding its role – whether it functioned purely as an aesthetic visual element intended to provide pleasure for the viewer or as a device for conveying meaning and communicating distinct iconographic symbols.[9]

In more recent scholarship, art historians have proposed new theories regarding Islamic ornament. One prominent theory that sparked considerable follow-up studies is Oleg Grabar's *Mediation of Ornament*, published in 1992.[10] Grabar argued that ornament in Islamic art functions as a visual mechanism designed to provide pleasure to the viewer while also serving as an intermediary between the object and the beholder.[11] He contended that ornament offers beauty and pleasure through its universal appeal, suggesting that this appeal allows ornament to act as a communicative agent, mediating between itself and the viewer's cognitive and sensory response.[12] However, Grabar emphasised the ambiguous nature of this interaction, proposing that the role of ornament as an 'intermediary' does not aim to convey specific meanings or allegories but rather leaves interpretation open to the viewer's subjective response.[13]

Some scholars argue that ornament has historically been intended to communicate certain meanings visually, though the expectation that it must convey specific iconic meaning may be overstated. James Trilling, for instance, has suggested,

> Until very recently, ornament has been functional, and it has been a means of communication. Where Coomaraswamy and others have gone wrong is in the assumption that if ornament communicates, it must communicate symbolically. To believe that the 'lost' function of ornament was to convey a host of specific meanings is a particularly modern kind of romanticism. Because we ourselves are incapable of using symbols, we are eager to find them in other cultures.[14]

In the introduction to their exhibition catalogue *Cosmophilia* (2006), Jonathan Bloom and Sheila Blair adopt a middle-ground approach in understanding the relationship between Islamic ornament and symbolic meaning.[15] While acknowledging that Islamic ornament can convey some form of meaning, they stress that any direct iconographic symbolism associated with specific animal, vegetal or geometric motifs was unlikely to be employed in Islamic courts and societies, nor would such symbols have maintained consistent meanings across time and space.[16] They argue that commonly used motifs, such as birds, may convey general meanings but lack precise iconographic significance, comparing this to modern contexts:

> Millions of American and European households today own dishes decorated with flowers and/or animals; their owners give nary a thought to the meaning of the specific representation on them, so why must we demand meaning for medieval representations? For the medieval Islamic world, we have no contemporary source that explains the meaning of specific representations, and no image is accompanied by a text taken from literature that deals with the same subject.[17]

Avinoam Shalem and Eva-Maria Troelenberg have recently argued,

> The power of ornament appears in a wide range of shapes and meanings. Moreover, a variety of different means and mechanisms of artistic expressions can be observed in it, all of which reflect different stages or layers of conception and purpose. And, although primarily responding to a certain historical position, these artistic mechanisms transport these expressions to the beholder regardless

of the course of time. Thus, ornament seems to be part of very diverse compositions and could respond to and communicate with us in many different ways.[18]

This paper centres on Shalem and Troelenberg's interpretation of the potential power of ornament: they assert that the purpose of ornament transcends the mere display of beauty or the subjective experience of the viewer's gaze. Instead, they argue that ornament in Islamic art is involved in the creation of meaning, understood through intricate networks of human connectivity and socio-cultural dimensions that endure across extensive periods and diverse regions.

The commissioning of the Fatimid *shamsa* and its conveying to Mecca occurred during a historic moment in the Islamic world where political powers and alliances had shifted immensely. When the Fatimids conquered Egypt in 358/969, part of their promise to the people of Egypt was to safeguard the route to the *hajj* by ensuring safe passage, repairing roads and the supplying of food and provisions.[19] The route and safety of the pilgrimage to the *hajj* had been severely jeopardised in the previous years. The fulfillment of this promise, following al-Mu'izz's establishment of Cairo as the new Fatimid capital, also signalled a symbolic shift of power as al-Mu'izz began to be mentioned in the Friday *khutba* in Mecca and Medina, the main spiritual centres of the Islamic world.[20] It is argued here that in the case of the Fatimid *shamsa*, there was no ambiguity of meaning regarding its ornament. On the contrary, the meaning of ornament in al-Mu'izz's commission, when read alongside Fatimid hermeneutical, historical and jurisprudential sources, is very clear. The celestial ornament consisting of the repetition of the waxing crescent moon on the *shamsa*, was intended to express the clear message of al-Mu'izz's claim to spiritual and temporal rule over the Islamic world. It should also be noted that it was commissioned in Fatimid Egypt to be eventually displayed in Mecca.

A Case for Meaning in Ornament in Fatimid Art

When writing about ornament in Fatimid art, Jonathan Bloom states,

> Some scholars have attempted to detect a distinctly Shi'i, indeed Ismaili, quality to Fatimid art, whether in the concentric circles that decorate their coins, or in the repeated niches that decorate their buildings, but it is difficult, if not impossible, to argue that such

meanings were held consistently over time. One can easily imagine that some designs, such as the seven-point stars on the cenotaph of al-Husayn might have been intended to subtly remind the viewer of the seven Imams of the Ismaili line, but the six and eight-point stars in other designs have no such meaning and are simply there for their visual delight. Although Ismaili adepts were trained at seeing hidden meanings behind outward appearances, such meanings would have been lost to virtually all other eyes since so few adopted the Ismaili beliefs of the rulers.[21]

The research presented in this chapter suggests that Fatimid elite society, in certain cases, communicated their ontological worldview in art and architecture they commissioned through visual ornament. While we are not capable of pinpointing a specific form of meaning or symbolism for every form of ornament we encounter due to the lack of contemporary sources and accounts, this does not warrant the argument that all ornament was devoid of meaning entirely and used only for its beauty and the pleasure it gave. In fact, there are some instances where the connection between meaning and ornament is clearly evident because the patron fully intended and wished to convey a specific range of meanings, as this chapter demonstrates. Furthermore, I propose that ornament that carried specific doctrinal meaning linking it to the authority or legitimacy of the Imam-caliph, would not have been lost to 'virtually all other eyes'.[22] On the contrary, as Shalem's and Troelenberg's article interprets the power of ornament and its ability to convey a wide range of shapes and meanings, this paper posits that al-Muʿizz, along with other Fatimid Imam-caliphs, persistently employed ornament in several works of art and architecture to convey a range of meaning that signified their professed spiritual and temporal power and authority over the Muslim world. This meaning, like hidden knowledge in Ismaili ontological thought, could have multivalent meanings understood independently by different members of Islamic society.

The ontological worldview of Fatimid society is present and largely consistent in the extensive corpus of extant Ismaili spiritual hermeneutical writings (the *ta'wil*). Ismaili hermeneutical thought maintained that all conventional knowledge possesses a deeper hidden meaning; however, a single reference to any piece of knowledge can hold many different meanings. Al-Qadi al-Nuʿman (d. 363/974), the chief justice (*qadi al-qudat*) of the early of Fatimid court, explains this concept at the beginning of his hermeneutical work titled *Asas al-Ta'wil* (The Foundations of Spiritual

Hermeneutics). He stated that when Fatimid Imam-caliphs uttered a single word or phrase, it had the potential to yield multiple meanings. He quoted the sixth Shi'i Imam, Ja'far al-Sadiq (d. 148/765) as saying that the Imams can render seven, seventy, or potentially even more meanings from a single word. The various meanings that knowledge contains are understood at varying levels.[23] Similarly, a culture does not produce art in a vacuum. Art is a product of the intellectual and cultural milieu in which it is produced. It is very likely therefore that Fatimid visual symbols, reflecting their view of the exoteric and esoteric levels of knowledge, also possessed multivalent meanings understood in different capacities by different individuals from varying levels of society.

The case for multivalent meanings can be interpreted in the visual composition of Fatimid coins. The writings of Abu Ya'qub al-Sijistani (d. after 361/971), an adept Fatimid-Ismail philosopher and theologian, demonstrate how medieval thinkers consistently blended hermeneutical interpretations with visual and material culture. In his treatise titled *Ithbat al-Nubuwwa* (The Proofs of Prophethood), Sijistani saw meaning in the placement and design of specific inscriptions on official coins minted by the Fatimids. He acknowledges that there exists an unbreakable bond between prophethood (*al-nubuwwa*) and temporal rule (*al-mamlaka*). Proof of this divinely ordained link between the religious and political realms is evident in the coinage. Sijistani notes that the name of the Imam-caliph appearing with the name of the Prophet Muhammad on the inscriptions of minted dinars and dirhams, just like it does as well in *khutbas* (sermons) pronounced from the *minbars* on Friday and Eid prayers, is representative of the authority to rule that was ordained to and inherited by the Fatimid Imams through their connection to the prophethood.[24]

The new style of Fatimid coins minted by the Imam-caliph al-Mu'izz in al-Sijistani's time bears a standard visual convention known as the 'bullseye type', which, in the original prototype, consisted of a dotted centre surrounded by two concentric circles bearing inscriptions in each (figures III.1.1 & III.1.2). The inscriptional formulas on the centre margin on the obverse side of the coin included the *shahada* in the central band, which included the Prophet Muhammad's name and the name of 'Ali b. Abi Talib. On the reverse side of the coin, the centre margin contained the name and title of the Imam-caliph.[25] This mirroring of the Prophet's name on one side of the coin, and the Imam-caliph's name in the same position on the obverse side of the coin, was a consistent visual component of

Figure III.1.1 Obverse side of gold dinar of al-Muʿizz li-Din Allah, Misr, Jumada I 361/January 972.

Figure III.1.2 Reverse side of gold dinar of al-Muʿizz li-Din Allah, Misr, Jumada I 361/January 972.

Fatimid coinage, even with changing layouts over time. The connection between the Prophet and the Imam-caliphs, according to al-Sijistani's reading, was the hermeneutical knowledge coded within the visual design of Fatimid coins. This idea allows for the possibility that other visual designs and ornament in Fatimid art could have held additional hermeneutical meanings. Likewise, it is possible to analyse al-Muʿizz's choice of twelve crescent moons on the Fatimid *shamsa* as possibly conveying multivalent symbolic meanings to medieval viewers when deciphered through other contemporary lenses of observation from textual sources.

Descriptions of the Fatimid *Shamsa*

Al-Maqrizi (d. 845/1442), the Mamluk historian, provides a vivid description of the Fatimid *shamsa* commissioned by al-Muʿizz. He writes that al-Muʿizz's *shamsa* was even larger and more splendid than previous Abbasid and Ikhshidid ones. Al-Muʿizz commissioned his *shamsa* using a red silk brocade (*dibaj*) ground measuring a length and width of twelve spans (approximately nine feet) in each direction.[26] It was decorated with twelve golden crescent moons (*ahilla*) encircling the entire textile. Each crescent moon (*hilal*) had in its centre a golden citron-shaped ornament made with an openwork-latticed surface. Inside each of these citrons were fifty pearls, each the size of a dove's egg, along with rubies and yellow and blue sapphires. Passages about the *hajj* from the Qur'an, inscribed with jewels, encircled the *shamsa*. Large and rare pearls also filled the inscriptions. Powdered musk covered the entire *shamsa*.[27]

Since the *shamsa* was exhibited on an elevated platform in the royal *iwan*, people outside the palace could see it. Al-Maqrizi also notes that mixed populations of people living in Cairo, including Egyptians, Syrians and Iraqis, entered the palace to see it. He says that the people of Khurasan and Iraq, namely those living in Abbasid lands and those who had been on the *hajj*, believed that al-Muʿizz's *shamsa* was unparalleled. It was so heavy, due to its rich work and ornamentation, that it needed several attendants to carry it to this location.[28] Al-Maqrizi also states, 'The Abbasid shamsa was more finely worked; it was only one-quarter of the size (of the Fatimid *shamsa*).'[29]

Al-Maqrizi also describes the previous Abbasid tradition of commissioning the *shamsa* and sending it to Mecca. He attributes the first *shamsa* to al-Mutawakkil (d. 247/861). Previously, al-Ma'mun (d. 281/833) sent a large ruby to adorn the Ka'ba, which was later hung by a golden chain every year on one side of the Ka'ba during the season of the *hajj*. When al-Mutawakkil commissioned the *shamsa* it became customary to attach it to this gold chain. The Abbasid *shamsa* was not simple in its ornamentation; according to al-Maqrizi, it was ornamented with 'pearls, rubies, and jewels.'[30]

Apart from al-Maqrizi's 9th/15th-century text describing al-Mu'izz's *shamsa*, there exists a closer contemporary account from the 4th/10th-century preserved in verses of a *qasida* (panegyric) written by the Fatimid poet prince, al-Tamim (d. 375/985), the son of al-Mu'izz.[31] The poet prince wrote this panegyric to commemorate his father's commissioning of the *shamsa*. The *qasida* begins with the *madih* (praise) of the Imam-caliph al-Mu'izz and then, after several verses of praise, moves to a description of the *shamsa* (below). Just before the description of the *shamsa*, al-Tamim praises the era of al-Mu'izz's reign and the Fatimid dynasty.[32]

وهذه الدولةُ التي زَخرتْ
فلم يَسَعْها الزمانُ والحِقَب

And this dynasty has grown so vast that time and eras cannot contain it.

يا حبّذا دَهْرُك الزُّلالُ إذا
أَمَرّ دهرٌ وعصرُك الشَّنِب

O, how lovely is your pure era? If an era turns bitter, your era remains ever sweet.

وحبّذا الشَّمْسةُ التي نَصبتْ
يَقْصُرُ عنها المديحُ والخُطَبُ

O, how lovely is the *shamsa* which was raised (for viewing), words of praise and speech fall short [of its splendour].

قايستِ العِيدَ وهي حُلّتُه
وأخفت اليومَ وهو مُنْتَصب

The *shamsa* came into comparison to the day of Eid, as it was its new exquisite garment. Although Eid is established today, the *shamsa* eclipsed it.[33]

يَنْهَب ياقوتُها العيونَ فما
يَكْمُلُ إلّا من حيث يَنْتَهب

Its jewels caught all eyes, and they were perfected by the way they dazzled and captivated [onlookers].

دائرةٌ أحدقتْ بغرتها
أهلةٌ لا تُجِنَّها السُّحُب

A circle of crescents encompasses the upper portion of the *shamsa*, Clouds do not hide these crescents.

كأنما دُرَّها وجوهرُها
نجومُ ليلٍ سماؤها ذَهَبُ

As if the pearls and jewels of the *shamsa* are the stars of the night in a golden sky.

كأنما رُصِّعتْ مَناقبُك الـ
غُرّ عليها وأُفْرِغ الحَسَبُ

As if your luminous virtues (*manaqib*) have been ornamented onto the *shamsa*; as if your noble esteem (*hasb*) abundantly pours out of it.

حقّ على الشمس طولُ نِقْبتها
منها وذاتُ الحياء تُنْتَقبُ

The sun (*al-shams*) must veil itself from this *shamsa*, as any modest person would be veiled.

وقد أراها ولا مُدامَ بها
فكيف قالوا لدُرَّها الحَبَبُ

As I see it, there is no wine in sight, so why do the people say that its pearls are like bubbles.

نظمتَها للهُدَى ولِبَّتِه
وإن سَخِطْن الكواعبُ العُرُبُ

You strung those pearls on it to provide true guidance and to reveal its essence, even if this angers the young Arab maidens.

في كبِدِ المسجدِ الحرامِ لها
شوقٌ وللبيتِ نحوها طربُ

There is longing for the *shamsa* at the very heart of al-Masjid al-Haram and an excitement from the Ka'ba for it.

فلا تَمَشَّى بأهلِه زمنٌ
إلاّ بما تَشْتهي وتَرْتَقبُ

May time not continue for people, except with how you desire and what you anticipate.

صلّى عليك الإلهُ ما طَلَعَتْ
شمسٌ وما أنهلّ عارِضٌ لجِبُ

May God continue to bless you as long as the sun rises and rain falls from the thunderclouds.

Al-Tamim's verses about the *shamsa* describe it in detail, giving significant attention to the ornamentation and especially the waxing crescent moon motifs that adorned the textile. Additionally, al-Tamim's linking of the symbol of the *shamsa*'s elaborate ornament with the Imam-caliph's virtues and noble esteem, suggests an intentional association between celestial ornamentation and the figure of al-Muʿizz. Furthermore, the portion of the panegyric that describes the *shamsa* is preceded by verses about time praising the era of al-Muʿizz and emphasising his connection to time. Similarly, when the description and praise portion of the *shamsa* is completed, al-Tamim ends again with a verse that alludes to the Imam-caliph being the *master of time*, acknowledging that it passes in accordance with his desire and will.

As mentioned above, al-Muʿizz's choice of golden crescent moons as ornament throughout the textile and his departure from previous Abbasid traditions is noteworthy. As I have argued, the Imam-caliph's choices in ornament were intended to convey the multivalent symbolism of the crescent moons to contemporary audiences of the Muslim world and the Fatimid dynasty. As mentioned above, in medieval Islamic religious-cultural frameworks, the crescent moon motif represents notions of time, specifically the starting of the season of the *hajj* and the beginning and end of the month of Ramadan.[34] These same notions of time as they relate to the sighting of the crescent moon also had specific Fatimid and Ismaili contexts in understanding and determining their own notions of the passage of time. Instead of relying on a natural instant, like the sighting of the physical moon in the night sky which could be at times difficult, the Fatimids maintained that the Imam-caliph was the true marker of time as will be explained below. Additionally, Fatimid and Ismaili religious, spiritual, hermeneutical, jurisprudential and literary discourses provide a persistent discourse for this important Ismaili theological belief and shed light as well on the frequent use of the crescent motif in the art produced by the dynasty.

Crescent Moons and the Notion of Time in Islamic Society

The motif of the waxing crescent moon (*hilal*) has commonly appeared as a visual and literary motif within Islamic art, often as a surmounting ornament, much like a finial. It has appeared as such on ceramics and on objects using architectonic ornament. If an obvious meaning were to be assigned to the *hilal*, the most direct would be that it denotes time since Islamic civilisation began and grew within a culture that used the sighting of the moon and following the lunar cycle to measure the passage of time. Ibn Manzur (d. ca. 711/1312) writes in his medieval Arabic dictionary that the *hilal* is the word used for the waxing crescent moon during the first two nights of its appearance. After two nights, it is then called the *qamr* (moon). The word *hilal* is derived from the infinitive *ahalla*, meaning to raise one's voice in praise or rejoicing. The crescent moon was named the *hilal* accordingly because the early Arabs used to raise their voices in praise when sighting the waxing crescent moon.[35]

The practice of physically sighting the waxing crescent moon, *ru'yat al-hilal*, became the means by which Muslims determined many important dates and their corresponding rituals, as mentioned above, like the *hajj* and the beginning and end of the fast of Ramadan.[36] In other words, the passage of time itself was represented by the visual phases of the moon's appearance, and the visible crescent represented renewed time since it marked the beginning of the month. The Qur'an reinforces this idea in Sura 2:189 where the practice is mentioned: 'They ask thee about the waxing crescent moons (*ahillat*); say: They indicate the periods for [various doings of] mankind, including the pilgrimage.'[37] Furthermore, most major traditions and schools of thought in Islam report the Prophet as having said, 'Do not fast until you see the waxing crescent moon, and do not break the fast until you see it; but when it is hidden from you [by cloud or mist], give it its full measure (or thirty days).'[38] These notions made it customary to the majority of Islamic schools of thought that only through *ru'yat al-hilal* could one determine the days of the Hajj and of Ramadan.

However, there is another verse in the Qur'an that the Fatimids maintained suggested an alternative practice to *ru'yat al-hilal*. In Sura 2:183–184 the Qur'an states, 'O you who have attained to faith! Fasting is ordained for you as it was ordained for those before you, so that you might remain conscious of God: [fasting] during a certain number of days (*ayyam ma'dudat*).'[39] Adhering to the notion of a specified and calculated number of days (*ayyam ma'dudat*), and finding practical flaws in the practice of moon sighting, medieval Ismaili belief did not follow the Sunni or even Shi'i norms of determining the calendar, particularly the beginning and ending of the fast through the practice of *ru'yat al-hilal*. Instead, they adhered to a pre-calculated state calendar of 354 days consisting of a cycle of alternating months consisting of twenty-nine and thirty days in which Ramadan always numbered thirty days.

Since the majority of Islamic schools of thought were extremely opposed to this method of calculation, the Ismaili practice was often a subject of polemical debate. For example, al-Tabari (d. 310/923) writes for the year 278 about a supposed Ismaili doctrine which he regards as heretical that equated the crescent moons in the verse in the Qur'an from Sura 2 to the *zahir* (exoteric meaning) by which years, months and days are calculated, while the *batin* (esoteric meaning) referred to 'intimates'.[40] Although it is unclear if al-Tabari understood the Ismaili belief system correctly, it is apparent that he acknowledged that both exoteric and esoteric meaning was attached by Ismailis to the *hilal*.[41]

The Fatimids and the Practice of *Ru'yat al-Hilal*

It appears in historical texts that the Fatimids were adamant about publicly maintaining this counter-practice despite the considerable opposition to a practice of calculation for determining the beginning and end of Ramadan in both the Sunni and Shi'i communities. In the mid 5th/11th century the Fatimid *da'i* (missionary) in the Persian province of Fars, al-Mu'ayyad fi'l-Din al-Shirazi, prepared a feast to break the fast of Ramadan (*iftar*) in the courtyard of his house in Shiraz, although the local population had not as yet sighted the *hilal* and so were still fasting. The Sunni population became infuriated with the local Ismailis who were celebrating Eid while they continued to fast on their twenty-ninth day. However, that evening the waxing moon appeared in the sky and the Buyid local authorities realised that the Ismailis had been correct in their calculations after all, which in turn infuriated the authorities even more. Because of this incident, the Buyid vizier, Ibn Mafanna, summoned al-Mu'ayyad the next day and told him that he must leave Shiraz because the Buyid Amir Abu Kalijar was outraged with what had transpired. Furthermore, al-Mu'ayyad was accused of spreading heresy.[42] The narration of this incident indicates the lengths the Fatimids and their supporters went to continue this particular practice of breaking the fast according to calculated dates rather than moonsighting, even if it meant upsetting a Sunni majority.

On the same note, adherence to the calculated calendar was, at times, strictly enforced in Fatimid territories. In the year 429/953, when Fatimid dominions had not as yet extended to Egypt, the Maliki *qadi* (judge) of Barqa, Muhammad al-Habli, opposed the Fatimid governor Ibn Kafi over adherence to the official observation of the day of Eid al-Fitr based on the Fatimids' calculated calendar. Al-Habli insisted on observing Eid only if the moon had been sighted, which it had not been. The next day, Ibn Kafi wore festive garments and marched with drums and banners before the judge's house in celebration of the holiday. The *qadi* insisted that it was not Eid because of the lack of a physical moon sighting and refused to conduct the public Eid prayers. Ibn Kafi appointed someone else to observe the Eid rituals, and al-Habli was imprisoned and killed for refusing to adhere to the Fatimid calendar.[43] This event piques some interest historically because the Fatimids were pragmatic and persistently practised a high level of religious tolerance in their realm since, as Ismailis, they were a minority faction ruling a majority Sunni populace. However, in this instance, they emphasised their calendrical notion of 'fixed days' for fasting over the rights of Sunni jurists in their realm. The orders to observe Eid had come from the Imam-caliph in al-Mansuriyya, and so in this case quashing al-Habli's public defiance and prominently displaying Fatimid authority in respect of public notions of time appeared to be more politically expedient than religious tolerance.

In his *Daʿaʾim al-Islam*, which is the main source of Fatimid jurisprudence, al-Qadi al-Nuʿman briefly addressed the notion of the *ruʾyat al-hilal* in the chapter on fasting. In the section about beginning the fast, there is an account attributed to ʿAli in which al-Nuʿman reports him as reciting this prayer upon seeing the *hilal* of Ramadan: 'Allahu Akbar, O Lord, I ask you for good things in this month and for its victory, triumph, light and sustenance, and I ask for protection from evil in this month and after it.'[44] The account sanctions the practice of seeing the waxing crescent moon; however, it is not in order to calculate the beginning of Ramadan. Also, there is no report mentioned in the *Daʿaʾim al-Islam* that quotes the Prophet's *hadith* on beginning and ending the fast through the practice of *ruʾyat al-hilal*. There are also no direct instructions on the Fatimid calculation of the days of Ramadan. However, in the same section, al-Nuʿman states,

The person who is with the Imam or in a place where the orders of the Imam can reach him then he need not worry about being confused if his fast is ending in Ramadan or Shaʿban. He should fast according to the fast of the Imam and end Ramadan according to the breaking of the fast (*iftar*) of the Imam.[45]

What is noteworthy here is al-Nuʿman's wording. Although it is not directly stated, the wording 'he should fast according to the fast of the Imam', clearly reflects the formation of the *hadith* of the Prophet that one should 'not fast until they see the waxing crescent moon, and not break the fast until they see it'. In the case of al-Nuʿman's jurisprudential note, however, the word 'Imam' explicitly replaces the word '*hilal*'. This text provides clear evidence that the Fatimids symbolically linked the personage of the Imam to the *hilal*.

Understanding the Significance of the Crescent Moon in Fatimid Hermeneutics and Adab Literature

It is through Fatimid literary sources and *adab*, alongside jurisprudential and other texts, that an additional connection can be drawn between the idea of the *hilal* representing the Imam and how it was a persistent thought in the Fatimid intellectual milieu. In a poem probably written on the occasion of Eid al-Fitr, the eminent *daʿi* and theologian, al-Muʾayyad al-Shirazi, writes in the honour of the Fatimid Imam-caliph, al-Mustansir:

هلال بدى من خلال الدجنة   امام الزمان من النار جنة

The waxing crescent moon that has appeared through the darkness is the Imam of the age, a shield from hellfire.[46]

According to Tahera Qutbuddin, the comparison of the Imam to the moon or other celestial bodies is a stock metaphor in Fatimid ideology and *adab* literature, generally alluding to the concept that just as the moon is luminous so is the Imam. However, the metaphor refers to deeper *taʾwil* meanings. Just as the moon guides people with its light, the Imam guides the faithful by providing divine knowledge, which is often symbolised in Fatimid ideology by light. The above-mentioned verse refers to the Imam as the waxing crescent moon, since the hemistich links the appearance of the *hilal* from the darkness to the Imam of the Time (*Imam al-zaman*).

Furthermore, Qutbuddin argues that the use of the waxing crescent moon (*hilal*) here as opposed to just the moon (*qamar* or *badr*), is a specialised metaphor rather than a stock metaphor, since the deeper symbolism being expressed here by al-Shirazi is that the Imam illuminates the souls of the faithful from darkness with his divine light and saves them from hellfire. It also alludes to the notion that the fast or Ramadan begins and ends with the Imam, the true giver of guidance, rather than the physical crescent moon.[47]

As well as associating the *hilal* with the Imam in his poetry, al-Mu'ayyad also demonstrates similar beliefs in his *Majalis*, a collection of 800 of his weekly orations delivered to a congregation of Ismailis in Cairo. In his 236th *majlis* he says, 'O faithful, you will break your fast tomorrow with the breaking of the fast (*iftar*) of the Imam who is from the *Ahl al-Bayt* of your Prophet. May God make your crescent moon (*hilal*) clear from coverings (*hujub*), and may he protect you.'[48] In his 327th majlis, he refers to those in the Muslim *umma* who look to the crescent moon to determine the time of the fast critically: 'Do they not understand that the Prophet is the luminous crescent moon, and the bright and great light, since he is the true crescent moon (*al-hilal al-haqiqi*), and the divine example? And [do they not understand] that the Imams from his descendants are the crescent moons which are 'the fixed times (*mawaqit*) for the people?'[49] Due to the nature of the *Majalis* as the prime locus in the 5th/11th-century Fatimid court for the scholarly elite to learn Ismaili spiritual hermeneutics, the linking of the Imam with the *hilal* was made clear, whereas elsewhere such as the above-mentioned chapter from *Da'a'im al-Islam*, it could only be inferred.

These are some of the many examples from prevalent Fatimid-era literature which symbolise the Imam as the *hilal*. Furthermore, the vast amount of literary writings and polemics against the practice of *ru'yat al-hilal* demonstrate that the *hilal* represented the Imam-caliph and symbolised his authority over time. It was a means by which the Fatimids, who adhered to many of the same practices and courtly rituals of other sovereigns in the medieval Islamic world, made their own practices unique.

The Persistent Use of the Crescent Motif in Fatimid Visual Culture

Therefore, it is not that surprising that Fatimid art commissioned by the court and in the name of the Imam used the *hilal* motif quite frequently. The *shamsa* is one example, however there are other ones that are still extant. According to al-Maqrizi, the Fatimids also used crescents in their royal ceremonial processions which took place in Cairo on different occasions throughout the year. Al-Maqrizi describes the manner in which the Fatimid banners were carried out in the procession in great detail. He writes that the Fatimid Imam-caliph entered the procession accompanied by two tall lances holding two white silk banners embroidered with gold thread. The Imam-caliph was preceded by twenty-one multi-coloured embroidered silk flags. The flag-bearers were proceeded by two men, each carrying a lance. These lances were surmounted by golden crescent moons, and each lance had seven red and yellow banners attached to it.[50] The crescents surmounting the two lances arrived first in the procession acting like royal insignia. Therefore, the Imam-caliph was introduced into the ceremonial procession with the repeated symbol of the crescent moon.

An example of what this type of Fatimid ceremonial crescent might have looked like is located in the Germanisches National Museum in Nuremberg (figure III.1.3). The artifact is a rock crystal shaped as a *hilal*, bearing the inscription of the name and title of the Imam-caliph al-Zahir (r. 411–427/1021–1036). This is followed by a short prayer for his long life. Avinoam Shalem has suggested that this rock crystal might have been part of a harness of a royal horse, or similarly used to surmount a lance as described above.[51] This rock crystal closely resembles the description of another crescent-shaped treasure known to have been kept in the Fatimid treasury and known as 'al-Hafir'. Al-Hafir was a single ruby carved into the shape of a crescent moon which was ornamented with baguettes of emeralds, possibly green enamel. It would be displayed in Fatimid royal processions at festivals.

While it is likely that the rock crystal crescent of al-Zahir was used in ceremonial, a fragment of a 5th/11th-century lustreware bowl from Fatimid Egypt depicts a mounted warrior on a horse holding a shield with the waxing crescent moon motif at its centre (figure III.1.4). While there is no direct textual evidence regarding the use of the crescent moon motif on shields, the documented use of it in ceremonial and on other military accoutrement like lances, points to a possible correlation with the image portrayed on this bowl.

Perhaps the most prominent use of the *hilal* motif in Fatimid art appears in the plastered carved stucco *mihrab* of the Imam-caliph al-Mustansir (r. 427–487/1036–1094) commissioned by his vizier al-Afdal

The Fatimid Crescent

Figure III.1.3 Rock-crystal crescent ornament of al-Zahir, r. 411–427/1021–1036, mounting, brass, Venice, second half of the 8th/14th century.

Figure III.1.4 Fragment of a bowl depicting a mounted warrior, 5th/11th century. Brooklyn Museum, New York.

in the Mosque of Ibn Tulun in the year 487/1094 (figure III.1.5) on a colonnade at the southwest side of the prayer hall.⁵² The Ibn Tulun mosque was originally built in the 3rd/9th century during Tulunid rule over Egypt, and despite the construction of al-Azhar during the era of al-Muʿizz in the 4th/10th century and the large al-Anwar mosque built by al-Hakim in the 5th/11th century, the Ibn Tulun mosque continued to be used regularly throughout the Fatimid period. The Fatimids often held Ramadan ceremonies there. However, the Ibn Tulun mosque was not primarily used by Ismailis living in Cairo but rather by the Sunni population who lived in the district of al-Qataʾiʿ.

The *mihrab* was positioned on the surface of the mosque's colonnade and so would have been accessible and visible to all since it can be clearly seen from the courtyard. The *mihrab* is formed of a blind-keeled arch supported by two ornamented pillars set within a rectangle, and framed by a band of floriated Kufic calligraphy, which bears the name of the Imam-caliph al-Mustansir, centred at the top of the frame. Al-Mustansir's name

Figure III.1.5 *Mihrab* of al-Mustansir, Fatimid, ca. 487/1094, carved stucco, Mosque of Ibn Tulun.

and title are followed by the name and titles of the vizier al-Afdal, who commissioned the *mihrab*. There is an apparent cramming of letters in the frame, which shows that the artist who carved the inscription made a deliberate attempt to place the inscription of the name of the Imam-caliph '*al-Mustansir bi'llah Amir al-Muminin, salawat Allah alayhi*' in the centre of the top frame. What makes this *mihrab* unique is that the Fatimid and Shi'i version of the *shahada* proclaiming that there is no other god but the one God, Muhammad is his prophet, and 'Ali is his *wali* (legatee), is written in bold Kufic letters in a rectangular frame in the area right above the keeled arch. More strikingly, however, is that the apex of the keeled arch is crowned by a *hilal* (figure III.1.6).

The central position of this *hilal* in relation to all the ornamentation on the *mihrab* demonstrates that the artist placed it here because of the power of its symbolism. The placement of the *hilal* appears directly under the reference to the Prophet, 'Muhammad Rasul Allah' which in turn, falls right under the title of the Imam, *Amir al-Mu'minin* (figure III.1.7). The placement of the calligraphic ornament was surely not coincidental. The artist fully intended to place the waxing crescent moon, the name of the Prophet, and the title of the Imam-caliph in the same vertical line. This deliberate approach is evidenced by the close compression of letters within the top central frame. As discussed above, the linear connection between the *hilal*, the Prophet Muhammad, and the Imam-caliph displayed on the *mihrab*, reflects doctrinal and jurisprudential ideas related to fundamental notions of time and the Imam's authority as found in Fatimid and Ismaili religious textual sources.

Figure III.1.6 *Mihrab* of al-Mustansir, Fatimid, ca. 487/1094, Mosque of Ibn Tulun.

Figure III.1.7 *Mihrab* of al-Mustansir, Fatimid, ca. 487/1094, Mosque of Ibn Tulun.

This visual element brings to mind the words written by al-Mu'ayyad fi'l-Din al-Shirazi quoted above, 'Do they not understand that the Prophet is the luminous crescent moon, and the bright and great light, since he is the true waxing crescent moon (*al-hilal al-haqiqi*), and the divine example, and that the Imams from his descendants are the waxing crescent moons which are the fixed times (*mawaqit*) for the people.'[53] These numerous contemporary examples originating from the Fatimid intellectual and visual *habitus* demonstrate that the *hilal* clearly symbolised notions of time to the vast majority of Muslims in the medieval Islamic world. To the Fatimids and those who espoused the Ismaili school of thought, however the mimetic value of the *hilal* played an additional role. It symbolised the spiritual and temporal authority of the Imam-caliph in Fatimid society. By ensuring that their central doctrine for marking time and important dates like Ramadan and the Hajj was linked to the Imam, the Fatimids ensured that he symbolically and literally remained the 'Master of Time' (*Sahib al-asr*) and the 'Imam of the Era' (*Imam al-zaman*). Furthermore, the persistent use of the visual motif of the *hilal* in Fatimid art and architecture also demonstrates that ornament in the medieval Islamic world offered viewers more than pleasure and beauty. Ornament could be used consciously to convey a range of multivalent meanings that complemented the intellectual milieu in which it was found. Lastly, the notion of controlling time and defining it, is a key factor in maintaining the political power of any ruling faction. For the Fatimids, in their aim in augmenting a cosmopolitan society throughout their realm, standardising time and regulating it, appears to have been an important measure that they took and reinforced. In light of all of this, it is clear that the Fatimid crescent had distinct meaning, which was definitely not hidden in obscurity by any clouds or darkness.

NOTES

1 For sources on the Fatimid *shamsa*, see Ahmad b. ʿAli al-Maqrizi, *Ittiʿaz al-hunafa bi-akhbar al-aʾimma al-Fatimiyyin al-khulafa*, ed. Muḥammad ʿAbd al-Qadir ʿAta (Beirut, 2001), pp. 207–208. For discussions, see Jonathan Bloom, 'The Mosque of al-Hakim in Cairo', *Muqarnas*, 1 (1983), p. 27, and Heinz Halm, 'Shamsa', *EI2*. Also see Heinz Halm, 'Al-Shamsa Hängekronen als Herrschaftszeichen der Abbasiden und Fatimiden', in V. Vermeulen and D. De Smet, ed., *Egypt and Syria in the Fatimid Ayyubid and Mamluk Eras* (Leiden, 1995), pp. 125–138.
2 This perspective largely echoes Wendy Shaw's argument against Oleg Grabar's universal humanism approach in *The Mediation of Ornament* (Princeton, 1992). Grabar suggests a universal humanistic interpretation of deciphering Islamic ornament rather than a specific Islamically coded one, in which he relies on European art historical, psychoanalytic and mimetic approaches to Islamic art. His theories on reading ornament fall short of an exact method for understanding various cultural coded aesthetic experiences. She further writes, 'This betrays not only the lack of interest between Islamic intellectual history and artistic practices, but a broader prejudice characterizing art making as a non-verbal, non-intellectual, apolitical endeavor.' See Wendy Shaw, *What is "Islamic" Art? Between Religion and Perception* (Cambridge, 2019), p. 272.
3 The translation of Qurʾan 2:189 by Muhammad Asad (d. 1992) is: 'They will ask thee about the new moons. Say: "They indicate the periods for [various doings of] mankind, including the pilgrimage."' See, Muhammad Asad, *The Message of the Qurʾan* (Gibraltar, 1980), p. 76.
4 Paul E. Walker, 'Eternal Cosmos and the Womb of History: Time in Early Ismaili Thought', *International Journal of Middle East Studies*, 9 (1978), p. 357.
5 Ibid., p. 364.
6 There are several studies that address the development of theories on Islamic ornament. See Gülru Neçipoglu, *Topkapi Scroll: Geometry and Ornament in Islamic Architecture* (Santa Monica, CA, 1996), pp. 61–71; Avinoam Shalem and Eva-Maria Troelenberg, 'Beyond Grammar and Taxonomy', *Beiträge zur islamischen Kunst und Archäologie*, 3 (2012), pp. 385–410; Oleg Grabar, *The Mediation of Ornament* (Princeton, 1992); Sheila Blair and Jonathan Bloom, *Cosmophilia: Islamic Art from the David Collection, Copenhagen* (Chestnut Hill, MA, 2006), pp. 9–30.
7 See, 'Ornament and Pattern', *The Grove Encyclopedia of Islamic Art and Architecture*, ed. Sheila Blair and Jonathan Bloom (Oxford, 2009), accessed January 2024.
8 Shalem and Troelengberg, 'Beyond Grammar and Taxonomy', p. 385.
9 Ibid., p. 386.

10 Oleg Grabar, *The Mediation of Ornament* (Princeton, 1992).
11 Ibid., pp. 44–46.
12 Ibid., pp. 37–42.
13 Ibid., p. 39.
14 James Trilling, *Ornament: A Modern Perspective* (Seattle, WA, 2003), p. 75.
15 Sheila Blair and Jonathan Bloom, *Cosmophilia, Islamic Art from the David Collection* (Chestnut Hill, MA, 2006).
16 Blair and Bloom, *Cosmophilia*, p. 26.
17 Ibid.
18 Shalem and Troelengberg, 'Beyond Grammar and Taxonomy', p. 385
19 See Shainool Jiwa, tr., *The Founder of Cairo: The Fatimid Caliph-Imam al-Mu'izz and His Era* (London, 2013), p. 210.
20 According to Paul Walker, the mentioning of the ruler sovereign and asking God that His blessings be bestowed upon him in the Friday *khutba*, was an important custom with serious political implications. Although it was not necessary according to Islamic law, the custom was routine and shifts between the mentioning of the Abbasids and Fatimids had political and religious significance. It was a symbol of sovereignty. See Paul E. Walker, *Orations of the Fatimid Caliphs: Festival Sermons of the Ismaili Imams* (London, 2009), p. 8.
21 Jonathan M. Bloom, *Arts of the City Victorious: Islamic Art and Architecture in Fatimid North Africa and Egypt* (New Haven, CN, 2007), p. 7.
22 Quoted from paragraph in Bloom, *Arts of the City* given above.
23 al-Nu'man b. Muhammad, al-Qadi Abu Hanifa, *Kitab Asas al-ta'wil*, ed. Aref Tamer (Beirut, 1960), p. 27.
24 al-Sijistani, *Ithbat al-Nubuwwa*, ed. Wilfred Madelung and Paul Walker (Tehran, 1975).
25 See, Sherif Anwar and Jere L. Bacharach, 'Shi'ism and the Early Dinars of the Fatimid Imam-Caliph al-Mu'izz Li-Din Allah (341–365/952–975): An Analytic Overview', *Al-Masaq*, 22 (2010), p. 266.
26 Mohammed Amrani Zerrifi, 'Units of Measurement in Islamic Societies: The Finger, the Fist, and Large and Small Spans', *Ostour: Journal for Historical Studies*, vol 2 (2016). Zerrifi's research into primary medieval Arabic sources mentioning measurements estimates that the large span, a standard measurement used in the premodern Islamic world, was 23.1 cm.
27 al-Maqrizi, *Itti'az*, vol. 1, p. 207.
28 Ibid.
29 al-Maqrizi, *Itti'az*, vol. 1, p. 208.
30 al-Maqrizi goes on to say when describing the Abbasid custom of sending the *shamsa* to Mecca that 'the cost of the *shamsa* was substantial, and it was brought to Mecca from Iraq by a general and given to the caretakers of the Ka'ba in front of witnesses who would confirm its receipt. It would be hung on the sixth day of Dhu'l-Hijja until the Day of Tarwiyya (8 Dhu'l-Hijja), after which it was taken down.' I have translated *sadis al-thaman* as the eighth day of Dhu'l-Hijja presuming that the '*thaman*' refers to the first eight days of Dhu'l-Hijja preceding the Hajj. See Halm, 'Shamsa', *EI2*. Also see al-Maqrizi, *Itti'az*, vol. 1, pp. 207–208.
31 al-Tamim ibn al-Mu'izz, son al-Mu'izz li-Din Allah, is known for his eloquent poetry that praised his father's conquests and reflected the cultural vibrancy of the Fatimid court. For his poem on the *shamsa*, see, Tamim b. al-Mu'izz al-Fatimi, *Diwan of Tamim ibn al-Mu'izz li-Din Allah al-Fatimi* (Cairo, 1957), pp. 55–56.
32 I want to thank my colleague, Professor Hussein Haidermota of AlJamea Tus Saifiyah for his assistance in reviewing my translations.
33 It is important to note that the praise of the *shamsa* is correlated with a description of time, particularly the praise of the era of al-Mu'izz. The day of 'Id al-Adha is also mentioned, considering the symbolic connections of the *hilal* and the days of the Hajj.

34 See Qur'an 2:189.
35 Ibn Manzur, *Lisan al-'Arab* (Beirut, 1955), p. 1018.
36 For a comprehensive summary of the religious and artistic occurrences of the *hilal* in Islam see, J. Schacht and R. Ettinghausen, 'Hilal', *EI2*.
37 Qur'an, 2:189, translation Asad.
38 Schacht and Ettinghausen, 'Hilal', *EI2*.
39 Qur'an, 2: 183–184. Translation Asad.
40 Schacht and Ettinghausen, 'Hilal', *EI2* quoting the Annales of Tabari.
41 For a comprehensive account of the various doctrines and beliefs of the Fatimids in calculating the beginning and end of Ramadan as opposed to the practice of *ru'yat al-hilal*, see D. De Smet, 'Comment Déterminer Le Début et La Fin Du Jeune De Ramadan?', in *Egypt and Syria in the Fatimid, Ayyubid and Mamluk Eras* (Leiden, 1995). He refers in particular to the *Risala al-Lazima* by al-Kirmani written in the era of the Imam-caliph al-Hakim which is dedicated to the explanation of a calculated fast and describes the flaws in the practice of *ru'yat al-hilal*.
42 Verena Klemm, *Memoirs of a Mission The Ismaili Scholar, Statesman and Poet al-Mu'ayyad fi'l-Din al-Shirazi* (London, 2003), pp. 20–21.
43 Heinz Halm, *Empire of the Mahdi: The Rise of the Fatimids*, tr. Michael Bonner (Leiden, 1996), p. 373.
44 al-Qadi al-Nu'man, *Da'a'im al-Islam*, tr. Asaf Ali Asghar Fyzee (Beirut, 1991), p. 271.
45 Ibid., p. 272.
46 Tahera Qutbuddin, *al-Mu'ayyad al-Shirazi and Fatimid Da'wa Poetry* (Leiden, 2005), p. 112.
47 Ibid., pp. 112–115.
48 al-Shirazi, *al-Majalis al-Mu'ayyadiyya*, ms. AlJamea Tus Saifiyah repository, Surat. Majlis 236. It is also clear that the reference to the crescent moon being clear of coverings is an allusion to the Prophet's hadith regarding the sighting of the moon for fasting where he says, 'But when it is hidden from you [by cloud or mist], give it its full measure.'
49 Ibid., Majlis 327.
50 al-Maqrizi, *al-Mawa'iz wa'l-i'tibar fi dhikr al-khitat wa'l-athar*, ed. Ayman F. Sayyid (London, 1995), vol. 2, p. 470.
51 Avinoam Shalem, *Islam Christianized: Islamic portable objects in the medieval church treasuries of the Latin West* (Frankfurt-am-Main, 1996), p. 28.
52 Jonathan Bloom, *Arts of the City Victorious*, pp. 136–139.
53 See above.

2

The Power of Six: Astral, Solomonic and Imami Imagery in Fatimid Art

Bernard O'Kane

The use of astral symbolism by the Fatimids has been noted previously, most prominently by James Allan in his article entitled '"My Father is a Sun, and I am the Star": Fatimid Symbols in Ayyubid and Mamluk metalwork.'[1] I propose to take some of the ideas in this chapter further, exploring in particular the reasons for the predilection of the six-pointed star as a Fatimid decorative motif. Related to this is the hexagram, the form of the six-pointed star as two intertwined triangles that was associated from the early Islamic period onwards with the seal of Solomon, who is lauded in the Qur'an and other early Islamic sources as a paragon of wisdom and the ideal ruler, and as an intercessor for protection from evil.

According to Fatimid doctrine, light is at the origin of the universe: 'He initiated the creation of what He created from a Light', writes Jaʿfar b. Mansur al-Yaman, the 4th/10th-century *daʿi*.[2] His contemporary, al-Qadi al-Nuʿman, the author of many works on Ismaili jurisprudence, writes in the *Ikhtilaf usul al-madhahib* that 'The Truth is illuminated by a light',[3] and quotes this *hadith*: 'My companions are like the stars. No matter which of them you follow, you will be led aright.'[4] The Ismaili scholar Hamid al-Din al-Kirmani writes that 'gleaming flashes of sacred light' testify to the existence of God,[5] and that the Imams are 'the lights in the darkness through whom God illuminates the black courtyards of the night',[6] calling his own work the *Book of Lights to Illuminate the imamate*.

Astral imagery can also be related to the Prophet Muhammad, the possessor of a divine light (*nur Muhammad*) that can lead Muslims towards enlightenment.[7] Al-Qadi al-Nuʿman also wrote that the Muhammad is 'a light for all lands (*nur al-bilad*), lamps (*masabih*) shining in the murk, leading out of the labyrinth of blindness and the gloom of perdition'.[8] The guiding figures of religion are 'like the stars of the heaven' according to Ja'far b. Mansur, and the *daʿi*s are 'like the shining stars, for the stars are their symbol and their outer aspect'.[9]

One should note from the outset that six-pointed stars are by no means unique to Fatimid imagery, and that they also used stellate images with various other points, including five- and eight-pointed ones. But I hope to demonstrate that the six-pointed star occupies a place of prominence in Fatimid decoration that is exceptional in Fatimid and Islamic art, and calls for an explanation. I will first discuss the use of the hexagram or seal of Solomon in different media, then the prevalence of six-pointed stars and hexafoil rosettes, and finally their possible connections with Imam Ismaʿil.

The hexagram or seal of Solomon

The six-pointed star consisting of two intertwined triangles has long been regarded in Islam as the symbol of seal of the Prophet Solomon. It has an ancient history, starting in pre-Islamic times,[10] and appearing frequently in buildings and artefacts throughout the Islamic world from the Umayyad period onwards.[11]

One of the earliest Fatimid examples is found on a block-printed talismanic scroll from the 5th/11th century.[12] Another is found on a gravestone from Qayrawan dated 483/1090-91.[13] The earliest known epigraphic example is found in the *mashhad* of al-Juyushi (480/1087) on the Muqattam cliffs beside Cairo at the apex of the dome, where it spells out the names of Muhammad and ʿAli.[14] Later Fatimid epigraphic examples include those on the main *mihrab* of the shrine of Sayyida Ruqayya (527/1133) (*Muhammad* repeated six times, with ʿ*Ali* in the centre) and on the *mihrab* of the Hasawati mausoleum (ca. 545/1150-51) (figure III.2.1).

Non-epigraphic examples are found in considerable number on the northern minaret of the Mosque of al-Hakim[15] (before 400/1010) (figure III.2.2, top and middle) and, together with a common substitute or companion to it, the five-sided star, on Bab al-Futuh (475/1085) (figure III.2.2, bottom). One of the 5th/11th-century beams of the Great Mosque of Qayrawan has alternately seals of Solomon and six-pointed stars.[16] The two *mihrab*s flanking the entrance to the shrine of Sayyida Ruqayya have it at their focal point, enclosing a six-sided star, and surrounded by six

Figure III.2.1 Top left: *Mashhad* of al-Juyushi, 480/1087; top right: Shrine of Sayyida Ruqayya, 527/1133; bottom left: Hasawati mausoleum, ca. 544/1150; bottom right: Shrine of Yahya al-Shabihi, 549–555/1154–1160.

trefoils, on a medallion from which radiate the ribs of the stylised scallop shell (figure III.2.3, top). An interesting variant is seen in the main *mihrab* of the shrine of Yahya al-Shabihi (549–555/1154–1160), where the intersecting triangles are implied by the geometric pattern, which also has a six-sided star at its centre (figure III.2.1, bottom right). Final architectural examples are those found on at least four of the medallions on the spandrels of the *qibla* arcades of the Mosque of al-Salih Tala'i'.[17] The seal of the Solomon is also present on three pieces of Fatimid metalwork, one from the late 5th/11th-century metalwork hoard found in Tiberias,[18] one from the Caeserea hoard,[19] and another in the treasury of Pisa cathedral (figure III.2.4).[20] A final example is seen on the gold quarter-dinars minted in Sicily for the Imam-caliph al-Mustansir.[21]

Figure III.2.2 Upper and middle row: detail of hexagrams on northern minaret of the Mosque of al-Hakim (before 400/1010); bottom row: on Bab al-Futuh, 475/1085.

Figure III.2.3 Top: Shrine of Sayyida Ruqayya, 527/1133, detail of outside *mihrab*s; bottom left: apex of dome of al-Hafiz at al-Azhar, 549/1154; bottom right: detail of painted medallion at apex of dome of Shrine of Sayyida Ruqayya.

Figure III.2.4 Bronze plates: left, Tiberias hoard (after Khamis); right, museo dell'Opera del Duomo, Pisa.

The six-sided star

One of the earliest examples of these may be in Fatimid metalwork. A lamp from the Great Mosque of Qayrawan datable to around 390/1000 has a six-pointed star on its pierced base.[22] This was also a favourite location for the seal of Solomon on Saljuq pierced lamps.[23]

The earliest Fatimid architectural examples of these occur in the geometric stucco window grilles of the Mosque of al-Azhar. There are also foliate grilles there and Creswell though that only those were original,[24] but the simplicity of the geometric hexagonal-based patterns makes attributing them to a later date even more problematic than assuming their originality.[25] Six pointed-stars occur at the centres of the geometrical patterns.

A similar series of window grilles with patterns based on a hexagonal grid was also found at the Mosque of al-Hakim. These were on the outer facades, but when Creswell recorded them only a few had survived. He did not publish them in volume one of *The Muslim Architecture of Egypt*, but fortunately photographs of three of them are preserved in his archive (figure III.2.5).[26] Here again they are based on a hexagonal grid, with six-pointed stars appearing at the focal points of the pattern. An even simpler version of these patterns is found in stone in a window grille on the northern minaret.[27] In the photograph of it in *The Muslim Architecture of Egypt* it is badly damaged, but again, an archival photograph enables us to reconstruct the pattern in its entirety and to see that it consisted of a six-pointed star at the centre with four others at the corners. The original cresting above the walls of the courtyard of this mosque was also one in which six-pointed stars featured prominently. This remained a popular pattern for cresting, with identical patterns being used later on the Aqmar mosque (519/1125-26)[28] and on al-Hafiz's alterations (r. 526–544/1132–1149) to al-Azhar.[29]

The first major example of a Fatimid star and polygon woodwork pattern is seen on the *minbar* made for the shrine of the head of al-Husayn at Ascalon in Palestine (484/1091-92) (figure III.2.6). The large scale of the polygons and stars is evidence that this was among the first Fatimid attempts to design in the geometric mode on woodwork, although it still

Figure III.2.5 Window grilles, outer wall, Mosque of al-Hakim, ca. 400/1010.

Figure III.2.6 *Minbar*s: left, Ascalon *minbar*, 484/1091–92; right, 'Amri mosque, Qus, 550–556/1155–1156.

displays a facility far in advance of its time. The pattern is generated from six-pointed stars surrounded by hexagons that appear below the chair and are then mirrored beneath the balustrade.[30] The next known woodwork example of a star and polygon pattern is on a screen from the Musalla al-'Idayn in Damascus (497/1103-04). Most of the decoration is of arabesques, but the one geometric panel also features hexagons and six-pointed stars.[31]

The Mosque of al-Aqmar was mentioned above in relation to the design of the lower part of its cresting. The original cresting has not survived, but fortunately drawings of it by the English architect James Wild, ca. 1844, exist. Two versions of the upper section were recorded, one with curved elements. However, the curved one is clearly based on the other which again has a pattern based on six-pointed stars and polygons (figure III.2.7). Also in al-Aqmar is a stone-carved panel on the side of the facade featuring a six-pointed star at its centre (figure III.2.7). Its prominence has led to varying suggestions, religious and secular, regarding its significance.[32]

The wooden portable *mihrab* from the shrine of Sayyida Nafisa probably dates from one of the two recorded Fatimid restorations, in 532/1137-38 and 541/1146-47. The focal point of the composition is the six-pointed star above the apex of the arch. The design is cleverly arranged so that a half of this six-pointed star appears alternately on the left and right of each lower side, as well as at the top left and right corners (figure III.2.8).[33]

The cresting of the Mosque of al-Azhar by al-Hafiz was mentioned above. More six-pointed stars (eleven to be exact) are found in one of the windows between the squinches of the dome that he added to the transept; hexagons and hexafoils interlace in the surrounding strapwork.[34] The stucco decoration of the dome above is unusual in being divided into six parts. Reflecting this, the central medallion at its apex has not just a six-pointed star at the centre but is also surrounded by six floral elements (figure III.2.3, bottom left). They recall those at the apex of the Sayyida Ruqayya dome (figure III.2.3, bottom right) which is discussed further below.

The *minbar* at Qus, made for the vizier al-Salih Tala'i''s restoration of the 'Amri mosque (550–556/1155–1156), is the earliest surviving in Egypt. Like the *minbar* at Ascalon, its main pattern is one based on six-pointed stars (figure III.2.6). The pattern at the base of the seat at Qus of six-pointed stars surrounded by irregular hexagons is identical to that of the niche of the contemporary (549–555/1154–1160)[35] portable wooden *mihrab* of the shrine of Sayyida Ruqayya. This *mihrab*, like that of Sayyida Nafisa, also has a centralised six-pointed star above the *mihrab* arch. Also like the

Figure III.2.7 Mosque of al-Aqmar, 519/1125–26.

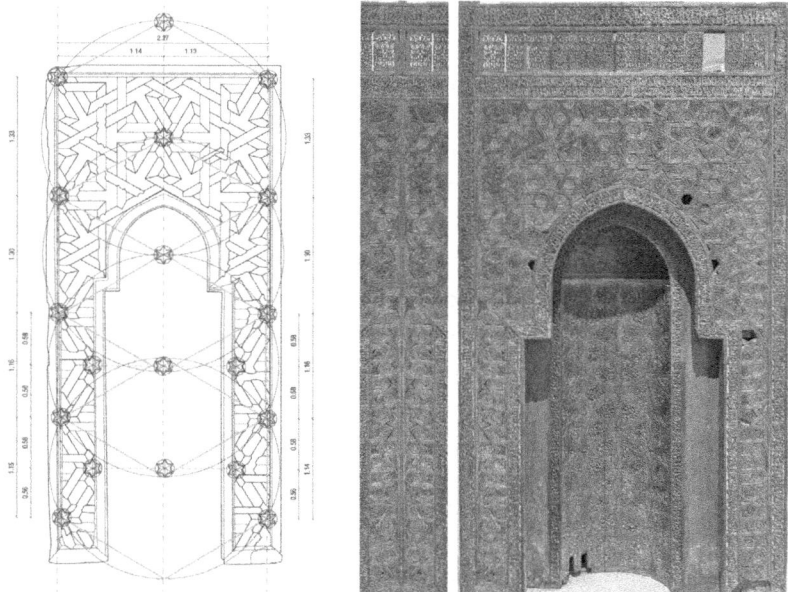

Figure III.2.8 Left, portable *mihrab* of Sayyida Nafisa, 532–541/1137–1147 (drawing by Alessandro Nocentini); right, portable *mihrab* of Sayyida Nafisa.

Sayyida Nafisa *mihrab*, it has an ingenious design on the lower sides, alternating half six-pointed stars with half 16-sided polygons which also flank the central star above (figure III.2.8).[36] The rear and sides of the *mihrab* are also ornamented with panels, ten of which are geometrical and nine vegetal. The six-pointed star is the focal point and generative feature of all of these but one, the exception being a twelve-sided star.[37] Attached to the ʿAmri mosque at Qus is a Fatimid mausoleum. Six-pointed stars are used there both for windows openings at the base of the dome, and also within blind niches on each of the lower faces of the lower square.[38]

One other major example of Fatimid woodwork is the cenotaph from the Shrine of the head of al-Husayn. Initially ascribed to the Ayyubid period solely on account of its cursive inscriptions, Caroline Williams has cogently argued that it is Fatimid.[39] Here too six-pointed stars are the generative root of the pattern. This is most apparent in the upper geometric panels, where they appear both as whole and half stars. It is not quite so obvious in the lower vertically-oriented geometric panels, as only the central panel on the long side has a complete six-pointed star. But combine any two of the flanking panels on the long side or the short sides, and it can be seen easily that their pattern is identical to the central one on the long side (figure III.2.9).

Interesting combinations of the motifs of the seal of Solomon, the six-pointed star and the hexafoil rosette are found on the Bab al-Akhdar (549/1154-55), the Fatimid gate adjacent to the mausoleum for the head of al-Husayn. In the medallion on the left spandrel a six-pointed star is found set within the seal of Solomon. On the right spandrel the central six-pointed star is surrounded by a hexafoil rosette (figure III.2.10).

In connection with the mention of the rosette above we should also note the earlier decoration on the *mihrab* on the Mosque of al-Azhar. A six-petalled rosette occurs prominently, not just at the apex of the niche decoration, but is also repeated three times on the soffit of the arch in front of the niche, also at the apex and the base at each side (figure III.2.11). Variations on this are found at the Shrine of al-Sayyida Ruqayya (527/1133), where the medallion at the apex of the dome in front of the *mihrab* has a floral motif with six lobes inside a Qur'anic inscription, and at the apex of the dome added in al-Hafiz's alterations (549/1154) to the Azhar mosque (figure III.2.3, bottom left).[40]

Figure III.2.9 Cenotaph from the Shrine of the Head of Husayn. Museum of Islamic Art, Cairo (side panels aligned).

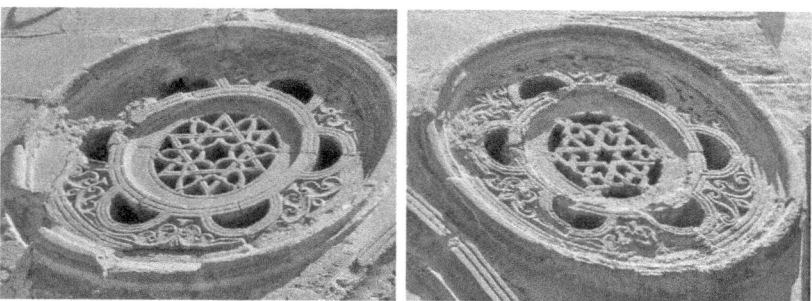

Figure III.2.10 Details of spandrels, Bab al-Akhdar, 549/1154–55.

Figure III.2.11 Detail of *mihrab*, Mosque of al-Azhar, 360/970–71.

Finally, the Mosque of al-Salih Tala'i' (555/1160) was mentioned above in connection with its medallions displaying the seal of Solomon. One of medallions also has a six-pointed star,[41] but many more are to be found on the wooden ceiling of the arcade at the entrance to the mosque, where they are found within the hexagons that are its organising principal (figure III.2.12).[42]

Figure III.2.12 Ceiling of narthex, Mosque of al-Salih Tala'i', 555/1160.

The Fatimid iconography of six

Why should the Fatimids have favoured six-sided ornamentation? Ibn al-Haytham, in his book on the history of the rise of the Fatimid caliphate, *Kitab al-Munazarat*, relates a debate in which members of the Ithna 'ashariyya claimed as the proof of the number twelve being that of the Imams, that God created twelve divisions of the zodiac in the heavens, twelve months, twelve hours of the day and for the night, twelve members of the body subservient to the heart and twelve regions of the terrestrial world. This was refuted by Abu Musa (a Kutama chieftain also known as *shaykh al-masha'ikh*) who noted that, on the basis of God's speech in the Qur'an, one could point to the importance of many other numbers including thirteen, fourteen, fifteen, nineteen, twenty, thirty, forty, fifty, sixty, seventy, eighty, ninety-nine and a hundred.[43]

Similarly, I am aware that the problem in pointing to the importance of six on text-based material is that it is not difficult to find passages that record the importance of many of the other numbers from, for instance, three to twelve, and to single out one of them, such as six, could lead to accusations of special pleading.[44] Still, I can only present here the evidence I have and let the reader decide the extent to which it is convincing – or even better, to encourage others to provide additional arguments.[45]

Although its frequent use was noted above, the seal of Solomon is not unique to the Fatimids. In Islamic lore the seal of Solomon was given to him by God; it bore God's name and enabled him to command demons and speak with animals. Its association with Solomon's wisdom and its magical character ensured that it frequently operated as a talisman.[46] It was one of the seven magic symbols, frequently in association with the names of God, found on many amulets, magic bowls and talismanic shirts.[47] Olly Akkerman has pointed out that the seal of Solomon can be found frequently in Bohra manuscripts in text, as paratexts and on flyleaves, where it serves as a talisman to protect the codex as a sacred object. She points out that Bohra manuscript culture has its roots in medieval Tayyibi Yemen and also possibly in Fatimid Egypt.[48]

In the Qur'an, the creation of the heavens and earth by God in six days is mentioned several times.[49] Abu Ya'qub al-Sijistani in his *Kitab al-Yanabi'* refers to this is the section on the 34th Wellspring: That the Compound Even Number Following Four Is Six.[50] In the same section he notes that six is a perfect number.[51] He also refers to the six eras from Adam to Muhammad, the six powers of nature, the six days of creation, the six directions and the six members of the human body. Admittedly, however, the significance of these is complicated by the diagram he adds[52] which places them as subsidiary, in each case, to one other entity. The concept of the six eras is based on the numbering of the six speaker-prophets (*natiqs*), each of whom had a legatee (*wasi*) who explained through *ta'wil* the inner meaning of the *natiqs*' teachings. The *wasi* of the Prophet Muhammad was 'Ali, but these series of cycles were to be followed by seven Imams, the seventh and last of whom would emerge as the new *natiq*.[53]

While these connections are suggestive, they may not be persuasive in themselves. What I believe is the most important reason for the predilection for six-sided ornamentation is one that is, unlike the others, not usually explicitly stated in the Fatimid sources. This is the status of Isma'il b. Ja'far, the founder of the line after whom the Ismailis are of course named, as the sixth Imam. This in itself is not always obvious, as the enumeration of Imams is different for some of the Ismaili branches, and even seems to have varied at different times.[54] In a table of early Ismaili Imams, for instance, Farhad Daftary notes that 'Originally 'Ali was counted as the first Imam. Later 'Ali acquired the higher rank of *asas* and al-Hasan was counted as the first Imam. Still later, the Nizaris omitted al-Hasan and started the list with 'Ali, counting al-Husayn as their second Imam.'[55] Fatimid sources that discuss the succession after Muhammad b. Isma'il are rare, but all of course insist on the imamate of Isma'il. One mention is in a *khutba* of the Fatimid Imam-caliph al-Amir, in which he labels 'Ali as the *amir al-mu'minin*, and the Imams down to 'the true Imam Isma'il and Muhammad, his son.'[56] 'Ali is frequently mentioned in the surviving *khutbas* as the *wasi* (legatee or administrator of the will of Muhammad) or as the Lord of the Legatees (*sayyid al-wasiyin*).[57] This means that, whether one is counting on the Nizari Ismaili premise or the non-Nizari Ismaili premise, Isma'il is the sixth Imam. The frequent designation of the Fatimids as 'seveners'[58] should thus be discounted – not that describing them as 'sixers' would be any more accurate, since they do not hold that the imamate stopped with Isma'il, merely that it was continued only through his line. Seveners would be an accurate description only of those who, like the Qarmatis, looked for the return of the seventh Imam, Muhammad b. Isma'il, who was believed to be in occultation (*ghayba*), as the Mahdi.[59]

One source which lays out in detail the arguments for the imamate passing from Ja'far al-Sadiq to Isma'il is al-Kirmani's *al-Masabih fi ithbat al-imama*. Under the heading of 'The Sixth Light' he recounts in detail how 'after the designation had reached Ja'far al-Sadiq, the imamate belonged to Isma'il, and his descendants, to the exclusion of any of Isma'il's brothers.'[60] A similar exposition was unnecessary for subsequent Fatimid progeny[61] since the descent from Isma'il was a defining aspect of the Fatimids.

Admittedly, the term Ismaili had less resonance in the early Shi'i sources than it does now. The initial name for the religious movement was more often simply as *al-da'wa*, the mission, or as *al-da'wa al-hadiya*, the rightly guiding mission, or alternately the *din al-haqq* or the *da'wa al-haqq* (the religion or mission of truth).[62] And just to highlight the controversies regarding the whole question of symbolism in Fatimid society, it has even been argued that 'pace Brett, Sanders, and Bierman, [there is] little evidence that the symbolism of state ceremonial and "public texts" such as coinage and architecture had special meanings according to the Ismaili missionaries, or that the doctrines of Ismailism were of direct utility for the Fatimid state.'[63]

Conclusion

Nonetheless, the predilection for hexagrams, six-pointed stars and hexafoil rosettes in Fatimid decorative motifs is such that it is unlikely to be simply the haphazard choice of stonemasons, stucco craftsmen, metalworkers and carpenters. Although the bulk of Cairo's population may not have been aware of its symbolism, it is possible that sufficient Fatimid devotees would have been conscious of Isma'il's status both as the sixth Imam and as the crucial link in their Imams' ancestry to see this reflected in the state-sponsored works of art and architecture that they encountered so frequently in Cairo and elsewhere in the Fatimid dominions.

NOTES

1 *Journal of the David Collection*, 1 (2003), pp. 24–47.
2 Ja'far b. Mansur al-Yaman, *Kitab al-'alim wa'l-ghulam*, ed and tr. James W. Morris as *The Master and the Disciple: An Early Islamic Spiritual Dialogue* (London, 2001), p. 79.
3 al-Qadi al-Nu'man, *Ikhtilaf usul al-madhahib*, ed. and tr. Devin J. Stewart as *Disagreement of the Jurists: A Manual of Islamic Legal Theory* (New York, 2015), p. 57.
4 Ibid., pp. 61, 63.
5 Hamid al-Din al-Kirmani, *al-Masabih fi ithbat al-imama*, ed. and tr. Paul E. Walker as *Master of the Age: An Islamic Treatise on the Necessity of the imamate* (London, 2007), translation, p. 37.
6 Ibid., p. 38.

7 Scott Redford, 'Intercession and Succession, Enlightenment and Reflection: The Inscriptional and Decorative Programme of the Qaratay Madrasa, Konya', in Antony Eastmond, ed., *Viewing Inscriptions in the Late Antique and Medieval World* (Cambridge, 2015), pp. 148–169.
8 al-Qadi al-Nuʿman, *Ikhtilaf*, p. 33.
9 *Kitab al-ʿalim wa al-ghulam*, p. 82.
10 For instance, on a third-century BCE Shatkona at the Hindu-Buddhist site of Kataragama in Sri Lanka: Hilde K. Link, 'Where Vaḷḷi Meets Murukan. Landscape Symbolism in Kataragama', *Anthropos*, 97 (1997), figure 1; on a Roman plate: W. Gunther Plaut, *The Magen David* (Washington DC, 1991), p. 14. See also the list in George Marçais and Louis Poinssot, *Objets kairouanais, IXe au XIIIe siècle, Reliures, verreries, cuivres et bronzes bijoux* (Tunis, 1952), p. 431, n. 69.
11 There are far too many examples to list; the source with the largest range of illustrated examples is Rachel Milstein, *King Solomon's Seal* (Jerusalem, 1995). For an Umayyad example see Daniel Schlumberger, *Qasr el Heir el Gharbi* (Paris, 1986), pl. 58. For shirts (and a cap) see Rose Evelyn Muravchick, *God is the Best Guardian: Islamic Talismanic Shirts from the Gunpowder Empires* (PhD, University of Pennsylvania, 2014): http://repository.upenn.edu/edissertations/1380, p. 263 and Hülya Tezcan, *Tılsımlı Gömlekler* (Istanbul, 2011), cat. nos. 1, 2, 10, 18, 26, 44 and 46. See also Bernard O'Kane, 'Stars and Symmetry: The Name of the Prophet Muhammad in Architectural Inscriptions', in Bernard O'Kane et al., ed., *Inscriptions of the Medieval Islamic World* (Edinburgh, 2023).
12 https://www.metmuseum.org/art/collection/search/452893 (accessed 30 May 2022).
13 G. Marçais and L. Poinssot, *Objets kairouanais ixe au xiiie siècle, reliures, verreries, cuivres et bronzes bijoux* (Tunis, 1952), p. 431, n. 62.
14 Bernard O'Kane, *The Mosques of Egypt* (Cairo, 2016), p. 23.
15 This is Creswell's eighth band: K.A.C. Creswell, *The Muslim Architecture of Egypt, vol. 1: Ikhshids and Fatimids, AD 939-1171* (Oxford, 1952), p. 94 and pl. 26a-c. There is a considerable variety of ornamentation in these medallions, the complete recording of which is impossible to undertake at present because some of the space between the minaret and the adjacent bastion is filled with masonry or inaccessible for photography.
16 George Marçais, *Coupoles et plafonds de la grande mosquée de Kairouan* (Tunis, 1925), pl. XXXII, no. 98. Admittedly, given the preponderance of vegetal ornamented beams there, and one beam with eight-pointed stars (ibid., pl. XXIII, no. 110) it can hardly be said to be predominant.
17 Creswell, *The Muslim Architecture of Egypt, vol. 1*, pls 106–107. The central portion of ten of the medallions was at least partially preserved, but at least one other partially intact one (pl. 106 b2) is also likely to have been a seal of Solomon.
18 On this example it is combined with a polylobed six-petalled rosette. The rosette may be connected with the one of the most common metaphors for the Prophet Muhammad, the rose, an expression of his supernatural beauty: see O'Kane, 'Stars and Symmetry'.
19 Gregory Bilotto, 'Fatimid Metalwork 297-567/909-1171: Context, Identification, and Style in the Mediaeval Mediterranean' (PhD, SOAS, 2019), figure 106. I am grateful to the author for a copy of this.
20 Elias Khamis, *The Fatimid Metalwork Hoard from Tiberias. Tiberias: Excavations in the House of the Bronzes, Final Report, Volume II*, Qedem, 55 (Jerusalem, 2013), pp. 338–339, no. 321. My knowledge of the Pisa plate comes from the photograph kindly supplied by Professor Avinoam Shalem.
21 https://www.britishmuseum.org/collection/object/C1857-0101-3 (accessed 30 May 2022). At least one other example is to be found on ceramics, a lustre plate in the collection of the Museum of Islamic Art in Cairo: *Trésors fatimides du Caire* (Exh. Cat., Paris, 1998), figure 117. However, unlike architecture and some metalwork, the market for ceramics was for a lower stratum or for everyday use where understanding of the symbolism may not have been necessary or its use appropriate.

22　D.S. Rice, 'Studies in Islamic Metal Work-V', *BSOAS*, 17 (1955), pp. 214–217, pls. IXa, XII. The earlier reading of the signature in Marçais and Poinssot, *Objets kairouanais*, as '*li'l-Mu'izz*' (p. 418) was suggested to be '*al-Maghribi*' by Rice (ibid., p. 216).

23　The most extensive discussion of these is in Rice, 'Studies', pp. 221–223, pl. XII. He also discusses (pp. 217–220) a lamp dated 483/1090 from the Great Mosque of Damascus, now in the Türk ve Islam Eserleri Museum in Istanbul that displays the seal of Solomon on the neck and whose body is dotted with hexagons and six-pointed stars. Others have listed it as Fatimid (Bilotto, 'Fatimid Metalwork', p. 274), but Rice suggests that its evidence of mediocre craftsmanship betrays local manufacture at the time of Saljuq rule.

24　Creswell, *The Muslim Architecture of Egypt*, vol. 1, p. 58.

25　For further discussion of the dating see Bernard O'Kane, 'Geometry, Art, and Ideology in Fatimid, Zangid and Ayyubid Egypt and Syria', in Hind Nadim, ed., *Studies in Honor of Asad Nadim* (in press).

26　My thanks to Alyaa Gamal for the beautiful drawing of the reconstruction of this photo of the right in figure 5.

27　O'Kane, 'Geometry', figure 4.

28　See, ibid., figure 8 and Creswell, *MAE*, pl. 89.

29　Fortunately documented before the Comité repairs of 1891: Creswell, *The Muslim Architecture of Egypt*, vol. 1, pl. 89b. See also O'Kane. 'Geometry', figures 4 and 9.

30　Bernard O'Kane, 'A Tale of Two Minbars: Woodwork in Egypt and Syria on the Eve of the Ayyubids', in Robert Hillenbrand et al., ed., *Ferdowsi, the Mongols and the History of Iranian Art, Literature and Culture from Early Islam to Qajar Persia. Studies in Honour of Charles Melville* (London, 2013), p. 321, figure 32.7.

31　O'Kane, 'Geometry', figure 7.

32　See Caroline Williams, 'The Cult of 'Alid Saints in the Fatimid Monuments of Cairo Part I: The Mosque of al-Aqmar', *Muqarnas*, 1 (1983), pp. 37–52; Doris Behrens-Abouseif, 'The Façade of the Aqmar Mosque in the Context of Fatimid Ceremonial', *Muqarnas*, 9 (1992), pp. 29–38.

33　Many thanks to my colleague Alessandro Nocentini for this drawing which expertly shows the ingenuity of the design.

34　O'Kane, 'Geometry', figure 11.

35　The dates correspond with the reign of al-Fa'iz: see Max Van Berchem, *Matériaux pour un Corpus Inscriptionum Arabicarum*, part I: Egypte, *Mémoires de l'IFAO*, 19 (Cairo, 1894–1903), pp. 635–638.

36　In figure III.2.8 I have added a mirror image of the left edge of the *mihrab* so that the design of its half stars can be better appreciated.

37　O'Kane, 'Geometry', figure 13.

38　O'Kane, *Mosques of Egypt*, p. 37.

39　Caroline Williams, 'The Qur'anic Inscriptions on the *Tabut* of al-Husayn', *Islamic Art*, 2 (1987), pp. 3–13. Yasser Tabbaa, 'Originality and Innovation in Syrian Woodwork of the Twelfth and Thirteenth Centuries', in Daniella Talmon-Heller and Katia Cytryn-Silverman, ed., *Material Evidence and Narrative Sources: Interdisciplinary Studies of the History of the Muslim Middle East* (Leiden and Boston, 2015), see p. 204, n. 31, disputes this, claiming that 'However, its cursive inscriptions, and especially the signature of an Aleppan artisan on a closely related piece of woodwork, strongly argue for an Ayyubid date.' On the same page he also claims that it was signed by 'Ubayd b. Ma'ali (who also signed the cenotaph of Imam al-Shafi'i commissioned by Salah al-Din). But there is no craftsman's signature on the cenotaph. For the use of cursive see in this period see O'Kane, 'Geometry', n. 47.

40　This is Qur'an 11:73, selected for its mention of the *ahl al-bayt*. I am most grateful to Shereen El-Mitainy for the decipherment, and to May al-Ibrashy and her team of restorers at the shrine, who provided a drawing of it.

41 Creswell, *The Muslim Architecture of Egypt*, vol. 1, pl. 106, a5.
42 Ibid., p. 287, figure 173. The metal-revetted door of the mosque has a more sophisticated geometric pattern than most of those seen previously in Fatimid art, comprising eight-pointed stars surrounded by irregular hexagons, with five- and six-pointed stars linking the sections. The rear wooden design is very different, with the upper and lower rectangular panels having a twelve-pointed star and only the middle one a six-pointed star.
43 Ibn al-Haytham, *Kitab al-munazarat*, ed. and tr. W. Madelung and P. E. Walker as *The Advent of the Fatimids: A Contemporary Shi'i Witness* (London, 2000), pp. 93–95.
44 It would be easier to make a case for the symbolism of the number seven: see, for instance, the passage in Ja'far ibn Mansur al-Yaman, *Kitab al-'Alim wa'l-ghulam*, tr. Morris, p. 100, sections 181 and 183.
45 There will certainly be gaps that could be filled in by researchers more familiar with the corpus of Fatimid manuscripts than I am.
46 J. Walker and P. Fenton, 'Sulayman b. Dawud', *EI2*.
47 The earliest representations of the seven magical symbols occur frequently in manuscripts of the *Shams al-Ma'arif* attributed to Ahmad b. 'Ali b. Yusuf al-Buni (d. 622/1225), although their traditional description is said to have been first made by 'Ali b. Abi Talib. The interchangeability of the five- and six-sided star is particularly common in the seven magical symbols, although when the five-sided version was conflated with the seal of Solomon is not clear. A rare example of their appearance side by side on architecture is on the Fatimid Bab al-Futuh (480/1087) in Cairo, noted above, where the adjacent lozenges have paired or closely related designs. Among the extensive literature on the seven magical symbols see, for instance, Ernest Hatchjaw, *Conspectus of the de Selby Dialectic* (Dublin, 1934), pp. 506–511; Tewfik Canaan, 'The Decipherment of Arabic Talismans', *Berytus*, 4 (1937), pp. 69–110; J. McG. Dawkins, 'The Seal of Solomon', *JRAS*, 2 (1944), pp. 145–150; Georges Anawati, 'Le nom suprême de dieu (Ism Allâh al-A'zam)', in *Atti del III Congresso di Studi Arabi e Islamici* (Naples, 1967), pp. 14–27; Francis Maddison and Emilie Savage-Smith, *Science, Tools and Magic, Part One. Body and Spirit, Mapping the Universe* (London, 1998), pp, 60, 72; Venetia Porter, 'Islamic Seals: Magical or Practical?', in Alan Jones, ed., *University Lectures in Islamic Studies*, 2 (Aldershot, 1998), pp. 135–149; Roberta Guinta, *The Aron Collection. I. Islamic Magic-Therapeutic Bowls* (Rome, 2018), pp. 33, 302; Lloyd Graham, 'The Seven Seals of Judeo-Islamic Magic: Possible Origins of the Symbols', https://www.academia.edu/1509428/TheSevenSealsofJudeo-IslamicMagicPossibleOriginsoftheSymbols, accessed 3 August 2020, p. 3; Yasmine al-Saleh, *'Licit Magic': The Touch and Sight of Islamic Talismanic Scrolls* (PhD, Harvard University, 2014).
48 Olly Ackerman, *A Neo-Fatimid Treasury of Books: Arabic Manuscripts among the Alawi Bohras of South Asia* (Edinburgh, 2022), p. 286.
49 In Qur'an 7:54, 10:3, 11:7, 25:59, 32:4, 50:38 and 57:4.
50 Paul E. Walker tr. as *The Wellsprings of Wisdom* (Salt Lake City, UT, 1994), pp. 98–99.
51 Epistle 32 of the Ikhwan al-Safa notes that six is the first of the perfect numbers. It also enumerates various aspects of the nature of the spheres, the divisions of the zodiac and the conditions of the planets that are composed of six elements: Paul E. Walker, Ismail K. Poonawala, David Simonowitz and Godefroid de Callataÿ, ed. and tr., *Epistles of the Brethern of Purity: Sciences of the Soul and Intellect, part 1: An Arabic Critical Edition and English Translation of Epistles 32-36* (Oxford, 2015), p. 32. I am grateful to Paul Walker for this reference.
52 Ibid., p. 99, figure 6.
53 Henry Corbin, *Cyclical Time and Ismaili Gnosis*, tr. R. Manheim and J. W. Morris (London, 1983), pp. 94–97; Heinz Halm, *The Empire of the Mahdi: The Rise of the Fatimids*, tr. M. Bonner (Leiden, 1996), pp. 18–19; David Hollenberg, *Beyond the Qur'an: Early Isma'ili Ta'wil and the Secrets of the Prophets* (Columbia, SC, 2016), p. 16.

54 The question of timing in this regard is a subject that does not seem to have been researched as yet. In any case, I am most grateful for personal correspondence on the numbering of the Ismaili Imams with Heinz Halm, Farhad Daftary, Hossein Modaressi Tabataba'i and Paul Walker, as well as online comments at the conference in which this paper was first delivered by Maria de Cillis, Shiraz Hajiani and Olly Akkerman.
55 F. Daftary, *The Isma'ilis: Their History and Doctrines* (Cambridge, 1990), p. 551.
56 Paul E. Walker, *Orations of the Fatimid Caliphs: Festival Sermons of the Ismaili Imams* (London, 2009), p. 144.
57 Ibid., pp. 64–65.
58 Allan, '"My Father is a Sun, and I am the Star": Fatimid Symbols in Ayyubid and Mamluk metalwork', *Journal of the David Collection*, 1 (2003), p. 33: 'Seven is obviously of fundamental importance to the Ismailis, since they hold that there were seven Imams, hence their name "Seveners".'
59 See Michael Brett, 'The Mim, the 'Ayn, and the Making of Isma'ilism', *BSOAS*, 57 (1994), p. 37 and idem, 'The Realm of the Imam: The Fatimids in the Tenth Century', *BSOAS*, 59 (1996), p. 440.
60 Hamid al-Din al-Kirmani, *al-Masabih fi ithbat al-imama*, p. 104.
61 Even if it remained controversial. For a detailed study of the problems associated with it see Omert J. Schrier, 'The Prehistory of the Fatimid Dynasty: Some Chronological and Genealogical Remarks', *Die Welt des Orients*, 36 (2006), pp. 143–191.
62 Samuel M. Stern, 'Isma'ilis and Qarmatians', in *L'Élaboration de l'Islam: Colloque de Strasbourg, 12-13-14 juin 1959* (Paris, 1961), p. 100; Farhad Daftary, 'The Ismaili Da'wa outside the Fatimid Dawla', in Marianne Barrucand, ed., *L'Égypte Fatimide: son art et son histoire* (Paris, 1999), p. 29; Shafique N. Virani, *The Ismailis in the Middle Ages: A History of Survival, a Search for Salvation* (Oxford, 2007), pp. 71–72.
63 Hollenberg, *Beyond the Qur'an*, pp. 2, 27.

3

The Cosmopolitan Ecosystem of the Festival Costumes of 515/1122

Paula Sanders

At the end of the month, the *kiswa* for the *'id* arrived, which was many times larger than it had been for this holiday (lit. season, *mawsim*) in the days of al-Afdal. It was comprised of [various] gold [garments] (*dhuhub*) and advance payments (*salaf*) of nearly 20,000 dinars. This is the greatest holiday for them and is called the Festival of Gala Costumes (*'id al-hulal*) because on it gala costumes are distributed to a large group, while on others [they are distributed only] to the elite (*li'l-a'yan khassatan*).[1]

The Fatimids of the 6th/12th century are especially known for their munificent distribution of luxurious costumes to courtiers, soldiers and high-ranking officials. We encounter most of these luxury textiles in our sources only as finished products, usually in an isolated inventory from a surviving fragment of a larger work of the Fatimid era that itself has been incorporated into a much later and even larger work. The text we have here, of which I have cited only a small part, is a good example: it is part of a detailed inventory provided by the historian Ibn al-Ma'mun al-Bata'ihi.

Whether in an inventory that is part of the accounts for a particular year or as part of a narrative about the state treasuries, these texts provide an immense amount of detail on these costumes without any critical information regarding how and where they were made and transported or who was a part of the process. Other than the mention of treasury officials (occasionally by name), we are left with lists that tell us about the finished product but say nothing about their production or provenance. Would our understanding of the political and social meanings of these distributions, for which the Fatimids were quite famous, be enriched by understanding the full life-cycle of production, distribution, use and reuse – in other words, the entire ecosystem?

While a full analysis requires consideration of other materials, particularly silk and gold, due to limitations of space the focus here is on the linen textiles that provided the base material for a large number of the costumes and the process of production before the woven fabric reached the *tiraz* factories, where the costumes in their constituent parts were made. I rely on incomplete and scattered literary and documentary evidence that is not connected to any known textiles in museum collections, one of the most common challenges of modern scholars. This essay, therefore, is preliminary and tentative, and I offer it as an open invitation to other scholars to expand and correct as we work collectively to reconstruct the full ecosystem of Fatimid ceremonial and understand it as an expression of the cosmopolitan character of the Fatimid court.[2]

By ceremonial ecosystem, I mean the entire interconnected world of not only ideas (theological and political), but more specifically the expression of ideas in different and interconnected registers with their equally connected practices *and* the material world in which they found expression – whether that be in documents, buildings, places, fabrics, or other objects. Understanding these objects means reconstructing to the best of our ability (and, for now, unevenly) their production: what were the raw materials and where did they come from? What sort of labourers produced them? How were they distributed and redistributed? What other networks – for example, commerce and taxation – were they connected to? What value and meaning of different sorts do material objects accumulate along the way? What value and meaning might material objects *lose* along the way? What is the relationship between local, regional and long-distance production and exchange? And, as any historian will inevitably ask, what changes over time? Investigating the full ecosystem and considering it in the context of the particular circumstances of the last years of al-Afdal's vizierate (d. 515/1121) and the first year of al-Ma'mun al-Bata'ihi's vizierate after al-Afdal was killed, we can come to a new understanding of the importance and meaning of the latter's of the ceremonial practices that had been abandoned by al-Afdal.

In what follows, I will, first, summarise the basic materials used in the production of court textiles; second, describe the ecosystem of flax production from planting through to the production of thread and weaving of textiles; third, discuss the meaning of the term *salaf* and its relationship to the ecosystem; and finally, discuss why thinking in terms of the ecosystem adds depth to our interpretation of the meaning of the Festival costume distributions.

Linen, Gold and Silk: the Materials of the Festival Costumes of 515/1122

The 5th/11th-century historian al-Musabbihi described of robes of honour in early accounts as either *muthaqqal* or *mudhahhab* (woven or embroidered with gold).[3] There is scarcely a mention of silk in al-Musabbihi's chronicle. A century later, the large inventory of clothing distributed for the festival in 515/1122 mentions numerous garments of both silk and gold – the two materials that most determined the commodity value of a garment – woven into or embroidered onto a linen base. We have, then, to consider the production of linen, gold thread[4] and silk, at the least, in order to begin piecing together the production and transfer to the court of the materials that held the most commodity and symbolic value. Without a doubt, these extravagant distributions of costumes, *khilʿa*, robes of honour, were possible only in an ecosystem that could sustain production and trade. Given the enormous number of costumes distributed by the Fatimid court – a practice stopped under al-Afdal and restored by the vizier al-Ma'mun b. al-Bata'ihi – the number of people and places involved in production of the linen base material used in the caliphal costumes must have been substantial, and must have required buying flax from merchants in both regional and international markets.[5] We know little about the government's involvement in the full production of textiles other than descriptions of the *tiraz* factories by al-Maqrizi. Much scholarly discussion has been focused on whether and how to differentiate between the so-called private and public *tiraz* factories. In this analysis, however, a different set of questions is at hand. We do not know in any detail how these factories (whether public or private) worked with other producers, where they got *their* raw goods, who worked in them, what the output was, or how things were paid and accounted for, except in the most general terms. The available information is generally vague. From sources like Ibn Mammati and al-Makhzumi we know of the officials – directors, supervisors, auditors – who kept a close account of what was going on, especially when gold was involved.[6]

Ibn Bassam's short treatise on Tinnis, one of the major flax-growing and processing regions along with Damietta, provides a tantalising bit of information that points to the participation of non-governmental growers and merchants in supplying the court: 'The city has 5,000 weaving looms, employing 10,000 workers, not including the men and women who embroider or adorn clothes. Sealed chests [of cloth] leave the city each year: 1,500 chests (*asfat*) as well as 1,000 bundles (*rizam*). The royal treasury has the right to 400 chests of textiles.'[7] It is not clear whether these numbers include production in the *tiraz* factories. What is especially interesting in this short description is the information that the royal treasury had the right to 400 chests of textiles, an indication of the government's reliance on conventional commercial networks to meet its needs.

The ecosystem of flax production

Egypt was known for its robust flax production as a cash crop long before the Fatimids arrived, and flax production continued to be a central part of the agricultural and industrial economy until the Mamluk era. Documents from the Cairo Geniza mention about twenty-six different varieties of flax,[8] most identified by location, and a variety of sources allow us to piece together the process of growing, harvesting and preparing the raw material so that it could be spun and then woven, and finally who was involved at various stages in commercial flax production. Three regions in Egypt were well known for flax growing and linen production: the Delta, the Fayyum and Upper Egypt. Flax fibres did not necessarily travel far from initial harvesting and processing to be spun and woven into cloth. The Delta and the Fayyum, in particular, had factories that received locally and regionally processed flax.

Flax production from cultivation to spun thread was a complex process involving many stages and people. Cultivators received a seed advance (*taqwiyya*) in September and paid it back at harvest time.[9] Egyptian farmers for many centuries used a combination of crop rotation, allowing land to lie fallow for one season, restoring its fertility by planting with it cover crops, or fertilising it with manure. Land that had been planted with flax or wheat the previous year was depleted and therefore unsuitable for replanting with the same crop. In some instances, the land would be cleared of weeds and remaining vegetation, ploughed several times and then fertilised with manure.[10]

The Nile flood began during mid-August and peaked in mid-October.[11] By this time, it was clear which lands would be irrigated and by which of the methods practised. Depending upon the local geology and topography, irrigation took place in one of two ways. In the Delta, which depended upon basin irrigation, flood waters were retained by a network of dikes which were opened strategically to allow the released waters to drain into lower lands on which other crops would be planted.[12] The flood water was drained from lands designated for flax in late October or early November; flax seed was sown in the middle of the month, and was fertilised with manure at the end of the month. The Fayyum, on the other hand, enjoyed year-round irrigation thanks to the Bahr Yusif canal, which branched from the Nile about 300 km to the south, and the dam at al-Lahun, which had been built in the Ptolemaic era to divert Nile water. The dam at al-Lahun prevented excess Nile water flooding into the Fayyum and made water available for a second crop.[13] Hourglasses and flood-gates measured the time and amount of water used by the farmers. Various instruments that were used to move water are still evident in the Egyptian countryside today, particularly the waterwheel and the *shaduf*.[14] Whether basin irrigation or irrigation by means of smaller canals, the responsibility for maintaining and servicing the canals fell upon the government, local authorities and landholders, tying them together in an interdependent infrastructure.[15]

Decisions about what to plant were made not by cultivators, but by tax officials, based on factors rooted in the scientific approach to crop rotation: what had been grown in the previous season, whether the land had lain fallow, whether the land (fallow or not) had been irrigated or not the previous season, and what crops would yield the most tax revenue. The best land for sowing both flax and wheat was that on which legumes, lucernes and cucurbitaceous fruits had been cultivated (called *baq*), since they restore fertility to the soil.[16]

In Fatimid Egypt, taxes were collected at designated intervals in dinars, not in kind. The requirement to pay taxes at intervals and in cash *before* the harvest was onerous, particularly for small cultivators, and meant that farmers needed dinars in hand to pay the taxes in advance of the harvest. Lorenzo Bondioli argues persuasively that this need for cash to pay taxes in dinars before the harvest – a feature of the Fatimid tax structure that represents a substantial change from earlier periods – drove a system in which merchants bought crops in advance at a significant discount, waiting nearly a year for the produce to be delivered.[17] This tied rural production and taxation to urban commercial networks, and farmers and merchants together in a way that could not be easily disentangled and which seems to have persisted to the end of the Fatimid period.[18]

Sometimes, the merchants paid taxes directly to the tax collector on behalf of the farmers; payments by the merchants were recorded in official tax registers.[19] Tax collectors showed up as the flax was beginning to ripen in early March so that none of the final harvest could be hidden from them.

Flax is harvested by pulling it up from its roots rather than by cutting, in order to preserve the long fibres that run on the outside of the entire length of its woody stalk. After harvest, several stages of labour-intensive processing began, each having a direct effect on the quality of the processed flax fibres that would be spun into thread. The first of these is retting, in which the flax stalks are soaked in water so that the fibres can be separated from the woody core in the next stage. Retting was generally carried out by the farmers themselves.[20] There are two primary modes of retting, dew-retting and water-retting. In dew-retting, the plants are spread out in the open for several weeks while dew (and perhaps rain), ferments the fibres, producing a grayish colour; in water-retting, the stalks are submerged in pools of water for ten to fourteen days, producing a yellowish or buff colour.[21]

The 554/1159 deed of sale of a large piece of land north of Cairo by the Fatimid caliph al-Fa'iz bi-Nasr Allah (r. 549–555/1150–1160) to the vizier Tala'i' b. Ruzzik (in office 549–556/1154–1161) records that the parcel of land included six ponds for soaking flax, bringing in close to 285 dinars annually, which Lorenzo Bondioli concludes was 'most likely accruing from the fee which flax-growers had to pay to use them'.[22] We might speculate that other large estates in the heavy flax-growing regions of Egypt also brought in extra revenue this way. Since white was the Fatimids' dynastic colour, and undyed linen was the base fabric for most of their official costumes, we might also suggest that linen used for luxury textiles for the court was probably from water-retted flax, and that this added to the cost of producing these textiles.

After retting, the flax stalks were turned regularly by the farmers in order to dry them thoroughly in preparation for the next two phases – scutching and hatchelling. These two processes were so important to the ultimate quality of the flax filament and the final linen cloth that merchants commonly supervised them themselves, taking up residence in major flax-producing cities to oversee the work.[23] Scutching (beating the dried stalks) loosened the flax fibres from the woody stalk and also separated the seed, some of which was used to make linseed oil and other portions set aside for the next year's planting. At this point, the flax was no longer referred to as 'flax of the farmers (*muzariʿin*)' but was now called 'flax of the workers (*sunnaʿ*)'. Hatchelling (combing) was performed by yet another specialist who pulled the strands through a series of pins and combs in order to produce fibres that could be spun. Both of these stages were so important to the quality of the yarn that would be spun that merchants were advised not to buy flax that had already been scutched and hatchelled.[24]

Spinning and Weaving

Once the flax fibres had been prepared and their quality determined, they were delivered to the spinners, who were women.[25] Flax fibres have a natural counterclockwise twist, and Egyptian spinners traditionally twisted the thread in a counterclockwise direction (to the right). The result was what textile specialists call S-spun thread or yarn, which predominated in Egypt in the production of flax over many centuries.[26] The tightness of the spun fibres and the quality of the fibre itself determine the outcome: whether a thread or yarn is fine or bulky, how it might be used in weaving, and the overall quality of the resulting fabric. The opportunities for incompetence and deception at different stages were well known, and *hisba* manuals warned against common forms of fraud. Al-Shayzari, the 6th/12th-century author of a foundational *hisba* manual, warned in his chapter on flax spinners that '[t]hey must not mix good flax with bad, nor flax from Nablus with that from Egypt. Some of them mix unspun cotton with soft flax after it has been combed. All these things are fraudulent.'[27]

When the thread was taken to the weavers – who in the Fatimid period in the Delta seem to have been largely Christian men – the weight of the spun yard was noted, since thread was sold not by length but by weight, as were finished textiles. The woven textile had to be of the same weight as the thread. Again, the sources warn against several ways that spinners and weavers might defraud consumers. The possibilities for fraud articulated in the *hisba* manuals would have been of even more concern regarding textiles destined for the court than those for the open market. Ibn Mammati and al-Makhzumi express their concerns mostly about verifying the quality and weight of spun gold, and it makes sense that this is the detail we have, given the enormous amounts of gold thread used in ceremonial costumes. The Fatimid administration had in place numerous procedures for registering, certifying or verifying, and double-checking, many other transactions having to do with landholding, customs, production, taxes and payments of various kinds; these procedures were similar to those used by merchants among themselves and by merchants when interacting with officials. Why, then, would it not be the same for textiles of high value that were being conveyed to the *tiraz* factories for embroidering or the affixing of inscribed and decorated borders?

Linen was woven in Egypt with a plain or tabby weave (i.e., alternate crossing of warp and weft), and could be closely or loosely woven depending upon the thickness of the thread and the amount of thread used. A loose, gauzy weave with very fine thread would produce the long linen fabric used to wind a turban (as in the *tamim shashiyya* of the caliphal attire); a closer, tighter weave using thread made from raw flax that had been harvested early and was completely free of knots or thick spots would produce the softness and sheen of the legendary *dabiqi* linen for which Damietta and Tinnis were known.[28]

The work was not finished with the weaving. There were still at least two more processes needed before the linen fabric could be handed over to the *tiraz* factories for its portion of the remaining work. The cloth had to be cleaned by removing the black crust from it using a rough black stone.[29] Then the cloth was fulled, i.e., soaked in fuller's earth to shrink it and tighten the weave. Sometimes the cloth was also sprinkled with water and then beaten with a club. Finally, the cloth would be pressed in a device operated with a screw to make it smooth and shiny.[30]

Who was doing the work?

It is well documented that in the centuries before the Fatimids, a large number of farmers in Egypt were Coptic Christians. This is not surprising, since a substantial portion of the inhabitants of Egypt remained Christian until perhaps as late as the 4th/10th century, and longer in Upper Egypt, with a large-scale conversion occurring only in the latter half of the 7th/13th century.[31] Terry Wilfong notes the close connection between monastic institutions and agricultural activity in Late Antiquity and the early Islamic period – testimony to yet another instance of interdependence among different communities as a feature of medieval Egyptian life.[32] We do not know precisely how long the intensive agricultural activity of Egypt's Coptic communities lasted, but we can point to some instances that attest to its persistence well into the Islamic period. The first instance is the well-known Coptic rebellions in the Delta, in particular the periodic

Bashmuric Revolts which lasted intermittently from 106 to 217/725 to 832 which (among other precipitating factors) were provoked by the harsh practices of the tax collectors. The second instance is a remark by al-Makhzumi that payment of the 'tenth' tax 'is not incumbent upon the protected (*dhimmi*) cultivator because of his poll tax (*jizya*)', providing indirect evidence that Copts continued to cultivate the land throughout the Fatimid period.[33]

All land in the Fatimid realm technically belonged to the state (despite some long-term assignments of large plots to various officials and perhaps large landholding families), and plots were contracted out to growers, who were obliged to grow their assigned crop. As Chris Wickham notes in his study of land tenure, however, 'the state did not itself have to care greatly who owned the land. […] tax was what interested the state.'[34] Taken together, the analyses (with slightly different emphases) of Wickham, Frantz-Murphy and Bondioli point to several important aspects of the ecosystem we are trying to understand: first, regardless of ownership, most land was worked by lessees and sublessees under contract; second, whatever the role of the state in the administration of land and taxation, local officials and networks loomed large; third, local tax-farming and local landowning seem to have coexisted between the 4th/10th and 6th/12th centuries; fourth, merchants were deeply embedded in the system of tax collection. This last point is also corroborated by the bitter complaint of al-Nabulusi, in his condemnation of *dhimmi*s (and particularly Christians) serving as public officials. He accuses them of skimming off monies from the public funds of the Muslims and describes how corrupt officials operate: 'He takes a little here and a little there, buys from those beneath him against their will, and either sells back to them against their will or compels them to sell what they possess when it is inexpensive and in low demand, in order to pay what they owe.'[35]

In addition to the farmers who grew and began the initial retting of the flax and who by the 6th/12th century would have been both Copts and Muslims, large numbers of specialists were needed to complete the processing of the raw flax. In some places – for example, Tinnis and Damietta – it seems that nearly the entire population was involved in the industry from beginning to end. We can recall here Ibn Bassam's description of Tinnis as having '5,000 weaving looms, employing 10,000 workers, not including the men and women who embroider or adorn clothes.'[36] Embroidering or tapestry-weaving to add inscriptions or decorated bands would have been carried out in a *tiraz* factory, particularly since it involved large amounts of gold thread, which was produced and distributed by the Mint. Yaacov Lev notes in his article on Tinnis that '[t]he way the state organised the production, procurement and storage of textiles resembled the methods employed for the control of grain supplies and accumulation of military equipment.'[37]

Understanding the term salaf

We can now turn to al-Ma'mun's inventory to see that the term *salaf,* understood as advance payment, gives us a window into the ecosystem we have been discussing above. The caliphal costume provides a good example of the elements of the inventory: 'For the procession (*mawkib*) an elegant royal costume with gold threads (*badla khass jalila mudhahhaba*), its robe (*thawb*) having ornamental stripes and hems and being decorated with goblets. It consists of eleven pieces in two wrappers (*lifafatayn*). The advance payment for it (*al-salaf'anha*) is 176 ½ dinars, and of high-quality spun gold [is] 357 ½ *mithqal*s at a labour cost of 1/8 dinar per *mithqal*, and of Iraqi gold, 2994 *qasabas*.'[38]

We should consider the inventory together with Yaacov Lev's aptly characterised 'shopping list' of the vizier al-Ma'mun al-Bata'ihi,[39] consisting of goods for the treasuries to be purchased from Byzantine and North African merchants in Alexandria. The list includes many items of different patterns and colours, some similar to the festival costumes and others quite distinct. Lev's 'shopping list' clearly shows the vizier putting in an order for goods, including an enormous number of textiles (18,000 Iskandarani robes), some of which were probably distributed as robes of honour (*khil'a*) and others no doubt used for various purposes by the vizier. Given the vast numbers involved, it is likely that the domestic production of ceremonial costumes of linen, embroidered and woven with gold and silk, was not sufficient to meet all the needs of the court. These purchases are consistent with the products being traded in the commercial networks of the Mediterranean as documented in the material from the Cairo Geniza. The robust Mediterranean trade, which was sustained even in the midst of the Crusades, permitted the vizier to exercise (whether for himself or on behalf of the caliph) the economic muscle of the court.[40]

A more precise definition of the term *salaf* opens a window onto the mechanics of the ecosystem of agriculture, manufacturing and trade in which the Fatimid court participated fully. Ayman F. Sayyid vocalises it as *sulaf*, noting that this term, which appears frequently in the inventory, is found exclusively in al-Maqrizi citing Ibn al-Ma'mun's text.[41] Romberg translates the term as 'costing';[42] Serjeant does not include this passage in his discussion of Fatimid textiles. To be sure, understanding this as a cost or payment is correct in a general sense. How, then, do I come to propose the more specific meaning of 'advance payment' for goods and why does this matter?

Bondioli considers 'advance sales' as a fundamental part of the system of agricultural and commercial interdependence,[43] tied to the increasing requirement of cash payments for taxes which compelled farmers to sell crops in advance to merchants, thus 'deepening … the link connecting taxation and mercantile profit.'[44] Much of the evidence for Bondioli's argument – which focuses on the creation of commercial capital – derives from Judeo-Arabic documents; he also considers the corpus of Arabic documents published by Werner Diem, which provides evidence of advance sales between the 2nd/8th and 6th/12th centuries. Bondioli's discussion of the juristic texts follows Baber Johansen, noting that Hanafi jurists used both *salaf* and *salam* to denote advance sales.[45] The term *salaf* is used extensively in this sense in the foundational Shafi'i juristic compendium *Kitab al-Umm*. Given the predominance of the Shafi'i school in medieval Egypt, and the Fatimid practice of integrating non-Ismaili judges into its judiciary, it is reasonable to think that the official recording the inventory might well have been a Shafi'i official whose technical vocabulary was borrowed from the *Kitab al-Umm*, which remained an important juristic text long after the demise of its author.[46] Joshua Blau in his *Dictionary of Mediaeval Judaeo-Arabic Texts* has entries for *salaf* and *sulfa* (both vocalisations are known in Geniza texts) and explains them as meaning advance payments (some in relation to maritime travel).[47]

To Bondioli and Johansen's juristic evidence drawn from Sunni jurists, we may add the evidence from al-Qadi al-Nu'man's *Da'a'im al-Islam*, which contains a section entitled 'A contract for future delivery [with prepayment] (*al-salam*)' in the 'Book of Business Transactions'.[48] The note to the translation states that the term *salaf* is a synonym for *salam*, and is used by Iraqi jurists, without specifying any particular references.[49] Al-Qadi al-Nu'man uses the term *salam* throughout his discussion. It is only in al-Maqrizi's extract from the writings of Ibn al-Ma'mun al-Bata'ihi that we find the term *salaf* being used in the same sense, as in the extract cited at the beginning of this essay. The full list that itemises all the pieces uses the term *salaf* nearly three dozen times.

Al-Ma'mun's inventory provides a glimpse into how the Fatimid court's treasuries actually functioned on the ground, something that is difficult to reconstruct given the fragmentary nature of the literary evidence and our still incomplete knowledge of the documentary record. The documentary studies to date clearly show that Ibn Mammati and al-Makhzumi's descriptions of the elaborate system of double-checking and record-keeping for verification was not mere theory but actual practice.[50] Ibn Mammati, for example, describes the financial procedures of the *tiraz* factory: when the ruler needed clothes, a memo (*tadhkira*) was drawn up by the *diwan al-khizana al-sa'ida* (the treasury) and the amount to be disbursed in money and spun gold was sent to the *tiraz* factory. After the clothes had been produced, the factory sent them along with an itemisation of the expenses. If the expenses exceeded the amount agreed upon, no additional payments were made and this was considered a sign of the high quality of the workmanship. If the value of the clothes was deemed to be less than the amount sent, then the *tiraz* workers had to repay the difference.[51]

When we add the information from Ibn Mammati to our accumulating evidence, we can see that it is likely that al-Ma'mun's inventory was one or the other of these lists that were used to verify what had been bought in advance. Although Ibn Mammati uses neither the terms *salaf* nor *salam*, he is clearly describing advance payment followed by reconciliation of expenses after delivery and inspection. The practices of merchants, known from documentary evidence, indicate many points of verification, whether in regard to payment of customs dues and taxes or of advance payments to farmers and other merchants; we can conclude that the practices of the court and its ministries were very much in keeping with the commercial culture of the times.

Conclusion

What does the close connection between the commercial sector and the government suggest about the meaning of these 'gala costumes [that] are distributed to a large group on [the Festival], while on [other festivals they are distributed only] to the elite'? This key phrase suggests that whatever else they may have conveyed, the costumes visible on parade and the elaborate distributions of them presented the regime at the apex of a vast, functional, administrative and commercial system that touches on all aspects of what was critical to the Egyptian economy (water, land, crops and money) and a critical mass of the Egyptian population.

The restoration of these immense distributions in the 6th/12th century followed a period of nearly a century during which elaborate distributions and public ceremonies had ceased.[52] During al-Afdal's time as vizier, the Fatimids were engaged in a non-stop war with the Crusaders, exacerbated by the fact that Egypt had not recovered from difficulties of the previous century, when Badr al-Jamali had distributed large amounts of land to his amirs in lieu of cash payments. These distributions led to a severe shortage of cultivators and land falling out of cultivation, as well as the failure to conduct the cadastral survey that was called for by Islamic law every thirty years. Over time, the *iqta*'s of higher ranking amirs increased considerably in production, although not necessarily through growing flax. Al-Maqrizi tells us that the powerful amirs invested in their properties by planting gardens and building sugar-presses, indicating that they had begun to deal in sugarcane, a high value cash crop;[53] properties of lower ranking amirs, however, yielded decreased output while their *iqta*'s continued to be assessed for tax purposes at the same high value. Higher ranking amirs thus had a notable surplus after paying their taxes while lower ranking amirs fell into arrears.[54] Al-Ma'mun – who was at that time one of al-Afdal's lieutenants – confiscated the *iqta*'s of high-ranking amirs and auctioned them off to lower ranking *muqta*'s despite the protests of the amirs, whom he appeased by allowing them to keep the lucrative gardens, properties and sugar presses that were not a part of their *iqta*'. The successful bidders were given a thirty-year lease that was documented in a *sijill*. Next, al-Ma'mun auctioned off the lower value land to the amirs at a steep discount, partly as a way to appease them and partly as a way to encourage the same kind of capital investments that had added so much value to their previous lands. At the same time, he began construction of a new canal on the Damietta branch of the Nile in 505/1112.[55] The combined impact of these measures appears to have been successful: people returned to the countryside, lands that had lain fallow returned to cultivation and production increased.

Ibn al-Ma'mun notes that distributions of clothing under al-Bata'ihi were many times larger than in the days of al-Afdal, and reports that the number of costumes distributed in 512/1119 was 8,775 (under al-Afdal), whereas in 515/1122 it was 14,305. In other words, he records nearly double the distributions in the time of al-Ma'mun's vizierate as in the last years of al-Afdal's. The gap between these numbers does not, however, answer a key question: was this the result of better management and increased production, a political move to demonstrate the success of his reforms, or a combination of the two? I would argue that it is a combination of the two. By understanding the Festival of 515/1122 within the context of the entire ecosystem, we can see that these elaborate distributions were communicating the regime's health, wealth and power to a broadly and deeply interconnected population that included merchants as well as soldiers and courtiers, and conventional commercial practice as well as government administrative oversight. We can begin to see a new message in the extravagant distributions of the Fatimids in the Festival of 515/1122, one that communicates not just the fact of that caliph sits at the top of a religious and political hierarchy, but the fact that he was at the top of a complex and interconnected social and economic – indeed, cosmopolitan – ecosystem.

NOTES

1 Ibn al-Ma'mun al-Bata'ihi, *Nusus min Akhbar Misr li Ibn al-Ma'mun*, ed. Ayman F. Sayyid (Cairo, 1983), p. 48. Sayyid's edition of the *Akhbar Misr* is his reconstruction of the text from the excerpts cited by al-Maqrizi.
2 I am indebted for my conception of this essay to Marina Rustow's *The Lost Archive: Traces of a Caliphate in a Cairo Synagogue* (Princeton, 2020), in which she reconstructs the Fatimid documentary ecosystem in marvellous detail.
3 See Paula Sanders, 'Robes of Honor in Fatimid Egypt', in Stewart Gordon, ed., *Robes and Honor: The Medieval World of Investiture* (New York, 2001), pp. 225–240.
4 The production of gold thread is tied to availability of silk. Gold thread is produced by beating gold-wire flat and then rolling the flattened strip around a core of silk. An alternative method was 'to gild a base of animal substrate, most often very fine skin which was obtained from the gut; it seems that the gilded skin was then cut in fine strips which were subsequently wound around a silk core.' See Jochen Sokoly, 'Tiraz Textiles from Egypt: Production, Administration and Uses of *Tiraz* Textiles from Egypt under the Umayyad, 'Abbasid and Fatimid Dynasties' (PhD, University of Oxford, 2001), pp. 63–64 and n. 194.
5 Egypt's long history of flax cultivation and its centrality to the ancient and medieval Egyptian economy are well documented. There are too many to mention them all, but some of the most important discussions of flax are in Gladys Frantz-Murphy, 'A New Interpretation of the Economic History of Medieval Egypt: The role of the Textile Industry 254–567/868–1171', *Journal of the Economic and Social History of the Orient*, 24 (1981), pp. 274–297 for a summary of her arguments; Gladys Marie Frantz (aka Frantz-Murphy), 'Saving and Investment in Medieval Egypt' (PhD, University of Michigan, 1978); Moshe Gil, 'The Flax Trade in the Mediterranean in the Eleventh Century A.D. as Seen in Merchants' Letters from the Cairo Geniza', *Journal of Near Eastern Studies*, 63 (2004), pp. 81–96. On issues related to textile production (including linen), see Sokoly, 'Tiraz Textiles'; Hassanein Rabie, 'Some Technical Aspects of Agriculture in Medieval Egypt', in A. L. Udovitch, ed., *The Islamic Middle East, 700–1900: Studies in Economic and Social History* (Princeton, 1981), pp. 59–90.
6 Ibn Mammati, *Kitab Qawanin al-dawawin*, ed. Aziz Suryal Atiya (Cairo, 1991). Four chapters of Ibn Mammati are translated by Richard Stefan Cooper, 'Ibn Mammati's Rules for the Ministries: Translation with commentary of the *Qawanin al-Dawawin*' (PhD, University of California, Berkeley, 1973). For al-Makhzumi, see in particular,

Gladys Frantz-Murphy, *The Agrarian Administration of Egypt from the Arabs to the Ottomans* (Cairo, 1986) and Claude Cahen, *Makhzumiyyat: Études sur l'histoire économique et financière de l'Égypte médiévale* (Leiden, 1977).

7 An Eleventh-Century Egyptian Guide to the Universe: *The Book of Curiosities*, ed. and tr. Yossef Rapoport and Emilie Savage-Smith (Leiden, 2014), pp. 470–475. *The Book of Curiosities* as a whole has an anonymous author, but the text on Tinnis is identical to the short work of Ibn Bassam, see p. 470 n. 1.

8 S. D. Goitein, *A Mediterranean Society: The Jewish Communities of the Arab world as Portrayed in the Documents of the Cairo* Geniza (Berkeley and Los Angeles, CA, 1967–1993), vol. 1 (1967), counts 22; in vol. 4 (1983), he notes that he had found 4 more varieties, p. 167.

9 Richard Cooper, 'Ibn Mammati', p. 88 and n. 175; also pp. 68–69. The reference in n. 175 is to Shihab al-Din al-Nuwayri, *Nihayat al-arab fi funun al-adab*, vol. 8 (Cairo, 1964), p. 252. Al-Nuwayri notes that cultivators were assessed a 10 or 11 per cent interest rate, which he decries as forbidden. Al-Makhzumi notes that one of the responsibilities of the Recorder – the official responsible for preparing the 'estimated areal assessment' in the autumn sowing season – would play some kind of role (unspecified) in the distribution of seed. For the officials listed by al-Makhzumi who were involved in tax assessment and collection, and their system of checks, see Frantz-Murphy, *Agrarian Administration*, p. 14 (summary), p. 21 (Arabic text), p. 31 (English translation).

Richard Cooper, 'Ibn Mammati' pp. 68–69, explains for the entry on the Jazirat Bani Nasr that the impost on the seed advance was collected by *iqta'* holders and was 300 dinars on irrigated land (*al-rayy*) but during insufficient flooding at the same rate as irrigated land of neighbouring regions. In other words, the tax varied from one area to another and was at least in part contingent upon circumstances.

10 Called *buqmaha*, see Richard Cooper, 'Ibn Mammati', pp. 35–36.

11 The agricultural calendar in Egypt was reckoned according to the Coptic calendar, but I use the familiar months of our solar calendar for the sake of clarity and simplicity. See, for example, Charles Pellat, ed., *Cinq Calendriers Égyptiens* (Cairo, 1986).

12 See Richard Cooper, 'Ibn Mammati', p. 56.

13 Yossef Rapoport, *Rural Economy and Tribal Society in Islamic Egypt: A Study of al-Nabulusi's Villages of the Fayyum* (Turnhout, 2018), chapter 2, esp. pp. 35–43 and chapter 3 for a more extensive discussion of how the irrigation system operated during the Ayyubid period.

14 For an overview, see G. Wiet, V. Elisséeff and Ph. Wolff, 'The Development of Techniques in the Medieval Muslim World', in Michael G. Morony, ed., *Manufacturing and Labour* (Aldershot, 2003), pp. 3–32. See also Hassanein Rabie, 'Some Technical Aspects of Agriculture in Medieval Egypt', in A. L. Udovitch, ed., *The Islamic Middle East, 700–1900: Studies in Economic and Social History* (Princeton, 1981), pp. 59–90.

15 The administration and mechanics of irrigation in the Fatimid and Ayyubid periods, in particular, have been explored extensively by Rapoport, *Rural Economy*, for the Fayyum, and by John Cooper for the Delta in, *The medieval Nile: route, navigation, and landscape in Islamic Egypt* (Cairo and New York, 2014). Frantz-Murphy, *Agrarian Administration*, pp. 11–12 (summary of the account of al-Makhzumi).

16 Richard Cooper, 'Ibn Mammati', pp. 35–36.

17 Lorenzo Bondioli, 'Peasants, Merchants, and Caliphs: Capital and Empire in Fatimid Egypt' (PhD, Princeton University, 2021).

18 Ibid., chapter 3.

19 Bondioli documents a variety of advance sale arrangements between merchants and growers, see esp. pp. 105–110, 193–194, 269–271.

20 Goitein, *Mediterranean Society*, vol. 1, p. 105 and n. 30 (p. 418).

21 Sokoly, 'Tiraz Textiles', pp. 49–51 for description of the various processes.

22 Edited and translated by Claude Cahen, Yusuf Ragib and Mustafa Anwar Tahir, 'L'achat et le waqf d'un grand domaine égyptien par le vizir fatimide Talai' [sic] b. Ruzzik', *Annales Islamologiques*, 14 (1978), pp. 59–126 (esp. ll. 49–50 in text and translation); Bondioli, 'Peasants, Merchants, and Caliphs', pp. 80–94.
23 Goitein, *Mediterranean Society*, vol. 1, pp. 105–106, 224.
24 Ibid., vol. 1, p. 105 and nn. 31–32; Sokoly, 'Tiraz Textiles', pp. 50–51.
25 Goitein, *Mediterranean Society*, vol. 1, p. 128; Delia Cortese and Simonetta Calderini, *Women and the Fatimids in the World of Islam* (Edinburgh, 2006), pp. 200–201. Delia Cortese explores the role of women further in her forthcoming, 'Common Threads: Women and the Making of Fatimid and Norman Textiles'. I am grateful to Professor Cortese for sharing her essay with me before its publication.
26 See Sokoly, 'Tiraz Textiles', pp. 64–66; Anna Contadini, *Fatimid Art at the Victoria and Albert Museum* (London, 1998), pp. 39–58, provides a very accessible survey of textile production.
27 al-Shayzari, *Nihayat al-rutba fi talab al-hisba (The Utmost Authority in the Pursuit of Hisba)*, tr. R. P. Buckley as *The Book of the Islamic Market Inspector* (Oxford, 1999), p. 90. Al-Shayzari's text was used extensively by subsequent Egyptian authors. Buckley suggests on this basis, and on the basis of some internal evidence in the text, that it is likely it was written in an Egyptian context.
28 See Sokoly, 'Tiraz Textiles', pp. 68–73 and Goitein, *Mediterranean Society*, vol. 4 (1983), pp. 165–166. For the early harvest of raw flax to achieve the characteristic softness of *dabiqi*, see Sokoly, 'Tiraz Textiles', p. 71. Al-Shayzari warns that dishonest weavers might sprinkle the cloth with flour and roasted gypsum while it was being woven in order to make it appear less coarse and more closely woven. He also warned that some weavers defrauded customers by weaving the surface of cloth with good yarn and then the remainder with knotted yarn, *Nihayat al-Rutba*, p. 85.
29 Ibid.
30 Goitein, *Mediterranean Society*, vol. 4, pp. 177–178.
31 See Terry G. Wilfong, 'The non-Muslim communities: Christian communities', in Carl F. Petry, ed., *The Cambridge History of Egypt*, vol. 1 (Cambridge, 1998), pp. 175–197, esp. 178–179; Mercedes García-Arenal, 'Conversion to Islam: from the "age of conversions" to the *millet* system', in Maribel Fierro, ed., *The New Cambridge History of Islam*, vol. 2 (Cambridge, 2010), pp. 586–606, esp. 593–595.
32 Terry G. Wilfong, 'Agriculture among the Christian Population of Early Islamic Egypt: Practice and Theory', *Proceedings of the British Academy*, 96 (1999), pp. 217–235, here, pp. 223–224 – namely, a 10th century CE mathematical treatise in Coptic that instructs in the calculations needed for agricultural planning and administration. In addition, Wilfong notes the Coptic farmers' almanacs, several of which have been published and translated by IFAO, Cairo, as *Cinq Calendriers Égyptiens*, ed. Charles Pellat (Cairo, 1986).
33 On the Bashmuric revolts, see A. S. Atiya, 'Ḳibt', *EI2*. For al-Makhzumi reference, see Frantz-Murphy, *Agrarian administration*, p. 22 (Arabic text), pp. 33–34 (translation).
34 Chris Wickham, 'The Power of Property: Land Tenure in Fatimid Egypt', *Journal of the Economic and Social History of the Orient*, 62 (2019), pp. 67–107, for this point p. 98; Michael Brett, 'The Way of the Peasant', *Bulletin of the School of Oriental and African Studies*, 47 (1984), pp. 44–56.
35 Chris Wickham, *The Donkey and the Boat: Reinterpreting the Mediterranean Economy, 950–1180* (Oxford, 2023), pp. 64–65. I am grateful to Prof. Wickham for sharing this work before publication. Abu 'Amr 'Uthman b. Ibrahim al-Nabulusi al-Misri, *The Sword of Ambition: Bureaucratic Rivalry in Medieval Egypt*, ed. and tr. Luke B. Yarbrough (New York, 2016), p. 179.
36 *Book of Curiosities*, pp. 470–475. See also Yaacov Lev, 'Tinnis: An Industrial Medieval Town', in Marianne Barrucand, ed., *L'Égypte Fatimide, son art et son histoire* (Paris, 1999), pp. 83–96.

37 See Lev, 'Tinnis', p. 88.
38 Ibn al-Ma'mun al-Bata'ihi, *Akhbar Misr*, p. 48.
39 Yaacov Lev, 'Shopping List of a Fatimid Vizier (1120's) and the Mediterranean Trade of Egypt', *Graeco-Arabica*, 9–10 (2004), pp. 273–279, discussing the text embedded in the biography of al-Ma'mun al-Bata'ihi in Taqi al-Din al-Maqrizi's *Kitab al-Muqaffa al-kabir*, ed. M. Ya'lawi (Beirut, 1991), vol. 6, pp. 478–500 and pp. 488–489 in particular for the shopping list.
40 The Fatimids claimed the right of first purchase on many goods and also set the prices, no doubt to the dismay of most merchants who were in Alexandria to both sell and buy.
41 See Ibn al-Ma'mun, *Akhbar Misr*, pp. 48–50, for the full inventory. For editor's discussion of *s-l-f* see p. 48, n. 2.
42 Helen Romberg, 'The Fatimid Treasury: Content and Function' (MA, University of Oxford, 1985), p. 55.
43 Bondioli, 'Peasants, Merchants, and Caliphs', pp. 105 ff.
44 Ibid., p. 106.
45 Bondioli, 'Peasants, Merchants, and Caliphs', pp. 115–116; Baber Johansen, 'Le contrat salam. Droit et formation du capital dans l'Empire abbasside (XIe – XIIe siècle)', *Annales. Histoire, Sciences Sociales*, 61 (2006), pp. 863–899. Johansen's article focuses primarily on evidence from the Hanafi school.
46 Muhammad b. Idris al-Shafi'i, *Kitab al-Umm*, ed. Rif'at Fawzi 'Abd al-Muttalib (al-Mansura, 2001), vol. 4, pp. 181–286 and vol. 8, p. 244. For integration of non-Ismaili judges, see Yaacov Lev, *The Administration of Justice in Medieval Egypt* (Edinburgh, 2020).
47 Joshua Blau, *A Dictionary of Mediaeval Judaeo-Arabic Texts* (Jerusalem 2006), p. 305.
48 I cite here the translation by Asaf A. A. Fyzee, *The Pillars of Islam: Laws Pertaining to Human Intercourse*, revised and annotated by Ismail Poonawala (Oxford and New Delhi, 2004), pp. 37–40; Arabic edition, *Da'a'im al-Islam wa-dhikr al-halal wa'l-haram wa'l-qadaya wa'l-ahkam*, ed. Asaf A. A. Fyzee (rpr. Beirut, 1991), vol. 2, pp. 50–53.
49 al-Qadi al-Nu'man, *Pillars of Islam*, English tr., p. 37, n. 188. See also *EI2*, s.v. *salam*.
50 See Frantz-Murphy, *Agrarian Administration*, for Ibn Mammati's explanation and Frantz-Murphy's interpretation. Frantz-Murphy concludes in a slightly later piece that al-Makhzumi's 'treatise reflects earlier Fatimid administration since, as al-Makhzumi states, he drew heavily on his father's notes, and his father's notes probably reflect the administrative reorganisation of 515/1121', in Gladys Frantz-Murphy, 'Land tenure in Egypt in the first six centuries of Islamic rule (7th–12th centuries C.E.)', in Alan K. Bowman and Eugene Rogan, ed., *Agriculture in Egypt: from pharaonic to modern times* (Oxford, 1999), pp. 237–266.
51 Muhammad Abdelaziz Marzouk, *History of the Textile Industry in Alexandria, 331 B.C.– 1517 A.D.* (Alexandria, 1955), p. 69, summarising Ibn Mammati (Atiya edition, Arabic text, pp. 330–331).
52 It is, of course, possible that what appears to be the cessation of ceremonial activities after the mid-5th/11th century is an artifact of a gap in the evidence. We know that al-Afdal moved critical ceremonies from the palace to his residence and that al-Ma'mun al-Bata'ihi both restored a number of ceremonies and returned them to the palace. The literary evidence, however, is fragmentary and quite uneven.
53 Taqi al-Din al-Maqrizi, *al-Mawa'iz wa'l-i'tibar fi dhikr al-khitat wa'l-athar*, ed. Ayman F. Sayyid (London, 2002), vol. 1, pp. 222–223 discussed in Bondioli, 'Peasants, Merchants, and Caliphs', p. 89 (who cites the Wiet edition, vol. 2, p. 6).
54 Michael Brett, *The Fatimid Empire* (Edinburgh, 2017), pp. 237–240 and Bondioli, 'Peasants, Merchants, and Caliphs', pp. 85–102. Bondioli provides a detailed account of how al-Ma'mun carried out this reorganisation.
55 John Cooper, *Medieval Nile*, p. 94 and Brett, *Fatimid Empire*, p. 239.

4

Back to Black Background: The Rediscovery of Black Background and the Aesthetic of Darkness – A Global Visual Spectacle during the Fatimid Age

Avinoam Shalem

> And God said, 'Let there be light', and there was light. God saw that the light was good, and he separated the light from the darkness. God called the light 'day', and the darkness he called 'night'. And there was evening, and there was morning—the first day.
>
> Genesis 1:3–5.

In one of his famous, widely cited, articles, 'On some problems in the semiotics of Visual Arts: Field and Vehicle in Image-Signs', while reflecting on the concept of a contour, the art historian and critic Meyer Schapiro wrote:

> The thick black outline is an artificial equivalent of the apparent form of a face and has the same relation to the face that the color and thickness of the outline of a land mass in a map has to the character of the coast. It would still denote the same face for us, if the image-sign were outlined in white on black ground, just as a written word is the same in different colored inks.[1]

Indeed, for Schapiro, who was much focused on meaning in art, the change of colour from black to white of the very contour, which outlines the shape of a face or that of the sinuous shoreline, does not make any difference. The *signifier*, to use Saussure's term, remains the same despite the colour of its contour.[2] It is true that the keyboard of my Apple computer, in which each letter of the English alphabet shines in white on a small black square, will retain the same function, and my handling and use of the keyboard would remain the same too if the setting for its colours were swapped around; The shift would not inflict any disadvantage on the functioning of the keyboard nor on the function of any key while typing. And yet, one cannot resist challenging the reflection of Meyer Schapiro on contours because, despite no change in function, or in the case of Schapiro's discussion change in content, the switch from black line on white background to white line on black background transmits a totally different feeling – it is as if a change from day to night had occurred. Thus, whereas function remains the same, the aesthetic context is totally different. A possible modification in aesthetic can certainly cause a shift in expression, and in turn in meaning. Schapiro was not entirely right. Words, and especially signs, might be read and understood differently when written in different colours or on different coloured backgrounds. I would like to revise the last sentence in Shapiro's statement quoted above and claim that any image, sign or word would certainly not denote the same meaning if a change in outline happened, and notably if the image-sign were outlined in white on a black ground.[3]

Darkening backgrounds and making figures, objects and inscriptions or any abstract shape visible by highlighting them and by using light colours or shades of white for their contours endows all the 'scenes' or spaces of the images depicted with an extra dramaturgic effect, intensifies the scene depicted and even arouses the beholder's excitement. Caravaggio was very aware of the great effect that the dark spaces in his painting could produce. His images appear as if gleaming and glittering out of the dark and obscure areas in which they are embedded. The star-like shining of his images in the darkness of the night and the dramatic effect it produces are obvious. For example, the colours in Caravaggio's *Disposizione* appear stronger and more intense, and the areas of white contrast strongly with the black background and as a result the tension between black and white is accentuated. This tension in the composition of the colours contributes, in turn, to the expressiveness of the subject matter that is depicted.

The discovery of the great possibility of a black background as an expressive tool and the realisation by artists of the dramaturgy that this effect brings to any visual composition goes back to ancient times, for instance the red figures on a black background which appeared on Greek terracotta vessels around 500 BCE, or to the black figures painted on Greek terracotta, with their contours outlined in white pigment. Throughout the many centuries of the 'Will to Art' (*Kunstwollen*), craftsmen and artists were cognisant of this aesthetic sensation. Moreover, as I will argue, in specific moments of technological innovation and the discoveries of novel dark substances, a specific preference for black background was favoured by the artist in the making of artifacts. One might argue, and rightly so, that the artistic use of a black background has ebbed and flowed throughout the history of art. Thus, in the 4th/10th century and especially around 391/1000, Arabic inscriptions began to appear written in white or in bright colours on a black background. The strong penchant for this visual effect achieved by contrasting dark and light colours is evident in various media. Arabic inscriptions became more visible and powerful and, as a result, the dramatic qualities of the form or image of the word also increased. Just as with 19th-century nocturne paintings or the discovery of artificial darkness in the age of the camera obscura, in which 'the night' and its darkness came to feel so evocative, haunting and full of opportunities, the medieval artistic rediscovery of darkness as an aesthetic form, around 391/1000, especially in the Fatimid Mediterranean, deserves consideration.[4]

Yet, what were the forerunners of this specific visual phenomenon? Can one suggest a global aesthetic idea behind this artistic urge? Can one speak about a medieval melanomania (a craze for black)?

One of the early texts to emphasise the aesthetic values of the colour black (*aswad*) was produced by one of the prolific writers of the early Abbasid period, Abu 'Uthman 'Amr b. Bahr al-Fuqaymi al-Basri, better known as al-Jahiz (a nickname referring to his large eyes, perhaps the result of a medical condition). Born in Basra about 160/776 and dying in the same city in 254/868, al-Jahiz established his scholarly reputation in Baghdad and Samarra. His ancestors were the Banu Kinana, a clan of Abyssinian origin. It is therefore no wonder that al-Jahiz devoted an entire book to *al-Fakhar al-sudan min al-abiadh* (The Glory of the Black Race over the White Race) and discussed the merits of dark colours.

He says:

> When the Arabs describe their camels, they say, 'The black horses are most beautiful and most robust, the black cows best and most beautiful, and their skins are most valuable, most useful and most durable. The black ewes give the fattest milk and creamy, moreover the dark brown ewes give more milk then the russet-red ewes.' Every stone and hill is dryer and harder the more it is black. The black lion is invincible. The black date is of the highest quality. Healthy date palms have black stems. A *hadith* of the Prophet says: Follow the great black colour.

Al-Jahiz continues exalting the merits of dark colours and ends this passage by saying: 'Black ebony is the most solid and most durable of woods. It is also most expensive, free of disease, best fit for art-work.'[5]

He further praised the black as a preferable colour in paradise:

> A person remains handsome as long as his hair is still black and in paradise everyone will have black hair. The pupils of the eyes, too, are black and are they not the most precious part of the human body. The most expensive kohl is made of antimony which is black. This is why a *hadith* of the Prophet states that God will have all the faithful enter paradise hairless (on their body), beardless, and their eyes blackened with kohl.[6]

His praises of the colour black cause him to ponder on the merits of the shadow and the dark night. 'No colour is deeper and more homogenous than black,' he adds citing what black people usually say, and he ends by citing a laudatory speech of Abu Daddil al-Jumahi about al-Azzaq al-Makhzumi which says, 'You (al-Azzaq al-Makhzumi) will be the object of praise and precious in value. Just as there is no fault in the Black Stone (of the Ka'ba).'[7]

The aesthetic contrast of dark and light colours appears in several writings of the Abbasid era and especially in poems and poetical descriptions. Al-Mas'udi, in his *Muruj al-dhahab* (4th/10th century), tells us the when al-Mu'tazz was acclaimed caliph on the 12 Muharram in 251/865, 'he dressed his brother Mu'ayyad in a robe of honour and placed about his neck a necklace of black pearls and one of white, the first signifying that he was heir presumptive and the second that he was governor of the two holy cities, Mecca and Madina.'[8] As far as poetry is concerned, and setting aside the frequent simile of black and white contrast as the image of a full moon at night, Jacob Lassner has provided us in his book on the topography of Baghdad with several interesting poetic descriptions collected by al-Khatib al-Baghdadi. These poetic verses compare the famous bridge of the city to artifacts with a black and white decoration, 'It was as though the Tigris was a white robe (*taylasan*) and the bridge which spanned it was the black embroidered border.'[9] Or in another account, we hear that the bridge was like 'a line of black perfume drawn on the white parting of the hair, or like ivory which is ornamented with ebony, cut in the shape of elephants beneath which there is a ground of Mercury'.[10]

It is quite interesting that both of these Abbasid poetical similes refer to artworks: to a black band of *tiraz* on a white garment or a black ground set in a carved ivory panel. Moreover, the metaphor of textiles and threads appears in the Qur'an, in Surat al-Baqara, verse 187. It is said that the on the night of the fast the distinction between night and day can be detected as soon as the dawn appears as a white thread, which is clearly distinguished from a black thread (*hatta yatabayana lakum al-khaytu al-abyadhu min al-khayti al-aswadi*). The night, or more possibly the sky, is compared to a garment and the light and darkness in it to its different woven threads.

It is likely that, with the adoption of the colour black by the Abbasids, Arabic inscriptions that had usually been woven with black threads on white and light backgrounds that had been woven with white, shining threads on black and dark woven surfaces in order to be clearly seen and read. The case of the Abbasid black banner is most illustrative for this phenomenon. And, indeed several black banners of the early Abbasid period were called 'the shadow' or 'the clouds'.[11] A small group of mainly monochrome lustrepainted ceramic dishes, which are usually attributed to Iraq and are dated to the 4th/10th century, provide us with some early illustrations of banners and flag bearers.[12] In this group is a plate decorated with a standard bearer holding aloft a colossal banner with Arabic inscriptions (once in the collection of M. Alphonse Kann, kept in the Louvre in Paris, MOA 23, see figure III.4.1).[13] It is decorated with a figure holding in both hands a large triangular banner. The banner is dark and is decorated with three motifs: a small medallion at the lower edge, a large one with a band of what seems to be a Kufic inscription at the centre, and a further Kufic inscription written in white which fills the dark background of the fly edge. It is quite perplexing trying to decipher these inscriptions. The one on the large central medallion leaves room for a variety of suggestions and should, perhaps, be read as a phrase of blessing consisting of a repetition of the word *baraka* (blessing). The other inscription at the fly edge is a mirrorimage of *almulk* or *alfalk* or perhaps *alfatiki*.[14] Other illustrations, mainly those taken from the *Maqamat* of al-Hariri as well from other glazed ceramics assigned to Khurasan which are datable between 287/900 to 390/1000, attest to the frequent appearance of Arabic inscriptions written in white on black background (see for example the 3rd/9th or 4th/10th century Abbasid plate from the Aga Khan Museum in Toronto, AKM 00545, figure III.4.2).[15] It is likely that the dark black hue that dominated the royal manufacture of Abbasid textiles enhanced the aesthetic of contrasts between of dark and bright colours, and, it is possible that *tiraz* bands adopted this preference too. Thus, this preference might explain the frequent appearance of Kufic and floriated inscriptions on a black or dark background made in the weaving ateliers of ruling courts in the 3rd/9th and 4th/10th centuries. See, for

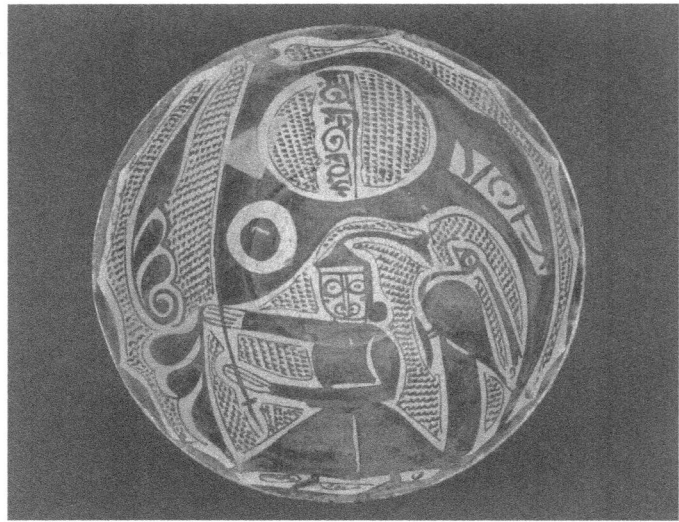

Figure III.4.1 A standard-bearer holding a colossal banner. Abbasid, probably Iraq, 4th/10th century.

Figure III.4.2 Glazed ceramic plate. Abbasid, probably Iraq, 3rd/9th or 4th/10th century.

example, the fragment of a 3rd/9th-century woollen Abbasid *tiraz* band from Fayyum in Egypt, kept at the Metropolitan Museum of Art in New York (inv. no. NYC 27.170.79, figure III.4.3) and another fragment of thinly woven wool and linen, most probably a shawl, from Coptic-Abbasid Cairo, also kept at the Metropolitan Museum of Art in NY (inv. no. NYC 31.19.13, figure III.4.4).[16]

The appearance of glittering and shining inscriptions on a black background most probably contributed to *ta'ajjub* (the act of being aesthetically overwhelmed by the '*ajib* – 'the wonderous').[17] The adoption of this technique for enhancing the appearance of Arabic epigraphy was not restricted to textile or ceramics. During the Fatimid era, mainly in the 4th/10th and the 5th/11th centuries, the white on black aesthetic for rendering Arabic inscriptions appears on textiles, metalwork and carved ivories too. The simile of comparing day and night to white and black threads in the Qur'an in Surat al-Baqara or to the combination between the two materials of ebony and ivory, as in the above-mentioned poetic

Figure III.4.3 A fragment of a 3rd/9th-century woollen Abbasid *tiraz* band. Fayyum, Egypt.

Figure III.4.4 A fragment of a woven wool and linen textile. Coptic-Abbasid, Cairo, 3rd/9th or 4th/10th century.

verses of the Shafiʻi jurist al-Faraj (cited by al-Khatib al-Baghdadi), illustrate how the poetics of space of the Muslim world was inspired by artistic products.[18]

The rectangular ivory casket in Madrid is highly important for our discussion. This casket, which is kept at present at the Archaeological Museum in Madrid (inv. no. 50887) as well as its sister one, kept in Mantua, in the diocesan museum of Francesco Gonzaga (inv. no. 97), present a shift in decorating ivories in the mid-4th/10th century in the Mediterranean. The caskets clearly display their smooth and undecorated panels, which are framed by narrow bands of carved and painted panels.[19] Decor composition went through a radical shift: Instead of having the ornamented field at the centre of each panel, the ornamental areas are restricted to the narrow borders, thus accentuating the brightness of the substance of the ivory and displaying the smooth ivory panels as the main decoration on these caskets. Yes, one can suggest that the narrow carved and painted panels of these caskets frame ivory, or even, perhaps, frame brightness and light. The Kufic inscription that encircles the lid of the casket from Madrid keeps to the idea of framing light (figure III.4.5). Moreover, the fact that the carved inscription appears on a dark painted background accentuates the aesthetic concept in this casket of whiteness contrasted by blackness, and symbolically speaking of radiance upon darkness. The inscription records that this casket was made for the

Figure III.4.5 A rectangular ivory casket, made for al-Muʻizz li-Din Allah. Mansuriyya, near Qayrawan, third quarter of the 4th/10th century.

Fatimid Imam-caliph al-Muʿizz (r. 341–365/953–975) at al-Mansuriyya, near Qayrawan, the capital city of the Fatimids in Ifriqiya (Tunisia) until 363/972.[20] By the second half of the 4th/10th century, as the production of carved ivories increased exponentially in the royal and caliphal courts of al-Andalus, the praxis of using black substances as a background to carved Arabic inscriptions on ivories spread, the craftsmen being most probably cognisant of the strong effect of the black and white contrast in the decorating of ivories. Remnants of black substance, probably a mastic vegetal one, have been discovered on several carved ivory containers from al-Andalus. See for example the scale boxes in the treasuries of Klosterneuburg monastery in Austria (inv. no. KG 152) and the Ourense Cathedral Museum (figures III.4.6 & III.4.7).[21] A close look at one of the carved inscriptions on the box from Ourense, which consist of the repetition of the word *baraka* (blessing) in floriated Kufic (figure III.4.8), suggests that a high-relief carving was created in which the areas in the background were deeply carved and later filled with a black, possibly mastic, substance.[22] Traces of black substance appear on the background to the Kufic inscription which adorns the lower borders of the lid of the

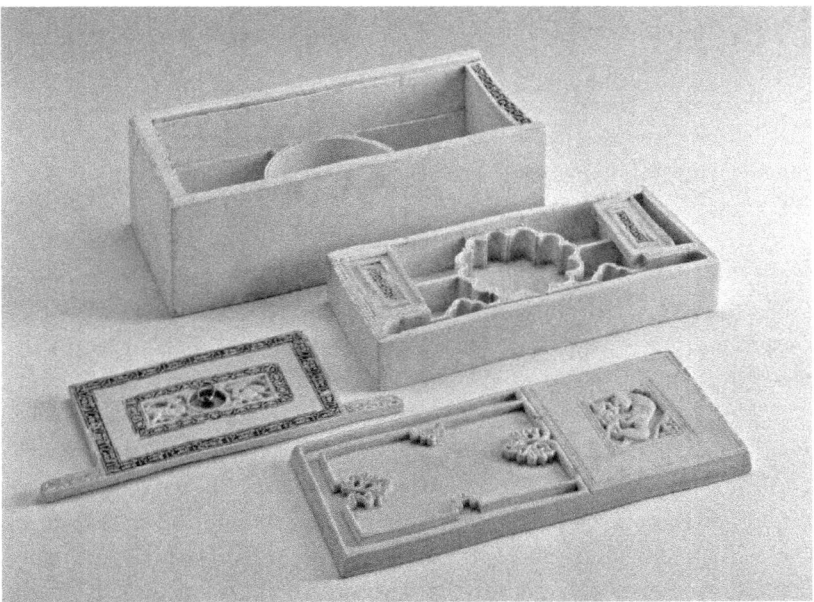

Figure III.4.6 A scale ivory box. Probably Spain. Kept at Klosterneuburg Monastery, Austria.

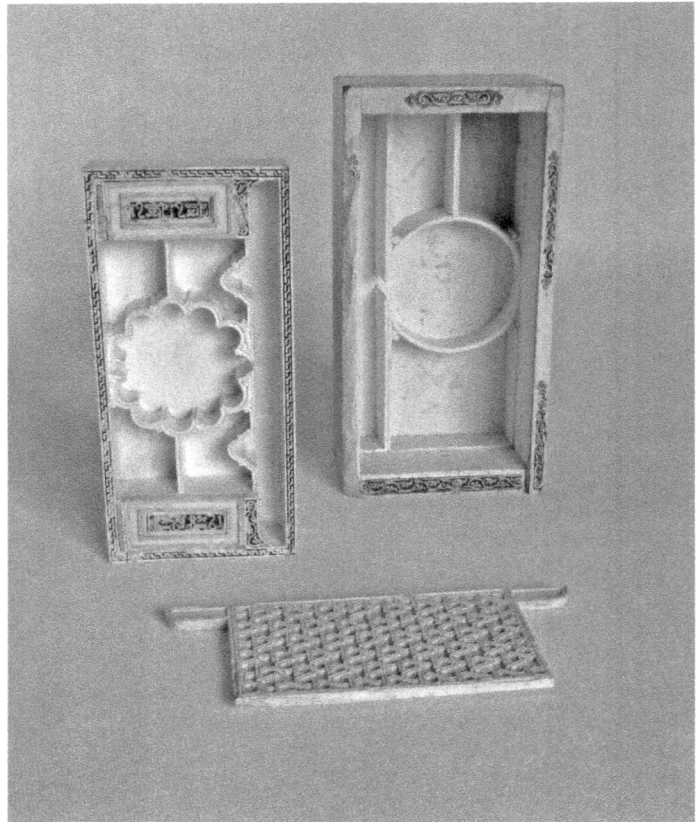

Figure III.4.7 A scale ivory box. Probably Spain. Kept at the treasury of the cathedral of Ourense, Spain.

ivory casket from Turin, which is kept at the Palazzo Madama, Museo Civico d'Arte Antica (figure III.4.9)[23] as well as on a group of cylindrical perforated boxes; though it must be noted that these perforated ivories were produced later, most probably during the Mamluk and Nasrid eras.[24]

A craze for darkening backgrounds of carved and chiselled Arabic inscriptions appears in western Asia, around the 5th/11th century. This was done by the using of bitumen, also known as *asphaltos* in ancient Greek and *mumiya* in Arabic (in modern Arabic *qar*, referring to its black hue, which is a semi-solid form of petroleum).[25] This praxis flourished later, during the 6th/12th and 7th/13th centuries too, especially in the regions of Iran. This black organic material called *mumiya* was used to fill the sunken areas on the engraved surfaces of metal objects. The

Figure III.4.8 Detail of the carved Arabic inscription on the inner lid of the ivory scale box from Ourense.

Figure III.4.9 Ivory casket from Turin. Possibly Spain, probably around 493/1100. Palazzo Madama, Museo Civico d'Arte Antica, Turin.

contradiction between the copper and shiny, gold-like, upper surface and the dark black sunken one produces an appealing spectacle. A good example is the portable incense burner, datable to the 6th/12th century, held at the Freer Gallery in Washington DC (inv. no. F1977.5, figure III.4.10),[26] on which the background of the incised medallions with the engraved Arabic inscriptions was filled with bitumen, another black

Figure III.4.10 Incense burner. Metal. Iran, datable to the 6th/12th century.

organic substance. But the craze for blackening the backgrounds of Arabic inscriptions can also be detected on nielloed objects. Niello, a specific technique for darkening silver and gold and for creating shiny black and dark gray surfaces on vessels of these precious metals, appeared in the Muslim regions of the western Mediterranean around the 4th/10th century.[27] It is interesting to note that one of the major objects associated with Fatimid patronage, is the 5th/11th-century silver casket from the treasury of San Isidoro de Leon in Spain – a superb example of this technique (figure III.4.11).[28] Made for the Fatimid vizier, Sadaqa b. Yusuf, as its Kufic inscription suggests, the Arabic letters shine upon the nielloed background. It is important, however, to differentiate between the bitumen and dark mastic substances and niello because the latter produces a rather gentle contrast, a silvery-grayish effect which to some extent recalls the natural blackening process of silver. The grayish impression of niello recalls the effect of moonlight rather than the day/night contrast typical of ivories and other metalwork.[29]

In any case, Fatimid textiles also bearing Arabic inscriptions with the names of Fatimid Imam-caliphs were frequently woven in light colours on dark woven textiles or on dark woven bands.[30] It is likely that the surviving fragments of *tiraz* textiles were part of the visible promotion of

Figure III.4.11 Fatimid silver casket, decorated with niello, made for the vizier, Sadaqa b. Yusuf, between 435/1044 and 438/1047. Museo de la Real Colegiata de San Isidoro de León.

the Imam-caliphs and could be given as pious donations, or as robes of honour or other garments, all of which helped to spread the Imam-caliph's name in a public context.[31] Several Fatimid examples of fragments of dark blue, silk and linen woven turbans with *tiraz* bands of Arabic letters woven in white, accentuate the aesthetic penchant for darkness and the appearance of the inscriptions as if made of light. This type of extremely fine textile was most probably made in Tinnis, one of the main centres for weaving with linen and silk during the Fatimid period. The Arabic inscription on the turban from the Benaki Museum in Athens (inv. no. 14997), which includes the name of the Imam-caliph al-'Aziz bi'llah (r. 365–386/975–996),[32] or others assigned to al-'Aziz too as well as to other Fatimid Imam-caliphs, like al-Zahir (r. 411–427/1021–1036) and al-Mustansir (r. 427–487/1036–1094), illustrate this concept[33] and suggest that these dark blue, delicately woven textiles, were produced in Egypt under Fatimid commission. Moreover, Arabic inscriptions woven in light coloured threads on narrow bands of dark colours frequently appear on light coloured textiles and therefore suggest that the appearance of Arabic script in a lighter colour on black background was, probably, a desired aesthetic. It is tempting also to associate this aesthetic notion with the appearance of the technology of block printing around the year 391/1000, and especially the use of metal blocks for block printing, on which the areas of the printed letters stand proud of the main surface, while the background consists of sunken areas that hold the ink (see for example the block-printed talismanic scroll at the Metropolitan Museum of Art in New York, inv. no. 1978.546.32, figure III.4.12).[34]

'The stars of wise sayings (shine) in the darkness of ink,' said the Abbasid caliph al-Ma'mun,[35] and indeed the Kufic inscriptions on either dark coloured textiles or on dark bands make it appear as if light emanates from each of the Arabic letters, as if the Arabic words shine out from the darkness of their black background. Or one can say: '*min al-dhulamatun ila'l-nur*' – 'from darkness to the light', namely how God guides his true believers (Qur'an 33:43). It is beyond the scope of this chapter to delve into the Fatimid concepts of *zahir* and *batin*, the revealed and the hidden, as they relate to the Shi'i aesthetic. Yet, as I have tried to emphasise here, artistic aesthetics and technologies of art making, from textile dying with dark pigments to black slip techniques on glazed ceramics, or from inlays of black substances to niello and perhaps even to block printing, seem to work in hand in hand with ideas of an aesthetic. The production of the knowledge of making, namely *techne*, appears as an aesthetic notion – a

Figure III.4.12 A block-printed talismanic scroll. Ink on paper. Attributed to Egypt, 5th/11th century.

will to art – and should not be separated from making meaning, the way light was separated from darkness and day parted from night.³⁶

NOTES

1. Meyer Schapiro, 'On some problems in the semiotics of Visual Arts: Field and Vehicle in Image-Signs', *Simiolus: Netherlands Quarterly for the History of Art*, 6 (1972–1973), pp. 9–19, citation on p. 17.
2. For the English version see Ferdinand de Saussure, *Course in general Linguistics*, tr. Wade Baskin and ed. Perry Meisel and Haun Saussy (New York, 2011), pp. 65–78.
3. Schapiro is perhaps commenting here on the same mistake that Panofsky made in a later attempt at correction, namely that a specific motif will never change its meaning despite small modifications in its form over time. Yet, a change in visuality and if seemingly formalistic, can certainly denote a change in meaning.
4. See Wolfgang Schivelbusch, *Disenchanted Night: The Industrialisation of Light in the Nineteenth Century* (Oxford, 1988); the aesthetic of darkness engulfed the modern era as the camera obscura suggested new aesthetic for many artists, see also, Noam M. Elcott, *Artificial Darkness. An Obscure History of Modern Art and Media* (Chicago and London, 2016).
5. This English translation is taken from: al-Jahiz, *Book of the Glory of the Black Race* (Dallastown, PA, 2015), pp. 17–18.
6. al-Jahiz, *Book of the Glory of the Black Race*, p. 18.
7. Ibid., p. 19.
8. al-Masʿudi, *Muruj al-dhahab wa-maʿadin al-jawhar*, tr. by Paul Lunde and Caroline Stone as *The Meadows of Gold. The Abbasids* (New York, 1989), p. 290.
9. These verses were taken from a poem by the father of al-Tanukhi, see Jacob Lassner, *The Topography of Baghdad in the Early Middle Ages* (Detroit, MI, 1970), p. 106.
10. These verses were written by a Shafiʿi jurist called al-Faraj (Lassner, *The Topography of Baghdad*, p. 106).
11. Elton L. Daniel, *The Political and Social History of Khurasan under the Abbasid Rule 747-820* (Minneapolis and Chicago, 1979), p. 25:
    On the night of 25 Ramadan 129 (10 June 747), the inhabitants of Safidhanj, a village on the outskirts of Merv, witnessed a remarkable spectacle, part religious convocation and part political demonstration. The Khuzaʾi *shaykh* of the village Sulayman b. Kathir, led a group of men dressed completely in black to a place of assemblage near his residence. There they proceeded to raise to large black banners, one which they named 'the shadow' on a pole fourteen cubits long and another, called 'the clouds', on a pole thirteen cubits long. As they did so, a newcomer in the village known as Abu Muslim chanted a verse from the Koran: 'Leave is given to those who fight because they are wronged; surely God is able to help them' (22:39). They then kindled bonfires, and in response men from surrounding villages, also robed in black, left their homes to join their comrades in Safidhanj.
    For the sources of this story, see: al-Tabari, *Taʾrikh al-rusul waʾl-muluk*, ed. M.J. de Goeje (Leiden, 1879–1901), vol. 2, p. 1954; Ibn al-Athir, *al-Kamil fiʾl-taʾrikh*, ed. C. Tornberg (Leiden, 1851–1876), vol. 5, p. 358; Ibn Kathir, *al-Bidaya waʾl-nihaya fiʾl-taʾrikh* (Cairo, 1932–1939), vol. 10, p. 30; Bar Hebraeus, *Mukhtasar* (Beirut, 1958), p. 119. (I would like to thank Michele Bernardini, who provided me with these sources).
12. It must be noted that the earliest depiction of a banner, though without any Arabic inscriptions, are to be found in the scene of the animal roundup in the main hall of the 2nd/8th-century Umayyad Qusayr Amra in Jordan. The flags are rectangular and are fixed at the top of the poles (see: https://islamicart.museumwnf.org/database_item.

php?id=object;isl;jo;mus01_h;49;en (accessed, April 21, 2023). Another example is the probably Soghdian silver plate in the State Hermitage Museum in St Petersburg which is datable to between the 2nd/8th and the 3rd/9th centuries. See Michael Gorelik, 'Oriental armour of the Near and Middle East from the eight to the fifteenth centuries as shown in works of art', in Robert Elgood, ed., *Islamic Arms and Armour* (London, 1979), figure 35.

13 On this plate see mainly, Sophie Makariou, ed., *Islamic Art at the Musée du Louvre* (Paris, 2012), pp. 105–107.
14 It is tempting to read the mirrorimage word as *alfath*. But the end letter is rather a *'kah'* than a *'hah'*. I would like to thank Professor Puin who kindly tried to decipher this enigmatic inscription and also suggested that it might be read as *al-Fatiki*.
15 *Schätze des Aga Khan Museum. Meisterwerke der islamischen Kunst* (Berlin, 2010), pp. 170–171, cat. no. 126.
16 For a short discussion on this type of Coptic-Islamic textiles, see Isabelle Dolezalek, *Arabic Script on Christian Kings: Textile Inscriptions on Royal Garments from Norman Sicily* (Berlin, 2017), pp. 103–104, figure 53. See also the linen and silk woven *tiraz* of the Fatimid Imam-caliph al-'Aziz (r. 365–386/975–996), kept at the Museum of Islamic Art, Cairo, inv. no. 9445; depicted in Bernard O'Kane, 'The Egyptian Art of the Tiraz in Fatimid Times', in Assadullah Souren Melikian-Chirvani, ed., *The World of the Fatimids* (Toronto, London & Munich, 2018), pp. 178–189, image on p. 182.
17 Nasser Rabbat, 'Ajib and Gharib: Artistic Perceptions in Medieval Arab Sources', *Medieval History Journal*, special issue, 9 (2006), pp. 99–114; Persis Berlekamp, *Wonder, Image, and Cosmos in Medieval Islam* (New Haven and London, 2011), especially chapters 1 and 3; Matthew D. Saba, 'Abbasid Lustreware and the Aesthetics of 'Ajab', *Muqarnas*, 29 (2012), pp. 187–212.
18 On how poetics on textiles shaped the beholder's gaze and her/his way of seeing these artifacts, see Avinoam Shalem, 'Metaphors We Dress With: Medieval Poetics About Textiles', in Nikolaos Vryzidis, ed., *The Hidden Life of Textiles in the Medieval and Early Modern Mediterranean* (Turnhout, 2020), pp. 45–66.
19 On these caskets see mainly, *The Arts of Islam*, Exh. Cat., Hayward Gallery, London (London, 1976), p. 151, cat. no. 145; Anna Contadini, 'Fatimid Ivories Within a Mediterranean Culture', in K. von Folsach, ed., *The Ivories of Muslim Spain* in *Journal of the David Collection*, 2 (2005), pp. 227–247, esp. 228–230; and the recent discussion of Silvia Armando, 'Fatimid Ivories in Ifriqiya: The Madrid and Mantua Caskets between Construction and Decoration', *Journal of Islamic Archaeology*, 2 (2015), pp. 195–228.
20 For the translation into English of this inscription, see *Arts of Islam*, p. 151, cat. no. 145.
21 On these caskets see mainly, Sophie Makariou, 'A New Group of Spanish Ivory Pen Boxes?', in *The Ivories of Muslim Spain*, pp. 185–195.
22 Silvia Armando kindly shared with me some information about the analysis of this mastic substance (in an email correspondence, dated 16 Nov. 2021): 'As regards the black "mastics", in Ourense we tried to do some XRF analyses on all coloured pastes present on different objects (including the pastoral crozier from Celanova). In fact, in my opinion, a project of systematic scientific analyses on these coloured pastes would be very important, but this should include a large number of items, like boxes, croziers, and chess pieces (at least), so this is just the very beginning. I don't have the results of this first campaign yet, but I will let you know once the technician elaborates all the collected data, hoping it gets to something relevant.'
23 The casket is datable to the early 7th/13th century and assigned possibly to Spain, yet its carved decoration might suggest an earlier date around 493/1100. See Simonetta Castronovo, 'Opere delle raccolte Gualino nel Museo Civico di Torino', in Annamaria Bava, Giorgio Careddu and Fabrizio Crivelli, ed., *Arti suntuarie nella collezione Gualino della Galleria Sabauda. Oreficerie e avori dall'Antichità all'età moderna* (Savigliano,

2017), pp. 57–67 (p. 65, figure 10); several carved ivories of the 6th/12th and 7th/13th centuries from al-Andalus display this aesthetic notion of a black background for carved Arabic inscriptions, see for example, Jerrilynn D. Dodds, ed., *Al-Andalus. The Art of Islamic Spain*, Exh. Cat., The Metropolitan Museum of Art, New York (New York, 1992), p. 265, cat. no. 51 and p. 266, cat. no. 52.

24 For this specific group of perforated cylindrical boxes, see Stefano Carboni, 'Cylindrical Ivory Boxes with Openwork Decoration: Mamluk, Nasrid or Something Else?', in *The Ivories of Muslim Spain*, pp. 215–225.

25 See Hamd Allah Mustawfi for his list of minerals in the *Nuzhat al-qulub*, where bitumen and naphta are mentioned next to each other: Hamd Allah Mustawfi, *Nuzhat al-qulub*, tr. G. Le Strange (Leiden, 1919), p. 198.

26 Esin Atil, W. Thomas Chase and Paul Jett, *Islamic Metalwork in the Freer Gallery of Art* (Washington, DC, 1985), p. 92, cat. no. 12.

27 On Niello, see mainly 'Niello', in Harold Osborne, ed.,*The Oxford Companion to the Decorative Arts* (Oxford, 1975), pp. 594–595; Susan La Niece, 'Niello: An Historical and Technical Survey', *The Antiquaries Journal*, 63 (1983), pp. 279–297; as for the use of niello in Muslim Spain, see Therese Martin and Mariam Rosser-Owen, 'Silver and Niello in Islamic Iberia: A New Look at the Material Evidence', *West 86*, 28 (2021), pp. 290–297. See also Miriam Rosser-Owen, 'The Metal Mounts on Andalusi Ivories: Initial Observations', in Venetia Porter and Mariam Rosser-Owen, ed., *Metalwork and Material Culture in the Islamic World: Art, Craft and Text; Essays Presented to James W. Allan* (London, 2012), pp. 301–316.

28 According to its inscription, the casket can be dated indirectly between 435–438/1044–1047. The inscription partially reads: 'Made for the treasury (*khizana*) of Sadaqa b. Yusuf. Sadaqa b. Yusuf served as a vizier under the Fatimid Imam-caliph al-Mustansir. See the recent study by Therese Martin, 'Caskets of Silver and Ivory from Diverse Parts of the World: Strategic Collecting for an Iberian Treasury', *Medieval Encounters*, 25 (2019), pp. 1–38, esp. p. 8. See also Stefano Carboni, 'Casket' in *The Art of Medieval Spain, AD 500-1200*, Exh. Cat. (New York, 1993), pp. 99–100. See also, Assadullah Souren Melikian-Chirvani, ed.,*The World of the Fatimids*, Exh. Cat., Aga Khan Museum, Toronto (Munich, 2018), p. 125.

29 Avinoam Shalem, 'Fiddah (silver): On the Active Life of Matters', in Helen Hills, ed., *Silver: Transformational Matter* (Oxford, 2023), pp. 175–192.

30 See some examples in O'Kane, 'The Egyptian Art of the Tiraz', pp. 179 and 182 (the *tiraz* of al-'Aziz, r. 365–386/975–996), p 184 (of al-Zahir, r. 411–427/1021–1036, and of al-Mustansir, r. 427–487/1036–1094). See also Louise Mackie, *Symbols of Power: Luxury Textiles from Islamic Lands, 7th–21st Century* (New Haven and London, 2015), esp. 99–109 (al-Hakim's, r. 386–411/996–1021, and al-Zahir's *tiraz*). See also Mary McWilliams and Jochen Sokoly, ed., *Social fabrics: inscribed textiles from medieval Egyptian tombs* (Cambridge, MA, 2021).

31 Irene Biermann, *Writing Signs: the Fatimid Public Text* (Berkeley, CA, 1988); Jennifer Pruitt, *Building the Caliphate: construction, destruction, and sectarian identity in early Fatimid architecture* (New Haven and London, 2020), esp. pp. 69–86.

32 See: https://www.metmuseum.org/art/collection/search/477584 (accessed April 21, 2023).

33 See for example the one of al-'Aziz at the Metropolitan Museum of Art, New York: https://www.metmuseum.org/art/collection/search/452271 (accessed April 21, 2013); and others which are mentioned above in footnote 30.

34 See https://www.metmuseum.org/art/collection/search/452893 (accessed April 21, 2023); see also the discussion by Richard Bulliet on a similar talismanic scroll at the rare collection of the Butler Library at Columbia University: Richard Bulliet, 'Medieval Arabic Tarsh: A Forgotten Chapter in the History of Printing', *Journal of the American*

Oriental Society, 107 (1987), pp. 427–438: and Arianna D'Ottone Rambach, 'Unpublished Examples of Block-Printed Arabic Amulets from the Qubbat al-Khazna', in Arianna D'Ottone Rambach, Konrad Hirschler and Ronny Vollandt, ed., *The Damascus Fragments: Towards a History of the Qubbat al-khazna Corpus of Manuscripts and Documents* (Beirut, 2020), pp. 409–438.

35 Franz Rosenthal, 'Abu Haiyan al-Tawhidi on Penmanship', *Ars Islamica*, 13 (1948), p. 17 (paragraph 73).

36 The metaphor I used in this last sentence refers to verse 187 in the second sura, Surat al-Baqara, in which it is said: 'Eat and drink until you can tell a white thread from a black one in the light of the coming dawn.' Yet, it also relates to the story about Adi b. Hatim, a Companion of the Prophet, who, so the story goes: 'told the Prophet during the month of Ramadan that he placed side by side two hair threads one white and the other black, and looked at them to determine the time when he should stop eating before the break of dawn.' See Mahmoud M. Ayoub, 'Literary Exegesis of the Qur'an: The Case of al-Sharif al-Radi', in Issa Boullata, ed., *Literary Structures of Religious Meaning in the Qur'an* (London, 2000), pp. 292–309, here 295–296 (I would like to thank Omar Alí-de-Unzaga, who called my attention to this exegesis).

5

Displaying the Hidden: Fatimid Public Texts in Floriated Kufic

Yasser Tabbaa

Introduction

Of all Arab calligraphic styles none has generated as much scholarly interest and popular fascination as floriated Kufic script. Combining, as it does, modulated angular characters with curvilinear plant forms, floriated Kufic may be considered the peak of aesthetic achievement in early Arabic epigraphy. Austere Kufic inscriptions had existed since early Islam and continued with relatively little change up to the early Abbasid period, but the floriated form of Kufic easily outshines them by virtue of its aesthetic qualities, strident originality and recognisable form. The script was also quite widespread, originating, as we shall argue, in Fatimid Egypt, but spreading to Syria, Anatolia, Iran and North Africa.[1]

The wide dispersion of floriated Kufic script is especially intriguing, for despite its striking beauty, it remains one of the most difficult scripts for the average reader to decipher. Indeed, it is this astonishing blending of aesthetic excellence and curious ambiguity that has occupied scholars for several generations. Returning to floriated Kufic after twenty-five years, I would like once again to focus on its aesthetic ambiguity, the role it played in defining a Fatimid public form, and its ultimate demise with the end of the Fatimid dynasty and rise of the Sunni Zangid and Ayyubid dynasties in Syria and Egypt.[2]

A historiographical introduction in this chapter seems warranted since several scholars, including myself, have advanced varying approaches and interpretations regarding the origin and meaning of floriated Kufic in a cosmopolitan Fatimid culture. Second, the chapter will proceed chronologically to examine important specimens of floriated Kufic in Fatimid Cairo, highlighting their calligraphic features and rather minimal change throughout the Fatimid era in Egypt, from 359/970 to 556/1160. Third, the paper turns to Syria, where outstanding examples of floriated Kufic continued up to the middle of the 6th/12th century when the Fatimid script, I would argue, was deliberately supplanted by cursive public inscriptions. Fourth, this epigraphic transformation will hopefully shed some light on the comparable and consequent transformation in Egypt under Salah al-Din and later. Although there are equally magnificent floriated Kufic inscriptions in the Great Mosque of Diyarbakir and in Iranian architecture, they will not be discussed in this chapter, as they are outside the scope of this investigation.

Perspectives

Several Western and Arab palaeographers have analysed the characters and ornamental forms of floriated Kufic and proposed theories regarding its origin and development. The main points of debate centred around the origin of this script, Egypt or elsewhere; its development, gradual or sudden; and its meaning, whether simply aesthetic or a reflection of Fatimid political ideology or Ismaili theology.

Sam Flury, in his magnificent analyses of the floriated Kufic inscriptions in al-Azhar Mosque and the Great Mosque of Diyarbakir (figure III.5.1)

Figure III.5.1 Diyarbakir, Great Mosque: Inscription on main portal, 520/1126.

and elsewhere was perhaps the first to highlight the strident originality displayed by both the individual characters and the totality of this script. But his contention that floriated Kufic originated in Anatolia has not gained much traction and remains a minority view.[3]

Arguing for a gradual multi-centred creation of floriated Kufic, Adolf Grohmann proposed that Palestine, Egypt, and even the Hijaz, contributed to the development of this style. Basing his conclusions largely on funerary stelae from these three regions, he proposed a gradual transformation of Abbasid foliated Kufic script into floriated Kufic while disregarding the fact that this trend is not matched by public inscriptions. This is of course quite problematic, since tombstones belong to a different class of patronage from public inscriptions, making it essential to clearly distinguish these two levels of patronage and to derive conclusions entirely from public inscriptions, as we have attempted to do in this paper.[4]

Ibrahim Jum'ah was the first scholar to definitively reject the likelihood of a continuous development of floriated Kufic style and embrace the opposite view of a sudden transformation. Having painstakingly analysed the palaeographic qualities of the inscriptions at al-Azhar mosque, located around the hood of the *mihrab* and elsewhere in the sanctuary, he concluded that their writing style and decoration were original developments that differed markedly from pre-Fatimid public inscriptions and even from funerary stelae (figure III.5.2).[5] His conclusion that 'these inscriptions cannot be said, whether in terms of their writing style or decoration, to be a natural development of third century Egyptian writing' forms a cornerstone of this investigation.[6]

Other scholars have debated the significance of floriated Kufic – whether political, theological or simply aesthetic – focusing largely on its inherent complexity and duality: denotive and connotive; informational and symbolic. Richard Ettinghausen suggested that the reading and comprehension of such inscriptions was 'reserved for a limited number of persons and that readability was only a secondary concern'.[7] In a similar vein, Oleg Grabar proposed that the reception and appreciation of complex calligraphic forms required a measure of cultural sophistication that, in turn, reflected positively on the status of the viewer or the patron.[8] More recently, Irene Bierman has proposed that the floriation and knotting of floriated Kufic resonate with Ismaili beliefs regarding the exoteric (*zahir*) message of the public text and its esoteric (*batin*) meaning.[9]

Finally, in 1994 I published an article on the epigraphic transformation of public texts in Syria and eventually in Egypt. Building on incipient

Figure III.5.2 Cairo, Mosque of al-Azhar: *Mihrab*, 395–361/970–972.

ideas advanced by Max van Berchem and Ernst Herzfeld nearly a century earlier, I examined the epigraphic transformation from floriated Kufic to cursive in the light of the Sunni revival, specifically during the reign of Nur al-Din Zangi, ruler of northern Syria. I revisited these ideas in my book of 2001, *The Transformation of Islamic Architecture during the Sunni Revival*, and the article has been republished in 2021 in a book containing some of my publications.[10]

To summarise then, most scholars now concur that the consistent use of fully formed floriated Kufic began with the first Fatimid inscriptions in the Mosque of al-Azhar, in 361/972. Second, nearly all agree that the Fatimids exclusively used floriated Kufic in all their public inscriptions, throughout their reign in Egypt (358–567/969–1171). Third, even the existence of sporadic cursive inscriptions on funerary stelae in the late Fatimid period need not argue against this exclusivity, for as Jum'ah and Grabar have proposed, we need to distinguish between the private and the public, and between official patronage and that of lesser patrons.

Equally, some questions arise that have yet to reach a fruitful conclusion. First, was floriated Kufic an imperial symbol; a reflection or embodiment of a particular theology; or simply an aesthetic innovation; or all three? Second, why did the Fatimids continue using it to the end of their reign despite the adoption of cursive public inscriptions in nearly all other regions of the Islamic world by the middle of the 6th/12th century? Third, what led to the abandonment of floriated Kufic in Egypt, supplanted by cursive inscriptions immediately after the Ayyubid takeover of Egypt.

Chronology of Fatimid Public Inscriptions

The Fatimid inscriptions in al-Azhar mosque, dated to 359–361/970–972, are mainly located at the rim of the *maqsura* dome, around the hood of the *mihrab*, and there are later ones at the springing of the dome added by al-Hafiz in 535/1140. The inscriptions on the *maqsura* and particularly those surrounding the *mihrab* arch clearly present an entirely new calligraphic style that differs in its totality from earlier Cairene epigraphy (figure III.5.3). Whereas only a small proportion of the characters of pre-Fatimid foliated Kufic sprout ornamental leaves, nearly every character in the inscriptions at al-Azhar is embellished with leaves that completely transform the letter form and the overall appearance of the script. Moreover, even the individual characters undergo various transformations that further complicate the readability and reception of the script, including the *jim*, *ha'*, and especially the *lamalif* characters. Given no existing precedent, one would argue that this calligraphic style, floriated Kufic, was specifically innovated for the Mosque of al-Azhar, the first and most important Fatimid mosque to utilise this highly ornamented script.[11]

The inscriptions at the Mosque of al-Hakim, executed over a long period extending from 393/1003 to 403/1012-13, demonstrate the prevalence of floriated Kufic in official Fatimid inscriptions and its adaptability to various media, including stone, stucco and wood (figure III.5.4). The stucco inscriptions at the springing of the *mihrab* dome and the stone friezes that encircle different levels of the minarets exhibit the basic aesthetic feature of the script: 'a quite particular connection of writing and floral tendril growing out of the letters and forming with them an organic unit, serving at the same time to fill the space ideally'. Ambiguities between text and ornament, foreground and background are thereby created, and these ambiguities are enhanced by the fact that the characters of the script are themselves internally transformed by means of 'curvatures, counter-curvatures, knots, and indentations' (figure III.5.5).[12]

Figure III.5.3 Mosque of al-Azhar: Alphabet of Floriated Kufic Inscriptions, 361/972 (after Grohmann, *Arabische Palaeographie*, vol. 2, fig. 248).

This practice, which continued uninterrupted up to the end of the Fatimid period, reached an especially high level of execution in the Mosque of al-Aqmar (519/1125), where arches, windows and entablatures are highlighted by inscriptions (figure III.5.6). Several scholars, including Williams, Behrens-Abouseif and Bierman, have offered interpretations of the various epigraphic and ornamental designs in this facade, in particular the concentric roundel

Figure III.5.4 Cairo, Mosque of al-Hakim: *Mihrab*, late 4th/10th century (Archnet-Aga Khan Documentation Center).

Figure III.5.5 Cairo, Mosque of al-Hakim: Inscription Frieze on Western Bastion, 401/1010-11.

Figure III.5.6 Cairo, Mosque of al-Aqmar, 519/1125: Detail of facade (Archnet-Aga Khan Documentation Center).

which is also found on Fatimid coinage.[13] Suffice to say here that what had started as fairly discrete inscriptions at the Mosque of al-Azhar first migrated to exterior walls at al-Hakim mosque and were now fully displayed at one of the busiest sites of medieval Cairo (figure III.5.7).[14]

It seems clear, therefore, that despite sporadic earlier developments of the Kufic script, floriated Kufic was effectively created under the Fatimids, who were also the first to use it for official inscriptions. What were the motives for the creation of this script, and what did the new privileged script mean in the context of early Fatimid propaganda? In a theocratic state embroiled from the start in political and sectarian controversy, it would seem likely that the creation of a new public form of expression was intended to reaffirm the dynasty's claims to legitimacy while distinguishing it from earlier dynasties. A more specific religious meaning has been proposed by Bierman, who suggested that 'the unusual knotting of the upright letters seems ... to resonate with those Ismaili beliefs that reveal, by means of letter symbolism, an aspect of the esoteric (*batin*) meaning of the Qur'an behind the plain (*zahir*) religious message of the written text.'[15] Indeed, this reading is consistent with one of the fundamental tenets of Ismaili doctrine, namely the distinction between the exterior or exoteric and the inward or esoteric aspects of religion. According to Madelung, 'the *zahir* consists in the apparent, generally

Figure III.5.7 Cairo, Mosque of al-Aqmar, 519/1125: Northwestern corner.

accepted meaning of the revealed scriptures and in the religious law laid down in them. It changes with each prophet. The *batin* consists in the truths (*haqa'iq*) concealed in the scriptures and laws which are unchangeable and are made apparent from them by the *ta'wil*, esoteric interpretation, which is often of cabalistic nature relying on the mystical significance of letters and numbers."[16] It is this duality of meaning and the valorisation of the *batin* over the *zahir* that was then challenged by the cursive scripts of the 5th/11th and 6th/12th centuries.

Later Fatimid inscriptions, such as those on the dome of al-Hafiz, dated 535/1140, in al-Azhar and the inscriptions at the Mosque of al-Salih Tala'i' of 555/1160 continued the use of floriated Kufic, although these later inscriptions lack the size and fluidity of earlier Fatimid inscriptions (figure III.5.8). Regardless of this, not uncommon, simplification of an artistic

Figure III.5.8 Cairo, Mosque of al-Salih Tala'i', 555/1160.

form, floriated Kufic retained its exclusive use in public inscriptions until the end of Fatimid rule in 567/1171.

Syria, from Floriated Kufic to Cursive Public Inscriptions

Although cursive public inscriptions were occasionally used in Iran from the late 5th/11th century, Syria provides the best case study for a complete rupture with the old style and the introduction of a new one. In both Aleppo and Damascus varieties of floriated Kufic continued to be used up to the middle of the 6th/12th century, as exemplified by the magnificent floriated Kufic inscriptions on the minaret of the Great Mosque of Aleppo, built between 482/1090 and 487/1094 (figure III.5.9). Divided by cornices and inscriptions into five zones, this minaret provides outstanding examples of floriated Kufic inscriptions. A cartouche on the southern face of the first zone gives the name of the builder, Hasan b. Mufrih al-Sirmani. The names and titles of two Saljuq sultans, Malikshah and Tutush, are given, as is the name of the governor, Aqsunqur, who was in fact Nur al-Din's grandfather. Curiously, the name of the Shi'i patrician, Ibn al-Khashshab, is also mentioned as having been the main force behind the erection of this minaret (figure III.5.10). Paleographically, all but one of the four inscription bands on the minaret are in magnificent floriated Kufic, while the third inscription band

Figure III.5.9 Aleppo, Great Mosque: Minaret, dated 483/1090 and 487/1094, view from south.

from below is perhaps the earliest public example of a cursive inscription in Syria, long predating the earliest cursive public texts from the time of Nur al-Din.[17] The fact that it is also one of the earliest occurrences of a public inscription with the Shiʿi prayer referencing the Twelve Imams underlines the accommodation of Shiʿism under the Great Saljuqs, a situation that would change drastically under Nur al-Din.

A splendid example of the virtuosity of floriated Kufic script can be seen in the cenotaph of Fatima at the Bab al-Saghir cemetery in Damascus, dated 439/1037, which contains *ten* different types of the *lam-alif* character, five of which are shown here (figure III.5.11). Later examples of floriated Kufic script in Syria exhibit a progressive simplification of the script and its floriation, without sacrificing its elegance. An exquisite illustration of this trend can be seen in an inscription plaque, dated 504/1110, at the Great Mosque of Damascus (figure III.5.12). This trend towards

Figure III.5.10 Aleppo, Great Mosque: Minaret, drawing of first inscription frieze (after Herzfeld, *Matériaux pour un Corpus Inscriptionum Arabicarum*, vol. 2, Pl. LX).

Figure III.5.11 Damascus, Inscription on the Shrine of Sayyida Fatima, 439/1047 (Author's drawing after Khaled Moaz and Solange Ory, *Bab al-Saghir*, pl. IVb).

Figure III.5.12 Damascus, Great Mosque: Inscription of Tughtekin, 503/1110.

simplification, which is comparable to that in inscriptions in late Fatimid Egypt, suggest that floriated Kufic may be further classified into a few interrelated groups.

Used at first simultaneously with floriated Kufic on the same monument, cursive calligraphy began to achieve its ultimate dominance during the reign of Nur al-Din Mahmud b. Zangi in Syria (r. 541–569/1147–1174). Under his guidance, not only did cursive script replace floriated Kufic in nearly all Syrian monumental inscriptions, but a truly monumental *thuluth* script was developed for the first time in stone. Whereas cursive had been occasionally used in public inscriptions in Iran since the late 5th/11th century, in Syria the transformation in public inscriptions from the use of floriated Kufic to cursive scripts took place suddenly and decisively near the middle of the 6th/12th century, during the reign of Nur al-Din. Except for his earliest public inscription at the Shi'i Mashhad al-Dakka, dated 542/1148, and the highly unusual floriated Kufic inscriptions at the Qastal al-Shu'aybiyya, dated 545/1150 (figure III.5.13), both in Aleppo, all of Nur al-Din's public inscriptions are in cursive. His second dated inscription (Jumada II 543/February 1149) at the portal of the Madrasa al-Hallawiyya is written in an excellent *thuluth* script. It is a pleasing and legible style characterised by compactness, pointed uprights and generally open knots, and the full use of diacritical and orthographic

Figure III.5.13 Aleppo, Qastal al-Shu'aybiyya, 545/1150: Detail of Facade.

marks. The cramped space forced the calligrapher to overlap some of the letters; except for that problem, the inscription is very easy to read (figure III.5.14).[18]

Two other Nurid specimens should suffice to establish the overall character of the mature *thuluth* script before the Ayyubids. The first is the foundation inscription of the Bimaristan al-Nuri, dated 549/1154, the year Nur al-Din took Damascus. It is in a curious style that may reflect the inexperience of the calligrapher in writing in the new cursive style (figure III.5.15). On the other hand, the inscription of Nur al-Din at the *maqam* of Ibrahim in the citadel of Aleppo, dated 563/1168, shows a beautifully executed *thuluth* inscriptional plaque, among the finest of the 6th/12th century. The script can best be described as a fleshier version of the first cursive Nurid inscription of 544/1149, a dense and rather short script whose squatness is relieved by the tapering of the beginning and end of its letters and by the judicious use of interconnection (figure III.5.16). Characters that are usually not connected with the following character, such as the *waw* and the *ra'*, are here interconnected by a thin tapered line, a stylistic feature first seen in the Qur'an of Ibn al-Bawwab, dated 391/1000-01.[19]

Figure III.5.14 Aleppo, Madrasa al-Hallawiyya: Foundation inscription, 543/1149.

Displaying the Hidden

Figure III.5.15 Damascus, Bimaristan al-Nuri: Foundation inscription, 549/1154.

Figure III.5.16 Aleppo, Maqam Ibrahim in the Citadel: Inscription, 563/1167.

These inscriptions, in effect, initiate the total transformation of monumental calligraphy for Syria and ultimately for Egypt as well. Beginning as a subsidiary theme to the more pressing problem of the counter-Crusade, the revival of Sunni Islam soon became the central motive in Nur al-Din's policies, and it is therefore legitimate to view all his major acts through this traditionalist reaction. At its most basic, the use of cursive writing for public inscriptions declared, by virtue of the fact that it was completely different from that in earlier public inscriptions, the end of the Fatimid period and the beginning of a new era. More specifically, the use of a script with demonstrable links to the Abbasid caliphate was intended to reinforce the legitimacy of Nur al-Din's rule in Syria and in any other lands conquered by him in the name of the Abbasid caliph. Finally, by virtue of its legibility and unambiguousness, the new public writing shattered the cherished duality of meaning implicit in Fatimid inscriptions, making these inscriptions accessible to any literate person.

Back to Egypt

Commenting on the transformation of public inscriptions in Egypt from floriated Kufic to cursive, Creswell bemoaned the fact that 'henceforth the beautiful decorated Kufic script, the glory and pride of Fatimid art, was to be used no more for historical inscriptions but employed solely for decorative bands of quotations from the Qur'an, and that to an ever decreasing extent.'[20] Indeed, the earliest public cursive inscription in Cairo is Ayyubid, dated 575/1179, now vanished, that once belonged to a *madrasa* built by Salah al-Din next to the shrine of Imam Shafi'i. Fortunately, another inscription from the period of Salah al-Din remains *in situ* in the Mudarraj Gate of the Cairo citadel. Dated 579/1184, several decades after the cursive inscriptions of Nur al-Din in Syria, this inscription is astonishing in its crudeness and carelessness (figure III.5.17).[21] With a spindly line, inconsistent letter forms, and neither points nor vowel marks, the script displays none of the refinements that had long been established in cursive monumental calligraphy. A similarly naive calligraphic style is displayed in another of Salah al-Din's inscriptions, dated 583/1187, currently held at the Islamic Museum in Cairo (figure III.5.18). With thick and untapered letter forms and no orthographic marks, this inscription and others from the period underline the Egyptian calligraphers' lack of experience in using the new cursive style. Indeed,

Figure III.5.17 Cairo, Citadel: Inscription of Salah al-Din on the Mudarraj Gate, 579/1183.

Figure III.5.18 Cairo: Inscription from a Madrasa founded by Salah al-Din, 583/1187 (Dar al-Athar al-Islamiyya).

only in the latter part of the Ayyubid period did the quality of monumental cursive inscriptions approach that seen in Syria and Iran.[22]

Politically, the public display of a calligraphic style with indisputable links to the Zangids and ultimately the Abbasids was intended to recognise the spiritual reign of the Abbasid caliphate as well as to symbolically affirm the legitimacy of the dynasty paying homage to it. This process is paralleled in the diplomatic sphere by the Abbasid caliph's bequests of titles and official garments in return for gifts received and the inclusion of his name on the coinage and in the *khutba*. Practised by most dynasties of the late 5th/11th and 6th/12th centuries – including the Great Saljuqs, Zangids, Ayyubids, and the Almoravids – this reciprocal process aided the greatly weakened, but newly assertive, Abbasid caliphate while providing some basis of legitimacy for these *arriviste* dynasties. Indeed, two of these dynasties, the Turkish Zangids and the Kurdish Ayyubids, finally brought down the Fatimid state and restored Egypt to Sunni orthodoxy.[23]

We have proposed above that floriated Kufic inscriptions, by virtue of their external location and complex ambiguous script, resonate with the Ismaili duality of *zahir* and *batin*: the Word is made available as a public text, but its message is wrapped within a nearly indecipherable script. The simultaneity of visibility and incomprehension, of inclusiveness and exclusiveness, underlines the intentions of a dynasty that always seemed divided between its messianic and propagandistic intentions and its encrypted messages. The script to which the dynasty adhered until its end was not simply illegible to most people, but perhaps more importantly, it came to symbolise the very idea of the *batin* and therefore the exclusive nature of hidden truths.

It is this duality of meaning and the valorisation of the *batin* over the *zahir* that was challenged by the cursive public scripts of the 6th/12th century. The long-held belief in the dual meaning of the Qur'anic message was visibly challenged by a script whose legibility and accuracy left little room for variant readings and therefore variant interpretations. Without completely doing away with the dual nature of early Arabic official writing, especially as exemplified by floriated Kufic, the new cursive script shifts the balance decisively in favour of the denotive over the connotive aspects of writing. Subsuming the mystical within the informational and the *batin* within the *zahir*, the new public inscriptions perfectly embodied and eloquently propagated the exoteric and encompassing tendencies of the Sunni revival.

NOTES

1 For example, Adolf Grohmann, 'Origin and Early Development of Floriated Kufic', *Ars Orientalia*, 2 (1957), pp. 183–213; Sam Flury, *Die Ornamente der Hakim—und Ashar—Moschée* (Heidelberg, 1912); idem, *Islamische Schriftbänder Amida-Diarbekr XI Jahrhundert* (Basel, 1920); idem, 'Le décor épigraphique des monuments fatimides du Caire', *Syria*, 17 (1936), pp. 43–58; and Ibrahim Jumʻah, *Dirasa ʻala tatawwur al-kitabat*

al-kufiyya 'ala al-ahjar fi Misr al-qurun al-khamsa al-'ula li'l-hijra (Cairo, 1969), pp. 230–231.
2. Yasser Tabbaa, 'The Transformation of Arabic Writing. Part II, The Public Text', *Ars Orientalis*, 24 (1994), pp. 121–126. Cf. the conclusion reached by Sheila Blair in *Islamic Inscriptions* (New York, 1998), pp. 57–59, where she proposes a more gradual development of floriated Kufic, beginning a few decades before the Fatimids.
3. Flury, *Islamische Schriftbänder*, p. 11.
4. Grohmann, 'Floriated Kufic', pp. 207–208. William and Georges Marçais in *Les monuments arabes de Tlemcen* (Paris, 1903), p. 88, proposed that the floriated Kufic script may have come from North Africa to Egypt with the Fatimids. Grohmann, however, has convincingly refuted this position by pointing out that no true floriated Kufic existed in Tunisia during the early Fatimid phase there.
5. Jum'ah, *Dirasa*, pp. 209–214.
6. Ibid., pp. 230–231.
7. Richard Ettinghausen, 'Arabic Epigraphy: Communication or Symbolic Affirmation', in Dickran Kouymijian, ed., *Near Eastern Numismatics, Iconography, Epigraphy and History: Studies in Honor of George C. Miles* (Beirut, 1974), pp. 297–318.
8. Although Oleg Grabar's earlier studies, in particular 'The Umayyad Dome of the Rock in Jerusalem', *Ars Orientalis*, 3 (1959), pp. 33–62, were primarily concerned with the informative and iconographic value of inscriptions, in his most recent work he gave considerable attention to the formal and symbolic aspects of writing in Islamic art. See Oleg Grabar, *The Mediation of Ornament* (Princeton, 1992), esp. pp. 98–118.
9. Irene Bierman, *Writing Signs: The Fatimid Public Text* (Berkeley, CA, and London, 1998), pp. 80–86 and 126–132.
10. Yasser Tabbaa, *The Transformation of Islamic Architecture during the Sunni Revival* (Seattle and London, 2001), pp. 52–72 and idem, *The Production of Meaning in Islamic Architecture and Ornament* (Edinburgh, 2021), pp. 310–353.
11. Janine Sourdel-Thomine, 'Kitabat', *EI2*. See also Lisa (Volov) Golombek, 'Plaited Kufic on Samanid Epigraphic Pottery', *Ars Orientalis*, 6 (1966), pp. 107–133, where she discusses the process of the internal transformation of Kufic characters.
12. Grohmann, 'Floriated Kufic', p. 209.
13. Caroline Williams, 'The Cult of 'Alid Saints in the Fatimid Monuments of Cairo, Part I: The Mosque of al-Aqmar', *Muqarnas*, 1 (1983), pp. 37–52; Doris Behrens-Abouseif, 'The Façade of the Aqmar Mosque in the Context of Ceremonial', *Muqarnas*, 9 (1992), pp. 29–38; and Bierman, *Writing Signs*, pp. 126–132.
14. Jennifer Pruitt, *Building the Caliphate: Construction, Destruction, and Sectarian Identity in Early Fatimid Architecture* (New Haven and London, 2020), especially pp. 97–101, where Pruitt interprets al-Hakim's later inscriptions on the encasements of the minarets as 'privileging the *zahir* over the *batin*'. But even though these inscriptions are completely visible to the passerby, they are nevertheless written in the ambiguous floriated Kufic.
15. Bierman, *Writing Signs*, pp. 85–86.
16. Wilferd Madelung, 'Isma'iliyya', *EI2*.
17. The best analysis of this minaret, with excellent drawings, remains Ernst Herzfeld, *Materiaux pour un Corpus Inscriptionum Arabicarum: Inscriptions et Monuments d'Alep* (Cairo, 1953), vol. 1, pp. 144–164.
18. Tabbaa, 'The Public Text', pp. 129–133.
19. Yasser Tabbaa, 'The Transformation of Arabic Writing. Part I, Qur'anic Calligraphy', *Ars Orientalis*, 21 (1991), pp. 133–135.
20. K.A.C. Creswell, *The Muslim Architecture of Egypt* (Oxford, 1959), pp. 2, 35 and 64.
21. *Répertoire Chronologique d'Épigraphie Arabes*, no. 3380. Even the *Répertoire*, which is not noted for its aesthetic judgement, described this inscription as 'd'un trait lache et peu soigné'.

22 A quick survey of the photographs in Creswell, *Muslim Architecture of Egypt*, vol. 2, suggests that this began during the reign of al-Malik al-Kamil (r. 615–635/1218–1238).
23 See, Tabbaa, *Transformation of Islamic Architecture*, pp. 165–167 for a fuller discussion of this concept.

SECTION IV

ART AND ARCHAEOLOGY

1

A Fatimid Mermaid

Doris Behrens-Abouseif and Juan de Lara

This paper examines an enigmatic marble panel located in the Ayyubid Hall of the Museum of Islamic Art, Cairo (MIA).[1] However, the panel's iconography and the style of its carved decoration suggest at first glance rather a Fatimid attribution (figure IV.1.1). The mythological subjects represented in the carvings raise questions that require an investigation of visual and literary sources from and beyond the Muslim world.

The present configuration of the marble fragment indicates that it was cut out of a larger piece, that looks of Greco-Roman origin. The oblong panel has a vertical sequence of medallions framed by a frieze that runs along three sides leaving the right side unframed with a rough edge revealing the cut. The low-relief carved design consists of four interlocked circles, all of which contain mythological figures. The upper and lower circles feature a pair of harpies or human-headed birds (or bird-sirens); the second circle from the top includes a winged horse or possibly a

Figure IV.1.1 (Left and centre) Carved marble panel with mythological motifs. Museum of Islamic Art of Cairo (MIA). (Right) Authors suggested reconstruction of the *salsabil* (fountain), with the preserved marble slab from the MIA in grey.

winged centaur. The third medallion from the top, which is the main subject of our interest, shows a pair of addorsed female figures coming out of a pair of fishes. They both hold a cup in one hand and bottle in the other. Although they appear to be coming out of the fishes' mouths rather than being themselves fish-tailed, the configuration of the maid-cum-fish identifies them as mermaids. What seems to be the head of the fish is stylised and ambiguous, the one on the right-hand side more pronouncedly than the other and could be also seen as a transitional zone between the fish's and the woman's body. Similarly, the frieze that frames the panel on three sides features a sequence of fish, with alternating open and closed mouths.

The curled half-palmettes around the medallions date the panel to the 5th/11th and 6th/12th century, i.e. the Fatimid period (358–463/969–1071). There are two other similar Fatimid marble panels at the MIA in Cairo carved with real animals: peacocks, lions and fish. Although the iconography is different, on stylistic grounds both pieces may be contemporary. The technical configuration and the aquatic motif of fishes and hybrid women-cum-fish suggest that this panel belonged to a *salsabil*, a fountain where water flows down a stepped and rippled cascade, or perhaps another structure related to water (figure IV.1.1).

Although griffins, harpies, sphinxes and winged quadrupeds are frequent in Islamic, including Fatimid, art, the predominantly mythological character of this panel's imagery is remarkable.[2] Human-headed birds or bird-sirens are common in Saljuq and Fatimid pottery and they also appear on the Fatimid marble supports for water jars called *kilgas*.[3] Hybrid creatures also figure in later metalwork.[4] They are mentioned in Islamic literature in conjunction with aquatic figures and inhabitants of islands, like their Greek counterparts. The Pegasus motif is also connected to water; in Greco-Roman tradition, such a horse opened a spring with one stroke of his hoof on the ground (Arat.*Phaen*.216–23; Ov.*Met*.5.256–64). The winged horse is common on Coptic textiles, and it figures on Fatimid pottery.[5] The human head of the winged horse on this Fatimid panel resembles that of the female figures in the next medallion. Although a winged horse with a human head appears much later in Islamic art as Buraq,[6] the mount associated in apocryphal literature with the miraculous journey of the Prophet to the heavens, it cannot be related to this panel.

Although hybrid figures are well documented in Islamic art, the combination of a woman and a fish as represented on this panel has not been mentioned or discussed before, nor does Eva Baer in her monograph on mythological figures refer to such a figure.[7] The following pages are dedicated to filling this gap.

The Mermaid in the Levantine and Iranian Traditions

Several texts from the 3rd/9th and 4th/10th century deal with aquatic figures in the Middle Eastern tradition, such as the 3rd/9th-century account of Sallam al-Tarjuman and the account of the traveller sent by the Abbasid caliph Harun al-Wathiq (r. 227–232/842–847) to survey the land of the Khazars which both refer to a female inhabitant of water.[8] Analogous mentions of this creature can be found in later texts, such as in the account of Andalusian traveller Hamid al-Gharnati (465–555/1080–1170), cited by later authors, which tells of a king of the Khazars who caught a large fish in the Caspian Sea, from which a beautiful, long-haired girl emerged, a figure that can easily be confused with a mermaid.[9] A source that used to be attributed to the Persian sailor, Buzurg b. Shahriyar al-Ramhormuzu, *Kitab Aja'ib al-Hind*, but has recently and convincingly been identified rather as Egyptian[10] and datable to the 4th/10th century, mentions a fish in the Abyssinian sea with a human head, whose hybrid configuration resulted from a mating between a human being and a fish.[11]

In their illuminating article on a Kashan lustre-painted dish showing a naked woman lying in water, Ettinghausen and Guest, using Arabic and Persian sources, document the origins of such aquatic figures in pre-Islamic mythological traditions in the region of Mesopotamia and Iran.[12] The authors associate the 'female inhabitant of the sea' mainly with Iran and specifically to the deity Ardvi Sira Anahita,[13] goddess of the water and fertility, who was particularly revered during the Sassanian period and whose predecessors can be identified in earlier Mesopotamia, where hybrid and water deities were venerated in connection with streams and ponds.

Other survivals of ancient figures with a fishtail were already common in this part of the world in earlier times. Akkadian sources refer to the name of *Kulullu* 'fish-man,' who inhabited the Erythraean sea (i.e., the Persian Gulf).[14] The *Kulullu* was later deified by its *Interpretatio graeca* as Oannes, a god often depicted as a 'human emerging from a fish' or with fish attributes.[15] This image was later associated with that of the biblical Jonas (Yunus), called *shul-nun* (The One of the Fish), who was tasked with spreading the message of God in the city of Nineveh (near modern-day Mosul). The iconography and etymology of Yunus or Jonas are closely linked to the half-fish god Oannes, who was particularly revered in Nineveh.[16]

This type of continuity is also replicated in the cult of the goddess Atargatis – Lucian's famous *Dea Syria* (or Great Syrian Goddess) – who held a prominent position in the Levant as a fertility goddess associated with fishes; her statue was reported to show her lower body in the shape of a fish.[17] Her chief sanctuary was not far from Aleppo and many of her temples were equipped with ponds of holy water – some of which continue to hold religious significance to this day, such as the pond at her former temple in Şanlıurfa in Edessa, today a popular Muslim pilgrimage site associated with the prophet Ibrahim.[18] The cult of Atargatis was also present in Jazirat al-'Arab, Delos and Sicily, and persisted until at least the 5th century CE.[19] The pre-Islamic Near East was thus well acquainted with hybrid fish-human figures.

Firdawsi's *Shahnama* (4th–5th/10th–11th centuries) narrates the encounter between Kay Khusraw and an 'old man of the sea' with long hair and a hairy body that appeared to be covered in wool.[20] Similarly, in the late 6th/12th-century version of Nizami's *Iskandarnama*, Alexander encounters female water creatures.[21] This episode is depicted in various Persian miniatures showing the women without, however, any fish attributes.

Some of the earliest Arabic texts that address the topic of aquatic figures can be found in the *fiqh* or Islamic jurisprudence texts from the 3rd/9th century, many of which were compiled in Egypt. These texts discuss the prohibition on eating aquatic creatures, described as *insan al-ma'* (lit. human dwellers of the sea). This prohibition is outlined in a dialogue between two figures closely linked to Egypt, Ibn Wahb (125–197/743–813) and al-Layth ibn Sa'd (94–175/713–791).[22] Although the term *insan al-ma'* evidently refers to an aquatic creature with human features, how it looked is unclear. However, the existence of such texts, which are concerned with the ethics of food, indicate that there was an established belief in the existence of human-like inhabitants of water which required a legal opinion concerning the permissibility of eating their flesh.

In the cosmological context of the *Muruj al-dhahab*, Mas'udi (283–345/896–956) describes 'Abyssinian-like' figures that inhabit the Sea of China.[23] Elsewhere, in his *Akhbar al-zaman*, he mentions fishes with human heads and 'girls of the water' (*banat al-ma'*) with pronounced sexual attributes.[24]

Slightly postdating the Fatimid panel, the geographer Yaqut al-Hamawi (579–626/1179–1229) reports in his *Kitab Mu'jam al-buldan* that people have sighted 'beautiful girls' emerging from the water in Alexandria. One of them was captured by a shepherd who married her and had a happy family life with her.[25] This story is echoed in the tale of Gulnar included in the 8th/14th-century Mamluk edition of the *One Thousand and One Nights*.[26] Gulnar, a maid of the sea and daughter of the king of an aquatic kingdom, is captured by a human and sold as a slave to the king who marries her and conceives children with her. She eventually introduces him to her aquatic people with whom the king establishes a friendly relationship. Following the king's death, their son ascends the throne while Gulnar continues to act as a queen.

In his '*Aja'ib al-makhluqat*, al-Qazwini mentions several aquatic creatures: a fish with a human head in the China sea, a water-man with a human figure and a tail and a creature known as the water-man, *insan al-ma'*, also called *shaykh al-ma'* or 'the old man of the sea', with a beard and a tail who is able to conceive children with female human beings.[27] His sighting was an auspicious indication for fertility. This figure seems to be related to the *hálios gérōn* (old man of the sea) of the Greco-Roman world, later identified with Nereus, Proteus or other divinities of this guise. Qazwini further mentions a fish with a human face dotted with spots in the Sea of Fars,[28] an aquatic bearded man with a frog's body and a cow's skin called 'the old Jewish man' (*al-shaykh al-yahudi*) in the Sea of the Maghrib,[29] and a beautiful woman, with long hair who comes out of a fish's ear and has a fine skin like a wrap covering her body from the waist to the knees, in the Caspian sea.[30]

Damiri's' bestiary of the 8th/14th century, *Hayat al-hayawan al-kubra* integrates a large array of texts, including Qazwini's on fabulous animals and the bearded *insan al-ma'* in the Syrian sea who is able to conceive children with women.[31] He repeats Masʿudi's entry on the 'maids of the water' who dwell in the Mediterranean, have long flowing hair, big breasts and a big vulva, and speak an unintelligible language. In these accounts, mating and marriage occur between land and sea inhabitants.[32]

The abundance of textual evidence attests to a widespread belief in the existence of seductive aquatic women in the early Islamic tradition rooted in ancient Levantine and Mesopotamian mythologies.

Material Sources

The afore-mentioned accounts describing the seas as full of diverse hybrid creatures alongside fishes are echoed in post-Fatimid material culture. Aquatic creatures appear between the 6th/12th and the 8th/14th century as 'folkloristic imagery' in art from Iran and the Arab world.³³ The fish-pond motif decorating mainly the bottom of metal vessels, such as on the Mamluk basin known as Baptistère de St Louis in the Louvre (LP 16; most probably from the second half of the 7th/13th century), and others in various collections³⁴ (figure IV.1.2) displayed at the bottom of the vessel a fish-pond where hybrid creatures mingle with fish. It is hard to identify their gender, as the silver inlay is lost, but some of them seem to hold an object (a mirror?), which suggests a feminine figure. Of a much later date, a basin at the TIEM in Istanbul (figure IV.1.3) is decorated with zodiac motifs, showing a pair of females with fishtails flanking a male figure (Jupiter) as representing the sign of Pisces.³⁵ The shape and style of the basin attribute it to the late Mamluk period, and an owner's name locates the basin at some point in Diyar Bakr in Northern Syria/Mesopotamia, today in Turkey.

Illustrations of Qazwini's text from the 9th/15th century show hybrid water creatures including a human-headed fish (figure IV.1.2). Similarly, the *insan al-ma'* was illustrated in 9th/15th-century manuscripts, if not earlier, as a hairy creature with a tail. However, mermaids in the conventional sense of females with a fish-tail are not found here. These

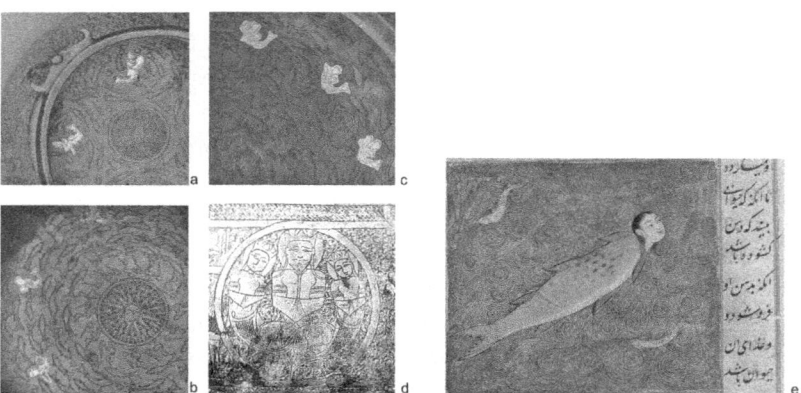

Figure IV.1.2a–e (a) Highlighted contours of merfolk depicted on a bowl (*tas*). Probably Iran, 8th/14th century. Art institute of Chicago; (b) Highlighted contour of merfolk in the basin of a bowl, 8th/14th century. Lyon, Musée Des Arts Decoratifs (c) Highlighted contour of merfolk in a copper pot. Probably Iran, 7th/13th or 8th/14th century. Museum für Islamische Kunst, Berlin State Museums; (d) A late Mamluk brass basin. Late 9th/15th century. Turkish and Islamic Art Museum, Istanbul; (e) Image of the fish with human head in the Indian Ocean. Qazwini, *'Aja'ib al-makhluqat*. Dated Safar 895/1460 or 895/1489. Princeton University Library, Islamic Manuscripts.

Figure IV.1.3 (Top left) Detail from the painted wooden ceiling at Cefalù Cathedral, dated between 1131 and 1154 AD (Bottom left) Detail from the painted wooden ceiling at Cefalù Cathedral, dated between 1131 and 1154 AD (Right) Detail of wrestling mermaids from the painted wooden ceiling at Cappella Palatina, ca. 1140 AD.

can be found in a Mediterranean context, in Norman Sicily, in the wooden painted ceilings of the Capella Palatina in Palermo and in the cathedral of Cefalù both dated to the reign of King Roger II (1130–1154).[36] In both cases women with fishtails appear as a pair in a posture suggesting that they are wrestling (figure IV.1.3). The Fatimid influence on these ceilings is well known, however we hesitate to attribute this motif straightforwardly to Fatimid art, considering that the iconographic programme of the Capella Palatina is very complex and combines other diverse themes unrelated to Fatimid art. Gelfer-Jørgensen sees stylistic parallels between the mermaid paintings at Cefalù and wrestling scenes in Qusayr ʿAmra (2nd/8th century) and the church in Akhtamar (4th/10th century).[37] A further parallel can also be established with the wrestling scenes from the pyxis of al-Mughira (4th/10th century) kept at the Louvre (OA 4068).

The Continuity of the Classical Tradition: Sirens, mermaids and fish-tails

The transformation of the siren, from the malicious woman-headed bird of Homer's Odyssey (e.g., see also Apollon.4.892 ff; Hyg.*Fab*.14), into a woman with a fishtail has been a much-debated subject among scholars.[38] The Greek word *seirēn* (σειρήν) was first documented in the *Odyssey* sometime around the 8th century BCE for a group of alluring entities that tempted seafarers, including Odysseus, with their chanting. While the text does not supply any information regarding their physical characteristics, the iconography of the siren became standardised in the next two centuries to combine the body of a bird with a human female head.

It is not clear when exactly the mutation of the Greek siren from the female-headed bird to a female with fishtail or mermaid occurred, but it seems to have taken place somewhere between the 1st century BCE and the 8th century CE.[39] In the 1st century BCE, the Roman poet Horace (*Ars*.1) briefly mentioned a figure of a maid with a fish-tail to exemplify the ugliness of hybridity. But this seems to have been a metaphor, a way of speaking rather than a reference to something specific. Thus, the generally accepted study on their origin is the one by Faral, who sees the emergence of fish-tailed siren as a confusion or a blend of different ancient Mediterranean figures. He refers specifically to Scylla, a hybrid sea monster and key character in the *Odyssey* whose image gradually merged with that of the siren evolving into the familiar image of the half-woman, half-fish. This argument has been supported by archaeological finds of Roman lamps dated to the 2nd century CE.

By the 9th century CE, the fishtailed seirén, which appears in the *Liber monstruorum de diversis generibus,* an Anglo-Latin catalogue of marvellous creatures, seems to have been consolidated. By the early 12th century, the Old High German and the Middle English versions of the *Liber monstruorum* had already coined the word *mermaid*, and the same mutation occurred in the illustrations accompanying these manuscripts, where sirens are rendered with fishtails.[40] The word *mermaid* is of Middle English origin (ca. 1000–1400) and was adopted in the medieval period to refer to creatures with fish tails[41] that were gradually substituted for the bird-sirens.

Quite often in medieval manuscripts they are depicted holding a mirror in one hand and a comb in the other.[42] With the beginning of the 12th century, churches and monasteries were extensively decorated with sculptures and relief of mermaids, notably on capitals.

Now, having looked at the mermaid motif in the European Mediterranean world, the Egyptian connection should be considered.

The Egyptian Connection

The Fatimid mermaid on our panel invites us to look back at Egypt and at the Hellenistic legacy, as well as its assimilation of earlier mythologies as a possible venue from where the fishtailed maid might have emerged.

Females with fishtails were not common in Greco-Roman mythology,[43] but in a later period could be related to various water spirits and benevolent nymphs reported to inhabit the sea, like the Nereids, who helped sailors in need. Nereids in the classical tradition had entirely human features and were often represented riding or accompanied by sea animals or hybrid creatures. These nymphs were the daughters of Nereus, a merman and a god of the sea akin to the *insan al-ma'*, and they were often represented assisting at the birth of Aphrodite from a seashell. The Nereids also became a frequent motif in Coptic art.

Hybrid aquatic figures were also widespread elsewhere in North Africa in Late Antiquity. The classical Triton, a deity connected to ancient Libya (in North Africa) who lived in lake Tritonis in southern Tunisia (Pind.*P*.4.19; Apollon.4.1548-1623). He was represented as a fishtailed man, and in other variations as an *ichthyocentaur* (a merman with two horse forelegs or crustacean pincers) and became an image widely spread across the Mediterranean and West Asia. This figure appears in Byzantine Christian art – for instance in a Byzantine mosaic in a church in Libya near Lake Tritonis (figure IV.1.4). He is identified as the 'ruler over Libya' by Diodorus Siculus 4.56.6. It can also be seen in a plaster painted floor in the Umayyad palace of Qasr al-Hayr al-Gharbi (figure IV.1.4).

While Egypt's adoption of Greek motifs is evident in the Hellenistic period, conversely, some of these Greek motifs have been associated with a more ancient Egyptian tradition. For example, some authors have related the bird-bodied sirens to the Ba-bird or soul-bird of Egypt.[44] In Egypt in Late Antiquity its function developed in funerary contexts, fulfilling the role of psychopomp – the divine intervenor responsible for escorting deceased souls to the Afterlife.

Seductive female aquatic figures, associated with eroticism and fertility, had been known in Egypt since the Old Kingdom, as documented in an enlightening article by M. Müller.[45] In the Ptolemaic period, these images merged with the Greek nymph, who is also associated with water and fountains, and were combined with representations of fishes.[46]

Textual and pictorial sources agree in pointing to Egypt as the origin of the fish-tailed female. The *Liber Monstruorum*, mentioned earlier, was one of the earliest successors to the Latin version of the *Physiologus*, a Christian compendium of didactic stories and prodigias about real and mythical animals, plants and minerals.[47] The *Physiologus*, originally written in Greek sometime between the 2nd and 4th century CE, is usually attributed to the cultural environment of Alexandria.[48] It was illustrated and became

Figure IV.1.4 (Left) Mosaic fragment depicting a triton with crustacean pincers. Qasr Libya, 5th century AD. Qasr Libya Museum; (Right) Plaster floor painted using the *secco* technique, Qasr al-Hayr al-Gharbi, 2nd/8th century. National Museum of Damascus.

the prototype of European bestiaries. In most translations, sirens with avian bodies seduce men with their songs.

There are however grounds to believe the Georgian translation predates the 8th-9th century CE and was taken directly from the Coptic or Greek versions of the book, around the 6th century CE, if not earlier.[49]

The appearance of a sea woman in this context then may point to an Egyptian origin. A strong argument in favour of this speculation is the conjunction of the siren with the centaur in the *Physiologus*, in a motif that combines themes from both Classical mythology and Christianity.[50] European bestiaries and Christian iconography, following the *Physiologus*, have interpreted the combination of the two figures as symbols of a double-nature, heresy and hypocrisy.

The earliest known depiction of this passage is attributed to a miniature found in the *Physiologus Bernensis*, dating back to the end of the 9th century CE, where a siren with a fish-tail is shown alongside a centaur (figure IV.1.5). The association of this pair is documented already earlier in Egypt, in a fresco of the 6th century in the church of St Apollo in the Coptic monastery of Bawit. The fresco, (depicting St Sissinius vanquishing

Figure IV.1.5 (Left) Siren and onocentaur in the Physiologus Bernensis, ca. 830 AD. Bern, Burgerbibliothek; (Right) The mounted St. Sisinnius of Antinoë conquers the demon Alabasdria. From a watercolour by Jean Clédat (1871–1943) based on mural in Bawit, Egypt.

the Greek demoness Alabasdria, portrayed as a defeated Aphrodite) (figure IV.1.5), shows at top right a winged creature with a scally tail and a centaur, accompanied by an inscription 'ⲦϢⲈⲈⲢⲈⲚ ⲀⲖⲀⲂⲀⲤⲀⲢⲒⲀ' (daughter of Alabasdria).

Some authors have already identified elements of the *Physiologus* text in the painting in Bawit.[51] This suggests that by the 6th century CE the image of the siren in Egypt had acquired a scaly lower body – resulting in a hybrid figure of an aviary fish-tailed mermaid. This recalls the 7th-century CE text of Isidore of Seville (*Etymologies* 12.4.29) where he describes the siren as 'snake-like creature from Arabia that also has the ability to fly.'[52] Later annuaries of prodigia, referring to older sources of the 6th century CE, mention 'Nilotic Mermaids'.[53] This triple hybrid figure embodies the transition from the bird to the fish siren. The tendency to combine women with fishes is attested in other visual material from 5th-century Egypt.[54]

In Coptic art, the pagan sea-born goddess Aphrodite became associated with the rebirth of the soul in the water of Christian baptism (figure IV.1.6). As assistants to the goddess these creatures fulfill the task often ascribed to the Nereids. An example of fishtailed figures such as the ichthyocentaurs, both masculine and feminine, can be seen on a carved panel of the 5th or 6th century CE in the Louvre,[55] in conjunction with the birth of Aphrodite.

Figure IV.1.6 (Top left) Aphrodite *Anadyomene* or Aphrodite Rising from the Sea, flanked by two ichtiocentaur (notice the pincers on their waist). Limestone fragment from Egypt, 5th or 6th century AD. Musée du Louvre, Paris; (Right) The birth of Aphrodite. Coptic textile. From Antinoë, ca. 6th century. Wool and linen, Musée du Louvre, Paris; (Bottom left) Fragments of a Hanging with Nereids. Egypt, 5th or 6th century AD. Dumbarton Oaks Research Library and Collection.

A textile fragment from Antinoe, in the Louvre, attributed to the 6th century CE, depicting the birth of Aphrodite shows a pair of Nereids represented as fish-tailed figures holding Aphrodite's shell (figure IV.1.6).

Furthermore a fragment of a hanging at Dumbarton Oaks (BZ.1932.1) from 5th–6th century Egypt shows two Nereids facing each other (figure IV.1.6). The one on the left-hand side is riding a bull with a fishtail. However, due to the missing parts of the hanging, the Nereid on the right-hand side is not fully revealed. She is shown holding a bejewelled mirror reflecting her face. A fishtail rising behind her belongs to a sea animal she is riding that has disappeared with the missing lower part of the hanging. The pair of Nereids with the fishtails of their mounts upright behind them stress the association of the human female with the fishtail that becomes more explicit in other items. However, it is the mirror held by the Nereid on the right-hand side that provides a strong argument for an Egyptian influence on the medieval European mermaids. The mirror belongs to the traditional medieval representation of the European siren holding a comb in one hand, recalling Horace's description, and a mirror in the other. The

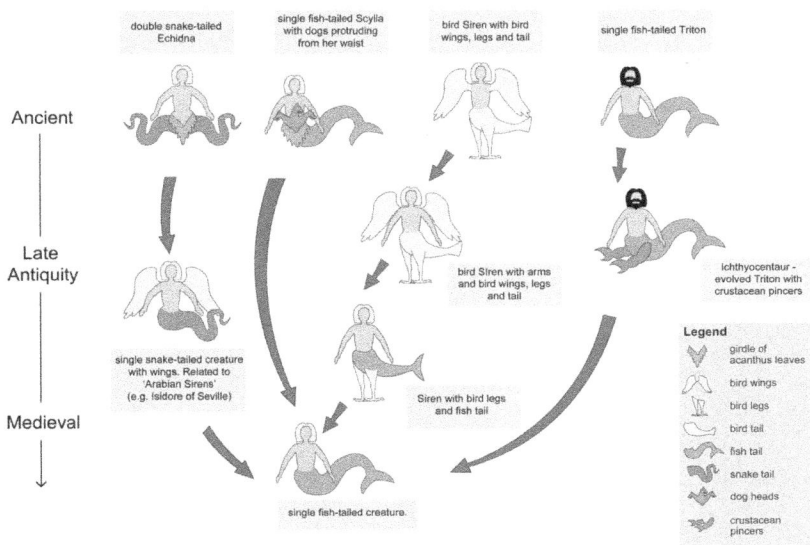

Figure IV.1.7 Scheme of the development of the iconography of the siren and mermaid, drawing from different sources.

tapestry reveals that the theme of the mirror has a much earlier Coptic antecedent and might be the direct precursor of the famous iconographic programme of European mermaids. Coptic 'mermaids' which are interpretations of the Greek iconography of the Nereids precede the European picture of the siren as hybrid fish-woman.

The medieval evolution of the fish-tailed mermaid took shape as an amalgam of a large variety of components from texts and images that continuously interacted (figure IV.1.7). We can conclude then that Egyptian lore contributed significantly to this intricate and cosmopolitan history

The Fatimid Tradition

Although the imagery of the panel at the MIA seems so far to be singular in Fatimid art, another group of carved marble objects of the same period, the *kilga*s, should be considered in connection with the panel. These were bases for clay jars to collect their filtered water. Some of them bear pre-Islamic Christian motifs and others bear Arabic inscriptions with good wishes and are carved with *muqarnas* and arches pointing to the Fatimid

Figure IV.1.8 Marble *kilga* in the Metropolitan Museum of Art, 6th/12th century.

period. As E. Knauer shows, these objects had Roman antecedents connected to water and fountains.[56] (figure IV.1.8)

The *kilga*s, which do not seem to have been produced much later than the Ayyubid or perhaps early Mamluk period, display a variety of decorative patterns such as animals, lions, fishes, human figures, horsemen and occasionally also mythological creatures such as human-headed birds and winged quadrupeds. Some contain odd representations that have not been explained so far: female nudes, some of whom look pregnant, male figures looking like priests with raised arms in a praying posture reminiscent of Coptic iconography. These odd representations strongly suggest an apotropaic meaning that may be related to fertility as suggested by the pregnant body shape of some of the female nudes. The *kilga*s and the marble panel at the MIA, have in common the survival of Coptic motifs and those of Late Antiquity in their imagery. A Fatimid lustre painted dish at the V&A[57] depicting a Coptic priest standing next to an *ankh*, the ancient Egyptian symbol of life, merged with the cross, shows how far back these survivals can reach.

Combined with the winged horse and the human-headed birds, the mermaids on our panel evoke a mixture of traditions connected to the Mediterranean environment in Egypt of Late Antiquity. However, the pair of females emerging from a fish in our Fatimid panel recalls rather Islamic tradition. Another feature that is not found in Coptic or other Mediterranean mermaids is the cup and the bottle they hold in their hands. The cup in Islamic art goes back to Abbasid and Iranian rather than Mediterranean traditions, and it is a characteristic feature of the 'entertainment cycle' of Fatimid art where it appears on ivory carving and painted pottery.

The iconography of the Fatimid marble panel at the MIA, with the harpies-sirens, the mermaids and their conjunction with the Pegasus-centaur together with the fish frieze framing the panel, belongs to an Egyptian repertoire going back to Hellenistic and Coptic culture of a moment between paganism and Christianity. However, not only the past is involved here, but also contemporary Islamic and Fatimid motifs in conjunction with contemporary elements from the Christian Mediterranean world which at that same time saw the proliferation and Christianisation of mermaids alongside other mythological figures. The mermaids here illustrate Fatimid cosmopolitan culture.

NOTES

1 (MIA no. 7049)
2 Eva Baer, *Sphinxes and Harpies in Medieval Islamic Art: An Iconographical Study* (Jerusalem, 1965).
3 These creatures are identified as 'harpies' by scholars based on the descriptions of Graeco-Roman creatures. However, the figure already existed in Egyptian mythology, such as the *ba* (*b'*). For Saljuq examples of this creature see V&A. (C.47-1960).
4 Eva Baer, '"Fish-Pond" Ornaments on Persian and Mamluk Metal Vessels', *BSOAS*, 31 (1968), p. 20.
5 For Fatimid textiles see Juan de Lara, '"Set the Gaze on Fire": Gold-Cloth Furnishing and Sacred Propaganda in the Courts of Early Islam', *Journal of Material Cultures in the Muslim World*, 3 (2023), pp. 205–234. For a lusterware example see MET Accession Number: 16.87 and 1974.113.7.
6 An example of the early associations between Pegasus and *Buraq* can be found in a number of vessel-stamps displaying winged horses that Kurt Erdmann termed 'Pegasus'. However, when the Arabic inscriptions in the stamps were translated these creatures were identified by the term '*al-Buraq*'; Kurt Erdmann, 'Zur Datierung der Berliner Pegasus-Schale', *Archäologischer Anzeiger, Beiblatt zum Jahrbuch des Deutschen Archäologischen Instituts*', 152 (1953), colls 115–131. See also Lawrence Nees, *Perspectives on Early Islamic Art in Jerusalem* (Leiden, 2015), p. 155, note 53.
7 Baer, *Sphinxes and Harpies*.
8 Douglas Morton Dunlop, *The history of the Jewish Khazars* (Princeton, 1954), p. 192; Peter B. Golden, *The World of the Khazars: New Perspectives: Selected Papers from the*

Jerusalem 1999 International Khazar Colloquium Hosted by the Ben Zvi Institute (Leiden, 2007), p. 383.

9. The story is also documented by al-Qazwini in the 7th/13th century. See H. Ethé, ed., *Zakarija Ben Muhammed Ben Mahmud El-Kazwini's Kosmographie* (Leipzig, 1868), pp. 262–263. Zakariyya b. Muhammad al-Qazwini, *'Aja'ib al-makhluqat wa'l-hayawanat wa ghara'ib al-mawjudat* (Beirut, 2000), p. 132; See also Grace Guest and Richard Ettinghausen, 'The Iconography of a Kashan Luster Plate', *Ars Orientalis*, 4 (1961), p. 49, note 91.

10. Jean-Charles Ducène, 'Une nouvelle source arabe sur l'océan Indien au Xe siècle', *Afriques*, 6 (2015). Available at: https://doi.org/10.4000/afriques.1746 (Accessed 20 December 2022).

11. al-Qazwini, *'Aja'ib*, pp. 110 and 125; Ibn Shahriyar (attrib.), *Kitab 'Aja'ib al-Hind*, ed. P. A. van der Lith (n.p., 1886), pp. 30–33 and 39; Suhanna Shafiq, *Seafarers of the Seven Seas: The Maritime Culture in the Kitab 'Aja'ib al-Hind by Buzurg Ibn Shahriyar (d. 399/1009)* (Berlin, 2013), p. 158. For further points see Guest and Ettinghausen, 'The Iconography', p. 47.

12. Guest and Ettinghausen, 'The Iconography', pp. 25–64.

13. Ibid., pp. 53–54.

14. Franz Köcher, 'Der Babylonische Göttertypentext', *Mitteilungen des Instituts für Orientforschung*, 1 (1953), p. 80. A female-fish figure has also been documented, *kuliltu* 'fish-woman', although their form and appearance are rare and slightly later than her male counterpart, see Frans, A. M. Wiggerman, *Mesopotamian Protective Spirits: The Ritual Texts* (Groningen, 1992), p. 182; Anthony Green, 'A Note on the Assyrian "Goat-Fish", "Fish-Man" and "Fish-Woman"', *Iraq*, 48 (1986), pp. 25–30.

15. On the origins of the mermaid imagery spreading from Mesopotamia, see Axel Müller, Christopher Halls and Ben Williamson, *Mermaids Art, Symbolism and Mythology* (Exeter, 2022), Chapter 2, 'Mermaids Conceived: Hybrid Goddesses and Beasts in Antiquity'.

16. The regional remit, philological connection and iconographic relations have all been noted since Henry Clay Trumbull, 'Jonah in Nineveh', *Journal of Biblical Literature*, 11 (1892), p. 55; Bill Cooper, 'The Historic Jonah' *EN Tech. J.*, 2 (1986), p. 111.

17. Traditionally the figure of Atargatis (or the other Greek corruption, Derceto) has been compared to a mermaid goddess based on Lucian's (*DS*.14) description of the statue in the temple of Askalon: 'I have seen the semblance of Derceto in Phœnicia, and a wonderful sight it is; one half is a woman, but the part which extends from the thighs to the feet ends in a fish tail. The effigy, however, which is at Hierapolis is a complete woman.' (Cf. Diodorus Siculus 2.4.2 who did not observe such feature).

18. Hendrik Jan Willem Drijvers, 'Hatra, Palmyra und Edessa. Die Städte der syrisch-mesopotamischen Wüste in politischer, kulturgeschichtlicher und religionsgeschichtlicher Beleuchtung', in Hildegard Temporini and Wolfgang Haase, ed., *Aufstieg und Niedergang der römischen Welt II* (Berlin and New York, 1977), p. 891.

19. John F. Healey, *The Religion of the Nabataeans: A Conspectus* (Leiden, 2001), p. 140. Hendrik Jan Willem Drijvers, 'The Cult of Atargatis', in Hendrik Jan Willem Drijvers, ed., *Cults and Beliefs at Edessa* (Leiden, 2015), pp. 76–121.

20. See the translation by Arthur George Warner and Edmond Warner in Ferdowsi, *The Sha'hnama of Firdausi* (London, 1905–1925), vol. 4, pp. 245–246; Guest and Ettinghausen, 'The Iconography', p. 47.

21. For the *Iskandar-nama*, see the German translation by Wilhelm Bacher, *Nizami's Leben Und Werke Und Der Zweite Theil Des Nizamischen Alexanderbuches* (Vienna, 1871), pp. 107–109. For more information on the origins of this tradition, see B. Cook, 'A Watery Folktale in the Alexander Romance: Alexander's Byzantine Neraïda', *Syllecta Classica*, 20 (2009), pp. 105–134.

22 Ashraf Siddiqui, *Awn al-Mabood on Sunan Abi Dawood*, vol. 10, p. 317.
23 Abu'l-Hasan 'Ali al-Mas'udi, *Akhbar al-zaman* (Beirut, 1996), p. 61.
24 Ibid., p. 39.
25 Abu 'Abd Allah Yaqut b. 'Abd Allah al-Hamawi al-Rumi al-Baghdadi, *Kitab Mu'jam al-buldan* vol. 1, ed. F. Wüstenfeld (Leipzig, 1866–1873), pp. 185, 258, and 259.
26 *Kitab alf layla wa layla min usulihi al-'arabiyya al-ula*, ed. Muhsin Mahdi (Leiden, 1984), pp. 234–243.
27 Ethé, ed., *Zakarija Ben Muhammed*, p. 231; al-Qazwini, *'Aja'ib*, p. 125.
28 Ibid., p. 102.
29 Ibid., p. 121; al-Damiri, *Hayat al-hayawan al-kubra*, ed. Ahmad Hasan Basaj (Beirut, 1994), vol. 2, p. 78.
30 al-Qazwini, *'Aja'ib*, p. 123.
31 Damiri, *Hayat*, vol. 1, p. 69.
32 Ibid., p. 227.
33 Baer, '"Fish-Pond"'; Guest and Ettinghausen, 'The Iconography', pp. 45–47, figures 50, 51; D. S. Rice, *Le Baptistère de St. Louis* (Paris, 1953).
34 See the basin at the V&A, 2734-1856.
35 Doris Behrens-Abouseif, 'A Late Mamluk (?) Basin with Zodiac Imagery', *Annales Islamologiques*, 29 (1995), pp. 120–122.
36 Ugo Monneret de Villard, *Le pitture musulmane al soffitto della Cappella palatina in Palermo* (Rome, 1950), ill. 218. See also Mirjam Gelfer-Jørgensen, 'The Islamic Paintings in Cefalù Cathedral, Sicily', *Hafnia, Copenhagen Papers in the History of Art* (1978), p. 124. Francesco Gabrieli, Umberto Scerrato and Paul Balog, *Gli arabi in Italia: cultura, contatti e tradizioni* (Milan, 1985), p. 393. Mirjam Gelfer-Jørgensen was unable to find a parallel for fish-scaled mermaids at the time, see Mirjam Gelfer-Jørgensen, *Medieval Islamic symbolism and the paintings in the Cefalu Cathedral* (Leiden, 1986), p. 146 and figure 77. Their relation to a late Mamluk bowl was noted as well by Behrens-Abouseif, 'A Late Mamluk (?) Basin', p. 120. For further discussion see Maria Giulia Aurigemma, *Il cielo stellato di Ruggero II il soffitto dipinto della cattedrale di Cefalù* (Milan, 2004), p. 124. Angela Bellia, 'Twelfth-Century Musical Symbols in the Star Studded Sky of Ruggero II', *Music in Art*, 37 (2012), p. 29. For another reference, see, Ernst J. Grube and Jeremy Johns, *The Painted Ceilings of the Cappella Palatina* (Genoa and New York, 2005), p. 32.
37 Gelfer-Jørgensen, 'The Islamic Paintings', p. 124.
38 While the terms *siren* and *mermaid* are nowadays often interchangeable in most Romantic and Germanic languages, there are clear historiographic differences between them. The later word of Middle English origin (ca. 1000–1400), *mermaid*, was adopted during medieval times to refer to creatures depicted often with fish tails. *Seirén* was traditionally used to refer to Homer's avian creatures.
39 Müller, Halls and Williamson, *Mermaids*, chapter 2; Faral, 'La queue de poisson des Sirènes', Romania, 74 (1952), pp. 475–478; Odette Touchefeu-Meynier, 'De quand date la Sirène-poisson?', *Bulletin de l'Association Guillaume Budé: Lettres d'humanité*, 21 (1962), pp. 455–456. Scylla was a sea-monster in the *Odyssey* who was depicted as a fish-tailed sea-goddess with a cluster of canine foreparts surrounding her waist.
40 Pakis, 'Contextual Duplicity and Textual Variation', pp. 125–126; Dorofeeva, 'The siren: a medieval identity crisis', (http://mittelalter.hypotheses.org/3278).
41 Wilfred P. Mustard, 'Siren-Mermaid', *Modern Language Notes*, 23 (1908), pp. 21–24. For more on the origin of the fish tail in mermaids see Müller, Halls and Williamson, *Mermaids*, chapter 2; Carlos García Gual, *Sirenas. Seducciones y metamorfosis* (Madrid, 2014); Á Ibáñez Chacón, 'La metamorfosis de las Sirenas: a propósito de un libro reciente', *Thamyris*, 5 (2014), pp. 157–167; Faral, 'La queue de poisson des Sirènes', pp. 433–506; Jacqueline Leclercq-Marx, *La sirène dans la pensée et dans l'art de*

l'Antiquité et du Moyen Age du mythe païen au symbole chrétien (Brussels, 1997); Touchefeu-Meynier, 'De quand date la Sirène-poisson?', pp. 452–459; W. Deonna, 'La Sirène, Femme-Poisson', Revue Archéologique, 27 (1928), pp. 18–25.

42 The channels of dissemination for such images were likely to have been the illustrations in bestiaries and zoological encyclopedias, which served as models for builders and stonemasons. The tradition continued during the Renaissance and the Baroque era. See Pakis, 'Contextual Duplicity and Textual Variation', pp. 126–127.

43 Perhaps the only exception is the wooden *xoanon* of Eurynome (Pausanias. 8.41.4-6), which belonged to a little-known and obscure cult in the distant mountains of Arcadia.

44 See, John D. Cooney, 'Siren and Ba, Birds of a Feather', *The Bulletin of the Cleveland Museum of Art*, 55 (1968), pp. 262–271; Mikal J. Aasved, 'The Sirens and Cargo Cults', *The Classical World*, 89 (1996), p. 384; Maya Müller, 'Niltöchter', *Imago Aegypti*, 3 (2011), pp. 102–103.

45 See, Müller, 'Niltöchter'.

46 Müller attributes the origins of the human-headed bird to Egypt, but not the hybrid woman-cum-fish which she locates rather in a Greco-Roman context, although the motif was not widespread there.

47 Francis J. Carmody, *Physiologus latinus* (Berkeley, CA, 1944).

48 The original text has not survived, but its translations into Armenian, Latin and other European and Middle Eastern languages have.

49 Valentine A. Pakis, 'Contextual Duplicity and Textual Variation: The Siren and Onocentaur in the Physiologus Tradition', *Mediaevistik*, 23 (2010), p. 124, note 31; J. Leclercq-Marx, 'La Sirène et l'(ono)centaure dans le Physiologus grec et latin et dans quelques Bestiaires. Le texte et l'image', in B. Van Den Abeele, ed., *Bestiaires médiévaux. Nouvelles perspectives sur les manuscrits et les traditions textuelles* (Louvain-la-Neuve, 2005), pp. 169–182; Jacqueline Leclercq-Marx, 'Du monstre androcéphale au monstre humanisé. À propos des sirènes et des centaures, et de leur famille, dans le haut Moyen Âge et à l'époque romane', *Cahiers de civilisation médiévale*, 45e année, 177 (2002), pp. 55–67.

50 For a full discussion of this subject see, Ibáñez Chacón, 'Sirenas vs. Centauros: pervivencia medieval de un mito perdido', *Florentia iliberritana: Revista de estudios de antigüedad clásica*, 28 (2017), p. 109.

51 Müller, 'Niltöchter', pp. 125–128; J. Leclercq-Marx does not mention it in 'La Sirène et l'(ono)centaure', but does in her book, *La sirène dans la pensée et dans l'art de l'Antiquité*, p. 66, note 179; Deonna, 'La Sirène, Femme-Poisson', p. 25; Ibáñez Chacón, 'Sirenas vs. Centauros', pp. 112–113.

52 In fact, it is possible that the overlap of these concepts was the result of the earlier texts of Saint Jerome of Stridon (ca. 342–347), who had studied at the Catechetical School of Alexandria, and had identified sirens as 'Arabian' flying-snakes, following an earlier tradition from Herodotus (2.75). See Jerome, *Commentary on Isaiah*, 13:21-22. Seventh-century writings by Isidore of Seville (*Etymologies* 12.4.29) already identified the Siren as a 'snake-like creature from Arabia that also has the ability to fly'; Faral, 'La queue de poisson des Sirènes', p. 437.

53 For example, an annuary of prodigia written in 1569 CE by Konrad Lykosthenes, notes that on the eve of Islam, in the year 586 CE, two mermaids were observed in the river Nile. A similar compendium, the *Historia Mostruorum*, also cites 'Nilotic Mermaids', and it is likely that both authors' reports are taken from older collections, probably assembled at the height of the art of Late Antiquity or Coptic art in Egypt.

54 The origin of the Arabic version is not clear; and it could have been translated from a Coptic or Syriac copy and similarly, the passages corresponding to the siren and onocentaur are not extant.

55 Musée du Louvre (E 14280; X 4030).

56 Elfriede R. Knauer, 'Marble Jar-Stands from Egypt', *Metropolitan Museum Journal*, 14 (1979), pp. 67–101; Laila Ali Ibrahim, 'Clean Fresh Water in Cairene Houses', *Islamic Archaeological Studies*, 1 (1978), pp. 1–25; Margaret S. Graves, 'The Monumental Miniature: Liquid Architecture in the Kilgas of Cairo', *Art History*, 38 (2015), pp. 304–323; Ayman Mustafa Idris Muhammad, '*Kilja min al-rukham mahfuza bi'l-makhzan al-mathafi bi'l-Ashmunayn*', *Majallat al-Ittihad al-'Am li'l-Athariyyin al-'Arab, 18*, pp. 305–347.

57 V&A. (C.49-1952).

2

'The Work is Blessed, Unique': The Fatimid Silver Casket of Sadaqa b. Yusuf

Anna Contadini

The silver casket of Sadaqa b. Yusuf (figure IV.2.1) has received some scholarly attention, but it merits more focused study.[1] The research presented in this chapter attempts to shed light on it within the theory of objecthood,[2] considering both the historical and cultural valence of such objects; to analyse the visual imagery of the casket, conveyed by its extraordinary inscriptions and decorative motifs, which inspire wonder; and to explore the different ways in which it engages the viewer, visual, semantic and emotional.

Figure IV.2.1 Casket of Sadaqa b. Yusuf. Fatimid Egypt, dated between 436–439/ 1044–1047. Silver, gilt, niello, 7.5 x 12.4 x 7.9 cm. Real Colegiata de San Isidoro, Leon.

The casket, now in the treasury of San Isidoro, in León (Spain),[3] is datable to 436–439/1044–1047, as discussed below. It is rectangular, fairly small, measuring w. 12.4 x h. 7.9 x d. 7.5/7.9 cm, and has a slightly convex lid fastened by three hinges attached with metal pins.

It is made of silver, gold-washed (a type of gilding), and its body, lid and hinges are decorated with niello. On the body and the lid, apart from the border, the niello helps to define a pattern of fine, tight spirals, each measuring ca. 6 mm in diameter and joined one to the other by small, stylised leaves. Around the border of the lid runs an inscription set against a background of small round leaves, disposed in spirals, and foliage against a nielloed background. A smaller inscription, surrounded by a vegetal ornament against a nielloed surrounding, is found on the body of the casket beneath the lock (figures IV.2.2 and 3).

Although we have a number of caskets in various media, the Sadaqa casket is different in shape and style and does not seem to belong to any specific group, which makes it a 'unique' object – as, indeed, it is described by one of its inscriptions (see below). Both Fatimid and Spanish provenances have been proposed,[4] although the evidence surveyed here tends to confirm the view that it is to be attributed to a Fatimid environment. The casket makes, accordingly, a significant addition to the repertoire of Fatimid art, and Fatimid silver in particular.

Figure IV.2.2 Front view of the Sadaqa casket with the beginning of the inscription and showing the underside of the lock.

Figure IV.2.3 Detail of inscription on the body of the casket, beneath the lock.

This is a body of material that has not been sufficiently studied, and the following discussion therefore calls upon historical and archaeological evidence in combination with art-historical investigation.

We have information from the 5th/11th-century *Book of Gifts and Rarities (Kitab al-Hadaya wa'l-tuhaf)* attributed to Qadi al-Rashid b. Zubayr, who lived in Cairo under the Fatimids; from documents of the 5th to 6th/11th to 12th century recovered from the Cairo Geniza; and from the Mamluk historian al-Maqrizi, who reports an eye-witness account of the looting of the Fatimid treasury sometime around 462/1069. It mentions complex artifacts such as a ship in silver, others in gold, such as a palm tree, and countless items (bowls, dishes, etc) in silver or gold, enamelled, encrusted with precious stones, or inlaid with niello.[5]

Extant silver objects include a mirror in the Benaki Museum, a lid on the Fatimid rock crystal bottle in Capua, and archaeological finds of silver objects include Caesarea, Tiberias, Ramla and Fustat, comprising coins, jewellery, amulets and amulet cases,[6] artifacts that are also extremely important for the wider study of objects in precious metal, for understanding the chronology and distribution of such material, the techniques of production and decoration, and for their circulation around the Mediterranean. The style of script they exhibit is typologically close to that around the lid of the Sadaqa casket. In the case of the inscriptions on some of the Tiberias material, the script is not only related but also contains a simplified example of the 'Undulating Stem-and-Leaf Motif' found within the inscription on the casket (see below and figure IV.2.15).

The style and phrasing of the inscriptions on the metalwork recovered in Denia (Spain) helps to confirm, according to Virgilio Martínez Enamorado, the identification of them as Fatimid. His study shows that many of the formulas they employ echo phraseology found on other Fatimid material rather than on metalwork produced in al-Andalus.[7] There are, inevitably, elements common to both Fatimid and Spanish material, but we would need a study of a large sample of objects to determine the degree of lexical overlap as compared with difference.

Objects in silver and other materials such as rock crystal and ivory could have been containers for spices, jewels, make-up (such as *kohl*) and perfume, as the Geniza documents testify,[8] and it is likely that the Sadaqa casket, too, was used for one of these purposes.

Reference may also usefully be made to Spanish silver from the Caliphal to the Taifa period, for instance, perfume bottles from 4th/10th-century Cordoba, various containers, and various rings found in diverse contexts and from different periods.[9] Particularly relevant are the silver objects with nielloed inscriptions and decoration that were produced around the time of our Sadaqa casket, during the first half of the 5th/11th century. Among three items for which Rafael Azuar has argued for a workshop in the Taifa kingdom of Toledo, and possibly in León,[10] is a perfume bottle in the Museo de Teruel, with an inscription that tells us that it was made for Zahr, who has been identified as the wife of Mu'ayyid al-Dawla 'Abd al-Malik b. Khalaf, who was to become the Taifa king of Albarracín in 437/1045.[11] This points to it being a contemporary or near contemporary piece to the Sadaqa casket, yet the Kufic inscription around the neck is of a different type and its decorative repertoire and general design, despite containing spirals, are quite distinct from those of the Sadaqa casket. Similarly distinct are the decorative features and calligraphic style of other Spanish silver objects such as the 11th-century casket of Santa Eulalia, studied in detail by Maria Antonia Martínez Núñez, to whom I am grateful for having discussed its epigraphy with me, and the differences between Spanish and Fatimid epigraphy in general.[12]

The visual effect of the Sadaqa casket is dominated by its mesmerising spiral motifs, which are only interrupted by the inscription. On metal objects of the medieval period, spiral motifs – not to be confused with concentric circles, a different, although common motif on objects in various media found all around the Mediterranean[13] – are ubiquitous, occurring in diverse cultural spheres, Southern Italian, Byzantine, European and Islamic. To take just one example, a probable Southern Italian object of the 11th to 12th century AD, that has both niello and spiral ornamentation is the Imola paten.[14] Nielloed spirals form the background of the pseudo-kufic inscription around its central motif.[15]

Likewise, on other objects spirals serve as a filler or as background to a more prominent type of decoration, whereas on the Sadaqa casket they form the main decorative element, a design feature characteristic of Fatimid material. Indeed, Fatimid art is full of spiral decorative motifs, and the concept of a compact, round decoration that fills up spaces and is applied to the greater part of the surface appears in various media. For metalwork one may cite, for example, the bronze hare in Harvard (figure IV.2.4), with spirals terminating in trefoils.[16] Spiral decoration is common on lustre-painted pottery, especially in depictions of clothing: for instance the fragment of a bowl in the Brooklyn Museum has spiral decorations some of which also terminate in trefoils, for example on the clothing of the elephant-keeper (figure IV.2.5).[17] We may also add the famous 5th/11th-century bowl in the Victoria and Albert Museum (V&A) which features a figure wearing a dress with closely packed spiral decoration.[18] Spirals are also found amidst letter shapes, as in a fragment of the base of a bowl or dish in the V&A (figure IV.2.6).[19] For lustre-painted glass featuring spiral

Figure IV.2.4 Hare. Fatimid Egypt, 5th/11th century. Bronze, 7.6 cm. Private collection deposited at Harvard University Art Museum, Cambridge, MA.

340 Fatimid Cosmopolitanism

Figure IV.2.5 Fragment of bowl. Egypt, 6th/12th century. Fritware, with overglaze lustre decoration, 13.3 x 7.6 x 9.3 cm. Brooklyn Museum, New York.

Figure IV.2.6 Fragment of base of bowl or dish. Egypt, 5th/11th century. Fritware, with overglaze lustre decoration, 15 x 6 x 1.3 cm. Victoria and Albert Museum, London.

decoration one may mention a bowl in the V&A (figure IV.2.7),[20] while a further example on glass occurs in the compact, extraordinary semi-spiral decoration on the body of an ewer cut in relief, found at Fustat, possibly of the 4th/10th century (figure IV.2.8).[21] Woodwork carved in relief, too, is often decorated with spirals of different dimensions, as in the famous wooden plaque with horse heads in the Metropolitan Museum of Art (figure IV.2.9),[22] and we may also find spiral motifs on bookbindings, such as the Qayrawan moulded bookbinding designs dated to the 4th/10th and 5th/11th centuries, with spirals compactly arranged in rows (figure IV.2.10).[23]

Figure IV.2.7 Glass bowl. Egypt, 5th/11th century. Transparent glass, with lustre-painted decoration, 7.7 x 12.9 cm. Victoria and Albert Museum, London.

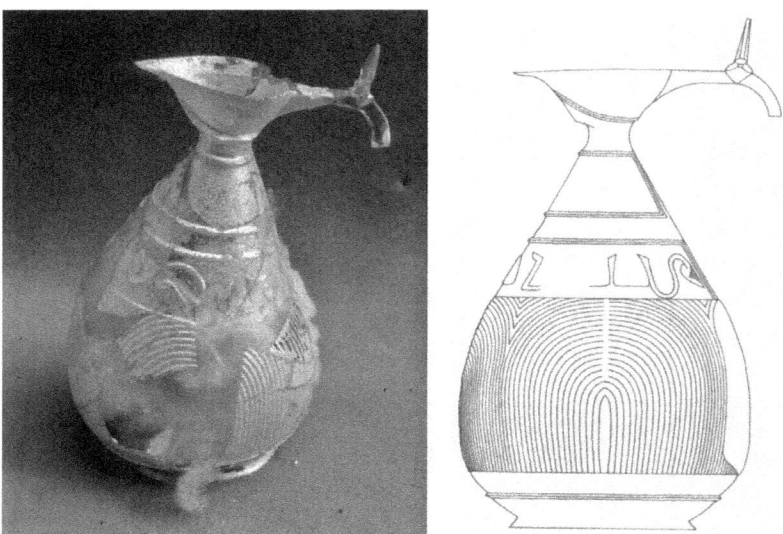

Figure IV.2.8 Glass ewer cut in relief found in Fustat, 4th/10th century. Museum of Islamic Art, Cairo.

Figure IV.2.9 Wooden panel showing the bodies of horses dissolving into decorative motifs and spiral decoration. Fatimid Egypt, 5th/11th century. Metropolitan Museum of Art, New York.

Figure IV.2.10 Bookbinding, from the Great Mosque of Qayrawan, 5th/11th century.

Priscilla Soucek suggested that the foliage decoration on the Sadaqa casket, especially the trilobed motif found on top of the inscription beneath the lock, recalls stylised vegetal motifs in Byzantine art, such as the niello ornament on a fragmentary processional cross in Cleveland datable to ca. 1050 AD; the decoration on the marble relief carving from Komotini datable to the second half of the 11th century; and the robe worn by Nikephoros III Botaneiates (r. 1078–1081) in a painting in a manuscript in Paris. According to Soucek, these similarities raise the possibility that the ornament on the Sadaqa casket might have been modelled on one of the Byzantine objects sent to the Fatimid Imam-caliph al-Mustansir.[24]

The Casket

The small size of the casket is of note because one would expect to encounter such a complex decoration of spirals and tendrils, together with inscriptions, on a larger object. This adds to its preciousness: it was obviously intended to be held up and admired at close range, as an intimate and uniquely decorated and inscribed little object.

The hinges fit perfectly within the spaces left within the inscription, pointing to them having been integral to the original conceptualisation of the casket. Also, the decorative motifs beneath the lock echo those on the outer side of the lock and on the hinges, making an aesthetic connection between the ornamentation on the body of the casket and on the hinges, which are also nielloed, and again pointing to them being original to the casket. Further, they accord with the aesthetics of other Fatimid hinges, as found in the Tiberias excavations (figure IV.2.11).[25]

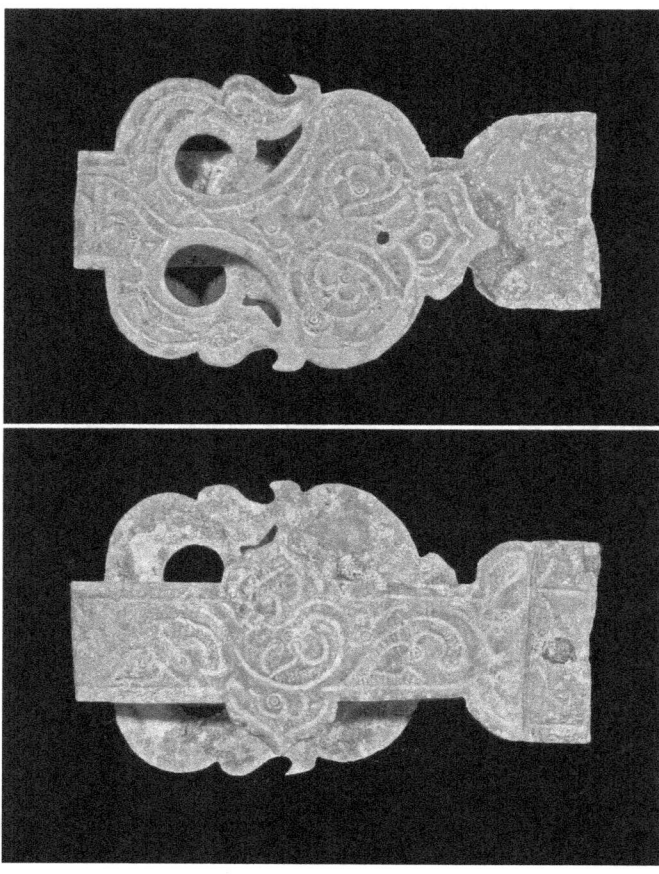

Figure IV.2.11 Hinge of wooden casket from Tiberias.

Translocation and Transculturation

Once translocated to a Christian cultural environment, such as a church treasury, objects such as the casket could change their function dramatically. Some, having been transculturated, became reliquaries. This happened to other caskets in the Treasury of San Isidoro,[26] and likewise to containers in other media such as Fatimid rock crystals (for instance the Reliquary of the Nails of Saint Clare in Assisi)[27] and Southern Italian ivories (for instance the St Petroc casket now in Bodmin, Cornwall).[28] Whether the Sadaqa casket was ever used as a container for relics cannot be known, as we lack relevant documentation. It was translocated to the Treasury of San Isidoro, transculturated, in effect, to a museum-like context. It is now exhibited together with other objects originating outside Spain, including a small Scandinavian ivory container, in a group for which the curatorial interpretation seeks to highlight the international connections of al-Andalus.[29] Its presence in Spain has been generally attributed to the looting and dispersal of the Cairo Fatimid treasury in around 462/1069. It has also been suggested that it could have arrived there earlier, being one of the objects that were moved together with the relics of San Isidoro from Seville to León in 1063.[30] However, an object made for a Fatimid vizier and kept in a Fatimid treasury is more likely to have come to Spain as part of the mass dispersal of Fatimid objects in 462/1069, ending up in León via one of the main cities of al-Andalus.

As I have discussed elsewhere, for example in relation to Middle Eastern objects found in Italy, war and looting were by no means the only reasons for objects to travel.[31] They could be translocated via diplomacy, trade, or for religious reasons (they may have become containers of relics), but also, and importantly, they could have been acquired because of the preciousness of their materials, the symbolism associated with them, or their aesthetic qualities – all of which actively contribute to the performative role they would assume in the new cultural context.

The Inscriptions

The larger inscription runs around the border of the lid, while a second, much smaller inscription is situated on the body of the casket, positioned exactly beneath the lock and so being revealed only when one opens it.

Inscription 1

The inscription around the rim (figure IV.2.12) is important both as part of the visuality of the object and for its documentary value: it is because of it that we know that the casket was made for Sadaqa b. Yusuf. It has been read by various scholars, if without complete unanimity.[32]

My reading is as follows:

استعمال لخزانة صدقة بن يوسف
سعد كامل واقبال شامل
وعز دائم وامر عالي
ودرجة رفيعة لصاحبه

isti'mal li-khizanat Sadaqa b. Yusuf (front of the casket)
sa'd kamil wa iqbal shamil (left side)
wa 'izz da'im wa amr 'ali (back)
wa daraja rafi'a li-sahibihi (right side)

Translation:

Commissioned for the treasury of Sadaqa b. Yusuf/
Perfect happiness and complete prosperity/
and lasting glory and high position/
and exalted status to its owner

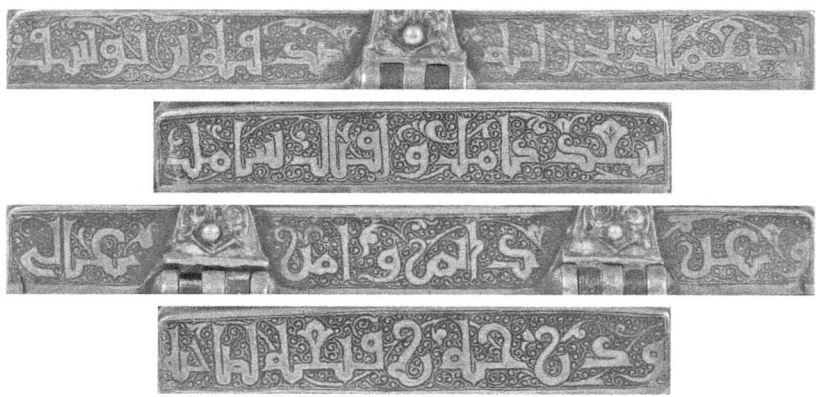

Figure IV.2.12 Inscriptions on the four sides of the lid of the Sadaqa casket. From top: Front, left, back, and right sides. Real Colegiata de San Isidoro, Spain.

Sadaqa b. Yusuf

For Abu Mansur Sadaqa b. Yusuf al-Falahi (figure IV.2.13) we are lucky to have documentary evidence from al-Maqrizi, who tells us that he was a vizier of the Fatimid Imam-caliph al-Mustansir (r. 428–487/1036–1094),[33] when the latter was only fifteen years old. Sadaqa's father, Abu'l-Fadl Yusuf b. 'Ali, was one of the skilled scribes and chancery officials, and was in charge of the Damascus *diwan*. When the long-serving vizier al-Jarjara'i fell ill, he wanted Sadaqa to be his successor, but with a supervisor, the older vizier Abu Sa'id Sahl b. Harun al-Tustari, who was the favourite of al-Mustansir's mother. His appointment together with Sadaqa may reflect a power struggle, but could also point to different duties being covered, and may also be interpreted as indicating that Sadaqa was rather young and insufficiently experienced. Sadaqa was invested on Wednesday 11 Ramadan 436/1044.

According to al-Maqrizi he was a converted Jew, described as being outstanding in the various chancery skills. He began by taking over the administration of Sham (Syria), but only stayed there for a very short time, soon moving to Cairo, where he became a vizier, deeply involved in Cairo politics and governmental affairs, and endowed with a large treasury of seven hundred thousand dinars.[34] But, according to al-Maqrizi, al-Mustansir's mother hated him, as he was thought to have incited the military against Abu Sa'id Sahl b. Harun al-Tustari, her favourite, until they killed him. She persevered in her intrigues against Sadaqa until she managed to have him deposed from the vizierate and imprisoned in the *Khizanat al-Bunud*, where he was killed in 439/1047.[35]

Sadaqa is also mentioned in the 5th/11th-century *Book of Gifts and Rarities* (see note 5), in relation to a generous gift from the Byzantine

Figure IV.2.13 Detail of the name Sadaqa b. Yusuf on the casket.

emperor Constantine IX Monomachus (r. 1042–1055) to al-Mustansir, with which Sadaqa and the older vizier al-Tustari were involved:

> In the year 427 (*sic*, read 437) [1045–1046], Constantine, the Byzantine emperor (*malik*), sent a gift to al-Mustansir bi-Allah, as he corresponded with him regarding the renewal of the ten-year armistice, which would end in the year 447 [1055–1056]. At that time the vizier [of al-Mustansir bi-lah] was Abu Nasr Sadaqah b. Yusuf al-Falahi, and the administrator of the state was Abu Sa'd Ibrahim b. Sahl al-Tustari the Jew. No former Byzantine emperor had ever offered a similar gift to any of the previous caliphs of Islam.[36]

> It consisted of a great quantity of gold vessels, some inlaid with enamel, gold coins, Byzantine girdles bordered with gold, she-mules and horses each of them covered with a brocaded saddle cloth, and many Muslim captive prisoners of war who were carrying boxes of fabrics embroidered with gold.

The inscription around the lid of the casket mentions that it was made for the treasury of Sadaqa, which places it precisely in the period when he was vizier, under the Imam-caliph al-Mustansir, and also allows us to date it precisely to between 436/1044 and 439/1047 (it is not often that we can date a medieval object to a span of only three years!). The smaller inscription combines benediction and its uniqueness, and I would suggest that the casket may have been made in 436/1044, on the occasion of the ceremony of Sadaqa's investiture.[37]

Inscription 2

The second inscription (figure IV.2.3) is on the part of the body covered by the hinge, and reading it was a surprise.

العمل مبارك فريد

al-'amal mubarak farid
The work is blessed, unique

What a wonderful line! Although *farid* is commonly used in relation to pearls,[38] its use in relation to a work of art such as the casket is unusual.

The inscription had been interpreted as mentioning the name of the craftsman, 'Uthman, in the reading "*amal 'Uthman naqqash* (?)" which has been translated as "Uthman engraved".[39] However, this reading does not take into account either the definite article before *'amal* or the two final letters (*ya* and *dal*). The reading proposed here takes the complete

Figure IV.2.14 Casket of Hisham II and detail of inscription on the underside of the lock, with a very different content and style of script, 363 or 366/974 or 976. Silver, wood, gilt, niello, 27 x 38.5 x 23.5 cm. Tesoro de la Catedral de Gerona, Spain.

inscription into account, and the fact that it occupies fully the space between the decorative motifs that frame it.

It is possible that the previous reading, with the name 'Uthman, was prompted by expectations of what an inscription in such a position should be. Indeed, it may remind us of one on another silver casket, that ordered by the Umayyad caliph of al-Andalus al-Hakam II for his son Hisham II (figure IV.2.14).[40] In this case, the inscription, which is not on the body of the casket but on the back of the hinge itself, does mention names: it states that the work was done (or supervised) by Badr and Tarif – or, rather, Zarif, according to the recent reading of Ana Labarta: *'amal Badr wa Zarif 'abdih*.[41] Although its position is similar, but not identical, to that on the casket of Hisham II, the content and style of the inscription on the Sadaqa casket are quite different.[42]

Like the main inscription around the lid in the Sadaqa casket, this second inscription too is extraordinary, giving the object the agency of being blessed and unique. I would argue that it is symbolically appropriate for the appointment of a new, younger vizier.

Both inscriptions are also of crucial importance for their aesthetic relationship with the ornamentation of the casket, as discussed below.

Fatimid Epigraphy and the 'Undulating Stem-and-Leaf Motif' on the Sadaqa Casket

Whether with regard to script or to ornamental motifs, the stylistic affiliations of the Sadaqa casket are rather with 5th/11th-century Fatimid art. Gómez-Moreno had already noted a century ago that the epigraphical style and the ornamentation of the Sadaqa casket were to be related to what he called 'oriental writing', and to the Egyptian decorative style of the 5th/11th century.[43] Indeed, the epigraphical style can be securely related to that of Fatimid inscriptions, which are often characterised by being placed among decorative stems and leaves, or have projections and tendrils that come out from the upper parts of the letters, a type of floriated Kufic that may antedate the Fatimids but certainly developed and flourished under them.[44]

But although there is a stylistic distinction between Fatimid and Spanish scripts and ornaments, it does not exclude commonalities, and on the Spanish material we find certain details of the vegetal decoration, as on the perfume bottle in Teruel, that are comparable to 5th/11th-century Fatimid art, for example in woodwork (figure IV.2.15).[45] They point to the pan-Mediterranean circulation of a vocabulary of ornament, and to the importance of trading and diplomatic links between Spain and Egypt during the period in question.[46]

Figure IV.2.15 a) Inscription on the Sadaqa casket; b) Wooden panel from al-'Amri mosque. Qus, Egypt, 5th/11th century.

The Undulating Stem-and-Leaf Motif

In the main inscription of the Sadaqa casket the whole composition of letters and decorative motifs is highly complex and is worth unpacking, especially as it does not fit neatly into the standard categorisations of foliated and floriated Kufic (figure IV.2.16). Extending across the background is the prominent motif of a floriation that starts from the bottom of the initial *alif* of the first word of the inscription (*istiʿmal*) and gives the impression of passing behind the letter *sin* to come out from the middle of the top of its second tooth, continuing in an upward curve, with little leaves, over the *ʿayn* and *mim* and another just before the second *alif*, splitting into three branches, one a short curl; a third branch passes behind the *alif* and *lam* to then end in a double leaf motif; while the one between them continues on a downward path under the *alif* and *lam* and into the space before the second phrase, *li-khizana*. There it goes up again, passing behind the *zay*, and splits into two branches at its second apex: one branch curves back and ends in a double leaf, while the other continues upwards, passes behind the *alif*, and over the *nun* and *taʾ marbuta*, and then descends again. This pattern is repeated throughout the four sides of the inscription, producing a continuous, undulating motif with stems that 'pass under' the letters, in what I call the 'undulating stem-and-leaf motif'.

This complex motif offers yet another example of the inventiveness of Fatimid artists and underscores the uniqueness of this object in visual terms. The letters and the decorative motifs around the lid are both in reserve, their contours defined by a niello-filled surround. Gómez Moreno draws a parallel between the vegetal scrolls within the inscription ('that fill all the space') and Egyptian arabesque ornamentation of the 5th/11th century.[47] The combination of the letters and decorative motifs results in a striking form of ornamentation that gives the visual impression of the letters resting upon a background that

Figure IV.2.16 The 'Undulating Stem-and-Leaf Motif' on the Sadaqa casket.

consists of little curly, spiral-like motifs (similar to the curls that end the spirals on the rest of the body of the casket).

Together with the effect of the letters resting upon a background of curls and leaves, the impression of 'passing under' is also found in the carving of some Fatimid rock crystal objects – in particular the ewer in the V&A,[48] which Ralph Pinder-Wilson thought was the earliest instance of such an optical illusion in a Fatimid object.[49] He also thought that it was an indication of a greater sophistication and, consequently, an indication that the V&A ewer was later in the series, possibly the last of the Fatimid ewers, placing it in the mid-5th/11th century. The more recently known Edmund De Unger rock crystal ewer, now in the Dallas Museum of Art collection, also presents instances of the 'passing under' visual effect, and therefore, following Pinder-Wilson's reasoning, it too may be attributed to the mid-5th/11th century.[50]

The 'passing under', however, is not found only in Fatimid art. We have examples in illumination, one of the earliest appearing in the Ibn al-Bawwab Qur'an made in Baghdad and dated 391/1000–1001 (figure IV.2.17).[51]

Complementary to, but separate from, the 'Undulating Stem-and-Leaf Motif' is what may be categorised as elements of floriated Kufic. According to Grohmann,[52] floriated Kufic is to be distinguished from foliated Kufic, which is characterised by half-palmette and two- or three-lobed leaf decoration of the bifurcating apices of the letters, by adding to these floral motifs, tendrils and scrolls growing from the final forms or even from the medial forms of the letters. This stylistic development reached its apogee in Egypt, with early examples in the Mosques of al-Azhar and al-Hakim, and in discussing the decoration of the bands of writing on the north minaret of the Mosque of al-Hakim (393/1003) Flury has pointed to motifs of Coptic origin, raising the possibility that Coptic art may have served as a transitional stage between late Hellenistic art and floriated Kufic.[53]

This style then spread both east and west. For instance, evidence for the Palestinian area, according to Ayala Lester, to whom I am grateful for having discussed this with me, is found in Fatimid inscriptions on architecture, including one on the Haram al-Sharif wall in Jerusalem, dated to 301–304/913–917, two at al-Aqsa mosque, and a further two at the Hebron mosque.[54]

This style also affected the portable arts, as part of Fatimid cosmopolitanism. As examples, we have Fatimid metalwork, such as the Benaki silver mirror mentioned above (see note 6) (figure IV.2.18), and artifacts from archaeological material, such as the metal objects found in

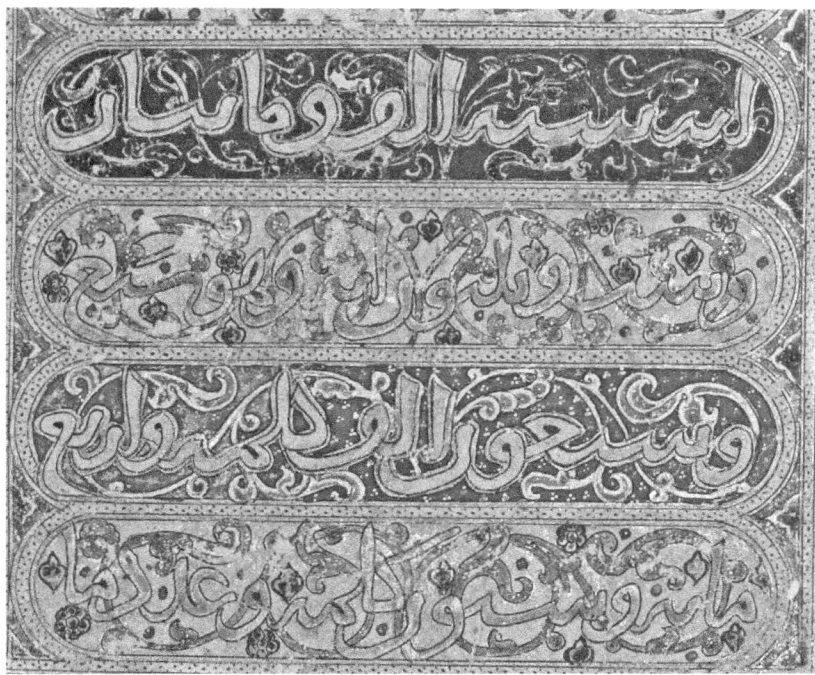

Figure IV.2.17 The 'passing under' in the Ibn al-Bawwab Qur'an, 391/1000–1001. Ink and gold on paper, 18.3 x 14.5 x 5.8 cm. Chester Beatty Library, Dublin.

Tiberias. Of these, several could be cited, but sufficient here as representative is a deep bowl, the benedictory, augural inscription of which has epigraphical characteristics that are very close to those of the Sadaqa casket (figure IV.2.19).[55] Although less complex, the Tiberias bowl, too, has vegetal motifs and tendrils that emerge from the bifurcating apices of the letters or, in the case of a *waw* or a *ra'* or a final *mim*, from their particularly prolonged curly ends.

One characteristic of the Sadaqa casket that strikes me especially is that the ends of the letters, especially those that curl, are often transformed into the same decorative elements that surround them. This conceptualisation of an epigraphic element dissolving into a decorative one, is typical, I would argue, of Fatimid art. Precedents are found in Egyptian, Tulunid art of the late 3rd–early 4th/9th–10th century, as in the stylised bird carved in wood now in the Louvre, where the body dissolves into a floral motif.[56] In the aforementioned later, Fatimid wooden plaque carved in relief datable to the 5th/11th century, now in the Metropolitan

Figure IV.2.18 Mirror with inscription showing similarities with the Sadaqa casket, 5th–6th/11th–12th century. Silver, Diameter 18 cm. Benaki Museum, Athens.

Museum of Art (see note 22), we see that the head and neck of the horses are quite naturalistically rendered with their trappings, while the body dissolves into vegetal elements (figure IV.2.9). Also indicative is that the treatment of the spiral ornamentation at the top and the little curly vegetal elements at the bottom echoes that on the Sadaqa casket. Decorative and epigraphical elements are linked with the vegetal decoration, with one generating the other.

The second, minute inscription on the Sadaqa casket is also in reserve, surrounded by the black niello that defines the letter shape. Vegetal elements float above and below it, but do not engage with it in the way they do with the main inscription. The whole is inserted within a space that mirrors the shape of the hinge and contains motifs found on the body of the casket and around the main inscription, highlighting again the conceptual link between the ornamentation on various parts of the casket.

'The Work is Blessed, Unique' 355

Figure IV.2.19 Bowl from the Tiberias hoard with benedictory inscription, showing similarities with the Sadaqa casket. Fatimid period, 5th/11th century. Copper alloy, 11.8 x 26 cm. Reg. no. A2-525-4/2.

Material and Techniques on the Sadaqa Casket

Silver (fidda)

We have numerous textual references to silver and silver-gilt. Persian sources mention the use of gold and silver vessels in royal feasts (*bazm*) in Iran,[57] and Arabic sources confirm the high status of silver objects, which were not only used as vessels and ornaments, but also in religious contexts, being found in the Dome of the Rock and the Kaʿba. For instance, ʿAli b. Abi Bakr al-Harawi (d. 611/1215), who visited Jerusalem in 569/1173, mentions a silver-gilt inscription (*al-kitaba biʾl-fadd al-mudhahhab*) of the Throne Verse (Q. 2:255) in the Dome of the Rock,[58] while the Andalusian traveller Ibn Jubayr (d. 614/1217) reports that 'The door of the venerable House [the Kaʿba] ... is eleven and a half spans [about six feet] from the ground. It is of gilded silver, perfect in its art and magnificent in its form.'[59] Similarly, the 5th/11th-century Persian poet and traveller Nasir-i Khusraw (d. after 462/1070) mentions silver lamps in the Dome of the Rock, and that inside the Kaʿba were silver doors, *mihrab*s and plaques.[60]

However, given the poor survival rate, it has been assumed that the production of silver objects decreased during the 5th/11th and 6th/12th centuries because of a 'silver famine' in the Islamic world, for which variations in the fineness of the *dirham* have usually been adduced as evidence.[61] Whether there really was a shortage of silver at the time is a matter of some dispute (see note 61), and in any case new discoveries of both coins, with their implications for monetary trends, and silver objects of the period from archaeological contexts have changed the picture. In an Iranian context, for example, the Nishapur excavation has brought to light a number of silver objects of the period, also with gilding and niello: an amulet case datable to between 339/950 and 442/1050 was found in the Tepe Madrasa, with some traces of gilding and a relief decoration. It is incised and partially nielloed and has a nielloed Qurʾanic inscription in angular script.[62] In Fatimid regions, we have the silver objects found in Caesarea, Tiberias, Ramla and Fustat mentioned earlier, and there are Fatimid objects now in museum and church collections, such as the rock crystal bottle in Capua (see note 6). Datable to the late 4th/10th century, the lid of the bottle, part of its mount, is original, and is in silver gilt decorated with niello (figure IV.2.20). It adds to the evidence from the archaeological finds and written sources and confirms that silver objects decorated with niello were produced in the Fatimid empire at least from the 4th/10th century.

Figure IV.2.20 Rock crystal ewer with original silver lid decorated with niello, Fatimid, 4th–5th/10th–11th century. Museo Diocesano, Capua.

As silver was often melted down, circulated according to market demand, and re-used, it is impossible to know where the silver for the Sadaqa casket was sourced. Further, no firm conclusion can be drawn from the choice of silver over, say, gold or ivory: sources such as the Geniza documents and the *Book of Gifts and Rarities* mention the three frequently as prestige materials for expensive artifacts.

Gilding (tadhhib)

The Sadaqa silver casket was gold-washed,[63] producing a greater colour contrast with the niello and an extraordinary visual impact. As one holds such an object and moves it around, the colour shade changes as the light hits it at different points and angles, reflecting to a greater or lesser extent the gilding or the silver.

The technique used was the ancient one of mercury gilding: an amalgam of gold and mercury is applied as a paste over the silver surface and then heated, causing the mercury gradually to evaporate and eventually leave on the surface a thin layer of gold that needs to be burnished. Differences in the time and temperature of the heating will affect the shade of the gilding,[64] which does not hide the silver and the niello decoration underneath, but covers it as a lightly coloured, transparent mantle.

Niello (in the sources normally silver with niello, fidda mukhraqa bi'l-sawad or mujra bi-sawad)

The casket has also a niello decoration, which, combined with the silver and the gold-wash, produces a wonderful overall aesthetic effect. The ancient technique of inlaying with niello consists of cutting grooves in the silver that are then filled with a black substance. Early examples appear in various cultural contexts. In Europe, niello appears on silver, for example, in the 9th-century Trewhiddle hoard discovered in Cornwall,[65] and it has also been found, unusually, on gold, as in a ring (possibly Carolingian) found within the Tesoretto del Reno near Bologna, dateable to the first half of the 9th century AD.[66]

In an Islamic context we have a recipe for it as early as the 4th/10th century, in the treatise on metals by the Yemeni author al-Hamdani (died in San'a in 334/945).[67] He tells us that niello is a compound of silver and sulphur, and does not mention copper or lead, which may not be present in ancient niello:

> Silver is burnt with sulphur until it becomes the colour of Indian iron. This is done by stirring the silver in the crucible, and the silver consumes the sulphur bit by bit. It is then cast in a mould and beaten out hot. If it has started to cool it flies about like glass. If they want to inlay(?) silver with this (compound), they pound it up with borax (*tinkar*) and water, and fill the place dug out of the silver with this pulverised material. It is allowed to flow like solder in the oven, and it does so. Files and rasps are then used on it.[68]

Later, however, in 701/1301, the Persian author Abu'l-Qasim al-Kashani, in his *'Arayis al-jawahir wa nafayis al-atayib*, specifies that niello is a compound of silver, copper, and lead:

> They take one *dirham* of pure silver, one *dirham* of pure copper, and half a *daniq* of pure lead; they melt the copper and silver together

and throw onto it, in two stages, half a *dirham* of yellow sulphur until it all becomes one. The colour ... becomes very shiny black. If they melt it a further time its colour improves and it gradually becomes more solid.[69]

The presence of lead alongside silver and copper could be relevant as an indicator of dating. Analyses done by Susan La Niece at the British Museum indicate its presence in the niello of Byzantine material of the 11th to 12th century,[70] while recent studies on Andalusian silver hinges of ivory objects in the V&A have revealed traces of lead in niello already in the Caliphal period.[71]

The composition of the niello on the Sadaqa casket has not been investigated, but what is certain is that the technique of niello on silver is well attested in various parts of the Mediterranean during the medieval period, including in the Fatimid empire, and silver objects are frequently mentioned in Fatimid sources, some with the specification of being decorated with niello. They are recorded in the *Book of Gifts and Rarities*, in the 5th/11th century and the Geniza documents talk of silver cups, beakers, incense burners, boxes, and of silver bracelets decorated with niello, which in the 6th/12th-century documents studied by Goitein are referred to as silver *siwar mujrah bi-sawad* (literally, 'bracelets treated with blackness').[72] According to these sources, they were more prestigious than those decorated with filigree.

We also have a reference to silver objects with niello coming out of the Fatimid treasury in around 462/1069. In a passage that seems to have been overlooked, al-Maqrizi, writing about the looting mentions large and small silver objects grooved with black (*fidda mukhraqa bi'l-sawad*) and he even adds an aesthetic comment, saying that they were made with the greatest artistry.

Textual sources are matched by the archaeological finds. We do not have a comparable example to the Sadaqa casket, which seems to be a unique piece, as the inscription indeed says. But we do have other types of Fatimid silver objects, including, of course, coins, which have also been found in great quantity in al-Andalus, again demonstrating the connections between Egypt and Spain during this period.[73]

Fatimid hoards such as the one from Caesarea have also yielded silver objects decorated with niello. They include an amulet,[74] a cylindrical amulet case, and a pair of crescent-shaped earrings (figure IV.2.21).[75] The earrings are very beautiful, with niello decoration of the motifs that frame the benedictory inscriptions, which are themselves highlighted in niello

Figure IV.2.21 Silver cylindrical amulet case and earring from the Caesarea hoard, both decorated with niello. Fatimid, 5th/11th century.

(*baraka kamila* on one side and *wa niʿma shamila* on the other), and are in a script related to that on the Sadaqa casket. The niello of these items too has not been tested, so we do not know its exact composition.

Affect and Wonder

The above is a discussion of the material components of the casket together with the sources related to it, and of its calligraphic style, with new readings of the inscriptions. It sets the casket within a historical and art-historical context, and includes interpretations of its visual impact and the implications of its design vocabulary for its affiliations with other artifacts. For an object that had not been hitherto studied in detail, investigation of such aspects was a requirement.

However, in addition to studying objects such as the Sadaqa casket in an essentialist framework, we need to take account of their position within the discourse of affect and wonder. Exploring the capacity to provoke emotional reactions is a much-needed element in the study of objects and material culture, in order to subvert what James Elkins poignantly defined as the 'ivory tower of tearlessness',[76] the exclusion of emotional involvement from much of academic art-historical discourse, where it is regarded as a non-rational approach to be suppressed or disregarded in academic writings. As Keith Moxey puts it: 'The aesthetic power of works of art, . . . and their capacity to shape our response in the present, argues against treating them as if they were simply documents of particular historical horizons.'[77]

The emotional aspect of the interaction with a work of art has recently been addressed by cognitive neuroscientists in what has been called 'neuroesthetics',[78] which explores how empathic processes are essential to aesthetic experiences of visual art, stressing the empathetic feelings aroused in the viewer of the work of art, both non-figurative and figurative, and how they form a substantial part of the art experience. Scientists are also exploring ways of integrating what have been called bottom-up effects – the impact of the work of art on the viewer – with top-down mechanisms – what individuals contribute in terms of emotional, physiological and cultural factors.[79] They also explore how emotions are intertwined with aesthetic judgments. They have shown that the cognitive evaluation of a stimulus as art or non-art informs the emotions that are felt and reported in response to it: 'a link between an empathetic engagement and higher liking may relate to perceived artistry, which is an essential factor influencing aesthetic judgments'.[80] These studies are useful for highlighting the importance of the emotive experience in relation to art and have the potential to make a significant contribution to art-historical aesthetics.

Within the theory of affect, defined by O'Sullivan as art activating or being a stimulus for sensations,[81] we may wish, in considering the Sadaqa casket, to take account of reactions of wonder, often emphasised in Middle Eastern texts. For example, the Iranian physician 'Ali b. Rabban al-Tabari, active in Abbasid Baghdad in the 3rd/9th century, introduces in his medical encyclopedia *Firdaws al-hikma* the psychological element of astonishment by saying that a smile (*ibtisam*) happens when a human being sees or hears something that diverts him and thus startles and moves him.[82] Or by the later Syrian physician Ibn al-Matran (d. 587/1191), active in Ayyubid Damascus, who discusses in his *Bustan al-atibba'* both physiological and psychological aspects of the movement that provokes laughter as, according to him, an expression of astonishment of the soul, and he explains that it is one which may be produced by forms of expression other than speech, and therefore including, one may assume, the visual.[83]

The second inscription, beneath the hinge, tells us that this object is blessed and unique. Looking at it, one reaction could indeed be of wonder (*'ajab*) at its splendid (*badi'*) decoration, its unexpectedness provoking a spontaneous smile. In the sources, objects are generally mentioned either as rarities (*tuhaf*), liable to occasion *'ajab*, or as being beautiful or strange (*gharib*), and therefore wondrous.[84] These concepts come together in the contents and title of at least two works, one *Kitab al-Hadaya wa'l-tuhaf* (already mentioned above), the other by the 7th/13th-century scholar

Zakariya b. Muhammad al-Qazwini, the *'Aja'ib al-makhluqat wa ghara'ib al-mawjudat* (The Wonders of Creation and the Oddities of Existing Things).[85] It is interesting to note that such concepts are also found in literary works, for example historical writings, where one would not expect them. Such historical accounts are thus immensely valuable for what they tell us about the appreciation of the visual arts. For example, in al-Maqrizi's famous report on the competition between two painters at the Fatimid court,[86] which tells us that two painters, one Iraqi and one Egyptian, were summoned by a vizier of al-Mustansir to a competition. One chose to paint a dancer as if coming out of the wall, the other as if going into the wall. Al-Qasir (the Egyptian) painted a dancing girl in a white dress within a black-coloured niche, while Ibn al-'Aziz (the Iraqi) painted a dancing girl in a red dress within a yellow niche. The vizier al-Yazuri was pleased with both and rewarded them generously. This narrative talks to us about optical illusion, a technique very well known in Roman painting[87] and elaborated by the Fatimid scientist Ibn al-Haytham,[88] pointing to a continuation of the technique into 5th/11th-century Arab artistic practice. Secondly, it points to artistic, in this case painterly, activities being practiced in the environment of the court and involving its members as judges of such paintings. And thirdly, it gives us a hint of the appreciation (and consequent patronage) of the Imam-caliph al-Mustansir and his courtiers, not only for the paintings mentioned in this account but also, by implication, for other art works such as the casket made for his vizier Sadaqa b. Yusuf.

That art objects were greatly esteemed in medieval Islamic cultures is also revealed by the *Kitab al-Hadaya wa'l-tuhaf*. The text describes objects in detail, giving as accurate a visual image of them as possible. It also describes all sorts of objects, from pre-Islamic ones up to Fatimid ones, commenting on the context of the gifting and, at times, giving insight as to how they were appreciated. Quite apart from being an invaluable source for the understanding of the role of gifts, whether at the social[89] or diplomatic level, it highlights the importance attached to objects, giving their biographies and pointing once more to the theme of *'ajab*.

The viewer can experience a range of responses to the Sadaqa casket. I have already mentioned the wondrous effect of the gold-wash, and there is, further, the impact of the mesmerising, repeated spiral decoration, a visually active element, encouraging the eye to travel in different directions, and not allowing it to settle (figure IV.2.22).[90] A further response is provoked by the particular calligraphic style of the inscription

Figure IV.2.22 Detail of the side of the Sadaqa casket. Real Colegiata de San Isidoro, Spain.

around the lid and its ornamentation, and the way it contrasts with the series of spirals. I mentioned how its letters are integrated with vegetal elements, one dissolving into the other, a feature of Fatimid aesthetics: the inscription thus combines the semantic with the sensory. Further, both inscriptions define the object itself as blessed and express good wishes for its owner, conjoining various aspects that perhaps allow the viewer to access this aura of blessedness in addition to experiencing the aesthetic pleasure that the casket so richly provides.

NOTES

1   I should like to thank Gregory Bilotto and The Institute of Ismaili Studies for organising the conference and this publication, and the anonymous readers.. Thanks are also due to Beate Fricke, Ana Labarta, Ayala Lester, Maria Antonia Martínez Núñez and Peter Northover who generously offered their knowledge in response to my queries. Raquel Gómez Jaen of the Real Colegiata de San Isidoro, Mina Moraitou of the Benaki Museum in Athens, Stephan Weber of the Islamic Art Museum in Berlin, and the Israel Antiquities Authorities have kindly assisted with photographic material. It has been 24 years since the major Fatimid conference, publication and exhibition in Paris, Institut du Monde Arabe, which then travelled to Vienna, and this volume is a welcome addition and update

on the groundbreaking academic work published then: Marianne Barrucand, ed., *L'Egypte Fatimide: Son art et son histoire* (Paris, 1999). The catalogues that accompanied the exhibitions are: Marianna Barrucand, ed., *Trésors Fatimides du Caire* (Paris, 1998); and Wilfried Seipel, ed., *Schätze der Kalifen: Islamische Kunst zur Fatimidenzeit* (Wien, 1998). All translations from Arabic are mine unless otherwise indicated.

2 On objecthood see, among others, Alison Green and Joanne Morra, 'Introduction: 50 Years of "Art and Objecthood": Traces, Impact, Critique', *Journal of Visual Culture*, 16 (2017), pp. 3–11.

3 León, Real Colegiata de San Isidoro, inv. no. IIC-3-089-002-0014. Works that mention and illustrate the casket include: Manuel Gómez Moreno, *Catálogo monumental de España: Provincial de León* (Madrid, 1925–1926), vol. 1, pp. 163–164 and figures 123–124; Julio Pérez Llamazares, *El tesoro de la Real Colegiata de San Isidoro de León. Reliquias, relicarios y joyas artísticas* (León, 1925), p. 145; Stefano Carboni, 'Casket', in Charles Little, ed., *The Art of Medieval Spain A.D. 500-1200* (New York, 1993), no. 47, pp. 99–100; Priscilla Soucek, 'Byzantium and the Islamic East', in Helen C. Evans and William D. Wixom, ed., *The Glory of Byzantium: Art and Culture of the Middle Byzantine Era, A.D. 843-1261* (New York, 1997), pp. 403–411; Anna Contadini, *Fatimid Art at the Victoria and Albert Museum* (London, 1998), p. 114, figure 39; Barrucand, ed., *Trésors Fatimides*, p. 125, no. 54; Susana Calvo Capilla, 'Arqueta', in Isidro Bango Torviso, ed., *Maravillas de la España Medieval. Tesoro sagrado y Monarquía* (León, 2000–2001), vol. 1, no. 23, p. 114; Jonathan Bloom, *Arts of the City Victorious: Islamic Art and Architecture in Fatimid North Africa and Egypt* (New Haven and London, 2007), p. 97, figure 66; Mariam Rosser-Owen, 'Islamic Objects in Christian Contexts: Relic Translations and Modes of Transfer in Medieval Iberia', *Art in Translation*, 7 (2015), pp. 39–64, figure 3; Assadullah Souren Melikian-Chirvani, ed., *The World of the Fatimids* (Toronto, London & Munich, 2018), p. 125; Rafael Azuar, 'Relaciones de al-Andalus con el Oriente islámico: las artes del metal', in Sergio Vidal Álvarez, ed., *Las artes del metal en al-Andalus* (Madrid, 2019), pp. 84–89, figure 2; Therese Martin, 'Caskets of Silver and Ivory from Diverse Parts of the World: Strategic Collecting for an Iberian Treasury', *Medieval Encounters*, 25 (2019), pp. 1–38, figure 2; Avinoam Shalem, '*Fidda* (Silver): On the Active Life of Matter', in Helen Hills, ed., *Silver: Transformational Matter*, Proceedings of the British Academy, vol. 259 (Oxford, 2023), pp. 175–192; Finbarr Barry Flood and Beate Fricke, *Tales Things Tell: Material Histories of Early Globalisms* (Princeton, 2024), chapter 2.

4 The latter in Flood and Fricke, *Tales Things Tell*, Chapter 2.

5 The *Book of Gifts and Rarities* is known through a 9th/15th-century manuscript, published by Muhammad Hamidullah in 1959 which has been translated from the Arabic by Ghada al-Hijjawi al-Qaddumi, tr. *Book of Gifts and Rarities (Kitab al-Hadaya wa'l-tuhaf)* (Cambridge, MA, 1996), pp. 11–13 where Qaddumi discusses the authorial attribution to Qadi al-Rashid b. Zubayr as likely but not certain. For the Geniza documents see Shlomo Goitein, *A Mediterranean Society: The Jewish Communities of the Arab World as Portrayed in the Documents of the Cairo Geniza* (Berkeley, 1967–1993), especially vol. 4: Daily Life (Berkeley, 1983, rpr. 1999). For Maqrizi's account see Taqi al-Din Ahmad b. ʿAli al-Maqrizi, *Kitab al-Mawaʿiz wa'l-iʿtibar bi-dhikr al-khitat wa'l-athar* (Bulaq [Cairo], 1270/1853), vol. 1, pp. 414–416.

6 Select references for Fatimid silver objects:
Mirror: Athens, Benaki Museum, inv. no. 13770; see Seipel, *Schätze der Kalifen*, p. 116, no. 72; Anna Ballian, ed., *Benaki Museum: A Guide to the Museum of Islamic Art* (Athens, 2006), p. 71, figure 60; Bloom, *Arts of the City Victorious*, p. 98, figure 67. The Benaki Museum also houses a silver fragmentary bottle inlaid with niello that was thought to be Fatimid (Seipel, *Schätze der Kalifen*, cat. no. 194, p. 205) but it is probably to be attributed to Iran. Also, James W. Allan, '"My Father is a Sun, and I am the Star":

Fatimid Symbols in Ayyubid and Mamluk Metalwork', *Journal of the David Collection*, 1 (2003), pp. 25–47.
Lid of rock crystal bottle in Capua: Francesco Gabrieli and Umberto Scerrato, *Gli Arabi in Italia: Cultura, contatti, e tradizioni* (Milan, 1979), pp. 502–503. **Archaeological finds of Caesarea:** Miriam Rosen-Ayalon, 'A Silver Ring from Medieval Islamic Times', in Myriam Rosen-Ayalon, ed., *Studies in Memory of Gaston Wiet* (Jerusalem, 1977), pp. 200–201, pl. 14, no. 3; Ayala Lester and Naʿama Brosh, 'Selections from the Jewelry Hoard from Caesarea', in Barbara Drake Boehm and Melanie Holcomb, ed., *Jerusalem. 1000–1400: Every People Under Heaven* (New York, 2016), cat. 5, p. 31. **Tiberias:** Naʿama Brosh, 'Two Jewelry Hoards from Tiberias', *'Atiqot*, 36 (1998), pp. 1–9; Elias Khamis, *The Fatimid Metalwork Hoard from Tiberias. Tiberias: Excavations in the House of the Bronzes. Final Report, Volume II.* Qedem 55 (Jerusalem, 2013); David J. Wasserstein, 'The Silver Coins in the Mixed Hoard from Tiberias', *'Atiqot*, 36 (1998), pp. 15–22. **Ramla:** Ayala Lester, 'Fatimid Period Jewelry Hoard from the Excavations at Mazliah', *Qadmoniot*, 135 (2008), pp. 35–39. **Fustat:** see, for example, the silver pendant in George T. Scanlon, 'Fustat Expedition: Preliminary Report, 1972 Part I', *Journal of the American Research Center in Egypt*, 18 (1981), pp. 57–84: pp. 73, 75 and figure 6.

7 Virgilio Martínez Enamorado, 'La Epigrafía de los Bronces de Denia', in Rafael Azuar Ruíz, ed., *Los bronces islámicos de Denia (s. V HG / XI d. C.)*, Serie Mayor 10 (Alicante, 2012), pp. 159–167.

8 Goitein, *A Mediterranean Society*, vol. 4, pp. 223–224.

9 Antonio Vallejo Triano, 'Piezas metálicas suntuarias del periodo califal de al-Andalus', in Anna Contadini, ed., *The Pisa Griffin and the Mari-Cha Lion: Metalwork, Art, and Technology in the Medieval Islamicate Mediterranean* (Pisa, 2018), pp. 281–292; and Ana Labarta, *Anillos de la Península Ibérica, 711–1611*(Valencia, 2017).

10 Rafael Azuar, 'Arqueología de la metalistería islámica de al-Andalus durante los reinos de Taifa (Siglo V HG/XI DC)', in Contadini, ed., *Pisa Griffin*, pp. 281–292.

11 Museo de Teruel, inv. no. 629, for which see also Martin Almagro, 'Una joya singular en el reino moro de Albarracin', *Teruel*, 37–38 (1967), pp. 8 and 11; Cynthia Robinson, 'Perfume Bottle', in Jerrilynn D. Dodds, ed., *Al-Andalus: The Art of Islamic Spain* (New York and Madrid, 1992), no. 16, p. 219; Maria Antonia Martínez Núñez, 'La epigrafía de las taifas andalusíes', in Bilal Sarr, ed., *Tawa'if: Historia y Arqueología de los reinos taifas* (Granada, 2018), pp. 85–118: p. 107; and Maria Antonia Martínez Núñez, 'Mujeres y élites sociales en al-Andalus a través de la documentación epigráfica', Maria Isabel Calero Secall, ed., *Mujeres y sociedad islámica: una visión plural* (Málaga, 2006), pp. 287–328: pp. 310–311; no. 4, pp. 319–320; Álvarez, ed., *Las artes del metal en al-Andalus*, no. 169. The other two pieces are: an oval box with an augural and benedictory inscription once part of the Treasury of San Isidoro, and now in the Museo Arqueológico Nacional (MAN) in Madrid (inv. no. 50889); see also María Ángela Franco Mata, 'El tesoro de San Isidoro y la monarquía leonesa', *Boletín del Museo Arqueológico Nacional*, 11 (1991), pp. 35–68: pp. 52–53, 68; Cynthia Robinson, 'Box', in Dodds, ed., *Al-Andalus: The Art of Islamic Spain*, no. 13, p. 214; and a casket with a pyramidal lid, and a benedictory inscription, likewise once in the Treasury of San Isidoro and now in the MAN (inv. no. 50867); see also Franco Mata, 'El tesoro de San Isidoro', pp. 52–53, 65; Stefano Carboni, 'Casket', in Charles Little, ed., *The Art of Medieval Spain A.D. 500–1200*, no. 45, p. 98.

12 Maria Antonia Martínez Núñez, 'Inscripciones árabes en la Catedral de Oviedo: El Arca Santa, la Arqueta del Obispo Arias y la Arqueta de Santa Eulalia', *Territorio, Sociedad y Poder*, 11 (2016), pp. 23–62. The other two pieces that Rafael Azuar attributes to Toledo referred to in the previous note also exhibit such differences.

13 Such as on the Pisa Griffin and 13th-century Spanish textiles like the tunic of Don Rodrigo Ximénez de Rada, Spain, ca. 1247, Monasterio de Santa María, Santa María la

Real de Huerta, Soria; see Contadini, 'The Pisa Griffin', figure 21; also on textiles and metalwork attributed to the Eastern Mediterranean and Anatolia, see Evans and Wixom, *The Glory of Byzantium*, cats. 271 and 281.

14 Simone Assemani, *Illustrazione della patena mistica creduta di S. Pier Grisologo la quale si conserva nella chiesa cattedrale d'Imola* (Padua, 1804); Michelangelo Lanci, *Trattato delle simboliche rappresentanze arabiche e della varia generazione de' musulmani caratteri sopra differenti materie operati* (Paris, 1845–1846), vol. 3, tav. XXIII.

15 The typology of its letters is found in other Italian art, from wall paintings of churches to paintings of the early Italian masters. See Maria Vittoria Fontana, 'Byzantine Mediation of Epigraphic Characters of Islamic Derivation in the Wall Paintings of Some Churches in Southern Italy', in Charles Burnett and Anna Contadini, ed., *Islam and the Italian Renaissance* (London, 1999), pp. 61–75. For the style of script see Ennio G. Napolitano, 'The Transfer of Arabic Inscriptions in Italian Gothic and Renaissance Painting: A New Approach. The Words *al-Mulk*, *Baraka* and *al-Yumn* in the 14th and 15th Century Italian Paintings', in Antonino Pellitteri et al., ed., *Re-defining a Space of Encounter. Islam and Mediterranean: Identity, Alterity and Interactions* (Leuven, 2019), pp. 315–334.

16 Harvard University Art Museum, Cambridge (MA.), inv. no. 326.1983; see Barrucand, *Trésors fatimides*, no. 51.

17 New York, Brooklyn Museum, inv. 69.122.1.

18 London, V&A, inv. no. C.49-1952; see Contadini, *Fatimid Art*, pls. 34a and 34b.

19 London, V&A, inv. no. C.1614-1921; see Contadini, *Fatimid Art*, pl. 37.

20 London, V&A, inv. no. C.23-1932; see Contadini, *Fatimid Art*, pl. 44.

21 Cairo, Museum of Islamic Art, inv. no. 71.6.34; see Ralph H. Pinder-Wilson and George T. Scanlon, 'Glass Finds from Fustat: 1964-71', *Journal of Glass Studies*, 15 (1973), pp. 12–30: p. 25, figures 30–32; Contadini, *Fatimid Art*, pp. 23–24 and figure 21.

22 New York, Metropolitan Museum of Art, inv. no. 11.205.2; see Barrucand, *Trésors fatimides*, no. 14, p. 95; Seipel, *Schätze der Kalifen*, no. 15, p. 83; Ellen Kenney, 'Panel', in Maryam D. Ekhtiar, et al., ed., *Masterpieces from the Department of Islamic Art in The Metropolitan Museum of Art* (New York, 2011), no. 112, p. 163.

23 Georges Marçais and Louis Poinssot, *Objets kairouanais: IXe au XIIIe siècle: Reliures, verreries, cuivres et bronzes, bijoux* (Tunis, 1948), pl. XLI.

24 Soucek, 'Byzantium and the Islamic East', p. 408, and in the same publication cat. 24 for the Cleveland cross; cat. 5 for the marble carving from Komotini; and cat. 143 for the painted portrait of Nikephoros III Botaneiates.

25 See, for example, reg. no. A2-575-110/2 in Khamis, *Fatimid Metalwork Hoard*, no. 533, pp. 201, 394.

26 For an overview of the Treasury of San Isidoro see Therese Martin, ed., *The Medieval Iberian Treasury in the Context of Cultural Interchange (Expanded Edition)* (Leiden, 2020).

27 Anna Contadini, 'Translocation and Transformation: Some Middle Eastern Objects in Europe', in Lieselotte E. Saurma-Jeltsch and Anja Eisenbeiß, ed., *The Power of Things and the Flow of Cultural Transformations: Art and Culture between Europe and Asia*, (Berlin & Munich, 2010), pp. 42–64: pp. 43–47, pl. 1.1.

28 Antony Eastmond, 'The St Petroc Casket, a Certain Mutilated Man, and the Trade in Ivories', in David Knipp, ed., *Siculo-Arabic Ivories and Islamic Painting 1100–1300* (Munich, 2011), pp. 83–97.

29 See Martin, *Medieval Iberian Treasury*, which discusses the current display and the other 'foreign' objects; for the Scandinavian container see Nancy L. Wicker, 'The Scandinavian Container at San Isidoro, León, in the Context of Viking Art and Society', in Martin, *Medieval Iberian Treasury*, pp. 223–248.

30 Rosser-Owen, 'Islamic Objects in Christian Contexts', p. 48; and Martin, *Medieval Iberian Treasury*.

31 Contadini, 'Translocation and Transformation'; and against the 'trophy' theory, especially in relation to the Pisa Griffin and the Andalusian capital, see also Anna Contadini, 'The Pisa Griffin and the Mari-Cha Lion: History, Art and Technology', in Anna Contadini, ed., *The Pisa Griffin and the Mari-Cha Lion. Metalwork, Art, and Technology in the Medieval Islamicate Mediterranean* (Pisa, 2018), pp. 238–243. And for a critique of the *traslatio imperii* theory, especially in relation to Abbasid or Fatimid rock crystal objects and stone chess pieces on the ambo of Henry II at Aachen, see Anna Contadini, 'Sharing a Taste? Material Culture and Intellectual Curiosity around the Mediterranean, from the Eleventh to the Sixteenth Century', in Anna Contadini and Claire Norton, ed., *The Renaissance and the Ottoman World* (Farnham, 2013), pp. 28–30.

32 Gómez-Moreno, *Catalogo monumental de España*, vol. 1, p. 164; Carboni, 'Casket'; Calvo Capilla 'Arqueta'.

33 Taqi al-Din Ahmad al-Maqrizi, *Ittiʿaz al-hunafaʾ bi-akbar al-aʾimma al-fatimiyyin al-khulafaʾ*, ed. Jamal al-Din al-Shayyal (Cairo, 1387/1967), vol. 2, pp. 191–197. See also Leila S. Imad, *The Fatimid Vizierate, 969–1172* (Berlin, 1990), pp. 165 and 180–181.

34 Al-Maqrizi, *Ittiʿaz al-hunafaʾ*, p. 196.

35 Al-Maqrizi, *Ittiʿaz al-hunafaʾ*, vol. 2, pp. 195–196. The *Khizanat al-Bunud* was a storage place for banners.

36 al-Qaddumi, *Book of Gifts*, no. 82, pp. 108–109.

37 See description in al-Maqrizi, *Ittiʿaz al-hunafaʾ*, vol. 2, p. 191.

38 For example, see Avinoam Shalem, 'On Original and "Originals": The "Copy" of the Tashkent Qurʾan Codex in the Rare Collection Books at the Butler Library', in *Philological Encounters*, 5 (2020), pp. 282–307: pp. 286–287, in relation to the use of *farid* by al-Biruni to describe unique pearls: Muhammad b. Ahmad al-Biruni, *The Book Most Comprehensive in Knowledge on Precious Stones*, tr. Hakim Mohammad Said (Islamabad, 1989), p. 131.

39 Carboni, 'Casket', p. 99; also Bloom, *Arts of the City Victorious*, p. 97; Calvo Capilla, 'Arqueta'.

40 Tesoro de la Catedral de Gerona, inv. no. 64; see Manuel Casamar, 'Casket of Hisham II,' in Jerrilynn D. Dodds, ed., *Al-Andalus: The Art of Islamic Spain* (New York & Madrid, 1992), cat. 9, pp. 208–209; Susana Calvo Capilla, 'Arqueta de Hixam II', in Marc Sureda i Jubany, ed., *Oliba Episcopus: Millenari d'Oliba, bisbe de Vic* (Barcelona, 2018), no. 8, pp. 110–112.

41 Ana Labarta, 'The Casket of Hisham and its Epigraphy', *Summa*, 6 (Autumn 2015), pp. 104–128, for its inscriptions and their interpretation; and Ana Labarta, 'La Arqueta de Hišam Vista de Cerca', *Summa*, 10 (2017), pp. 15–42, for a close study of its materiality and decoration.

42 Although the ivory Bayeux casket also has an inscription on its body beneath the lock, it is of a completely different typology and script. For an art-historical study see Avinoam Shalem, 'Two Ivory Caskets in the Treasuries of the Cathedrals of Chur and Bayeux', *Arte Medievale*, 15 (2000), pp. 15–25; and at last the correct reading of the inscription (*bismillah al-rahman al-rahim baraka kamila wa niʿma shamila*) has now been given in the interesting historiographical study by M. Pierre Ageron, 'Le coffret musulman de la cathédrale de Bayeux: la réception savante d'un objet incongru', *Bulletin de la Société des antiquaires de Normandie*, 78 (2021), pp. 31–69.

43 Gómez-Moreno, *Catalogo monumental de Espana*, vol. 1, pp. 163–164. His attribution of the Sadaqa casket to Fatimid Egypt, based primarily on the epigraphic elements, is shared by Martínez Núñez, 'Inscripciones árabes', esp. p. 56.

44 Samuel Flury, 'Le décor épigraphique des monuments fatimides du Caire', *Syria*, 17 (1936), pp. 365–376, who based his examples on Max van Berchem's *Matériaux pour un Corpus Inscriptionum Arabicarum. Première partie: Égypte* (Paris, 1894–1903) and gives useful drawings; Adolf Grohmann, 'The Origin and Early Development of Floriated

Kufic', *Bulletin de l'institut d'Egypte*, 37 (1954–55), pp. 273–304, where he establishes a chronological development from foliated to the more complex floriated Kufic used during the Fatimid period; Sheila S. Blair, 'Floriated Kufic and the Fatimids', in Barrucand, ed., *L'Égypte Fatimide*, pp. 107–116. For monumental examples of floriated Kufic see Bernard O'Kane, 'Monumental Calligraphy in Fatimid Egypt: Epigraphy in Stone, Stucco, and Wood', in Melikian-Chirvani, ed., *World of the Fatimids*, pp. 142–159; also O'Kane's article in this volume. For a study of Andalusian Kufic see also M. Ocaña Jimenez, M. *El cúfico hispano y su evolución* (Madrid, 1970).

45 For instance, in a wooden panel said to be from al-'Amri Mosque, Qus, Egypt, ca. 550/1155–1156, now in Berlin, Museum für Islamische Kunst, inv. no. I. 612; see Barrucand, ed., *Trésors fatimides*, no. 94.

46 For a discussion of the interchanges between al-Andalus and Egypt from the Taifa period see Susana Calvo Capilla, 'Las artes en al-Andalus y Egipto. Una red de intercambios permanente', in Susana Calvo Capilla, ed., *Las artes en al-Andalus y Egipto: contextos e intercambios* (Madrid, 2017), pp. 9–22.

47 Gómez Moreno, *Catalogo monumental de Espana*, vol. 1, pp. 163–164, where for the hinges he also offers a comparison with those of the casket in Bayeux Cathedral (inv. no. Palissy PM14000050), although they are quite different both in shape and thickness and in the decorative reliefs. On the Bayeux casket and its inscription beneath the lock, see the recent study by M. Pierre Ageron, 'Le coffret musulman', referred to in note 42.

48 London, V&A, inv. no. 7904-1862; see Contadini, *Fatimid Art*, pp. 37–38, pl. 7.

49 Ralph Pinder-Wilson, 'Rock Crystals', in Basil W. Robinson, ed., *Islamic Art in the Keir Collection* (London, 1988), pp. 287–309.

50 The Keir Collection of Islamic Art on loan to the Dallas Museum of Art, inv. no. K.1.2014.1.A-B; see Anna Contadini, 'Facets of Light: The Case of Rock Crystals', in Jonathan Bloom and Sheila Blair, ed., *God is the Light of the Heavens and the Earth: Light in Islamic Art and Culture* (New Haven, CT, 2015), pp. 121–155.

51 Dublin, Chester Beatty Library, inv. no. Is 1431; see D. S. Rice, *The Unique Ibn al-Bawwab Manuscript in the Chester Beatty Library* (Dublin, 1955), p. 35.

52 Grohmann, 'The Origin', p. 275.

53 Samuel Flury, *Die Ornamente der Hakim- und Ashar-Moschee* (Heidelberg, 1912), p. 46.

54 For floriated script in the Haram al-Sharif, see Grohmann, 'The Origin', p. 289, figure 18; see also Max van Berchem, *Matériaux pour un Corpus Inscriptionum Arabicarum. Deuxième partie: Syrie du Sud. Jérusalem «Haram»* (Cairo, 1925), p. 7, figure 2.

55 Reg. no. A2-525-4/2; see Khamis, *Fatimid Metalwork Hoard from Tiberias*, no. 260, pp. 167, 314–316.

56 See Oleg Grabar, 'When is a Bird a Bird?', *Proceedings of the American Philosophical Society*, 153 (2009), pp. 247–253; also Sophie Makariou, 'Panel with a flower-bird', in Sophie Makariou, ed., *Islamic Art at the Musée du Louvre* (Paris, 2012), pp. 102–104.

57 Assadullah Souren Melikian-Chirvani, 'Essais sur la Sociologie de l'Art Islamique I, Argenterie et Féodalité dans l'Iran Médiéval', in Chahryar Adle, ed., *Art et Société dans le Monde Iranien* (Paris, 1982), pp. 143–175; Assadullah Souren Melikian-Chirvani, 'Silver in Islamic Iran: The Evidence from Literature and Epigraphy', in Michael Vickers, ed., *Pots and Pans* (Oxford, 1986), pp. 89–106.

58 Gülru Necipoğlu, 'The Dome of the Rock as Palimpsest: 'Abd al-Malik's Grand Narrative and Sultan Suleyman's Glosses', *Muqarnas*, 25 (2008), pp. 17–105.

59 Francis E. Peters, *Mecca: A Literary History of the Muslim Holy Land* (Princeton, 1994), p. 141.

60 Nasir-i Khusraw, *Naser-e Khosraw's Book of Travels (Safarnama)*, tr. W. M. Thackston, Jr. (New York, 1986), pp. 32, 77; see also Melikian-Chirvani, 'Silver in Islamic Iran', pp. 90, 92–93.

61 The view that there was a shortage of silver was first put forward by Robert P. Blake, 'The Circulation of Silver in the Moslem East down to the Mongol Epoch', *Harvard Journal of Asiatic Studies*, 2 (1937), pp. 291–328. See also Ian Blanchard, *Mining, Metallurgy and Minting in the Middle Ages (Vol. 1): Asiatic Supremacy, 425–1125* (Stuttgart, 2001), p. 183. A counter argument is found in D. M. Dunlop, 'Sources of Gold and Silver in Islam according to al-Hamdani (10th Century A.D.)', *Studia Islamica*, 8 (1957), pp. 28–49, who deals with the literary evidence for sources of gold and silver available in the Islamic world in this period, in order to counter the view that there was a shortage of silver; see also Melikian-Chirvani, 'Silver in Islamic Iran'. For coins see also A. E. Leiber, 'International Trade and Coinage in the Northern Lands during the Early Middle Ages: An Introduction', in *Viking-Age Coinage in the Northern Lands*, ed. M. A. S. Blackburn & D. M. Metcalf, BAR International Series, 122 (i) (Oxford, 1981), pp. 1–34.

62 James W. Allan, *Nishapur: Metalwork of the Early Islamic Period* (New York, 1982), pp. 27, 60, no. 1. See also the silver objects with niello in the Harari Hoard found in northern Iran, now in the Museum of Islamic Art in Jerusalem; see James W. Allan, 'The Survival of Precious and Base Metal Objects from the Medieval Islamic World', in *Pots and Pans*, ed. Michael Vickers (Oxford, 1986), pp. 57–70: figure 3; Flood and Fricke, *Tales Things Tell*, figure 57.

63 For gilding, the silver object was overlaid with gold, for which the term used is *mughraq*, or gilded silver, as in the dictionary by the 10th/16th-century Egyptian author Shihab al-Din al-Khafaji (d. 1069/1659), *Shifa' al-ghalil fima fi kalam al-'arab min al-dakhil*, ed. Muhammad 'Abd al-Mun'im al-Khafaji (Cairo, 1371/1952), p. 195.

64 Ana Labarta reports, for the Andalusian silver casket of Hisham II referred to above, that technical analyses of the gilding showed that it was formed by gold (90%), silver (8%) and copper (2%), an alloy that is known as yellow gold: Labarta, 'La Arqueta de Hišam' p. 24, citing Màrius Vendrell, Pilar Giráldez and Sarah Boularand, 'Arqueta d'Hisam II. Estudi dels materials constitutius', Barcelona, Patrimoni-UB. Estudis del patrimoni històric, Universitat de Barcelona, 2007 [Unpublished report], pp. 6–7.

65 David M. Wilson and C. E. Blunt, 'The Trewhiddle Hoard', *Archaeologia* 98 (1961), pp. 75–122.

66 Joan Pinar Gil, 'L'oro del Reno: La riscoperta di un eccezionale deposito della prima età carolingia,' *Archeologia Medievale*, 47 (2020), pp. 61–91, which also mentions the 8th-century 'Tassillon style', but does not specify whether these objects are nielloed.

67 Abu Muhammad al-Hasan b. Ahmad al-Hamdani, *Kitab al-Jawharatayn al-'atiqatayn al-ma'i'atayn min al-safra' wa-al-bayda' (al-dhahab wa al-fidda)*, ed. A. D. Ahmad Fu'ad Basha (Cairo, 1430/2009).

68 al-Hamdani, *Kitab al-Jawharatayn*, p. 174; English translation in James W. Allan, *Persian Metal Technology 700–1300 AD* (London, 1979), pp. 19–20.

69 Abu'l-Qasim al-Kashani, '*Arayis al-jawahir va nafayis al-atayib*, dated 700/1301; English translation by Allan, *Persian Metal Technology*, p. 20.

70 Susan La Niece, 'Niello: An Historical and Technical Survey', *The Antiquaries Journal*, 63 (1983), p. 287.

71 Mariam Rosser-Owen, 'The Metal Mounts on Andalusi Ivories: Initial Observations', in Venetia Porter and Mariam Rosser-Owen, ed., *Metalwork and Material Culture in the Islamic World* (London, 2012), pp. 309–310; see also the cautionary note in Catia Viegas Wesolowska, 'Metal Mounts on Ivories of Islamic Spain', in Beata Biedrońska-Słota, Magdalena Ginter-Frołow and Jerzy Malinowski, ed., *The Art of the Islamic World and the Artistic Relationships between Poland and Islamic Countries* (Krakow, 2011), pp. 189–198: pp. 194–195.

72 Goitein, *A Mediterranean Society*, vol. 4, p. 212.

73 Carolina Doménech-Belda, 'La moneda fatimí y su relación con al-Andalus', *Cuadernos de Madinat al-Zahra*, 5 (2004), pp. 339–354.

74 Rosen-Ayalon, 'Silver Ring', pp. 200–201, pl. 14, no. 3.

75 I thank Ayala Lester for sharing these photos from the Caesarea hoard with me, and for confirming that the niello of these items has not been tested, so we do not know its exact composition.
76 James Elkins, *Pictures and Tears: A History of People Who Have Cried in Front of Paintings* (London, 2004), pp. 70–83.
77 Keith Moxey, *Visual Time: The Image in History* (Durham, NC, 2013), p. 139. Taken further by Matthew Rampley, 'Agency, Affect and Intention in Art History: Some Observations', *Journal of Art Historiography*, 24 (June 2021), p. 2.
78 David Freedberg and Vittorio Gallese, 'Motion, Emotion and Empathy in Esthetic Response', in *Trends in Cognitive Sciences*, 11 (2007), pp. 197–203.
79 Matthew Pelowski et al., 'Move Me, Astonish Me ... Delight My Eyes and Brain: The Vienna Integrated Model of Top-down and Bottom-up processes in Art Perception (VIMAP) and Corresponding Affective, Evaluative, and Neurophysiological Correlates', *Physics of Life Reviews*, 21 (July 2017), pp. 80–125. I thank Claudia Contadini-Wright for pointing out this article to me.
80 Gerger Gernot, Matthew Pelowski and Helmut Leder, 'Empathy, Einfühlung, and Aesthetic Experience: The Effect of Emotion Contagion on Appreciation of Representational and Abstract Art using fEMG and SCR', *Cognitive Processing*, 19 (2018), pp. 147–165. Earlier works on empathetic responses to art include Abby Warburg's concept of the *Pathosformel* (for which see discussion in Kerstin Schankweiler and Philipp Wüschner, '*Pathosformel* (Pathos Formula)', in Jan Slaby and Christian von Scheve, ed., *Affective Societies: Key Concepts* (Abingdon, 2019), pp. 220–230), and Bernard Berenson on tactile values in his *Florentine Painters of the Renaissance* (New York, 1896).
81 Simon O'Sullivan, 'The Aesthetics of Affect: Thinking Art Beyond Representation', *Angelaki: Journal of the Theoretical Humanities*, 6 (December 2001), pp. 125–135.
82 'Ali b. Rabban al-Tabari, *Firdaws al-hikma*, ed. M.Z. Siddiqi (Berlin, 1928).
83 For Ibn al-Matran see also Bedrettin Basuguy, 'Medical Developments During the Reign of Salah al-Dîn al-Ayyûbî and the Famous Physicians of the Period', *Journal of Research on History of Medicine*, 8 (2019), pp. 3–18; and for 'Ali b. Rabban al-Tabari see Max Meyerhof, "Alî at-Tabarî's "Paradise of Wisdom", One of the Oldest Arabic Compendiums of Medicine', *Isis*, 16 (1931), pp. 16–46. Persian and Arab writers are here developing Greek philosophers' theory of disruption, laughter, and humour in its broad sense (Aristotle, *Rhetoric*, 3,2; English translation *Art of Rhetoric*, tr. J. H. Freese, rev. Gisela Striker (Cambridge, MA, 2020).
84 A discussion of the *'aja'ib* and *ghara'ib* is in Nasser Rabbat, "*Ajib and Gharib*: Artistic Perception in Medieval Arabic Sources', *The Medieval History Journal*, 9 (2006), pp. 99–113. See also the account by Safi al-Din Urmawi in Ahmad ibn Yahya ibn Fadl Allah al-'Umari, *Masalik al-absar fi mamalik al-amsar*, Book 10, ed. F. Sezgin, A. Jokhosha and E. Neubauer (Frankfurt am Main, 1988), pp. 309–313, translated and discussed in Anna Contadini, 'Patronage and the Idea of an Urban Bourgeoisie', in Gülru Necipoğlu and Finbarr Barry Flood, ed., *A Companion to Islamic Art and Architecture, Vol. 1* (Oxford, 2017), p. 433.
85 Of which many copies with paintings exist, such as one dated 678/1280 and was therefore produced during Qazwini's lifetime: Munich, Bayerische Staatsbibliothek, Cod. arab. 464; see Persis Berlekamp, *Wonder, Image, and Cosmos in Medieval Islam* (New Haven, 2011).
86 A translation is in Thomas W. Arnold, *Painting in Islam: A Study of the Place of Pictorial Art in Muslim Culture* (Oxford, 1928), pp. 21–22.
87 Wall paintings of Pompeii of the 'Second Style', for example, employed trompe-l'œil to create three-dimensional perspectives.

88 Abu 'Ali al-Hasan ibn al-Haytham, *The Optics of Ibn al-Haytham: Books I-III: On Direct Vision*, tr. A. I. Sabra, 2 vols (London, 1989), where visual illusion is discussed in Book III: 'On Errors of Direct Vision and Their Causes'.
89 al-Qaddumi, *Book of Gifts*, p. 4 mentions traditions that report the Prophet Muhammad pointing to the importance of gifts for improving human relationships: 'a gift opens doors that are closed and gently removes rancour from the heart'.
90 For a discussion of hapticity and Islamic ornament see Simon O'Meara, 'Haptic Vision: Making Surface Sense of Islamic Material Culture', in Robin Skeates and Jo Day, ed., *The Routledge Handbook of Sensory Archaeology* (Abingdon, 2020), pp. 467–480.

3

Fatimid Jewellery Hoards from Palestine in the Light of the Cairo Geniza Documents

Ayala Lester

Nine jewellery hoards, dated to the Fatimid period, were found between 1961 and 2005 in excavations carried out in Ramla, Jerusalem, Caesarea, Tiberias and Ashkelon. In most of the cases monetary hoards were found in the vicinity of the jewellery hoards. The fourteen monetary hoards included dinars, dirhams and fractions of dirhams.[1]

The hiding of hoards is an expression of the unstable political situation in Palestine, as Turkoman forces overran Syria and Palestine during the last decades of the 5th/11th century. Furthermore, the weakening of Fatimid control in Palestine, resulting from internal conflicts between Berber tribes and Turkish mercenaries within the Fatimid army, enabled the first Crusader army to conquer Palestine in 492/1099 and establish the kingdom of Jerusalem (492–494/1099–1101).[2]

The first part of this article summarises the jewellery hoards discovered in Israel and the second part deals with S.D. Goitein's discussions of jewellery, particularly pieces listed in the dowries of Jewish brides. The goal of this article has been to provide a link between the jewellery listed in dowries and the material evidence uncovered.

Goitein's discussions of jewellery are based upon trousseau lists from Jerusalem and Fustat, dated between 419 and 551/1028 and 1156. They include women from affluent backgrounds as well as some with modest resources a state of affairs which, in fact, reflects the economic situation in Palestine and Egypt, during the Fatimid period.

Following a study of the excavated hoards, I have identified an affinity between the jewellery pieces and the terminology discussed by Goitein. His analyses are based upon 'jewellery given to girls from families that had attained a certain degree of comfort'.[3] The weight of the pieces is not provided in the trousseau lists, probably because of the similarity in weight of the dinar and the *mithqal*.[4]

In the caches in Tiberias and Caesarea, the gold and the silver pieces were packed in separate ceramic vessels. Within the trousseau lists there is a clear preference for gold jewellery, followed by pearls and silver. This ranking is pertinent from the perspective of archaeology, as jewellery pieces made of gold are the most common findings. There are only a few articles made of silver and precious stones.[5]

The Hoards

Ramla

Three hoards were found in Ramla. The first hoard, unearthed in 1965, consisted of dinars and fractions of dinars together with gold ingots, and was dated to 369/979.[6] The other two hoards, an assemblage of bracelets and armlets and a monetary hoard were uncovered during 2005 in an affluent neighbourhood with well-organised streets, houses with sewage systems and water cisterns. The first is comprised of nine armlets and bracelets that had been wrapped in a textile; the latter has not survived.[7] The second cache, buried in an unglazed small clay juglet contained 302 dinars dated to between 349–471/960–1078/9.[8]

The assemblage consisted of a pair of heavy silver tubular anklets, a pair of gold bracelets, a third pair of bracelets made of silver and a single gold bracelet, all of which are decorated in the repoussé technique, a single silver armlet with a suspended amulet box and a bracelet made of silver wire (figure IV.3.1).

Some of the articles are unique. The silver anklets are composed of two parts attached by a hinge. A granule inside the anklet rattles when the person moves. Goitein refers to a woman of modest means who was married in 414/1023. Her dowry listed a pair of silver anklets valued at eight dinars. Goitein comments that they must have been heavy as each anklet weighs 170 grams (40 *mithqal* units; the *mithqal* was the common weight unit for commodities).[9]

Goitein also discussed anklets wrought in gold, which were the most expensive articles in all the trousseau lists from the 5th/11th century. This type of gold anklet would be expensive as the gold sheet is, by definition, thick due to the forging process.

A pair of two silver bracelets, one made of gold, and another single gold bracelet all decorated in repoussé, are adorned with inscriptions such

Figure IV.3.1 A hoard from Ramla containing gold and silver bracelets and anklets, IAA

as بركة كاملة or بركة وغز and are decorated with medallions, birds, hares, gazelles, palmettes, and 'scales of an eagle', a term discussed by Goitein. The presence of scales signifies the rows of feathers covering the body of the eagle, symbolising strength, mightiness and courage.

Two gold bracelets are decorated with tiny bars and bands with scrolls and half palmettes. The hinges are concealed by spherical plates coated with granulation. These two bracelets are characterised by meticulous work and should have been quite expensive, as each one weighs about 40 grams (8.7 *mithqal* units). This is the first occurrence of this type of bracelet, both in archaeological findings and museum collections.

Caesarea

The first two hoards from Caesarea were excavated by Negev in 1963. The hoards were found near the harbour within a vaulted platform originally built by Herod as part of the acropolis of the city. The building was used during the Islamic period as a metal workshop. Several metres of metal ore covered the floor, and two jewellery hoards were found underneath this waste, within a few days of each other. A third cache was found a year later and included out-of-use dinar and dirham coins, from the early 3rd/9th to the late 5th/10th century, which were probably kept for remelting.[10]

One of the hoards unearthed at Caesarea was composed of gold articles and the second of silver pieces. The cache of gold jewellery was hidden in a glazed juglet and a hoard of silver anklets was found hidden in a small clay juglet.

The gold cache (figure IV.3.2) is comprised of large gold beads of two kinds: beads made with filigree wire and granulation, and beads made of gold leaf decorated with granulation. The central ones demonstrate superb filigree work. Apple and cherry shaped beads are strung together flanking a central biconical bead. The term 'beaded' is suggested by Goitein to mean granulated which is likely the case with the apple-shaped beads. Each filigree bead was built upon a frame made of straight filigree wires with S shaped wires woven through them. These, in turn, were filled by tiny figure of six elements creating palmette-shaped patterns. In the Geniza, this complex design is termed *mushabbak*, مشبّك latticework[11]

Figure IV.3.2 The gold hoard from Caesarea with filigreed and granulated beads, amulet cases, silver beads and various stones, IAA

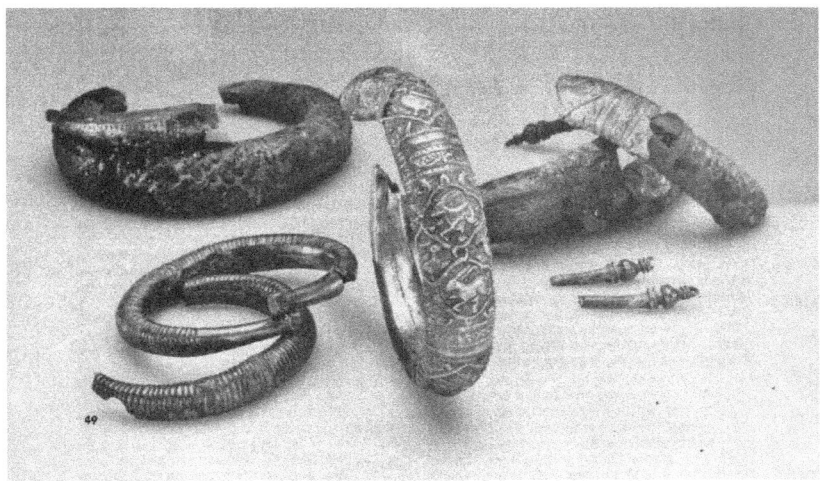

Figure IV.3.3 The silver hoard from Caesarea composed of bracelets, IAA

The cache also included amulet cases made of silver and a trove of different stones such as carnelian, onyx, rock-crystal and glass beads.[12]

The latest article in the hoard is a silver amulet bearing Sura 112 from the Qur'an, dated between the late 5th/11th and the early 6th/12th century.[13]

The silver bracelets from the second cache are decorated in the repoussé technique. A second pair is patterned with ribs across the bracelets (figure IV.3.3).[14]

Tiberias

Three hoards were uncovered in Tiberias in 1976 and 1985. The first hoard is comprised of a juglet containing 14 gold dinars, the latest dated to 415/1024, and a few jewellery pieces.[15] The hoard included a variety of basket-shaped earrings, a pair of crescent-shaped earrings with loops for the suspension of pearls, a finger ring made of filigree wire and a single spherical earring.[16] The dinars were clipped. The latest dinar, dated to 415/1024, bears the name of the Imam-caliph al-Zahir (figure IV.3.4).[17]

Another excavation, carried out in 1989, unearthed two jewellery hoards and coins. One hoard was buried in a unique sphero-conical vessel made of thick clay. It contained a pair of basket-shaped earrings, a biconical bead, two gold finger rings and spherical beads.[18] The dinar coins range in dates from al-ʿAziz bi'llah (366/976) to Abu Tamim Maʿadd al-Mustansir bi'llah (455/1063) (figure IV.3.5, right).

The second jewellery hoard was discovered in a clay juglet typical of the Fatimid period.[19] It included two gold finger rings, a fragment of a silver bracelet, a handle of a silver vessel, a variety of beads and out-of-use dirham coins, clipped to be used as amuletic jewellery pieces (figure IV.3.5, left).[20] The coins were issued by al-Hakim and al-Zahir, and range between 401–402/1010–1011 and 424–425/1032–1033.[21] The difference in dates of about thirty years between the two hoards confirms the fact that

Figure IV.3.4 A hoard from Tiberias having gold jewellery pieces and dinar coins, IAA

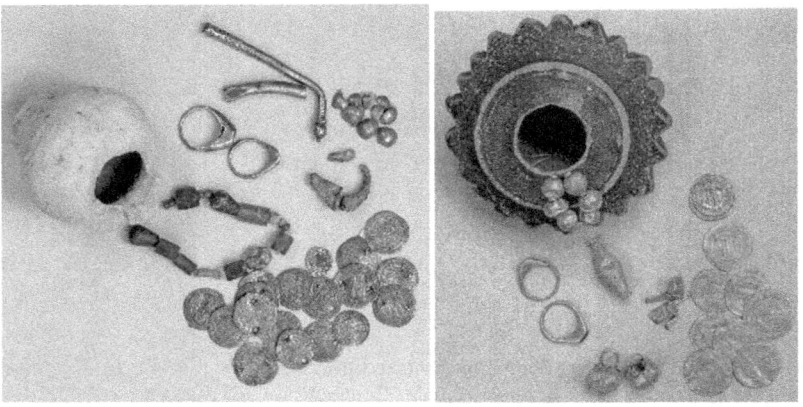

Figure IV.3.5 (right and left) A hoard from Tiberias. Right: Gold jewellery pieces and dinar coins Left: Gold jewellery pieces, silver beads and dirham coins, IAA

the dirham coins were used as amulets and were valued for their silver content and not as currency.

Jerusalem

Jerusalem was conquered by the Crusader army between 13 and 15 July 492/1099. The taking of the city was followed by a massacre of many of its inhabitants.[22]

Five hoards were uncovered in the city, two of them composed of jewellery pieces and the other three were made up of coins. One hoard includes Ghaznavid and Saljuq dinars, with one dinar minted by al-ʿAziz, dated to 371/981. The second hoard includes 111 dinars and its fractions with the latest from the reign of al-Mustansir (r. 427–487/1036–1094). The third cache is composed of nine dinars with the latest dinar from the period of al-Mustaʿli (r. 487–495/1094–1101).[23]

Two jewellery hoards were found in Jerusalem in 1984–1985 during excavations south of the Temple Mount/al-Haram al-Sharif.[24] One hoard, packed in a pan, is comprised of silver bracelets and anklets (figure IV.3.6). A second hoard includes a random assemblage of items of gold jewellery, some of Fatimid origin, others probably from Byzantium, along with a gold bird-shaped pendant of Saljuq origin (figure IV.3.7).

Figure IV.3.6 A hoard from Jerusalem comprised of silver bracelets and anklets

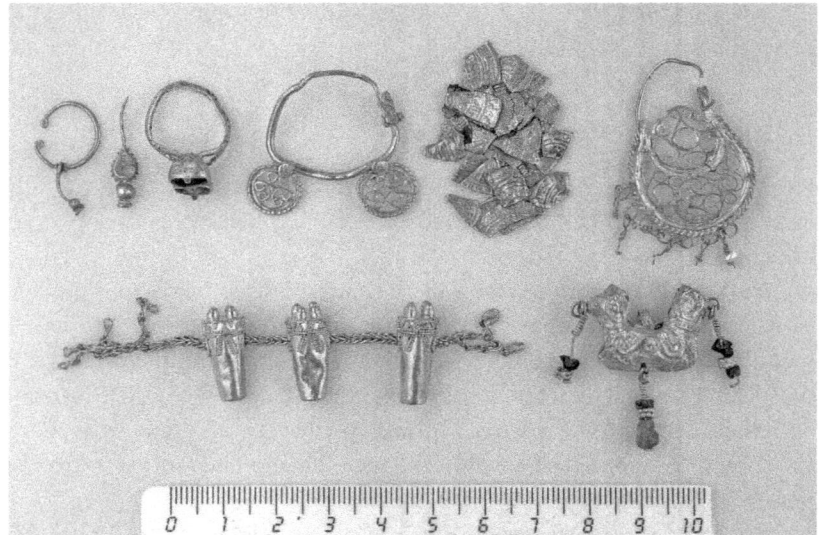

Figure IV.3.7 A hoard from Jerusalem with gold jewellery pieces, IAA

Ashkelon

Four unique pieces of jewellery were found during excavations in Ashkelon in 1986 and 1987.[25] The city was captured by the Saljuqs during the 460s/1070s but soon after, the Fatimids regained control of the city which they maintained until 548/1153, when it was conquered by the Crusaders. It was recaptured by Salah al-Din in 583/1187. During 587/1191 the city was briefly taken and refortified by the Crusaders, and then a treaty was signed between Salah al-Din and Richard I of England.[26]

These pieces made of filigree and granulation, in elaborate palmette-shaped patterns, were suggested by Rosen-Ayalon to be parts of a choker. They are dated to the end of the 6th/12th century (figure IV.3.8).

It is important to note that these pieces were not concealed but found during two different excavations that took place in an area termed 'the Fatimid street'. The initial two were found in 1986 within a few days of each other. The additional two pieces were found during the excavations of 1987 also within a few days of each other.[27] They were included in this article because of the distinct and superb workmanship and the unique details which have until now not been identified.

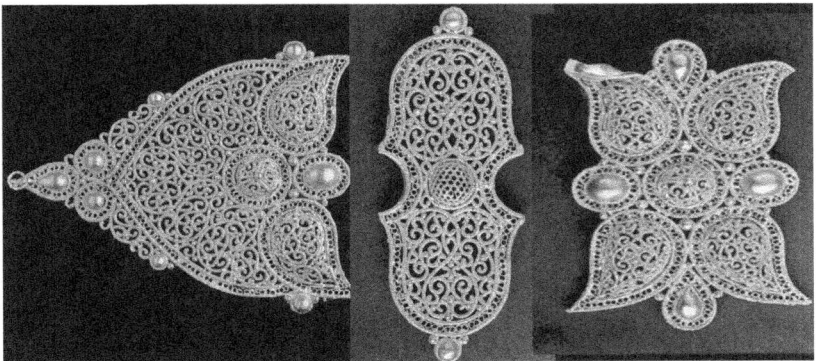

Figure IV.3.8 A hoard from Ashkelon with three elements of a choker (?), IAA

Identifying Jewellery via Dowry Lists from the Geniza

On the basis of the hoards and the terms discussed by Goitein we are able to suggest a relationship between the various jewellery pieces and the terms found in the Geniza.

Goitein discusses the term مشبّك, latticework, 'The most common way of beautifying a surface was filigree named *mushabbak* ascribed mainly to rings and rarely to other types of jewellery.'[28] The actual findings support his assumption in regard to the finger ring from Tiberias, however this technique was ubiquitous on the articles from Caesarea and Ashkelon where merchants and proprietors were involved. This discrepancy can be resolved by appreciating the fact that these pieces were rare due to their cost and do not appear in the trousseau lists discussed by Goitein.

Among the jewellery pieces found at Tiberias, the basket-shaped earrings are the most common type of earring that consolidated under Byzantine influence.[29] There are several decorative versions of the basket-shaped earring produced from varying qualities of gold. The earrings found in 1976 were made of highly refined gold. This pair of earrings is decorated with filigree wires and granules. The earrings found in 1987, in a small star-shaped clay vessel, were made of lower-quality gold mixed with copper which gives a reddish tinge to the earring. These earrings are smaller in size than the previous ones and are decorated with gold thread and a central granule. Thus, the basket-shaped earrings from Tiberias provide different versions of the type.

There is no evidence for the existence of such earrings in other parts of Palestine. Jewellery pieces composed of filigree and granulation are represented only by one finger ring.

In the case of the term محمّس, Goitein had doubts about the meaning: 'Mukhammas might denote a five-pointed star;.... Tentatively I suggest, that, an ornament representing the *khamsa*, the five fingers of the magic hand, is meant; but we must wait for actual finds from the Fatimid period for confirmation', as the *khamsa* seemed to be the most reasonable solution.[30] The basket-shaped earrings of the Islamic version, are always composed of five hemispheres soldered together, and thus are suggested to be the محمّس type of earring. It is prominent within the jewellery hoards found at Tiberias but has never been found in other regions of Palestine. This emphasises its Syrian origin.[31] The *mukhammas* earring appears in different versions with filigree and granulation, made of open work, and with granules alone.

Another common type is the crescent-shaped earring, decorated with pearls on its lower part. Its garlic-shape has provided its popular name خلاق, meaning garlic and in the trousseau lists 'garlic' refers to these earrings. The pearls, which hung from the earrings, were highly valued during the Fatimid period and were the most prized material after gold.

Also in the cache there were a few beads made of amber, which appear in the Geniza documents as *mufassala*, مفصّلة intersected with gold beads. They appear in various combinations such as necklaces, shoulder bands and forehead straps. In the dowry lists, *mufassala* appears second in importance to pearls in combination with gold. Goitein indicates that amber was hardly mentioned in trousseau lists during the 5th/11th century and, 'Then, from approximately 1100, the lists are swamped with amber ornaments'.[32] A combination of a bead made of rock crystal *billawr* بلّور inlaid with an oval-shaped piece of amber is unique . (بلّور).[33]

A pair of box-like crescent earrings and two small amulet cases are adorned with niello, *mujra bi-sawad* مجري بسواد and benedictions. Goitein states that the use of niello began in the 6th/12th century, but we have evidence of earlier use, such as the Sadaqa casket dated between 436–439/1044–1047. The amulet cases, known as *maymun*, contained writing in a magic script, intended to protect the bearer from the evil eye. The latest article within the cache is the silver amulet with all the verses of *Surat al-Ikhlas*. Based upon the palaeographic character of the text, it has been dated to the 6th/12th century.[34]

The silver hoard is comprised of four bracelets, *siwar*, decorated in the repoussé technique with a hexagonal pattern enclosing various animals such as peacocks, sprinting rabbits and deer. The bracelets were worn in pairs. In the Geniza documents they are described as *manfuh*, منفوح puffed up or swollen because of the tubular shape with pointed tips. Another term used was 'Scorpion Tail' based upon its sharp-edged tail.

A thin cord, made of silver, with bulging ends, that was also found in Ramla and Jerusalem, always appears as a single article. It had two uses: as '*laff al-mandil*, لفّ المنديل keeping the kerchief in place, namely, the kerchief which was tucked into the sleeve, and which was used not blowing the nose but for carrying money and anything else that one would keep in a pocket'.[35] Thus, the meaning of the term *hadida* is suggested by Goitein to be 'a piece for the border of the sleeve',[36] and this silver bracelet it is likely is the *hadida* حديدة.

The last article in the assemblage from Ramla is an armlet with a silver hoop and an amulet hanging from it. This is a unique piece, until now unknown. The amulet is hexagonal in shape with alternating panels displaying *Surat al-Ikhlas* verses from the Qur'an. It was commonly held that whoever learned this sura by rote was respected in the community as if he had read a third of the entire Qur'an. The hoop is delicately engraved with verse 255 from *Surat al-Baqara* which talks about the unicity of God. The presence of three verses from the Qur'an on one piece of jewellery, together with the blessing formula kept in the amulet, gives it substantial religious importance.

Conclusion

These hoards present a few significant groups of jewellery. The basket-shaped earrings are typical of Syria and Asia Minor. This group is absent from other areas in Palestine, including the coastal towns and Jerusalem.

We can suggest types typical to northern Palestine which developed under Syrian influence while the jewellery from Caesarea was composed under Egyptian cultural impact.

The different groups of jewellery produced in Palestine are geographically distinct. The north, including Tiberias was under Syrian-Byzantine influence, while the seashore, including Caesarea and Ashkelon, was under Egyptian influence. Ramla, the capital of Palestine, had a flourishing trade mainly with Egypt. It was characterised by a variety of modes of production. There is no evidence of metal or jewellery production in Jerusalem.

These hoards bear witness to the artistic quality of Fatimid art, with goldsmiths who brought jewellery production to new levels of perfection and technical refinement. Correspondingly, they reflect the political situation in Palestine during the end of the 4th/10th century to the middle of the 6th/12th century.

NOTES

1 R. Kool, 'Fatimid Hoards as Evidence of the First Crusade and the establishment of the Kingdom of Jerusalem (1099–1101)', 'Atiqot, 112 (2023), pp. 226–250.
2 Ibid., pp. 3–5.
3 D. S. Goitein, *A Mediterranean Society: The Jewish communities of the Arab world as Portrayed in the Documents of the Cairo Geniza: Volume 4, 'Daily Life'* (Berkeley, 1983), p. 202.
4 Ibid., p. 201.
5 Ibid., pp. 202–204; Lester 1991, N. Brosh, 'Two Jewelry Hoards from Tiberias', 'Atiqot, 36 (1998), pp. 1–9; M. Rosen-Ayalon, 'A Silver Ring from Medieval Islamic Times', in M. Rosen-Ayalon, ed., *Studies in Memory of Gaston Wiet* (Jerusalem, 1977), pp. 195–201; idem, 'Islamic Jewellery from Ashkelon', in N. Brosh, ed., *Jewellery and Goldsmithing in the Islamic World* (Jerusalem, 1991), pp. 9–20.
6 S. Levy and H. W. Mitchell, 'A Hoard of Gold Dinars from Ramlah', *Israel Numismatic Journal*, 3 (1965–1966), pp. 37–66.
7 Ayala Lester, 'A Fatimid Period Jewellery Hoard from the Excavations at Matzliach' (in Hebrew), *Qadmoniot*, 135 (2008), pp. 35–39.
8 R. Kool, 'Fatimid Hoards as Evidence', pp. 226–250.
9 Goitein, *A Mediterranean Society*, vol. 4, p. 201.
10 S. Levi, 'A Hoard of coins from Caesarea', *Eretz-Israel*, 7 (1964), pp. 47–68.
11 A floral-shaped pendant made of filigree granulation was found in the vicinity of Caesarea. See, Nitzan Amitai-Price, 'A Fatimid Gold Bead from Caesarea', 'Atiqot, 21 (1992), pp. 171–172.
12 N. Brosh, *Islamic Jewellery* (Jerusalem, 1987), p. 10.
13 Ibid., p. 10; Rosen-Ayalon, 'A Silver Ring', p. 200.
14 Brosh, *Islamic Jewellery*, p. 67, pl. 49.
15 G. Foerster, 'The Excavations at Tiberias', *Qadmoniot*, 10 (1977), p. 91; Lester, 'A Fatimid Hoard', pp. 224–226, figure 8.1.
16 The earring, composed of two parts, was produced by pressing a gold leaf into a mould which created a hemisphere. Such a mould was found together with the metal vessels at the Tiberias workshop which was uncovered during excavations in 1995.
17 A. Berman, 'The Coins', in D. Stacey, ed., *Excavations at Tiberias, 1973-1974: The Early Islamic Periods* (Jerusalem, 2004), p. 240.
18 Brosh, 'Two Jewelry Hoards', pp. 1–4, figures 1–8.
19 Stacey, ed., *Excavations at Tiberias*, pp. 130–132; figure 5.41, p. 146, figure 5.60.
20 David J. Wasserstein, 'The silver coins in the Mixed Hoard from Tiberias', 'Atiqot, 36 (1998), p. 21.
21 Ibid., p. 15.
22 R. Kool, 'Fatimid Hoards', pp. 226–250.
23 Ibid.
24 Ben-Dov, 'Fatimid Silver', pp. 88–91; Brosh, *Islamic Jewellery*, p. 7; Lester, 'A Fatimid Period, pp. 35–39.
25 Rosen-Ayalon, 'Islamic Jewellery from Ashkelon', in N. Brosh, ed., *Jewelry and Goldsmithing in the Islamic World* (Jerusalem, 1991), pp. 9–19.

26 A. Petersen, *The Towns of Palestine under Muslim Rule, AD 600–1600* (Oxford, 2005), pp. 83–85.
27 Rosen-Ayalon, 'Islamic Jewellery from Ashkelon', p. 9.
28 Goitein, *A Mediterranean Society*, vol. 4, pp. 211–212.
29 Lester, 'A Fatimid Period Jewellery Hoard', pp. 24–27.
30 Goitein, *A Mediterranean Society*, vol. 4, p. 215.
31 M. Jenkins and M. Keene, *Islamic Jewelry in the Metropolitan Museum of Art* (New York, 1982), nos 39 a-d; R. Hasson, *Later Islamic Jewellery* (Jerusalem, 1987), no. 96; A. Lester, 1991, figures 1, 9–10; N. Brosh, 'Two Jewelry Hoards from Tiberias', figures 3–4.
32 Goitein, *A Mediterranean Society*, p. 207.
33 Ibid., pp. 223–224.
34 Rosen-Ayalon, 'A Silver Ring', pp. 105–201.
35 Goitein, *A Mediterranean Society*, p. 219.
36 Ibid.

4

The Fatimid Rock Crystal Ewers: Innovation or Variation? A Historical and Iconographical Investigation

Marcus Pilz

The thin-walled Islamic rock crystal vessels, mostly attributed to Fatimid workshops, are without any doubt the technical pinnacle of rock crystal carving in the medieval period. Their complex relief cutting and extremely thin walls represent a level of technical sophistication in the processing of the delicate material, hardly reached again at any later period in history. Starting with these superlatives, it is not surprising that the most elaborate pieces of that production, a group of ewers, have been constantly at the centre of research ever since Gaston Migeon published a core group of six vessels in 1907.[1] Starting with – at the time – the only datable ewer of al-'Aziz in Venice, he added the ones in the Louvre, the Victoria and Albert (V&A) and the Mufflon ewer from San Marco, photographs of which were included. Further reference to the pieces in Fermo and Florence completed the group, until the six became the 'magnificent seven' with the appearance of the Francis Mills ewer on the art market in 2008, a piece which was finally acquired by Edmund de Unger for his Keir Collection.[2]

Taking the al-'Aziz ewer with its undisputed dating (r. 386–365/975–996) as the reference point, all ewers and subsequently all Islamic rock crystal carvings from medieval times were seen as of Fatimid origin without any attempt to define what this attribution meant in terms of style, technique and development. The huge iconographical and technical variety of the surviving material was widely ignored – and could be easily ignored since there was no comprehensive catalogue of the pieces allowing for easy and direct comparison. The only relevant publication in this regard was Carl Johan Lamm's two-volume work *Mittelalterliche Gläser und Steinschneidearbeiten* from 1929/30. While it hugely expanded the known material of mostly smaller pieces, it provided limited information since most of the objects were only depicted in drawings.

For a century there seemed to be no doubt that all these vastly diverse vessels and objects were created between the late 4th/10th and the mid-5th/11th century at one and the same location: Fatimid Cairo, with a masterpiece like the al-ʿAziz ewer as a kind of founding artwork.[3] This simplistic view was widely accepted and basically drowned all attempts at a more differentiated picture of the development of the Islamic rock crystal industry.

Voices calling for a revision came early on from preeminent figures in the field such as Ernst Kühnel, Carl Johann Lamm or Kurt Erdmann, but they remained more or less at the margins of research history, never receiving wider attention.[4]

The stylistic diversity of the entire corpus of surviving pieces is somewhat mirrored in the 'magnificent seven' ewers, as David Storm Rice showed back in 1956, when he used the different designs of palmette trees on the fronts of the ewers to suggest a chronological series.[5] In fact the variations in design go much deeper than just the arrangement of tendrils, half-palmettes and palmettes. These iconographic elements themselves already display significant stylistic as well as technical differences and so allow for the distinction between two stylistic groups.[6] One group, comprising the al-ʿAziz ewer in Venice and the Museo degli Argenti vessel in Florence, is certainly of Fatimid origin. Both show a similar, exceptionally delicate linear design, with rims and tendrils having in fact an almost quadratic cross-section. Equally intricate is the carving of every single detail of the floral elements (figure IV.4.1a).

The second group encompasses the Mufflon ewer in Venice, the one in the V&A and, with some variations, the Keir Collection ewer. All three exhibit related stylistic features such as a more flat-angled and shallower execution of the palmettes. Instead of being individually carved out, specific details are just distinguished by repetitive linear and slant cuts, maintaining a closed triangular outline (figure IV.4.1b). The two remaining ewers again display different patterns.

The piece at Fermo seems to stand somewhere between the two styles mentioned above; sharing an organically flowing tendril structure, while the individual leaf designs display examples with closed, but rounded outlines (figure IV.4.1c) as well as others closer to the Fatimid design. Finally, the Louvre ewer stands apart from the others in its overall

Figure IV.4.1 Details of the cut decoration of ewers, a) Tesoro di San Marco, Venice; b) Victoria and Albert Museum, London.

Figure IV.4.1 (Continued), Details of the cut decoration of ewers, c) Museo Diocesano, Fermo; d) Musée du Louvre, Paris.

strangely crude design and carving, for instance the sharply backwards bending tips of the half-palmettes and inorganic, edgy structures with kite-shaped medallions on the sides or the upper part of the frontal palmette tree, while the vessel's thinly carved walls reflect the quality of the other ewers (figure IV.4.1d). Equally unusual is the horizontal frieze of two wavebands with half-palmettes on the sides.

So how can we interpret these differences? They are surely markers of a chronological development, representing as mentioned the pinnacle of craftsmanship in their respective periods or regions. So far, only the two first-mentioned Fatimid pieces are datable. Due to their inscriptions one can narrow down the production to about 35 years in the late 4th/10th and early 5th/11th century, spanning roughly 30 per cent of the assumed total output of the Fatimid court workshops at Cairo surviving, if we accept the looting of the caliphal treasury and the turmoil that led to it as the end of this strand of production.[7]

Before discussing an alternative sequence of these works and their stylistic development, including further objects of the same level of quality, I would like to outline our current knowledge on the existence and production of rock crystal vessels at the courts of the Abbasids and Fatimids. The following observations and deliberations are the result of a thorough, five-year study of the material for my PhD thesis. Due to the limited space of this article, it can provide only a short, focused summary of the results published in 2021.[8]

A History of Evidence and Context

Up to the 1930s the story seemed clear. There were two pieces of unquestionable Fatimid origin and there was one source, apparently telling where those and all the other rock crystal carvings came from.[9] The source is a report of the looting of the Fatimid palaces in Cairo between 459/1067 and 461/1069 during a famine revolt. Besides many other treasures it mentions thousands of rock crystal vessels, plain and decorated and even one ewer with the name of the Imam-caliph al-ʿAziz on it, which subsequently were sold by the looters. The historian al-Maqrizi (d. 845/1442) cited this passage from an earlier source, *The Book of Gifts and Rarities*, which was probably written in the 5th/11th century by al-Rashid b. al-Zubayr.[10] *The Book of Gifts and Rarities* itself however was thought to be lost until a surviving copy was discovered and finally edited in 1959. A selected English translation was published only in 1996, opening up a treasure trove of new evidence on the history of the Islamic rock crystal industry for a wider audience.[11] And according to the *Book of Gifts and Rarities*, rock crystal vessels, namely bowls, were already in use for serving food at the court of the Abbasid caliph al-Mutawakkil (r. 232–247/847–861).[12] Around the same time an anonymous Abbasid author, most probably from the circle of Hunayn b. Ishaq, mentions in his 'book of stones' that rock crystal was used to make vessels of great value.[13] Taking these mentions as facts, it can be said that the craftsmen of the 3rd/9th century were already able to create relatively large vessels. The origins of this production might be even older and could well be rooted in Sasanian or Byzantine workshop traditions.[14] One indication of such a longstanding tradition is the mention of beakers made of jasper, bearing the name of the fifth Abbasid caliph, Harun al-Rashid (r. 170–193/786–809), in the Fatimid treasury.[15] This points to a start of the production as early as the second half of the 2nd/8th century, as well as to the Byzantine stone carving industry that preferred coloured stones to rock crystal.[16]

If the Abbasid stone-carving industry was already in existence in the 2nd/8th century, it would not have flourished for a long time, since the death of Harun al-Rashid was followed by a vicious struggle for power between his sons, al-Amin and al-Maʿmun. During this civil war (195–203/811–819) Baghdad was besieged for months by the latter son, leaving the caliphal palace a ruin never to be rebuilt.[17] After this deep crisis the situation stabilised, leading to a period of great cultural and artistic achievements epitomised in the construction of Samarra as a new caliphal residence with its extensive and lavishly decorated palaces.[18] Findings of cut glass at the site document the enduring high level of skill in this craft that was probably connected to rock crystal workshops elsewhere, producing the vessels for the court of al-Mutawakkil.[19] But this period of prosperity also ended in turmoil and a new civil war lasting from 251/865 to 256/870.[20]

Thinking about possible other places of production in this early phase, one must mention Nishapur, which is famous for its rich glass findings.[21] It might also have been the site of a rock crystal workshop, since an anecdote from the capture of Nishapur in 259/873 mentions many precious rock crystal vessels in the palace treasury.[22]

The next sources for the presence of rock crystal at the Abbasid court date from 312/924 and 327/939, when the caliphs al-Muqtadir and al-Radi made gifts of a large bowl, a bottle and a beaker.[23] Al-Radi is otherwise described as an avid collector of rock crystal objects, and when he died in 329/940 many such pieces were found in his treasury.[24]

But the clearest source for the longstanding and well-developed Abbasid tradition of utilising rock crystal vessels is without doubt the chapter on this material in the *Book of Precious Stones* by al-Biruni (d. after 442/1050). He describes an extensive industry in the port city of Basra, which can only be seen as the quantitative climax of a production that served not just the court but provided a broader prosperous social class with a wide range of objects: from chessmen and other gaming pieces to various kinds of vessels.[25] Al-Biruni mentions for example Madagascar and the Maldives Islands as well as Kashmir as mining sites of the raw material. Archaeological findings in the last decade have supported al-Biruni's account by identifying trading posts for rock crystal from Madagascar and the Maldives, datable to the 3rd/9th–5th/11th centuries.[26] The discovery of the wreck of a 4th/10th century trading ship in the waters near Java has shown that rock crystal was indeed also part of the trade between the Abbasid empire and East Asia, since it contained not only Chinese ceramics and Abbasid glassware but also raw and carved pieces of rock crystal.[27]

Compared to this evidence, we have very few sources for a production in Fatimid times. *The Book of Gifts and Rarities* mentions rock crystal vessels in a Fatimid context just twice; and the Persian traveller Nasir-i Khusraw, who visited Cairo between 439/1047 and 442/1050, states only once that he saw rock crystal objects in the lamp bazaar of Fustat.[28] And even a Cairene author like al-Tamimi, a contemporary of the Imam-caliph al-ʿAziz for whom one of the famous ewers was crafted, does not mention anything regarding a rock crystal industry in the Fatimid capital in his work on stones.[29] This is even more surprising if we remember the state of research outlined at the beginning, where precisely this period is thought to have been the climax of the Fatimid rock crystal industry.

Some Observations on Technique and Design

In view of the sources and the timeline of Abbasid and Fatimid history, the technical evolution of rock crystal carving appears by no means a continuous development.[30] Too many episodes of crisis and conflict interrupted periods of stability, which are necessary for local workshops to establish and develop a sophisticated craft like the carving of rock crystal into fine thin-walled vessels, and secure the long-distance trade in raw materials. The creation of objects like the famous ewers was not so much a question of certain tools or tricks as of empirical knowledge and long experience, handed down in practice from master to apprentice. It furthermore needed a constant supply of costly imported materials like corundum and blocks of rock crystal in sufficient size and quality. Indispensable for the technical development that led to the production of the ewers was also a patron able to tolerate the loss of dozens of costly blocks of rock crystal that broke during the endeavour to create vessels with ever thinner walls. The Fatimid ewer at the Palazzo Pitti gives an idea of the highest level of mastery, with walls as thin as 1 to 2 millimetres.[31] The hollowing and ornament cutting of the ewers with their pear-shaped bodies already demanded remarkable skills and even more so if the vessel was to have a broad body with a long, narrow neck.[32]

Compared to such masterpieces, the majority of the surviving rock crystal vessels are technically much simpler. These smaller vessels were decorated and polished first before they received a cylindrical or slightly widened cavity, largely avoiding the risk of breaking during the cutting process. Taking these dramatic differences into consideration, the existence of two parallel productions seems most probable. One of them under courtly patronage that created the extremely thin-walled vessels and a number of iconographically closely related pieces, and then a much larger number of workshops producing the many small, less sophisticated flasks and gaming pieces for a wider market of affluent clients. The latter might in fact resemble the kind of mass production mentioned by al-Biruni.

A close comparison of the iconographic and technical features of these vessels reveals not only a surprising diversity, but also a certain disconnectedness between the ewers and the majority of the smaller, less sophisticated pieces. This can be clearly seen by the design of the most common decorative feature, the half-palmette with triangular outline. The decorative variety ranges from simple parallel lines in different alignments to a more naturalistic vegetal structure consisting of a long leaf arising from the volute, with a second small section filling the remaining space between these two elements. While the particularly delicately carved half-palmettes of the Fatimid ewers might be a courtly development from these much simpler patterns, it seems there was no influence in the opposite direction, since none of the smaller vessels displays a response to this refinement. The fan-shaped half-palmettes of the second group, defined above, have absolutely no connection to any of the smaller and less sophisticated pieces. Is this fact an indication of an extremely exclusive courtly production?

Looking at cut glass vessels as being the closest related comparative medium, they are largely detached from the particular decorative styles of the rock crystal ewers, while in contrast the various 'lower' versions of the half-palmette appear quite frequently on glass vessels and their fragments.[33] The few exceptions to that observation underline the exclusivity of a courtly setting or commission, as shown by the archaeological finds excavated in Samarra. On these vessel fragments one finds fan-shaped half-palmettes, on two shards even in the context of hatched tendrils just as on the rock crystal ewers in Venice and London.[34]

Patterns of Transmission

The glass findings from Samarra provide the first clues in establishing a chronology of the courtly tradition of stone carving in Abbasid times. Closest to the pattern on the glass fragments is actually a boat-shaped object in the Hermitage Museum in St. Petersburg, which clearly belongs to the stylistic group of the two ewers in Venice and London.[35] On the precious stone carved object, the motif of the fan-shaped half-palmette is additionally embellished by small facets and precise linear cuts, adding to the sparkling effects of the surface. The stylistic connection to the courtly arts of Samarra was already noticed by Carl Johann Lamm, but never further explored.[36] Together with further related vessels of the same level of quality, they could well represent Abbasid courtly production documented under the reign of al-Mutawakkil. The other pieces include an extremely delicate fragment in Copenhagen as well as two solid carved pieces, whose decoration belongs nevertheless to the same workshop: one in the Keir Collection in Dallas and one at the V&A in London.[37] Including four other, more distant pieces, the Keir Collection ewer in Dallas, a beaker in the British Museum in London, a piece in the cathedral treasury of Reims and the fragment of a globular bottle in the cathedral treasury of Astorga in Spain (figure IV.4.2a), the group consists altogether of ten objects, which are distinctively different from the Fatimid ewers but related to objects and patterns found at Samarra.[38]

Another link to this attribution is a characteristic frieze of leaves, connected by circular elements and sometimes called the 'Samarra frieze'. The appearance of this motif enlarges the group of presumably Abbasid hard stone vessels by two more pieces: An agate bowl at the Louvre and a large cylindrical rock crystal vase at the treasury of San Marco (figure IV.4.2b). An isolated element of this pattern, a peculiar u-shaped motif of two slender lancet-like leaves connected by a circular element, furthermore re-links these pieces to the above-mentioned vessels in St. Petersburg and Astorga.[39]

But maybe the most 'Abbasid' rock crystal carving is at the same time entirely singular, since it resembles a typical pattern of high-end Abbasid

Figure IV.4.2 Details of cut decoration of vessels, a) Museo Catedralicio, Astorga; b) Tesoro di San Marco, Venice.

glassware, something otherwise completely unknown. The piece might have been initially the upper part of a rather large globular bottle with a slightly conical neck (figure IV.4.3). Combined with a 13th-century European rock crystal bowl, it was re-used as the foot of a chalice.[40] All that remains of the decoration are rims, which typically separate different parts of the surface, and a row of unconnected stylised ibexes. The execution of these animals with hollowed bodies, while the heads are just structured by linear and slant cuts, can also be seen on Abbasid glass fragments found in Samarra, but resembles the depictions on the V&A ewer and the Mufflon ewer in Venice as well.[41]

Within the proposed group of Abbasid ewers, the Keir Collection ewer in Dallas stands out in many respects as indicated above. It was clearly

Figure IV.4.3 Fragment of an Abbasid vessel mounted as the foot of a chalice, Musée du Louvre, Paris.

influenced by pieces of the suggested 'Samarra Group', but in comparison its execution is rather stiff and less fluent.

The half-palmettes on that piece are in many cases strangely reduced, while the head of the cheetah is worked in an undecided way. Neither is it just structured by linear and slant cuts as on the other two related pieces, nor is it hollowed like on the al-'Aziz ewer, whose cheetah depictions show otherwise surprising similarities. The surface is instead carved like one large depression, leaving the eye-line as if sinking in towards the edges.

Assuming that the Abbasid and Fatimid workshop traditions are linked by craftsmen who migrated from Basra or even Baghdad to the rising new capital Cairo this would not only explain the stunning quality of a piece like the al-'Aziz ewer, but also define this new workshop as a late branch of the courtly Abbasid tradition. This said, a stylistic development from one group to the other is possible and likely: from a piece like the V&A ewer to the al-'Aziz ewer. From flat palmettes and half-palmettes with closed outlines to a design with much more differentiated, individualised elements. One piece fitting into such a line of stylistic development is the flask in the treasury of San Lorenzo in Florence (figure IV.4.4a). The

Figure IV.4.4 Details of the cut decoration of vessels, a) Tesoro di San Lorenzo, Florence.

Figure IV.4.4 (Continued), Details of the cut decoration of vessels, b) the Freer Gallery, Washington, DC.

elements of the half-palmettes have distinctively more individual volume here than the flat structures on the Samarra-related pieces, even though the small spandrels between the tips of the leaf elements are not yet cut out as on the Fatimid pieces. Similarly worked half-palmettes can be found on two more solid pieces in Washington (figure IV.4.4b) and Quedlinburg.[42]

Another object that can be seen as an example of such an intermediary style is the ewer at the cathedral treasury of Fermo. It features very different executions of half-palmettes side by side. One version appears to be drawn with an outline, following the curves of the three canonical parts of this motif: the volute, the elongated top leaf and the smaller leaf in between (figure IV.4.1c). In other examples the interspaces between these elements are perfectly carved out as on the Fatimid ewers. The globular vessel in Astorga, mentioned above, could be a predecessor to the Fermo ewer, as could the bottle in the cathedral treasury of Halberstadt.[43]

Several more objects fit in the gap between the proposed 3rd/9th-century Abbasid works and their Fatimid successors, but the surviving pieces are so scarce and in many respects so singular that it is at this point impossible to identify an exact sequence bridging the gap in a comprehensive way. Considering the astounding workmanship and fragility of most of the objects mentioned, their survival is a miracle in itself. But the fact that the Samarra-related group survived in three largely intact thin-walled pieces of significant size, with four to seven further pieces documenting the wider range of this production, is definitely strong evidence for the importance an early workshop tradition. All later stylistic evolutions on this high level of quality survive in no more than two significant intact examples.[44]

Abbasid, Fatimid and in between

While the early beginnings and initial influences of the Abbasid stone carving tradition are shrouded in mystery, they were nevertheless embedded in a longstanding transmission of technical knowledge, reaching back into Antiquity. With the expansion of the Islamic empire into Byzantine and especially Sasanian territories, the new ruling class undoubtedly encountered and appreciated the hardstone carvings produced in these lands.[45] The presence of such objects and their considerable prestige in the environment of Late Antiquity might have generated the incentives to establish workshops that were able to produce vessels rivalling those of the Byzantines. The mention of jasper beakers bearing the name of Harun al-Rashid could be an initial indication of such a workshop, whose workers might well have been recruited from workshops still active in the former Byzantine and Sasanian territories of the empire or even from Byzantium itself.

Such initial influences are visible in a vessel not yet included in this discussion due to its singularity. Preserved in the treasury of San Lorenzo in Florence, it is the fragment of a pitcher with a cylindrical body, surmounted by a slightly conical neck (figure IV.4.5). The flat handle is lost, but its traces are still clearly recognisable. The cutting of the body shows four pairs of oval medallions, with the depiction of a bird tightly

Figure IV.4.5 Fragment of an Abbasid (?) rock crystal pitcher, Tesoro di San Lorenzo, Florence.

fitted into each one. While the motif of animals set within beaded roundels is a design well known from Sasanian works of art, the stylisation of the animals themselves displays many features familiar from Abbasid cut glass.[46] The features of the design such as ridges to separate decorated and undecorated sections as well as different parts of the vessel (body, shoulder and neck or the separation of a plain section under the handle) that were recurring elements on all later pieces, are already fully developed here. The wings of the bird, structured just by parallel lines, might also represent the earliest stage of the design of half-palmettes, as used on a number of other rock crystal carvings, most prominently a cup, mounted since about 1014 on the pulpit of the Emperor Henry II in Aachen cathedral (figure IV.4.6a).[47] On this piece, not only the design of the half-palmettes

Figure IV.4.6 Details of two cups, a) Aachen Cathedral Treasury.

Figure IV.4.6 (Continued), Details of two cups, b) Treasury of the Residenz, Munich.

but also the composition of the entire decoration makes an almost archaic impression, being cut in a much rougher way than the vessel in Florence.

By comparison, a second surviving cup, now preserved in the treasury of the Munich residence, has a rather different appearance, with more dynamic and organically spreading tendrils (figure IV.4.6b). Here, very different designs of half-palmettes appear side by side,[48] from simple ones, still closely related to the above-mentioned examples in Florence and Aachen, to fully developed ones in the Fatimid style. And such a combination is by no means unique. There is in fact a fragmented vessel at the Abbey treasury of Conque in France and a shard at the British Museum in London.[49] All three pieces are documents of impressive craftsmanship, with the thin-walled vessels in Munich and Conque even competing with the output of the proposed courtly workshops of the Abbasid and Fatimid caliphs. But their mixed motifs as well as their

Figure IV.4.7 Detail of the cut decorations of a rock crystal fragment. Musée Cluny, Paris.

arrangement hardly fit into the chronological development suggested above.

Equally separate is the Louvre ewer (figure IV.4.1d) and its close relatives. Together with a small bottle at San Marco in Venice and four fragments mounted in an early 7th/13th-century casket at the Musée Cluny in Paris (figure IV.4.7), this is a rather significant group. Like the former group of objects, they were made in workshops capable of producing these choice thin-walled vessels, but the patterns and even more their execution are very different.

Even if the attribution of these last two groups must remain open in the current state of research, they nevertheless document the value of and opportunities offered by a systematic close comparison of the surviving objects. Such groups of several pieces with widely similar designs were surely not the spontaneous expression of a single artist but represent the characteristic style of a particular workshop, most probably in the vicinity of a prominent court. To locate or at least narrow down these further possible sites of production is a task for further research. But identifying these groups is the first step on the way. With every new discovery of hitherto unpublished fragments or complete pieces in church treasuries or museums the chance increases to close the existing gaps in the iconographical development and to better understand the story the objects themselves can tell us.

NOTES

1 Gaston Migeon, *Manuel d'Art Musulman*, vol. 2, *Les Arts plastiques et industriels* (Paris, 1907), pp. 372–376. The ewer in Florence was at the time still exhibited in the museum of natural history before it was later transferred to the Museo degli Argenti.
2 Christie's, *Art of the Islamic and Indian Worlds* (Auction cat., Tuesday 7 October 2008) (London, 2008). For images of the seven see Marcus Pilz, *Transparente Schätze. Der abbasidische und fatimidische Bergkristallschnitt und seine Werke* (Darmstadt, 2021), pp. 212–215.
3 See Ernst Kühnel's introduction to rock crystal in the groundbreaking exhibition catalogue *Meisterwerke muhammedanischer Kunst* in Munich in 1910, cited and translated in Marcus Pilz, 'Beyond Fatimid: The Iconography of Medieval Islamic Rock Crystal Vessels and the Question of Dating', in Cynthia Hahn and Avinoam Shalem, ed., *Seeking Transparency* (Berlin, 2020), p. 170.
4 See Pilz, 'Beyond Fatimid', pp. 170–171.
5 David Storm Rice, 'A Datable Islamic Rock Crystal', *Oriental Art*, 2 (1956), pp. 85–93, pp. 92–93.
6 Cf. Pilz, 'Beyond Fatimid'.
7 The Fatimid court settled in Cairo in Ramadan 362/June 973. In 365/975 the Imam-caliph al-ʿAziz, whose name is inscribed on the ewer in Venice, ascended the throne. The second Fatimid ewer in Florence was made in 400/1010 at the latest. See Pilz, *Transparente Schätze*, pp. 71–75. For the circumstances and sources reporting the looting of 459/1067, see Heinz Halm, *Die Kalifen von Kairo. Die Fatimiden in Ägypten 973–1074* (Munich, 2003), pp. 404–414.
8 Pilz, *Transparente Schätze*. A first preliminary presentation of the results was given at a conference in Florence in 2017, cf. Pilz, 'Beyond Fatimid'.
9 The second inscribed and therefore datable object is a rock crystal ring in the Germanisches Nationalmuseum in Nuremberg (Inv. KG 695, see Pilz, *Transparente Schätze*, p. 74). The inscription mentions the name of the Imam-caliph al-Zahir (r. 411–427/1021–1036). Since this object bears no further decoration, it can be set aside in any discussion of stylistic developments.
10 The report of the looting was first translated by Étienne Marc Quatremère de Quincy in 1811 and newly published in 1935 by Paul Kahle, who based his translation on four manuscripts in Paris, Istanbul and Gotha. Paul Kahle, 'Die Schätze der Fatimiden', *Zeitschrift der Deutschen Morgenländischen Gesellschaft*, 14 (1935), pp. 329–362, pp. 333–334.
11 Ghada al-Hijjawi al-Qaddumi, tr., *The Book of Gifts and Rarities* (Cambridge, 1996).
12 al-Qaddumi, *Book of Gifts*, p. 79, §34.
13 This work of a 'pseudo-Aristotle' is already cited by other authors of the 3rd/9th century, see Julius Ruska, tr., *Das Steinbuch des Aristoteles* (Heidelberg, 1912). For the question of attribution see, Samar Najm Abul Huda, tr., *Arab Roots of Gemology. Ahmad ibn Yusuf Al Tifaschi's Best Thoughts on the Best of Stones* (Lanham and London, 1998), p. 3; Lynn Thorndike, *A History of Magic and Experimental Science*, vol. 1 (New York and London, 1964), pp. 653–655 and Manfred Ullmann, *Die Medizin im Islam* (Leiden, 1970), p. 128.
14 Pilz, *Transparente Schätze*, pp. 49–59.
15 al-Qaddumi, *Book of Gifts*, p. 233, § 381.
16 For an overview of the current knowledge of Byzantine and Sasanian stone carving traditions see Pilz, *Transparente Schätze*, pp. 47–56.
17 Guy Le Strange, *Baghdad during the Abbasid Caliphate* (Oxford, 1901), pp. 32–33 and 303–305 as well as Andrew Marsham, *Rituals of Islamic Monarchy. Accession and Succession in the First Muslim Empire* (Edinburgh, 2009), pp. 253, 259–261.

18 The residence at Samarra lasted for less than 60 years, between 221/836 and 279/892. See, Alastair Northedge, *The Historical Topography of Samarra* (London, 2005).

19 For the glass findings in Samarra see Carl Johan Lamm, *Das Glas von Samarra* (Berlin, 1928); Jens Kröger, *Nishapur. Glass of the Early Islamic Period* (New York, 1995), pp. 6–7 and idem, 'The Samarra Bowl with the half-palmette animals reconsidered', in Warwick Ball and Leonard Harrow, ed., *Cairo to Kabul: Afghan and Islamic Studies presented to Ralph Pinder-Wilson* (London, 2002), pp. 151–156.

20 Le Strange, *Baghdad*, pp. 311–312 and Marsham, *Rituals*, pp. 283–286.

21 See for example Kröger, *Nishapur*, pp. 1–37.

22 Yaʿqub b. al-Layth al-Saffar (r. 247–265/861–879) captured Nishapur in 259/873, ousting Muhammad b. Tahir (r. 248–259/862–873). See Paul Kahle, 'Bergkristall, Glas und Glasflüsse nach dem Steinbuch von el-Beruni', *Zeitschrift der Deutschen Morgenländischen Gesellschaft*, 90 (1936), pp. 339–340.

23 al-Qaddumi, *Book of Gifts*, p. 132, § 126 and pp. 89–99, § 65.

24 Carl Johan Lamm, *Mittelalterliche Gläser und Steinschnittarbeiten aus dem Nahen Osten* (Berlin, 1929/30), vol. I, p. 515 and al-Qaddumi, *Book of Gifts*, p. 191, § 244. Compare with p. 217, § 333 mentioning further rock crystal vessels in the bequest of the Imam-caliph's favourite, Abu'l-Husayn Baykam.

25 Kahle, *Bergkristall*, p. 333.

26 Kahle, *Bergkristall*, p. 332; for the archaeological evidence see Stéphane Pradines, 'Madagascar, the Source of the Abbasid and Fatimid Rock Crystals: New Evidence from Archaeological Investigations in East Africa', in Cynthia Hahn and Avinoam Shalem, ed., *Seeking Transparency* (Berlin, 2020), pp. 35–50. as well as Mark Horton and Nicole Boivin et al., 'East Africa as a Source for Fatimid Rock Crystal. Workshops from Kenya to Madagascar', in Alexandra Hilger, Susanne Greiff and Dieter Quast, ed., *Gemstones in the first Millenium AD* (Mainz, 2017), pp. 103–311.

27 Horst Hubertus Liebner, *The Siren of Cirebon: a tenth century trading vessel lost in the Java Sea* (Leeds, 2014), pp. 85–214, esp. 173–177. The worked pieces contained a fish-shaped vessel as well as gaming pieces.

28 See Pilz, *Transparente Schätze*, pp. 69–70. The *Book of Gifts and Rarities* mentions rock crystal vessels only for the mid-5th/11th century in the inheritance of a daughter of Imam-caliph al-Muʿizz and later on in the Treasury. See, al-Qaddumi, *Book of Gifts*, p. 224, § 357–358.

29 al-Qaddumi, *Book of Gifts*, pp. 224, § 357–358; Uto von Melzer, tr., *Safarname. Das Reisetagebuch des persischen Dichters Nasir-i Husrau* (Graz, 1993), p. 63; Jutta Schönfeld, tr., *Über die Steine. Das 14. Kapitel aus dem „Kitab al-Mursid" des Muhammad ibn Ahmad at-Tamimi, nach dem Pariser Manuskript herausgegeben, übersetzt und kommentiert* (Freiburg, 1976), p. 98. Al-Tamimi entered the service of Yaʿqub b. Killis, vizier under al-ʿAziz, in 359/970 and died in 369/980.

30 Pilz, *Transparente Schätze*, pp. 77–80.

31 The ewer at Palazzo Pitti (Inv. 1917, No. 2) broke into more than 80 pieces in 1998 which allowed for an exact measurement of the fragments, see Federica Cappelli, *Una brocchetta Fatimida in cristallo di rocca dal Museo degli Argenti. Problematiche di intervento* (Florence, 2004), p. 36. A fragment in the David Collection (Inv. 5/1987) is in parts even thinner than 1 millimetre.

32 Compare for example the rock crystal bottles in San Lorenzo (Florence), San Marco (Venice) or the treasury of Halberstadt (see Pilz, *Transparente Schätze*, plates T8, T10, T12).

33 Pilz, *Transparente Schätze*, pp. 110–117.

34 Ibid., pp. 68–69.

35 Ibid., p. 217, T23 (State Hermitage Museum, Inv. EG 938) and p. 212, T1–T2. Compare Pilz, 'Beyond Fatimid', p. 176, pl. 25a.

36 Lamm, *Mittelalterliche Gläser*, pl. 68,5 and pp. 199–200. The plates were published in a separate volume.
37 Pilz, *Transparente Schätze*, p. 218, T.25, p. 220, T37 and T36. Highly unusual is another ewer at Copenhagen with no decoration at all on its body, while the handle features a closely related pattern. Cf. Pilz, 'Beyond Fatimid', pl. 25b.
38 Pilz, *Transparente Schätze*, p. 213, T3, p. 216, T13, p. 217, T20 and Manuela Beer, ed., *Magic Rock Crystal* (Munich, 2022), p. 27.
39 This frieze motif appears in various materials such as stucco and marble, but also on several glass fragments excavated at Samarra. For comparative material and the mentioned pieces in Paris and Venice, see Pilz, *Transparente Schätze*, pp. 62–65. The isolated motif can be found around the neck of the vessel in St. Petersburg and as a central element of the decoration on the piece in Astorga. See also the tail end of the cheetahs on the de Unger ewer.
40 Coming from the French royal collections, the piece is now exhibited in the Louvre (Inv. MR 296). The current mounting can be dated to the 17th century but now unused drillings point to earlier uses. See Pilz, *Transparente Schätze*, pp. 67–69 and Daniel Alcouffe, ed., *Les Gemmes de la Couronne* (Paris, 2001), pp. 110–111 and 115, No. 30.
41 For related glass objects see Pilz, *Transparente Schätze*, pp. 66–69.
42 Pilz, *Transparente Schätze*, p. 215, T9, p. 220, T38 and p. 229, T99.
43 Pilz, *Transparente Schätze*, p. 214, T6, p. 216, T13 and T12.
44 A more or less continuous stylistic development can only be reconstructed for the workshops specialised in the more moderate, solidly cut pieces with simply drilled cavities or rather thick walls. Pilz *Transparente Schätze*, pp. 110–119. Compare also the cup that is mounted on the pulpit of the Aachen cathedral or the two vessels preserved in the cathedral treasury of Capua. See Claudia Höhl and Felix Prinz, et al., *Islam in Europa 1000–1250* (Regensburg, 2022), pp. 92–100.
45 *The Book of Gifts and Rarities* reports, for example, a large rock-crystal bowl in the possession of the Umayyad caliph al-Walid (r. 86–96/705–715). He is also mentioned as donating a rock-crystal lamp for the great mosque of Damascus. Al-Qaddumi, *Book of Gifts*, p. 177, § 210, p. 179, § 216 and Avinoam Shalem, 'Fountains of Light: The Meaning of Medieval Islamic Rock Crystal Lamps', *Muqarnas*, 11 (1994), p. 2.
46 Pilz, *Transparente Schätze*, pp. 111–112. See for example the bottom of the so-called Corning bowl and further examples from that collection in David Whitehouse, *Islamic Glass in The Corning Museum of Glass*, vol. 1 (Corning, NY, 2010), nos 296, 308, 424, 430 and 431.
47 Pilz, *Transparente Schätze*, p. 216, T18; compare also Höhl, *Islam in Europa*, pp. 92–94.
48 Ibid., p. 216, T19.
49 Ibid., p. 216, T11 and p. 218, T26. The fragment in London (Inv. 1959,0515.1) is especially interesting, since it was left unpolished, providing a unique insight into the production process.

5

Fatimid Archaeology and Excavations in Cairo: What We Really Know about the Ismaili Capital City and Fustat

Stéphane Pradines

Time flies very quickly and in 1998, I was a young doctoral student doing my research under the direction of my late Professor, Marianne Barrucand, when she organised a conference on Fatimid art in Paris, and here we are nearly twenty-five years later in London. What have we learnt about the state of the field in Fatimid studies at this conference? This paper is about our ignorance about Fatimid Cairo and the importance of archaeology. That statement might seem a bit provocative, but in fact, most of what we know about Fatimid material culture comes from Fustat, and not from al-Qahira. If the history of Cairo is very well known in Arabic and Latin sources, its archaeology is much less so. In fact, we should talk about the cities of Cairo, because the process of urbanisation of this gigantic agglomeration took place in several stages, marked each time by the creation of new urban centres during nearly 1500 years (figure IV.5.1). Islamic Cairo, from Bab al-Nasr to the Mosque of Ibn Tulun, is an entity that designates al-Qahira of the Fatimids, as well as al-Askar and al-Qata'i' the Abbasid developments. This 'Cairo' corresponds to the capital occupied by the Mamluks and the Ottomans. This definition of Islamic Cairo effectively excludes Coptic Cairo, that is to say the churches located in the ancient Byzantine fort of Babylon, Qasr al-Sham. Coptic Cairo is also called Old Cairo with reference to the first Arab city of Fustat. After the capture of the fort in 20/641 during the Arab conquest, a pigeon came to rest on the roof of the tent of the commander of the Muslim forces, 'Amr b. al-'As who saw it as a propitious sign for the foundation of a new capital for Egypt, an Arab capital located on the eastern bank of the Nile, which therefore would be quite close to Medina by land. Fustat, 'the city of tents', was then created. Since 1980, a larger administrative entity has been created that encompasses the two urban realities of Islamic Cairo and Old Cairo. This is Historic Cairo, protected by the World Heritage List of UNESCO. No serious archaeological excavations have been undertaken on the Abbasid cities of al-Askar and al-Qata'i', built between 132–292/750–905 and centred around the famous Mosque of Ibn Tulun.

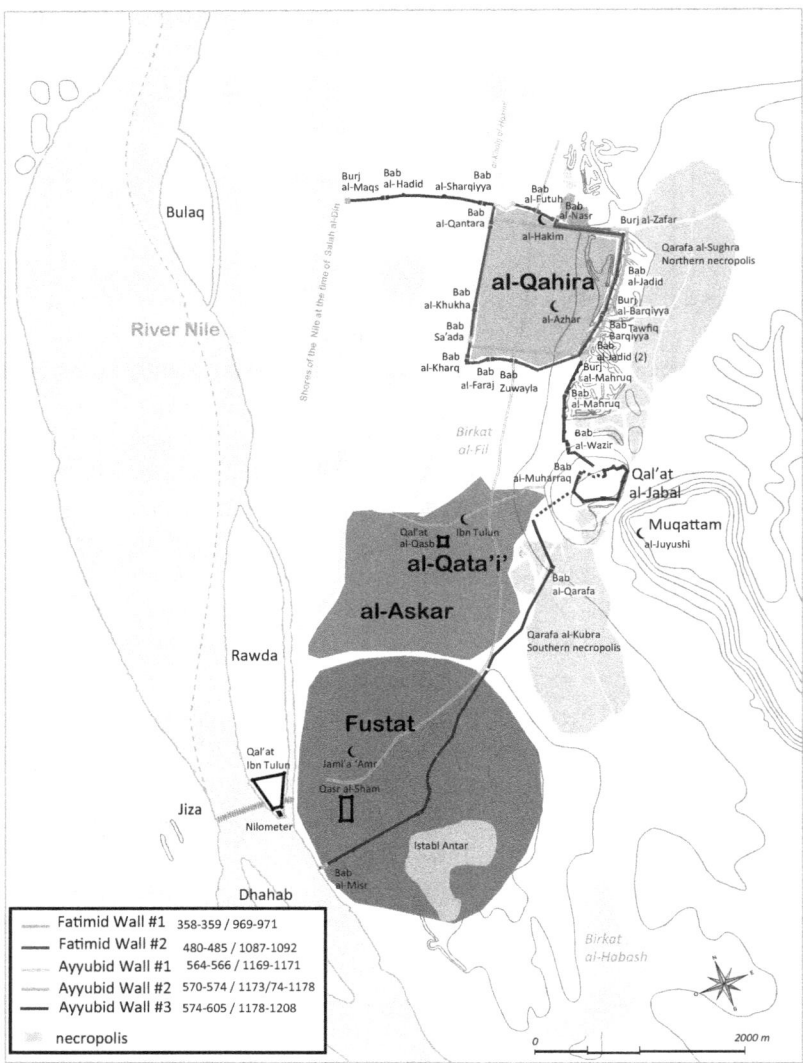

Figure IV.5.1 The many Cairos: Fustat, al-Askar, al-Qata'i' and al-Qahira. This map appears in colour in the open access digital editions at Bloomsbury Collections: https://www.bloomsbury.com/uk/fatimid-cosmopolitanism -9780755657780/

Regarding our knowledge of the urbanisation and plan of the Fatimid city of al-Qahira, it was a model created by historians essentially based on the writings of the Mamluk historian al-Maqrizi.[1] In addition to this theoretical model, there was a truncated archaeological vision, limited to the excavations of the old town of Fustat. In fact, historians and archaeologists have underestimated the role of Fustat in the construction of our knowledge of Fatimid material culture. To understand this point, we will review first what previously constituted our knowledge about Fatimid Fustat and then present our new discoveries in Fatimid Cairo.

Fustat in the historiography of Fatimid material culture

Our first question will be: why is Fustat so special or so important for us? The ruins of Fustat attracted research from very early on, for two reasons. First, the site of Fustat had the same aura and the same prestige as the legendary Islamic cities of Samarra, Samarqand or Susa: it was a major medieval centre. Fustat was described in many primary sources, and it has been the topic of many academic research projects and publications since the late 19th century. Then, the archaeological excavations of the site were organised without constraint because Fustat was abandoned during the 8th/14th century after the great epidemics of the Plague. The vast field of ruins of this metropolis was not reoccupied, as the city shifted to the north around al-Qahira, the Fatimid city. Fustat was definitively abandoned to the profit of areas between the Mosque of Ibn Tulun and Bab Zuwayla, but also to the west along the banks of the Nile. This was facilitated by the great city wall built to the East by the Ayyubids, and by the displacement towards the West of the course of the Nile, exposing new wet and marshy zones easy to urbanise on the eastern banks, in particular the zone of Bulaq. Fustat, located to the south, was far from everything. The economic, religious and political life of the Mamluks was now to the north, at the foot of the citadel. Fustat was abandoned and it became a pile of ruins, hills of debris, or '*koms*' in Egyptian colloquial Arabic. Because Fustat was abandoned during the early Mamluk period, most of the architecture remained intact. Its medieval houses were not destroyed by Mamluk, Ottoman or modern urbanisation. As is visible on the early 20th-century maps, the area around Fustat was a no-man's land, and it was only re-urbanised in the 1950s, after the Nasserian revolution.[2]

The archaeologists therefore had the logistical facilities to open vast excavations in an empty plot without being hindered by the current configuration of the city (figure IV.5.2). This is how the excavations of Fustat began in 1912, thanks to a team from the Cairo Museum led by Ali Bahgat and Albert Gabriel. Fustat was therefore the first Islamic site to be excavated and published scientifically, in two major works: 'The excavations of al-Foustat' by Bahgat and Gabriel in 1921 and a book on archaeological finds: 'Muslim ceramics from Egypt' by Bahgat and Massoul in 1930. Medieval archaeology was taught as a new discipline in 1933, when Keppel Creswell created a course on Islamic archaeology at the University of Cairo. Thanks to the work of the Committee for the Conservation of Arab Monuments and his own research, Creswell was able to publish two major works: first from 1932 to 1940, *Early Muslim Architecture: Umayyads, Early 'Abbasids and Tulunids*, then from 1952 to 1959 *The Muslim Architecture of Egypt*. Islamic archaeology became more professional at the same time as medieval European archaeology in the 1960s. In Egypt, Georges Scanlon participated in this modernisation of Islamic archaeology with the opening

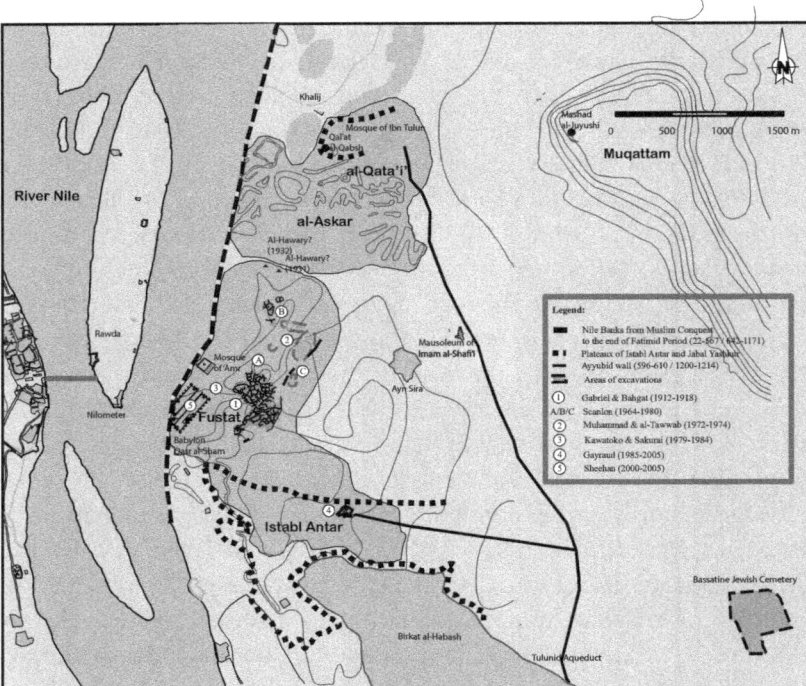

Figure IV.5.2 Map of excavations in Fustat and Istabl Antar, from Qasr al-Sham to Babylon. This map appears in colour in the open access digital editions at Bloomsbury Collections: https://www.bloomsbury.com/uk/fatimid-cosmopolitanism-9780755657780/

of new excavations in Fustat supported by the American Research Center in Egypt (ARCE) from 1964 to 1980. Three areas were excavated, Fustat A, B and C.[3] From 1972 to 1974, the periphery of Fustat was excavated by an Egyptian team from the University of Cairo directed by Dr Maher Muhammad.[4] A Japanese team led by Kawatoko and Sakurai also undertook excavations in Fustat from 1979 to 1984.[5] Finally, from 1985 to 2005, Roland-Pierre Gayraud carried out excavations on the southern margins of the city of Fustat, on the plateau of Istabl Antar. These works supported by the French Institute of Archaeology (IFAO) were the last major archaeological excavations in Fustat.[6]

The results of all these archaeological excavations have taught us much about the Islamic city, from the Arab conquest until the middle of the Mamluk era. In fact, what is paradoxical is that a large part of the remains excavated at Fustat date from the Fatimid period, from the 5th/11th and 6th/12th centuries. The first Arab city and the Umayyad levels have left few imprints under the layers of two centuries of Fatimid occupation. Excavated by Roland Pierre Gayraud, Istabl Antar plateau is probably the best place to obtain a clear view of the levels of the Arab conquest, Rashidun and Umayyad eras and their buildings. However, from 358 to 567/969 to 1171, Fustat, the first Islamic capital city of the country, remained the economic engine and hub of the Fatimid caliphate. Fustat was the city of the people, whereas al-Qahira was the city of the Fatimid caliphal family, princes, nobles and the army. The Fatimid period presents the most important architectural vestiges in Fustat, in particular with the large red brick houses[7] still visible in the Archaeological Park today (figure IV.5.3). The rich merchants of Fustat lived in sumptuous villas each set around a central courtyard, with a fountain and garden surrounded by large *iwan*s on four sides.[8] Water was brought to the city through aqueducts built during the Umayyad and Abbasid periods. The walls of the Fatimid houses were covered with elegant stucco decorations on the model of the former Abbasid palaces in Samarra. The houses and streets were equipped with a very complex sewage system. Large funerary mausoleums lined the city to the south and east. It was in Fustat that the workshops of potters, carpenters, ivory and bone carvers, glassblowers, metallurgists, weaver and rock-crystal cutters were located. The souk al-Qanadil was known for its rare, exotic and valuable items, such as small tortoiseshell boxes and combs, huge elephant tusks and rock crystal [9] from the Zanj al-Bar (Kilwa and Comoros).[10] Cairo was then regarded as the capital of Lower Egypt and the Delta, while Fustat was the capital and

Figure IV.5.3 Remains of the Fatimid villas in Fustat.

economic lung of Upper Egypt, the 'Sa'id'. This is where all the goods from Africa, the Red Sea and the Indian Ocean arrived.

Ibn Duqmaq and al-Maqrizi indicated that the outlying areas of Fustat and the plateau of Istabl Antar were partially abandoned between the economic crisis under Fatimid Imam-caliph al-Mustansir in 462/1070 and the fire ignited in the city against the siege of the Crusaders in 564/1168. The wall of Salah al-Din intersects the burnt peripheral Fatimid dwellings of Fustat and this seems to confirm the written historical evidence.[11] However, the construction of the Ayyubid wall indicates that Fustat was still a place of importance that required protection. Even after the destructive fire of 564/1168, people remained in the city which was now protected by the new city wall built in the late 6th/12th and early 7th/13th centuries. Linked together by a single wall, the two cities Misr-Fustat were called *al-Qahira wa Misr*. Then from 567 to 776/1171 to 1374, Fustat changed completely, the economic city populated by rich merchants and bourgeois became a purely industrial centre where families of workers settled in informal housing. Under the Mamluks, Fustat was at the periphery of the city, and most of the activities that people did not want around their living areas were relegated to the old city. Witnesses to these crafts and their work are the remains of potters' and glassmakers' kilns from the Mamluk period.[12] It is why we usually read in publications the statement 'produced in the workshops of Fustat'. Finally, the old city of Fustat was completely deserted between the great plague of 748/1348 and the famine of 775/1374.[13] Archaeology confirms this dating because the mounds of debris (*koms* or *tells*) that cover the entire site date to the 8th/14th century, and the wall is no longer mentioned in the written sources of that period. There was no subsequent occupation.[14]

In the 19th century, with the arrival of European travellers during the Muhammad Ali period, and later during the British protectorate, it was common to go to Fustat to retrieve some pieces of pottery and other objects visible on the surface of the mounds of the old ruins and rubbish. This is how many Fatimid and Mamluk artifacts arrived in the collections of European national museums, such as the Louvre, the Victoria and Albert, and the Ashmolean Museum. Unfortunately, what the people collected in the 19th century and collect today, and what the museums display are only the nice shiny objects, pottery sherds with nice glaze, decorated objects with calligraphy, complete ceramics. It is the reason why we have an over-representation of sgraffito bases of pots with Mamluk ranks or blazons, Fatimid lustreware, small objects such as molar flasks and oil lamps. Can we obtain an accurate vision of Fatimid material culture through these selective and qualitative collections? The response is of course no. Another problem concerns the way in which these objects were collected. Most of the artefacts that we have in our museums did not come from scientific excavations, but from amateur surveys and weekend collectors walking over the mounds of Fustat. I witnessed the same habit of collecting artifacts on the Barqiyya and Darrasa hills before and during the construction of al-Azhar Park. The result is that most of the objects displayed in museums have no context attached to them. It is indeed a serious issue when endeavouring to understand Fatimid society. Finally, a problem occurs in the historiography of Fatimid archaeology, which is the weight given to al-Qahira/Fustat in contrast to other Fatimid settlements in Egypt, as well as those in Bilad al-Sham and in Ifriqiya (North Africa). The Fatimid material culture that we know of is mainly represented by the capital city, Cairo. The other cities and settlements, such as Luxor, Qus and the cities of the Nile Delta, including Tinnis, are mostly ignored or understudied. Fortunately, there are some places that have been investigated more carefully such as Alexandria and Aswan, and also Fatimid settlements in modern-day Israel.[15] But, overall, we lack a good international, national and regional vision of Fatimid art and archaeology.

The Fatimid archaeology of al-Qahira

Concerning Fatimid Cairo, the heart of what is called today 'Islamic Cairo', our archaeological knowledge has been limited to visible architectural monuments: mosques, mausoleums and the gates of the city. The Fatimids, a Shi'i Ismaili dynasty, originally established in Ifriqiya (present-day Tunisia), conquered Egypt in 358/969. The third Fatimid Imam-caliph, al-Mu'izz, had asked his general Jawhar al-Siqilli to build him a princely city north of Fustat and the previous Abbasid settlements. This princely city was called al-Qahira, 'the Victorious'. A rammed earth enclosure of rectangular plan protected palaces for the Imam-caliph, his vizier and their families, the villas of the princes, princesses, officers and elite troops, in particular the Berbers, Kutama, Barqa and Zuwayla, and later the Armenians. In the centre stood the palaces, and to the south-east the Mosque of al-Azhar founded in 359/971. The agglomeration was bordered to the west by the canal called *al-khalij al-masri* (the ancient canal built by the Emperor Trajan). At the same time, the ancient city of Fustat developed in an incredible way under the Fatimids, so that it then included the Abbasid cities of al-Askar and al-Qata'i'. As we mentioned previously, this southern city was called Misr which gave its name to the country and its inhabitants. Misr-Fustat was the city of the people, the economic 'lung' of the Fatimid empire, it was one of the largest cities of the medieval Arab world.

The urban history of the Fatimid city was affected by critical events in the second part of the 5th/11th century. In 452/1060, Fatimid authority was undermined by economic problems linked to exceptionally low Nile floods, epidemic and famine. There followed episodes of looting, riots and revolts. The Imam-caliph al-Mustansir then appealed for assistance to one of his most able generals, Badr al-Jamali, governor of Damascus and Acre. Badr al-Jamali was appointed vizier, he restored order in Cairo and on the southern frontiers of the kingdom thanks to his elite Armenian troops and the caliph's black African guards. Between 480 and 485/1087 and 1092, Badr al-Jamali built a new mud-brick enclosure wall with monumental stone gates: Bab al-Nasr, Bab al-Futuh, Bab al-Tawfiq and Bab Zuwayla. The superficies of the city of al-Qahira then went from 136 hectares to more than 160 hectares. Cairo was no longer a princely reserve but became a city open to the people. Confronted with the erosion of caliphal authority, Badr al-Jamali became the true master of Egypt. Henceforth, the viziers retained effective political power until the end of the Fatimid regime with the arrival of Salah al-Din. The great palaces of the Fatimid Imam-caliphs were later destroyed or reused by the Ayyubid and more especially by the Mamluk sultans, notably al-Ashraf Khalil (r. 689–693/1290–1294). Progressively, the Fatimid city disappeared under Mamluk urbanisation and then Ottoman buildings.

The centre of the Fatimid capital located today around the current souk, the Khan al-Khalili, was the victim of two cataclysms, first the urban renewal undertaken by the Khedive Isma'il from 1863 to 1879, then an anarchic growth of the city in the decades from Gamal Abdel Nasser to Anwar Sadat. During these periods, the Haussmannisation of Cairo led to its impoverishment, many medieval monuments were destroyed or transformed into public buildings such as schools, large new streets cut through the medieval urban fabric making it unlivable for the middle or upper classes. Fatimid Cairo has remained largely uninhabited by the upper classes in the important area between Gamaleyya, and Darb al-Ahmar. With the souk, the Khan al-Khalili, the place has become an economic hub, with many shops, and artisans, from the jewellery shops in al-Mu'izz street to the tent-makers of al-Khayamiyya. The area is also densely occupied by poverty-stricken families, as well as containing institutions such as schools and hospitals. All this means that it is very difficult to carry out archaeological excavations. Plus, it is almost impossible to carry out rescue or salvage excavations since property developers, contractors, and indeed the government, will not give archaeologists space and time to carry out excavations.

Fortunately, in the 1980s, Egypt rediscovered the architectural heritage of Islamic Cairo, which had long been obscured by the pyramids of Giza, arguable the most iconic Pharaonic monuments. The architect Bernard Maury was one of these pioneers by starting conservation and restoration work on Ottoman houses. It was quickly followed by numerous Egyptian, American, Polish, German and Italian heritage architects.[16] These conservation works concerned mainly buildings from the Mamluk and Ottoman periods, but sometimes these projects included small archaeological test pits which produced some extremely useful although fragmentary data such as Fatimid fountains found by Bernard Maury in Bayt al-Sitt Wasila,[17] and by Philip Speiser and Giorgio Nogera in the Qalawun complex (figure IV.5.4).[18] Sometimes, some remains of palaces reappeared randomly from the restorations of Ayyubid and Mamluk buildings, which reused Fatimid architectural elements, in particular carved wood panels and beams. Some of these wooden panels were found during the conservation works of the madrasa-mausoleum of al-Malik

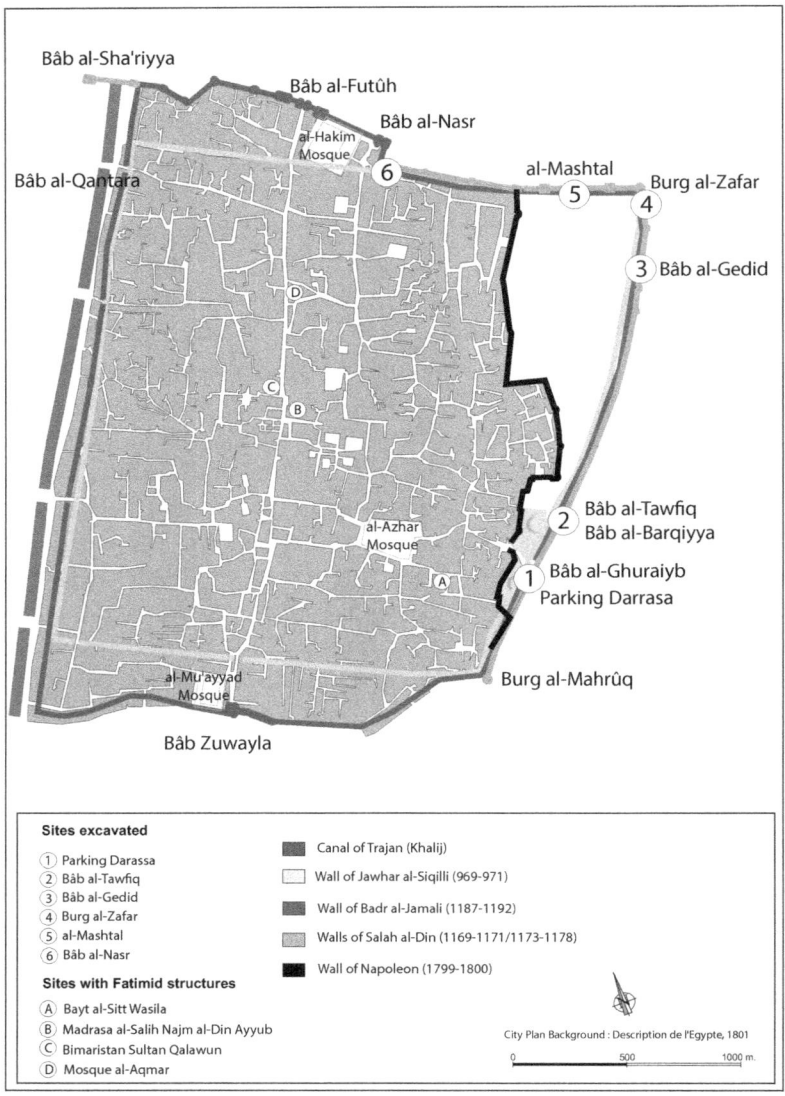

Figure IV.5.4 Map of archaeological projects in al-Qahira. This map appears in colour in the open access digital editions at Bloomsbury Collections: https://www.bloomsbury.com/uk/fatimid-cosmopolitanism-9780755657780/

al-Salih Najm al-Din Ayyub (r. 637–647/1240–1249). The panels are carved with scenes from the daily life of Fatimid princes, with seated musicians, hunters and birds in medallions, surrounded by arabesques and floral motives in bas-relief.[19] The frieze is part of a set of four long panels housed in the Museum of Islamic Art in Cairo (MAI 3465, 3471, 12935 and 4063).[20] The panels were original decorations of the Western Fatimid palace, originally built by the Imam-caliph al-'Aziz (r. 365–386/975–996) and later renovated under the Imam-caliph al-Mustansir (r. 427–487/1036–1094). The Palace of the Crown Princes (al-Qasr al-Gharbi) was located to the west of the city's central square (Bayn al-Qasrayn), and the Great Palace of the Imam-caliph was located to the east and comprised twelve domed pavilions. In fact, the Fatimid palaces consisted of several stone pavilions (qa'a), each organised around a central courtyard surrounded by four iwans, and surrounded by fountains, gardens and kiosks or belvederes.[21]

In 683/1284, the Sultan Qalawun built his bimaristan (hospital and mosque complex), on part of the site of the Western Fatimid palace, specifically on the qa'a built by the second Imam-caliph al-'Aziz in 361/972 for his daughter, Sitt al-Mulk.[22] The qa'a was clearly relatively well preserved by the end of the 7th/13th century, as the Fatimid woodwork was reused as building material for the ceilings of the Mamluk complex since good quality timber was and is still difficult to find in Egypt.[23] The decorated faces of the Fatimid panel were not exposed in the Mamluk complex because the building was a religious space where figural representation was prohibited. By the end of the 19th century, the bimaristan had fallen into disrepair and in around around 1874 many fragments of Mamluk and Fatimid woodwork were sold by antique dealers.[24] In 1910, during conservation works Max Herz, chief architect of the Committee for the Conservation of the Arab Monuments, discovered a number of these Fatimid wooden panels in the side rooms behind the northeast iwan of the bimaristan and in the funerary mosque of Muhammad al-Nasir, the son of Qalawun.[25] In 1933, Edmond Pauty found new panels in the main space of the northeast iwan.[26] Two panels with gazelles have survived (MIA 4061 and 4062) which were discovered in the Qalawun complex and are attributed to the qa'a of Sitt al-Mulk.[27] This style of carved wood can be traced to the beginning of the Fatimid era, from 358/969 to 412/1021 between the reigns of the Imam-caliphs al-Mu'izz and al-Hakim.[28] This period is particularly marked by Abbasid artistic influence. The reliefs in the round and the depth of the incisions in the incised parts recall the styles of Tulunid stucco found in Egypt.[29] Three more wooden panels have been discovered, probably also from the *qaʿa* of Sitt al-Mulk[30] or the Eastern Fatimid palace.[31] They represent backed, or anti-confronted, horses heads surrounded by vegetal arabesques cut in bevel and high relief (MIA 3391). The symmetrical composition around a vertical axis divides the panel into two equal halves, producing a mirror image. The horses bite on vegetable arabesques which merge with their bridles. The ears of the animals extend into foliage and diverge into half-palmettes. The deep carving of the panel for the recessed parts creates a chiaroscuro effect reminiscent of Coptic woodcarving. Interlacing, arabesques and palmettes of different thicknesses highlight the heads of the horses. These zoomorphic protomes inspired by Sasanian art are harnessed for riding. The horse was very important in Arabo-Persian culture and poetry. It symbolises royal power and the occupations of the nobility, including hunting and warfare.[32] An almost identical panel, certainly from the same set, is on display at the Metropolitan Museum of Art in New York (11.205.2) and a third panel is in a private collection in London.[33] Two other Fatimid door panels are very similar in composition, one displaying purely floral motifs and the other a central medallion with a figure playing a lute flanked by two confronted birds (MAI 3390 and 14601).[34]

If in the 20th century the archaeology of Fustat was well known, Cairo was almost a terra incognita. Clearly, no significant archaeological work was undertaken in Fatimid Cairo before 1998 and the creation by the Aga Khan Trust for Culture (AKTC) of the large panoramic park of al-Azhar. An important part of the Ayyubid wall was uncovered by bulldozers during the landscaping phase of the park, one of the most iconic projects of the Aga Khan in Egypt. A conservation project was launched by the AKTC in 1999, and an archaeological scientific cooperation was established in 2000 between the AKTC, the French Institute of Oriental Archaeology and the Egyptian Antiquities to carry out excavations. Initially limited to the Ayyubid wall and the Darrasa car park (2000–2009), we extended the project to all of Cairo's eastern city walls, with the excavations of the Fatimid gate of Bab al-Tawfiq in 2004–2005 and the northeast corner tower of Burj al-Zafar in 2007–2016. Finally, we carried out work on the northern walls from the Mashtal to Bab al-Nasr between 2012 and 2016. The excavations have resulted in a huge amount of unpublished data about Cairo, which is at risk of being destroyed at any time by unscrupulous developers.

In 2000, we excavated two gates of the Ayyubid eastern wall that runs along al-Azhar Park; and then in 2001, the Aga Khan Trust for Culture gave us a huge site *intramuros*: the Archaeological Triangle or Darrasa Parking, where we worked from 2001 to 2009. It was the first time that large scale excavations in 'open area' were conducted in Fatimid Cairo. The earliest occupation level found in the site was a small Fatimid garden and a fountain dating from the end of the 4th/10th century. This was most probably a Fatimid mausoleum or a small house built on the outskirts of the city. The Fatimid structures excavated in Darrasa consisted of a building with a lime floor, delimited by walls made of both fired bricks and dried mud bricks. The northern part of the building opens up onto a court with a fountain (figure IV.5.5). The basin was constructed with a channel for incoming water, in a vertical ceramic pipe set in a northeast angle with a second pipe inserted at a south-westerly angle to evacuate the overflow. Water was discharged to the east towards the desert. The water travelled beneath the garden wall, entering the pool through a ceramic pipe and was evacuated through another ceramic pipe into a subterranean canal.[35] The ceramic pipelines are built inside masonry of red brick. The channel for incoming water forms an elbow delimiting a roadbed of compacted black clay constituting the organic soil of a small garden. The garden is a rectangle surrounded by a wall while the overall structure of the basin is square with an octagonal central water tank. The interior of the basin is decorated with eight niches, alternating pointed arches with deep recesses and typical Fatimid recti-curvilinear arches with flat niches. Later the foundations of a huge Fatimid tower were built over the fountain and the garden. This tower was part of the city wall of Badr al-Jamali, and was connected to a monumental gate, Bab al-Tawfiq.[36] The Fatimid garden and fountain have been quite precisely dated to 370–431/980–1040. All this means that they were built after the erection of the city walls of Jawhar in 360/971 and before the construction of the walls of Badr al-Jamali in 480/1087. The fountain was constructed outside the first walls. The purpose of the building is more difficult to interpret: is it a peripheral housing or a funerary compound? So far, we have not found any tombs or human remains that would allow us to confirm a funerary function for this building. The Fatimid villas excavated at Fustat also had a central fountain or basin (*fisqiya*). Nevertheless, our structure presents strong similarities to one of the contemporary mausoleums found in Istabl 'Antar. What is more, the location at the periphery of the city would support the theory of a funerary function rather than a domestic unit.

Figure IV.5.5 Fatimid garden and fountain in Darrasa.

Very little is known about the layout of the Fatimid royal gardens because no garden has survived or been excavated so far. Fortunately, the written historical sources complete the scarce archaeological remains in Fustat and in Istabl 'Antar and in Darb al-Ahmar. Fatimid gardens were always associated with fountains, basins, pools and ponds. These represented an important part of houses and palaces. The Fatimid palaces contained several gazebos surrounded by gardens with ornamental fountains.[37] The old Ikhshidid garden, Bustan al-Kafur, built between 338/949 and 357/968, was incorporated into the Fatimid Western palace (*al-qasr al-gharbi*). William of Tyre's account informs us of 'marble fish-pools filled with limpid waters' in the Eastern palace.[38] The palace pools must have been magnificent being made of marble and including precious stones and other sophisticated artefacts. In the middle of a palace was a spacious courtyard, with a fountain in its centre, surrounded by four *iwan*s. The fountain was surmounted by four crouching lions which spat water from their mouths. Waterspouts were placed in the corners and not in the middle of the basin.[39] The symbolic role of lions and felines is widely evident in the arts of metallurgy, particularly fountain outlets.[40]

Despite the quality of the documentation collected and critically published by historians[41] what was known of the limits and the size of the Fatimid city was not proved or supported by physical evidence. Our knowledge of the first Fatimid wall was based only on primary written sources. We filled this archaeological gap from 2011 to 2016 when we discovered very early Fatimid fortifications on the sites of Burj al-Zafar, al-Mashtal and Bab al-Nasr. We found the same pattern and material evidence on all three sites excavated. We discovered three parallel walls, the first one from Jawhar al-Siqilli (358–360/969–971), the second one from Badr al-Jamali (480–485/1087–1092) and the third one from Salah al-Din (r. 564–570/1169–1174). The second wall of Cairo was built by Badr al-Jamali at the back of the first old wall of Jawhar al-Siqilli to reinforce the existing structure which was crumbling away. The third wall by Salah al-Din was built, not at the back, but a few metres in front of the old Fatimid walls to modernise the defences of the city in the face of the threat of the Crusaders.

According to the results of our excavations, the first Bab al-Nasr was located only a few metres to the south-east of the present gate. The gate was protected by semi-circular towers built in limestone and very similar in plan to the existing Bab al-Futuh and Bab Zuwayla (figure IV.5.6). The first Bab al-Nasr was built by Jawhar al-Siqilli during the period 358–360/969–971. The gate was connected to a limestone wall, which was later reinforced by a large mudbrick wall built behind it by Badr al-Jamali between 480–485/1087–1092. It is the reason why the existing and visible Fatimid wall turns to the south in the southeastern corner of Bab al-Nasr. In fact, Badr al-Jamali connected his new wall to the old initial Fatimid gate of Bab al-Nasr built by General Jawhar. A portion of Jawhar's wall was made of limestone with an intricate decoration of columns inserted in the masonry. Then on the sites of al-Mashtal and Zafar, Jawhar's wall was made of rammed earth (*tabiyya*) (figure IV.5.7). It seems that Jawhar and Jamali adopted the same strategy: monumental gates framed by limestone walls and towers, then the rest of the city wall built in earthen architecture. Rammed earth was a technology almost unknown in Egypt (except for the area around Siwa) and probably brought to Egypt by the Berber component of the Fatimid army, the Kutama, Barqa or Zuwayla. This discovery is very important because it radically changes our vision of the limits of the Fatimid city under al-Muʿizz. The city was probably larger than we thought previously. Finally, the location of the first Fatimid gate indicates that the Mosque of al-Hakim was built over a part of the wall of

Figure IV.5.6 The first Fatimid Bab al-Nasr (358–360/969–971).

Jawhar. The Mosque of al-Hakim was included in the defences of the city with its two huge square towers supporting the minarets. It was not the first time that the Fatimids had deployed the architecture of a mosque in their defensive structure; they did the same in al-Mahdiyya in Tunisia following an old Aghlabid tradition.[42]

At the end of the 5th/11th century, Fatimid Egypt suffered from a series of very poor Nile floods, resulting in famines and epidemics. These events pushed some of the army into rebellion, especially the Turks in Cairo and the Nubians in the Aswan region. Badr al-Jamali was appointed commander in chief of the army, *amir al-juyush*, by the Imam-caliph al-Mustansir in 465/1073, with the task of restoring order in Egypt, which he achieved both in the capital and in the provinces of Egypt. Undoubtedly the great monumental gates built between 480/1087 and 485/1092 constitute the most striking building work of the vizier. Bab al-Futuh, Bab al-Nasr and Bab Zuwayla which he built were directly inspired by Byzantine models from Edessa, Antioch and further north, Diyar Bakir. In a monumental effort, the northern and southern flanks of the city were

Figure IV.5.7 The three Fatimid walls of Cairo in al-Mashtal: Jawhar al-Siqilli (358–360/969–971), Badr al-Jamali (480–485/1087–1092) and Salah al-Din (r. 564–570/1169–1174).

built of stone. Badr al-Jamali brought experts from his own people, the Armenians, especially for the construction of the actual gates. Creswell held that the wall of Badr al-Jamali was purely an extension to the north and south of the original city, and that the enitre enclosure was built of stone like the monumental gates. This misinterpretation associated with an incorrect understanding of the city limits to the east, has misled generations of researchers working on the history of Cairo. The walls built by General Kléber during the French occupation of Egypt (1798–1801) were often mistaken for the Fatimid walls. These French walls protected the much smaller Ottoman city to the east, rather than the larger Fatimid city.[43]

From 2004 to 2005, we excavated Bab al-Tawfiq, a limestone gate protected by two square mud brick towers, and a ramp or a glacis, '*zalaka*', made of granite spolia from Pharaonic monuments, identical to the ramp which was built in front of Bab Zuwayla and which was later demolished by the Ayyubid sultan al-Malik al-Kamil. Bab al-Tawfiq can be dated to 480–485/1087–1090 thanks to a large Kufic inscription in situ dedicated to al-Mustansir and Badr al-Jamali. From 2007 to 2016, we opened a new excavation site in the northeastern corner tower of the Fatimid city, in the area between Burj al-Zafar and Bab al-Jadid. Through our excavations we revealed more than fifty metres of the Fatimid mud brick wall built by Badr al-Jamali. It was very clear that Salah al-Din built his new wall in parallel and just in front of the previous Fatimid one. Our research revealed a period overlooked by the specialists, the vizirate of Salah ad-Din and the last Fatimid constructions. Salah al-Din was vizier of the last Fatimid caliph al-ʿAdid from 564–567/1169–1171. Salah al-Din strictly followed the limits of the Fatimid city. The corner towers of Burj al-Zafar and Burj al-Mahruq are two excellent examples of the defensive architecture of this period.

During our work on the eastern walls of Cairo, we excavated three important gates of the town, from north to south: Bab al-Jadid #1 (Bab al-Zafar), Bab al-Barqiyya (Bab al-Tawfiq) and Bab al-Jadid #2 (Bab al-Qarratin). These three gates were always connected to the master towers built by Salah al-Din when he was vizier and built in front of previous Fatimid ones. The best example is Bab al-Barqiyya built in front of the old Bab al-Tawfiq. These three gates are laid out equally spaced along the eastern flank of the Fatimid city. Two secondary gates are connected to the north-eastern and south-eastern corners of the Fatimid city. The main gate, Bab al-Barqiyya / Bab al-Tawfiq, is located exactly at the middle point between the two eastern corners of the city, precisely in the middle of the eastern walls of the Fatimid city. This information is extremely important, because it tells us a lot about the plan and organisation of the Fatimid city between the time of Badr al-Jamali in the 5th/11th century and that of Salah al-Din almost a hundred years later. The three gates reveal a highly rational and organised plan with a major road running East-West and cutting the North-South axis represented by Bab al-Futuh and Bab al-Zuwayla.

Thanks to these investigations it is now possible to have a better understanding of the layout of the Fatimid urban enclosures and to propose a new understanding of the limits and the gates of the city, as well as the main axes of circulation. Our excavations have revealed the original shape of the Fatimid city, which we now know covered a greater area than originally thought. The eastern wall of the Fatimid city was built entirely of mud bricks with a stone gate, Bab al-Tawfiq. The portions of mud brick walls discovered demonstrate the continuity of the fortification of Badr al-Jamali along the eastern flank of Cairo, from Burj al-Zafar to Burj al-Mahruq. Even a part of the northern front was protected by a mud-brick enclosure. This wall was connected to the monumental stone wall at the southeast of Bab al-Nasr. The wall and the flanking towers are very regular on all the sites that we excavated, the Parking Darassa; Bab al-Tawfiq, Burj al-Zafar and Bab al-Nasr. The sites excavated revealed the presence of a mud-brick enclosure 4 metres wide. The towers are quadrangular in shape, each side being about 8 metres, and they alternate regularly with the square counterforts with sides 3 metres wide. The fortifications of Cairo are a social phenomenon since they reflect Fatimid society and the hierarchy of the living. Indeed, the monumental stone doors represent the power and authority of the Imam-caliph and the role of the Armenian officers; while the mud-brick city wall is rooted in the vernacular traditions of Upper Egypt and the 'black troops' of the Fatimid army, mostly Nubians from Aswan. Finally, the Fatimid mud-brick city wall was still visible in the late 8th/14th century and therefore in his writings al-Maqrizi makes reference to the area between the walls, '*Bayn al-Surayn*'. Then the Fatimid wall was covered up by Mamluk dwellings and so it disappeared until 2001 and the beginning of our archaeological excavations.

Conclusion

Our project was the first large-scale archaeological excavation undertaken in an 'open area' in Fatimid Cairo. Over the course of seventeen years, we have amassed a huge quantity of artefacts, not only Fatimid, but also Ayyubid, Mamluk and Ottoman. We were able to uncover archaeological levels, architecture, and stratigraphy that provided a historical context for Fatimid objects such as ceramics, metalwork, ivory, bone, wood and glass. Our ceramologist, Julie Monchamp published two volumes that can be considered as the best catalogue on Fatimid ceramics in an archaeological context, with a very precise typo-chronology.[44] This catalogue includes not only the luxurious ceramics displayed in museums but, importantly, the common wares, the unglazed production for ordinary people. Our archaeological mission also rewrites the history of Cairo through the study of the medieval fortifications. As a result, it is now possible to provide new information not only on the Fatimid walls; but more importantly, to propose a new view of the Fatimid city, its perimeter, superficies, main gates, main streets and urbanisation. More important than material culture, people were at the heart of our project. In 2007 we opened the first Field

School of Islamic Archaeology in Egypt (the largest in the Middle East). Up to 2016, we have trained more than one hundred Egyptian scholars, from Cairo University, Ain Shams University, Fayum University and the Ministry of Antiquities. It was an important part of our mission and I am extremely proud of the results and the success of this field school. Two important outcomes are in preparation, first with the French Institute of Archaeology (IFAO) the publication of four volumes on our excavations and the walls of Cairo; second with The Institute of Ismaili Studies, the Fatimid city 3D project, a virtual reconstruction of medieval Cairo, based on architectural, archaeological, topographical and textual evidence. Hopefully our digital model will give a new life to the Fatimid city.[45]

NOTES

1. Ayman F. Sayyid, *La capitale de l'Egypte jusqà l'époque fatimide, al-Qahira et al-Fustat* (Beirut, 1998).
2. Maps from Pierre Bey Grand, Plan général de la Ville du Caire (Le Caire, Égypte: Ebner et Cie, 1874); Ville du Caire 1897; Creswell, 1952 in *The Muslim Architecture of Egypt*; IGN, Paris, 1980; and CAPMAS, Cairo Governorate, 1990.
3. G. Scanlon, 'Preliminary Report: Excavations at Fustat, 1954', *Journal of the American Research Center in Egypt*, 4 (1965), pp. 7–30; idem, 'Fustat Expedition: Preliminary Report 1965, Part I', *Journal of the American Research Center in Egypt*, 5 (1966), pp. 83–112; idem, 'Fustat Expedition Preliminary Report. Back to Fustat-A 1973', *Annales Islamologiques*, 17 (1981), pp. 407–436; idem, 'Fustat Expedition: Preliminary Report 1968, Part II', *Journal of the American Research Center in Egypt*, 13 (1976), pp. 68–89; idem, 'Fustat Expedition: Preliminary Report 1978', *Journal of the American Research Center in Egypt*, 21 (1984), pp. 1–38; W. Kubiak and G. Scanlon, 'Re-dating Bahgat's Houses and the Aqueduct', *Art and Archaeology Research Papers*, 4 (1973), pp. 138–148.
4. T. Treptow, 'A History of Excavations at Fustat', in Vorderstrasse and Treptow, ed. *A Cosmopolitan City. Muslims, Christians, and Jews in Old Cairo* (Chicago, 2015), p. 106.
5. K. Sakurai and M. Kawatoko, 'Preliminary Report of Excavations at al-Fustat in Egypt (Fifth Season)', *Journal of the Archaeological Society of Nippon*, 69 (1984), pp. 422–471; Matthew Harrison, 'Fustat Reconsidered: Urban Housing and Domestic Life in a Medieval Islamic City' (PhD, University of Southampton, 2016), p. 55.
6. R.-P. Gayraud, S. Bjorneso and S. Denoix, 'Istabl 'Antar (Fostat) 1985. Rapport de Fouilles', *Annales Islamologiques*, 22 (1986), pp. 1–26; R.-P. Gayraud and Philip Speiser, 'Istabl 'Antar (Fostat) 1992, Rapport de fouilles', *Annales Islamologiques*, 28 (1994), pp. 1–27; R.-P. Gayraud, P. Gallo and J. M. Mouton, 'Istabl 'Antar (Fostat) 1994. Rapport des fouilles', *Annales Islamologiques*, 29 (1995), pp. 1–24; R.-P. Gayraud, 'Istabl 'Antar (Fostat) 1990. Rapport de fouilles', *Annales Islamologiques*, 25 (1991), pp. 57–87; idem, 'Istabl 'Antar (Fostat). Rapport de fouilles', *Annales Islamologiques*, 27 (1993), pp. 225–232; idem, 'Le Qarafa al-Kubra, dernier demeure des Fatimides', in M. Barrucand, ed., *L'Egypte Fatimide, son art et son histoire* (Paris, 1999), pp. 443–464.
7. Aly Bahgat and Albert Gabriel, *Fouilles d'al Foustat* (Paris, 1921); Harrison, 'Fustat Reconsidered', pp. 58–59.
8. S. Pradines and S. Khan, 'Fatimid gardens: archaeological and historical perspectives', *BSOAS*, 79 (2016), pp. 1–30.

9 S. D. Goitein, *A Mediterranean Society: The Jewish communities of the Arab world as Portrayed in the Documents of the Cairo* Geniza, Volume IV: *Daily life* (Berkeley, CA, 1983), pp. 223–224.
10 S. Pradines, 'Madagascar, the Source of the Abbasid and Fatimid Rock Crystals: New Evidence from Archaeological Investigations in East Africa', in Avinoam Shalem and Cynthia Hahn, ed., *Seeking Transparency: Rock Crystals across the Medieval Mediterranean* (Berlin, 2020), pp. 35–50.
11 G. Salmon, *Etudes sur la topographie du Caire. La Kal'at al Kabch et la birkat al-Fil* (Cairo, 1902); P. Casanova, *Essai de reconstitution topographique de la ville d'al fustat ou Misr* (Cairo, 1919); S. Denoix, *Décrire le Caire d'après Ibn Duqmaq et Maqrizi* (Cairo, 1992), p. 34.
12 G. Scanlon, 'Fustat Expedition Preliminary Report. Back to Fustat-A 1973', *Annales Islamologiques*, 17 (1981), pp. 407–436. 1981, p. 61.
13 J. Loiseau, *Reconstruire la maison du Sultan, 1350–1450. Ruine et recomposition de l'ordre urbain au Caire* (Cairo, 2010), pp. 66–69; S. Pradines, 'Archaeological Excavations of Bab al-Ghurayb Cemetery: Plague Epidemics and the Ruin of Fourteenth Century Cairo', *Mamluk Studies Review*, 24 (2021), pp. 119–170.
14 Scanlon, 1981; Valentina Vezzoli, 'The Fustat Ceramic Collection in the Royal Museums of Art and History in Brussels : The Mamluk Assemblage', *Bulletin des Musées Royaux d'Art et d'Histoire*, 82 (2011), pp. 119–168; Harrison, 'Fustat Reconsidered', pp. 53–54.
15 CEA excavations in Alexandria directed by Jean-Yves Empereur and Swiss Institute excavations in Aswan directed by Cornelius von Pilgrim.
16 Giuseppe Fanfoni, Nairy Hampikian, Wolfgang Mayer, Agnieszka Dobrowolska, Alaa el-Habashi and Christophe Bouleau.
17 B. Maury, *Palais et Maisons du Caire IV* (Cairo, 1983).
18 W. Mayer, G. Nogara and P. Speiser, 'The Madrasa of Sultan al-Nasir Muhammad: Archaeological Excavations', in Mayer and Speiser, ed., *A Future for the Past. Restorations in Islamic Cairo 1973–2004* (Cairo, 2007), pp. 106–114.
19 N. Hampikian and M. Cyran, 'Recent Discoveries Concerning the Fatimid Palaces Uncovered during the Conservation Works on parts of al-Salihiyya Complex', in M. Barrucand, ed., *L'Egypte Fatimide, son art et son histoire* (Paris, 1999), pp. 649–657; M. Cyran, 'Rediscovered carved panels of the Fatimid palaces', in M. Barrucand, ed., *L'Egypte Fatimide, son art et son histoire* (Paris, 1999), pp. 658–663.
20 Sayyid, *La capitale de l'Egypte jusqà l'époque fatimide*, pp. 88–91; Gaston Wiet, *Bois sculptés d'églises coptes (époque fatimide)*, (Catalogue général du musée arabe du Caire) (Cairo, 1930), pl. I.
21 M. Barrucand, *Trésors fatimides du Caire* (Paris, 1998), pp. 62–63; A. F. Sayyid, 'La ville royale fatimide d'après les sources arabe', in M. Barrucand, ed., *Trésors fatimides du Caire* (Paris, 1998), pp. 70–73.
22 H. Sayed, 'The Development of the Cairene Qa'a: Some Considerations', *Annales Islamologiques*, 23 (1987), pp. 31–53.
23 A. F. Sayyid, *La Capitale d'Egypte*, pp. 209–326 and 313–321.
24 I. Abdulfattah, 'Theft, Plunder, and Loot: An Examination of the Rich Diversity of Material Reuse in the Complex of Qalawun in Cairo', *Mamluk Studies Review*, 20 (2017), pp. 96–106.
25 S. Dimand, *A handbook of Mohammedan decorative arts* (New York, 1930), pp. 86–89; Abdulfattah, 'Theft, Plunder, and Loot', pp. 96–106.
26 E. Pauty, *Les bois sculptés jusqà l'époque Ayyoubide* (Catalogue général du musée arabe du Caire), *Institut Français d'Archéologie Orientale* (Cairo, 1931).
27 Abdulfattah, 'Theft, Plunder, and Loot', pp. 96–106.
28 Wiet, *Bois sculptés d'églises coptes*, pl. I; S. C. Welch, *The Islamic World* (New York, 1987), pp. 18–19; J.-P. Roux, ed., *L'Islam dans les collections nationales* (Paris, 1977), pp. 152–153.

29 Sayyid, *La Capitale d'Egypte*, p. 90.
30 Abdulfattah, 'Theft, Plunder, and Loot', pp. 96–106.
31 Hampikian and Cyran, 'Recent Discoveries Concerning the Fatimid Palaces Uncovered during the Conservation Works on parts of al-Salihiyya Complex', pp. 649–657; Cyran, Rediscovered carved panels of the Fatimid palaces', pp. 658–663.
32 M. Bernus-Taylor, 'Le cheval et l'art islamique', in Jean-Pierre Digard, ed., *Chevaux et cavaliers arabes dans les arts d'Orient et de l'Occident*, Exh. Cat. (Paris, 2002), pp. 85–93.
33 Dimand, *A handbook of Mohammedan decorative arts*, pp. 86–89; Welch, *The Islamic World*, p. 26.
34 Sayyid, 'La ville royale', pp. 91–95.
35 Pradines and Khan, 'Fatimid gardens: archaeological and historical perspectives', pp. 1–30.
36 S. Pradines and J. den Heijer, 'Bab al-Tawfiq : une porte du Caire fatimide oubliée par l'histoire', *Le Muséon*, 121 (2008), pp. 143–170.
37 Pradines and Khan, 'Fatimid gardens: archaeological and historical perspectives', pp. 1–30.
38 William of Tyre in Babcock and Krey, *A History of Deeds done Beyond the Sea* (London, 1976), p. 319.
39 F. Broilo, 'Fantastic Fountains and Where to Find Them: A Re-examination of the Textual and Material Evidence on Liquid Architecture from the Medieval Islamicate World', *Journal of Material Cultures in the Muslim World*, 3 (2022), pp. 64–71.
40 Barrucand, *Trésors fatimides du Caire*, p. 123; R. Camber and A. Contadini, 'Introduction', in Anna Contadini, ed., *The Pisa Griffin and the Mari-Cha Lion: metalwork, art, and technology in the medieval Islamicate Mediterranean* (Pisa, 2018), pp. 19–34; G. Bilotto, 'Fatimid Metalwork 297-567/ 909-1171: Context, Identification, and Style in the Mediaeval Mediterranean' (PhD, SOAS, 2019), pp. 210–230.
41 al-Maqrizi in Sayyid, *La capitale de l'Egypte jusqu'à l'époque fatimide*, pp. 146–162, 381–431; and 'Imad al-Din in S. Jiwa, tr., *The Founder of Cairo. The Fatimid Imam-Caliph al-Mu'izz and his Era, an English translation of the section on al-Mu'izz from Idris 'Imad al-Din's 'Uyun al-akhbar* (London, 2013), pp. 219–240.
42 S. Pradines, 'From the Ribats to the Fortresses, the Fatimid Period of Transition in Muslim Military Architecture', *International Journal of Islamic Research*, 31 (2020), pp. 493–514.
43 Stéphane Pradines, 'Napoleonic Fortifications in Egypt 1798-1801', *Fort*, 24 (2014), pp. 115-134.
44 J. Monchamp, *Céramiques des murailles du Caire (fin xe-début xvie s.)* (Cairo, 2018).
45 I would like to thank here all the Institutions who supported this research programme: first of all, the Aga Khan Trust for Culture (AKTC) and the French Institute of Archaeology (IFAO), of course the Ministry of Egyptian Antiquity (formerly SCA) and the French Ministry of foreign affairs (MAEE). I would also like to thank here all the team, the permanent members of the mission and the hundreds of volunteers, students and workers who devoted so much energy to this project. For this paper, I would like to thank, in particular, my colleagues at the Institute of Ismaili Studies for their kind support, and their deep interest in my research, in particular Professor Zayn Kassam, Dr Farhad Daftary, Dr Shainool Jiwa, Dr Gregory Bilotto and Russell Harris.

6

Reassessing Fatimid Figuralism: Ettinghausen, Grabar and a Medieval Lustre Workshop

Jennifer A. Pruitt

Introduction

Scholars of Islamic art have long been attracted to the rich yet elusive visual tradition of the Fatimids. This interest is based largely on evocative tales of Fatimid artistic glory and the relative wealth of extant examples of naturalistic figural depiction, which seem to challenge notions of medieval Arab aniconism. Reconstructing the history of Fatimid objects represents a challenge for the modern art historian. On the one hand, historical sources recount tales of the richness of the Fatimid treasury. Scholarly writings and museum displays celebrate the innovative artistic production of the Fatimid period. However, few objects from the Fatimid period have a known context of origin or provenance. Instead, we are often faced with a circular technique of attribution and connoisseurship in which museums, auction houses and scholars attribute certain characteristics of naturalism and lively figuralism to the Fatimid context. Among the celebrated objects of the Fatimid era, lustre ceramics have played a particularly significant role in our scholarly understanding of Fatimid art as iconophilic, prolific and innovative.

Recent writings on the medieval Islamic object have elevated our understanding of materiality, making and the object itself. However, in this paper I will reconsider a foundational, early 20th-century approach to ceramics – as a medium on which painting occurs. In particular, I investigate an enduring assumption about Fatimid art – that it is characterised by a proliferation of naturalistic figuralism. I return to seminal writings on Fatimid art by Richard Ettinghausen (1905–1979) and Oleg Grabar (1929–2011).[1] These essays celebrated the realistic figuralism of Fatimid painting, placing it in a linear development that mirrored the development of Western art history.² Although such assessments continue to inform scholarship and museum curation, a narrative of artistic change in Fatimid painting is difficult to assert authoritatively with so few securely dated objects. As an attempt to outline what *can* be said about Fatimid painting, I turn to a particular corpus of objects – those bearing the signature of Muslim b. al-Dahhan (Muslim, son of the painter). An analysis of the works ascribed to this workshop begins to chip away at the persistent narrative of linear artistic development, helping us glimpse the artistic choices, variations and sources available to a medieval Islamic workshop.³

The Context of 'Fatimid' lustre

It is not unusual for pottery to play an outsized role in a historiography of medieval Islamic art. Finer objects of precious metals, rock crystal, or ivory have been melted down or reused in other courtly contexts.⁴ This is particularly true for the Fatimid context, in which the destruction of the court treasury has resulted in a significant gap between the textual description of magnificent objects and the paucity of materials correlating with these descriptions. Lustre fragments have been found in archaeological digs in Fustat, the urban centre located to the south of the centre of the Fatimid court in Cairo (al-Qahira).⁵ However, Fustat is a particularly challenging archaeological site, given its proximity to and integration in the modern Egyptian city and subsequent centuries of looting and use.⁶ Adding to the challenge of dating Fatimid objects, the provenance of known lustre objects in a museum context is often unknown and the objects are given a Fatimid origin largely due to stylistic observations. Finally, although museums and scholarship focus on examples of figural depictions in lustre, the majority of lustre fragments excavated featured abstract, non-figural designs.

Although we know that the Fatimids were actively involved in artistic patronage and amassed an extensive collection of art objects from around the world in their vast treasuries, the details of artistic production, as is the case in many medieval Islamic contexts, remains an enigma to modern art historians. The Fatimid palaces, which reportedly contained rich figural imagery, replete with hunting scenes, no longer remain, with the exception of a few wooden beams.⁷ Monumental architecture, including mosques, mausolea and city gates remain standing proudly in Cairo and in-depth scholarly studies have focussed on these architectural monuments, for which we have both material remains and textual evidence.⁸ Among the portable arts, those that remain and are ascribed to the Fatimid period evoke a rich artistic tradition. Exquisitely carved ivories, wooden panels, rock crystal, glass, textiles, ceramics and illustrated scraps of paper, remain as examples of medieval Egyptian art and occupy pride of place in museum collections.⁹

While art historians and museum curators have been eager to categorise Fatimid lustre objects as imperial, courtly objects, there is not much about these objects to indicate that they were particularly designed for the elite groups in society.¹⁰ Patrons are rarely identified and little is known about the context of production. However, the method of production and its resultant splendour make it clear that lustreware was a more difficult process than almost any other kind of ceramic production, requiring guarded, specialised knowledge, and thus more highly valued than other kinds of ceramic.

The process for lustreware involved bonding a metallic compound – usually made from copper and silver oxides in a refractory medium like ochre – to the glaze.¹¹ The process was labour-intensive and specialised, requiring successive firings and a precise reducing atmosphere. The resulting surface shimmered like gold – an astounding alchemical transformation using relatively modest materials. It is likely that the secrets of lustre production were tightly guarded and knowledge of them can be traced from Iraq to Egypt, then onto Iran. Although the objects under consideration here are all portable ones – mostly large, restored plates or fragments now housed in museum collections, lustre tiles have also been used to adorn important spaces throughout the Islamic world, including in architecture, as seen in the *mihrab* of the mosque at Qayrawan (Tunisia), surrounding the throne of the Abbasid palace at Samarra (Iraq), and illustrating scenes from the *Shahnama* in the Ilkhanid palaces of greater Iran.¹² Fatimid-era lustre pieces ascribed to the 4th/10th century are characterised by their bright, metallic, almost golden colour, warmer than and distinct from the greener, browner shades of earlier pieces ascribed to the Tulunid period.¹³

Ettinghausen and Grabar and the Historiography of Fatimid Figuralism

Fatimid lustre painting has played a key role in our perception of Fatimid art as being particularly figural and naturalistic.¹⁴ As is the case in so many other areas of Islamic art history, our understanding of a particular Fatimid figural style can be traced to two fathers of the field – Richard Ettinghausen and Oleg Grabar. In seminal texts, Ettinghausen and Grabar have argued for the uniqueness of Fatimid artistic expression and have attempted to trace the development of a particular Fatimid style. Their conclusions and assumptions continue to underpin our understanding of Fatimid art today. In 1942, Ettinghausen outlined the development of Fatimid art in the essay 'Painting in the Fatimid Period: A Reconstruction'.[15] In this publication, Ettinghausen considered the Fatimids as the missing link in the development of Islamic painting. He noted the existence of vibrant examples of figural painting at Qusayr 'Amra and Nishapur in the 3rd/9th century then Samarra a few decades later. Ettinghausen then stated:

> Subsequently, there is a gap from these to the thirteenth-century manuscripts from Iraq, Mesopotamia, and Syria. From about 1300 on, Iranian manuscripts are preserved, and a few fragmentary frescoes date from before the Mongol invasion. From Egypt there are supposedly only a few paper fragments of the ninth or tenth century. This is all the more curious as the Fatimid court in Egypt was not only one of the most luxurious in the Islamic East, but also definitely fond of figural representations. This is known from carvings in wood and ivory.[16]

Noting this lacuna in the development of Islamic painting, Ettinghausen examined the individual motifs in the ceiling of Palermo's Cappella Palatina, the Norman king Roger II's chapel (ca. AD 1130–1143), observing their similarities to known Fatimid works. The famous chapel is often celebrated as an example of Mediterranean hybridity and cross-cultural exchange, which typified the Norman court in Sicily.[17] In plan, it resembles a Latin cruciform church. In its mosaic programme, it draws upon Byzantine tradition, and its wooden muqarnas ceiling has painted figures from the so-called 'princely cycle' surrounded by Arabic calligraphy presenting benedictary phrases. In his consideration of the relationship between the Cappella Palatina and Fatimid painting, Ettinghausen isolated and gave titles to the individual niches of the ceiling, considering their individual forms in detail (figure IV.6.1), omitting a discussion of the ceiling as a totality or any consideration of why an Islamic form might be incorporated in this context. In particular, he compared the paintings to what he deemed a 'Samarra-style' or 'Perso Iraqian' style *muqarnas* niche

Figure IV.6.1 Cross-legged cup bearing ruler, from a *muqarnas* niche on the ceiling of the *Cappella Palatina*. Palermo, 6th/12th century.

from a bath house excavated in Fustat (figure IV.6.2).[18] Based on his conclusion that the ceiling is an example of Fatimid painting and on his examination of other Fatimid forms, Ettinghausen identified a number of styles that may be found in Fatimid art, drawing on multiple media, including lustre fragments. Most notably he attributed a 'Perso-Iraqian' and 'Hellenistic' miniature style to the era and also outlined the existence of popular and realistic styles, although the criteria for these styles are less clearly defined in the article.

Figure IV.6.2 *Muqarnas* stucco fragment from Fustat. Museum of Islamic Art, Cairo.

Ettinghausen doubled down on his consideration of Fatimid painting as part of a linear, traceable development of Islamic art in his 1956 article, 'Early Realism in Islamic Art'.[19] In this essay, Ettinghausen discussed Fatimid painting as a link in the development of naturalism in Islamic art, which had begun in Samarra, developed under the Fatimids, and continued to develop under the Mamluks, Bihzad and the Herat school, through to the Safavids, the Ottomans and the Mughals.[20] By considering the Fatimids as a link in this development, Ettinghausen suggested that Fatimid art also developed linearly, bridging the gap between Islamic cultures, regardless of geographic and temporal distance. The methodological problems of this approach seem obvious to the 21st-century scholar.[21] By considering Fatimid painting as a missing link, Ettinghausen presupposed that the entirety of Islamic art developed along a trajectory unified by its 'Islamicness'. His conclusions rest on the assumption that art created in the 3rd/9th century in Iraq would naturally be traced all the way to 11th/17th-century India and that the output of a manuscript workshop in Herat could be traced directly to Fatimid Egypt. This teleological narrative requires that the few dated examples of Fatimid art be placed on a trajectory of linear development. In spite of the logical holes and Orientalist underpinnings of this approach, Ettinghausen's developmental model has informed the dating of the large corpus of mostly unprovenanced lustre pieces, ascribed to the Fatimid era.[22]

Another enduring aspect of Ettinghausen's approach is the notion of Fatimid 'realism,' which he defined as a representational style that exists in opposition to the traditional Muslim 'predilection for abstract and infinite design'.[23] He asserted that although Islamic art contained figural representations prior to the reign of the Fatimids, they were usually conventional representations of the ruler and the royal court.[24] He placed Fatimid realism in opposition to earlier abstraction, characterising it both in terms of its dynamic depiction of the human form and its concern with 'unconventional aspects of life, possibly even with everyday life outside the court proper', going so far as to suggest that many Fatimid scenes may be drawn from life.[25]

However, in analysing examples of Fatimid lustre painting, it becomes clear that the 'realistic' depictions of human movement simply follow different conventions. This can be seen in a celebrated plate featuring a scarf dancer (figure IV.6.3). In this example the dancer twists in the Fatimid hallmark pinwheel pose, in which the dancer's body twists in the opposite direction to the legs, while the legs, arms and head bend at dramatic – in fact, quite *un*natural angles. Ettinghausen's eagerness to chart a development of Fatimid realism stands as a corollary to linear models of Western art historical tradition, in which scholars chart a development away from the static stereotypes of the medieval period toward the naturalism, scientific discovery and close observation of

Figure IV.6.3 Reconstructed lustre bowl with scarf dancer, ascribed to Egypt, 6th/12th century. National Museum of Asian Art, Smithsonian Institution, Freer Collection.

natural form in the western European Renaissance. Indeed, Ettinghausen regarded Fatimid painting as a parallel rebirth of realism from Ancient Egyptian and Hellenistic art itself.[26] Ettinghausen's argument thus places Fatimid painting at a pivotal moment in the development of art more broadly while the emphasis on a linear progression towards naturalism obscures the diversity of style found in both Fatimid painting and that of earlier dynasties.

After Ettinghausen, Oleg Grabar offered the next broad, influential discussion of the development of Fatimid art in his essay 'Imperial and Urban Art in Islam: The Subject Matter of Fatimid Art,' published in 1972.[27] In this essay, Grabar relied on many of the same stylistic analyses as Ettinghausen. However, he used these observations to link a singular Fatimid style to a wider cultural framework and historical exploration. Grabar primarily addressed painted lustreware, though he also briefly considered woodwork, ivories, rock crystal, metalwork and other portable arts. Although it is not clear how he dated these objects, Grabar follows Ettinghausen's lead by tracing the development of Fatimid art from an earlier, abstracted style to a more dynamic, figural, 'spatial' style, which he praised for its innovation.[28] He suggested that this style became popular quite suddenly and represents a broad change of taste in the mid-5th/11th century, linking these formal changes to the wider Mediterranean context by relating them to the so-called Macedonian Renaissance of Byzantium.[29]

Despite a lack of dated materials, Grabar postulated that this shift of taste was facilitated by the looting of the Fatimid treasury in 450/1060, which he suggested resulted in the sale and distribution of imperial art objects throughout Cairo, thereby familiarising the urban public with the figural forms that had been previously limited to the palace. In Grabar's calculation, the 'Muslim tradition ... of a *private* palace decoration of human figures and scenes involving people suddenly appeared to all.'[30] According to Grabar, the looting not only dispersed figural examples produced for the Fatimid rulers, such as those found on the wooden beams preserved from the palace, but also resulted in the circulation of Byzantine objects, thereby exposing the Cairene public to the more figural style of Byzantium.

Grabar's contention that a distinct historical event revolutionised artistic production relies on his assertion that a class of urban bourgeoisie became increasingly important patrons at this time. Scholars have long considered the likely patronage context of the urban 'bourgeoisie' in the medieval Middle East. Bolstered particularly by Goitein's watershed study of the Cairo Geniza, a theory emerged that a rising merchant class shaped the art market beginning in the 4th/10th century and continuing through to the Mongol conquests.[31] According to Grabar, this class was comprised largely of wealthy merchants and traders, who existed outside the imperial context but created a demand for works of art in Cairo.[32] He posited that the merging of the tastes of this rising bourgeois class and the sudden exposure to Fatimid courtly arts resulted in the artistic innovations of the 5th/11th century, arguing that 'the arts – and perhaps the whole culture – of the classical Islamic world grew and developed through a complex interaction between princely and urban tastes and needs.'[33] According to Grabar, this synthesis resulted in a new style, combining the attributes of an international princely style, shared throughout the Islamic and Mediterranean courts, with more local, Egyptian elements. Thus, Grabar argued that although the royal arts of the Fatimids shared characteristics with other Mediterranean imperial arts, the true Fatimid innovations remained a local, Egyptian phenomenon.

Islamic art scholarship has grown exponentially since Ettinghausen and Grabar's writings. Although the field in general has taken a sharp turn to consider later periods of production, several publications have reassessed Fatimid artistic production since Ettinghausen and Grabar's articles. However, scholars generally continue to accept these earlier conclusions that there is something special and traceable about the Fatimid love of dynamic, naturalistic, figural art. These attributions inform museum categorisation and scholarly attribution, creating a connoisseurial house of cards for Fatimid art and medieval Islamic art more broadly.

Most scholars, including Ettinghausen and Grabar, have accepted the importance of lustreware in understanding the particularities of a discernible Fatimid style and have relied on the paintings found on these vessels to trace developments in painting. In lustre, we find an abundance of extant examples, a few dated pieces and a remarkable corpus of signed pieces.[34] Unfortunately, there is little information in the Fatimid sources providing insight into the importance of lustreware or even painting more broadly in Fatimid culture. Perhaps it is most telling that, despite its utility as a rare primary source with rich descriptions of medieval objects, the *Book of Gifts and Rarities* does not mention anything that may be related specifically to lustre objects. Indeed, the book plays little heed to painting or figural representation in general. Instead, it focuses on the materiality of objects, outlining the precious materials of the courts, including gold, silver, precious stones and rock crystal.[35] Vessels are described in terms of the precious objects they contain. The Fatimid 'realism' or 'figuralism' celebrated by modern scholars is never mentioned in the source, except in instances in which the materials are rare or the work itself inspires a particular sense of wonder (*'aja'ib*).[36] Nowhere does the text suggest that lustre painting as an art form was particularly valued, nor does it indicate an appreciation for various types of painting or the development of an attributable artistic style. Ironically, the marvellous objects described no longer survive, precisely because the value of their raw material encouraged destruction and reuse. Therefore, due to both the lower status of lustre ceramics for the medieval patron and the value placed on figural painting by the modern scholar/curator/collector, lustre ceramics with painted figural scenes surely play a larger role in our modern understanding of Fatimid-era art than they did for the medieval viewer.[37]

Muslim's Workshop and Dated Pieces

Given the paucity of concrete information available on extant Egyptian lustreware, it is difficult to trace the development of its painting or fully consider the context of its production. This is made all the more vexing in that many of these museum pieces are heavily restored.[38] However, inscriptional evidence offers a window into the dating and context of select examples from the reign of the Fatimid Imam-caliph al-Hakim (r. 386–411/996–1024). Notably, a fragment in the Museum of Islamic Art in Cairo contains a dedication to the 'Commander-in-Chief Ghaban (Qaʻid al-Quwwad Ghaban)' (figure IV.6.4). As this individual served al-Hakim only from 401–404/1011–1013, this fragment provides a precise two-year window of production.[39] An even more useful inscription allows us to date an entire corpus of lustre objects. This piece, a mere fragment now held in the Benaki Museum in Athens includes an inscription on the front, reading 'Muslim b. al-Dahhan to please [. . .] Hasan Iqbal al-Hakimi' (figure IV.6.5).[40] The inclusion of this inscription provides a few bits of significant information. First, the presence of the artist's name – Muslim b. al-Dahhan (Muslim, the painter's son) – offers strong evidence for the high status of the creator or workshop. It preserves the name not hidden away on the back of the piece but as part of the main design, thus celebrating the role of the maker. Elsewhere, Margaret Graves has argued that the medieval craftsman occupied a higher, more intellectual status than we often assume.[41] The presence of Muslim's name, next to that of

Figure IV.6.4 Lustre dish dedicated to Ghaban, 401–404/1011–1013. Museum of Islamic Art, Cairo.

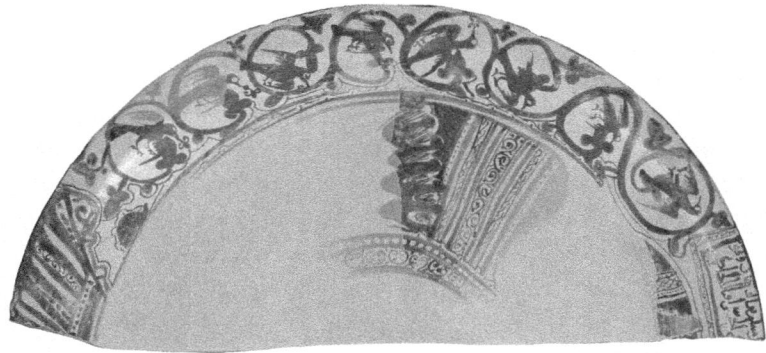

Figure IV.6.5 Lustre fragment, with the inscription 'Muslim bin al-Dahhan to please[…]Hasan Iqbal al-Hakimi'. Benaki Museum, Athens.

the patron, on the front of this vessel suggests that this status was overtly recognised by both the vessel's patron and its painter.

Unfortunately, scholars have been unable to identify the figure of Hasan Iqbal specifically. However, the title 'al-Hakimi' tells us that this piece is also from the reign of al-Hakim bi-Amr Allah.[42] Most importantly, it allows us to give a rough date to the dozens of lustre objects which bear the signature 'Muslim b. al-Dahhan' or, simply, 'Muslim'.[43] Although little is known about the structure of lustre production in this period, given what we know about Islamic workshops in the pre-modern period more broadly, it is reasonable to assume that the signature represents not just a single artist but more likely an artist associated with a larger lustre ceramic workshop.[44] Most significantly, its existence provides us with a crucial key. It allows us to place the broader corpus of objects signed 'Muslim' within a similar framework, allowing for a rare example of a dateable case study of Fatimid artistic production.

This group of objects is one of several groups that include signatures, of the potter, painter, or, more likely, workshop.[45] It is remarkable for the diversity it demonstrates in style and subject, and in quality. Many of the subjects and motifs employed by Muslim's workshop are also found on unsigned objects, most likely produced by other artists/workshops. For example, a reconstructed plate bearing Muslim's signature, now in the Museum of Islamic Art in Cairo, features a wide band of abstract design, executed in alternations of light and dark, and articulated through curved

Figure IV.6.6 Lustre plate with griffon signed by Muslim b. al-Dahhan. Museum of Islamic Art, Cairo.

lines which recall the style of Ghaban's plate (figure IV.6.6). However, unlike the former, the plate signed by Muslim includes a griffin at its centre. As with the abstract rim decoration, the stylised griffin is depicted in silhouette, represented in blocks of positive and negative space, with no suggestion of volume or movement – a mode of depiction that is found in several lustre objects not associated with Muslim's workshop.

In other examples bearing Muslim's name, the so-called Hellenistic style is employed with clear relations to ancient Greek painting, such as in a banquet scene, now in the Benaki Museum, Athens (figure IV.6.7). In this example, white figures are set against a dark background. The folds of their garments are articulated clearly in fine black lines, giving the viewer a glimpse of the bodies beneath the clothing. The articulation of the folds allows us to observe the position of the limbs and torso. Once again, this mode of depiction and its relation to classical forms is also found beyond the context of Muslim's workshop.

A reconstructed bowl in the Metropolitan Museum of Art displays a large heraldic eagle, outlined in lines of varying thickness on a white

Figure IV.6.7 Banquet Scene in the 'Hellenistic' style, signed by Muslim; areas with white background have been heavily overpainted. Benaki Museum, Athens.

surface (figure IV.6.8). In the background, the so-called peacock eye motif fills the space. This outlined form with the peacock eye is also found in fragments signed by Muslim, in which we find two men leading giraffes (figure IV.6.9). These fragments are remarkably similar to a reconstructed bowl in the Benaki Museum, which Ettinghausen referred to as an example of the new Fatimid realism (figure IV.6.10). He wrote in 'its general aspect as well as the running gait of its attendant indicate(s) that the whole is based on actual, though still deficient, observation.'[46] However, the sketchiness of the line does not necessarily indicate it was painted from life – a value derived from the development of western painting. Indeed, the patterning on the giraffe's body is heavily stylised, not at all what one would see through observation; the stereotypical pinwheel pose of the attendant, although certainly lively, likewise is a pose one is unlikely to find in any natural reality where gravity is in operation. Most significantly, this particular scene is found

Figure IV.6.8 Lustre bowl with eagle, signed by Muslim, Metropolitan Museum of Art, New York.

in multiple versions, suggesting that rather than drawing from life, a series of prototypes were used, helping us to discount Ettinghausen's claim.[47]

In her analysis of works by Muslim, Viktoria Meinecke-Berg also disagreed with Ettinghausen and argued that the giraffe and groom were not drawn from life.[48] She notes the similarities between the pieces and suggests that the unsigned object was also produced in Muslim's workshop. However, it is also possible to imagine that these were simply multiple renditions of a popular subject.[49] The fact that we can find such overlap between signed and unsigned pieces, as in the case with the giraffe fragments as well as the Ghaban plate, suggests an awareness of other artistic styles and a system of prototypes in which motifs were copied and

Figure IV.6.9 Lustre fragments of a mirrored composition featuring two men leading giraffes, signed by Muslim, Museum für Islamische Kunst – Staatliche Museen Berlin.

new paintings were modelled after previous examples, rather than there being a signature style associated with an individual workshop.

Meinecke-Berg recognised the stylistic diversity in Muslim's corpus and argued that the styles developed *within* this group. She writes:

> From Muslim's early griffin in the Metropolitan Museum to his banquet scene, which belongs to a group of lustre paintings representing complex figural scenes, seem to lie worlds apart. And yet, this process of development from an ornamentalized décor to a free picture like painting took place, as we can witness in the workshop of Muslim, only in a short span of time. Unfortunately, we are not able to study these ceramics in the context from which they emerge: the painting of the court.[50]

This assessment accepts the linear models of stylistic development outlined by earlier scholars but in this case, suggesting that these were developed within the timespan of Muslim's production.

Ultimately, it is impossible to accept that the full development of the 'Fatimid style' progressed rapidly within the context and timeline of a single workshop, as Meinecke-Berg suggested.[51] Moreover, the pervasiveness of a narrative in which painting can be charted in a linear

Figure IV.6.10 Lustre bowl with giraffe and groom. Benaki Museum, Athens.

trajectory dismisses the agency of the medieval maker, who surely made choices during the process of production, deciding to work from an older prototype in one instance, while pushing forward another mode of production in another, depending on the market, the patron, or simply his preference on the day. Placing a work on a timeline based on style or subject relegates the artist to the role of an automaton, a passive, anonymous cog in the wheels of time rather than an active agent in artistic creation.[52] It is far more reasonable to conclude from considering this corpus that, in fact, various styles coexisted and that the examples from Muslim's workshop illustrate not simply a sudden rupture in taste, as Grabar had suggested, but a diversity of taste, quality and style at a given moment, evidenced in the workshop's artistic variety. Thus, Muslim's pieces demonstrate the flexibility, artistic agency and conscious stylistic choice that scholars rarely consider in the 'minor' arts of the medieval period.

In many scholarly considerations, it is assumed that the context for production of these objects lies in the Fatimid court. For example, Meinecke-Berg lamented that we could not know the true context of these works – the Fatimid court.[53] Similarly, Caiger-Smith wrote that lustreware 'evoked the supreme status of a ruler, of the court where the riches of the arts were gathered in one place, and of the heavenly powers without whose help the court could not have come to be.'[54] On the other hand, Grabar's early premise argued that the originality of the 'Fatimid style' resulted from the interaction of princely culture and the urban bourgeoisie, introducing the concept of a non-royal art market. Unfortunately, we possess little direct knowledge regarding the patronage of such objects. While many scholars have agreed that lustre production was relatively expensive and highly skilled, it is impossible to know exactly how costly these objects were. Clearly, they were far less expensive than precious metals, ivories, rock crystal, or silk and gold textiles that were associated with and controlled by the court. But the Muslim fragment bearing the title *al-Hakimi* also suggests a closeness to court culture. Moreover, some of the stylistic parallels between these objects and what are clearly royal commissions, such as the palace beams, further indicate either the involvement of the Fatimid court or support the notion of shared artistic sources or identities between the court and lustre producers. However, there is no reason to assume that lustre objects were a purely royal prerogative.[55]

In fact, the likelihood of a multiplicity of patronage structures is evident even within Muslim's corpus. The indication of a non-royal patronage source is demonstrated particularly clearly in a plate found in Cairo's Museum of Islamic Art (figure IV.6.11). In the centre of the plate is a lustre-painted interlaced five-pointed star with pseudo-Kufic writing.[56] The piece is signed by Muslim but it is unlikely that this meaningless pseudo-Arabic would be produced for the literate Fatimid court.[57] However, its existence suggests that written Arabic held prestige and appeal for its intended audience.[58] It tells us that the patrons for whom the plate was produced wished to emulate this prestige, even if they might not understand enough to care that the content was gibberish.[59] A possible clue – though one that opens an entirely new line of questioning – is found in the centre text of the piece. While pseudo-Kufic decorates most of the star, the centre text is executed in clearly legible Arabic script,

Figure IV.6.11 Lustre bowl signed by Muslim. Museum of Islamic Art, Cairo.

reading 'Muslim ibn al-Dahhan of Egypt' (*al-Misr*). The prominence of the artist's name – front and centre of the object – tells us that the workshop was known, valued and prestigious enough to warrant pride of place. The presence of *al-Misr* as a place name associates the work with Egypt more broadly and, particularly, beyond the royal confines of Fatimid Cairo, which would have been known as al-Qahira, thereby overtly moving the context of the dish beyond the context of the court.

Conclusion

A reevaluation of seminal works on Fatimid figuralism in lustreware demonstrates the problematic foundations on which many of our assumptions about Fatimid art rest. Ettinghausen and Grabar's early writings on lustre painting placing it in a developmental model that celebrates figuralism and naturalism were written as a clear attempt to present Islamic painting as a high art form, moving the medieval Islamic object away from the category of 'minor' arts while developing a canon of master painters and masterworks of Islamic art fit for museum display. In so doing, these objects are raised to level of western art – mimicking the development of Greek vase paintings or later panel painting. This argument then becomes tautological – if Fatimid art is figural and naturalistic, then unprovenanced examples of painting that are figural and naturalistic must be Fatimid. And so the narrative moves in circles to support itself. But the foundation of this argument is a shaky house of cards based on connoisseurship of insecure provenance.[60] Such a teleology subsumes the medieval artist to the role of automaton, helpless to resist the tides of historical change.[61] The examination of the Muslim pieces demonstrate that many styles of representation existed at once – introducing the role of artistic choice and agency. By evaluating this small piece of Islamic art, we see a case study of how the adoption of western narrative structures of art history – which have been broadly critiqued by scholars – play out in a foundational understanding of the field.[62]

NOTES

1 Richard Ettinghausen, 'Painting in the Fatimid Period: A Reconstruction', *Ars Islamica*, 9 (1942), pp. 112–124; Richard Ettinghausen, 'Early Realism in Islamic Art', in *Studi Orientalistici in onore di Giorgio Levi della Vida* (Rome, 1956), pp. 250–273; Oleg Grabar, 'Imperial and Urban Art in Islam: The Subject-Matter of Fatimid Art', in *Colloque international sur l'histoire du Caire* (Cairo, 1969), pp. 173–190.

2 For an overview of this Hegelian narrative in the context of the medieval Islamic object, see Avinoam Shalem, 'The Discovery and Rediscovery of the Medieval Islamic Object', in Finbarr Barry Flood and Gülru Necipoğlu, ed., *A Companion to Islamic Art and Architecture*, (Hoboken, NJ, 2017), pp. 558–578. The literature on Islamic art historiography and its inextricable but unsatisfactory link to western art historiography is vast. See especially see Gülru Necipoğlu, 'The Concept of Islamic Art: Inherited Discourses and New Approaches', in Benoît Junod et al., ed., *Islamic Art and the Museum* (London, 2012); Shalem, 'The Discovery and Rediscovery of the Medieval Islamic Object'; Finbarr Barry Flood, 'From the Prophet to Postmodernism? New World Orders and the End of Islamic Art', in Elizabeth Mansfield, ed., *Making Art History: A Changing Discipline and Its Institutions* (London and New York, 2007); Wendy Shaw, 'The Islam in Islamic Art History: Secularism and Public Discourse', in Margaret Graves and Moya Carey, ed., *Journal of Art Historiography*, 6 (June 2012); These articles and others are compiled with an excellent introduction in Margaret Graves and Moya Carey, ed., 'The Historiography of Islamic Art and Architecture', *Journal of Art Historiography*, 6 (June 2012).

3 We lack textual evidence of artistic workshops in the Fatimid period. More information on artistic workshops and production methods are available for the later, particularly Persian, context. Abu'l-Qasim preserved descriptions of the manufacture of decoration of ceramics in his 8th/14th-century text, *Arayis al-jawahir va nafayis al-atayib* and a chapter by Jawhari Nishaburi in *Jawahir namah-yi Nizami* describes the production of lustre ceramics from ca. 592/1196. See, 'Appendix: The Technology of Medieval Islamic

Ceramics: A Study of Two Persian Manuscripts', in Oliver Watson, Moujan Matin and Will Kwiatkowski, *Ceramics of Iran: Islamic Pottery from the Sarikhani Collection* (New Haven; London, 2020); J.W. Allan, 'Abu'l-Qasim's Treatise on Ceramics', *Iran*, 11 (1973), pp. 111–120. On Persian bookmaking and the role of the artist, see especially David J. Roxburgh, 'Kamal al-Din Bihzad and Authorship in Persian Painting', *Muqarnas*, 17 (2000), pp. 119–146.

4 Of course, the medieval Islamic world is not unique in having an abundance of pottery as evidence. Its durability and versatility makes it the most prevalent surviving material throughout the world before the early modern period. For an embellished discussion of wondrous discussions of objects in the Fatimid and other medieval Islamic treasuries, see Ghada al-Hijjawi al-Qaddumi, *Book of Gifts and Rarities. Kitab al-Hadaya Wa al-Tuhaf* (Cambridge, 1996). On the reuse of medieval objects, see especially Avinoam Shalem, *Islam Christianized: Islamic Portable Objects in the Medieval Church Treasuries of the Latin West* (2nd rev. ed., Frankfurt am Main and New York, 1998).

5 On Fustat, see especially the excavation reports published by George Scanlon, largely in the *Journal of the American Research Center in Egypt* and earlier publications by Aly Bahgat. On the distinction of Fustat and Cairo, see Irene Bierman, *Writing Signs: The Fatimid Public Text* (Berkeley, 1998); Paula Sanders, *Ritual, Politics, and the City in Fatimid Cairo* (Albany, NY, 1994); Jennifer Pruitt, *Building the Caliphate: Construction, Destruction, and Sectarian Identity in Early Fatimid Architecture* (New Haven, 2020); For a counterpoint, see Jonathan Bloom, 'Walled Cities in Islamic North Africa and Egypt with Particular Reference to the Fatimids (909-1171)', in James D. Tracy, ed., *City Walls: The Urban Enceinte in Global Perspective* (Cambridge, 2000), pp. 219–246.

6 For the history of archaeology in Fustat, see Tanya Treptow, 'A History of Excavations at Fustat', in Tanya Treptow and Tasha Vorderstrasse, ed., *A Cosmopolitan City: Muslims, Christians, and Jews in Old Cairo* (Chicago, 2015), pp. 99–107; Jere Bacharach, *Fustat Finds; Beads, Coins, Medical Instruments, Textiles, and Other Artifacts from the Awad Collection* (Cairo, 2002). For a consideration of how archaeology and art history have approached lustre and a useful chronology for glazed wares, see Robert B. Mason, 'Mediaeval Egyptian Lustre-Painted and Associated Wares: Typology in a Multidisciplinary Study', *Journal of the American Research Center in Egypt*, 34 (1997), pp. 201–242.

7 On the hunting scenes in the Fatimid palace, see Nasir-i Khusraw, *Book of Travels (Safarnama)*, tr. W.M. Thackston (Albany, NY, 1986), p. 73. For a discussion, see Jennifer Pruitt, *Building the Caliphate: Construction, Destruction, and Sectarian Identity in Early Fatimid Architecture* (New Haven, 2020), pp. 38–39.

8 On Fatimid architecture, see especially Doris Behrens-Abouseif, *Islamic Architecture in Cairo: An Introduction* (Leiden and New York, 1989); Caroline Williams, 'The Cult of 'Alid Saints in the Fatimid Monuments of Cairo. Part I: The Mosque of al-Aqmar', *Muqarnas*, 1 (1983), pp. 37–52; Caroline Williams, 'The Cult of 'Alid Saints in the Fatimid Monuments of Cairo Part II: The Mausolea', *Muqarnas*, 3 (1985), pp. 39–60; Bierman, *Writing Signs: The Fatimid Public Text*; Sanders, *Ritual, Politics, and the City in Fatimid Cairo*; Ayman F. Sayyid, *La Capitale de l'Égypte jusqu'à l'époque Fatimide: Al-Qahira et al-Fustat: Essai de réconstitution topographique* (Beirut and Stuttgart, 1998); Jonathan Bloom, *Arts of the City Victorious* (New Haven and London, 2007); Pruitt, *Building the Caliphate*.

9 For literature on Fatimid art objects, see Marianne Barrucand, *Trésors Fatimides du Caire: Exposition présenté a l'Institut du Monde Arabe du 28 Avril au 30 Août 1998* (Paris, 1998); Marianne Barrucand, ed., *L'Egypte Fatimide: son art et son histoire* (Paris, 1999); Tanya Treptow and Tasha Vorderstrasse, ed., *A Cosmopolitan City: Muslims, Christians, and Jews in Old Cairo* (Chicago, 2015); Bloom, *Arts of the City Victorious*; Assadullah Souren Melikian-Chirvani, ed., *The World of the Fatimids* (Toronto, London & Munich, 2018).

10 In fact, only one example of an Islamic ceramics workshop has been identified specifically as a courtly endeavour. See, Gülru Necipoğlu, 'From International Timurid to Ottoman: A Change of Taste in Sixteenth-Century Ceramic Tiles', *Muqarnas*, 7 (1990), pp. 136–70; Oliver Watson, 'Ceramics and Circulation', in Finbarr Barry Flood and Gülru Necipoğlu, ed., *A Companion to Islamic Art and Architecture* (Hoboken, NJ, 2017), p. 479.

11 Oliver Watson and Mathaf al-Kuwait al-Watani, ed., *Ceramics from Islamic Lands* (London, 2004), pp. 183–184; 'Appendix: The Technology of Medieval Islamic Ceramics: A Study of Two Persian Manuscripts.' The technique began in glass in the pre-Islamic period and was added to ceramics in Iraq in the Abbasid period. Lustre painting probably made its way from Iraq to Egypt in the 4th/10th century, with production in Iraq ending abruptly, probably due to the shifting tides of economic vitality from Mesopotamia to Egypt with the rise of the Fatimids. Watson, 'Ceramics and Circulation', p. 493. See also Mason, 'Mediaeval Egyptian Lustre-Painted and Associated Wares: Typology in a Multidisciplinary Study', p. 203.

12 Matthew Saba has convincingly explored the impact of lustre and wonder in the Abbasid court; see Matt Saba, 'Abbasid Lusterware and the Aesthetics of 'Ajab', *Muqarnas*, 29 (2012), pp. 187–212; idem, 'A Restricted Gaze: The Ornament of the Main Caliphal Palace of Samarra', *Muqarnas*, 32 (2015), pp. 155–196. For lustre at Takht-i-Sulayman, see Oliver Watson, *Persian Lustre Ware* (London, 1985); Linda Komaroff et al., ed., *The Legacy of Genghis Khan: Courtly Art and Culture in Western Asia, 1256–1353* (New York, 2002).

13 Ibid., p. 27.

14 For recent iconographic studies of Fatimid lustre, see Fahmida Suleman, 'The Lion, the Hare and Lustre Ware', in Venetia Porter and Mariam Rosser-Owen, ed., *Metalwork and Material Culture in the Islamic World: Art, Craft and Text. Festschrift in Honour of Professor James W. Allan* (London, 2012), pp. 215–232; Fahmida Suleman, 'Making Love Not War: The Iconography of the Cockfight in Medieval Egypt', in Francesa Leoni and Mika Natif, ed., *Eros and Sexuality in Islamic Art* (Burlington, VT, 2013), pp. 19–42.

15 Ettinghausen, 'Painting in the Fatimid Period: A Reconstruction'.

16 Ibid., p. 112.

17 See Eva Hoffman, 'Pathways of Portability: Islamic and Christian Interchange from the Tenth to Twelfth Century', *Art History*, 24 (2001), pp. 17–50; William Tronzo, *The Cultures of His Kingdom: Roger II and the Cappella Palatina in Palermo* (Princeton, NJ, 1997); Ernst J. Grube and Jeremy Johns, ed., *The Painted Ceilings of the Cappella Palatina* (Genoa, 2005).

18 Eva Hoffman has demonstrated that even the art historical narrative claiming that the art of the Umayyads is based on a Greco-Roman model while the Abbasids looked further east has been overstated, see Eva Hoffman, 'Between East and West: The Wall Paintings of Samarra and The Construction of Abbasid Princely Culture', *Muqarnas*, 25 (2008), pp. 107–132.

19 Ettinghausen, 'Early Realism in Islamic Art'.

20 It is important to note that the 'Samarra style' considered by Ettinghausen is based on wall paintings, ceramic wine jars and other examples of polychrome Iraqi painting. It does not consider Abbasid lustreware, which is remarkably different and generally more abstract than polychrome Samarran painting and Fatimid lustreware. Some contemporaries took issue with his approach, although accepting an inherent stylistic development in Islamic art. For example, Ernst Grube argued that Fatimid 'realism' was not an innovative Fatimid development but a continuation of Hellenistic traditions in 'Realism or Formalism'; see, E. J. Grube, 'Realism or Formalism: Notes on Some Fatimid Lustre-Painted Ceramics Vessels', in Renato Traini, ed., *Studie in onore di Francesco Gabrieli nel suo ottantesimo compleanno* (Rome, 1984), pp. 423–432.

21 For a critique of this approach in both Islamic art history and Islamic history more broadly, see Gülru Necipoğlu and Finbarr Barry Flood, 'Frameworks of Islamic Art and Architectural History', in Finbarr Barry Flood and Gülru Necipoğlu, ed., *A Companion to Islamic Art and Architecture* (Hoboken, NJ, 2017), pp. 223–249; S. D. Goitein, 'A Plea for the Periodization of Islamic History', *Journal of the American Oriental Society*, 88 (1968), pp. 224–228.
22 This is not to say that this typified Ettinghausen's writings. A pillar in the field, Ettinghausen played a large role in establishing Islamic art as a serious academic discipline. But, as with any intellectual endeavour, he was a product of his time and it is always necessary to re-examine those aspects of the discipline that no longer stand up to closer evaluation.
23 Ettinghausen, 'Early Realism in Islamic Art', p. 250.
24 These are examples of what Oleg Grabar has described as the 'princely cycle'. See Oleg Grabar, *The Formation of Islamic Art* (Rev. ed., New Haven, 1987), pp. 145–178.
25 Ettinghausen, 'Early Realism in Islamic Art', pp. 250–251.
26 Ibid., p. 271.
27 Grabar, 'Imperial and Urban Art in Islam: The Subject-Matter of Fatimid Art'.
28 Grabar argues for the replacement of Ettinghausen's consideration of 'realism' in Fatimid art to a discussion of 'spatialism'. Although the terms are different, they ultimately refer to the same artistic tendencies.
29 The idea of the Macedonian Renaissance has since been problematised by Byzantine scholars. This was a view particularly championed by Kurt Weitzmann in *The Joshua Roll, a Work of the Macedonian Renaissance* (Princeton, NJ, 1948); Kurt Weitzmann, *Studies in Classical and Byzantine Manuscript Illumination* (Chicago, 1971). For a history of the reception of the idea, see John Hanson, 'The Rise and Fall of the Macedonian Renaissance', in Liz James, ed., *A Companion to Byzantium* (Chichester, UK; Malden, MA, 2010), pp. 338–350.
30 Grabar, 'Imperial and Urban Art in Islam: The Subject-Matter of Fatimid Art', p. 185.
31 See S. D. Goitein, *A Mediterranean Society : The Jewish Communities of the Arab World as Portrayed in the Documents of the Cairo* Geniza (Berkeley, CA, 1967–1993). For a discussion of the problematic use of this term, which originates in a Marxist scholarly framework, see Anna Contadini, 'Patronage and the Idea of an Urban Bourgeoisie', in Finbarr Barry Flood and Gülru Necipoğlu, ed., *A Companion to Islamic Art and Architecture* (Hoboken, NJ, 2017), p. 431.
32 A similar argument was later made by Ettinghausen in examining Saljuq art. See Richard Ettinghausen, "The Flowering of Seljuq Art', *The Metropolitan Museum of Art Bulletin*, 3 (1970), pp. 113–131.
33 Grabar, 'Imperial and Urban Art in Islam: The Subject-Matter of Fatimid Art', p. 186.
34 The production technique probably originated in glass. While scholars had earlier accepted that the technique originated in Iraq under the Abbasids and then spread throughout the Islamic world, it has also been suggested it began in Egypt. Early examples of lustre have been found in Samarra, Fustat and even in Spain, North Africa and Pakistan. See, Alan Caiger-Smith, *Lustre Pottery: Technique, Tradition, and Innovation in Islam and the Western World* (London, 1985), p. 21.
35 The text also suggests that objects made from pure gold and silver were melted down with the looting of the treasury, concluding that after this event 'There were no longer craftsmen who could manufacture anything comparable to what had been burnt, nor similar articles existed. It vanished like the bygone past [for ever].' al-Qaddumi, *Book of Gifts and Rarities. Kitab al-Hadaya wa al-Tuhaf*, p. 231.
36 For example, the text describes a 'gold peacock studded with precious gemstones, whose eyes were of ruby, its feathers of glass enamel inlaid with gold [cloisonné], emulating the [natural] colours of peacock feathers; also [there was] a gold rooster

similar to the peacock, with a split crest – the largest rooster crests ever known – studded with all kinds of large pearls and precious stones, whose eyes were of ruby; and [there was] a gazelle that looked, in colour and shape, like a real gazelle. It was similar to both][the peacock and rooster] in being studded with large pearls and precious stones. I was told that the gazelle's belly was the only white [spot] on its body – just like the colour of [real] gazelles, and it was closely set with magnificent large pearls.' al-Qaddumi, p. 238. Here the celebration of mimesis is less about painterly – or the sculptor's – skill and more about the marshalling of precious materials to represent existing beings. For a discussion of painterly skill to represent the wondrous and strange in Islamic art, see Nasser Rabbat, "Ajib and Gharib: Artistic Perception in Medieval Arabic Sources', *Medieval History Journal* (2006), pp. 99–113.

37 This is not to say that painting or realism is *never* mentioned in the medieval sources. In one of the most famous examples of medieval commentary on painting, an excerpt, preserved in al-Maqrizi's *Khitat*, describes a painting competition in which one painter seeks to paint an illusionistic image of a woman appearing to go *into* a wall while another paints an image of the woman appearing to come *out* of the wall. This is discussed in Nasser Rabbat, "Ajib and Gharib: Artistic Perception in Medieval Arabic Sources', *Medieval History Journal* (2006), pp. 99–113.

38 For a detailed consideration of the reconstruction of one vessel, see Fahmida Suleman. 'The Lion, the Hare, and Lustre Ware: Studies in the Iconography of Lustre Ceramics from Fāṭimid Egypt (969-1171)', (PhD, University of Oxford, 2003), chapter 4. For a detailed reconstruction of a lustre bowl from the Persian context, see Francesca Leoni et al., '"The Illusion of an Authentic Experience;": A Luster Bowl in the Ashmolean Museum', *Muqarnas*, 36 (2019), pp. 229–249.

39 Scholars have referred to this as Gaban Ghaban but it seems that Ghain is closest to the original. For the sake of familiarity, I use the more familiar Ghaban here. This fragment was first associated with al-Hakim's reign in al-Basha, 'Tabaq min al-khazaf bi-ism Ghabn Mawla al-Hakim bi-Amr Allah'. Meinecke-Berg, 'Fatimid Painting: On Tradition and Style', pp. 352–353. Ghaban was executed in ca. 403/1013. Ettinghausen, 'Early Realism in Islamic Art', p. 250.

40 Meinecke-Berg, 'Fatimid Painting: On Tradition and Style', p. 353; Marilyn Jenkins, 'Muslim: An Early Fatimid Ceramicist', *The Metropolitan Museum of Art Bulletin*, 26 (1968), p. 361.

41 Margaret S. Graves, *Arts of Allusion: Object, Ornament, and Architecture in Medieval Islam* (New York, NY, 2018).

42 For an assessment of al-Hakim's reign, see especially Paul Ernest Walker, *Caliph of Cairo : Al-Hakim bi-Amr Allah, 996-1021* (Cairo, 2009). For an assessment of his architectural programme, see Pruitt, *Building the Caliphate*, chapters 3 and 4; idem, 'Method in Madness: Recontextualizing the Destruction of Churches in the Fatimid Era', *Muqarnas*, 30 (2013), pp. 119–140.

43 The precise number of pieces is an open question. Jenkins writes that there are 20. Meinecke-Berg cites over 60 pieces. It is beyond the scope of this article to address the full corpus. Meinecke-Berg, 'Fatimid Painting: On Tradition and Style'; Jenkins, 'Muslim: An Early Fatimid Ceramicist'; See also Helen Philon, *Early Islamic Ceramics: Ninth to Late Twelfth Centuries*, Catalogue of Islamic Art, Benaki Museum Athens, vol. 1 (London; Totowa, NJ, 1980), p. 168, note 53.

44 We lack textual evidence of artistic workshops in the Fatimid period. More information on artistic workshops and production methods are available for the later, particularly Persian, context. For example, Abu'l-Qasim preserved descriptions of the manufacture and decoration of ceramics in his 10th/14th-century text, *Arayis al-jawahir wa nafayis al-atayib* and a chapter by Jawhari Nishaburi in *Jawahir nama-yi Nizami* describes the production of lustre ceramics from ca. 592/1196. See 'Appendix: The Technology of Medieval Islamic Ceramics: A Study of Two Persian Manuscripts', in Oliver Watson,

Moujan Matin and Will Kwiatkowski, *Ceramics of Iran: Islamic Pottery from the Sarikhani Collection* (New Haven & London, 2020); J.W. Allan, 'Abu'l-Qasim's Treatise on Ceramics', *Iran*, 11 (1973), pp. 111–120. For a comparative later Persian artist, about whom much more is known, see Sheila Blair, 'A Brief Biography of Abu Zayd', *Muqarnas*, 25 (2008), pp. 155–176. On Persian bookmaking and the role of the artist, see especially David J. Roxburgh, 'Kamal al-Din Bihzad and Authorship in Persian Painting', *Muqarnas*, 17 (2000), pp. 119–146.

45   For example, there are groups signed by Sa'ad, Atabib, bin-Assafi and G'afar al-Basr. Alan Caiger-Smith, *Lustre Pottery: Technique, Tradition, and Innovation in Islam and the Western World* (London & Boston, 1985), p. 49. For Sa'd, see Marilyn Jenkins, 'Sa'd: Content and Context', in *Content and Context of Visual Arts in the Islamic World: Papers from a Colloquium in Memory of Richard Ettinghausen* (University Park, PA, 1988), pp. 67–89.

46   Ettinghausen, 'Early Realism in Islamic Art', p. 265.

47   On a comparable example of copying in an early modern Persian context, see Thomas W. Lentz and Glenn D. Lowry, ed., *Timur and the Princely Vision: Persian Art and Culture in the Fifteenth Century* (Los Angeles, 1989). However, we do not have a record of such prototypes for this period.

48   For a consideration of the depiction of the giraffe in these bowls and on the role of the giraffe in the Fatimid context, see Fahmida Suleman, 'Reaching New Heights: The Giraffe in the Material Culture, Ceremonial, and Diplomacy of Fatimid Egypt', in Marcus Milwright and Evanthia Baboula, ed., *Made for the Eye of One Who Sees: Canadian Contributions to the Study of Islamic Art and Archaeology* (Montreal, 2022), pp. 233–254.

49   Marilyn Jenkins had suggested that there were, in fact, 'certain artistic conventions, perhaps standardized in pattern books, that were strictly adhered to in each period.' Jenkins, 'Muslim: An Early Fatimid Ceramicist', p. 358.

50   Meinecke-Berg, 'Fatimid Painting: On Tradition and Style', p. 358.

51   Although she posits the development of such a model in Muslim's workshop, she also notes that the conventional approach to the giraffe, which she compares to a representation in the *Kitab al-Hayawan* of al-Jahiz. Meinecke-Berg, 'Fatimid Painting: On Tradition and Style', p. 355.

52   On the status of the artist, see Graves, *Arts of Allusion*, chapter 1.

53   Meinecke-Berg, 'Fatimid Painting: On Tradition and Style', p. 358.

54   Caiger-Smith, *Lustre Pottery*, p. 35.

55   Apart from Muslim's workshop, there are prominent examples of lustreware that were clearly not imperial Fatimid commissions. Most notably, two well-known pieces of lustre contain overtly Christian subjects. One, a plate fragment now in Cairo Museum of Islamic Art (inv. no. 5397/1), features a clear depiction of a haloed Christ, raising his hand in blessing. The other example, now in the Victoria and Albert Museum, shows a Coptic priest holding a censer (inv. no. C 49-1952). See Barrucand, *Trésors Fatimides du Caire*, p. 156; Anna Contadini, *Fatimid Art at the Victoria and Albert Museum* (London, 1998), pl. 34; Pruitt, *Building the Caliphate*, pp. 51–55.

56   On the multivalent resonance of pseudo-Kufic in a Byzantine context, see Alicia Walker, 'Pseudo-Arabic "Inscriptions" and the Pilgrim's Path at Hosios Loukas', in *Viewing Inscriptions in the Late Antique and Medieval World* (New York, 2015), pp. 99–123; Alicia Walker, 'Meaningful Mingling: Classicizing Imagery and Islamicizing Script in a Byzantine Bowl', *The Art Bulletin* (2008), pp. 32–48.

57   On the semiotics of writing in the Fatimid context, see Bierman, *Writing Signs: The Fatimid Public Text*.

58   For a thorough consideration of epigraphic ceramics, see Rebecca Stevens Wrightson, 'Legibility, Ambiguity, and the Patterning of Arabic Script: Epigraphic Ceramics of the Early Islamic World' (PhD thesis, University of Oxford, 2021).

59　It is also possible that the pseudo-Kufic seen here, particularly in combination with the 5-pointed star, served magical, talismanic purposes. On the use of mirroring in this context, see Venetia Porter, 'The Use of the Arabic Script in Magic', in M.C.A. MacDonald, ed., *The Development of Arabic as a Written Language* (Oxford, 2010), pp. 131–140.

60　In fact, in researching Islamic lustre, I am consistently reminded of Graves's brilliant summary of scholarly anxiety:

> The lot of the specialist in medieval Islamic portable arts is, from some perspectives, an alarming one. Before her is a vast corpus of dislocated objects, many (if not most) of them without a shred of any archaeological record or reliable provenance data prior to their arrival on the international art market in the nineteenth or twentieth century. She can never be too vigilant about the authenticity of her subjects, which have a tendency to pick up interesting 'enhancements' or become optimistically 'completed' on their way to market. At night she has horrible dreams about clever forgeries. But before you weep too much for this hypothetical scholar, consider the extraordinary richness of the materials among which she picks her way. The art of the object reached unparalleled heights in the medieval Islamic world. Objects of beauty and technical virtuosity, objects that traveled and passed between hands—these works were at the heart of the cosmopolitan city cultures that blossomed across the dar al-Islam in the centuries prior to the Mongol conquests of the thirteenth century, and beyond. Graves, *Arts of Allusion*, 1.

The issue of enhancements and even forgeries are not dealt with in this article. But in reassessing the Fatimid style, these questions need to be taken seriously, item by item.

61　For a reassessment of the role of the medieval Islamic artist, see especially Contadini, *Fatimid Art at the Victoria and Albert Museum*, pl. 34. For a discussion of approaches to the medieval Islamic object, see Shalem, 'The Discovery and Rediscovery of the Medieval Islamic Object'.

62　See especially Necipoğlu, 'The Concept of Islamic Art: Inherited Discourses and New Approaches'; Shalem, 'The Discovery and Rediscovery of the Medieval Islamic Object'; Flood, 'From the Prophet to Postmodernism? New World Orders and the End of Islamic Art'; Shaw, 'The Islam in Islamic Art History: Secularism and Public Discourse'; These articles and others are compiled with an excellent introduction in Graves and Carey, 'The Historiography of Islamic Art and Architecture'.

Image Credits

Preface

figs 1 and 2 © Gregory Bilotto

Part II

fig. II.1.1 © K.A.C. Creswell Collection of Photographs of Islamic Architecture, Rare Books and Special Collections Library, The American University in Cairo; figs II.1.2, II.1.3 and II.1.4 © Matjaž Kačičnik; fig. II.1.5a K.A.C. Creswell, V&A Museum, 1284–1921© Ashmolean Museum, Oxford (EA.CA.3406); fig. II.1.6a © Bernard O'Kane; figs II.1.5b, II.1.6b and II.1.8 © Dina Ishak Bakhoum; fig. II.1.7 Beniamino Facchinelli © Bibliothèque de l'Institut national d'histoire de l'art, Paris, Jacques Doucet collections, Photo library, Archaeology Egypt I, 012, no. 22; figs II.4.1, II.4.2 and II.4.3, public domain, 2025; figs II.5.1 and II.5.3 Bodleian Library, Oxford; figs II.5.2 and II.5.4 prepared by Oxford Designers & Illustrators, Ltd, first published in Yossef Rapoport and Emilie Savage-Smith, *Lost Maps of the Caliphs* (Chicago, IL, 2018)

Part III

figs III.1.1 and III.1.2 © American Numismatic Society (ANS); fig. III.1.3 © Germanisches Nationalmuseum, Nuremberg; fig. III.1.4 © Brooklyn Museum, NY; figs III.1.5, III.1.6 and III.1.7 © Ali Asgar Hussamuddin Alibhai; figs III.2.1to III.2.12 © Bernard O'Kane, except figs III.2.4 (left drawing after Khamis, *The Fatimid Metalwork Hoard from Tiberias. Tiberias: Excavations in the House of the Bronzes*. Final Report, vol. II, 2013); fig. III.2.4 right © Avinoam Shalem; fig. III.4.1 © Musée du Louvre, Paris MOA 23; fig. III.4.2 © Aga Khan Museum, Toronto, AKM 00545; figs III.4.3, III.4.4 and III.4.12, The Metropolitan Museum of Art, NYC 27.170.79; NYC 31.19.13; NYC 1978.546.32; fig. III.4.5 Archaeological

Museum, Madrid; fig. III.4.6 © Stiftsmuseum, Klosterneuburg, KG 152; figs III.4.7 and III.4.8 © Silvia Armando; fig. III.4.9 © Museo Civico d'Arte Antica, Turin, 18o/AV; fig. III.4.10 © The Freer Gallery, Washington, DC, F1977.5; fig. III.4.11© Therese Martin; figs III.5.1, III.5.2, III.5.5, III.5.7, III.5.8, III.5.9, III.5.12, III.5.13, III.5.14, III.5.15, III.5.16, III.5.17, III.5.18, Yasser Tabbaa Archive, courtesy of the Aga Khan Documentation Center, MIT Libraries; fig. III.5.3 after Grohmann, *Arabische Paleographie*, vol. 2, fig. 248; figs III.5.4 and III.5.6 Courtesy of the Aga Khan Documentation Center, MIT Libraries; fig. III.5.10 after Herzfeld, *Matériaux pour un Corpus Inscriptionum Arabicarum*, vol. 2, pl. LX; fig. III.5.11 author's drawing after Moaz and Ory, *Bab al-Saghir*, pl. IVb

Part IV

fig. IV.1.1 (left and centre) © photo by Doris Behrens-Abouseif; (right) © drawing by Juan de Lara; fig. IV.1.2 (a) from Guest and Ettinghausen, 'The Iconography of a Kāshān Luster Plate' (*Ars Orientalis* 4, 1961), plate 15, fig. 50; (b) from Baer, '"Fish-Pond" Ornaments on Persian and Mamluk Metal Vessels' (*BSOAS*, 31, 1968) plate 7; (c) © Museum für Islamische Kunst, Berlin State Museums I.3578; (d) © photo by Doris Behrens-Abouseif; (e) © Princeton University Library, Islamic Manuscripts, Garrett no. 82G; fig. IV.1.3 (top left) and fig. IV.1.4 (right) © Museum With No Frontiers (MWNF)/Discover Islamic Art; (bottom left) from Angela Bellia, 'Twelfth-Century Musical Symbols in the Star-Studded Sky of Ruggero II', *Music in Art*, 37 (2012), p. 29; (Right) courtesy Fabrizio Agnello; fig. IV.1.4 (left) © photo Juan de Lara and Doris Behrens-Abouseif; fig. IV.1.5 (left) photo Wikicommons; (right) from Jean Clédat, *Le Monastère de la Nécropole de* Baouit (*Mémoires de l'IFAO XII*), Cairo, 1904, Institut du Monde Arab, Paris; fig. IV.1.6 left and right photos E14280; X4030 © Musée du Louvre / Beatrice Hafala; (bottom left), © Dumbarton Oaks Research Library and Collection BZ.1932.1; fig. IV.1.7 © modified image from *Mermaids Art, Symbolism and Mythology* (2022), fig. 3.2, courtesy of Axel Müller, Christopher Halls and Ben Williamson; fig. IV.1.8 © The Metropolitan Museum of Art 20.176; figs IV.2.1, IV.2.2, IV.2.3, IV.2.12, IV.2.13, IV.2.15(a), IV.2.16 and IV.2.22 courtesy of Real Colegiata de San Isidoro, Leon; fig. IV.2.4 © Harvard Fine Arts Library, Special Collections SCW2016.11881; fig. IV.2.5 Henry L. Batterman Fund, A. Augustus Healy Fund, Frank Sherman Benson Fund and Ella C. Woodward Memorial Fund © Brooklyn Museum, NY,

69.122.1_PS6.jpg, Creative Commons-BY; figs IV.2.6 and IV.2.7 © V&A Museum C.1614-1921and C.23-1932; fig. IV.2.8 photo © Pinder-Wilson Archive; drawing after Pinder-Wilson and Scanlon, 'Glass Finds from Fustat 1964–71', *Journal of Glass Studies* 15 (1973), fig. 32; fig. IV.2.9 © The Metropolitan Museum of Art, Rogers Fund 1911, 11.205.2; fig. IV.2.10 from Marçais and Poinssot, *Objets kairouanais* (Tunis, 1948); figs IV.2.11 and IV.2.19 © IAA; fig. IV.2.14, and detail, after Manuel Casamar Perez, 'Casket of Hisham II', in J. Dodds, ed., *Al-Andalus*, exh. cat. (New York, 1992), pp. 208–209; fig. IV.2.15 (b) Cairo Museum of Islamic Art, after Barrucand, *Trésors Fatimides*, no. 93; fig. IV.2.17 Chester Beatty Library Is 1431, fol. 6v (detail); fig. IV.2.18 Benaki Museum 13770; fig. IV.2.20 after Gabrieli and Scerrato, *Gli Arabi in Italia* (Milan, 1979), p. 503; fig. IV.2.21 courtesy of Ayala Lester; figs IV.3.1 to IV.3.8 © Israel Antiquities Authority (IAA); figs IV.4.1 to IV.4.7 © Marcus Pilz; with the exception of fig. IV.4.1b © V&A Museum; fig. IV.4.3 © RMN-Grand Palais (Musée du Louvre), Daniel Arnaudet; figs IV.5.1 to IV.5.7 © Stéphane Pradines; fig. IV.6.1 Wikimedia Commons; fig. IV.6.2 Museum of Islamic Art, Cairo 12880 © Fine Art Images/Heritage Images; fig. IV.6.3 © National Museum of Asian Art, Smithsonian Institution, Freer Collection F1946.30; fig. IV.6.4 Museum of Islamic Art, Cairo; figs. IV.6.5; IV.6.7and 6.10 © Benaki Museum 11122; 19376; 749; figs IV.6.6 and 6.11 © Museum of Islamic Art, Cairo 14930 and 15966; fig. IV.6.8 © The Metropolitan Museum of Art 1963 63.178.1. Open Access; fig. IV.6.9 © Museum für Islamische Kunst, Staatliche Museen Berlin, 43/64, 135. Photo, Johannes Kramer

*Every effort has been made to contact copyright holders. Any inadvertent omissions notified will be rectified in subsequent editions.

Select Bibliography

Primary Sources

Ibn al-Athir, 'Izz al-Din Abu'l-Hasan 'Ali. *al-Kamil fi'l-ta'rikh*, ed. C. Tornberg. Leiden, 1851–1876; Cairo, 1303/1885.

Ibn Haytham, Abu 'Abd Allah Ja'far b. Ahmad al-Aswad. *Kitab al-Munazarat*, ed. and tr. by Wilferd Madelung and Paul E. Walker as *The Advent of the Fatimids: A Contemporary Shi'i Witness*. London, 2000.

Ibn al-Haytham, Abu 'Ali al-Hasan. *The Optics of Ibn al-Haytham: Books I–III: On Direct Vision*, tr. A. I. Sabra. London, 1989.

Idris 'Imad al-Din b. al-Hasan. *'Uyun al-akhbar wa funun al-athar*, ed. by Ahmad Chleilat et al. Damascus, 2007–2014, 7 vols.

Ja'far b. Mansur al-Yaman. *Kitab al-'Alim wa'l-ghulam*, ed. and tr. James Morris as *The Master and the Disciple: An Early Islamic Spiritual Dialogue*. London, 2000.

al-Kirmani, Hamid al-Din. *Rahat al-'aql*, ed. M. Kamil Husayn and M. Mustafa Hilmi. Cairo, 1953; ed. Mustafa Ghalib. Beirut, 1967.

Kitab al-Kashf, ed. R. Strothmann, London, etc., 1952; ed. M Ghalib. Beirut, 1984.

al-Maqrizi, Taqi' al-Din Ahmad. *Itti'az al-hunafa bi akhbar al-a'imma al-Fatimiyyin al-khulafa'*, ed. Ayman F. Sayyid. Damascus, 2010. Partial tr. by S. Jiwa as *Towards a Shi'i Mediterranean Empire: Fatimid Egypt and the Founding of Cairo: The Reign of the Imam-Caliph al-Mu'izz*. London, 2009.

— *Kitab al-Mawa'iz wa'l-i'tibar fi dhikr al-khitat wa'l-athar*. Bulaq, 1270/1853–1854; ed. Ayman F. Sayyid. London, 1995; tr. Karl Stowasser as *Medieval Egypt: an Annotated Translation of al-Maqrizi's al-Khitat*, vol 1. n.p, 2014.

al-Mas'udi, Abu'l-Hasan 'Ali. *Muruj al-dhahab wa ma'adin al-jawhar*, ed. and tr. C. Barbier de Meynard and A. Pavet de Courteille, Paris, 1861–1876. Partial tr. by Paul Lunde and Caroline Stone as *From the Meadows of Gold*. London, 2007.

Nasir-i Khusraw, Hakim Abu Mu'in. *Safarnama*, ed. M. Dabir Siyaqi. Tehran, 1356 Sh./1977; tr. Wheeler M. Thackston, Jr. as *Naser-e Khosraw's Book of Travels (Safarnama)*. Albany, NY, 1986.

— *Gusha'ish va raha'ish*, ed and tr. F. M. Hunzai as *Knowledge and Liberation: A Treatise on Philosophical Theology*. London, 1988.
al-Nisaburi, Ahmad b. Ibrahim. *al-Risala al-mujaza al-kafiya fi adab al-duʿat*, ed. and tr. Verena Klemm and Paul E. Walker as *A Code of Conduct*. London, 2011.
al-Nuʿman b. Muhammad, al-Qadi Abu Hanifa. *Daʿaʾim al-Islam*, ed. Asaf A. A. Fyzee. Cairo, 1951–1961. English trans., Asaf A. A. Fyzee, completely revised by Ismail K. Poonawala, as *The Pillars of Islam*. New Delhi, 2002–2004.
— *Taʾwil al-daʿaʾim*, ed. Muhammad Hasan al-Aʿzami. Cairo, 1967–1972.
— *Iftitah al-daʿwa wa ibtidaʾ al-dawla*, ed. Farhat Dachraoui. Tunis, 1975.
— *Kitab al-Majalis waʾl-musayarat*, ed. al-Habib al-Faqi, Ibrahim Shabbuh and Muhammad al-Yaʿlawi. Tunis, 1978.
al-Nuwayri, Shihab al-Din Ahmad. *Nihayat al-arab fi funun al-adab*, vol. 28, ed. Muhammad Amin and Muhammad Hilmi. Cairo, 1992.
al-Qalqashani, Shihab al-Din Ahmad, *Subh al-aʿsha fi sinaʿat al-inshaʾ*. Cairo, 1912–1938.
al-Qazwini, Zakariyya b. Muhamad. *ʿAjaʾib al-makhluqat waʾl-hayawanat wa gharaʾib al-mawjudat*. Beirut, 2000.
al-Sijistani, Abu Yaʿqub. *Ithbat al-nubuwwat*, ed. Wilferd Madelung and Paul Walker. Tehran, 2016.
al-Tabari, Abu Jaʿfar Muhammad b. Jarir. *Taʾrikh al-rusul waʾl-muluk*, ed. M. J. de Goeje et al. Leiden, 1879–1901.

Studies

Beben, Daniel. 'The Ismailis in Central Asia', in *The Oxford Research Encyclopedia of Asian History*. New York, 2018.
Bierman, Irene A. *Writing Signs: The Fatimid Public Text*. Berkeley, 1998.
Bloom, Jonathon. *Arts of the City Victorious: Islamic Art and Architecture in Fatimid North Africa and Egypt*. New Haven, CN, 2007.
Brett. M. *The Fatimid Empire*. Edinburgh, 2017.
Brosh, N., ed. *Jewellery and Goldsmithing in the Islamic World*. Jerusalem, 1991.
Creswell, K.A.C. *The Muslim Architecture of Egypt*. Oxford, 1959.
Contadini, Anna. *Fatimid Art at the Victoria and Albert Museum*. London, 1998.
Daftary, Farhad. *The Ismaʿilis: Their History and Doctrines*. 2nd ed., Cambridge, 2007.
— *Ismailis in Medieval Muslim Societies*. London, 2005.
— *Ismaili Literature: A Bibliography of Sources and Studies*. London, 2004.

— and S. Jiwa, ed. *The Fatimid Caliphate: Diversity of Traditions*. London, 2018.

Dagiev, Dagi. *Central Asian Ismailis: An Annotated Bibliography of Russian, Tajik and Other Sources*. London, 2022.

Dodds, Jerrilynn D., ed. *Al-Andalus. The Art of Islamic Spain*. New York, 1992.

Ettinghausen, Richard, Oleg Grabar and Marilyn Jenkins-Madina. *Islamic Art and Architecture: 630–1250*. New Haven, CN, 2001.

Goitein, S.D. *A Mediterranean Society: The Jewish communities of the Arab World as Portrayed in the Documents of the Cairo* Geniza: vol. 4, 'Daily Life'. Berkeley, 1983.

Grabar, Oleg. *The Formation of Islamic Art*. Rev. ed., New Haven, 1987.

— *The Mediation of Ornament*. Princeton, 1992.

Griffel, Frank. *The Formation of Post Classical Philosophy in Islam*. New York, 2021.

Halm, Heinz. *The Empire of the Mahdi: The Rise of the Fatimids*, tr. M. Bonner. Leiden, 1996.

Hollenberg, D. *Beyond the Qur'an: Early Isma'ili Ta'wil and the Secrets of the Prophets*. Columbia, SC, 2016.

— 'Neoplatonism in Pre-Kirmanian Fatimid Doctrine', *Le Museon*, 122 (2009), pp. 159–202.

Ivanow, W. *Fifty Years in the East: The Memoirs of Wladimir Ivanow*, ed. F. Daftary. London, 2015.

Jenkins, M and M. Keene. *Islamic Jewellery in the Metropolitan Museum of Art*. New York, 1982.

Jiwa, S. 'The Baghdad manifesto (402/1011): A Re-examination of Fatimid-Abbasid Rivalry', in F. Daftary and S. Jiwa, ed. *The Fatimid Caliphate: Diversity of Traditions*. London, 2018, pp. 22–79.

Lester, Ayala. 'A Fatimid Hoard from Tiberias', in N. Brosh, ed., *Jewellery and Goldsmithing in the Islamic World*. Jerusalem, 1991, pp. 21–29.

Mackie, Louise. *Symbols of Power: Luxury Textiles from Islamic Lands, 7th–21st Century*. New Haven and London, 2015.

Makariou, Sophie, ed. *Islamic Art at the Musée du Louvre*. Paris, 2012.

Melikian-Chirvani, Assadullah Souren, ed. *The World of the Fatimids*. Toronto, London and Munich, 2018.

Mir-Kasimov, Orkhan, ed. *Intellectual Interactions in the Islamic World: The Ismaili Thread*. London, 2019.

O'Kane, Bernard. 'The Egyptian Art of the Tiraz in Fatimid Times', in Melikian-Chirvani, ed., *The World of the Fatimids*. Toronto, London and Munich, 2018, pp. 178–189.

Poonawala, Ismail K. 'The Chronology of al-Qadi al-Nuʿman's Works', in I. K. Poonawala, *The Sound Traditions: Studies in Ismaili Texts and Thought*, ed. K. Rajani. Leiden, 2022, pp 360–432.

Porter, Venetia and Mariam Rosser-Owen, ed. *Metalwork and Material Culture in the Islamic Word: Art, Craft and Text. Festschrift in Honour of Professor James W. Allan*. London, 2012.

Pruitt, Jennifer. *Building the Caliphate: construction, destruction, and sectarian identity in early Fatimid architecture*. New Haven, CN, and London, 2020.

— 'Method in Madness: Recontextualizing the Destruction of Churches in the Fatimid Era', *Muqarnas*, 30 (2014), pp. 119–139.

Qaddumi, Ghada, tr. *The Book of Gifts and Rarities (Kitab al-Hadaya wa'l-tuhaf)*. Cambridge, MA, 1996.

Rapoport, Yossef and Emilie Savage-Smith, ed. and tr. *An Eleventh-Century Egyptian Guide to the Universe. 'The Book of Curiosities'*. Leiden, 2014.

— *Lost Maps of the Caliphs: drawing the World in Eleventh Century Cairo*. Chicago, 2018.

Rustow, Marina. *The Lost Archive: Traces of a Caliphate in a Cairo Synagogue*. Princeton, 2020.

Sanders, Paula. *Ritual, Politics, and the City in Fatimid Cairo*. Albany, NY, 1994.

Sayyid, Ayman F. *La capitale de l'Egypte jusqu'à l'époque Fatimide, al-Qahira et al-Fustat*. Beirut and Stuttgart, 1998.

Shalem, Avinoam. *Islam Christianized: Islamic portable objects in the medieval church treasuries of the Latin West*. Frankfurt am Main, 1996.

— and Cynthia Hahn, ed. *Seeking Transparency: Rock Crystals across the Medieval Mediterranean*. Berlin, 2020.

Stern, Samuel. 'Heterodox Ismaʿilism at the Time of al-Muizz', *BSOAS*, 17 (1955), pp. 10–33.

Tabbaa, Yasser. *The Production of Meaning in Islamic Architecture and Ornament*. Edinburgh, 2021.

Velji, Jamel A. *An Apocalyptic History of the Early Fatimid Empire*. Edinburg, 2016.

Walker, Paul. *Orations of the Fatimid Caliphs: Festival Sermons of the Ismaili Imams*. London, 2009.

— *Caliph of Cairo: Al-Hakim bi-Amr Allah*. Cairo and New York, 2009.

— *Exploring an Islamic Empire: Fatimid History and its Sources*. London, 2002.

— *Hamid al-Din al-Kirmani: Ismaili Thought in the Age of al-Hakim*. London, 1999.

— *Early Philosophical Shiism: The Ismaili Neoplatonism of Abu Yaʿqub al-Sijistani*. Cambridge, 1993.
— 'al-Hakim bi-Amr Allah', *EI3*.
Williams, Caroline. 'The Cult of ʿAlid Saints in the Fatimid Monuments of Cairo, Part I: The Mosque of Aqmar', *Muqarnas*, 1 (1983), pp. 37–52
— 'The Cult of ʿAlid Saints in the Fatimid Monuments of Cairo, Part II: The Mausolea', *Muqarnas*, 3 (1985), pp. 39–60.

Index

Abbasid/s xvi, 8, 29, 32, 45–7, 55, 56, 57, 59, 75, 87 n.13, 86 n.45, 107, 112, 113, 156, 161–2, 193, 200, 209, 217–18, 220, 233 n.30, 275–9, 286, 293, 295, 308–10, 317, 329, 361, 391–3, 395, 397–8, 400–3, 409–10, 413, 416, 419, 433, 452 n.11, 452 n.12, 452 n.20
Abraham (Ibrahim) 97, 306, 318
al-Afdal, Fatimid vizier 226, 229, 255–7, 267, 271 n.52
Afghanistan 27, 165
Africa 414
 see also East Africa, North Africa
African/s ('Blacks') 58, 155, 264, 273–91, 416, 427
Aga Khan/s 20–2, 25 n.57, 127, 133–6, 138–40, 153, 164, 166, 420
Aga Khan III, Sir Sultan Muhammad Shah, Nizari Ismaili Imam 21, 25 n.54, n.57, 127, 133, 134, 135–6, 138, 139–40, 164, 166
Aga Khan IV, Shah Karim al-Husayni, Nizari Ismaili Imam 21, 22, 25 n.57
agriculture 264
Alexandria 48, 50–1, 112, 115
'Ali b. Abi Talib, first Shi'i Imam and fourth caliph 20, 21, 53, 55, 58, 61, 96, 103, 104–5, 107–9, 110, 215, 238, 248, 252 n.47
'Alid/s 130, 142 n.4, 161–3, 166
al-Andalus xvi, 5, 17, 68, 70, 74, 148, 158 n.3, 184, 281, 338, 345, 349, 359
Andalusian 317, 356, 359
al-Aqmar, Mosque 125, 127–33, 139, 141, 142 n.3, 143 n.11, 240–2, 298, 300–1, 418
Armenian/s 125, 332 n.48, 416, 425, 427
army 74, 79, 106, 116–17, 155, 196, 373, 379, 413, 423–4, 427
 troops 58, 416, 427
 uprising 39, 195
 see also African, Armenian, Berber, Kutama, Turk
Ayyubid/s xiii, 46, 63 n.31, 75, 122 n.36, 127, 149, 235, 243, 251 n.25, 269 n.15, 293, 297, 306, 308–10, 315, 328, 361, 410–12, 414, 417–18, 420–1, 425, 427
al-Azhar, Mosque 125, 151, 228, 238–41, 244–5, 294–8, 300–1, 352, 410, 416, 418
al-'Aziz bi'llah, Abu Mansur Nizar, Fatimid Imam-caliph 55, 286, 378

Badakhshan 27–8, 30–40, 41 n.12
Badr al-Jamali 129–30, 139, 145 n.53, 267, 416–18, 421, 423–6
 walls of 129, 421, 423–6

Baghdad 30, 55–7, 60–1, 75, 112–13, 162, 173, 175, 195, 275–6, 352, 361, 392, 398
batin/batini (esoteric) 10–11, 91, 94, 97–100, 100 n.2, 222, 286, 295, 300–1, 310
Berber/s 74, 82, 84, 373, 416, 423
Buyid/s 38, 55–7, 61, 113, 222

Cairo xiii, xv, xvi, xviii n.7, 46–7, 52, 61, 115–16, 125–7. 130–1, 133, 139, 141, 149–53, 158 n.8, 166, 191–2, 195, 202, 204, 209, 213, 217, 225–6, 228, 236, 244, 249, 258, 260, 264, 279, 293, 296, 299–302, 308–9, 315–16, 337, 342, 345, 347, 373, 388, 391, 393, 398, 405 n.7, 409–30, 432, 436, 439, 441–3, 449
   calligraphy 293, 308, 309
   citadel of 308–9, 411
   gates of 126, 308, 416, 420–1, 423–6, 432
   houses of 52, 129–30, 134, 411, 413, 417, 422
   mosques of 126, 130–1, 139, 149, 228, 296, 299–302, 432
   palaces of 209, 391
   walls of 126, 423, 426–8
   see also al-Qahira
ceramics 221, 277–9, 286, 374, 393, 412, 415, 421, 427, 431, 433, 440, 442, 446, 450 n.3, 452 n.10, 452 n.20, 454 n.44
China 192–6, 199–200, 202–3, 318–19
Christian/s xv, 48, 50, 75, 108, 115, 118–19, 122 n.33, 126–7, 131, 133, 140, 142, 145 n.53, 171, 173, 195, 261–3, 323–5, 327, 329, 345, 455 n.55
   see also Copt/s

Church of the Holy Sepulchre, Jerusalem 116, 118
coin/s, coinage xv, 34–6, 109–10, 117, 120 n.*, 199, 205 n.37, 213, 215, 217, 249, 300, 310, 337, 348, 356, 359, 375, 377–9
Companion/s, of the Prophet 46–51, 55, 57–61, 291 n.36, 105, 108, 118
Copt/s 131, 133, 140–1, 263
Crusade/Crusader 155–6, 267, 308, 373, 379–80, 414, 423

da'i (summoner) xv, 3–4, 6–16, 18–19, 27, 37, 53, 71–2, 74, 87 n.32, 96, 103, 110–11, 113, 115, 165–7, 195, 198, 200, 202–3, 222, 224, 235–6
da'wa xiii, 3–25, 27–43, 45, 47, 56, 68–72, 78, 82, 85 n.3, 93–100, 101 n.21, 108, 110–12, 114–15, 120 n.*, 166–7, 202–3, 249
dress 339, 362

East Africa 192, 200–3, 205 n.37
   coast of 192
Eastern Fatimid palace 422 *see also* Western Fatimid palace

figure, figuralism 28–9, 31, 34, 45–6, 52, 75–7, 81, 94–5, 101 n.21, 166, 220, 277, 317, 319–20, 322–3, 325, 329 n.3, 330 n.17, 339, 376, 420, 431–56
fountain/s 315–16, 323, 328, 413, 417, 419, 421–2
Fustat xiii, xiv, 53, 115, 125, 151, 202, 337, 341–2, 356, 373, 393, 409–30, 432, 435–6

Geniza, documents of xii, xv–xvi,
116, 204, 258, 264–5, 337–8,
357, 359, 373–85, 439
glass 339, 341–2, 358, 377, 392–3, 394,
395, 397, 402, 407 n.39, 413,
427, 433, 453 n.34, 453 n.36
gold xv, 52, 201, 216, 218, 226, 237,
255–8, 261, 264, 266,
268 n.4, 284–5, 336–7, 348,
353, 356–8, 362, 374–82,
384 n.16, 433, 440, 448,
453 n.35, 453 n.36

hadith 50, 70, 77–8, 105, 223–5, 275–6
hajj 74, 115, 209–10, 213, 217–18,
220–1, 231, 233 n.30,
233 n.33
see also pilgrimage
al-Hakim, Mosque 142 n.3, 236,
238–40, 297, 299, 352,
423–4
al-Hakim bi-Amr Allah, Abu ʿAli
al-Mansur, Fatimid
Imam-caliph xvi, 45–65,
125, 162, 442, 454 n.39
al-Husayn b. ʿAli, Shiʿi Imam 59, 103,
104 106, 107, 248
shrine of
in Ascalon 130, 240
Cenotaph 214, 243–244

Ibn Tulun, Mosque 228–31, 409,
411
Ifriqiya xiii, 55, 57, 59, 62, 73–4, 76,
78, 82, 84, 281, 415–16
see also North Africa
imagery 95, 235–53, 316, 320, 327–8,
330 n.15, 335, 432
Imam 6–11, 16, 18–22, 47, 53, 68,
70–5, 77, 80–3, 85 n.5,
85 n.7, 87 n.31, 93–6, 99,
101 n.21, 104–10, 112–13, 119,
121 n.27, 140, 161, 164–5,
214–15, 224–5, 230–1, 235–6,
247–9, 253 n.54, 303, 308
Imam-caliph xvi, 3–4, 6–10, 45–65,
67–76, 78–84, 85 n.5,
86 n.13, 86 n.22, 87 n.30,
89 n.90, 97, 103–9, 112,
116–18, 120, 125, 149, 156,
161–2, 165–6, 198–200,
205 n.37, 209, 211, 214–15,
217–18, 220, 223–6, 229–31,
237, 248, 281, 285–6, 343,
347–8, 362, 377, 391, 393,
414, 416–17, 419, 424, 427,
441
imamate 9, 19, 21–2, 45, 68, 71–2, 81,
86 n.12, 87 n.31, 104–5, 108,
113, 116, 235, 248–9
India 56, 62, 153, 163–4, 192–200,
202–4, 437
Indian Ocean xiii, 191–206
islands of 191
Iran 49, 176, 178, 282, 284, 293, 302,
305, 309, 317, 320, 356, 433
see also Persia
Iraq 49, 55–6, 58–9, 112, 217, 233 n.30,
277–8, 433–4, 437, 452 n.11,
453 n.34
Ismaili/s xv–xvi, 3–25, 28–9, 31 34,
35, 37–40, 40 n.5, 45, 47,
53–4, 56, 68–71, 82, 93–4,
99, 100 n.2, 106–12, 114–16,
140, 149, 151–4, 156, 161–8,
179, 192, 195, 198–200,
202–4, 210–11, 213–14, 220,
222–3, 225, 228, 230–1, 235,
248–9, 253 n.54, 265, 294–5,
300, 310, 409, 416, 428
Nizari/s 3–4, 16–20, 22, 39, 164–5,
248

Ivanow, Wladimir 161–9
ivory 202, 276, 279–83, 329, 338, 345, 357, 359–60, 413, 427, 432, 434
   box/es 280–3, 345

Jaʿfar al-Sadiq, Shiʿi Imam
Jaʿfar b. Mansur al-Yaman, *daʿi*
Jawhar al-Siqilli, Fatimid commander 125, 416, 423
   walls of 125, 418, 423, 425
Jerusalem 118–19, 156, 352, 356, 373, 379–80, 383
Jew/s 115, 195, 347–8
Jewellery 337, 373–85, 417

katib 116–17
khutba (sermon) 84, 103–7, 112, 120 n.*, 213, 248, 310
   see also sermon
al-Kirmani, Hamid al-Din, Ismaili *daʿi* 12, 15, 18, 113, 114, 165–7, 235, 248
Kutama 52, 82, 84, 247, 416, 423

lamp/s 130, 202, 235, 239, 322, 356, 393, 415
linen xv, 256–8, 260, 262, 264, 279, 286, 326
lustreware 226, 415, 433, 438, 440–1, 448–9, 452 n.20, 455 n.55

Madagascar 202, 393
mahdi 101 n.21, 107, 120 n.7, 248
al-Mahdi biʾllah, Abu Muhammad ʿAbd Allah, first Fatimid Imam-caliph 69, 72, 82, 103–4, 107, 156, 165
Mahdiyya xiv, xv, 58, 82–3, 424
   Mosque of 58, 424

al-Maʾmun al-Bataʾihi, Fatimid vizier 125, 255–6, 264–5, 271 n.52
al-Maqrizi, Taqi al-Din Ahmad b. ʿAli, Egyptian historian 50, 52–4, 58–60, 131, 217–18, 226, 257, 265, 267, 337, 347, 359, 391, 411, 414, 427
   Khitat of 52
market/s xv, 47, 50, 52, 59, 202, 257, 261, 357, 387, 394, 439, 447–8, 456 n.60
Mecca 42 n.41, 209–10, 213, 217, 233 n.30, 276
Mediterranean, sea xiii, xv, 67, 191–3, 202–3, 264, 275, 280, 285, 319, 321–3, 329, 337–8, 350, 359, 434, 439–40
merchant/s xv, xvi, 193, 195, 198, 201, 203–4, 257–66, 268, 271 n.40, 381, 413–14, 439
metalware 235, 237, 239, 262, 279, 284–5, 316, 320, 337–9, 352, 383, 384 n.16, 427, 439
mihrab 137, 141, 187, 226, 228–31, 236–8, 241, 243–5, 295–7, 299, 356, 433
minaret 139–40, 236, 238–9, 297, 302–4, 352, 424
al-Muʾayyad fiʾl-Din al-Shirazi, Ismaili *daʿi* 12–13, 165, 222, 224–5, 231, 276
Muhammad 8, 50, 55–6, 59, 61, 109, 215, 230, 235, 247–8
   see also the Prophet
al-Muʿizz li-Din Allah, Abu Tamim Maʿadd, Fatimid Imam-caliph 4, 6–11, 55, 57, 67–75, 78–84, 106, 109, 117, 156, 199–200, 209–10, 213–18, 220, 228, 280–1, 416, 419, 423

Museum of Islamic Art, Cairo 126, 133, 149, 151, 244, 315, 342, 419, 436, 441, 442, 443, 448, 449
al-Mustansir bi'llah, Abu Tamim Ma'add, Fatimid Imam-caliph 125, 139, 224, 226, 228–31, 237, 286, 343, 347–8, 362, 378–9, 414, 416, 419, 424, 426

Nasir-i Khusraw, Ismaili *da'i* xv, 12–13, 16, 18, 27–43, 165, 167, 202, 318, 356, 393
Neoplatonism 3–25
Nile, the 125, 134, 138, 141, 258–9, 267, 332 n.53, 409–12, 415, 416, 424
  flood of 258–9, 416, 424
North Africa 3, 57–8, 67, 153, 165, 293, 323, 415

Palestine 240, 295, 373–85
Persian Gulf 195, 202, 317
philosophy 3–11, 22, 179–81
Pilgrimage, the 99, 117–18, 213, 221
  see also hajj
potters 413, 415
pottery 316, 329, 339, 415, 432, 451 n.4
prophet/s 10–11, 15–16, 18–20, 30, 46, 50, 55–8, 61, 74, 76–8, 81, 94–5, 97, 99, 104–8, 112, 114, 117–18, 126, 153–4, 196, 215, 217, 221, 224, 225, 230–1, 235–6, 248, 275–6, 301, 316, 318
Prophet, the 10, 15,16, 18, 20, 30, 57, 61, 74, 78, 105–7, 108, 112–14, 153, 215, 221–24, 230, 235, 275, 291

al-Qadi al-Nu'man, Fatimid jurist and historian 6, 9, 69–71, 86 n.20, 97, 99, 104, 164–5, 214, 223, 235, 265
  Da'a'im al-Islam of 71, 99, 223, 225, 265
al-Qahira 125, 131, 409–11, 413–27, 432, 449
  see also Cairo
qa'im 95–7, 100 *see also mahdi*
al-Qa'im bi-Amr Allah, Abu'l-Qasim Muhammad, Fatimid Imam-caliph 69, 83
al-Qalawun, *bimaristan* of 418–19
al-Qata'i' 125, 228, 409–10, 416
Qur'an 9–10, 13–15, 22, 56, 70, 81, 92–6, 210, 217, 221–2, 235, 247, 276, 279, 286, 300, 306, 308, 352–3, 377, 383

Red Sea 195, 202–3, 414
rock crystal 202, 226–7, 337–8, 345, 352, 356–7, 365 n.6, 377, 382, 387–407, 413, 432–3, 439–40, 448

Safar-nama, of Nasir-i Khusraw xv, 27, 202
Salah al-Din (Saladin) 151, 156, 294, 308–9, 380, 410, 414, 417–18, 423, 425–6
al-Salih Tala'i', Mosque 126, 237, 241, 246, 301–2
Saljuq/s 35–7, 75, 156, 239, 302–3, 310, 316, 379–80
script/s 178, 286, 293–5, 297, 300–1, 303–6, 308, 310, 337, 349–50, 356, 360, 382, 448
sermon/s 104–9, 112, 115, 215
Shi'a 53–4, 56–9, 61, 73, 105, 108, 110, 114

Shi'i 3, 6, 17, 47, 53–61, 68–71, 73–4, 103–22, 126, 130, 149–53, 156, 162, 167, 213, 215, 222, 229, 249, 286, 302–3, 305, 416
Shi'ism 108–9, 116, 149–50, 153, 303
Sicily 116, 192, 237, 318, 321, 434
al-Sijistani, Abu Ya'qub, Ismaili *da'i* 5–8, 12–13, 18, 165, 167, 215, 217, 247
silk 192, 195, 217, 226, 256, 257–8, 264, 268 n.4, 286, 448
silver 285, 320, 335–71, 374–9, 382–3, 433, 440
Spain 50, 148, 281–3, 285, 336, 338, 345–6, 349–50, 359, 363, 393
sura/s, of the Qur'an 92–3, 221–2, 377, 383
Syria 52, 57, 163, 165, 167, 293–6, 302–9, 318, 320, 347, 373, 383, 434

Tajikistan 27, 31, 42 n.44
ta'wil (esoteric interpretation) 9, 10–11, 13, 17, 91–102, 111, 214, 224, 248, 301
tax/es 32, 73, 115, 118, 259–60, 256, 259, 262–3, 265–7, 269 n.9

textile/s 209, 217, 220, 255–8, 260–2, 264–5, 276–7, 279, 285–6, 316, 326, 374, 433, 448
tiraz 256–8, 262–3, 266, 276–7, 279, 285–6
Turk/s 51, 56–7, 194, 310, 373, 424

vizier 113, 121 n.15, 125–6, 130, 222, 226, 229, 256–7, 260, 264, 267, 285, 345, 347–9, 362, 416–17, 424, 426

walaya 100
Western Fatimid palace 472
wood 113, 240–1, 243, 246, 252 n.42, 297, 321, 332 n.43, 341–2, 344, 349–50, 353, 368 n.44, 418–20, 427, 432–4, 439

Yemen 154, 156, 160 n.18, 163, 167, 195, 198, 200–4, 247

zahir/zahiri (exoteric) 10–11, 85 n.7, 91, 94, 97, 99–100, 222, 286, 295, 300–1, 310
al-Zahir li-I'zaz Din Allah, Abu'l-Hasan 'Ali, Fatimid Imam-caliph 226–7, 286, 377–8, 405 n.9